D1475283

Social Policy in the Third Reich

San Diego Christian College
Library
Santee, CA

San Diego Christian College
Library
Santee, CA

305.562 0943
M412 s

Social Policy in the Third Reich

The Working Class and the 'National Community'

BY TIMOTHY W. MASON

Translated by John Broadwin
Edited by Jane Caplan
With a General Introduction by Ursula Vogel

BERG

Providence/Oxford

First published in 1993 by

Berg Publishers

Editorial offices:
221 Waterman Street, Providence, RI 02906, USA
150 Cowley Road, Oxford, OX4 1JJ. UK

© Jane Caplan, Raphael Samuel, Simonetta Piccone Stella and
Ursula Vogel 1993

First published in 1977 as *Sozialpolitik im Dritten Reich. Arbeiterklasse und
Volksgemeinschaft.*
© *Westdeutscher Verlag GmbH Opladen*

All rights reserved.
No part of this publication may be reproduced in any form or by any means
without the written permission of Berg Publishers Limited.

Library of Congress Cataloging-in-Publication Data
Mason, Timothy W., 1940–
    [Sozialpolitik im Dritten Reich. English]
    Social policy in the Third Reich : the working class and the 'national
community' / by Timothy M. [sic] Mason : translated by Jim Broadwin;
    edited by Jane Caplan; with an introduction by Ursula Vogel and Simonetta
    Piccone Stella.
        p.   cm.
    "The main text of this book (the preface, and chapters i–iv) is a transla-
tion of Tim Mason's 'Sozialpolitik im Dritten Reich. Arbeiterklasse und
Volksgemeinschaft' (Opladen. Westdeutscher Verlag, 1977)"—P. 1.
    Includes bibliographical references and index.
    ISBN 0–85496–621–8 cloth   0–85496–410–X paper
    1. Labor policy—Germany—History. 2. Germany—Social policy—His-
tory. 3. Working class—Germany—History.   I. Caplan, Jane.   II. Title.
HD8450.M37213   1990   93–53
305.5'62'094309043—dc20   CIP

British Library Cataloguing in Publication Data
A CIP catalogue record for this book is available from the British Library

Printed in the United States by Edwards Brothers, Ann Arbor, MI.

Contents

General Introduction

Ursula Vogel

Sozialpolitik im Dritten Reich, which is here for the first time made available to English readers, was the cornerstone of Tim Mason's work and the greatest investment of his personal and professional life. It was originally written to introduce *Arbeiterklasse und Volksgemeinschaft* (1975), a collection of documentary material on the Nazi regime's policies towards the working class.[1] Although it was published separately in a paperback edition of 1977 and thus stood on its own, this introduction was never meant to be a finished product or last word on the subject. Together with the unpublished doctoral dissertation of 1971[2] it was a first attempt to locate the terrain for a future comprehensive analysis of National Socialism. This larger work remained unwritten. But Tim Mason always hoped that the results of his life-long engagement with the book might be published in English in some form. He was working on the Epilogue to a planned translation of *Sozialpolitik* when he died in March 1990.

Some of the obstacles that he encountered are familiar to scholars today. The boundaries of the project expanded and shifted under the impact of prolific research on the Nazi period; it was delayed by the burden of academic teaching and by the pressure of numerous and diverse publication commitments. In Tim Mason's case such barriers had a more paralysing effect because of his illness, which left him through all of his adult life with few periods of energy to confront the ever more daunting demands of a great synthesis. Visitors to the crammed study in the attic of 29 St John Street in Oxford will remember the overwhelming physical presence of 'the book': the giant rolls of documents from the Koblenz and Potsdam archives held by a broomstick between two chairs; the boxes with thousands of handwritten filing cards (this was before the time of the word processor) closing in on the desk; new literature on the subject taking over the floor and, in later years, winding down the staircase; with Fallada's *Little Man, What Now?* and the postcards of Heartfield illustrations (pinned to the lampshade) serving as a constant reminder that the social history of the Third Reich could not be told from official documents alone.

1. T.W. Mason, *Arbeiterklasse und Volksgemeinschaft. Dokumente und Materialien zur deutschen Arbeiterpolitik 1936–39*, Opladen, 1975.
2. T.W. Mason, 'National Socialist Policies towards the German Working Classes 1925 to 1939', unpublished PhD thesis, University of Oxford, 1971.

In the Epilogue Tim Mason looks back on a decade of struggling with a task that had by now grown beyond the hope of completion. Revisiting the main sites of the old building – class, domestic crisis, war – he restates the argument in the light of the advances and changed priorities of research on Nazi Germany. The enormous distance marked by the development of historical scholarship may help to explain why he believed that the old framework could no longer sustain the story which had to be told about the Third Reich. In his own judgement it was the burden of inadequacy that weighed most heavily in the decision to revise the earlier work rather than build it into a new, more wide-ranging study. But that choice could perhaps appear imperative only to someone who was so keenly aware that scholarly work is itself involved in the process of historical change and vulnerable to it.

Given the extent to which we prize the progression of knowledge in our academic disciplines it may be tempting to take the Epilogue as the more authentic statement on the subject. To approach the book from this angle – that is, to read the beginning from the perspective of the end – would be a mistake. It would then be difficult to see why *Sozialpolitik*, together with the essays of the preceding decade,[3] occupied a special place in the fascism debates of the 1970s. Tim Mason's earlier work will show more clearly how a distinct and original approach to the understanding of National Socialism developed under the influence of two traditions of historical scholarship. His close contact with German historians on the Left strengthened his natural propensity towards theory. It combined with an equally strong passion for the spadework of archival research that he owed to his undergraduate training at Oxford. Thus, in the book's interpretive framework class relations hold the key to the understanding of the Nazi regime. But their specific form is derived from the documentary material, not from the typical constellation of economic forces under capitalism. The theoretical model is recast to allow for the 'primacy of politics' over structural economic interests and antagonisms. The book deals extensively with the effects of the economic depression in the late 1920s, with developments in the labour market, with structural crises in different sectors of production. That even under a total dictatorship politics operated in a space bounded by the contradictions of a capitalist economy is not in question. But political rule had become primary in the sense that it extended into, and directly controlled, all spheres of social activity.

The primacy of politics determines where the story begins and where it ends. The first chapter traces the ideological origins of a fundamental

---

3. See T.W. Mason, *Essays on Fascism and National Socialism* (provisional title, Cambridge, forthcoming).

contradiction that was to divide the policies of the Nazi regime between incompatible priorities. The ultimate goal of a new European order based upon the political and racial supremacy of the German *Volk* required that all of the nation's resources be made subservient to the single imperative of military expansion. It demanded above all a unified society capable of bearing a future war effort of unprecedented scope. But the ideological fixation on the absolute priority of foreign policy was locked from the outset into the confines of a historical myth. Hitler's whole understanding of politics revolved around the experiences of Germany's defeat in the First World War. Like many of his contemporaries in the 1920s he perceived its causes through the distortions of the stab-in-the-back legend (which blamed Germany's military 'collapse' of 1918 upon internal subversion). Projected into the future the legend evoked the ever-present danger of the fighting community's vulnerability to conflict and betrayal from within. As the following chapters show, the legacy of the November Revolution was to have a profound and lasting effect upon the regime's attitude towards the German working class. A dictatorship whose ideology denied the very existence of classes became in its political practice the prisoner of an understanding of history in which class conflict had an all too real meaning. In targeting the trade unions and the socialist/communist parties as the wire-pullers behind Germany's social divisions, the lessons of 1918 foreshadowed the politics of terror. But the same fear of history repeating itself also fuelled the regime's obsessive concern with its own legitimacy. It stood behind the ceaseless efforts of re-education and behind the propagation of *Ersatz* communities that were to secure the integration of the working class into the nation. Most importantly, the haunting spectre of a war lost to social revolution manifested itself in the failure to pursue those domestic policies that should have laid the foundations for the successful venture of military expansion. By the end of the book, at the point where the pressures of an accelerating domestic crisis push the regime into the gamble of a premature war, the legacies of 1918 will have come full circle.

From the way in which the plot is set out it is clear that the history of class relations in the Third Reich has to be told from the vantage point of the regime and by reference to the documentary evidence amassed by its representatives. The dominance of political actors and processes is, however, not only dictated by considerations of methodological adequacy. Their vivid portrayal in the narrative owes much to Tim Mason's fascination with the high drama of politics – with the interplay between individuals and institutional structures, with personality clashes, power struggles and empire-building ambitions. Although his own active involvement in politics tended to be on the side of radical intervention –

in his student days the most direct knowledge of the state would have come from inside a police van, after a sit-in in Trafalgar Square – he had both a keen appetite and an unusually sharp eye for what was going on at the centre of the political stage. He loathed bureaucracy in all its guises and had the Marxist's amused contempt for the pretensions of upper-class politicians. Yet, for many hours of the day he would bury himself under pages of newsprint studying every move of the 'enemy'– and enjoying it. During the miners' strike of 1974 he lit his house with miners' lamps while talking most of the time about the political strategies of the government. This abiding interest in everything political is, in the book, reflected in an account of National Socialist rule that stays clear of moral generalizations and judgements. It is not moral evil that is seen to make history, even in this extreme case, but 'normal' politics (albeit under the constraint of abnormal conditions)

How could the Nazi dictatorship establish itself in a society whose democratic institutions and strong traditions of working-class mobilization should have offered sufficient guarantees against such invasion? Why was there no massive popular resistance either before or after 1933? The exceptional historical circumstances which any answer to such questions has to take into account are outlined in the second and third chapters of the book. The analysis details the massive transformation of class relations that followed upon the Nazi seizure of power and the physical destruction of the organizations of the German labour movement in the spring of 1933. The unprecedented constellation of a class war waged from above and by means of overt force confronts the social historian with intractable conceptual and methodological problems. If the German working class in this period is to be defined 'by what was done to it',[4] it must be doubtful whether we can relate the social policies of the Third Reich to 'class' in any meaningful sense, especially since the near-complete silence forced upon millions of disenfranchised and subjugated workers has had the effect of barring future generations from direct access to their experiences, actions and motivations.

That the story of the German working class could nevertheless be told against these odds is owed to Tim Mason's undogmatic understanding of class. On a basic level, and despite the difficulties of cogent definition, he took 'class' as given in the diverse expressions of human agency. While in some contexts his analysis affirms the determining power of socio-economic structures, in others it relies on the subjective dimensions of lived experience and on an intuitive grasp of the realities of the *Arbeitsalltag* (everyday life). Tim Mason had a rare ability to 'see' history in the concrete, material facets of daily life. I remember a

4. See below, p. xxii.

conversation in the late summer of 1989 about the crisis in the Soviet Union. Everybody was trying to fit events into a grand scheme of socialism's demise. He commented that if miners had to go on strike for soap, the experiment of a communist society must surely have failed. He similarly identified the German working class under the Nazi dictatorship with tangible instances of shared suffering – hunger, destitution, fear of unemployment. The weekly budget of a working-class household which leaves a family of five with 73 pfennigs after necessary deductions will, he assumed, speak for itself. The German text encapsulates those experiences in a recurrent combination of words: *Armut und Elend* (poverty and suffering), *Not und Entbehrung* (distress and deprivation). Curiously reminiscent of the austerity of Lutheran hymns, they convey an unambiguous sense of physical suffering and despair.

The book's main objective is to assert the subterranean political significance of class by tracing its reflections in the official documents of the regime. That the latter itself saw little reason to put its trust in the loyalty and co-operation of the working population is nowhere more clearly manifest than in the disjointed patchwork of its social policies. Designed to rid the German nation of class conflict they are the most eloquent testimony of its continued existence. Readers who approach the subject for the first time, and perhaps with textbook conceptions of 'totalitarian' rule in mind, will be unprepared for an account of policy-making that bears but little resemblance to the stereotype of dictatorial omnipotence. What emerges instead is the anatomy of a regime paralysed by incompatible goals and internal power struggles and unable to exact from its subjects the material sacrifices that the war governments of democratic England and America imposed upon their citizens. The exigencies of economic war preparation would have demanded the tight control of the labour market, the curbing of wage demands and job mobility as well as the extension of the working day and the ruthless enforcement of discipline on the shopfloor. Yet, the search for the enactment of these necessary measures leads to a trail of half-hearted measures, of delay and compromise, of fake solutions and, at decisive points, simple inaction. At issue is not, in the first instance, the incompetence of policy-makers. Rather, the documents reveal that the regime's failure to force its political priorities upon the working population resulted from an infectious concern with the possibility of widespread dissatisfaction. The need to secure at least the semblance of popular legitimacy in turn fuelled power rivalries between different groups within the Party and set the latter on collision course with the military leadership. In the formation and organizational expansion of the German Labour Front (Chapters 3 and 5) the book presents a paradigmatic case of Nazi social policy. Radical rhetoric, feverish activity, organizational quagmires masquerading as *Gemeinschaft* had to cover for the lack of any real purpose or direction. What is evident in this as in other cases is, on the one hand, the persistent hostility of the workforce and, on the other, the extent to which this attitude compelled the regime to retreat from those radical domestic policies upon which the success of its foreign policy was staked.

The last and longest chapter covers the period between 1936 and the winter of 1939/40. The contradictions that had built up from the fusion of a capitalist market economy with the command structures of the political dictatorship erupted in a 'spiralling crisis without end'.[5] In a situation where the economic preparations for a sustained war effort lagged behind strategic requirements and where the policies aimed at the pacification of Germany's working class had demonstrably failed, the pre-emptive strike of a war of territorial expansion and plunder offered the only escape route. Mason's analysis, which develops the regime's drift into war from the fusion of several processes of disintegration, offers perhaps the most compelling example of the book's narrative and explanatory power. While the structural imbalances of a capitalist economy are shown to play a crucial role in throwing political strategies into disarray, the dominant emphasis of Chapter 6 casts the institutional corrosion of those years as a crisis of politics. The regime had itself created the situation in which the political reliability of the working class could not be taken for granted and in which, as a consequence, policy decisions were caught in an uncontrollable cycle of repression and concession. Moreover, the ideological fixation of the leadership on the empty dynamic of interminable struggle resulted in a total incapacity to adapt goals to available means. In these circumstances the only way out of the crisis lay in the *Flucht nach vorn* (flight forwards).

A vital link connecting economic crises, political instability and the drift towards war was, finally, the 'opposition' of the working class. The assertion that German workers refused to collaborate with the regime – not merely by indifference or apathy but by identifiable forms of collective action – has always been the most controversial claim of the book. 'Opposition', as it is understood here, does not manifest itself in the heroic deeds of individuals nor in the form of politically motivated mass protest. Given that the dictatorship had destroyed the conditions of publicly visible and testifiable action workers could express their dissatisfaction only within the confined space of economic non-cooperation. Evidence for the massive occurrence of disruptive behaviour in the workplace can, the author claims, be pieced together from the sheer den-

5. See below, p. 184.

sity of such cases in the official records and, similarly, from the pervasive attitude of uncertainty and indecision with which the regime responded to the perceived threat of widespread insubordination. A third and decisive element that lends to the diffuse evidence of defiant behaviour the distinct quality of 'class' action is derived, in this context too, from an appeal to lived experience: favourable constellations in the labour market after 1936 provided workers with a space 'to set the conditions of their own political subjugation'.[6] That they used it in the way they did was, Tim Mason believed, due to residual traditions of practical solidarity – to memories of acquired rights and of collective political practice that reached back into the time before 1933. Although it figures prominently only in a few pages towards the end of the book, the reconstitution of working-class agency has in an important sense been part of the story from the beginning. This is not to say that it emerges as a foregone conclusion guaranteed by dogmatic certainty rather than empirical testimony. But his belief that German workers were not implicated in the politics of the National Socialist regime, nor merely its passive victims, does contain an imponderable element of hope in which the political concerns of the present bore on his engagement with the past. It reflects the dominant intellectual and emotional interest that guided Tim Mason's work in those years.[7]

The concluding section of the book maintains a precarious balance. It anticipates the final triumph of the *Volksgemeinschaft* in the fundamentally changed circumstances of a total war and the pervasive use of terror which only now became possible. It suggests that the labour policies of the dictatorship failed to force the working class into compliance. But it also indicates that a different story might have to be told once the factory-as-community turned into the factory-as-concentration camp. The last two sentences, furthermore, open the door on future developments that a history centred in class relations might no longer be able to explain: 'Only one further step could follow ...: the destruction of human beings in the production process for the sake of production. This fate was reserved for the foreign slave labourers'.[8]

In the twelve years that separate *Sozialpolitik* from the Epilogue Tim Mason worked and wrote on a wide range of subjects. The titles of his English, Italian and German publications indicate a broadening engage-

6. See below, p. 210.
7. For a further elaboration of this argument, see. T.W. Mason, 'The Workers' Opposition in Nazi Germany', *History Workshop Journal*, no. 11, Spring 1981, pp. 120–37; for a significant modification of the claim, see T.W. Mason, 'The Domestic Dynamics of Nazi Conquests: A Response to Critics', in T. Childers and J. Caplan (eds.), *Reevaluating the Third Reich*, New York, 1993, pp. 161–89, esp. pp. 171f.
8. See below, p. 274.

ment with European social history as well as new priorities of theoretical reflection that were to become the dominant concern of his last writings. The most substantive thematic expansion in his research on Nazi Germany was indebted to the influence of feminist scholarship. What he learnt from the editorial group of *History Workshop Journal* and from a large circle of feminist friends and colleagues in Italy, Germany and the United States brought him in touch with dimensions of everyday life that had played but a secondary role in *Sozialpolitik*. His 1976 article 'Women in Nazi Germany' was a pioneering attempt, undertaken at an early stage of the debates on feminist history, to come to grips with the challenge.[9] He responded to it not in the form of theoretical confrontation but, characteristically, by opening up a largely uncharted terrain of empirical research. Here as elsewhere the immersion in new material gave rise to general questions of historical method. The difficulties that he encountered in reconstructing women's experience and role in Nazi Germany led him to rethink the key presumption of a 'political social history' which tends to locate actions and actors in the domains of public relevance. The task then was not to add another piece – women's history – to the mosaic assembled so far but 'to break the tyranny of foreground actors over my historical perspective'.[10] In the course of the 1980s, and through his friendship with Simonetta Piccone Stella (whom he married in 1987), feminism came to change his personal and intellectual life in the most pervasive manner. To talk and listen to him was to be drawn into a dialogue in which divisions between work and personal experience, argument and feeling seemed not to exist. An example of how much this openness entered into his understanding of history is the beautiful essay on Rosa Luxemburg's letters to her comrade and lover Leo Jogiches.[11] Luxemburg's character and her vision of 'life in its fullness', undivided between passionate intimacy and political struggle, is cast as the promise of a socialist future that can only be realized from the core of transformed relationships between men and women: 'it was in its time distinctively a woman's conception of what life could be'.[12]

A different challenge to his earlier work – and a demand of reorientation more unsettling in its implications for the book that Tim Mason planned to write – was bound up with a major paradigm shift in the approach to German history. An intense process of reflection on the

9. T.W. Mason, 'Women in Nazi Germany, Part I', *History Workshop Journal*, no. 1, Spring 1976, pp. 74–113; 'Women in Germany, 1925–1940: Family, Welfare and Work. Conclusion', *History Workshop Journal*, no. 2, Autumn 1976, pp. 5–32.

10. Mason, 'Women in Germany', p. 26.

11. T.W. Mason, 'Comrade and Lover: Rosa Luxemburg's Letters to Leo Jogiches', *History Workshop Journal*, no. 13, Spring 1982, pp. 94–109.

12. Ibid., p. 106.

foundations of Germany's national identity and the preoccupation with the German *Sonderweg*, which exploded in the *Historikerstreit* of 1986/7, threatened to divest the fascism-model of the previous decade of much of its explanatory force. It became doubtful whether an analysis that accorded priority to social conflict and institutional structures would still be adequate once the incommensurable nature of the Nazi dictatorship and its manifestation in genocide ('the most extreme peculiarities of German Nazism')[13] had moved into the centre of professional and public debates.

Tim Mason's own research on Italian fascism pointed towards similar conclusions.[14] For it established a vantage point of comparative evaluation which rendered the dominant emphases in his interpretation of National Socialism increasingly problematic. Not only had the resistance movement of the Italian working class played a decisive part in the defeat of the Mussolini regime, but anti-fascism had become constitutive of the post-war Italian republic in a way for which there was no equivalent in the reconstitution of the German state after 1945. The observed disparities were bound to reopen the question why the Nazi dictatorship lasted as long as it did and why it was at no point threatened by massive resistance.

Would it not have been possible to respond to these challenges by expanding the scope and reordering the architectonic design of the earlier work? The new Introduction to this volume, and the first section of the Epilogue revolve around this question. What is at issue is the historian's capacity to confront those defining features of National Socialist rule that became fully apparent only towards the end of the Third Reich – the drive beyond politics that accounts for the survival of the regime 'until the bitter end' of May 1945, and genocide. As Tim Mason saw it now, the foundations on which his work had built contained no space for those facts: 'my story has no place for the very real ending'.[15] Neither the self-destructive logic that locked the regime's policies into the alternative of total victory or total defeat nor the enormity of suffering inflicted upon millions of people by the politics of biological racism could come into view from the starting-point of class relations.

Given the demands that Tim Mason made on himself and on scholarly work in general this judgement must have had devastating implica-

---

13. T.W. Mason, 'Whatever Happened to Fascism?', in Childers and Caplan (eds.), *Reevaluating the Third Reich*, p. 255.

14. See T.W. Mason, 'Massenwiderstand ohne Organisation. Streiks im faschistischen Italien und NS-Deutschland', *Gewerkschaftliche Monatshefte*, vol. 35, 1984, pp. 518–32; and 'Gli scioperi di Torino del Marzo '43', in *L'Italia nella seconda guerra mondiale et nella Resistenza*, Milano.

15. See below, p. 278.

tions. For him the study of history was inseparable from the desire to understand particular phenomena in the whole context of meaning. He had hoped that his research on the labour policies of the Nazi regime would enable him to move outwards towards a comprehensive interpretation of National Socialism which would connect with the broader history of European fascism and thus capture a decisive moment in the experience of modernity. These were not ambitions of theoretical speculation. Unwillingness 'to get one's hands dirty' in the pursuit of primary research would in his eyes condemn any piece of scholarship. Yet, without a vision capable of integrating such material into a meaningful story, empirical research would have seemed to him pointless. The passion of wanting to understand the whole was what made him a historian.

The Introduction to the present volume identifies the task of telling the history of National Socialism 'in the broadest possible context' as a demand of moral and political responsibility.[16] This emphasis is easily misunderstood. It is not a call to moralize about the past, to pass judgement on the intentions and actions of historical agents. The challenge that the historian must answer, Tim Mason believed, derives from an imperative of public morality – to establish the priority of genocide for our knowledge. It entails the moral obligation that we owe to those who suffered persecution and extermination and, at the same time, a political obligation because we have to assume that the understanding of the past will bear on the circumstances of future choices. For his own work these demands seemed to leave only one choice – to start all over again and build from new foundations, or to abandon a project to which the original design was no longer adequate. He no longer had the strength to write the larger book that he believed had to be written about National Socialism. He told the story of what may be involved in writing it.

16. See below, p. 4.

Editor's Note

Jane Caplan

The main text of this book (the Preface and Chapters 1–6) is a translation of the Tim Mason's *Sozialpolitik im Dritten Reich. Arbeiterklasse und Volksgemeinschaft* (Opladen: Westdeutscher Verlag, 1977). The translator and editor have reproduced this text virtually unchanged, apart from minor editorial amendments. Note references are also unchanged from the original; but where new or English-language editions of books cited are available, these are now noted in the Bibliography. The Bibliography follows the style of the original German edition in not giving page references for articles and chapters.

I have assembled the Introduction to the English Edition and the Epilogue from later texts written (in English) by Tim Mason over a period of years in preparation for an English translation of the original book. These texts were only partially completed before Tim Mason's untimely death, and their preparation for publication here presented some editorial difficulties. The Introduction bore the handwritten annotation '1978/9?', and was apparently a draft to which Mason intended to return. In the interests of legibility, I have omitted the author's shorthand and marginal notations, as also his few draft references, and have made minor editorial changes. (Readers interested in an unedited version of the text are referred to the version published in *History Workshop Journal*, no. 30, Autumn 1990).

The Epilogue, apparently written in 1988–9, was intended by Mason as a substantial review of the considerable scholarly literature on the economic and social history of Nazi Germany that had accumulated in the thirteen years since the publication of *Sozialpolitik*. Some of this new literature directly addresses Mason's arguments and interpretations, and it has filled in many of the gaps in knowledge that he had noted in his book. Rather than attempting to revise the text of the book itself, Mason prepared this epilogue as a discussion of scholarly responses to his arguments, and of the implications of new research for his earlier interpretations.

The Epilogue published here consists of four sections, which were found in various states of completion. The texts and notes of section 1 (Introduction) and section 2 (Class), were complete, but sections 3 and 4

(Domestic Crisis; 1939–45) were incomplete and appear to have been the sections on which the author was working at the time of his death. Section 3 is a heavily revised and extended version of a previously published paper. For this version, I have followed Mason's own method of working from the previously published version, in order to complete the notes as far as possible and to bring the section to a conclusion. In order to maintain the integrity of the text, a certain amount of overlap between sections 3 and 4 was unavoidable.

The first three sections of the Epilogue review the arguments of the original book in the light of other historians' criticisms and new research. Mason evidently planned to write three further essays which would expand the original book substantively and chronologically, as well as interpretively. Only the first of these essays, entitled '1939–45', was completed; it appears here as section 4 of the Epilogue. This text was an early draft and lacked full notes, but appeared more or less complete as an essay. In preparing it for publication, I have integrated the author's marginal notes where appropriate, and I have attempted to render the references as completely as possible from his preliminary jottings. No texts for the remaining two essays – one provisionally titled 'Attitudes and Experience' and the other a comparison of Nazi Germany and Fascist Italy – were found, and presumably they were never started. Preliminary notes on the 'Attitudes and Experience' essay show that Mason planned to divide this discussion into three parts: 'Generations'; 'Work, Income, Household, Wives'; and 'Depth of Left Commitment pre-1933'. (The reader interested in Mason's approach to the comparative history of Nazism and fascism can consult two of his previously published essays: 'Massenwiderstand ohne Organisation. Streiks im faschistischen Italien und in NS-Deutschland', in Ernst Breit (ed.), *Aufstieg des Nationalsozialismus, Untergang der Republik, Zerschlagung der Gewerkschaften*, Cologne, 1984, and 'Whatever Happened to "Fascism"?', *Radical History Review*, no. 49, Winter 1991, pp. 89–98, reprinted in Thomas Childers and Jane Caplan (eds.), *Re-evaluating the Third Reich*, New York, 1993, pp. 253–62.)

John Broadwin translated the original text, except for Chapter 2, which was translated by Sara Lennox. I am grateful to both for their insightful translations and willingness to assist in a complex editorial process. I would also like to thank Volker Berghahn and Michael Geyer for help with some troublesome references; Pamela Swett and Jessica Reynolds for revising the Bibliography; and Jeanmarie Alls, Allyn Bensing and Lorraine Kirschner for assistance with typing. I could not have completed my work on the project without the support and friendship of Simonetta Piccone Stella and Ursula Vogel.

Editor's Acknowledgements

Tim Mason's executors (Simonetta Piccone Stella, Raphael Samuel, Ursula Vogel and myself) owe a tremendous debt of gratitude to those of his friends and colleagues whose contributions funded this translation. Without their generosity, the book could not have been published. We hope that they will see in this translated and expanded version of Tim's work a fitting tribute to the memory of a distinguished and much-loved scholar and teacher.

Volker and Marion Berghahn
Renate Bridenthal
Dieter Buse
Roger Chickering
Frederick Cooper
Geoff Eley
Richard Evans
Gerald Feldman
P. Foster
Celia Fox
Robert Gellately
Michael Geyer
John Gillis
Victoria de Grazia
Atina Grossmann
Bernard and Jane Guyer
J.C. and G. Harriss
Peter Hayes
Patricia Hilden
Jonathan Hyslop
David Kahn
Cora Kaplan

Carolyn Kay
Paul Kennedy
Ian Kershaw
Barbara Miller Lane
Magali Sarfatti Larson
Vernon Lidtke
Charles Maier
Arno Mayer
David Midgley
David Morgan
Jeremy Noakes
Mary Nolan
Dietrich Orlow
David Painter
Robert Paxton
Andrew Purkis
Jim Reed
Eve Rosenhaft
David Schoenbaum
Henry Ashby Turner, Jr
Alan Wigley

Versions of several sections of the book have previously appeared in different form, and permission to draw on these versions here is gratefully acknowledged: Introduction to English edition as 'Ends and Beginnings', in *History Workshop Journal*, no. 3, Autumn 1990, pp. 134–50; Chapter 2 as 'National Socialism and the Working Class, 1925–May, 1933', in *New German Critique*, no. 11, Spring 1977, pp. 49–93; Epilogue, section 3, as 'The Domestic Dynamics of Conquest: A Response to Critics', in Thomas Childers and Jane Caplan (eds.), *Reevaluating the Third Reich*, New York: Holmes and Meier, 1993, pp. 161–89.

From the standpoint of the existing (capitalist) social order, the National Socialist State is stronger than the liberal state, and it is irrelevant whether the owners of the means of production and property rule directly, i.e., politically; or indirectly, without wielding visible political power; or are even politically mutilated, but allow their economic power to operate like a natural force.

Bertolt Brecht, *Platform for Leftist Intellectuals*

War is nothing more than an evasion of the responsibilities of peace ... The contradiction between nationalism and socialism is implicit in the contradiction between war and peace. A 'triumphant' regime, successful in its foreign policy, need not concern itself with domestic reform.

Thomas Mann, *The Coming Victory of Democracy*

Preface to the German Edition

Timothy W. Mason

This book is a revised version of my introduction to the documentary collection titled *Arbeiterklasse und Volksgemeinschaft: Dokumente und Materialien zur deutschen Arbeiterpolitik, 1936–1939* (Opladen: Westdeutscher Verlag, 1975).

For this revision, I have almost completely rewritten and considerably expanded Chapter 2. In addition, I have used this opportunity to make a number of minor improvements and to supplement the Bibliography. To a large degree, though, the book still remains an introduction. It is, of course, a self-contained and coherent whole, to the extent that the main points of the narrative and the argument emerge clearly even without the documents. I hope, however, that the reader will be inspired to go to the collection of source documents, for they provide the kind of comprehensive, detailed and graphic picture of the social history of National Socialist Germany that no scholarly monograph can adequately reproduce. This is why the chapter notes refer not to the original document and its location, but rather to source materials published in *Arbeiterklasse und Volksgemeinschaft*: For example, 'Cf. Doc. 154' means that Document No. 154 can be found in that collection. To facilitate the use of these references, a complete index of the 244 documents and of the tables in the Statistical Appendix (Statistischer Anhang) published in the source book is included as an appendix to this volume.

This work is also an introduction in the sense that a comprehensive analysis of the economic and social history of Nazi Germany cannot be undertaken until many individual studies have laid the groundwork, for we still know very little about many aspects of this chapter of German social history. This is the reason I make repeated reference in the following chapters, as I did in *Arbeiterklasse und Volksgemeinschaft*, to the considerable gaps in our knowledge and to questions that still call for focused empirical research before any well-founded general interpretation can be ventured. Whether we are dealing with the history of farmers and rural workers, or the intricacies of price changes and living standards; whether we focus on the tricky but crucial questions of social mobility and population movement, or the structure of the family, the status of women, health and living conditions – there are still a great many topics which scholarship has barely touched, including such problem areas as the regime's tax and finance policies, the function and effect of its demagogic social and political policies, the status and effectiveness of individual Nazi institutions, such as Strength through Joy (*Kraft durch Freude*), Beauty of Labour (*Schönheit der Arbeit*), the National Vocational Competition (*Reichsberufswettkampf*), and so on. Finally, we must above all study the working class in the context of the production process, meaning not only that corporations and companies must make their archives more accessible to scholars, but that we must also learn better to appreciate the importance of these materials for social history.

Hence, this work is to be considered a prolegomenon and an introduction. Yet the awareness of large gaps in our knowledge and thus of the tentative nature of any attempt at interpretation should not inhibit the historian from hypothesizing. It is, after all, hypotheses that enable us to identify major gaps in our knowledge and to properly prioritize those issues that have yet to be investigated. I therefore intend this 'introduction' to be a full-scale historical interpretation which seeks to establish a frame of reference but makes no claim to being definitive; on the contrary, I hope it will inspire further research and analysis.

The interpretation that is attempted below presupposes that class relations are *the* constitutive element in the history of industrialized capitalist states, and that where no account is taken of class, basic political and ideological phenomena remain unintelligible or fall victim to misinterpretation.

By 'working class' I do not mean a positivist abstraction or the sum of all wage-earners and their dependants as they are tallied in statistically rigorous (and not so rigorous) national censuses and economic surveys. In economic and social histories of the last hundred years the working class is viewed, on the one hand, as the victim of the developmental laws of capitalist production and distribution and, on the other, as individual human beings who because of shared experiences seek to defend their common interests (in the widest sense of the term). In this latter type of social history the concept of class is always the experiential condition of conflict and struggle; the working class can be defined only in terms of its struggle against the ruling classes. Thus the historian is obliged to try and understand it from the perspective of this dynamic conflict.

Both of these interpretations are tightly interwoven into the history of the working class. However, it is not the intention of this work to get involved in reconciling them. In the present connection the use of the term 'working class' does not imply a commitment to any one theory: class, in the dual sense noted above, is simply a tool of the historian. It should be emphasized that the German working class, as the workers themselves defined it during their struggle against the ruling classes and the state, was not coterminous with the labour organizations that were destroyed in 1933, and it did not continue to exist solely in exile abroad or within persecuted political opposition groups inside Germany. As for those who were silenced or who gave up the struggle after 1933, we know precious little about the memories they retained of political parties, trade unions or workers' councils, or of their lost hopes for a socialist, democratic or at least peaceful future. But the documentary evidence we do have indicates the powerful persistence of the memories, past hopes and experiences of the working class.

We are concerned here primarily with two aspects of the class struggle: the unorganized, daily struggle of the workers over wages and working conditions; and the mounting repression by the ruling classes and the state. The latter aspect – class warfare as conducted from above – is treated in particular detail in the chapters that follow. This is in line with one of the basic characteristics of the Nazi system of government, that is, that the working class was defined during these years through its intensified exploitation and repression; in a certain sense, the working class was shaped by what was done to it. It is precisely the state's labour and social policy (*Sozialpolitik*) and Nazi propaganda – both of which seemed to deny the very existence of the working class – that, upon closer examination, reveal its special status, its all too precarious survival after 1933. From its inception to its demise, the regime of the Third Reich acted as though the working class was something special, with its own particular experiences and interests: experiences and interests which might one day serve as the basis for collective action that could imperil the system. This is clearly reflected in the documents on social and economic policy collected in the source book, which enable us to identify the working class as an entity and to study its behaviour, even though it was prevented during this period from engaging in any political activity.

The dynamic relationship among classes may have changed as a result of the elimination of the working-class parties and trade unions, yet the relationship itself continued to have a decisive influence upon politics. As both a target of repression and an object of fear on the part of those in power, the working class played a crucial role in the history of the Third Reich. Neither fear nor repression were incidental or mysterious components of the regime's policies: they were an integral part of the system's economic structure, a natural and necessary outgrowth of the preceding history of the labour movement and of German capitalism. It is here, in this one-sided and yet fierce struggle, not in abstract definitions or labyrinthine theories, that we must seek to find the German working class of the 1930s.

I spent the most important period in preparing this study as a research assistant at the Zentralinstitut für sozialwissenschaftliche Forschung (formerly the Institut für politische Wissenschaft) of the Free University of Berlin, which published my documentary collection as Volume 22 of its series. No author could wish for more active support than I received from the Institute. First and foremost, I would like to express my gratitude to Gilbert Ziebura, who, in his capacity as director of the Historical Section of the Institute, facilitated the publication of this work, and upon whose advice, patience, and support I could always rely. Of crucial importance was the considerable editorial assistance I received from Frauke Burian and Albrecht Schultz at every stage in the preparation of this book. I would also like to express my thanks to Ursula Thilo, director of the Institute's library, and to her colleagues for their generous and knowledgeable support. Finally, I am deeply obliged to the Institute for granting me permission to issue this revision of my introduction as a separate publication.

I am grateful to my many colleagues for their suggestions and comments. The commencement of this work was greatly encouraged as a result of my discussions with James Joll and Alan Flanders. Friedrich Kahlenberg, Rudolf Vierhaus, David Schoenbaum, Klaus Hildebrand, Lutz Niethammer, and Dörte Doering read portions of the manuscript, forcing me to hone a number of my arguments. This book would not have been completed without the committed and critical support of my wife, Ursula Vogel.

Last but not least, I would like to thank the archivists of the Federal Archives (Bundesarchiv) and the German Central Archives (Deutsches Zentralarchiv); they were always ready to respond to my numerous requests and facilitate access to source material. Their broad knowledge and constant readiness to help cause me to look back fondly to my time spent in the archives.

List of Abbreviations

ADAP	Akten zur Deutschen Auswärtigen Politik
ADGB	Allgemeiner Deutscher Gewerkschaftsbund; German Trade Union Federation; Free Trade Unions
AwI	Arbeitswissenschaftliches Institut (of the DAF)
BA Koblenz	Bundesarchiv Koblenz
BA/MA Freiburg	Bundesarchiv/Militärarchiv Freiburg
DAF	Deutsche Arbeitsfront; German Labour Front
DNVP	Deutschnationale Volkspartei; German National People's Party
Doc.	Document
DRA	Deutscher Reichsanzeiger und Preussischer Staatsanzeiger
DVO	Durchführungsverordnung; executive order
DZA Potsdam	Deutsches Zentralarchiv Potsdam
Gestapa	Geheimes Staatspolizeiamt; Secret State Police Office
Gestapo	Geheime Staatspolizei; Secret State Police
GNP	Gross National Product
GPSA	Geheimes Preussisches Staatsarchiv
ILR	International Labour Review
IMGH	Internationaler Militärgerichtshof Nürnberg (International Military Tribunal, Nuremberg)
IML/ZPA	Zentrales Parteiarchiv im Institut für Marxismus-Leninismus beim ZK der SED
KdF	Kraft durch Freude; Strength through Joy
KPD	Kommunistische Partei Deutschlands; Communist Party of Germany
LAA	Landesarbeitsamt

List of Abbreviations

OKW	Oberkommando der Wehrmacht
NSBO	Nationalsozialistische Betriebszellen-Organisation; National Socialist Factory Cell Organization
NSDAP	Nationalsozialistische Deutsche Arbeiterpartei; National Socialist German Workers' Party
NS-Hago	Nationalsozialistische Handwerks-, Handels- und Gewerbeorganisation
NSV	Nationalsozialistische Volkswohlfahrt
RAM	Reichsarbeitsministerium; Reich Labour Ministry
R. Arb. Bl.	Reichsarbeitsblatt
Rep.	Repertorium
RFM	Reichsfinanzministerium; Reich Finance Ministry
RGBl.	Reichsgesetzblatt
RVA	Reichsverteidigungsausschuss; Reich Defence Committee
RWM	Reichswirtschaftsministerium; Reich Economics Ministry
SA	Sturmabteilung; Stormtroopers (of NSDAP)
SD	Sicherheitsdienst; Security Service (of SS)
SPD	Sozialdemokratische Partei Deutschlands; Social Democratic Party of Germany
SS	Schutzstaffel (of NSDAP)
Stat. Anhang	Statistischer Anhang; Statistical Appendix (to *Arbeiterklasse und Volksgemeinschaft*)
Stat. Handbuch	Statistisches Handbuch
Stat. Jahrbuch	Statistisches Jahrbuch
Vertrauensrat	Council of Trust
VO	Verordnung; decree
WTB	Wolff's Telegraphisches Büro

Introduction to the English Edition

All good history writing begins at the end. However artfully it may be disguised, however unthinkingly it may be assumed, the end of the story is there at the beginning. Where the end is judged to lie in time, what its character is, how it is defined – in taking these decisions about any piece of work, historians necessarily make their judgement about the general significance of their particular theme or period. And this judgement in turn determines where they start. If the end of the Third Reich was Hitler's suicide in the air-raid shelter of the Reich Chancellery on 30 April 1945, if the significance of the Third Reich lay in his personal predominance, in the mark which he stamped upon the politics of Germany, Europe, the world, then the story must begin with his birth. If the end of the Third Reich was Auschwitz, if the great fact about Nazi rule was genocide, the story must begin at the latest with the development of modern anti-Semitism in the 1870s. If the end of the story is the elimination of the German nation state after 1945, if the historical significance of National Socialism lay in the fact that it was German, the beginning must be taken back still further, at least to the failure of the national liberal revolution of 1848, probably to the Reformation and the foundation of Prussia. If, on the other hand, the end of the story was the military and political defeat of European fascism in 1945, if the significance of Nazi rule lay in defining an 'epoch of fascism' (Nolte) which was characterized above all by distinctive attitudes towards politics and public life, then the beginning is the emergence of fascist political groups in the immediate aftermath of the First World War.

Two further and quite different schools of thought doubt whether the history of National Socialism really has a chronological end and suggest that it is part of an unfinished story. If the real import of the Third Reich lay in the breakthrough of a completely new type of modern dictatorial politics – totalitarianism – historical understanding must be informed by an awareness that this form of domination can recur, under different guises, in all modern societies. The story must then begin with the first development of those specifically modern forms of political activity which contribute to the possibility of totalitarian rule – mass participation in politics, the rapid communication of political ideas, the emergence of powerful political organizations, and so on – developments which took shape in most European countries in the last two decades of the nineteenth century. The history of the Third Reich is also part of a possibly unfinished story if its real import is located in the class struggle. On this reading the imposition of fascist rule is a political alternative generated by major crises of industrial capitalism and by violent class conflict, which serves the function of both rescuing and developing further the modern capitalist economic system by means of wars of imperial expansion. Such a need could recur. The beginning of this story goes back to the first major political and economic crises of modern capitalism, to 1848 once more, but this time to the 1848 of Karl Marx and Louis Napoleon.

These examples are intended simply to illustrate the nature of the problem. The problem is not peculiar to writing about National Socialism and fascism: in a more or less acute form it faces all historians. Underlying the differences between the various histories which we have, for example, of the British working class or the British Empire, are different judgements about the end of the respective stories, and these judgements largely determine where each story begins, and what it is about – which themes are given particular significance. Was the British Empire a prelude to the national independence of the colonies (to the formation of new nation states), or was it a prelude to neocolonial economic exploitation? If it was a prelude to both, which of these endings matters more? Did the first stage of the making of the English working class end with Chartism, in the sense that later developments were new departures, or was there a continuity of causes, goals and forms of action from the 1830s to the formation of the Labour Party? These questions are of the same kind as those posed above about National Socialism. In each case, the answer about the end of the story in question will inform the beginning of the work, and strongly influence its structure and its interpretation. But historians of modern Britain can, and often do, get by without self-consciously posing themselves this kind of question. The high degree of continuity in modern British political history, without civil wars, revolutions or coups, has helped to nurture an indifference or scepticism towards questions of this kind, a distinctive admixture of professional scholarly caution and intellectual sloth (philistinism) which is hostile to reflection about the framework within which a work of history is written. Beginnings and ends seem very indistinct, the middle ground large and rich, wherever one stands in time. There are strong pressures, strong temptations to let the big questions look after themselves, or to leave them to the collective responsibility of the profession at large, whose accumulating wisdom will (perhaps) in time assign a place and significance to individual pieces of research. Many English historians write as though they were contributing to a mosaic, for which there is no design.

There are many intellectually compelling reasons for not writing history in this way. The approach skates over every important problem raised by modern theories of knowledge; the particular subject which is researched is not conceived of as part of a whole social, economic and political system, but is left to stand on its own; and the precision of the research becomes the main yardstick for assessing the objectivity of historical work, with the consequence that the ideological presuppositions which determine the choice of most topics of research are rarely considered by the individual historian or remarked upon by colleagues. What is missing is discussion of the meanings of past human experience, and how we can interpret it. Methodology is better practised than preached, and others have written more exactly than I can about the theoretical and philosophical issues involved in trying to write history (e.g. Jürgen Habermas, E. H. Carr and Pierre Vilar). Historians do better to try to work them out in their own specific studies, than to write about them as general issues. But it must be emphasized that the questions of ends and beginnings, and therewith the question of definition, are simply inescapable for the historian of Nazi Germany. Their priority is beyond taste, temperament or argument. While many historians of England have proved, at least to their own satisfaction, that it is possible to write about many aspects of the social and cultural development of the country in the nineteenth century, without even noticing that Britain was the greatest imperial power in the world (because this did not seem to be directly relevant to their own particular topic; the absence of mind with which the Empire was acquired has been inherited by its scholars), such myopia is quite impossible in the case of National Socialism. There is no aspect of the history of the movement and its supporters, no aspect of the history of Germany under Nazi rule that can have historical meaning, unless it is firmly related to the end of the story – however that end may be defined and described, wherever it may be located. This is so, not only because the Third Reich was a total dictatorship, which, by virtue of the comprehensive political power which it exercised brought all spheres of public life into some sort of relationship with each other – after 1936 people were authoritatively told, for example, that what they chose to eat was directly relevant to the development of Germany's military and economic power. The imperative to assess the whole is above all a moral and political imperative. The suffering and destruction of life that the Nazi regime brought about was on so vast a scale and of such novel quality, that any study of a part of the story that fails to confront this central fact must, at least by implication, trivialize the whole. If this study of the working class in Germany were a piece of labour history in the conventional sense, it would be an intellectual, moral and political evasion, however accurate it might be in detail. This obligation to attempt to interpret the whole through one of its constituent parts is not, in the end, different in kind from that which faces all historians working on all subjects. It is just more massively obvious. Casting a small, finely finished stone onto a heap which might one day transform itself into a mosaic is here an unmistakable capitulation. Elsewhere this is just less obviously the case.

The moral and political obligation to interpret the whole must not be confused with the task, now almost completed, of assigning moral and juridical responsibility for specific crimes. The latter approach focuses of necessity upon the intentions and actions of individuals. It is clearly nonsensical to exclude this dimension and to think of Nazi politics simply in terms of the working out of blind impersonal forces, but to concentrate solely upon individual responsibility both narrows and confuses our understanding. The causes of great historical changes are never the same as the intentions of the actors, however powerful they may have been; as a system of domination and conquest the Third Reich was more than the sum of its specific crimes, and the categories of individual moral responsibility are of only limited use in trying to account for the conditions which made policies of military aggression and genocide possible. The moral and political obligation of the historian has a broader and much less well defined focus. It is an obligation to the millions who were shot, gassed, crippled, tortured, imprisoned, uprooted, and, if the story is indeed unfinished, to people anywhere who may in the future be victims of another organized mass destruction of life.

This is the reason why the debate about the end and the essential character of National Socialism is no mere scholastic dispute. The debate is the form in which the discussion about the precise nature of the historian's moral and political obligation is cast and furnishes the vocabulary in which judgements are made. For the obligation is not an invitation to moralize about the past, but a command to understand in the broadest possible context. Understanding and explaining are themselves moral and political acts, and the communication of better interpretations of past history is in principle capable of modifying the grounds on which moral and political choices can be made in the future. These last words are chosen particularly carefully, for it is of course not the case that expert knowledge and understanding are in any sense a substitute for or superior to moral and political choices, nor that such choices can be reduced to questions resolvable by a special competence. But in the complex modern social order with its dense network of interdependencies between different sectors of public life, these choices must be heavily mediated by difficult calculations of probable consequences: the road to 1933 in Germany was paved with many intentions, which many people now, both in Germany and outside, consider good.

Thus a great deal hangs on where the story begins and where it ends. The meaning of the campaign of death, destruction and terror which the Nazi regime unleashed upon the world differs greatly, according to where the beginning and where the end is placed. Was it the most brutal chapter to date in the history of modern capitalist imperialism? Was it the culmination of generations of European anti-Semitism? Did it mark the conclusion, perhaps the necessary conclusion of specifically German political traditions? Could something like it recur? Or does the Third Reich confront us as an absolutely unique (in the trivial sense, everything in history is unique) historical phenomenon, which was wholly dependent for its development on a singular conjunction of long-term social change, short-term political and economic crises, of the legacy of the First World War and the presence of the one man, Hitler, who alone was able both to orchestrate and to set his personal stamp upon the whole? Historians do not agree about the answers to these questions, and they thus invest National Socialism with different political and moral meanings. From this it follows that they differ in the significance which they attach to the economic, administrative or military aspects of recent German history and in their assessment of the personal role of Hitler and his aims. They focus their attention and efforts on the different questions which seem to them to be of greatest importance in interpreting the whole phenomenon, and they often put different constructions upon the same piece of evidence. These basic disagreements will continue; they will not be resolved, first because the processes of research and argument are fundamentally open-ended, and second because the disagreements, like all such historical debates, contain an irreducible ideological component – the historian's own society (narrower and wider) and his perception of his role in society will always inform the questions that he asks and the modes of argument that he adopts in exploring these questions.

We need an end before we can begin. The history of the Third Reich as written hitherto offers many different ends, more than have been sketched in above. It is not a matter simply of choosing among them, for not all of them are mutually incompatible; modifications are possible and the attempt can be made to construct new versions. This part of the work is both inescapable and always provisional; abstinence and conclusiveness of proof are both impossible. But provisional conclusions are not wholly arbitrary. The provisional picture of the whole must be constantly open to modifications demanded by the study of the parts; and its validity will depend upon how comprehensively it can encompass, order and make intelligible all of the relevant parts. It is open both to empirical checks and to criticism on grounds of faulty reasoning.

This introduction is not going to take the form of yet another critical review of all the different possible approaches to the subject. The task of acknowledging intellectual debts and of pointing to the inadequacies of some views concerning the ends of National Socialism will be attempted in passing. This strategy has been chosen in the belief that the appropriateness of general historical theories needs above all to be demonstrated through the writing of history, rather than argued out at the level of theoretical discussion. These are not, of course, alternative methods of working and thinking: prior to the stage of writing, theoretical argument and the detailed reconstruction of past realities are complementary parts of a single intellectual effort. But in the presentation of historical work, the theoretical argument should be no more (and no less) than a visible ground-plan, sufficiently clear for readers always to be able to keep their bearings as they move through the different rooms of the completed structure, but not an independent set of outbuildings through which it is necessary to pass in order to reach the main structure. In terms of composition, the theoretical prolegomenon is a distraction, the more so if its main purpose has to be to invalidate general arguments or interpretations other than those actually adopted. These arguments are better conducted in other publications. Repeated reference to these debates over general interpretation ought to suffice as one type of check on the arbitrariness of the specific interpretation put forward; the other check is the adequacy of the account offered to the evidence available – are there omissions, misreadings, mistaken assessments of the importance of some themes? The discussion will go on. It is both a political and moral discussion and a set of rational arguments about the internal coherence of different approaches to the subject and about the relationship between evidence and interpretation. It can only attain its full political and moral import it if is conducted as a rational discussion in this sense.

The organizing principle of National Socialist politics was competition and struggle. That human life consisted of eternal struggle and competition and derived its meaning from struggle and competition was the basic axiom of Nazi thought and practice. It was the only ideological axiom that consistently informed all political practice. This seems to be the right way to formulate the observation, for it was not the case here that an 'idea' was systematically and self-consciously translated into political practice, or that an ethic of struggle and competition was enforced upon the German social and political system. Rather, the axiom was a practical assumption, a self-validating mode of experiencing the world and of acting in it. It had the status of an obvious truth, both about the processes of all social life and about the goals of politics.

The language of struggle was the only language in which National

Socialists gave an account of themselves which was not wholly mislead-ing: it was neither metaphor nor propaganda, but the vehicle of an undis-guised self-image which was acted out in a compulsive manner. This fact is most clear in the one partial qualification which Nazi leaders appeared to make to their vision of life as struggle: in their incessant invocation of the community and solidarity of all Germans. This nation-al-racial community (*Volksgemeinschaft*) was in no sense a goal in itself. Its informal structure was the product of the 'selection of the fittest', and was determined by the struggle of competing interests, orga-nizations and individuals. The purpose of communitarian solidarity was the efficient prosecution of the struggle against other peoples and states, and the Nazi vision of the future held out no prospect of conditions under which this struggle for imperial superiority might come to an end and thus make way for the construction of a new community of all Germans as an independent goal of policy. Whatever one makes of Hitler's speculations before 1941 about a future war of world domina-tion against the United States, the conquest of 'living space' in European Russia was never even conceived of as being a finite goal, and Hitler ruminated repeatedly about the danger of degeneration setting in, if the German people should ever find themselves in a situation in which they did not have to struggle against adversaries.

Hitler's one denial that he contemplated a regiment of eternal war for the German people, in his *Second Book*, reads like a rhetorical flourish, designed to anticipate the criticism that this was indeed the necessary consequence of his conception of life and politics. It is clear now that it was. The community of all ethnic Germans was only a fighting commu-nity. It was not the antithesis of the organizing principle of struggle; on the contrary, in its structure, its purpose and in its distinctive lack of finite political goals, the people's community was the instrument of struggle, the proof of its realization as a principle. That this community could be made to appear to many Germans as the antithesis of the omnipresent struggle, as a practical and moral compensation for its rigours, is evidence merely of their own yearnings, of the skill of Nazi propaganda in playing on this source of self-deception, and of the great difficulty which all people who live under dictatorships have in making sense of the world they live in. It was not easy for them to appreciate that the reality was quite different from that invoked by the sentimental slogans.

The outcome of the struggle best demonstrates its absolute quality. It is not a hindsight-wise criticism of the Allied demand for unconditional surrender to remark that it defined the terms of the last stages of the war in a manner that was exactly appropriate to the dynamic of the Nazi struggle: 'All or nothing', 'total victory' (a meaningless phrase, describing a strictly inconceivable goal) or 'total defeat' had been the sole alternatives around which Hitler's thinking revolved since long before the war-aim of unconditional surrender was agreed by Churchill and Roosevelt at Casablanca in January 1943. This conclusion to the war was not simply forced upon the Nazi leadership. Even if it had been, the precise form of the concluding stages would be no less revealing of the origins and character of the struggle. The manner in which defeat is experienced is always revealing in this sense; the extreme pressures of certain defeat strip regimes and individuals down to the bare skeleton of irreducible perceptions, motives and modes of action. Under these pressures the Nazi regime fell apart at the centre. Of solidarity, dignity, unity of purpose in defeat there was no trace. The bitter institutional and personal conflicts within the leadership, which in the past had done so much to drive the regime forward to ever greater achievements, burst through the constraints which Hitler's authority placed upon them. The latent incoherence and barely balanced rivalries at the centre of the Third Reich broke through to the surface, and the last weeks were weeks of intrigue, confusion, mutual recrimination and boundless hate and disillusionment; old scores were finally settled.

Where in the past these modes of political action (leavened with ambition) had been the raw material of policy-making, pushing the regime as a whole into a process of cumulative radicalization, there could no longer be any outcome in terms of policy. The fact of rivalry and struggle within the leadership stood alone, naked of any higher purpose. Speer contemplated assassinating Hitler, and then did his best to subvert the order that the retreating German forces should scorch the earth and destroy the means of survival for the population. (His willingness to tell Hitler that he had acted in this way on 23 April 1945, and Hitler's acceptance of this insubordination, without reproach or retribution, was one of the very few moments of honesty and elementary human sympathy among the Nazi leaders in these last weeks.) Göring, indecisive to the last, asked Hitler's permission to sue for peace. Bormann then finally settled scores with Göring by persuading Hitler to dismiss him from all his offices and have him arrested for treason. Five days later, on 28 April, when the Red Army was already fighting within the city of Berlin, news came through to the bunker that Himmler had been conducting unauthorized negotiations with the Western powers. He too was denounced, and stripped of all his posts, and, in an act which throws as much light as any other on the pattern of relations among the leading Nazis, Hitler ordered two fliers to leave Berlin and arrest Himmler; distrust spilled over into surreal vengeance and his adjutant in Berlin was shot. Of Hitler's old guard only two men stayed with him and maintained his confidence to the end: Goebbels and Bormann. But these two were acting out their own particular roles, not trying to bring order into the process of ultimate defeat. Goebbels, propagandist to the last, instinctively began to stage-manage the inferno in Berlin in order to turn it into a media-event which would, he hoped, inspire later generations; and Bormann continued compulsively to eliminate all rivals for supreme political influence in the Reich, even as the Reich was reduced to ill-defended and scattered patches of rubble. 'Disloyalty and betrayal have undermined resistance throughout the war', proclaimed Hitler in his last message to the armed forces, and General Jodl, one of the men closest to him until 22 April 1945, noted that Hitler 'spoke all the time of treachery and failure; of corruption in the leadership and in the ranks'.

Self-exculpation, the need to pass responsibility for defeat on to others, was only a minor motif in these ruminations; what they document much more powerfully is the utter lack of sympathy and mutual respect of leading Nazis for each other. Their most powerful bond had been the corporate self-aggrandizement of the Third Reich, on which their individual self-aggrandizement rested. Competition had always been the essence of this bond, and it was overlaid mainly by the prospect of success, less reliably by varying degrees of personal devotion to Hitler on the part of the other leaders, and not at all by a totally abstract rhetoric of common loyalty (which served the function of a necessary self-deception, both public and private). The imminence of complete defeat deprived co-operation among the leaders of its purpose (individual success) and deprived their disunity of its mask. At the end there was only rivalry, distrust and bitterness, an incoherent confusion utterly devoid of common purpose and even of common sentiment. Only Hitler's designation of Admiral Dönitz as his successor as Head of State and Supreme Commander allowed the – purely symbolic – ritual of surrender to be carried out, and it is most improbable that Hitler had this aim in mind when he made his choice of Dönitz. He may well have hoped that Dönitz would have the military authority necessary to continue resistance after the defeat, and the choice of an admiral was certainly yet a further act of vengeance against the army leaders, by whom he believed he had been consistently thwarted. The struggle *within* the Third Reich went on until the very end, and indeed, as we shall see shortly, beyond the end. It was all that was left.

At the peripheries of its networks of power, the dissolution of the Third Reich conformed to similar, if less dramatic, patterns. While escape and self-preservation were, for various reasons, not a realistic alternative for most of the top leaders, in the localities Party bosses were frequently observed quietly making off in their cars, taking with them the transportable fruits of office, and leaving behind them stirring injunctions to the people to resist to the last man. In this crisis, the ethic of leadership and responsibility, which the Party had so insistently proclaimed, ceded priority to that principle of struggle by which the local leaders had selected themselves; but it was now a simple struggle for survival, and the fittest were those who had cars, petrol and civilian clothes. Remarkably few of the functionaries, propagandists and policemen, who had owed their power in provincial Germany to the Nazi regime, showed any disposition to act heroically in its last defence. (Some of those who did, or who attempted to terrorize others into doing so, were forcibly restrained by the many anti-fascist resistance groups which sprang up in March-May 1945.)

Political and economic institutions continued to act according to type, playing the roles which they had carved out for themselves, or had been assigned, and unconcerned about the overall situation or the overall policy of the regime, in which context alone their particular activities might have made sense, or not. Thus in March 1945 the deputy head of one of the largest heavy industrial combines in the Ruhr reported to the head of the firm that the factories and offices had been destroyed; production had ceased, and he was writing from the cellars of the old administration building, where the board's grand piano and some of its wine had been saved; the workers no longer clocked on to clear the debris, but tried to save what they could of their own homes; in the preceding quarter, however, profits had remained satisfactory at 5 per cent. In April 1945 the chancellery of the NSDAP in Munich was still sending replacement membership cards, together with warnings about carelessness, to Party comrades who had lost them. The armed forces went on promoting men to higher ranks and, more obviously exemplary of the ethic of struggle, shooting deserters whom they could lay hands on and even holding courts-martial over those who managed to get away (this latter practice continued after the capitulation).

Such actions expressed something more than an over-adequate sense of duty, something more than the clinging to routines of men utterly disoriented by events: they threw into stark relief the complete fragmentation of politics under the dictatorship, that progressive disaggregation of the component parts of the power structure which the struggle for dominance within the regime had both fed on and accelerated. The businessman, the Party officials, the military officers were not thinking about the context of their actions, and this self-serving narrowness had long been tried and tested as the mentality most appropriate to the conflicts for power within the Third Reich. Someone else was looking after context, overall policy, the meaning of parts – just keep making the profits, issuing the Party cards, promoting the lieutenants and shooting the deserters, for there was no mercy for those who stopped or failed: someone else would push them to one side. The anticipated consequences of failure, inaction, lack of initiative, formed a powerful motive force in the politics of the Third Reich: the vague threat to each component institution that it would lose power, to each office-holder that he might be demoted (or worse), was among the most powerful mechanisms of competition within the Nazi system.

The mechanism was the more powerful for the fact that the threat was vague and the incentive to action thus unspecific. What was at stake here was not the capacity of an institution or an individual to execute orders, for frequently there were no orders. The component parts operated under a diffuse but heavy pressure to act, and because it was rarely clear precisely which action in any given situation would conform to the overall policies of the political leadership, self-defence against actual or potential competitors and self-aggrandizement at their expense was the one unquestionable goal of all such action. The vagueness of the pressure thus enhanced the disintegrative qualities of the struggle for predominance within the Nazi system: it spurred the component parts on to a restless dynamic activity and a harsh resilience, but the ends of this activity remained partial, self-serving and, in political terms, uncoordinated.

When they bothered to think about the question at all, the leaders of subordinate institutions could only hope that the leadership was moulding their actions into a coherent whole. Given the continuous overwhelming pressure of work on the particular tasks, and in the face of fragmentary but mounting evidence that the leadership was not fulfilling this function, most subordinate leaders preferred not to think about the question. They filtered out of their perceptions the problem of the larger purpose of their activities and got on with the job of competing, struggling. The utterly fragmented, robot-like activity of the various public agencies and business firms in the spring of 1945 was the grotesque finale of this internal struggle.

That the finale took this form in the domestic politics of the Third Reich was both a cause and a consequence of the external struggle. The complex relationship between the competition for power within the Third Reich, and the struggle of the Third Reich against the other powers and people of Europe, will be discussed in detail later. In this introductory context one fact about the external struggle is of overwhelming significance: it was fought through to a hopeless destructive conclusion, as an end in itself. The Second World War was lost for Germany before it was started. An awareness that it was lost forced itself upon the consciousness of individual military and political leaders by stages from late 1941 on, in a process of evaluation which was made random by the impossibility of conducting informed and co-ordinated discussions of the situation. It was not only that any such perspective upon policy-making and strategy were ruled out by Hitler's authoritative veto on all defeatist talk, for Hitler could enforce this veto only because the disintegrative competition for power had by now gone so far that no institutional framework now existed within which the responsible military, political and economic leadership groups could possibly collaborate in assessing the deteriorating situation in a comprehensive manner. By January 1945, with the failure of the Wehrmacht's Ardennes offensive and the simultaneous beginning of the massive thrust to the west by the Red Army, it was obvious to everyone in Germany that military defeat within a matter of months was absolutely certain.

Whatever ambiguities may attach to the interpretation of German strategy during 1944, it is only possible to make sense of it after January 1945 on the assumption that hopeless defiance, struggle to the last man and boy, had become the overt and single goal of 'policy'. Military resistance was a goal on its own account. It served no specific, defined strategic or political goals. The only point was that the Third Reich should go down fighting, taking down with it to death and destruction as many Allied troops and as many German troops and civilians as possible. It was a 'policy' of revenge against both the victors and the subject German people. Hitler was determined that, in its death throes, the Third Reich should prove him right on one point, which had been a central preoccupation throughout his political career: there should be no repeat of November 1918, no revolutionary stab-in-the-back, no capitulation. Resistance to the bitter end would prove something about the regime, prove that at least in this respect it was superior to the Wilhelmine Empire. Hence his boundless bitterness over the attempts of Göring and in particular of Himmler to negotiate a surrender to the Western powers; hence the use of methods of open terror by flying 'courts-martial' to conscript people off the streets for the last defence of Berlin. Defying the odds, preventing capitulation brought out in a final and unmistakable form Hitler's murderous contempt for the people whom he had flattered as a master race: because the imminent defeat had proved that the German people were not worthy of victory and thus not worthy of their leaders, millions more of them than necessary were to die, in order to prove that the National Socialist regime at least had the resilience to struggle to the very end. If the chimera of total victory was impossible, at least defeat could be total. The last struggle was a struggle against capitulation – those Germans who wanted to capitulate (whether they were footsoldiers, generals, political leaders, bishops) fused with the Allied armies into a single enemy of the regime.

There is a sense in which this reading of the last months of the war is 'beyond politics', and it is indeed not possible on the basis of the evidence to attribute to Hitler and his advisers any intelligible political purposes in their conduct of Germany's resistance. The last intelligible hope of this kind (and it was no more than a hope) was, that by concentrating the remaining armed forces heavily on the western front, the German leaders would be able to inflict such heavy losses on the United Kingdom and the United States that these powers would be willing to sue for a separate peace. (This attempt to bludgeon the Western powers into negotiations was perhaps coupled with the threat, at least implied, that this disposition of German forces would make it relatively easy for the Red Army to overrun the whole of Germany from the north-east: a development which could not be in the interests of the United States and the United Kingdom.) The defeat of the Ardennes offensive destroyed this hope. After this, speculations about the possibility of splitting the Allies continued to serve as short-lived morale-boosters in the bunker of the Reich Chancellery: Roosevelt's death on 12 April furnished one occasion, news of friction between the first American and Russian units which met at Torgau on the Elbe on 25 April another. But no consistent policy to this end can be discerned, for the end could only have been pursued after January 1945 by means of a complete capitulation to the Western powers (i.e. not to Russia). After Hitler's suicide Dönitz did try to inject some sort of rationale into the continued resistance of the German army, in that every day that the fighting was prolonged enabled more refugees to flee from the feared and hated Russian forces towards the west; and it may well be that some army commanders had been quietly pursuing this goal for some time before 30 April. But there is no hint in the sources that this consideration ever impressed itself upon Hitler.

His personal role in conducting the last stages of the struggle was very great, and in a whole variety of ways he consistently emphasized the trans-political character of the struggle, its symbolic, destructive and self-destructive purpose. He refused to allow the redisposition of the remaining German forces in ways which would both have held up to the advance of the Red Army and facilitated the movement of refugees to the west. His insistence that every German unit should simply hold out where it was and resist to the last showed clearly that the demonstration of defiant struggle was more important to him than practical results. Not only did the German forces have no defensive strategy at all in 1945 (a large part of the army stayed locked up in Bohemia); where Hitler could get his way, it was not to employ pragmatic defensive tactics either. He repeatedly commanded offensive action against the flanks of the Russian armies which moved to encircle Berlin. Although these commands were frequently clad in a rhetoric of fantasy about turning the tables and securing victory, they are really just further evidence of the self-validating quality which Hitler attached to the spring of 1945 as though it were a matter not of military strategy and tactics, but of will-power; of the assertion of will in a situation which he knew to be utterly lost. This, together with a still unrequited desire for vengeance against the officer corps on account of the Stauffenberg bomb plot, explains his repeated outbursts of hysterical hatred against field commanders who retreated or failed to achieve the breakthroughs he had ordered. He was not in fact interested in the practical task of defending Germany as effectively as possible. In terms of his radical ethic of either/or, there was nothing worth defending once the war was lost militarily, and so there was no set of practical tasks to which the practical reason of the General Staff could be applied. Tactical arguments became treasonable if they advocated withdrawals. Defiance, not defence, was the goal, and for this reason the question of the costs and effects of specific military decisions was simply irrelevant. The only imperative was that the Third Reich should go down fighting, for struggle was the law of life. At least in the manner of its defeat, the Third Reich could prove the truth of this law.

That these were indeed the terms in which Hitler saw the defeat of Germany is proved conclusively by two further and closely related facts: by his scorched earth orders of September 1944, which were repeated in a more draconian form on 19 March 1945, and by his comments that the outcome of the war had shown the German people to be unworthy of victory. In Hitler's intentions, nothing was to be left behind to make the Allied victory worthwhile, and nothing to facilitate the survival of the unworthy conquered people. In a world of remorseless struggle between peoples this was the necessary and only proper form which defeat could take. It was right, logical, that the defeat should be absolute, the victory costly in lives and of little political or economic profit. The German people would disappear as a great actor on the stage of history in consequence of the defeat; no lesser role was worth contemplating, and there could thus be no valid argument for trying to preserve the amenities of life in the ruins of defeat. Worse, such hopes and efforts could only serve as a breeding ground for defeatism and capitulation. The law of struggle dictated that the German people destroy themselves and their means of livelihood as they were being destroyed by the enemy.

This programme for the end of the Third Reich was devoid of politics in the conventional sense. Hitler was not attempting to achieve specific finite goals in the spring of 1945, and he was not even attempting to guide and control the flow of events towards an end which is accessible to normal empathetic understanding. He was compulsively seeking comprehensive destruction and self-destruction for the Third Reich in battle. This was neither a sudden whim, nor is it proof of his failing mental and physical powers. The programme antedated the collapse of the Ardennes offensive and the elimination of the last hope of playing power politics to the regime's advantage. There are vague anticipations of the programme much earlier: in addresses and speeches in the later 1930s Hitler frequently invoked 'the destruction of Germany' as a possible outcome of Nazi policy, if (as it was then always understood) his policies did not secure adequate support from army or business leaders, or whoever. The turn of phrase is no less significant than talk in *Mein Kampf* about the elimination of the Jews. The words convey, in each case, not a set intention but the mental possibility of utmost radicalism. 'The destruction of Germany' was a possible alternative outcome in Hitler's mind of the unending struggle for domination in the world, long before it became a programme. Long before it became a reality, another then still quite hypothetical alternative had also been ruled out by him time and again, and with the greatest vehemence: the Third Reich would never be forced to capitulate by a stab in the back. The German people were to go on fighting by all possible means until they were totally overwhelmed amid the ruins of their country.

In order to establish fully the distinctive qualities of the last goalless struggle, it is worth considering in a schematic manner what policies Hitler and his advisers could conceivably have adopted after mid-January 1945. First, a policy of conventional military defeat could have been pursued; that is, German forces could have been committed to a few carefully chosen major defensive battles, which, if successful, would have made the further continuation of the war seem realistic, at least for a time, and which, if lost, would have made 'surrender with honour' an acceptable solution within the peculiar utilitarian terms of the military ethic. The political leadership could have placed their own lives at risk in these battles. A week before his suicide Hitler regretted that he had not adopted this line, and had not had the army defend his East Prussian headquarters at Rastenburg to the end in November 1944. After mid-January there is no trace of this sort of strategic-political thinking in Hitler's orders. Under the impact of his insistence that every defensive position be held at once, defensive strategy collapsed into incoherence. Which parts of Germany were to be defended, how and by which units, was never the subject of realistic or, even in intention, pragmatic, planning. The scheme of fighting to the end in the mountainous terrain of Bohemia, Bavaria and Austria was never revised, although it became more and more clear that the Red Army was heading for Berlin and that it could not be stopped. Meanwhile the largest and best-equipped sections of the German army were locked up in Bohemia and in Denmark and Norway, where there was very little fighting, or had been surrounded and left behind by the Red Army in Courland. Even the plans for the evacuation of the Reich government from Berlin remained completely uncertain – as late as 25 April it was unclear which ministers were going where.

This confusion was by no means entirely due to the surprising rapidity of the advance of the Allied forces, nor to the worsening transport situation within Germany. Army leaders repeatedly pointed out tactical and strategic alternatives to Hitler, which might have concentrated and thus strengthened the military effort. The confusion, which certainly accelerated the collapse, was due in the first instance to Hitler's lack of interest in a 'policy of military defeat'. He behaved consistently as though military defeat was inevitable and uninteresting, as though he was determined that the defeat should be much more than a military defeat. The only thing that mattered was the spirit of total resistance, something quite different from a policy of maximum or optimum military resistance.

After mid-January 1945 the only policy which would have served the welfare of the German people was a negotiated surrender on both fronts, but the regime was interested in the welfare of the German people only in so far as it helped them to prove the regime's contention that they did indeed constitute a master race. The contention had been disproved (according to the logic of the argument from struggle), thus it was proper that the people should go under in every way – be killed, starve, die of disease, have their homes and workplaces destroyed. If a general surrender was quite out of the question, a serious attempt to split the Allied camp promised certain military advantages and at least held out a possibility of political advantage (if not for Hitler's Nazi regime). This policy, which was advocated in one form or another by almost all of Hitler's senior advisors during the spring of 1945, would, in order to have been realistic, have had to start with military surrender on one of the two fronts. Guderian, Army Chief of Staff, put it forward to Ribbentrop in January 1945, and later both Ribbentrop and another top official suggested that the regime should try to make common cause with the Soviet Union, and overrun Western Europe together. Getting on to terms with the Western powers on a platform of anti-bolshevism was the more popular alternative among the Nazi leadership, and some quite ingenious suggestions were made about ways in which the regime could prove its good faith and force the hand of the Western Allies – like releasing all of their prisoners of war, but not Russian prisoners. Hitler never took any of these proposals seriously, and although he gave his assent to some of the feelers put out to the Western powers, he was never prepared to contemplate the big step of surrender on one front, which alone would have given the policy even a slight chance of success. In respect of the Western powers, Hitler and Ribbentrop persisted in their decade-long struggle to bludgeon the United Kingdom into a perception of where its 'true interests' lay, namely in a joint struggle with Germany against bolshevism. Only force, not concessions, would open English eyes to realities. Thus the hints dropped with various representatives of the Western powers in the spring of 1945 met with incomprehending and angry rejection. Perhaps Hitler was right in his assessment that no initiative of this kind could have split the Soviet Union and the Western powers after January 1945. When Himmler finally tried it on 24 April, Churchill and Roosevelt insisted that they would only contemplate a simultaneous surrender to their forces and to the Red Army.

By January the Allies knew that they had won the war militarily, and their governments were not seriously threatened by war-weary populations, who would be embittered by the refusal of a German offer to surrender on one front. Yet, many Russian, British and American soldiers were to die in the last four months of fighting. The German government could have made this seem less than necessary; there were uncertainties in the Allied camp about the political future of Central Europe, and surrender to one side would have created many extremely difficult problems for the Allies. If, for example, the German armies in the west had surrendered after the failure of the Ardennes offensive, would the British and American forces have been able to stop German troops being moved across to the eastern front? Would they have marched across Germany, in order to attack in the rear the German armies which were still resisting the Red Army? Hitler was not willing to take the decisions which would have posed these questions. Such a policy would have been a gamble. He may well have thought that the news of his willingness to surrender on one front would have completely undermined the will to resist on all fronts, including the will of the civilian population. But he had taken bigger risks than this in the past, and no utilitarian calculation indicated that any of the alternatives was especially promising. It was not a policy which he himself could execute – he would have had to disappear as Führer at a very early stage in any such negotiations, since neither Stalin nor Roosevelt nor Churchill would have been willing to do business with him personally, But he was anyway going to lose his power, and in all probability his life too, either by his own hand or in battle or, least likely, by the hangman's rope.

Is it possible, one must ask, that a few more desperate weeks of his own life were more important to him than the chance of contributing (by surrender to the Western powers and by his own disappearance) to the continuing, future struggle against Russian bolshevism? This is possible, but it seems unlikely. By this stage his own life was probably not particularly dear to him, for all decisions to commit suicide are, in one sense or another, long prepared. The problem was the partial surrender which this line required. Hitler's machiavellianism knew no other limits than this, but this stratagem was outside of his repertoire. He had never at any time used surrender of any kind, however transparently dishonest, as a ploy to enhance his power or to gain his ends. This was not a matter of honour or dishonour, but of compulsive conviction that the struggle must always be fought as a struggle. Mendacious reassurances, false promises, tactical withdrawals, compromises which could later be undermined and dis- avowed – all these were possible modes of struggle, but any surrender which involved even a partial loss of independence was ruled out. This basic feature of the Party's struggle for power within Germany before 1933 and of the rise of the Third Reich to predominance on the continent of Europe after 1933 was maintained intact to the end.

It is not possible to prove from Hitler's recorded statements in the spring of 1945 that this was indeed the reason why no serious attempt was made to avert total collapse by means of a machiavellian partial sur- render, but this interpretation does fit with the basic patterns of Hitler's political actions from 1923 on. Struggle was only possible if he – the movement, the country – was dependent upon and beholden to no supe- rior power. Better to risk defeat than to sacrifice that independence. So the war continued on both fronts. The failure of the regime to explore any possible alternatives to complete collapse and destruction brings out what can only be described as an underlying determination among the leadership to lose totally.

1

The Legacy of 1918 for National Socialism

The total war of the future will make demands on the people on a scale we can hardly imagine. The moral and physical efforts of the First World War, which already placed really heavy burdens on our German people, will be exceeded by far in a future war.

Colonel Georg Thomas, at the fifth meeting of the Chamber of Labour, 24 November 1936

If you demand only sacrifices from a people – something the First World War showed us with all possible clarity: Hold out, hold out, stick it out, stick it out! – that's all well and good, but there is a limit to the endurance of every individual, and naturally of every people also. It's just as with an iron girder or any structure that is supposed to support a load. There's a limit and when that limit has been reached everything breaks. And for us, that was 1918, November 9 to be precise. We can be sad about it and embittered, we may curse and swear; but the fact is that the men in power then forgot to compensate the people for the enormous strain of those four-and-a-half years, forgot on the other hand to inject new sources of strength, to pump in new strength again and again.

Robert Ley, at the fifth meeting of the Chamber of Labour, 24 November 1936[1]

In November 1936 there was an extraordinary exchange of views between two of the leading representatives of the 'Third Reich'. At a meeting of senior officials of the German Labour Front (*Deutsche Arbeitsfront*, or DAF), Colonel Georg Thomas, the head of the War Economy Staff (*Wehrwirtschaftsstab*) in the War Ministry and Robert Ley, the leader of the DAF, had an open debate on the principles of National Socialist social policy, which was unusually frank given the regime's normal style of government. Thomas painted a dark picture. In his view the preparation for and conduct of future wars would call for great sacrifices by the entire nation. Only through hard work and simulta-

1. *Doc. 1.*

neous massive cutbacks in consumption could the foundation be laid for Germany's second bid for world power. He felt that the leadership's main task was to make the people understand the need for these efforts. To do this, he believed, required the government to establish a basis of public confidence by committing itself to tell the people the truth at all times and never to shrink from admitting the existence of economic bottlenecks and set-backs. Thomas warned that the desire to establish domestic unity by glossing over the truth was a dangerous tactic; on the contary, the people in the long run would give the government high marks for being brutally honest with them. It was not for nothing that both these warnings were directed to the DAF, since this mass organization was increasingly pressing for an increase in the workers' standard of living.

Thomas's comments on the role of political 'enlightenment and education' were also patently critical of the policies of Germany's leaders in the First World War. In his impromptu rebuttal of this point Ley showed remarkable tactical skill. A readiness to sacrifice and make massive efforts, he said, was indispensable to the attainment of the Führer's foreign-policy objectives; however, the government for its part had to compensate the workers for the privations and exertions demanded, by offering them the opportunity to refresh their energies. Ley maintained that it was in this area – in the neglect of the need to attend to the care and welfare of working people – that the old Imperial regime had committed its gravest error. With a directness uncharacteristic of the Nazi leadership, Ley attributed the revolution of 1918 to the physical collapse of the civilian population – that is, to material causes – which he meant of course in a strictly subjective and non-political sense.

This exchange of views did not have any immediate practical consequences. Yet the topics addressed are of enormous importance in the history of Nazi Germany. They constitute a fruitful, perhaps the best, point of departure for an analysis of the regime's policy towards the working class. It can be shown, for example, that the experience of defeat in the First World War and of the 1918 November Revolution represented a turning-point in the careers of a number of the leaders of the National Socialist German Workers' Party (NSDAP). The conclusions they drew from these experiences would leave a lasting impression on the policies they pursued both before and after 1933. The national fixation on November 1918, in the form of the so-called stab-in-the-back legend, offered them unique access to segments of the electorate that could not have been forged into a bloc or won over to National Socialism by any other political issue confronting the Weimar Republic.[2]

2. Cf. E. Matthias, 'The Influence of the Versailles Treaty', in A.J. Nicholls and E. Matthias (eds.), *German Democracy and the Triumph of Hitler*, London, 1971.

Even more important here, however, is the question of the political and economic problems confronting the ruling classes of Europe at the end of the First World War. The Bolshevik Revolution in Russia, far more than the November Revolution in Germany, thrust into prominence the question of the relation between war and radical social change. This issue had been anticipated by the policies of the imperialist powers before 1914; after 1917/18 it had become a matter of urgent importance. It seemed as though the expansionist military policies of two empires had been defeated by those who had borne the brunt of the suffering caused by the war. Thus the leaders of the Nazi movement – who had pledged themselves from the first to military expansionism – were intensely interested in the problem of fashioning a political and social structure that would minimize the threat to their plans for waging aggressive war and avoid a repetition of November 1918.

Although this issue was seldom formulated as clearly by the regime's representatives and practically never discussed openly, we can show that policies affecting rearmament and war were always influenced by the spectre of November 1918. Ley's spontaneous reaction to Thomas's challenge indicates that the former was quite conversant with the issue. Whenever the relationship of the working class to National Socialism appeared problematical or called for clarification, the end of the First World War was always eagerly seized upon to provide examples and guidelines. It therefore seems fitting to examine in greater detail the significance of the November Revolution to the politics of National Socialism.

The stab-in-the-back legend, which the NSDAP and all other nationalist groups vigorously supported, is extremely important for an understanding of Nazi policy. As an explanation of the defeat and the subsequent revolution it was, of course, a grotesque distortion of the facts, conveniently serving the interests of the moment. However, viewed apart from the circumstances surrounding its origins and propagation, the myth does contain a half-truth, reflecting the real fact of the high tension that existed between working-class interests, traditions and goals, on the one hand, and the prosecution of aggressive war on the other. The way Hitler diagnosed these tensions illuminates important characteristics of Nazi political strategy. For those who were aiming at a second bid for world power, the interpretation of 1918 had a programmatic function. The programmatic thread in Hitler's criticisms of Wilhelmine foreign policy has often been noted; however, the fact that this aspect of Hitler's critique clearly derived from an examination of Imperial domestic policy has been given less attention than it deserves.

Hitler's interpretation of the 'collapse' (*Zusammenbruch*), as he called it, combined two different, basically antithetical views of history.

On the one hand, he used a kind of metahistorical analysis, according to which defeat and revolution were the inevitable results of long-range developments in German public life: urbanization, the decline in morals, materialism, the growing influence of the Jews, the arrogance of the upper classes, the weak will and inconsistencies of the political leadership of the Second Empire, he asserted, were the chief causes of the catastrophe. Aside from trying to show that he was 'educated', Hitler also used these high-sounding phrases borrowed from the lexicon of the cultural pessimists to further two political goals. First, he sought to disassociate National Socialism from the older conservative forces, which were bound to Imperial traditions. Second, and more important, he wanted to establish the need for a total political regeneration, for only if the collapse could be shown to be the result of profound causes could the need for a profound regeneration appear plausible.

Hitler's other interpretation of 1918, on the other hand, was neither logically nor factually connected to his metahistorical reflections. But it appears so often and with such violence in his writings and speeches that it surely reflects his deep-rooted convictions. To Hitler the cause of the long-term degeneration of the German people was the leadership of the German working-class movement – those 'cowards', 'shirkers', that 'treasonous party rabble', that 'gang of despicable and depraved criminals', those 'Jewish-Marxist wire-pullers'[3] who in the midst of war had laid the groundwork for the socialist revolution, thereby stabbing in the back a nation that was fighting for its very survival. This was the classic version of the stab-in-the-back legend. But by subscribing to this conspiratorial theory of the 'collapse', Hitler necessarily cast doubt on the metahistorical inevitability of 1918.

Still, this historical explanation did have an important political function. A political ideology that called for the complete regeneration and unification of the existing corrupt society without seeking to change or even question the material (i.e. economic, social and political) foundations of the existing order required an 'enemy' or 'scapegoat'. However, again it must be emphasized that Hitler himself was convinced that these 'enemies' were real; nothing could shake his belief that certain individuals were responsible for all the woes plaguing modern society.

Hitler never understood the contradiction between these two interpretations of history. On the contrary, given his view of human beings, which was characterized mainly by contempt for their lack of will and judgement, these two theories complemented each other and combined to form a single analytical and programmatic concept. He was convinced that the mass of people were infinitely 'malleable' when it came

3. Adolf Hitler, *Mein Kampf,* Munich, 1941, vol. 1, ch. 7, pp. 641–5.

to politics. Thus he believed, for example, that 'far and away the majority' of newspaper readers 'believes everything it reads'. Elsewhere in *Mein Kampf* he wrote, 'The absorptive capacity of the masses is very limited, their ability to comprehend paltry'.[4] This is why he assigned such overriding importance to the role of ideology (*Weltanschauung*) in history. This is reflected with particular clarity in those passages in *Mein Kampf* where Hitler describes the root cause of Wilhelmine Germany's degeneration as a necessary consequence of its lack of moral and ideological fibre. He notes the German people's 'general decadence, cowardice, lack of principle – in short, unworthiness', its 'moral and ethical poisoning', all of which in Hitler's eyes were symptoms of the lack of 'a clear-cut, uniformly accepted *Weltanschauung*'.[5]

On the other hand, since the people were infinitely gullible and political philosophies were easily susceptible to manipulation, Hitler viewed the 'rotten party-political swindlers of the people' – that is, individual persons and their message – as a signficant political threat. They could, he believed, systematically dupe and seduce their unsuspecting followers and should therefore be put down with force or, better yet, be liquidated.

With regard to the November Revolution, Hitler saw two reasons for the existence of a conspiracy to undermine the army and the home front. On the one hand the old Imperial government had been unwilling to crush the labour movement; and on the other it had lacked an ideology capable of replacing Marxist-pacifist internationalism. Thus Hitler bitterly blamed the Kaiser for having failed to grasp the opportunity to liquidate the SPD and the unions, while at the same time he claimed that the time to do so had not been particularly propitious: 'What did they intend to give the masses, if ... Social Democracy had been broken? There was not one movement on the scene with any prospects for success in attracting the great host of more or less leaderless working people.'[6] In an earlier essay Hitler had ridiculed the political naiveté of those who in the 1880s had believed that Bismarck's Anti-Socialist Law and its attendant policy of intimidation and repression would suffice to drive the working masses into the arms of the bourgeois parties.[7] In fact, it was the old ruling class's inability to develop a programme appealing to the masses that signalled its decline and created favourable conditions for revolutionary agitators, the result of which was November 1918.

It is tempting to interpret Hitler's casuistic argument as a purely propagandistic attempt to give legitimacy to his own movement by falling

4. Ibid., pp. 262, 198.
5. Ibid., pp. 250, 252, 292.
6. Ibid., p. 190.
7. Adolf Hitler, 'Warum musste ein 8. November kommen?', in *Deutschlands Erneuerung*, vol. IV, 1924, p. 207.

back upon history: If only there had been an NSDAP in 1878 or 1914...! Nevertheless, it is worth noting that the direction he took in domestic policy after 1933 corresponded strikingly with his historical analysis. The outstanding feature of that policy was the heedless intermingling of violent, manipulative repression with an exaggeratedly idealistic world view. Thus those very groups Hitler blamed for the mismanagement of the Empire and for their role in bringing about the November Revolution gained in terms of immediate practical relevance. Hitler's theory of history was certainly not devoid of purely opportunistic and even cynical elements; however, to the degree that it later became a dogma that shaped the regime's policies, it also offers a valuable insight into the nature of Nazi rule.

History had shown, then, that the first condition for avoiding a repetition of the stab-in-the-back legend was the liquidation of the German labour movement, the elimination of its leaders and functionaries, and the radical suppression of its organizations. The 'liberation' of the basically patriotic but 'malleable' German worker from the demoralizing ideology of the 'November criminals' was the *sine qua non* for the coming aggressive war. Thus the NSDAP's campaign tactics from 1928 to 1932 led directly into the subsequent strategy for seizing power, for not only was the propaganda campaign against the 'November criminals' important programmatically; it also created the domestic conditions to carry out this part of the Nazi programme. The restive members of the petty bourgeoisie, who played such an important role in crushing the working-class parties and the unions in early 1933, seem to have been motivated largely by the call to avenge the treason of November 1918.[8]

In any event, the omission of August 1914 was made good with unparalleled thoroughness in the spring of 1933. The total destruction of organized labour was followed by the elimination, through systematic acts of terror, of all underground resistance groups that sought to spread social democratic or communist ideas. In terms of its remorseless efficiency and brutality, the repression surpassed anything the labour movement had encountered up to that point. The massive use of police force is ample proof of the importance the regime attached to this aspect of its rule. It had to totally eliminate any renewed threat of subversion to the 'domestic front'. The repression thus tallied with the conclusions Hitler had drawn in the 1920s from his wartime experience – that revolutionary and pacifist agitators were to be 'mercilessly rooted out'.[9]

On the other hand, the Party leadership's political self-image was not greatly affected by the fact that, as late as 1933, nobody had any idea

8. Cf. below, Chapter 2.
9. Hitler, *Mein Kampf*, p. 185.

about how to create a new social order that could withstand the strains of another world war. There were simply no realistic plans. And none could be expected, considering the basic contradictions inherent in the Nazis' programme – contradictions arising out of the necessity of disenfranchising and exploiting the working class in order to prosecute a war, while at the same time demanding their total political loyalty. Still, we cannot dismiss as mere wishful thinking the new rulers' hope that the destruction of the labour movement would in and of itself create the basis for developing a patriotic national-racial community (*Volksgemeinschaft*), thereby obviating the need for any additional political or organizational measures. It was precisely in this connection, according to Hitler, that ideology was of crucial importance. After the violent suppression of socialist ideas and the persecution of those who advocated them, the main task of the political leadership was to re-educate the people. In his Reichstag address of 30 January 1939 Hitler said, 'It must be admitted that this kind of community cannot be created chiefly by violent compulsion, but only by the compelling force of an idea, accompanied by a simultaneous and energetic process of permanent education'.[10]

Hitler never seems to have doubted that a unified political consciousness rooted in an unshakeable national will was the most important precondition for the success of his expansionist policies. As time passed he may have had some doubts about the practicality of achieving his educational ideal, as we shall see, but to the end he never ceased to assign it a central role. In Hitler's view of the nature of modern politics, faith in the omnipotence of political convictions *per se* was axiomatic. The political attitude of a people and the status of a nation among the other great powers were, in his eyes, ultimately a function of ideology: 'Only by a fanatically extreme nationalism with the highest social ethic and morality will Marxist internationalism be broken'.[11] In an address to the National Club in Hamburg in December 1930, Hitler expanded on this idea:

> [It is] because of the Communists, if for no other reason, that Germany is no longer able to fight beyond its borders. ... For the nation is paralysed by class divisions. ... My aim is to lead the many millions of workers back to the idea of the *Volk*. That will only happen when they sincerely believe in the ideal.[12]

10. Max Domarus, *Hitler. Reden und Proklamationen, 1932–1945*, Munich, 1965, p. 1050.

11. Hitler 'Warum musste ein 8. November kommen?', p. 107; in bold in the original.

12. Werner Jochmann (ed.), *Nationalsozialismus und Revolution: Ursprung und Geschichte der NSDAP in Hamburg, 1922–1933. Dokumente*, Frankfurt am Main, 1963, pp. 312f.

In its policy towards the working class the regime gambled a great deal on this ploy, especially during the years 1933 to 1936. Both the legislative organs and the DAF undertook a campaign of indoctrination that, together with institutionalized terror, was intended to ensure the loyalty of the workers. Even after it had become obvious that this domestic strategy had failed, Hitler continued to prattle on about the primacy of ideology, even in the company of his cronies and sycophantic advisors. He still saw the worker as a basically decent patriot who had been misled by unscrupulous Jewish-Marxist leaders. To those workers who had been hurled into a hostile world and had been exposed to the seductions of Marxism, he offered his full understanding, but not of course to those 'swine of theoreticians' like Hilferding and Kautsky.[13]

Occasionally he took pains to create the impression that the Nazi Party was directing most of its energy towards winning over the working class,[14] despite the fact that its failure in this regard before 1933 was notorious and had led to a bitter dispute with the so-called leftists in the Party. There is something patently grotesque about Hitler's remark that the regime had no more loyal supporters than its former enemies from the camp of the working-class parties.[15] Hitler saw himself in many roles, but he was especially proud of his achievements in political education and propaganda, to which he ascribed a large measure of the supposed success of his movement: 'My whole life was nothing but a constant effort to persuade others'. Adopting the tone of a high school civics teacher, he added an original perspective to the historiography of his regime: 'For goodness' sake, let's not run to the police because of every peccadillo. Let us rather stick to educative measures. Don't forget, after all, that it was not by using fear inspired by police methods that we National Socialists won over the people, but rather by trying to show them the light and to educate them'.[16]

It would be wrong to ascribe such an absurd explanation of his political success simply to the self-delusions of a dictator who tolerated no opposing points of view. This statement is the product of a kind of obsessive wish-fulfilment which informs the basic ideas in *Mein Kampf* so far as they deal with war and revolution. The success of our ideological efforts, Hitler said, is imperative or 'all [our] work will have been in

13. H.R. Trevor-Roper (ed.), *Hitler's Secret Conversations, 1941–1944*, New York, 1961, 1 February 1942. This passage does not appear in the new critical edition by Henry Picker and Ernst Schramm, *Hitlers Tischgespräche im Führerhauptquartier, 1941–1942*, Stuttgart, 1963.

14. Picker and Schramm, *Tischgespräche*, April 8, 1942.

15. Ibid., 8 April 1941 and 27 January 1942. Cf. Trevor–Roper (ed.), *Conversations*, 30 November 1941.

16. Picker and Schramm, *Tischgespräche*, 18 January and 23 June 1942.

vain, we will be forced to surrender'.[17] He professed his views with empty words, followed by deeds that were nearly as empty. At the end of 1936, for instance, he ordered the police to be more restrained in enforcing the Malicious Mischief Law (*Heimtückegesetz*), which made anybody who criticized the regime fair game for the Gestapo.[18] In the summer of 1939 he recommended a drastic reduction in the size of the regular police force (*Ordnungspolizei*) as a gesture to relieve the labour shortage.[19] Shortly before the beginning of the war, when the ministries introduced compulsory food rationing, Hitler again expressed himself in no uncertain terms; he 'flew into a rage over the [ration] cards. He wanted to get rid of them immediately, and was especially furious that once more everything was being carried out with the policeman's truncheon and threats of imprisonment instead of by an appeal to people's sense of honour'.[20] Of course, the best proof of the educational success of his National Socialist idealism would have been for people to cut back their consumption voluntarily in support of a criminal war of aggression!

This exaggerated idealism tended to ignore the limits of human endurance or socially determined modes of thinking and acting: any goal could be achieved through faith, devotion and will. Since the same rules that applied to the heroic fascist individual also applied to the whole nation, the education of an ideologically homogeneous people was bound to unleash unimagined collective energy. This thorough-going anti-materialism was manifested in the drive to 'humanize' all social relations and to stress again and again the the exemplary individual whose actions are motivated purely by idealism. The language of this ideal and its claim to ethical superiority[21] were not new; they had their origins in the nineteenth century and were an outgrowth of the long history of German bourgeois irrationalism. The radical expression of these views by the Nazis, however, was of more recent vintage; it arose from the front-line experience of the First World War, especially from the memory of the euphoria of August 1914, when a feeling of patriotic fervour seemed to sweep everything before it and to open up the prospect of a new future for the individual and the nation – a future unencumbered by the weight of past history or by social constraints.

17. See the quote at the beginning of Chapter 6 below.

18. *BA Koblenz*, R 58, file 243.

19. Report of the Reich Defence Committee (*Reichsverteidigungsausschuss*, or RVA) on the status of the Reich defence measures, 5 June 1939: *BA/MA Freiburg*, WilF5, file 560/1.

20. Elisabeth Wagner (ed.), *Der Generalquartiermeister: Briefe und Tagebuchauf-zeichnungen des Generalquartiermeisters des Heeres, General der Artillerie Eduard Wagner*, Munich/Vienna, 1963, p. 106. The cards were not scrapped.

21. Cf., for example, the sentence cited on p. 25 above from Hitler, 'Warum musste ein 8. November kommen?'; Hitler, *Zweites Buch*, Stuttgart, 1961, p. 53.

What counted were the primeval virtues of courage and sacrifice, of fortitude and comradeship – virtues which, after 1918, were to become the basic weapons in the arsenal of National Socialism. Like many others, Robert Ley expressed this feeling with a candour that left little to the imagination:

> The German Revolution began in those August days of 1914. ... It was there in the trenches of East and West that the nation discovered itself again; the grenades and mines never bothered to ask you if you were well-born or low-born, rich or poor, what your religion was or what class you belonged to; rather it was a monumental test of the meaning and spirit of this community.[22]

The viciousness with which the proponents of the stab-in-the-back legend attacked those who, in their eyes, were responsible for the November Revolution probably derived from the fact that the revolution had destroyed their own historical illusions, their pipe dreams of the perfect unity that had existed in August 1914. The desire to recover these lost illusions and seek revenge played no small part in motivating those who tended to build models for the future out of the national euphoria of the past.

The policy of Nazism can be viewed in part as an attempt to make the mood of 1914 a permanent condition and to fix in the political consciousness the chimera of a society held together by ideological bonds alone. This chimera, however, called for validation in the real world. Its believers wanted not only to preserve the memory of a sublime historical moment in the mind of the average citizen, but to convert this memory into active preparation for a future victorious world war. From their perspective, the Party's rise after the summer of 1930 seemed proof positive that ideology could move political mountains. This development was surely a repetition of the national euphoria of 1914. Given the NSDAP's weak start and the socially heterogeneous character of its growing constituency, it was obvious to the Party leaders that the political breakthrough could only be a consequence of the strength of National Socialist idealism. The Party's dramatic electoral successes appeared to confirm that antithetical interests and mutually hostile traditions could be reconciled solely by devotion to a higher ideal and that the persuasive power of such an ideal in the real world was the result of its own propaganda efforts.[23]

---

22. Robert Ley, *Durchbruch der sozialen Ehre*, Munich, 1935, p. 71. The original version of this address, delivered on 1 March 1934 to the diplomatic corps in Berlin, was worded somewhat differently: offprint with the title, *Die Deutsche Arbeitsfront, ihr Werden und ihre Aufgaben*, Munich, 1934. In this version the word 'community' (*Gemeinschaft*) appears twenty-three times.

23. These observations are to be regarded as a hypothesis. It would be valuable to study the NSDAP's self-image in this regard.

To anticipate any misunderstandings, we must mention the brutal cynicism and boundless opportunism that was an essential component of this interpretation of the relationship between ideology and politics. It was clear from the outset that the ideal of a unified national community was realizable only in the context of a major war. Furthermore, it was obvious that even the most elevating speeches about idealistic values and so-called higher tasks and responsibilities served very practical political ends: diverting attention from economic problems, obscuring class differences, committing the nation to absolute obedience and destroying the capacity for critical thinking. Finally, as Hitler himself clearly understood, this educational strategy presupposed the elimination through terror of stubborn, or ineducable, opponents.[24]

I am not concerned here primarily with passing moral judgement on the Nazis' *Weltanschauung*, determining the motives of Party leaders or enquiring into their integrity. What I wish to stress here is the specificity of National Socialist political thinking, rooted as it was in Germany's class structure, that is, its need to idealize *political* action and behaviour. This can perhaps be illustrated with an example drawn from the theme of this study. After 1933 the holders of power continually asserted that the regime's social policy aimed to substitute right-thinking for externally imposed norms of behaviour. This assertion was not only misleading in the sense that it suggested to the public that the definition of economic and social interests could be based solely on ideological maxims. It was also wrong because the pressure of external constraints was becoming increasingly severe. On the other hand, the assertion was in line with a domestic political goal that was essential to the regime, namely, the re-education of the working class. (This aim is not to be taken any less seriously simply because it was cynical or unrealistic.)

Thus from the experience of the First World War Hitler learned the conditions for prosecuting a second world war: enforced ideological unity, and terror. To understand the crisis atmosphere that gave birth to this policy after 1933, we must first consider those aspects of the defeat and revolution of 1918 which Hitler, at least in his public utterances, omitted to mention. He ignored anything that might indicate that Germany's collapse might have been due to the superior material strength of British, French and American imperialism. Doubts as to whether Germany's economic and population resources were adequate to the goals of her policy were likewise never raised. Such reflections were from the outset taboo in public, since they called into question the possibility of Germany's carrying out any second bid for world power.

24. Cf. his comments to his generals, 3 February 1933, quoted, for example, by Wolfgang Sauer in Karl Dietrich Bracher, Wolfgang Sauer and Gerhard Schulz, *Die nationalsozialistische Machtergreifung*, Cologne/Opladen, 1960, p. 863.

That Hitler none the less gave some weight to them is clear from his strategy of piecemeal conquest after 1937.

Even more revealing here are the meagre references in *Mein Kampf* to the motivations and attitudes of the revolutionary movement in 1918. It should come as no surprise that Hitler was unable to comprehend people rising in protest against a war which had become meaningless to them and against the politicians responsible for it. Nor could he understand the popular desire for a socialist society after the war. The only thing he saw in all this were the machinations of the 'enemy within'. Nevertheless, it is remarkable that he gave little or no weight to the intense privations suffered and the material sacrifices made by the working population during the final years of the war – mounting pressure in the workplace accompanied by a deterioration of working conditions and an increase in political repression. Only once did Hitler address this subject in *Mein Kampf*. While he was on sick leave in Berlin late in 1916 recovering from wounds received at the Somme, he noted his impressions: 'Bitter want was in evidence everywhere. The metropolis, with its teeming millions, was suffering from hunger. There was great discontent'.[25] But the point was swiftly passed over as the mere 'superficial effect..., superficial aspect' of the collapse, thus ignoring any causal connection. The only type of suffering for which Hitler showed any understanding was that of the man facing sudden death in the trenches; he had no feeling for the grinding, devastating routine of working people.

It is true, though, that in the course of the 1920s Hitler began to have doubts about the omnipotence of ideas. The reflections in his *Second Book* on the relation between national unity and economic prosperity show that he was coming to the conclusion that an 'appeal to beliefs or ideals' would not suffice in order to keep down the living standards of a 'cultured people...in the long run..... The broad masses especially will seldom show understanding for this. They experience the deprivation, curse those who are in their opinion responsible, which, at least in democratic states, is dangerous, since they thus become the reservoir for all attempts at revolt'.[26]

The attempt to come up with a solution to this problem, which was vital to any future rearmament programme, failed. Hitler's uncertainty here is reflected in his evasive and noncommittal arguments and the craven obscurity in his choice of words:

25. Hitler, *Mein Kampf*, pp. 211, 246.
26. Hitler, *Zweites Buch*, p. 121. Ten years later, at the so-called Hossbach Conference, he used the same words: *Akten zur Deutschen Auswärtigen Politik, 1918–1945*, series D, vol. 1, pp. 26f.

The struggle to earn one's daily bread is life's number one priority. A brilliant leader can concentrate a people's attention on goals that distract it from material things in order to serve higher spiritual ideals. ... A people can do without some material goods, so long as it gets powerful ideals in return. However, these ideals must never be purchased at the cost of material well-being, or they could have disastrous consequences for a people. Thus ideals are beneficial and good only so long as they increase the inner strength of a people and help them to carry on life's struggles.[27]

In short, by the end of the 1920s Hitler had calculated that a 'uniformly recognized *Weltanschauung*' could probably serve as a firm though temporary basis to prepare for war, provided it also offered genuine hope for improvement in the material conditions of life. His calculations also anticipated and justified the blitzkrieg strategy, and – with its corollary policy of conquest – a barbaric modern version of social imperialism as well. These plans pointed to the gamble that underlay the entire economic and social policy of the Third Reich. While leaving private ownership totally intact, the Nazis patronizingly called on workers to abandon their self-delusive belief in the ideology of the class struggle – an ideology developed as a result of decades of experience – and to sanction, indeed to celebrate as one of the regime's great achievements, their own immiseration, disenfranchisement, and loss of power.

However, as full employment gave the working class new economic clout this kind of fantastic speculation became irrelevant. The government's vacillation in the area of social and economic policy began soon after the seizure of power. After 1935/6 the grandiose invocation of a unified and harmonious society came to bear more and more the character of a stern warning against the threat of an economic struggle of all against all. The repeated appeals for national unity and harmony were addressed to a public which had never existed and could not exist. Classes were not the less real for the term having been banned. The ceaseless repetition of slogans about the 'common good' and about the overriding need for achievement, production and efficiency did not diminish the interest of industrial workers in higher wages, shorter hours and greater freedom. The slogans were even unable to extinguish the memory of the November Revolution or of earlier trade-union struggles.[28]

The fact that there was no repetition of the 'stab in the back' by the working-class movement during the Second World War was due above all to police terror – carried out mainly from 1933 to 1936 and from 1942 to 1945 – which claimed numerous victims among left-wing resis-

27. Hitler, *Zweites Buch*, p. 53.
28. Cf. *Docs. 28, 41 Part III d.*

tance groups. What was important here was not just the effectiveness of the Gestapo's operations, but the fact that, until 1943/4, terror alone was almost adequate to deter and stifle widespread, co-ordinated resistance. The regime found that it could not rely solely on the police, however. Living in fear of actual or potential worker dissatisfaction, the regime manoeuvred with a circumspection that became a dominant factor in shaping domestic policy after 1935. With the failure of the 'education' strategy, the social and economic aspects of class contradictions moved to the forefront. In other words, precisely those aspects of the November Revolution whose importance Hitler had denied came to play an ever greater role in the leadership's calculations. Although the dilemma was serious, it was also insoluble: to secure the domestic stability of the regime it seemed necessary to make concessions to the working class, concessions which would endanger the armaments programme and the major foreign-policy objectives. Albert Speer later gave a succinct summary of the problem:

> It remains one of the astounding experiences of the war that Hitler wished to spare his own people those burdens which Churchill or Roosevelt imposed upon their peoples without second thoughts. The discrepancy between the total mobilization of the labour force in democratic England and the sluggish treatment of this question in authoritarian Germany serves to characterize the regime's fear of a change in the people's loyalties. The elite wanted neither to make sacrifices itself nor to require sacrifices of the people; it was concerned to keep the mood of the people as good as possible by making concessions. Hitler and the majority of his political followers belonged to the generation which in November 1918 had experienced the revolution as soldiers, and they never got over it. Hitler often made it clear in *private* conversations that one could not be careful enough after the experience of 1918.[29]

In this connection Speer touched on certain other questions which will be the focus of the last chapter of this study: the lack of controls on consumer goods production from 1939 to 1940, the protected status of non-working German women, and the regime's drive to achieve popularity through a deceitful campaign of propaganda. As early as November 1936 Colonel Thomas had warned that all these matters would aggravate an already precarious war economy. In conclusion, Speer pronounced his verdict on the inconsistency of the regime's behaviour:'It was a confession of political weakness; it betrayed considerable anxiety that a loss of popularity could give rise to domestic political crises'.[30] In the conversations he had with Speer between 1942 and 1944, Hitler

---

29. Albert Speer, *Erinnerungen*, Frankfurt am Main, 1966, p. 229. Emphasis added.
30. Ibid.

again and again made clear his deep concern about the solidity of his power and his popularity.[31]

There is little more to add at this point. Suffice it to say this theme ran like a red thread though the domestic policy of National Socialism, even though explicit references are few and far between. Ley's frankness in dealing with sensitive subjects was characteristic of him personally,[32] not of the regime as such. He alone seemed prepared to rethink the lessons of the November Revolution for National Socialism and to use his insights for propaganda purposes. The reasons for his attitude were obvious: he bore no direct responsibility for military preparedness, and his experience as head of the German Labour Front prompted him to make a more realistic assessment of the relationship between the working class and the regime. The other Nazi leaders were more hesitant in this respect. Moreover, those who were charged with the responsibiity for preparing the economy and society for war and had a clear view of the shortfalls in industrial production and the lack of armaments for the military would have found small comfort in Ley's assurances that by acting on the lessons of 1918 and making timely concessions to the workers and consumers a second 'stab in the back' could be prevented. They had much more pressing problems to deal with: whether the Wehrmacht was in any way fit for action and whether industry had sufficient raw materials, labour, and machinery to support even a short campaign. At the same time, of course, they were also only too aware of the instability of the domestic political situation, and this did give Ley's strategy a certain credibility.[33]

This fundamental division within the Nazi hierarchy suggests why open discussion of the actual implications of the November Revolution was avoided. The following example of National Socialist labour-market policy illustrates how the spectre of 1918 continued to haunt those in power. When the armaments industry began in 1936 to hire cheap labour on its own initiative, the government intervened. It should be recalled that the system of leaving certificates (*Abkehrscheine*) favoured by employers during the First World War was bitterly resented by the workers, in whose eyes any diminution of their freedom served only to increase the wartime profits of industry. A less offensive system of regulations introduced by the government after 1936 to

31. W.A. Boelcke (ed.), *Deutschlands Rüstung im Zweiten Weltkrieg*, Frankfurt am Main, 1969, pp. 65, 74, 86, 91, 98, 109, 142, 315.

32. Cf. Chapter 3 below.

33. Cf., for example, the remarks of State Secretary Krohn on the question of paid holidays: *Doc. 54.*

replace the universally hated certificates proved to be relatively inefficient.[34]

The beginning of the socio-political preparations for war forced the politicians and officials concerned to be more blunt after 1936. During their secret work on drafting emergency legislation for the event of war (as it affected wages, working conditions, freedom of movement, taxes), they were relatively open about confronting the contradictory lessons of the First World War. As in the dispute over the leaving certificates, it was the Ministry of Labour that became the self-appointed advocate of a new interpretation of the stab-in-the-back legend, an interpretation in which economic class conflict played the decisive role. In the protracted negotiations on wartime measures, the representatives of the Ministry never wearied of insisting that the burdens of war be shared equally by all classes. Sparing the propertied classes while imposing burdens on the workers was a sure formula for repeating the disastrous outcome of the last world war.[35] Despite the scepticism of the other departments of government, which tended to support the interests of property, the Ministry of Labour persisted in its demands. It insisted that the principles underlying wage, tax and labour policy in wartime be 'psychologically bearable'. [36] Significantly, this phrase was used more and more during the period 1938/9, revealing, among other things, the dictatorship's anxiety regarding the mood of a people deprived of any avenue for free political expression; and the utter failure of the idealistic enthusiasm which Hitler had demanded and which had now degenerated into a mere technique for manipulation, with the negative aim of doing anything to avoid offending people. But above all it revealed the anxiety of those in power that drastic changes in social policy might disrupt the existing truce with the working class. What form such disruption would take – strikes or revolts, passive resistance or a decline in morale – was anybody's guess. But these were the kinds of concerns that caused the Ministry of Labour single-handedly to redraft the legislative contingency plans – and this three weeks before the outbreak of war.

The details of these disputes and the compromise solution of 4 September 1939, which lasted for less than a month, are analysed at the conclusion of this study.[37] In these introductory remarks special mention should be made of the fact that both Göring and Ley specifically cited the dangerous example of the First World War in their public statements on

---

34. Gerald Feldman, *Army, Industry and Labor in Germany, 1914–1918*, Providence/Oxford, 1992, pp. 211f., 307f., 327f., 384f., 412, 489; Ludwig Preller, *Sozialpolitik in der Weimarer Republik*, Stuttgart, 1949, pp. 24, 230f.; *Docs. 17–28*.

35. See especially *Doc. 161*.

36. *Doc. 169*.

37. See pp. 251–5, 269, 273 below.

the problem.[38] Although the question of a psychologically bearable social order that was also equal to the tasks required by the war machine was of paramount importance (both for the stability of the regime and for the operation of the armed forces), Hitler at first refrained from acting, and then in November 1939 came down heavily in support of the strategy of making concessions in domestic policy.[39] The otherwise sparse documentary sources provide some indication that this extraordinary inactivity was more the result of anxiety than of a desire to let subordinates deal with troublesome matters of secondary importance. Even a strong-willed leader could not resolve class conflict by such peremptory and *ad hoc* means. Hitler's personality was suited only to situations which called for either/or decisions; he could only focus on problems susceptible to immediate and dramatic solution. But no matter what decisions were made with regard to social policy, they turned out to be wrong: ruthlessness in resisting social and political demands only increased the danger of a new 'stab in the back', yet weakness in the face of the military's inadequate armament was unconscionable.

A discussion Hitler had with August Winnig in the summer of 1939, in which he asked Winnig the same question that was preoccupying officials in the Ministry of Labour, made clear that 1918 was very much on Hitler's mind: how could one ensure the loyalty of the working class in a coming war? Winnig, who had become a fascist in a peculiarly roundabout way via the Social Democrats and the Baltic Free Corps, advised Hitler to accept the old nationalist unions into the leadership of the DAF.[40] The suggestion was as absurd as the discussion was important. The crisis of the first few weeks of the war forced the government to go far beyond mere window-dressing in revising its social and economic policy, so as to prevent the home front from crumbling. Ley's advisors tried to justify the need for the continuation in wartime of the strategy of bribery practised before 1939. The experience of 1914–18, they wrote, had clearly shown that Germany's social system had been unable to stand up to the pressures of a world war and a blockade. They argued that these were 'well-known and undisputed facts, from which the general lessons ... have already long been drawn'.[41] Needless to say,

38. *Docs. 174 , 229.* The rulers' panicky fear during these months is reflected in Ley's complete distortion of the historical facts. Cf. also the perceptive warnings of a Kiel naval officer in November 1939: *Doc. 84.*

39. See pp. 253–4 below.

40. Albert Krebs, *Tendenzen und Gestalten der NSDAP*, Stuttgart, 1959, p. 156.

41. Arbeitswissenschaftliches Institut der DAF, 'Betriebliche Sozialpolitik in der Kriegswirtschaft', Manuscript, September 1939: *DZA Potsdam*. The authors paid lip-service to Hitler's interpretation of 1918 as above all a crisis of morale, adding empty phrases about the 'mental conditions' (*seelische Verfassung*) of the German people in the First World War, but this did not affect the substance of their analysis.

their analysis bore little resemblance to the views expressed in *Mein Kampf*. The consequences of these contradictory interpretations for the armaments programme and the war economy are the subject of the next chapter.

Summing up, we must ask, however, whether the paucity of documentary evidence on the relationship of the Nazi leaders to the November Revolution warrants this approach to the social and economic history of the Third Reich. Is there a danger of exaggerating the importance of this subject? The answer to this question lies in a clearer explication of the political circumstances surrounding statements regarding 1918, followed by a brief discussion of the general relationship between popular sentiment and policy in the Nazi state.

Speer's pointed remark about Hitler's reserving his utterances on the lessons of the November Revolution for *private* conversations is our most important guide in evaluating the passages quoted above. No other subject lent itself less to publicity, or even to detailed analysis within government circles than this one. The mere recognition that the version of the stab-in-the-back legend presented in *Mein Kampf* had no direct programmatic use in preparing for or fighting a second world war, did not somehow magically suggest a useful alternative strategy; it merely led to a brutal and unprincipled policy of *ad hoc* decisionism (*Dezisionismus*). An open and principled discussion of the political significance of the November Revolution would have been possible only within the framework of a pragmatic attempt to arrive at an alternative general strategy. The main reason that such a discussion never took place was that the regime did not and could not come up with a strategy that would promise success. Any attempt at persuasive (i.e. rational) planning in foreign affairs and military policy was bound to fail because of the internal contradictions in the domestic political structure and because of the social constraints on the regime. Economic 'appeasement' of the working class, which was imperative after 1936, could only be carried out at the cost of the economic preparations for war.

The regime, however, was incapable of giving up either objective. The weakness of the political leadership, as underscored by Speer, was rooted in the irreconcilability of two equally indispensable principles. It would have been equally difficult to implement either Ley's or Thomas's proposals of 1936. In a dictatorship whose political legitimacy depended increasingly on the success of power-politics, merely discussing these weaknesses involved certain dangers. The political leadership was bound to see this as a threat to its entire system of governance, the stability of which it equated with faith in its own infallibility. The generals and high-level officials for their part had good reason to fear for their jobs should they espouse a pragmatic view of the relation-

ship between aggressive expansionism and domestic political considerations, for that would have made them immediately vulnerable to
charges of defeatism. Thus they simply had to resign themselves to
doing the impossible; in these circumstances, even historically valid
doubts could only be expressed casually in private conversations. In any
event, such ideas could only have been used to form the basis for a new
and comprehensive foreign-policy strategy if the heedless drive towards
military expansion had been halted. As things stood, all that the generals
and top officials could do was to go for broke.

These are the reasons that the legacy of 1918 is to be found not so
much in the written record of the power holders as in the content of their
weak and contradictory decisions on domestic policy and in their wish
to close their eyes to even the worst economic conflicts. Any rational
explanation would have exposed the bizarre nature of their policy, its
incompatibility with their claims to be able to solve all problems by
power-politics alone. The regime's decisions, initiatives and omissions
with regard to the working class, which are the subject of the following
chapters, are all pervaded by a fear that is only at its most conspicuous
when the occasional direct allusion is made to 1918. What most distinguished nearly all the phases and aspects of the social and political
preparation for war was the vacillation of the power elite in the face of
the predictable unpopularity of their decisions and their acquiescence in
the demands of the people for peace and prosperity. Thus whether it was
dealing with wage and tax policy, workers' rights, civil conscription,
working women, consumer goods production or the price of food, the
regime only managed to come up with half-measures, which are the outward sign of the contradictions inherent in any modern policy of imperialist expansion – that is, the irreconcilability of the traditions and
interests of the working class with the demands imposed by a war of
conquest.

During the Second World War Germany's changed strategic situation
and the dictatorship's campaign of domestic terror ensured that this class
conflict, unlike that of 1917/18, would not be settled in the public eye.[42]
It would, in part, be quashed by the use of force and, in part, neutralized
by being mired in the anxieties and inconsistencies that plagued the
regime's own policies. The rhetoric of sacrifice only began to bite when
it became clear to all, despite official propaganda, that the war had
become a desperate war of defence. Fear of a Soviet invasion and resentment against Allied bombing created a kind of domestic political coun-

---

42. Judges did not hesitate to cite the example of 1918 against defendants who had
tried to express this conflict openly: Max Oppenheimer, *Der Fall Vorbote*, Frankfurt am
Main, 1969, pp. 96ff., 200–217.

terpart of the trench mentality of the First World War. With the failure of its expansionist policy, the regime's domestic policy enjoyed a short-lived 'success', because it was parasitic upon the need for national defence. This success was the basis for Speer's armaments policy. But even during this phase, the Gestapo was still indispensable, importing millions of foreign slave labourers and plundering the occupied territories not only to strengthen the military power of the nation but also in order to spare German workers the worst excesses of the war economy. This is why the legacy of 1918 for National Socialism must be sought in the principles and particulars of its social policy. It is when those in power reflect on the precedent of 1918 and the historian is able to detect shifts in their view of the stab-in-the-back legend that we begin to get a sense of what drives this policy.

A brief look at the NSDAP's attitudes and actions regarding these questions may also help counter criticism that the importance of the November Revolution has been exaggerated here. At the same time we can also get a clearer picture of how time and again the attention of the political leadership was brought back to the insoluble contradiction inherent in their policies. The position of the Gauleiters, of course, differed from that of the political and military leadership; as a group they were much less interested in the strategic relationship between economic policy and military preparation. Between 1930 and 1933 they had distinguished themselves primarily as election campaign managers. Except for the work of protecting their own jobs, they continued to consider electioneering their main task, even after the seizure of power, which had as it were institutionalized the idea of a permanent election campaign, without, however, providing any clear measure of success. In any case, while the NSDAP never stopped trying to indoctrinate the Germans in an ideology of idealism, the Gauleiters assumed a more practical attitude toward the people, viewing themselves as the guardians of the regime's popularity and thus as the interpreters of public sentiment. This signified a decisive shift of emphasis in policy towards the working class, the Gauleiters becoming the proponents of a softer line within the government's decision-making apparatus. They soon realized that draconian interference in the lives of working people could not be sustained with propagandistic sleight of hand. On the contrary, a policy of concessions to the workers, they felt, should be the basis of political re-education. Hitler was very favourably inclined to this suggestion, resulting as it did from the rough-and-tumble of every-day political life.

In opposing a further increase in food prices in November 1934, for example, Hitler in all likelihood was reflecting the Gauleiters' views. This development, he explained privately, might lead to a 'revolutionary situation'.[43] When the problem became acute again the following year, the Party came out even more forcefully in opposition, this time with greater success. At the same time, the Gauleiters, with the help of Hess, torpedoed a wage plan proposed by the Ministry of Labour which would have reduced the earnings of highly paid workers in the construction industry.[44] While these actions were largely defensive in nature, the DAF, again with the support of some of the Gauleiters, went over to the offensive in 1936, demanding social and political reforms, some of which were eventually carried out.[45] By the time the government launched its general offensive against the living and working conditions of the working class in September 1939, the position of the Party and of the constituency it represented had become strong enough to fend off the government.[46] During the war it was the Gauleiters who most doggedly opposed Speer's plans to concentrate the bulk of the economy's reserves in the armaments sector.[47]

This is an interesting phenomenon *per se*, not just as an example of the partial institutionalization of the economics of the class struggle within the political system, for the Gauleiters were most probably the first to recognize the fragility of the grandiose political ideals of National Socialism. It was their unvarnished reports and petitions that caused Hitler gradually to lose confidence in the solidarity of the *Volksgemeinschaft*. In the course of the 1930s he came to feel increasingly uncertain about domestic policy in general. He avoided dealing with the growing social crises, refused to give his ministers and Gauleiters clear guidelines, finding refuge in a field in which it was still possible to make earth-shaking decisions – foreign policy. It was Speer who first revealed the depth of Hitler's pessimism. In 1939 Hitler told him that the buildings Speer was designing to house the government on Adolf-Hitler-Platz would have to be 'capable of being defended like a fortress.' The reason: 'After all, it is not unthinkable that I may be forced to take some unpopular measures. Perhaps there will then be a revolt'.[48]

In the meantime he continued making decisions which he thought at the time were anything but unpopular, including the decision to launch a

43. Quoted in J.E. Farquharson, 'The NSDAP and Agriculture in Germany, 1928–1938', Ph.D. thesis, typescript, University of Kent, Canterbury, 1972, pp. 196–203; cf. also p. 153. His source: *BA Koblenz*, R43II, vol. 193.

44. Details below, pp. 136–8.

45. See pp. 160–78, 211–24, and *Docs. 53–5; 60–2; 64–5; 97–9; 130–1*.

46. See *Docs. 201–3, 208*. Sauckel was an exception: *Doc. 141*.

47. Cf. Alan S. Milward, *Die deutsche Kriegswirtschaft 1939–1945*, Stuttgart, 1966; Gregor Janssen, *Das Ministerium Speer*, Frankfurt am Main/Berlin, 1968.

48. Speer, *Erinnerungen*, p. 173.

war of conquest. Yet right down to the final stages of total defeat, he continued to be plagued by lingering fears that this criminal adventure might be too heavy a burden for the home front to bear. In the spring of 1945 the fiscal authorities drafted a long overdue bill to increase taxes. Hitler acceded but insisted that the law not be made public until the armed forces had won a battle somewhere, diverting public attention from the material sacrifices. The bill, by the way, was never enacted into law.[49]

The European revolutions that occurred between 1917 and 1919 had revealed the domestic political limits of military expansionism. The popular version of the stab-in-the-back legend denied the existence of these limits; the version specific to the Nazis went further and espoused a barbarous programme that promised, first, to suspend class conflict and then to eliminate it entirely by involving the whole nation in the building of a colossal imperial system. This programme, however, presupposed the use of terror and political education as the means to escalate the exploitation and repression of the working class during the period of rearmament and armed conflict while avoiding the risk of domestic turmoil. The programme failed mainly because of the socio-economic logic of the class struggle, and the consequences of that failure affected all areas of policy in Nazi Germany, not the least of which was foreign policy, which the original Nazi programme had sought to remove as far as possible from domestic political considerations. The consequent general crisis of the regime between 1938 and 1940, which is the focus of the remainder of this study, was thus the real legacy of 1918 for National Socialism.

In the meantime the starting point of this study has to be set back somewhat. According to the views Hitler formed in the 1920s of the First World War and its outcome, much depended on whether the Nazis could succeed in reducing the mass support of the working-class parties even before seizing power.

---

49. Fritz Federau, *Der Zweite Weltkrieg. Seine Finanzierung in Deutschland*, Tübingen, 1962, p. 28. For more examples, see Dietrich Orlow, *The History of the Nazi Party*, vol. 2: 1933–1945, Newton Abbot, 1973, pp. 263, 340, 407, 441, 456.

2

National Socialism and the Working Class, 1925 to May 1933

We want to conquer the soul of the worker and build him into the new state.

Ludwig Brucker, NSBO, in a discussion with representatives of the Free Trade Unions, 13 April 1933[1]

The following chapter is intended to illuminate the prehistory of the problems of National Socialist rule discussed in this book. A full perspective for the analysis of class relationships in Germany after 1933 can be gained only by first outlining the development and social composition of the National Socialist movement before the seizure of power, and by reconstructing the process that led to the destruction of working-class organizations in 1933. It is also extremely important to identify the changes in economic and political relationships produced by the world economic crisis. A thorough and differentiated treatment of these themes is of course impossible within the limited framework of this study. The discussion must therefore concentrate on those aspects of the rise of the NSDAP which were later to prove decisive for the development of the Nazi system after 1933.

The Nazi seizure of power denoted a marked shift of emphasis in the nature of domination in the capitalist system, a shift of emphasis from the labour process and the legal system to the realm of dictatorial political power. The class domination of the 1920s, which had been secured by the state, by law and by the cultural hegemony of the bourgeoisie, and which fell apart under the pressures of the world economic crisis, was replaced in 1933 by direct political domination *within* class society, domination resting upon the exercise of open violence. The new system did not involve general domination *over* class society, for, thanks to the massive repression of the working class, the capitalist economy was able to resume its course after 1933; and yet, the policies of the dictatorship were not primarily concerned with the task of perpetuating the cap-

---

1. A transcript has been published by Hannes Heer, *Burgfrieden oder Klassenkampf: Zur Politik der sozialdemokratischen Gewerkschaften 1930–1933*, Neuwied/Berlin, 1971, pp. 168–73; this quotation, p. 170.

italist economic order. Thus, the distinguishing characteristics of the new system of domination lay in the tendency for political violence to achieve an ever greater relative autonomy as against the driving forces of socio-economic development.

The most important preconditions for this rapid shift in the character of domination were, on the one hand, the development of the powerful National Socialist mass organizations in the years before 1933, which then destroyed or 'co-ordinated' all oppositional groupings, and on the other hand, the self-preservation and self-assertion, within their own special spheres of interest and competence, of certain powerful organizations of the ruling classes (trade associations, cartels, the civil service and armed forces) and their active co-operation with the new dictatorship. These two preconditions were closely linked with each other: they were interdependent basic features of the economic and political crisis. They were both more clearly present and more marked in Germany in the years 1932–4 than in any other society that produced a fascist regime.

In the process by which the capitalist order in Germany was stabilized in this purely fascist form, the Nazi mass movement played a doubly indispensable role. First, it robbed the conservative political forces of their own mass support, and then it destroyed the organizations of the working class. By the latter step, the NSDAP ruled out the only possible alternative resolution of the crisis of bourgeois society in Germany, that is, a political renovation of the social order through a more gradual co-optation of the Social Democratic Party (SPD) and the trade unions by non-terroristic means. A resolution of this kind would certainly have entailed a substantial loss of power for the organizations of the working class and their partial incorporation into an authoritarian corporative (*ständisch*) socio-economic order. But this would not have had the pure fascist quality of the National Socialist dictatorship. As late as 1933 this corporate resolution of the crisis was still the ideal of many of the old political and economic elites. They failed to realize their goal not least because of the independence of the Nazi mass organizations which, acting largely on their own initiative in March and April 1933, destroyed the working-class movement from the bottom up.[2]

Thus the Nazi mass movement has to be analysed in the specific context of the creation of a terroristic dictatorship – a dictatorship which did not seek to use administrative, legal and economic pressures to weaken the working-class presence, but which instead quite literally destroyed

2. There were at least three further reasons why this strategy for a resolution of the crisis failed: its supporters were not united; it had insufficient popular support; and it is very doubtful whether the KPD could have been broken in the same way that the non-Nazi Right hoped to break the SPD and the unions.

the working-class movement, and through this very act gained a far-reaching relative autonomy from the ruling classes. The causal nature of the connection between the elimination of independent working-class organizations and the relative autonomy of the regime in its subsequent relations with the ruling classes must be emphasized. The destruction of the working-class movement was of immediate short-term advantage to the ruling classes, and it served as the basis for their co-operation with the regime in the years after 1933 (hence the fact that the regime's autonomy was relative). Such wholesale repression and terrorism required, however, a concentration of power which set the mechanisms of 'normal' class domination out of action; and this requirement was met in the spring of 1933. It is in this overall context that the question of the relations between the NSDAP and the working class before May 1933 becomes so significant.[3]

After the refounding of the Party in 1925, the activists outside Bavaria devoted themselves with some energy to the task of breaking the political pre-eminence of the SPD and Communist Party (KPD) among the workers in large German cities. These activists, often erroneously termed the 'National Socialist Left', agitated for a rebirth of the German people based on a new unity of national purpose; it was to bind together all those who produced the wealth and power of the nation and thus reconcile the 'workers of the head' and 'workers of the hand' in the struggle against alleged common enemies: international communism, international finance capital, international Jewry. Communism was attacked because it rejected the national principle, and Social Democracy because it had capitulated to the 'Jewish' financial interests which, it was maintained, stood behind the fulfilment policy of the Weimar governments. At the same time, Nazis denounced the German National People's Party (DNVP) not only for being purely reactionary and backward-looking, and thus unrealistic in its political goals, but also as a party bound exclusively to the social interests it represented.[4]

This shrewd propaganda strategy was put into effect in the second half of the 1920s with great enthusiasm and remarkable persistence by

3. The general theoretical perspectives of these paragraphs remain largely implicit in the rest of this book, whose principal concerns are not of a theoretical order. I have drawn on theories of fascism mainly to identify and to elucidate central problems in empirical historical research. For concluding notes on violence and terroristic domination, see below, pp. 266–74. By far the most illuminating recent contribution to the debate on theories of fascism is Jane Caplan's essay, 'Theories of Fascism: Nicos Poulantzas as Historian', *History Workshop Journal*, vol. 3, 1977.

4. A detailed description of this propaganda is presented by Max H. Kele, *Nazis and Workers: National Socialist Appeals to German Labor 1919–1933*, Chapel Hill, 1972. Kele's analysis leaves much to be desired. Cf. the review essay by Timothy Mason, 'The Coming of the Nazis', *Times Literary Supplement*, 1 February 1974.

the Strasser brothers, Goebbels, Krebs and other 'old fighters' (*alte Kämpfer*) in the urban centres of western and northern Germany. But before 1930 they achieved very little success with it. The Hitler putsch of November 1923 had left no doubt that the NSDAP belonged in the camp of counter-revolutionary forces, and thus it is not surprising that the politically educated workers in the cities of the Ruhr saw through such demagogic endeavours and dismissed them as a new kind of reactionary confidence trick; the Nazis' political meetings were regularly disrupted by factory workers. Only in Berlin, and in a handful of industrial cities in the Rhineland, Westphalia, Saxony and Thuringia, could the NSDAP chalk up any gains at all in the ranks of the *organized* workers before 1930. These were, however, of only minimal significance in terms of numbers, and hence of election support and Party membership.[5] The SPD and the KPD remained the strongest representatives of the German working class, and their pre-eminence was never threatened in the slightest by the NSDAP before 1930.

This initial lack of success was of decisive importance in that it confirmed once and for all the relationship of National Socialism to the class structure of German society. If the NSDAP had won strong support among wage workers in the late 1920s, it would never have been able later to become the beneficiary of the massive political reaction against the Left which began with the world economic crisis. If, prior to 1928/9, the Party had unmistakably developed in a national-syndicalist or national-bolshevist direction, if its social and economic demands had emerged more clearly into the foreground, then in subsequent years the fears and ambitions of the German bourgeoisie would have found their political home in some other movement.[6] Although during the years of crisis many good German bourgeois considered the NSDAP too violent and vulgar and thus not trustworthy, it developed into a large national political movement precisely because it promised to side with the middle classes and to confront the economic and political power of the working class. The NSDAP did not emerge into the forefront of nation-

5. See above all the detailed and balanced study by Wilfried Böhnke, *Die NSDAP im Ruhrgebiet 1920–1933*, Schriftenreihe des Forschungsinstituts der Friedrich-Ebert-Stiftung, vol. 106, Bonn/Bad Godesberg, 1974, part C; Herbert Kühr, *Parteien und Wahlen im Stadt- und Landkreis Essen in der Zeit der Weimarer Republik*, Beiträge zur Geschichte des Parlamentarismus und der politischen Parteien, Düsseldorf, 1973, vol. 49, pp. 282ff.; Detlef W. Mühlberger, 'The Rise of National Socialism in Westphalia 1920–1933', Ph.D. Diss., University of London, 1975, pp. 297ff., 333f. Comparable studies of Saxony and Thuringia do not yet exist; short discussions in Kele, *Nazis*, pp. 108f., 161; and in Gerhard Schulz, *Aufstieg des Nationalsozialismus: Krise und Revolution in Deutschland*, Frankfurt am Main, 1975, pp. 479ff.

6. This was to some extent how things first developed; cf. the rise of the *Landvolk* movement, the *Wirtschaftspartei*, among other parties.

al politics between 1928 and 1930 as an alternative to the SPD and KPD, but rather as their most irreconcilable enemy.

This fact is widely known and is now scarcely disputed by scholars: each new study about the social composition and the activities of the Party before 1933 brings it out with greater clarity. However, for the complex of problems under discussion here this fact is of critical importance, and it is not enough simply to remark upon it: explanation is needed. In the late 1920s the socialist parties and the trade unions (in Catholic regions the Centre Party and the Catholic trade unions can be included) had firm support in the working-class population. Their strong position was based (except in the case of the KPD) on long practical experience, efficient organization, and on relationships of solidarity which had survived the confusion of the revolutionary period.[7] Within the framework of the Weimar Republic's political system these organizations were also in a strong position to represent the immediate interests of their members and supporters. Thus, after the stabilization crisis of 1923/4, wages and living standards again rose quickly, and governments responded positively to demands for moderate social reform. Moreover, in Prussia as well as in many of the big cities the SPD was a major force in government coalitions and in public administration. Although the working class in the late 1920s undoubtedly would have held a position of greater economic and political power if it had been united in a single movement, there was no evidence of decay, of inner weakness, or the sapping of political loyalty and morale – symptoms which would have provided the NSDAP with a bridgehead for successful agitation. Even the most plausible accusation drummed up by Nazi propaganda – that the leaders of the SPD and the Free Trade Unions had long given up the struggle for socialism and had abandoned their supporters for the sake of lucrative public offices – seems for the most part to have fallen on deaf ears.[8]

The extreme nationalism of the NSDAP – the most characteristic and distinctive aspect of its propaganda which set it apart from all other parties vying for the votes of the working class – also evoked little response.[9] This is due to the fact that in Germany aggressive nationalism had always been a programmatic point of the political parties supported by the middle and upper classes and had always been closely linked to reactionary domestic goals. In spite of numerous attempts by various Christian-national groups before and after 1914, no broad democratic

---

7. In some regions the KPD too was characterized by a trained and experienced core of members and voters who had moved from the SPD to the USPD and then to the KPD.

8. Cf. Kele, *Nazis*, p. 117 f.; Böhnke, *Ruhrgebiet*, part E, ch. 2.

9. In propaganda directed at workers, anti-Semitism played a subordinate role; cf. Böhnke, *Ruhrgebiet*, p. 219.

German nationalism had ever evolved with the capacity to integrate the essential economic and political interests of the working class. The contradiction between nation and class, around which the politics of imperial Germany revolved, continued after the November Revolution, if in new forms. To be sure, the struggle for national greatness and imperial expansion was no longer tied to the defence of an authoritarian constitution. But because of the complex of events in the winter of 1918/19 that contradiction reached a new level of emotional intensity for the German Right. Apart from short interludes in 1923, and then again in 1930 when the KPD assumed a decidedly nationalistic stance, the workers' parties resisted the temptation to adopt the slogans of their political opponents. On the other hand, they themselves, especially the Free Trade Unions, were patriotic enough in their own way to maintain the respect of those workers who were proud of their contribution to the war effort and who felt that the conditions of the peace treaty were unjust.[10] For all these reasons the extreme nationalistic demagoguery of the NSDAP found no response among factory workers before 1930.

This lack of success cannot be ascribed, however, only to the resistance that the NSDAP met in the shape of firmly established organizations and opinions. On several decisive issues the struggles of the Nazi Party for 'the soul of the German workers' were, despite their verbal bravado, half-hearted and smacked of dilettantism from the beginning. Thus the importance which Gregor Strasser and his supporters attached to the political conversion of the working class in the years between 1925 and 1928 elicited strong mistrust from the Munich leadership, particularly because of its likely effects on Party organization. Here two problem areas converged which were to have a decisive influence on the future development of the Party: the practical political question of its stance towards the trade-union organizations and, superimposed on this, the controversy about Hitler's personal power position and the *Führer* principle. In August 1929 Hitler essentially won both controversies, though making great tactical compromises in order to allow a certain freedom of action to those who still wanted to concentrate on attracting workers to the movement.[11]

10. This important theme deserves further scholarly investigation. The intense nationalism of the 1920s was certainly one of the weightiest political disadvantages for the workers' parties in their struggle for the preservation and expansion of their base. The unpublished dissertation by Ursula Hüllbüsch, 'Gewerkschaften und Staat: Ein Beitrag zur Geschichte der Gewerkschaften zu Anfang und zu Ende der Weimarer Republik', Heidelberg, 1958, provides important information about this, particularly about nationalist tendencies in the Free Trade Unions in 1932–3. Heer, *Burgfrieden*, relies strongly for detail on this analysis but ignores its historical perspective.

11. See Dietrich Orlow, *The History of the Nazi Party,* vol. 1: 1919–1933 Newton Abbot, 1971, pp. 102f., 168f.; Kele, *Nazis*, pp. 97–103.

But in many respects the line that Hitler represented set narrow limits to this kind of agitation. Hitler himself admitted openly that he knew of no solution which would resolve the dilemma for the Party. His remarks on 'the trade union question' in the second volume of *Mein Kampf* were totally inconclusive and predominantly negative, since he 'had not yet found the right man for the destruction of the Marxist trade unions'.[12] He conceded a legitimate function to the unions only as long as the state and employers failed to look after the workers' welfare. He denounced the class struggle, for which he made 'Marxism' (not the unions) responsible, and spoke out sharply against the founding of a Nationalist Socialist trade union because he had

> the steadfast conviction that it is dangerous to link an ideological (*weltan-schaulich*) struggle too soon to matters of economics. This could easily lead to economic aspects directing the political movement instead of the ideology forcing the trade unions into its course. ... A Nationalist Socialist trade union which sees it mission only in competition with the Marxists would be worse than none.[13]

Only seldom did Hitler question the unifying power of ideology in this way; the much-cited catch-all nature of the Nationalist Socialist movement, in good part the result of a calculated strategy, had its limits for Hitler at the point where it would have been necessary to institutionalize fundamental and deep-rooted conflicts of interest within the Party. Conflicts between artisans and large-scale industry, for example, or between agriculture and industry, could still be moderated within the Party because such groups had many other interests besides those that were mutually irreconcilable. In contrast, a trade union was only there to assert the claims of its members against an employer.[14] Class struggle within the Party, which Hitler correctly predicted as the unavoidable outcome of the founding of a class-specific organization, could only weaken the Party, complicate the position of its leadership and damage the plausibility of its central propaganda point, the call for an ideal national-racial community.

12. Hitler, *Mein Kampf*, p. 479. Hitler's irrational tendency to personalize structural problems is nowhere as clear as in the continuation of this thought: 'Anyone who at that time had really destroyed the Marxist unions in order to. . . aid the victory of the Nationalist Socialist conception of unions would in my eyes belong to the really great men of our people and his bust would some day be dedicated to posterity in the Valhalla at Regensburg. But I have come across no head which would belong on such a pedestal.' Ibid., printed in bold in the original, with the exception of the last sentence.

13. Ibid., pp. 680 f. The last two sentences are printed in bold in the original.

14. In contrast to the army supreme command in the First World War, Hitler refused to recognize that unions could also have other functions.

Hitler's readiness to address the working class separately in his own propaganda scarcely went beyond 'the German worker', who was patriotic, industrious and skilful, and 'the criminal functionaries' who dared to speak in his name. Thus he gave assurances that manual skills would be granted their full recognition in the coming Third Reich; he promised that a Nationalist Socialist government would do away with unemployment by destroying the Versailles System on which it was allegedly based; he made occasional denunciations of bank capital and expressed a vague anti-bourgeois and pseudo-egalitarian sentiment: Hitler had nothing but slogans to offer the working class. This rhetoric could no more satisfy the white- and blue-collar workers' wing of the Party, which finally organized itself in 1930, than Hitler's utterly vague projection of future Nationalist Socialist unions as occupational representatives in economic chambers and in a 'Central Economic Parliament'.[15] It is important to remember that the Party leadership never decided on a positive strategy either towards existing unions or with respect to founding their own trade-union organizations. There can be no doubt that this neglect essentially cut the Party off from a great number of wage-earners who saw trade unions as a critically important bastion of their rights and interests.[16]

The orientation of the emerging mass movement within the existing social structure was influenced far less by the negative stance of the Party leadership than by the fundamental transformation in Germany's economic and political situation – a transformation which took place quite independently of the activities of the NSDAP. Most important here were the first effects of the economic crisis and the radicalization of the DNVP. The Reichstag elections of 1928 showed unmistakably where the strongest voting potential for the NSDAP was to be found: among the farmers and in the old *Mittelstand* in the Protestant regions. As the crisis of German agriculture intensified in 1929, the Party redoubled its efforts in these regions. In the same year came the alliance with Hugenberg and the conservative Right in the Young Plan referendum. In view of the fact that the whole Party, including the so-called Left, pursued a ruthless opportunism in its efforts to attract new members and supporters, these new developments finally confirmed the position of the NSDAP at the

15. Hitler, *Mein Kampf*, pp. 675, 677. Kele, *Nazis*, pp. 110f., 176ff., does not emphasize clearly enough the importance of Hitler's own special line in these questions. See Henry Ashby Turner, Jr, 'Hitlers Einstellung zu Wirtschaft und Gesellschaft vor 1933', *Geschichte und Gesellschaft*, vol. 2/1, 1976, pp. 89–117.

16. Even for the white-collar workers this problem played an important role; thus the Party's basic anti-union position led to strong tensions between the NSDAP leadership and the leadership of the DHV, which, however, did not prevent the Nazi leadership from winning over numerous DHV members: Iris Hamel, *Völkischer Verband und nationale Gewerkschaft: Der Deutschnationale Handlungsgehilfen-Verband 1893–1933*, Frankfurt am Main, 1967, ch. 4.

extreme right of the political spectrum. As a consequence of this altered situation the Party acquired a social base which was fundamentally and totally hostile to the workers, not only in an ideological and political sense, but also as far as the central economic interests of the working class were concerned. There was no conceivable way that these interests could be reconciled with the demands of the Nazis' new nationalist following for lower taxes, higher prices for food, restrictions on department stores and consumer co-operatives, a reduction in social services and wages, and so on.[17] The social composition of the NSDAP membership, which grew by leaps and bounds between 1928 and 1930, decisively coloured the future character of the movement: the likelihood of any plausible efforts on behalf of the working class was constantly reduced, for all attempts of that sort now ran the risk of offending existing supporters.[18] With the intensification of the economic crisis – that is, with the intensification of the struggle over the distribution of a shrinking social product – this tension became steadily sharper.

There are two further reasons why, even at the beginning of the crisis, the NSDAP's orientation was determined so unambiguously by property interests (in the widest sense). The leadership of the local Party groups that developed in the years after 1925 came overwhelmingly from the bourgeoisie or the old *Mittelstand*. The rather loose structure of Party organization allowed these local functionaries great political independence and propagandistic initiative. Almost all regional and local research has emphasized the fact that workers were scarcely ever found in leading positions in the Party, even in larger cities: there were even reports that local groups sometimes resorted to dissimulation just to be able to display at least one worker in a responsible post.[19] Many analyses of the social composition of local leadership groups read like a roll-call of bourgeois occupations – government officials, school teachers, doc-

---

17. Of the wealth of literature on this theme, see especially Jeremy Noakes, *The Nazi Party in Lower Saxony 1921–1933*, London, 1971; Rudolf Heberle, *Landbevölkerung und Nationalsozialismus: Eine soziologische Untersuchung der politischen Willensbildung in Schleswig-Holstein 1918 bis 1932*, Stuttgart, 1963; Heinrich August Winkler, *Mittelstand, Demokratie und Nationalsozialismus: Die politische Entwicklung von Handwerk und Kleinhandel in der Weimarer Republik*, Cologne, 1972.

18. This risk was diminished by the fact that the movement displayed strong regional differences; thus, for example, it is questionable whether Nazis in East Prussia or in Bavaria even had to take notice of the Berlin Party's radical rhetoric. None the less, the need to hold on to members and voters already won represents a very imortant aspect of the development of the NSDAP to which too little attention has hitherto been given. All studies emphasize in a one-sided way the recruitment to the movement of ever wider circles. Schulz, *Aufstieg*, pp. 550, 585f., gives a summary of the very high turnover rate of Party membership before 1934.

19. See for example Albert Krebs, *Tendenzen und Gestalten der NSDAP Erinnerungen an die Frühzeit der Partei*, Stuttgart 1959, p. 44.

tors, clerks, self-employed businessmen, salesmen, retired officers, engineers, students.[20] These people were of course themselves dissatisfied with the existing authority structure in German society; without constant frustration and a profound distrust of the old ruling elite they would scarcely have come to National Socialism. But their newly awakened interest in politics was not in the least directed towards the improvement of the working class's living conditions. They were concerned first and foremost with their own advancement, with securing an advantageous position within a new elite.[21] The more the movement expanded, the more men of precisely this social background could solidify their positions within the local Party organizations, since they possessed both the education and often the experience in administration and organization which the increasingly complex bureaucratic structures of the Party demanded. Less-educated activists who had played a quite important role in the 1920s were now frequently relegated to the background by ambitious bourgeois newcomers. The latter were undoubtedly better equipped for active participation in a party which was at the point of transforming itself from a small sect to a mass movement.[22] The homogeneous non-proletarian character of the local leadership groups meant that the Party regarded the central economic and social demands of the workers with indifference at best. It further meant that the Party could only rely on the incomparably weaker weapons of a diversionary or nationalistic propaganda when it wanted to be heard in working-class quarters.

In addition to this there was a second important reason for National Socialism's ties to property interests. For the strategy which Hitler followed after 1924, attempting to gain power 'legally', it was imperative to be assured of at least the passive acquiescence of the old power elite, especially of the military and big industry. An open confrontation with these groups would not only have awakened the danger of a repetition of 1923 and thus the possibility of civil war, but it would further have overstrained the loyalty of those supporters of the NSDAP who viewed it as a genuinely conservative and restorationist movement. This strategic line by no means excluded fierce propagandistic attacks on the political

20. In addition to the works of Noakes, Böhnke and Kühr, see Geoffrey Pridham, *Hitler's Rise to Power: The Nazi Movement in Bavaria, 1923–1933*, London, 1973. That it was not outcasts from the bourgeoisie who were involved in these cadres is correctly emphasized by Theodore Abel, *The Nazi Movement: Why Hitler Came into Power*, New York, 1966, p. 315; cf. also Krebs, *Tendenzen*, pp. 45f.

21. Albert Krebs, for a time Gauleiter in Hamburg, was one of the very few exceptions in this regard. On the striving for recognition and upward social mobility in these circles within the NSDAP, see William Jannen, Jr, 'National Socialists and Social Mobility', *Journal of Social History*, vol. 9/3, 1976, 339–66.

22. See Orlow, *Nazi Party*, vol. 1, pp. 146f.; Pridham, *Bavaria*, pp. 85–115; Noakes, *Lower Saxony*, pp. 89–100; Krebs, *Tendenzen*, pp. 47ff.

organizations and spokesmen of older German conservatism. On the contrary, it practically demanded such tactics, since the 'legality' tactic made it necessary for the NSDAP to overtake all other bourgeois parties electorally in order then to approach the power elite in the role of the strongest political representative of a 'decent' (i.e. nationalist, non-socialist) Germany. But for the same reasons the Party could hardly risk lending support to political interests which this elite might have perceived as a direct threat to its own interests and power positions. This was ultimately the decisive reason why the NSDAP did not emerge in politics merely as the rival of the workers' parties, but rather as that power which was committed to crushing them. Hostility towards the working-class movement, closely combined with an aggressive nationalism, was hence the determining and common element that characterized all parties of the Right and conservative interest groups in the years after 1928. It was precisely the prospect that the NSDAP would act in accord with this basic position, and with more energy and success than any other political movement at that time, that lent the Party such attractiveness, and that also assured it the acquiescence of that elite with whose help alone the seizure of power could take place without profound turmoil.

The reaction of the working class to this threat was unequivocal but at the same time inadequate. Before the spring of 1933 remarkably few SPD supporters and union members converted to the cause of National Socialism. Though political loyalties were somewhat fluid on the boundary line between the KPD and NSDAP (especially in 1932), the growing strength of the KPD was still in every way more important than its occasional losses to the National Socialist movement. After 1930 both the KPD and the SPD understood themselves increasingly, if in different ways, as anti-fascist parties of the working class.[23] The fact that the KPD waged this battle with greater energy, or at least at greater volume, and the no less important fact that the acute distress of mass unemployment in industrial areas had a profoundly radicalizing effect, caused a big shift in electoral support, and a lesser shift in membership, from the SPD to the KPD between 1928 and 1932. But the number of voters for both parties taken together did not decline under the challenge of National Socialism: between 1928 and 1930 they rose by 700,000 and remained constant after that, at between 13 million and 13.1 million, up

23. Of Abel's group of 'old fighters' only 7 per cent had been members of left-wing organizations before they joined the NSDAP: *Nazi Movement*, p. 314. The classification of the KPD in these years as a 'totalitarian' party by emphasizing the anti-republican and anti-social democratic line of the Central Committee is unsatisfactory, among other reasons because it ignores the motivations of the members and particularly of the voters who supported the party. They were certainly more interested in the struggle against the NSDAP than in the struggle against the SPD.

to the last free Reichstag elections in November 1932, which once again confirmed this position. However, the electorate was growing steadily in these years, and in addition, the degree of voter participation rose. Thus, this figure of roughly 13 million voters represented a declining percentage of the total electorate. The voting strength of the SPD and KPD together fell from 40.4 per cent of all votes cast in 1929, to 35.9 per cent in July 1932.[24] These figures show that the workers' parties had reached the limits of their expansionary power, at least within the framework of the specific economic and political conditions of the time. To be sure, there were a series of more or less contingent factors which inhibited the further growth of the workers' parties: after 1928 both the SPD and the KPD lacked a decisive, convincing leadership, and both parties showed themselves incapable of responding to the economic and political crisis with new non-sectarian strategies.[25] But it is doubtful whether, even under the best leadership, the socialist parties could have succeeded in breaking through the sociological, ideological, religious and, not least, sex barriers which limited their expansion and thus their capacity for political integration after 1929. The election results indicate that those barriers were massive and firmly anchored. After 1929 only this kind of breakthrough would have been able to prevent by constitutional means the National Socialist seizure of power.[26]

In the course of the election campaigns between 1930 and 1932 there were certainly fluctuations between the workers' parties and the bourgeois parties (though these cannot be described with the requisite precision). But from the voting and membership statistics of the time one gets the general impression that the SPD and KPD together formed a political ghetto – a ghetto of considerable size, it is true, and one which, despite bitter internal struggles, was vigorously defended on the outside. It remained, nevertheless, a ghetto: after 1930 neither of the two parties was able any longer to make a convincing bid for hegemony in German politics. This derived partly from their inability to enter into political coalitions after the proclamation of the 'social-fascist' line by the Third International and after the collapse of the Great Coalition. But, of course, more important in the context of this study is the fact that millions of German wage-earners were entirely unreceptive to the political

24. See Alfred Milatz, *Wähler und Wahlen in der Weimarer Republik*, Schriftenreihe der Bundeszentrale für politische Bildung, no. 66, Bonn, 1965, pp. 90, 108, 126–50.

25. The strategies of the workers' parties were inappropriate both to their relationships with each other, and to the economic crisis. For the SPD's and the Free Trade Unions' conceptions of economic policy, see the articles by Robert Gates and Michael Schneider in Hans Mommsen, Dietmar Petzina and Bernd Weisbrod (eds.), *Industrielles System und politische Entwicklung in der Weimarer Republik*, Düsseldorf, 1974, pp. 206–237.

26. The SPD and the Free Trade Unions were not prepared to undertake extra-constitutional measures.

demands of the SPD and KPD, and remained immune to any attempt at political mobilization by the workers' parties. That in turn was one of the most important reasons why these parties were not successful in expanding and consolidating their power base in the last years of the Weimar Republic.

It is not possible here to enter into a thorough discussion of the electoral sociology of the period. Some brief remarks on this topic do seem necessary, however, both to illuminate the most prominent characteristics of National Socialism as a mass movement and to reconstruct with greater clarity the structure of political class conflict in the period between 1930 and 1933. Wage-earners and their adult dependants, including the relevant portion of the retired, constituted approximately half of the total electorate in these years: about 22 to 25 million of a total number of 42 to 45 million voters belonged to households whose main income consisted of the weekly wage of a manual worker. But when one considers that in this period the SPD also received considerable support from groups other than wage-earners, it appears that in the elections between 1930 and 1932 *at most half* of all wage-earners gave their votes to the workers' parties.[27] The statistical material allows only rough classifications and estimates. None the less, it is clear enough that, leaving aside the 1919 elections to the National Assembly, a very large proportion of the labouring population had never voted for a workers' party. The fact that these people did not change their position during the political and economic crisis which ended with the National Socialist seizure of power proved to be decisive. With the exception of those Catholic workers in the Ruhr, southern Germany and Silesia who voted for the Centre,[28] very little is known about the political opinions and affiliations of those millions of wage-earners who supported neither Social Democracy nor Communism; and we also know little about the range of their living and working conditions.

27. These figures represent rough estimates, based on statistics in Theodor Geiger, *Die soziale Schichtung des deutschen Volkes*, Stuttgart, 1967, pp. 22, 51; Milatz, *Wähler*, p. 128; *Statistisches Handbuch von Deutschland 1928–1944*, Munich, 1949, p. 32. If one counts the white-collar workers as well, the number of those entitled to vote who had to rely for sustenance on their labour power alone rises to a total of between 28 million and 32 million. For a precise picture of the social structure of the enfranchised population one would need a breakdown by age of employed persons and their dependants. Milatz, *Wähler*, ch. IV/4, does not pursue this question.

28. Johannes Schauff, *Das Wahlverhalten der deutschen Katholiken im Kaiserreich und in der Weimarer Republik*, ed. Rudolf Morsey, Mainz, 1975, provides no information about the social structure of the Centre or the BVP voters. Among them there were probably 2 million or 3 million wage-earners (including dependants). If one assumes that a good half of non-voters were likewise wage-earners (including dependants), the four groups KPD, SPD, Centre/BVP and non-voters thus counted 17.5 million to 19 million enfranchised voters from the working class. That would leave 5 million to 8 million.

Simply the number of workers not politically affiliated in this sense, and the importance which thus devolved upon them in the struggles of this period, indicate the fundamental and at the same time abundant ambiguity of the concept of class: it is a category which pertains both to socio-economic structures and to the historical process moved by human activity. The socio-economic dimension of the concept of class describes the general situation of all those who are dependent for their subsistence on their labour power alone. Here the emphasis lies on the general structures of capitalism and on the objective conditions of economic development which determine the position of the wage-earner in the production process. 'Class' in this sense indicates the forms of exploitation and oppression to which wage-earners are subject, their dependence on the law of supply and demand in the labour market, as well as the economically deprived living conditions that result from this. In the context of empirical research in social history this category is less precise than is generally assumed. The other meaning of the concept of class can only be determined with reference to the historical process, with reference to the history of the working-class movement. If one pursues the premise that underlies Edward Thompson's pioneering study *The Making of the English Working Class*, 'class happens when some men, as a result of common experiences (inherited and shared), feel and articulate the identity of their interests as between themselves, and as against other men whose interests are different from (and usually opposed to) theirs'.[29] Here the accent falls on the public activity that grows out of the common experiences of the workers, on active resistance to oppression, on solidarity as the class struggle creates it – in short, on the dynamic character of class conflict as the prime motor of historical development. When the concept of class is used in this sense, it draws attention to those individuals and groups who, by speaking and acting for their class, actively determine the framework of the political struggle.

For the historian it would be a senseless undertaking to try to draw a sharp distinction between these two dimensions of the concept of class. For a purism of definition, whether turned in the one or the other direction, will only mean that an essential part of historical reality is obscured from the beginning: an apolitical history of social structures is as uninteresting as the 'biography' of this or that workers' organization. But it must be admitted that all investigations that attempt to interpret the political history of a society as the history of class relationships will understand the working class primarily in the form of those workers who organized to represent the class interest. It was they, after all, who

29. E. P. Thompson, *The Making of the English Working Class*, London, 1963, p. 9.

challenged the propertied classes and drove them to counter-measures. In the period of the Weimar Republic German working-class leaders could in fact maintain with a high degree of conviction that they were speaking and acting for all wage-earners: not just for the active members of the class, but also for the unorganized, the indifferent, even the politically conservative workers.

This approach is not necessarily bound to a general teleology and it is not derived from a mechanistic determinism. It was only the unavoidable fact of class conflict that was determined by the class structure of capitalist society in Germany (and therein lay its central importance as a principle ordering all public life), but not the specific forms and configurations in which this conflict manifested itself at any point. For this reason it is not useful to discuss the political role of those wage-earners who supported neither the KPD nor the SPD in terms of the concepts of 'objective social situation' and 'false consciousness': this presupposes a narrow, rigid determinism, while the objective social situation of these people was itself almost certainly ambiguous. Few of them belonged to the industrial workforce in the strict sense of the word: it cannot be emphasized strongly enough that fewer than 8 million of the 16 million[30] classified as 'workers' in the occupational censuses of 1925 and 1933 were active in enterprises which could be classified as industries. The other 8 million to 8.5 million workers were employed in agriculture, public service, transportation, commerce and crafts, and private services. Apart from a few exceptions (notably the state railways and workshop trades like printing and some branches of engineering) the trade unions that constituted the hard core of the organized working class had little support in the non-industrial sectors of the economy. The working and living conditions of agricultural workers, craftsmen and tradespeople were considerably different from those of factory workers. Relationships to the employer, above all, were of a more individual than collective nature, since many of these workers lived in the countryside and in small and medium-sized provincial cities where the working-class movement had not been able to establish a stable and continuing

30. *Statistisches Handbuch von Deutschland*, Munich, 1949, p. 32; *Statistisches Jahrbuch für das Deutsche Reich*, 1936, p. 331. The figure of 16 million also includes those unemployed. The narrow category of industrial workers was not defined with perfect clarity: see *Stat. Anhang, Doc. I b.* Even if those employed by the Reichsbahn and in larger artisanal enterprises are included, one does not arrive at anywhere near 'ten million industrial workers' (Schulz, *Aufstieg*, p. 551). However, it must also be recognized that there was a constant and probably also relatively strong fluctuation within the industrial workforce, so that considerably more people possessed the basic experience of industrial labour than at any one point could be included in this occupational group – fluctuations due to change in occupation, rationalization, illness, retirement, marriage (for women), and so on.

presence. Conditions on the labour market were less extreme and less opaque: in many places the traditional hierarchical social order had still been preserved, and the Church also exercised a considerable influence over political culture. Thus, these people had little opportunity to develop class consciousness through confrontation and organization.

To the working class in the broad socio-economic sense belonged also a large number of women who were heavily under-represented in the electorate of the workers' parties. Their relationship to politics was decisively influenced by the fact that many left regularly paid employment, and thus a crucial arena of public experience, as early as age 20. For women in general it must be remembered that a long tradition of discrimination and subordination as well as restriction to purely familial responsibilities had militated against the development of that capacity for independent political decision and collective political activity which active participation in the working-class movement demanded.[31]

Lastly, there was that considerable group of people who can be characterized as the victims of the war and of the post-war crises, and as victims of economic competition in an era before the welfare state: people whose lives had been destroyed by the loss of family members, war injuries or impaired health, by long unemployment, inflation or the decline of their trade. In the late 1920s these people lived on the edge of poverty, dependent on public welfare and occasional work in order to eke out any existence at all. They were participants in a bitter individual struggle for mere survival, not in a political struggle for general goals.

For these and other reasons which were connected to the specific traditions of particular trades and occupations, the class experience (to employ Thompson's central concept again) of approximately half of those defined by the occupational census as 'workers' was fundamentally different from the experience of organized members of the class. For reasons which thus partly derived precisely from their objective social situation, they had not been able to develop that sense of solidarity in larger economic and political contexts which had become the real hallmark of the working-class movement.[32] The ambivalence that inheres in the concept of the working class may perhaps be expressed in the phrase that many workers were consigned to the working class without, however, belonging to it.

31. My essay, 'Women in Germany, 1925–1940: Family, Welfare and Work', *History Workshop Journal*, 1976, 1 and 2, contains some remarks on this question.
32. The category 'worker' here again includes adult family members. The tautological quality of the argumentation in the preceding paragraphs is obvious. The difficulty lies for the most part in the fact that unorganized workers have left so many fewer sources on the basis of which one could investigate their situation and their behaviour – not least precisely because they were unorganized. General statistics on those employed in trade and crafts: Winkler, *Mittelstand*, pp. 30f., Appendix I. Winkler could discover remarkably little about the wage-earners among them.

To say that they did not *yet* belong to it would be an oversimplification in two respects. Of course, one must take into consideration here the fact that those sectors of the economy where the organized working class was strongest were continually gaining workers from the provinces and from the handicraft sector, and that in the 1920s capitalist forms of economic organization were continuing to expand and subject more and more areas of economic life to their distinctive patterns of progress. But it was crucial that the dynamics of these socio-economic developmental tendencies were slower in pace than in the pre-war period, and that the proportion of the population that earned its sustenance by wage labour was as a whole no longer on the increase; it was white-collar jobs that were the major area of expansion.

It must, nevertheless, be borne in mind that the organized working class represented not only the immediate legal, social and material interests of the unorganized. [33] In its political practice it also anticipated their long-term future needs and interests by trying to transform the urban industrial world, dominated by big industry, big business and bureaucratic administration, so that the future generations drawn into this world by the continuing process of economic develement would experience less poverty, brutality and alienation. But the profound crisis which violently interrupted this developmental process in Germany between 1928/9 and 1933 thereby also robbed the working class movement of its anticipatory, future-directed role for the working class in general; to the degree that industry and trade shrank, the potential constituency of the workers' parties stagnated. Even more important was the narrowing of the political arena of the working-class movement. Reforms could no longer be undertaken and achieved, and the social revolution seemed still possible only to those whose power of critical judgement had been lamed by the demands which the Third International placed upon their loyalty.

If the argument is valid to this point, it is a mistake to pose the question in the following way: why did approximately one-half of the working-class electorate (to use the term in its sociological, positivistic sense) not vote for the workers' parties? There cannot be a simple, straightforward explanation. One could at best convey and describe the variety of relationships binding the different groups mentioned above into structures of political authority and culture that remained immune to the goals and forms of action of the organized working class. But what must be explained here is the fact that after 1929 the NSDAP gained considerable support from the ranks of those wage-earners who

---

33. For instance, by the reforms adopted in the area of labour and factory law, maternity protection and unemployment insurance, also by the effect of collective bargaining on the earnings of unorganized workers.

were neither organized in trade unions nor had regularly voted for the SPD or KPD in the preceding years. Thus in September 1930 roughly 26.3 per cent, and in January 1933 some 31.5 per cent of Nazi Party members described themselves as workers – about 75,000 and 300,000 people respectively. (In September 1930, only a third of these wage-earners were employed in industry.) These figures must be treated with great caution. First, the Party expanded rapidly in the period between the two counts, and there was a very high turnover rate among members, many of whom dropped out after belonging for only a short time; this fact is not adequately reflected in the social breakdown of the member-ship. Second, it is certain that among those members who identified themselves as 'workers' there was a considerable number of self-employed craftsmen, though it is not possible to say exactly how many. Despite these qualifications, the figures point to two clear conclusions. Workers were heavily under-represented within the movement, but they did constitute a minority which was in every respect significant.[34] Unfortunately, corresponding figures for the Nazi electorate cannot be obtained. But it can be concluded that among the 13.42 million Germans who voted for Hitler as Reich president in April 1932, and among the 13.77 million NSDAP voters in the Reichstag elections in July 1932, there must have been several million wage-earners and their family members – at least 3.5 million, probably more.

The pseudo-egalitarianism, together with the systematically ambiva-lent social rhetoric of the Party leadership and the novelty and dynamism which characterized its actions, provided the movement with access to this broad, heterogeneous and politically unstable sector of German soci-ety. Among the factors that influenced this part of the electorate, it is probably safe to ascribe particular importance to the extreme nationalism of the NSDAP, for the alleged 'anti-national' stance of the working-class parties – an accusation which conservatives and Nazis never tired of repeating – did act as a barrier between them and potential supporters among the wage-earning population. That nationalism and socialism, whether of the Social Democratic or the Communist variety, were funda-mentally incompatible was a major and recurrent theme of Nazi propa-ganda. In conjunction with the egalitarian pose of NSDAP, a conjunction which was new in German politics and for that reason doubly seductive, these nationalist slogans had considerable effect in the circles of unorga-nized and politically inexperienced workers. In the heavily ideological political culture of the Weimar Republic organized workers distinguished themselves from the unorganized above all by their ability to put the interests of their class before the so-called national or people's (*Volk*) interest; more precisely, to comprehend the latter in terms of the former.

As yet, little can be said about the specific sociological conditions for this effect. Wage-earners who voted for the Nazis were probably young rather than old; men were probably more strongly represented than women; in 1932 they could be found in all areas of industrial concentration but mostly not in large numbers; numbers were somewhat higher in individual industrial cities in Saxony, Thuringia, Westphalia and Silesia; they were most prominent and numerous in the medium-sized and small cities of the Protestant provinces.[35] Further detailed research will have to test the hypothesis that a large proportion of those wage-earners who were susceptible to the slogans of National Socialism were occupied in smaller businesses, in trade or handicrafts as well as in agriculture, and that they were strongly under the influence of their employers, who for their part had been among the most reliable supporters of the NSDAP since 1930/1. Wage-earners in industry seem to have given the Party little support before 1932. Hypotheses of this sort are difficult to test, for to date we know a great deal less about wage-earners in the provinces than about those in the cities, and much less about Nazi voters than about Party activists.

If we now turn to these activists, it becomes clear that especially in the sector of the unorganized wage-earners in industrialized areas and big cities the so-called National Socialist Left achieved a certain political importance. If one ignores its confused political rhetoric, which has been strongly emphasized in the scholarship of the past years, it is clear that the Nazi Left offers little more than a further example of the Party's strategic opportunism. It never constituted an independent political grouping of any significance. What it really amounted to was the workers' wing within the movement as a whole. The NSDAP appealed to various groups of potential supporters by telling them what they wanted to hear. Thus the Party tailored specific approaches to peasants, artisans, shopkeepers, civil servants, the self-employed, students, women, soldiers and big industrialists – and to workers as well.[36] This strategic

35. See Milatz, *Wähler*; Mühlenberger, 'Westphalia', ch. IX, iii; Böhnke, *Ruhrgebiet*, pp. 175–180. The best analysis of electoral support for the NSDAP is the article by Thomas Childers, 'The Social Bases of the National Socialist Vote', *Journal of Contemporary History*, 4, October 1976, pp. 17–42.

36. Cf. Goebbels's instructions for the Reichstag election campaign of June 1932, which prescribed totally different directions for the propaganda depending on which public was to be reached: quoted in Kele, *Nazis*, p. 206. On the 'National Socialist Left' in general see also the concise assessment of Ernst Nolte, 'Zur Phänomenologie des Faschismus', *Vierteljahrshefte für Zeitgeschichte*, vol. 10/4, 1962, pp. 395.

opportunism was expressed most forcefully in Goebbels's role as Gauleiter and newspaper boss in Berlin after 1927. His demagogic anti-capitalism, his energetic attempts to stir up social resentments and to portray the NSDAP as a movement of rough, simple, tough, rebellious young radicals were superficially much sharper in tone than those of his former boss Gregor Strasser. But Goebbels enjoyed an incomparably securer position within the Party leadership precisely because it was perfectly well known in Munich that he himself did not take his socio-political propaganda entirely seriously, because his loyalty belonged above all to the movement as a whole and to its leader, and not to the supporters he was able to win for the Party in Berlin.[37] The same fundamental opportunism reveals itself as well in the history of the great debates and schisms within the Party before 1933. From the Bamberg Party conference in February 1926, to the affairs of Otto Strasser, Stennes, Scheringer and Krebs, up to the (admittedly more complicated) case of Gregor Strasser's resignation – in every case, the men who found their positions untenable were those who sought to define the Party's role seriously as the motor of social change and did not consider political power a goal in itself.[38]

Although the Nazis' social demagoguery was thoroughly opportunistic and lacked any genuine commitment, the mere fact that it was allowed free rein after 1929/30 and was not suppressed by the Party leadership was of some importance for the future development of the movement. Through it the Party gained the appearance of non-exclusivity – an achievement which, so to speak, continually reinforced itself, for the more wage-earners joined the movement, the more it represented a plausible political alternative for others:[39] a popular movement (*Volksbewegung*) which distinguished itself precisely through this fact from the nationalist parties.

Those workers who identified actively with this variant of National Socialism formed, in accord with this opportunism, quite a heterogeneous body. Though much research must still be done on details here, it is nevertheless clear that they were less representative of their social class as a whole than those members of the old and new *Mittelstand* who before 1933 pursued their own anti-socialist variant of National Socialism. On the basis of existing studies it is possible to identify three totally different

37. This is well demonstrated by Kele, *Nazis*, pp. 91ff., 104ff., 131ff. Here he is building on the penetrating analysis of Martin Broszat, 'Die Anfänge der Berliner NSDAP 1926/27', *Vierteljahrshefte für Zeitgeschichte*, vol. 8/1, 1960, pp. 85ff.

38. This tendency intensified still more after 1933; for the repression of the NSBO, see below, pp. 95ff., 154ff.; the memoirs of Krebs, *Tendenzen*, pp. 69–71, are very useful here.

39. Among them, especially among the young, there were also genuine idealists: see e.g. Krebs, *Tendenzen*, pp. 50f.

groups of 'National Socialist workers'. First are those young men who composed the gangs of storm-troopers (SA) in the big cities. That this group has hitherto received the most attention, both at the time and in later scholarly investigations, can be explained on the one hand by the fact that their notorious street terror put them much more visibly in the public lime-light than other workers in the Party. Furthermore, they behaved like the bourgeoisie expected workers to behave, even though they were certainly not all workers. A statistical analysis of the composition of these SA groups is still lacking, and because of the high turnover among members it will not be easy to produce this kind of account. It seems improbable that wage-earners in the urban SA groups before January 1933 comprised more than half of the whole SA (about 300,000 men).[40] Reliable observers report that many of them were unemployed. The SA offered them soup kitchens, sometimes even clothes, shelter in SA homes, but above all activity, a superficial purpose in life and a perverse self-respect.[41] Some vacillated back and forth between the KPD and the NSDAP. Albert Krebs, who was familiar with this milieu in Hamburg and portrayed it with sympathy, described these people as the 'drift sand of the working-class movement'.[42] For them the SA gangs formed a point of order in the otherwise desolate, formless and decaying world of the big cities stricken by the crisis. Here could be found a chance to express destructive resent-ments, unbearable frustrations, despair and aggression. These aspects emerged most obviously in the capital. One of the major experts on the National Socialist movement writes aptly of the

> fatal confusion of mobilization and socialism which, more than its socio-political ideologies, occasionally led to the Berlin NSDAP's building a repu-tation as a party of socialist revolution. ... At the same time the mob's

40. Cf. Heinrich Bennecke, *Hitler und die SA*, Munich, 1962, pp. 213f. For the SA in gen-eral, see particularly the work of Sauer in Karl Dietrich Bracher, Wolfgang Sauer and Gerhard Schulz, *Die nationalsozialistische Machtergreifung. Studien zur Errichtung des totalitären Herrschaftssystems in Deutschland 1933–1934*, Cologne/Opladen, 1960, pp. 829–96.

41. Cf. Krebs, *Tendenzen*, p. 92; Rudolph Diels, *Lucifer ante Portas: Zwischen Severing und Heydrich*, Zürich, n.d. [1950], p. 55; Böhnke, *Ruhrgebiet*, pp. 154, 157, where the percentage of unemployed among SA men is estimated at 30–40 per cent – not a very high figure given the social structure of this region.

42. Krebs, *Tendenzen*, p. 74. The majority of urban unemployed probably went to the KPD without, however, being firmly integrated there. Along with the numerous eye-wit-ness reports of political fluctuations, the instability of their political ties to the KPD is attested to by various election results from 1932, particularly the second presidential elec-tion: see Kühr, *Essen*, p. 291; Kele, *Nazis*, pp. 205–8; Böhnke, *Ruhrgebiet*, p. 185; Henning Timpke (ed.), *Dokumente zur Gleichschaltung des Landes Hamburg 1933*, Frankfurt am Main, 1964, pp. 19–31. Böhnke, p. 192, stresses the return of these voters to the KPD in the course of the second half of 1932. It is probable that these circles of urban unemployed were likewise strongly represented among the numerous fluctuating mem-bers of the NSDAP in the crisis years.

propertylessness and lack of social interests, on which its lack of responsibility depends, lends it at times the positive image of social selflessness. Out of the selfless flight into the dynamism of political action grows the appearance of a martyr's dedication to the community.[43]

A second group of National Socialist workers was quite distinct from the volatile youthful *Lumpenproletariat*. This solid type was to be found mainly among those employed in public service – with the Reichsbahn and the post office, in municipal services and transportation.[44] Why the National Socialists received support from precisely this group cannot be readily explained. It is not yet clear whether it should be attributed to their consciousness of their special occupational prestige, or to political influence exercised by superiors in the administration, or else to anger about cuts in pay ordered by city and state officials (i.e. for the most part by Social Democrats). These two categories of National Socialist workers – the young unemployed in the big cities, and the 'uniformed workers' – found themselves in a political minority within their own social peer group and thus were continually subject to tough conflicts. In addition a third type of active 'worker-Nazi' can be identified whose situation was again different and, politically at least, less exposed: in the provinces numerous wage-earners obviously simply followed the political example of their social superiors, so that here the National Socialist organizations, including the SA, frequently reflected the hierarchical order of the local community.[45]

These are the three categories of active Nazi supporters among the labouring population recognized up to now. As the factory council (*Betriebsrat*) elections showed, the movement had little success before 1933 with those who had been able to retain their job in industry in the narrower sense defined above.[46] To be sure, these election results do not

43. Broszat, 'Berliner NSDAP', p. 91. It is possible that further investigation of this question will lead to the conclusion that the situation of the young unemployed people in the big cities was more marked by the collapse of social and familial ties or of political traditions than was the case with young unemployed people in the typical medium-sized industrial city which perhaps demonstrated greater homogeneity and unity.

44. See Noakes, *Lower Saxony*, pp. 175, 178; Böhnke, *Ruhrgebiet*, p. 71; William Sheridan Allen, *The Nazi Seizure of Power: The Experience of a Single German Town 1930–1935*, London, 1966, pp. 210f. The strike of the Berlin transportation workers might also be remembered here. Among these public sector workers the Free Trade Unions were by no means always weakly represented.

45. Cf. Allen, *Seizure*, pp. 29, 61, on the demonstrations in 'Thalburg' (Northeim) for which SA men from neighbouring villages were called into the city. The research of Richard Bessel (University of Oxford) on the SA in the eastern provinces, particularly in East Prussia, provides a similar picture. Useful general discussions about the origin and role of wage-earners in the National Socialist movement in Geiger, *Soziale Schichtung*, pp. 109–22; Martin Broszat, *Der Staat Hitlers*, Munich, 1969.

46. Böhnke, *Ruhrgebiet*, pp. 173f., 200.

provide conclusive proof, and there were also exceptions here: in individual firms and in some regions like Chemnitz-Zwickau as well as in a number of Westphalian mining and textile cities, the NSDAP achieved a certain entry into the structures of the politically-conscious working class. Even in these regions, however, the proportion of wage-earners in the Party by no means corresponded to their predominance in local population.[47]

This interpretation is confirmed by the fact that the single attempt undertaken by the Party itself to found a political organization of their own of workers – the National Socialist Factory Cell Organization (NSBO) – was long denied any noteworthy success. It is true that the NSBO came about as a consequence of the initiatives and demands of Party activists (among them some former Communists) whose political stance was essentially motivated by dissatisfaction with the inequality and inefficiency of the capitalist order.[48] None the less, from the beginning it was intended merely as a propaganda organization. Its founding in Berlin in 1928 and its recognition by Hitler in 1929 were no more than a gesture by means of which the Party leadership made concessions to those forces within the movement which had hitherto agitated in vain for a Party trade union. Although these latter groups had come in good part from the ranks of nationalistic white-collar workers' organizations and thus had trained and experienced officials among them, the concessions were of very limited nature and were accompanied by little enthusiasm. The NSBO was supposed to refrain from all trade-union activities and to limit itself to the role intended for it as a political shock-troop in the factories. The fact that until around the middle of 1932 the new organization received practically no financial support from the Party shows that even this drastic prohibition against all genuinely class-specific activity did not dispel the doubts of the Munich leadership.[49]

Up to this time the development of the NSBO had lagged far behind the development of the NSDAP itself. Before May 1932 it numbered scarcely 100,000 members. It thus did not include anything like all the Party members who classified themselves as workers. Even more

47. All of the local and regional studies available reach this same conclusion. See especially Mühlberger, 'Westphalia', pp. 363–81. It must always be remembered that the social structure of even the most completely industrialized cities was highly differentiated. Thus in Essen 40 per cent, in Chemnitz 42.8 per cent of the working population were *not* wage-earners in 1933: *Stat. Jahrbuch*, 1934, pp. 24f.

48. Noakes, *Lower Saxony*, p. 146. (The statement in Mason, *Arbeiterklasse und Volksgemeinschaft*, p. 20, note 9, that Johannes Engel, founder of the NSBO, had been a Communist, is mistaken.)

49. For a good general survey of the early stages of the NSBO see Hans-Gerd Schumann, *Nationalsozialismus und Gewerkschaftsbewegung*, Hanover, 1958, pp. 30–8; also Kele, *Nazis*, p. 149ff.

indicative is that fact that many of these members were not wage-earners at all but white-collar workers and artisans. Among the artisans there were also self-employed workers who were obsessed by organization and joined every possible group in the crisis years; in July 1932, they were ordered to leave the NSBO. More important in every respect were the white-collar workers. Their numerical importance is demonstrated by the NSBO's incomparably better results in the elections for employee committees than in those for factory councils in these years.[50] The egalitarian, nationalistic and state socialist slogans of the NSBO obviously struck a particular chord in this continually growing intermediate stratum, whose powerful non-socialist occupational organizations had long struggled for the realization of a series of contradictory aims. They attempted first of all to defend the special identity and the privileges of white-collar workers *vis-à-vis* manual workers; second, to gain for themselves as unions formal recognition and co-operation on the part of employers; and, third, together with the conservative parties supported by big industry, to agitate for the re-establishment of Germany's power status in Europe.

The interest-group elements in this programme were hardly compatible with those pertaining to national politics. After 1928 it became increasingly clear to the members of the largest white-collar organization, the anti-Semitic German National Salesmen's and Clerks' Association (DHV), that their aims could not be realized within the existing party system, at which point particularly the younger members joined the NSDAP and NSBO in great numbers, hoping to find fulfilment there for their vision of an 'organic popular democracy'. Gregor Strasser, for example, who along with Goebbels was one of the main supporters of the NSBO, directed special attention to these circles.[51] Moreover, workers in public service were strongly represented in the NSBO, while in industrial concerns their cells were often inspired and dominated by technicians, foremen, wage-earning artisans and, in mining, by pit-foremen.[52] In the second half of 1932, however, the NSBO seems to have succeeded in expanding its base, and in these months it also probably attracted more factory workers. In any case, its membership tripled within eight months.

50. Böhnke, *Ruhrgebiet*, pp. 173ff.; Noakes, *Lower Saxony*, p. 178; Kele, *Nazis*, pp. 202f.

51. See Hamel, *Völkischer Verband*, ch. 4; Krebs,*Tendenzen*, pp. 13ff.; Kele, *Nazis*, pp. 108f., 144, 202f.; Jürgen Kocka, 'Zur Problematik der deutschen Angestellten 1914–1933', in Mommsen, Petzina, Weisbrod (eds.), *Industrielles System*, pp. 797ff. The over-representation of white-collar workers in the Nazi movement was that much greater when one considers that 39 per cent of all white-collar workers were women, but that women were barely present at all in the NSDAP: see *Stat. Jahrbuch*, 1934, p. 19.

52. Noakes, *Lower Saxony*, pp. 174–82; this brief discussion is the sharpest and best researched analysis of the NSBO. See also Schumann, *Gewerkschaftsbewegung*, p. 34.

The NSBO now also began to behave increasingly like a trade union: it supported a series of strikes, talked about founding a united national trade union under its own leadership, and staked a claim to the leading role in the socio-policial arena once the Nazis had taken power. According to the propaganda, the goal of the NSBO remained the establishment of a social order organized by 'estates' (*Stände*): its line towards the end of 1932 left no doubt, however, that it considered the workers the most important estate. 'Through its practical experience', Schumann rightly observes, 'The NSBO slid further to the left'.[53] It may well be that this radicalization of rhetoric and tactics was an important factor in the growing popularity of the NSBO in these months. Yet it is equally probable that the hopeless situation of the labour market, together with increasing likelihood that the NSDAP would soon come to power, caused numerous workers to regard membership in the NSBO as a kind of insurance against the loss of their jobs.[54]

In spite of this surge in membership figures in 1932, in spite of the greater independence of the NSBO within the National Socialist movement and in spite of the radicalization of its propaganda and actions, the workers' wing in the NSDAP never became a weighty political force on its own account. First, the 300,000 members of the NSBO must be set against the 5.8 million blue- and white-collar workers who still belonged to the independent trade unions at the end of 1932, and against the million-plus membership of the *Reichsbanner*, the 650,000 wage-earners in the SPD, and the 250,000-strong KPD.[55] The NSBO as such represented no serious threat at all to the organized working class, whose loyalties remained for the most part unshaken until the spring of 1933. If the same point is now approached from another perspective, the chronology of the NSBO's development leaves little doubt that it owed whatever power it did have solely to the earlier, larger political gains of the Nazi movement as a whole. It seems to have profited more from the

53. Schumann, *Gewerkschaftsbewegung*, p. 38, also pp. 39ff., 167; and Kele, *Nazis*, pp. 198–201.
54. For further discussion of this thesis see below, pp. 86f. We do not yet know much about the social origins of the new members of the NSBO in the latter half of 1932. Some were self-employed craftsmen: cf. Noakes, *Lower Saxony*, pp. 180–2. It would be interesting to discover whether there were also many unemployed among them. In some areas industrial workers who joined the NSBO continued to pay their trade-union dues.
55. The figure of 5.8 million trade-union members includes members of the Free and the Christian Trade Unions (white- and blue-collar), but not those of the Hirsch-Duncker and other less independent organizations: Schumann, *Gewerkschaftsbewegung*, pp. 163f. See further Karl Rohe, *Das Reichsbanner Schwarz-Rot-Gold*, Düsseldorf, 1966, p. 73; Schulz, *Aufstieg*, pp. 554–9, 859f. Schulz's critique of the statistics on the social composition of SPD membership is plausible and useful, but his implicit conclusion that a very large proportion of the members belonged to the old or the new *Mittelstand* is less plausible. This topic also requires further investigation.

general success of the Party in 1932 than it contributed itself. Third, it must be strongly emphasized that, although the NSDAP was able in 1931/2 to increase its support among wage-earners not just absolutely but also relatively, workers in general still remained massively under-represented, both in the membership and among Nazi voters. In spite of the economic crisis and the resulting economic distress and political insecurity in industrial areas, the NSBO thus did not succeed in shifting the social base of the whole Party fundamentally and permanently: the NSDAP remained with almost 70 per cent of its membership a party of property-owners and salary-earners. Hence, it followed necessarily that the NSBO was quite incapable of calling the basic economic and socio-political line of the Party leadership into question. Developments in fact went in the opposite direction: in the course of 1932 the ties of Hitler and his closest advisers to existing property and power interests assumed even clearer and more definite forms, so that towards the end of this year the danger that the NSBO might institutionalize class con-flict within the movement became a burden, an uncomfortable hin-drance to efforts to win the trust of the old power elite at any price.[56]

The real political importance of the NSBO and of the wage-earners among the Party membership did not derive from programmatic aims and conscious intentions, nor from an independent position of power within the Nazi movement; rather, it was indirect and functional, a con-sequence of the heterogeneous nature of the mass movement and of the devious multiple strategies of the leadership. One of the most important functions of this group of activists was to make the bourgeois Nazis believe that they had joined a real 'popular movement', a movement that was more than just a new edition of the Pan-German League. There is much evidence of self-doubt, of a social and cultural guilty conscience, among the bourgeoisie at this time. The strong anti-bourgeois compo-nent in Party rhetoric resonated precisely with the bourgeois classes that Hitler himself despised as politically philistine and cowardly. The cate-gorical denial of ethical norms and the denigration of the intellectual and cultural values of the bourgeoisie, which was manifested in the Party's systematic use of violence and propaganda, found a wide response in these very circles. Brute force, ruthlessness, recklessness and loud self-assertion – all these qualities assiduously cultivated in the propaganda of the mass movement had an especially strong impact on those members of the old and new *Mittelstand* who, as a consequence of the practically uninterrupted series of political and economic crises

56. Schumann, *Gewerkschaftsbewegung*, pp. 38–48; Schulz, *Aufstieg*, pp. 550–4. Schulz draws quite different conclusions from the statistics on the composition of the Party, emphasizing above all its popular character.

since 1914, were losing all trust in bourgeois forms of public life. In this severe crisis of confidence raw youthful activism offered itself as the only attractive alternative; it seemed after all to be superior to the political institutions and modes of behaviour which had failed to protect bourgeois interests. These qualities of youthful strength and determination were in turn attributed to 'the worker'; many bourgeois Nazis, particularly the educated among them, attempted to accommodate themselves to this mythical figure. One can hardly assume that this form of bourgeois anti-bourgeois sentiment impressed real workers very much (even if it perhaps flattered some of them). Yet even such fantasies demanded some basis in fact. The workers in the National Socialist movement fulfilled just this function by helping to assure bourgeois members that they were struggling in the Party for a real social renewal, for a genuine national community, and so on. They attempted to establish their role of social and political leadership on a new basis of national solidarity within which all bourgeois inhibitions, educational privileges and status differences, now made responsible for their previous political powerlessness, would lose their legitimacy. The road to this singular goal led through violence, irrationality and mindless activism – modes of behaviour that seemed to transcend any class-determined model.[57]

With respect to the much larger group of passive Nazis – those who gave the Party their votes without working actively in it – the workers in the movement fulfilled a quite different function. Much suggests that they performed a large part of the strenuous, risky and dangerous Party tasks: demonstrations, distribution of propaganda literature and, above all, street battles. It was the foot-soldiers of the movement who in fact entered battle against Communists and Social Democrats, and while the bourgeoisie no doubt considered this task necessary, they showed little willingness to carry it out themselves. Still, one should not ignore the fact that within the Party there was no strict division of labour according to social class. A significant number of educated bourgeois members did take on thankless political activities, risking beatings in the process. But without the tens of thousands of wage-earners whom the Party had attracted by 1933, it would never have been able to assemble its civil-war army in Germany's big cities. After all, because of their physical constitution, origins and life-style these people were much better suited for rough, violent political confrontations than the inhabitants of bour-

---

57. The bourgeois cult of 'the worker' in the 1920s would be worth a detailed investigation. An especially striking example is cited in Noakes, *Lower Saxony*, p. 22. J. P. Stern, *Ernst Jünger: A Writer of Our Time*, Cambridge, 1953, pp. 43 ff., makes apt critical comments on the basic attitudes. On the general theme of bourgeois anti-bourgeois feeling, see especially Schoenbaum, *Hitler's Social Revolution*.

geois suburbs, and they were also more familiar with the practices of the common political enemy, 'the commune'. Among the Nazis who were arrested by the police in the period between 1930 and 1932 for crimes of political violence, wage-earners were heavily over-represented.[58] In the provinces the socio-political constellation looked different; in the big cities, however, these Nazi bands won the sympathy of broad non-proletarian strata primarily by putting pressure on the Social Democratic and Communist organizations. Thus before 1933 their tactical importance for the movement was probably much greater than their numbers alone might indicate.[59]

Here a further consideration is involved: even when the SA and NSBO threatened to become too radical with their populist demands and thus reinforced the fears of those circles for whose support Hitler was then striving, they could still fulfil useful functions for the Party leadership in the extremely unstable political situation after the fal! of the Brüning government. For Hitler, they represented in these months an instrument of political blackmail, albeit an uncertain one. On the one hand, they embodied the possibility of a development dangerous for conservative forces: the possibility that the whole Party might choose a radical course if the road to power should continue to be blocked by the economic and political elites. In the context of the growing political crisis between November 1932 and January 1933, another possible development seemed even more threatening: it was feared that the National Socialist movement would disintegrate if it were denied access to power, and that the KPD would then inevitably attract a large number of the earlier urban activists.[60] In the meantime, the brown mass movement had become a significant political fact in its own right; the question of its fate became increasingly acute for all political leadership groups in Germany (including the leadership of the NSDAP!).

In the spring of 1933 the NSBO performed a further important service to the Party. This service, too, was an unplanned by-product of the

58. Kühr, *Essen*, pp. 146, 154ff., particularly emphasizes the fact that the street battles were fought above all by the wage-earners in the NSDAP. Cf. also Diels, *Lucifer*, pp. 152 f. The Nazis called the strongly Communist areas of Berlin 'the commune'. It is not clear that the mass of bourgeois NSDAP voters in the big cities were ever direct witnesses of the violent actions of the movement they supported, since most of these incidents and attacks took place in the centre of the city or in the working-class districts. In this respect, too, the heterogeneous character of the National Socialist movement is striking.

59. To be sure, it is highly improbable that the SA and NSBO alone could have subdued the organizations of the working-class movement in a pitched battle; but it never came to that.

60. These threats were of course not expressed; strictly speaking it was a matter here of the fears of conservative circles. Neither development could have been desired by the Party leadership, but the formation of the 'cabinet of barons' by Papen compelled them to radicalize their rhetoric.

political situation, exploited by the Party leadership with ruthless opportunism. Through its very existence as a special workers' wing within the
movement, the NSBO intensified the confusion and insecurity of the
Free Trade Unions' leadership in those decisive days, as union leaders
tried to establish a political strategy *vis-à-vis* the new government. For
this and a number of other reasons, a strategy of adaptation and compromise seemed a lesser evil than unconditional confrontation and political
struggle; discussions with spokesmen of the NSBO still offered the
deceptive hope that, in spite of everything, room might perhaps still be
found in the new political system for some form of independent working-class organization equivalent to a trade union. That the NSBO had
such a solution in view is clear; so is the fact that this idea was categori-
cally rejected by the Party leadership. In the discussions with representatives of the NSBO the union leaders, it is true, reacted with
undisguised scepticism to the National Socialists' claim that they spoke
for the German workers (among their 'spokesmen' were a doctor and an
editor). They also expressed well-founded doubts about the real influence of the NSBO in government circles. But the mere presence of an
apparent alternative probably helped to unsettle the Free Trade Unions
further. As Leuschner remarked in discussions on 13 April 1933: 'The
members of your NSBO are in part still our own members'. Thanks to
the power that the Party leadership now possessed in the state, the narrow bridgehead that the NSBO had been able to erect among the industrial workers now achieved a certain tactical importance.[61] As these very
discussions were going on, the decisive phase in the creation of a fascist
dictatorship was taking place: the physical liquidation of the working-
class parties and the trade unions. In this process lay the final and most
important function of the Nazi mass movement.

The fact that the National Socialist movement could convince a portion of the wage-earning population that their interests demanded struggle against the independent organizations of the working class is not to
be denied. Yet, measured against the success with which the movement
mobilized and integrated the heterogeneous economic and political
interests of the propertied classes through its frontal attack on the KPD,
the SPD and the unions, this fact was of minor significance within the
overall development of class relationships between 1929 and 1932. The

---

61. Heer, *Burgfrieden*, pp. 172f.; Hans Mommsen, 'Die deutschen Gewerkschaften
zwischen Anpassung und Widerstand 1930–1944', in Heinz Oskar Vetter (ed.), *Vom
Sozialistengesetz zur Mitbestimmung: Zum 100. Geburtstag von Hans Böckler*, Cologne,
1975, p. 279; Gerhard Beier, 'Einheitsgewerkschaft: Zur Geschichte eines organisatorischen Prinzips der deutschen Arbeiterbewegung', *Archiv für Sozialgeschichte*, vol.
13, 1973; and Beier, 'Zur Entstehung des Führerkreises der vereinigten Gewerkschaften
Ende April 1933', *Archiv für Sozialgeschichte*, vol. 15, 1975.

promise that the NSDAP would sustain the economic, social and political prerogatives of the bourgeoisie with all means at its disposal seems to have been the decisive element in encouraging its growth, especially at the local level.[62] At the national level the Party was increasingly able to secure the sympathy of big industry because the latter began to view the Nazis as a useful instrument with which they could substantially undercut the political and economic power of the working class. The inability of all other conservative parties and groups to carry out this task formed one of the essential preconditions for the rise of National Socialism. Practically all German industrialists were in agreement after 1929 that this problem absolutely had to be solved if the existing capitalist order in Germany were to survive at all. This was far from being merely a question of a relatively short-term reduction of production costs (thus of wages), nor just of a temporary, crisis-linked redistribution of the social product in favour of capital. The much more fundamental question of the division of political and economic power in German society was at stake. To put it differently, small and large entrepreneurs, farmers, master craftsmen and house owners, commerce and big industry – they all demanded total affirmation of the power of property. They wanted to be assured with absolute certainty that the working class movement would never again possess the constitutional latitude that had permitted its considerable influence on the state's socio-economic policy in the 1920s. The National Socialist way out of this crisis of class society was not the one originally preferred by big industry. But with the collapse of all alternatives on the one hand, and with the openness of the Party leadership to the ideas of the industrialists on economic policy on the other, it won increasing plausibility in these circles as well.[63]

These class-specific needs and efforts were common to all important groupings within the National Socialist movement and among their supporters. They formed the foundation of the Party's political platform, and they were transmitted to the general public in the form of an

---

62. See especially Allen, *Seizure*.

63. Among the numerous contributions to the recent discussion of this quesion, see Eberhard Czichon, *Wer verhalf Hitler zur Macht? Zum Anteil der deutschen Industrie an der Zerstörung der Weimarer Republik*, Cologne, 1967; Heinrich August Winkler, 'Unternehmerverbände zwischen Ständeideologie und Nationalsozialismus', *Vierteljahrshefte für Zeitgeschichte*, vol. 17/4, 1969; Eike Hennig, 'Industrie und Faschismus', *Neue Politische Literatur*, vol. XV/4, 1970; Reinhard Vogelsang, *Der Freundeskreis Himmler*, Göttingen/Zürich/Frankfurt am Main, 1972; Henry Ashby Turner, Jr, *Faschismus und Kapitalismus in Deutschland*, Göttingen, 1972; idem., 'Grossunternehmertum und Nationalsozialismus 1930–1933', *Historische Zeitschrift*, vol. 221, 1975, especially p. 68; Dirk Stegmann, 'Zum Verhältnis von Grossindustrie und Nationalsozialismus 1930–1933', *Archiv für Sozialgeschichte*, vol. 13, 1973; idem., 'Kapitalismus und Faschismus in Deutschland 1929–1934', in H. G. Backhaus, *et al.* (eds.), *Gesellschaft: Beiträge zur marxschen Theorie*, Frankfurt am Main, 1976, vol. 6.

extreme nationalistic rhetoric. This propagandistic coupling of class interests with allegedly national interests increased the antagonism towards the organized working class. Hitler's programmatic statements in these years primarily referred to this large complex of class-determined needs and ambitions, since it provided the basic consensus on which the rise of the NSDAP rested. In its manifold outward forms the movement as a whole certainly moved beyond this basic platform: the violent anti-Semitism, the Führer-cult, the various and in part reactionary social and cultural utopias, above all the restless dynamism of Party activity, also contributed to the growing popularity of its *Weltanschauung*. But in the final instance it was class antagonism that represented the unifying and harmonizing element in the confusing multitude of sectional interests and dogmas which comprised National Socialism before 1933. Without this unifying bond of anti-Communist and anti-Social Democratic interests and ideas the movement would never have been able to develop so dynamic an integrative power. Without that, it would probably have disintegrated. Though they might agree on little else, all activists shared the same vision of the identity of the internal enemy.

These basic conceptions, moreover, found the support of broad circles in the government bureaucracy, industry, the army and among large property owners, although they otherwise regarded the unpredictable National Socialist mass following and its vulgar, politically inexperienced leadership with some scepticism. For, in contrast to the extreme components of National Socialist ideology mentioned above, this basic direction in social and in foreign policy did not appear as the arbitrary product of a fevered ideological imagination. Therein lay the real strength of the NSDAP in 1932/3: it was the most extreme and at the same time most popular political expression of a much broader economic, social and political reaction whose central aim consisted of forcing the working-class movement into retreat.

The history of class relationships in the last phase of the Weimar Republic is a more comprehensive theme than the rise of National Socialism alone. The changes in class relationships came about for the most part independently of the rise of the NSDAP, and were the effect primarily of the economic crisis. Indeed, these changes themselves produced one of the essential preconditions for the Party's rise: in the middle of 1932, workers' parties and trade unions were completely isolated, surrounded by a multitude of political forces and interest groups which, without exception, were out to reduce the power of the organized working class. To the right of the SPD there was not a single important grouping in German public life which was not determined to revise the Weimar Constitution in this direction. ('Constitution' must be understood here in the widest sense, including the areas of labour and industrial law as well as the legal status of the unions and the institutions of the welfare state.) Whether the talk was of restoring the monarchy or of strengthening the executive *vis-à-vis* the legislature, of establishing a corporate state or of clarifying the relationship between Prussia and the Empire, whether the demand was for the removal of economic policy from the Reichstag's jurisdiction or, in the most extreme cases, for total renewal by means of an as yet undefined, but doubtless dictatorial 'Third Reich' – the real tendency of all non-socialist political effort was directed towards the same general end. The organized working class did not have a single ally, whether in the political or in the economic arena.[64]

Closely linked to this was the additional fact that Germany's position in the international system altered swiftly between 1930 and 1932. After 1930 it was obvious both to government and to industry that the international consequences of the economic crisis – the progressive dissolution of the allied powers' common front, the economic collapse of neighbouring states to the east and south – created new and favourable conditions for the reassertion of Germany's position as a major power. But this general goal also presupposed the possibility of establishing military and economic priorities that were diametrically opposed to the political efforts of the working-class parties and equally to the basic interests of their members. Such a foreign policy was difficult to realize within the framework of a liberal constitution. Thus even Hitler's aggressive foreign-policy programme won, for the first time, a certain plausible reality-content. In this way the basis for possible co-operation between the NSDAP and the conservative elite was broadened.[65]

These observations pertain to the general framework of the political developments in the months between July 1932 and March 1933. But the specific events leading to Hitler's appointment as Chancellor and to the Reichstag elections of 5 March 1933 were not wholly determined by this framework. Much depended on these events, immeasurably more than most of those involved were then aware of. The open questions of this period – what concrete methods the political reaction would develop in order to secure the repression of the working class and what polit-

64. This approach is intended to indicate a possible way out of the cul-de-sac of conspiracy theories; it highlights questions about the inability of the economically dominant classes to consolidate their political power after 1930 and simultaneously emphasizes the essential harmony between National Socialism and the interests of big industry. The proof that this harmony was not a relationship of one-sided dependence has been provided by Henry Ashby Turner, but a new comprehensive interpretation of this is still lacking.

65. Dörte Doering, 'Deutsche Aussenwirtschaftspolitik 1933–1935', Diss., Social Science Faculty, Freie Universität Berlin, 1969; Alfred Sohn-Rethel, *Ökonomie und Klassenstruktur des deutschen Faschismus: Aufzeichnungen und Analysen*, Frankfurt am Main, 1973, part I; Edward W. Bennett, *Germany and the Diplomacy of the Financial Crisis, 1931*, Cambridge, Mass., 1962.

ical forms a new system of domination would work out – were even then far from trivial. Yet a one-sided concentration on the tactical struggles of this sort within the conservative camp runs the risk of distorting our perception of the larger constant factors in the development of the political crisis. It was these socio-economic factors that determined the framework of political possibilities. They were the basis of the NSDAP's popularity and finally conditioned the willingness of the old power elites to take the risk and allow the party to come to power. These factors can also explain why nationalist bourgeois Germany closed ranks behind the new regime between March and November 1933. For, in this respect, the consolidation of the National Socialist position of power was not primarily a result of intimidation and manipulation. Rather, it was tied to the fact that the regime had succeeded in asserting its own specific version of that general programme of goals to which all these groups adhered. The KPD, the SPD and the trade unions no longer existed.

The constellation of bourgeois forces on the one hand and the initially still intact organizations of the working class on the other thus determined the structure of the political crisis that reached its climax in the first four months of Hitler's chancellorship. The first and only decisive task of the new government consisted in the conflict with the workers' parties and the trade unions.[66] That this confrontation quickly took an unexpected turn is not surprising; the sources show quite clearly that the government was initially far from certain how they should wage this struggle, what methods and strategies they should employ in order to win.[67] Much depended on the form and extent of the repression that was now to be initiated, and in February 1933 no conclusive decisions were reached. However, these questions were solved shortly thereafter primarily by activists in the National Socialist movement, not by the government.

Much evidence suggests that the new government of the Reich wanted to proceed with caution in this conflict and was concerned above all to avoid a general strike or civil war. At the beginning of March, for example, Reich Labour Minister Franz Seldte had drafts of laws prepared with the aid of which the power of the independent economic organizations of the working class was to be gradually reduced. In these

66. This confrontation also offered the means by which the government overturned other obstructions to the establishment of a dictatorship – civil rights, the independence of the *Länder* governments. An especially clear example of this instrumentalization of the attack on the Left is documented by Timpke, *Hamburg*, pp. 35–41, 57f., 62ff.

67. With respect to the intention to dissolve and suppress the KPD violently, there was no lack of clarity at all. The following discussion centres primarily on the fate of the unions. On the destruction of the workers' parties, see Erich Matthias and Rudolph Morsey (eds.), *Das Ende der Parteien*, Düsseldorf, 1960; Bracher, Sauer and Schulz, *Machtergreifung*.

laws the 'yellow' trade unions, the *Stahlhelm* Self-Help Organization and the NSBO were to receive the right, denied them by earlier governments, to conclude collective wage agreements, and members of the factory councils were to be deprived of their strong legal protection against recall and firing.[68] These measures reflected views which had been current in conservative entrepreneurial circles for a long time, but they did not entail the immediate destruction of the working-class movement; for the trade union idea was 'rooted too deeply in the hearts of the German workers', as a leading social ideologue of the NSDAP confirmed in reference to the government's uncertainty in this matter[69] – a rare insight in those circles.

After the Reichstag fire, however, the government increasingly lost control over the entire political course of events. The National Socialist leadership backed itself into a situation in which only a 'go-for-broke' domestic policy was possible. The employment of SA units as auxiliary police to dissolve the KPD and persecute its members functioned as a blank cheque for the lower ranks of the Party, the SA, the NSBO and the SS, allowing them to attack all organizations of the working-class movement. As early as the first days of March several union offices were occupied by the SA, their furnishings destroyed, documents confiscated, burned or scattered, and functionaries mistreated in the most brutal way. This apparently spontaneous wave of terror spread in the course of March to all areas of the Reich so that by the middle of March the Free Trade Unions were scarcely able to function in the cities. The numerous and detailed letters of protest by the head of the Free Trade Unions were filed unread by the Reich President, Chancellor and all ministers to whom they were addressed. Everywhere union functionaries and members turned unsuccessfully to the police, who declared themselves totally without jurisdiction, even in the many cases where money and possessions were stolen by the SA groups, union members systematically tortured or even murdered.[70]

---

68. *BA Koblenz*, R43II, vol. 369; *DZA Potsdam*, RAM, vol. 6462. Further material on the tentative tactics of the government in these weeks in Hüllbüsch, 'Gewerkschaften und Staat', pp. 221–5.

69. Gerhard Starcke, 1934, cited in Schumann, *Gewerkschaftsbewegung*, p. 61.

70. Petitions of the Free Trade Unions, 8 March 1933, to Göring; 11 March to Papen; 13 March to Hindenburg: *DZA Potsdam*, RAM, vol. 6529, pp. 16–40 and *BA Koblenz*, R43II, vol. 531. Further documents, especially the petition to Hindenburg *et al.*, 29 March 1933: *GPSA Berlin*, Rep. 90 P, vol. 71/1. The petition to Hindenburg of 5 April 1933 has now been published by Gerhard Beier, *Das Lehrstück vom. 1 und 2. Mai 1933*, Frankfurt am Main, 1975, pp. 51ff.; see also pp. 37–9. Gerhard Braunthal, 'The German Free Trade Unions during the Rise of Nazism', *Journal of Central European Affairs*, vol. XV/4, 1956, pp. 350ff., lists a further series of similar documents from these weeks. Bracher, in Bracher, Sauer and Schulz, *Machtergreifung*, p. 178, is of the opinion that the organizations in Silesia and Saxony were 'unshaken to the last'. The Free Trade Unions included these regions among those hardest hit: petition to Seldte, 14 March 1933, *DZA Potsdam*, RAM, vol. 6529, p. 16.

It was not the numerical strength of the SA groups, but their violent fanaticism, their unpredictability and the lack of involvement of state officials that were decisive for the devastating effect of the wave of terror. By the end of March things had gone so far that the NSBO drew the attention of the Prussian Ministry of State to the need to permit unions to continue payment of unemployment benefits and so on to their members for social reasons (a function which they naturally could only carry out under the supervision of NSBO personnel).[71] The main task of the 'Action Committee for the Protection of German Labour', founded by the NSDAP leadership in those same days, was the preparation of a surprise attack on the whole union apparatus – a task, however, which for the most part had already been pre-empted by the wild excesses of the SA. The 'national uprising' in the factories took the same course. At the same time as experts in the Reich Labour Ministry were conferring on the legal formula for the recall of Communist factory council members, SA and NSBO gangs went into the plants, threw the elected councillors out into the street and took over their jobs and offices. A comparison of the results of the Berlin factory council elections of 2 March with those in the Ruhr of 7 April 1933 confirms the effects of the terror. In Berlin the Free Trade Unions could still assert themselves, but in the Ruhr mines the NSBO, with 30 per cent of the votes, had already achieved a relative majority.[72] The SA had previously proclaimed that union candidates would in any case not be allowed to assume office. The 'Law on Shop Representatives and Economic Associations', rewritten several times, had been far out-stripped by events before it was promulgated on 4 April.[73]

The attitude of the Reich government towards this violent uprising of fanatical National Socialist supporters is hard to interpret. In spite of certain similarities in individual attacks on the unions – destruction of files, inactivity of the police – it is virtually certain that the uprising was not centrally planned and executed. 'For whom should it [the SA] obey?' wrote Diels, head of the newly founded Gestapo Office. 'In reality nothing was commanded, nothing forbidden.'[74] As early as 10 March

71. GSPA Berlin, Rep. 320, vol. 10; this also happened in Westphalia, for example: Sauer, in Bracher, Sauer and Schulz, *Machtergreifung*, p. 870.
72. *DZA Potsdam*, RAM, vol. 502, pp. 130–40, pp. 219ff.; RWM, vol. 10285; Bracher, in Bracher, Sauer and Schulz, *Machtergreifung*, p. 180; Schumann, *Gewerkschafts-bewegung*, p. 66; Beier, *Lehrstück*, p. 32 f.; *RGBl, 1933*, I, p. 161.
73. *Gesetz über Betriebsvertretungen und wirtschaftliche Vereinigungen*. See also the decree by Göring of 17 February 1933, which prohibited the police from prosecuting criminal acts of the SA: Sauer, in Bracher, Sauer and Schulz, *Machtergreifung*, p. 865. But it is improbable that Göring wanted the unions included in the 'subversive organizations' that were defined no more closely in the decree. The government's interest lay initially in preserving a strict distinction between the KPD on the one hand and the SPD/Free Trade Unions on the other, as far as the measures of persecution and suppression were concerned.
74. Diels, *Lucifer*, p. 199; cf. also pp. 163f.

Hitler called the SA and the SS to the 'highest discipline' so that the 'process of the national uprising could be a planned one, directed from above'. Subsequently, leading figures in the state and the Party as well as in the Reich Association of German Industry issued similar appeals, warnings and instructions demanding the cessation of individual actions and the establishment of peace and order – for the most part, however, without success.[75] Although the government was accurately informed about the events and consciously refrained from employing state power against the terrorists, these appeals and warnings were not just propaganda intended to distance them from the excesses: they also bore witness to the well-founded concern that the leaders would lose hold of the reins of political power. Involved in addition was the fact that the individual actions were sometimes directed against industry, the state apparatus and foreign persons and interests, though in these cases in less violent a form. Finally, after the incomplete electoral victory of 5 March, the new government was not sure enough of its own power within the country to be prepared to accept the consequences of the uprising, which were at first totally unpredictable. When Göring and the leader of the police division in the Prussian Ministry of the Interior, Grauert, and Frick and Seldte discussed the problem with leading Party functionaries and industrialists on 28 March, the wave of terror against the unions represented for them a challenge from the outside. 'Immediate measures must be undertaken since the occupation of union offices drives things forward from the political side', Grauert remarked.[76]

Only when it became clear that the occupation and devastation of union offices was not being met with defensive responses, but instead seemed to increase the willingness of the union leadership to negotiate at the Reich level, did Hitler, Goebbels and Reich Organization Leader Ley decide to make use of the unexpectedly favourable and early opportunity to bring about a swift solution. But they were also forced to this decision by the violence of their supporters. Their own actions were to make clear that the leadership did not lag behind its following. (This interpretation is supported by the fact that in the origins of the boycott of department stores and Jewish businesses on 1 April 1933, wild, precipi-

---

75. *Schulthess' Europäischer Geschichtskalender*, 1933, p. 56; Schumann, *Gewerkschaftsbewegung*, pp. 63–5. Reaction of the SA to these warnings: Diels, *Lucifer*, p. 199. The vacillating position of Göring and Hitler: ibid., pp. 69f., 166f., 173, 183f. Schumann's assumption that these actions of the SA were 'easy . . . to control' by the Party and state leadership is scarcely justified: *Gewerkschaftsbewegung*, p. 63. Sauer too maintains this standpoint in Bracher, Sauer and Schulz, *Machtergreifung*, pp. 868 ff. See in contrast Pridham, *Bavaria*, p. 311.

76. Gutehoffnungshütte Sterkrade AG, *Historisches Archiv*, vol. 400101290/20. I would like to thank Professor Henry Ashby Turner for directing me to these documents. At the end of April 1933, Grauert was promoted to state secretary.

tate excesses stood in a similar relationship to the political decisions of the Party leadership as in the process just described.)[77]

The radical solution of 2 May 1933 was thus also in good part a sham action whose secretive organizational effort and military precision was utterly disproportionate to the expected opposition. It was intended to intimidate and impress the people and to satisfy the Party's own supporters rather than to carry out a carefully planned policy. A majority of the offices of the Free Trade Unions occupied at 10 a.m. on the morning of 2 May had for weeks operated only under the supervision of the NSBO.[78] Neither the government nor the Party leadership had even the beginnings of a clear answer to the now urgent question: what sort of social order could replace the one that had been demonstratively abolished by surprise attack? Yet the purely power-political, destructive success was initially satisfaction enough. The main thing was that the unions no longer existed.[79]

The uprising of the little Nazis to which the unions fell victim had its origin above all in boundless hatred of the working-class movement and of 'Marxism', and especially of the individuals who represented it. This hatred, in which the Party leadership had systematically indoctrinated its members, reached a new climax in the course of the election campaign and in the wake of the Reichstag fire. Here the opportunity was finally available to reckon up with opponents from earlier street battles without interference from the police and the law; even more important, the terrorists could also hope that, in the destroyed or neutralized organizations, they would themselves gain employment, security and power. But even this does not fully explain the intensity of the hatred or the long duration of the excesses; nor does the embittered, civil-war nationalism in the light of which union functionaries appeared to be traitors to

77. Heinrich Uhlig, *Die Warenhäuser im Dritten Reich*, Cologne, 1956, pp. 77–91; Helmut Genschel, *Die Verdrängung der Juden aus der Wirtschaft im Dritten Reich*, Göttingen, 1966, pp. 46–9.

78. The petition of the Free Trade Unions to Seldte on 5 April 1933 named over sixty cities in which the union offices had been occupied or destroyed, and described these cases: *DZA Potsdam*, RAM, vol. 6529, p. 8; Beier, *Lehrstück*. The petition to Hindenburg *et al.* on 20 March 1933 already estimated the total number at 200.

79. The above interpretation has a strongly hypothetical character, for the available documents yield little information about the political calculations of the state and Party leadership. Two requests of the SA supreme command for a free hand to destroy the unions were rejected by Hitler before the end of March: Arthur Schweitzer, *Big Business in the Third Reich*, Bloomington, 1964, p. 35. Cf. also Joseph Goebbels, *Vom Kaiserhof zur Reichskanzlei*, Munich, 1937, p. 284. Some evidence indicates that Hitler, Göring *et al.* wanted to separate the union question from that of the workers' parties. That was difficult from the outset because the union offices often occupied the same building as the local SPD leadership, and the SA could thus wipe out both simultaneously. The destruction of the SPD was also carried out largely from below, by attacks on the local offices, and so on: Matthias, in Matthias and Morsey (eds.), *Parteien*, pp. 171–3.

Germany. Particularly characteristic was the pervasive personalization of political and social relations by the SA storm-troopers, whose main goal consisted in the systematic humiliation and intimidation of individual people rather than in carrying out any kind of political-institutional restructuring in the real sense. They were less concerned with general issues and organizational structures than with what these persons allegedly embodied.

In the spring of 1933 the SA was utterly uninterested in social policy. This main characteristic of the wave of terror was a logical consequence of the endlessly repeated propagandistic assertion that Marxists, 'big time operators', Reds and Jews, had intentionally produced Germany's misery, and thus were personally responsible for it. Among the little Nazis there were many in 1933 who had experienced this misery in their own person in the form of the chronic unemployment, bankruptcies, dashed expectations, thwarted careers and embittering confusion of the post-war years.[80] To judge by their behaviour in these months, in their desperate resentment they believed literally in the words of their Führer and looked around for 'those who were responsible'. (In defining 'those who were responsible', they made no distinction between Communists and Social Democrats.) The movement seemed to have become everything for these men: an organized, self-contained fantasy world, inhabited only by 'friend and foe' and organized only by relationships of brute force.

The total ruthlessness which went with this attitude, together with the unpredictability of individual actions against unions and the SPD comprised both the strength and the weakness of the SA uprising: on the one hand it came quite unexpectedly, thus there were scarcely any defensive measures which could have opposed the massive but disorganized attacks.[81] On the other hand, the storm-troopers were not consciously attempting to establish their own power positions, so that Hitler, Göring, Goebbels and Himmler were able in general to keep the political initiative in their own hands – on condition that they went along with their atavistic following, but simultaneously distanced themselves politically from their deeds. This aspect of the seizure of power deserves much greater attention and emphasis than it has so far received. A thorough investigation of the behaviour of lower levels of the NSDAP in March

80. Cf. Krebs, *Tendenzen*, p. 92. The degree to which the SA leadership groups came from a different social milieu has not yet been adequately investigated.

81. The victims could not believe that the state machine would stand aside from the terror, and trusted to the protective intervention of the Reich government. Thus, union members and functionaries received no instructions to defend the offices by appropriate means. Because of the strong element of surprise in the SA attacks this also would not have been an easy task; yet it is still indicative that people waited for such instructions from above.

1933 and its political effects would probably produce fundamentally new insights into the beginnings of National Socialist rule and into the relationship of the mass base to the NSDAP leadership. [82]

If the working-class movement has appeared up to now in this discussion primarily as the object of a hostile policy which was only too successful, this corresponds in the broadest sense to the historical course of events.[83] Nothing can be added here to what has already been written about the political aspect of the capitulation or self-destruction of the workers' parties. As already mentioned, in 1932/3 the working-class movement was completely isolated politically. Beyond that, the three main organizations of the working class were moving increasingly further apart. The rivalry between the SPD and the KPD which lamed the defensive struggle, the passive legalistic stances of the SPD leadership, the equally unrealistic revolutionary tactics of the KPD Central Committee, and the increasing concern of the Free Trade Unions merely to preserve the trade union apparatus, a concern which determined its defensive political position as well as its disassociation from the Social Democrats and prepared its leading functionaries for one compromise after the other with the reactionary political forces – all these facts are taken for granted here.[84]

Behind the political history of the years from 1929 to 1933 stood, however, one over-riding fact: the international economic crisis, which within three years reduced the German national income by 40 per cent, put one-third of the working population out of work and brought public finance and the banking system to the very edge of a total breakdown. Neither agriculture nor industry could settle its debts. A continuing decline in prices held all branches of industry back from further investment, while the continuing high prices of critical investment goods still

---

82. Sauer, in Bracher, Sauer and Schulz, *Machtergreifung*, ch. III/2, gives much too great emphasis to the general rhetorical support of the terror by Hitler and Göring, by contrast with their political-strategic conception; he characterizes the terror as 'impulsiveness on command' but can cite only a few such commands. In contrast, he omits discussion of the decrees and appeals to halt the 'individual actions'. Cf. in contrast to this Bracher, ibid., pp. 148f., 179, who, however, mentions the questions only in passing; on the legal aspect of the terror see Schulz, ibid., pp. 427–42. Numerous aspects of the events remain unexplained; for example, it would be useful to know which institutions were in principle spared the wave of terror, especially whether the co-ordination of the Christian trade unions was accomplished by the same methods. The best descritption of the events is still the *Braunbuch über Reichstagsbrand und Hitler Terror*, Basel, 1933. On the mentality of the extraordinarily important, but probably not typical Berlin SA, see Diels, *Lucifer*, pp. 152f., 163f., 198.

83. Otto Wels, 22 August 1933 in Paris: 'We were really only objects of the development'; Matthias and Morsey, *Parteien*, p. 101.

84. Apart from the works already mentioned, see Karl Dietrich Bracher, *Die Auflösung der Weimarer Republik: Eine Studie zum Problem des Machtverfalls in der Demokratie*, Villingen, 1960.

bound by cartel agreements and the deflationary policies of the central government supported this tendency. More dismissals, which caused a further decline in purchasing power and thus a further decline in prices, were the result.[85] Until late 1932 the German economy seemed to move in an endless and hopeless downwards spiral.

The working-class movement's loss of power in the wake of the world economic crisis contains a dimension of social and economic history which is of critical importance both for an understanding of the relatively easy political victory of National Socialism in 1933 and for the social history of the Third Reich. Of all groups in the population the industrial workers were generally struck hardest by the crisis. On average in 1933, 40 per cent of all male industrial workers were unemployed, as against only 22 per cent of workers in public service, 15 per cent of agricultural workers and 13 per cent of white-collar workers.[86] The system of state unemployment insurance collapsed under the burden of mass unemployment. Despite repeated increases in contributions and reductions in benefits, the unemployed were increasingly 'steered out' of the insurance system into various relief organizations from which they drew less money, and even that only on the basis of a strict means test. Of the 5.8 million unemployed who were registered with the labour exchanges in December 1932, 1.3 million received no support at all; to them must also be added the so-called 'invisible' unemployed, estimated at over one million, who no longer registered. Of the rest, not quite 18 per cent enjoyed full insurance support, 29 per cent were supported by the state emergency relief scheme, and over half had already been steered out of these two state systems and had to live on the support of the regional relief organizations. Thus, of the 7 million unemployed, only the 792,000 recipients of full support from the unemployment insurance system got enough money to eke out a basic living.[87]

Of the 12.4 million who were still employed in December 1932, at least 2 million worked substantially shortened hours. The average working day declined sharply and remained in 1931 and 1932 at under seven

85. The best overview of the world economic crisis is given by the emigré trade unionist Wladimir Woytinski, *The Social Consequences of Economic Depression*, International Labour Office, Studies and Reports, Series C, no. 21, Geneva, 1936. On the problem of investments: Gerhard Kroll, *Von der Weltwirtschaftskrise zur Staatskonjunktur*, Berlin, 1958, p. 105; Dietmar Keese, 'Die volkswirtschaftlichen Gesamtgrössen für das Deutsche Reich in den Jahren 1925–1936', in Werner Conze and Hans Raupach (eds.), *Die Staats- und Wirtschaftskrise des Deutschen Reiches 1929/33*, Stuttgart, 1967.

86. Woytinski, *Consequences*, p. 151; Ludwig Preller, *Sozialpolitik in der Weimarer Republik*, Stuttgart, 1949, p. 168.

87. *Stat. Jahrbuch*, 1933, pp. 296 f. On so-called invisible unemployment, see Woytinski, *Consequences*, p. 175; Mason, 'Women in Germany', part I.

hours in most branches of industry.[88] Because of these conditions in the labour market and thanks to the Brüning government's imposition of wage reductions, the real wages of those still working sank substantially faster than the cost of living. Even the very global calculations of the Reich Office of Statistics attested to a 10 per cent decline in the per capita real income of all those employed between 1930 and 1933. The development in the case of the workers was estimated to be even less favourable. Indeed, a figure of 15 per cent or more for the average decline in the real income of those wage-earners still employed would correspond more closely to reality; to this must be added a rise in tax and insurance deductions of about 3 per cent of gross income. Many workers resigned themselves – if they could thereby avoid dismissal – to wages which fell short of the legal minimum.[89] A sure indication of this sudden impoverishment is given by consumption statistics: while the cost of living fell about 26 per cent from 1929 to 1933, retail turnover in groceries fell by about 30 per cent in the same period, and in clothing and furniture by about 40 per cent. Tobacco consumption declined by 15 per cent and beer consumption by almost 45 per cent.[90] At the same time, keeping a job demanded greater effort than ever before; workers found themselves in competition with each other because of the wave of dismissals. The consequence was a rise in productivity, for instance in coal mining.[91] The fate of the working class in these years was progressive immiseration, hunger, fear and hopelessness. They were the first victims of the death-throes of an apparently uncontrollable economic system which was quite indifferent to their interests and needs.[92]

88. The figures on short-time work are an estimate on the basis of figures in *Stat. Jahrbuch*, 1933, pp. 296, 308; the percentage statistics on short-time work etc. of union members produces a total far higher than 100 per cent. Average working week: Woytinski, *Consequences*, p. 310.

89. See Preller, *Sozialpolitik*, pp. 150–64; *Stat. Jahrbuch*, 1934, p. 502. The calculations of the *Stat. Handbuch von Deutschland 1928–1944* indicate a decline in average real income from 1929 to 1932 of just under 15 per cent. The data in Gerhard Bry, *Wages in Germany 1871–1945*, Princeton, 1960, pp. 189, 260, 304, 362, 409ff., 423ff., are somewhat unclear on this point. The figures cited by Sidney Pollard in his article in Mommsen, Petzina and Weisbrod (eds.), *Industrielles System*, are much too high.

90. *Stat. Jahrbuch*, 1934, pp. 333, 326f.

91. From 1929 to 1933 the number of mine workers declined by about 40 per cent, production in contrast by only about 31 per cent. Thanks to lowered wages and cartellized prices the profit margin per ton of coal sold rose sharply: *Stat. Jahrbuch*, 1934, pp. 115, 259, 271; Bry *Wages*, p. 405.

92. A social history of the economic crisis has not yet ben written: a brilliant sketch has been provided by Rudolf Vierhaus, 'Auswirkungen der Krise um 1930 in Deutschland: Beiträge zu einer historisch-psychologischen Analyse', in Conze and Raupach (eds.), *Staats- und Wirtschaftskrise*. Heinrich Bennecke, *Wirtschaftliche Depression und politischer Radikalismus*, Munich, 1969, contains some interesting details, but the interpretation is very schematic. For a contemporary report see especially Graf Alexander Stenbock-Fermor, *Deutschland von unten – Reise durch die proletarische Provinz*, Stuttgart, 1931.

The parallel between the economic and the political powerlessness of the working class during the international economic crisis was no coincidence, but it needs closer examination. It was not a simple matter of linear economic determination. None the less, the economic crisis did have certain inevitable consequences for political class relations. The first was the unions' loss of substance: unemployment was highest in precisely those branches of industry which were best organized. There were almost 1 million unemployed in the engineering industry alone; in each of the mining, textile and clothing industries and the building trades there were over 200,000. In 1932 an average of almost two-thirds of all union members were either unemployed or were forced to work reduced hours. The consequences for the financial and organizational strength of the unions must have been devastating.[93] Mass unemployment deprived the unions of their essential function: they could no longer represent the interests of their members. Without unions at all reductions in wages would certainly have been even greater, but their power to halt the process of immiseration was narrowly circumscribed, as is clearly demonstrated by the decline in real wages. Their most important lever in negotiations with the employers' organizations was, as the statistics on strikes and their outcome clearly demonstrate, no longer available to them.

Only in one case of some significance did the union movement succeed in putting up effective resistance in the area of wage policy: Papen's attempt, at the urging of industry, to do away with the binding nature of collective bargains and to legalize reductions below the standard minimum wage was frustrated mainly by a series of protest strikes and was rescinded three months later by the Schleicher government.[94] But that was an exception; otherwise the unions for the most part simply had to accept dismissals, reductions in wages, shortened hours, reorganization of the production line, and so on. Their demand that the available work be divided among the greatest number of workers possible was dismissed by the employers as unprofitable. To use Rosa Luxemburg's vivid metaphor, in these years the rock of Sisyphus rolled unchecked down the mountainside. The objective incapacity of the unions to represent the material interests of their members, their impotence with regard to the economic developments, explains to a great degree the political indeci-

93. *Stat. Jahrbuch*, 1933, pp. 291, 307. Cf. also note 88 above. The consequences of mass unemployment for the unions have not yet been investigated. Beier remarks that their liquidity was 'scarcely assured any more': *Lehrstück*, p. 10.

94. *Stat. Jahrbuch*,1933, p. 311; Preller, *Sozialpolitik*, pp. 416 f. Decree on Increasing and Preserving Opportunities for Work (*VO zur Vermehrung und Erhaltung der Arbeitsgelegenheit*), 5 September 1932, and repeal of this decree, 14 December 1932: *RGBl.I*, pp. 433, 545.

sion and lack of will of the leadership in the critical months between July 1932 and May 1933. Otherwise, considered in isolation from the oppressive burden of their insoluble problems as trade unionists, the fatal political stance of the leadership is completely incomprehensible.[95] The fear of individual leading union functionaries that, given mass unemployment and economic distress, a political general strike would end in a chaotic defeat indicates a certain lack of militancy, but their concern was by no means illegitimate. There could be no absolute assumption that members would be unanimously prepared to risk their jobs, especially not in the case of workers in public administration and transportation, whose actions would have been crucial in the event of a general strike. In addition, it was not as if there was a dearth of potential strike-breakers, a fact which also did not go unnoticed.[96]

If the international economic crisis necessarily produced a strengthening of the employers' power within the firm, it also affected the position of business within the political system – in both cases at the cost of the working-class movement. Here, too, objective economic necessity played an important role. As a consequence of the crisis, the state and business moved closer together and became more dependent on each other. That was expressed, among other things, in the fact that it was unquestionably in the state's interest to protect the economic system from even partial collapse. Examples of this are the reorganization of the large banking concerns after the 1931 crash and the purchase of Flick's Gelsenkirchen shares – both very costly undertakings. In addition, the direction of the government's economic policy became the deciding factor for the future of industry, and the direct political activity of business interests was thus increased accordingly. There is still much dispute about the political role of German industry in the years from 1929 to 1933, though one cannot really speak of industry as a monolithic unit in this context. But beyond all the tactical struggles within the business world, the political attitude of industry was characterized by two general tendencies. Both were directed against the working-class movement, and both came to full expression in National Socialism.

First, working indirectly against the working-class movement was the general retreat of industrial circles from a democratic form of gov-

95. Neither Schumann, *Gewerkschaftsbewegung*, nor Ursula Hüllbüsch, 'Die deutschen Gewerkschaften in der Weltwirtschaftskrise', considers this aspect. Pollard's approach is in every respect broader, and thus more convincing: Mommsen, Petzina and Weisbrod (eds.), *Industrielles System*, pp. 237-48.

96. Cf. Heer, *Burgfrieden*, pp. 131ff., 193; Braunthal, 'German Trade Unions', pp. 340f.; Beier, *Lehrstück*, p. 22. A thorough investigation of this complex of questions is needed. To be sure, not all aspects of the union leadership's policy can be attributed to their consciousness of weakness. On the opportunism of leading functionaries in Hamburg, see Timpke, *Hamburg*, pp. 85–8.

ernment, which was rationalized by the allegedly proven inability of democratic governments to base their general policy on the needs of private industry. The various conceptions of an authoritarian constitution which won many supporters in industrial circles in these years all had the reduction of working-class power as a central programmatic point.[97] Second, and closely linked to this, was industry's general attack on the form and substance of Weimar social policy. The Social Democrats and trade unions had won considerable concessions in this sphere. The employers, who in the crisis lost their freedom of manoeuvre and their capacity to make economic concessions, intensified their criticism of collective labour law, of the binding character of wage agreements, of the factory councils, of the state arbitration system as well as of the whole principle of social insurance, especially unemployment insurance. It was maintained, for the most part incorrectly, that social reforms had caused the rise in production costs of the late 1920s, which in turn were responsible for the extent of the crisis.[98]

The demand for a 'dismantling of social policy' (Preller) won economic and propagandistic credibility because of the crisis, but it was basically the disguised expression of a struggle for profit and power which could only be carried out at the expense of the working class. The fact that the Brüning government withstood this pressure, at least with respect to the institutions of social policy if not the level of benefits, in the long run weakened its position; it also explains the respect in which its successor was held in business circles. Schleicher's attempt to change the government's course again and to reach an understanding with the unions, which Papen had opposed, probably succeeded in dispelling industry's last reservations about National Socialism's accession to power.[99]

In Germany the international economic crisis led to a radicalization and politicization of class conflict on both sides. This development necessarily proceeded clearly in industry's favour, for its interests gained political weight, and this also increased its political power. This power was deployed systematically against the working-class movement, which could not defend itself in the arena of socio-economic policy. Only the public political arena remained. The defeat of the working-

97. Eberhard Czichon, *Wer verhalf Hitler zur Macht?,* Cologne, 1967; Wilhelm Treue, 'Die deutschen Unternehmer in der Weltwirtschaftskrise 1928 bis 1933', in Conze and Rapauch (eds.), *Staats- und Wirtschaftskrise,* especially pp. 82, 119; Bracher, *Auflösung,* pp. 438f.; Schweitzer, *Big Business,* pp. 89–96. See also the literature cited in note 63 above.

98. Karl Erich Born, *Die deutsche Bankenkrise 1931,* Munich, 1967, pp. 35f., 158.

99. Treue, in Conze and Raupach (eds.), *Staats- und Wirtschaftskrise,* pp. 123ff.; Preller, *Sozialpolitik,* pp. 196–204, 391–9, 512, 528; Turner, *Faschismus und Kapitalismus,* pp. 149ff.

class movement in 1931/2 was finally a political defeat and cannot be understood as just an epiphenomenon of changes in economic power relationships. Economic and political powerlessness developed parallel to each other, but were not identical. In the political stance of the workers' parties and the unions, a multitude of historical, sociological and strategic political factors played just as important a role as economic developments. These factors helped to determine their reaction to the crisis and mass unemployment. But if one presupposes this general political framework, it is possible to isolate specific effects of the economic crisis which likewise contributed decisively to the political weakening of the working class.

Thus the Prussian Prime Minister, Otto Braun, characterized as 'demoralizing' the fact that the crisis had forced 'us to dismantle ourselves what we had striven after in vain for decades, what we had fought for'.[100] Precisely in the area of state social policy, on the expansion and reform of which the SPD had focused its entire strategy, the international economic crisis robbed the SPD of all initiative: considerations of state and economic policy prevented it from fundamentally opposing cuts in welfare policy. On the other hand, the radicalization of its members and supporters, born of distress, precluded their party's assuming joint responsibility for the deflationary policy by participating in the government. The SPD was also unable to propose any economically viable alternative to deflation. Continuing election losses and superannuation of its cadres were not completely caused by this weakness, but probably derived in good part from it.[101] Together with the collapse of the party's general political strategy in the crisis years, this slow decline did not provide a good point of departure for a determined, aggressive-defensive struggle against National Socialism. Basically, the Social Democratic leadership no longer knew what they were struggling for. In contrast, mass unemployment worked immediately to the advantage of the KDP, which was able practically to double its voting strength in the Reichstag elections between 1928 and November 1932; but this relative success was fateful in that it seemed to confirm the correctness of the unrealistic revolutionary strategy of the party leadership, yet was not great enough to produce a decisive change in the balance of political power. For this reason the political struggle between the SPD and KPD continued unabated, laming the working-class movement until January 1933 and beyond. The increasing radicalization in the political mood of the industrial workers which could be observed everywhere thus found no united organizational expression.

100. Quoted by Matthias, in Matthias and Morsey (eds.), *Parteien*, p. 214.
101. On the age-structure of the SPD see Richard N. Hunt, *German Social Democracy 1918–1933*, New Haven, 1964, pp. 71f., 76, 86, 89f., 106f.

In the long run, mass unemployment ate away at the basic substance of the working-class movement. Anxiety about keeping a job, worry about finding a job, was not in the long term compatible with militant opposition to the existing social order. To be sure, this militancy had its immediate cause in impoverishment and mass unemployment, but in 1931/2 it was as little able to remedy these conditions as it was to prevent the advance of political reaction. Many employers had deliberately dismissed those workers who were active in politics and trade union affairs in the first lay-offs (in so far as they did not enjoy special protection as members of the factory councils). After the elections of July 1932, it must have become clear that in the future even stricter political criteria for the distribution of the scarce commodity, work, would be applied. In the frightful distress of this period the labour market, too, became politicized – the decision for political activism against National Socialism became more and more a decision for unemployment and hunger. The economic crisis thus provided the political and economic rulers with a potentially very strong weapon for disciplining the working class. However, it is not easy to estimate its effectiveness before 1933. Scarcely any widespread timidity and resignation can be detected in the working-class movement before January 1933. In contrast, the relatively limited resistance to the destruction of the workers' parties and the unions in the spring of 1933 cannot be fully explained by the hesitant and indecisive tactics of the leadership groups and by the unbridled SA terror. Many *Reichsbanner* and union members were certainly waiting hopefully in these months for the call to active resistance.[102] But the general impression remains that the political defeat in March-May 1933 highlighted the compelling material needs of the individual worker. This privatization, born of intense material deprivation and insecurity, undermined class solidarity. Given the lack of historical research into mass unemployment, this impression rests in good part on inferences drawn from the distribution of jobs by the new Reich government and the NSDAP in the second half of 1933, when work was systematically given to Nazi supporters.[103] It is also supported by the massive rush to join the NSBO, which by August almost tripled its membership, as well as by the numerous resignations from the SPD after the March elections

102. Examples in Allen, *Seizure*, p. 180, among others. The numerous examples of active resistance in *Geschichte der deutschen Arbeiterbewegung* ed. Institut für Marxismus-Leninismus beim Zentralkommitee der SED, E. Berlin, 1966, vol. 5, pp. 14–39, probably convey an accurate picture, although they are given without sources. The strike appeal of the KPD went out to an utterly unprepared membership. Without practical support from the Social Democrats and the unions it was also bound to be ineffective.
103. On this issue see below, pp. 118–9.

in 1933.[104] The pressures on individuals to behave in an opportunistic manner were very strong indeed. For instance, the charwoman who sympathized with the Communists but who voted for the NSDAP in 1932 so that her husband would be considered when jobs were handed out, illustrates the dilemma of the politically conscious working class.[105] In the capitalist economic system the socio-economic power of the working-class movement is directly dependent and its political power indirectly dependent on the law of supply and demand, on conditions in the labour market. The German working-class movement was broken on the wheel of the world economic crisis.

For the later history of the Third Reich it was of critical importance that working-class organizations were destroyed for just these reasons and in just this way. The new regime had not won the voluntary allegiance of the workers. It had conquered them with weapons of terror and mass unemployment and thus could not rely on their loyalty or co-operation. From the beginning the regime confronted millions of exploited workers, subjugated by force, who viewed its policies with deep, if impotent resentment; it had to reckon further with tens of thousands who, despite all repression, attempted to continue the struggle in illegal underground groups. The heritage of the November Revolution had not been overcome.

104. Schumann, *Gewerkschaftsbewegung*, p. 167; a portion of the 'converts' consciously wanted to infiltrate the NSBO. On the SPD, see Matthias, in Matthias and Morsey (eds.), *Parteien*, pp. 239ff. The new regime ruthlessly exploited its power as employer in all areas of public service: cf. Timpke, *Hamburg*, p. 82.

105. Personal communication to the author. The same resigned opportunism is documented by, among others, Böhnke, *Ruhrgebiet*, p. 158, note 101: Rudolf Heberle, 'Zur Soziologie der nationalsozialistischen Revolution: Notizen aus dem Jahre 1934', *Vierteljahrshefte für Zeitgeschichte*, vol. 13/4, 1965, pp. 438ff.; Bernhard Tacke, 'Erinnerungen um den 1 Mai 1933', *Gewerkschaftliche Monatshefte*, vol. 26/7, 1975, p. 433.

3

The Transformation of Class Relations

In a word, I was a greenhorn when I arrived on the scene and probably more surprised than anyone else as to why I was given this job. It wasn't as if we had a ready-made programme we could take off the shelf and use to build the Labour Front; I simply got an order from the Führer to take control of the unions, and then I had to work out what to do next.

Robert Ley, at the fifth annual meeting of the German Labour Front, September 1937[1]

The *coup de théâtre* of 2 May 1933 not only signified the destruction of the trade unions, but also put the Party leaders into the position of having at once to proclaim and to build a new social order, more or less from the ground up. 'Organic' development – the gradual subjugation and evisceration of the unions – which, as late as April, union leaders had considered the lesser evil,[2] was now out of the question. This, in turn, signalled the end of the short life of the NSBO, which might have served as a suitable vehicle to carry out a gradual co-ordination (*Gleichschaltung*) of the labour unions. But as a result of the 2 May coup the Party leadership, in the person of Reich Organizational Leader Robert Ley, had clearly wrested the political initiative (Ley was the successor to and fierce opponent of Gregor Strasser, who for his part had successfully defended the NSBO against the right wing of the Party up to the end of 1932). Thus, the only unambiguously National Socialist organization that had a socio-political vision even somewhat appropriate to an industrial society – the idea of a single labour union tied to the Party – was to be excluded from the social policy decision-making process. Even this vision was not enough to reassure conservative circles that social tranquillity, the rearmament programme, dominance by the Party leadership and, not least, the maintenance of private ownership would be guaranteed in the long run. It was probably because of such considerations that Ley announced as early

1. Robert Ley, *Der Parteitag der Arbeit vom 6. bis zum 13. September 1937. Offizieller Bericht über den Verlauf des Reichsparteitages mit sämtlichen Kongressreden*, Munich, 1938, pp. 264f.
2. Gerd Schumann, *Nationalsozialismus und Gewerkschaftsbewegung*, Hanover, 1958, pp. 56–9.

as 6 May the formation of a totally new organization, the German Labour Front (DAF). While retaining his position as Reich Organizational Leader, he assumed personal leadership of the DAF. In the space of four days, Ley organized a lavish founding congress to introduce his new organization (which still existed only on paper) to the general public. NSBO functionaries continued to be entrusted with the management of the seized union offices, but this was clearly a provisional arrangement.[3]

Up to the end of 1933 the leading groups in the government, economy and Party were in a state of confusion – almost impossible for the historian to disentangle – as to the goals of the provisional arrangement.[4] Ley rarely ever produced a realistic assessment of his own position, the excerpt from his 1937 speech quoted at the beginning of this chapter being an exception that does accurately reflect the facts, namely, the utter disorientation that marked the period surrounding the DAF's foundation.[5] Initially, in the summer of 1933 the debate over the desired social order was greatly influenced by the concept of estates or corporations (*Stände*). This model of society was quite widespread both inside and outside the Nazi movement, since 'corporate organization' (*ständische Aufbau*) could be used to envision a social order to suit anyone's special interests: increased economic protection for artisans and small businessmen; economic and social self-government via committees controlled by big industry; vertical or horizontal economic organizations; agencies with authority for economic policy or ones primarily for tasks of political education; or even a doctrine of political constitutionalism. All these ideas had a single and key aim in common – depriving the working class of power. This negative goal, however, no longer sufficed as a firm foundation on which to base a practical programme.[6] Yet the

3. Details on the founding of the DAF: ibid., pp. 76ff.; on the restraining of the NSBO, pp. 87–92. Cf. Ley's critical statements on the NSBO in Ley, *Parteitag der Arbeit*, pp. 266f.

4. The very incomplete documentary record of the economic and social policy of the second half of 1933 makes it still more difficult to bring out the essential features of these developments.

5. Cf. Note 1 above. Ley combined the crudest sort of lies with surprisingly truthful statements about the history of the DAF. The rhetorical solution of pseudo-problems was among the most important tactics of National Socialist propaganda.

6. Review of the literature in Raimund Rämisch, 'Die berufsständische Verfassung in Theorie und Praxis des Nationalsozialismus', D.Phil. diss., FU Berlin, 1957. Numerous petitions in regard to corporate organization from all levels of society: *DZA Potsdam* RAM, files 6462, 6463; documents on the discussion at the governmental level, April-June 1933: *BA Koblenz*, R43II, file 527b. On the Mittelstand movement, see Arthur Schweitzer, *Big Business in the Third Reich*, Bloomington, IN, 1964, chs. 2–5; Heinrich August Winkler, 'Unternehmerverbände zwischen Ständeideologie und Nationalsozialismus', *Vierteljahrshefte für Zeitgeschichte*, vol. 17/4, October 1969; idem, *Mittelstand, Demokratie und Nationalsozialismus*, Cologne, 1972, especially ch. VIII. 'Corporate organization' was *the* catchword of German *fascism*, but within the *National Socialist* movement it was just one current among others, though it went much further than the latter. Cf. Catholic social doctrine in the encyclical 'Quadragesimo Anno'.

debate over the possibility and configuration of a social order based on corporations continued for some time among the establishment, even after the Economics Minister had put a stop to all measures designed to translate slogans into practice,[7] for the most influential proponents of this idea – Thyssen, Papen and Feder – had not yet been excluded.[8]

Ley studied their plans for some time in the hope of finding guidance for building the DAF and developing a role for it. Later, though, he noted in this connection that he had 'never met two National Socialists who were of one mind about corporate organization. June and July 1933 were nothing less than a disaster. I can tell you I spent many a sleepless night wrestling with "corporate organization" [which] revealed itself to me to be an absolute chaos of ideas, a total confusion'.[9] However, the proponents of corporate organization did not fail because of the fuzziness of their ideas, which were no more confused than those of every other economic and socio-political school of thought,[10] but because of the opposition of two forces that were bound to fear a diminution of their own power in a corporatist social order – the ministerial bureaucracy and the NSDAP. Even Ley realized that a commitment to corporate organization would set limits on the growth of the DAF.[11]

In September 1933, then, all the institutional questions remained unresolved; but the social and economic constellation of forces had become much clearer. Not a single major industrialist had protested the destruction of the unions;[12] rather, after 2 May, industry circles were increasingly concerned about the future direction of social policy. After 2 May Ley felt compelled for tactical reasons to lie about the seizure of the union offices, saying that the takeovers only served to help create the single, centralized union so long desired by the working class.[13] This

7. Ban of 8 July 1933: *DZA Potsdam*, RWM, file 8964, pp. 3f.; further debates: ibid., vols 8920, 8932.

8. On Thyssen: *BA Koblenz*, R43II, files 527b, 531; *GPSA Berlin*, Rep. 90, file 1767; Papen's draft of a corporate order: *BA Koblenz*, R43II, file 348; Feder tried to push through his plans as early as November 1933: *DZA Potsdam*, RWM, file 8932, pp. 2–20.

9. Ley, *Parteitag der Arbeit*, pp. 265f.

10. Ideas on the form of corporate organization were nevertheless realized in that the transfer of social insurance to the corporations was discussed in great detail: *BA Koblenz*, R43II, file 534. See also below pp. 99f.

11. Reich Economics Minister Hugenberg and his successor Schmitt were both considered opponents of corporatist experimentation. Frauendorfer, who formulated the NSDAP's official party line, came out for a corporate order, but was opposed to all the major points in Thyssen's corporatist plan: Schumann, *Gewerkschaftsbewegung*, p. 83. Ley had a falling out with Frauendorfer and Thyssen in January 1934: *DZA Potsdam*, RWM, file 9018, pp. 3–7; *BA Koblenz*, R43II, file 527b.

12. On the positive attitude of some industrialists towards the anti-union plans of the Party leadership in 1932: Schweitzer, *Big Business*, p. 359. The activities of the employer associations in this regard in the spring of 1933 have not yet been studied.

13. Schumann, *Gewerkschaftsbewegung*, p. 79. The workers' and employees' associations were combined into the 'two pillars' of the DAF: p. 76.

move was prompted by his negative image among the working class. To his surprise, many of the NSBO officials entrusted with the management of the union offices took Ley at his word, and the next few months were marked by a number of radical populist acts, carried out in the name of the NSBO and DAF, aimed at improving working conditions. In the fight over the closure by the Mansfeld Corporation of the Sachsen mine in Hamborn, NSBO pressure tactics were still within legal limits. As a result of a large-scale propaganda campaign, the NSBO drew the attention of Hitler and Hugenberg to the case, and in July 1933 the proposal to close was withdrawn, even though workers and employees were forced to take a 9 per cent pay cut.[14] Disputes in other cities in the Ruhr were settled less peacefully. The NSBO overseer (*Obmann*) of Harpen Mining 'affronted' the director, threatening to send him to a concentration camp. A month later, in July 1933, the industrialist Poensgen lodged a complaint against the DAF because, he claimed, it had prevented him from laying off workers. The anti-capitalist radicalism of DAF branches was the subject of industry complaints in Bochum in July and Niederlausitz in September.[15] In August the Ministry of Labour's office in Silesia reported that the NSBO had been infiltrated by Marxists who, in defiance of government policy, were resolutely continuing the class struggle and brazenly organizing strikes.[16]

In their effort to participate in eliminating unemployment and at the same time to build strong shop-floor organizations (*Betriebsgruppen*), many local DAF groups sent out questionnaires to employers enquiring about wages, number of workers, workplaces, and so on – questionnaires the employers considered an unwarranted intrusion in their affairs. The Minister of Labour formally proscribed the sending of such questionnaires, yet the number of cases did not decline.[17] Many of the DAF and NSBO locals continued the union practice of conducting collective bargaining negotiations even though by mid-1933 collective bargaining was no longer considered a legal means for establishing rules governing work conditions. In August the leadership of the DAF pleaded in vain with the Ministry of Labour for a wage increase in all branch-

14. *DZA Potsdam*, RAM, file 105, pp. 55–153.
15. Harpener Bergbau AG: *DZA Potsdam*, RAM, file 105, pp. 46–51; Poensgen, Bochum and Niederlausitz: *GPSA Berlin*, Rep. 320, file 39.
16. *GPSA Berlin*, Rep. 320, file 16; copy of the report with subsequent correspondence: *BA Koblenz*, R43II, file 532. This impoverished region was already severely affected by the economic crisis. Labour disputes were temporarily prohibited throughout the country on 17 May 1933. On this whole question, cf. Martin Broszat, *Der Staat Hitlers*, Munich, 1967, pp. 184–92.
17. Intervention of the RAM in October 1933: *BA Koblenz*, R43II, file 550. Numerous complaints about these questionnaires during the period 1936–7: *DZA Potsdam*, RWM, file 10312.

es of the construction industry.[18] Individual representatives of the DAF and NSBO even tried, it seems, to bolster their demands by enlisting the aid of the Gestapo. A memorandum submitted to the Economics Minister at the end of August 1933 recommended that as a rule the arrest of an employer with more than fifty employees should take place only with the authorization of the Economics Minister; otherwise the continued state of insecurity in the Reich would only make economic reorganization more difficult, and without 'effective limits on interference in the affairs of management' the economic crisis could not be resolved.[19]

This discussion should not leave the impression that before and after 2 May 1933 the only thing that had happened was the violent removal of the former union leaders and their subsequent replacement by Nazis, without any basic changes in the social and politico-economic structure. The demands of the National Socialist leadership and the relationship of mutual dependence between it and the leaders of the economy – the details of which are still not clear – precluded any independent representation of workers' interests in the new social order.[20] Yet it was impossible to do away with class conflict – a basic structural component of capitalist society – either by rhetoric or the lash, especially during a period of material deprivation and misery. In the summer and fall of 1933, government and industry were confronted with the imminent threat of the revival, in a new political guise, of economic class struggle emanating from the very ranks of the Nazi movement, a struggle which to them was synonymous with the labour movement as such and which had in theory been eliminated. The fears of government and industry were a determining factor in the protracted development of the institutional principles of the new social order, a process that was temporarily halted between the end of 1933 and the beginning of 1934. This is why it is necessary to stress the uncontrolled, unplanned radicalism of the National Socialist workers' organizations during the latter half of 1933.[21]

The reconstruction announced in January 1934 not only affirmed the fundamental and complete abandonment by the new power elite of the

18. Wage negotiations: *DZA Potsdam*, RAM, file 2185, p. 305; file 2186, p. 83; letters of 4 and 13 October 1933 from the Düsseldorf industrialist Raabe to Poensgen: *GPSA Berlin*, Rep. 77, file 16. Petition of 9 August 1933 re miners' wages: *DZA Potsdam*, RAM, file 2185, pp. 230ff.

19. Anonymous memorandum of 29 August 1933: *DZA Potsdam*, RWM, file 9931, pp. 77–90. There is no indication as to the author's name, but we may assume it was an important person, since the other memoranda in this file were written by Goerdeler and Lautenbach.

20. Cf. Hitler's categorical statement during the cabinet meeting of 4 May 1933: *BA Koblenz*, R43II, file 537b.

21. A comprehensive discussion would also have to deal with other aspects: the corruption of many NSBO functionaries, their gross lack of qualifications, the organizational mess, etc.; outline in Schumann, *Gewerkschaftsbewegung*, ch. IV A.

supposed liberalism of Weimar society, but also clearly reflected the new conflicts of interest and the power struggles that arose after January 1933. In hindsight, these were clearly transitional phenomena, which became less important as the new regime gradually consolidated itself;. but to those involved at the time, it was not obvious what direction events would take. Indeed, their fear for their jobs was not entirely unfounded. The class struggle – in its 1933 manifestation as radical populism, which they were more or less able to suppress – reappeared later in different economic circumstances as a permanent structural element of the Third Reich. David Schoenbaum has described this as a situation in which social groups carried on their old struggles after 1933 under the guise of National Socialist ideology – like men who are forced to wrestle under a blanket.[22]

Generalizing broadly, we may say that the government bureaucracy and the leading industrialists distrusted any sign of political or economic independence in the people. Whether adherents of corporatist theories or not, they were all primarily interested in establishing an authoritarian, hierarchic organization of society, whose first commandment was to conform. It was these forces – not the NSDAP and its affiliated organizations – that determined the new social and economic order. In the beginning they succeeded in exploiting the 'national revolution' for the realization of their own goals, while at the same time striving to protect the old order, in the economy, government and public life, from the revolutionary encroachments of the Nazi movement that they felt were bound to lead to anarchy. The other side of their cynical and aggressive opportunism with respect to the labour movement was their authoritarian and defiant attitude towards the populist element in National Socialism. On both fronts the enemy was the politically active people, who refused to accept the role of the managed and the ruled. The mass of mobilized National Socialists turned out to be far less dangerous adversaries than the labour movement, since the former were extreme nationalists. Yet, despite their work in smashing the labour movement, they were a potential threat to industry and government, not an ally. Conservative forces had salvaged the machinery of government and society for National Socialism before the Nazis themselves had secured the state apparatus. The killing of Röhm was merely the culmination, the last crucial link, in the complex chain of events that led to the merging of the old elites with the new rulers, to the detriment of the masses of the people. The continuation of this process in the economic and sociopolitical arenas was the prerequisite for the 'final resolution' of the military-political question.

22. David Schoenbaum, *Die braune Revolution*, Cologne/Berlin, 1968, p. 336.

The successes of the politically conservative and capitalist forces were nowhere more noticeable by the end of 1933 than in the struggle to create new socio-political institutions. When it became obvious that none of the current corporatist theories offered a practical solution, the question of a new organization of society became purely a question of power, with the establishment having all the advantages on its side. A necessary consequence of Hitler's determination, expressed to his generals as early as 3 February 1933, to achieve the 'recovery of political power' for Germany along with the 'conquest of new living space in the East and its ruthless Germanization',[23] was a rearmament programme that militated against any revolution in the economy. The new regime also realized that its popular legitimacy depended greatly on its ability to solve the economic crisis and unemployment; socio-political experimentation was once again ruled out. Time and again in their petitions to Reich ministers the industrial associations emphasized this line of reasoning on behalf of 'tranquillity and order',[24] also pointing to the glaring lack of foreign exchange and to the absolute necessity of not allowing German exports to decline. The constellation of political forces was thus extremely unfavourable to the populist movements within National Socialism. These circumstantial political constraints were greatly enhanced and bolstered by the authoritarian model of the state and its mission that prevailed in nationalist conservative circles.

Significantly, the initial reaction of the bureaucracy, still largely intact after the Nazi seizure of power, was to assume direct responsibility for the work formerly done by the suppressed unions. The District Leaders for the Economy and Labour (*Bezirksleiter der Wirtschaft und der Arbeit*), who had been appointed on 16 May 1933 by Party authorities and given the task of supervising wage regulation, protective legislation (*Arbeitsschutz*) and the labour laws,[25] were soon dismissed. Three days later the government promulgated a Law on the Trustees of Labour, which delegated these tasks to Trustees who were solely responsible to the state; of the twelve Trustees appointed on 15 June

---

23. Gerhard Meinck, *Hitler und die deutsche Aufrüstung, 1933–1937*, Wiesbaden, 1959, p. 17.

24. For example, the Reichsverband der deutschen Industrie as early as March 1933: *BA Koblenz*, R43II, file 362. According to leading industrialists a new economic policy aimed at creating jobs could not be dealt with until the question of the unions had been 'solved'. I am grateful to Dr. F. P. Kahlenberg of the Bundesarchiv for this reference.

25. Decree by Ley and Wagener (Reich Commissar for the Economy); text according to *Wolff's Telegraphisches Büro* (W.T.B.), 17 May 1933: *BA Koblenz*, R43II, file 531.

1933, only two had been 'District Leaders'.[26] This solution was likewise strictly provisional – 'pending the total rearrangement of the social constitution' (para. 2/I) – but from the outset it was radically different from the placement of NSBO functionaries as administrators of the co-ordinated unions. The very reason for the establishment of the DAF had been to set limits to the power of these functionaries, whom Hitler, Ley and the industrialists tolerated only with the greatest distrust. In contrast, the office of Trustee was newly established by the central government and provided with direct state authority and juridical powers which represented a clear rebuke to those within the NSBO who were seeking to set up a single, centralized Nazi labour union.

The NSBO's condition continued to deteriorate during the second half of 1933. The massive influx of new Party members confronted the leadership with problems that were anything but simply organizational. Only a tiny minority of the NSBO's new members were convinced Nazis; the majority were probably opportunists motivated by the not unrealistic hope that swearing allegiance to a political creed might help them get a job. To this group of politically naive members must be added the other groups who joined with the express purpose of undermining the NSBO and reinforcing its inherent tendency to carry on the class struggle[27] – a tendency further encouraged by the very laws governing social change. Even naked terror did not relieve the NSBO functionaries of the need to win the trust of former union members. This called for concessions to union traditions that sometimes degenerated into the radical acts against employers described above. From the outset, Ley himself had recognized the enormous significance of the 'question of confidence'. It was Ley, after all, who had promised on 2 May that the new labour associations would continue to fulfil all the obligations of the defunct labour unions to their former members (for example, the payment of additional unemployment benefits).[28] The new regime still did not have sufficient means of coercion to prevent a possible mass

26. *RGBl. I*, p. 285. W.T.B., 15 June 1933: BA Koblenz, R43II, file 534. Schumann's claim (*Gewerkschaftsbewegung*, p. 82), that the Trustees were 'with one exception, all former legal advisors to the large employer associations' is not true. In the strict sense, only five qualified as such; four had been higher-level civil servants on the state (Land) level responsible for socio-political questions; in addition, there was one attorney (a specialist in political criminal law), one engineer, and the founder of the NSBO. In the first year several of the Trustees were replaced, but the corporation lawyers were never a majority: Schoenbaum, *Braune Revolution*, p. 319.

27. On the tactics of the KPD, cf. for example, *Geschichte der deutschen Arbeiterbewegung*, ed. Institut für Marxismus-Leninismus beim Zentralkommitee der SED, E. Berlin, 1966, vol. 5, pp. 40f.

28. Cf. Schumann, *Gewerkschaftsbewegung*, p. 78f. On the wage policy aspect of the question of confidence, see pp. 97–8 below.

exodus from the co-ordinated unions.[29] The NSBO became the victim of a contradictory policy that aimed to end class warfare but not to eliminate its causes, and that depended on the political support of the working class but could not furnish it with an organization of its own. The NSBO was prohibited from becoming involved in the structure of the new associations or from having anything to do with wage policy. At the beginning of 1933, a freeze on new members was imposed, limiting future membership to 1.1 million; there was also a cap of 300,000 set for candidate members. Current members were checked for their political reliability. To combat tendencies towards trade unionism, all employees and employers who were already Party members were invited to join the NSBO. From November 1933 the NSBO was left with only two responsibilities by the Party leadership: teaching Party ideology, and supplying the DAF, to which it had been subordinated, with new blood.[30]

The NSBO had lost the power struggle. However, its organizational subordination to the DAF, which was totally submissive to the Party leadership, merely papered over conflicts and did not represent any real progress towards a new social order. The future function of the DAF and its relation to industry, the ministries and, above all, the working class itself were totally unclear. Its identification – albeit reluctant – with the NSBO in the summer of 1933 was sufficient to make leading groups in the government and economy fearful, vigilant, and firm in dealing with the DAF. The business community, which was barely convinced of the need for *any* socially or politically oriented mass organization, was reluctant to acknowledge the fact that the government had even called on the DAF to restrain the NSBO. Thus Ley was in a difficult position in the autumn of 1933; he had no plans regarding the structure and function of the DAF and was suspected by the business community of being a populist proponent of a single, centralized union and by the populists in the NSDAP of being a tool of the old order. On 20 September 1933, he tried to make his case before the leading industrialists during the first session of the General Economic Council (*Generalrat der Wirtschaft*):

> ...a few words about the Labour Front. ... Gentlemen! I realize that as things were happening there were also differences of opinion in this group. Many

29. For example, membership in the DAF as a condition of employment, direct deduction of contributions from wages by the employer, etc.; see p. 157–8 below.

30. Details in Schumann, *Gewerkschaftsbewegung*, ch. IV A 4. The new division of responsibility in the Office of the State Secret Police (*Gestapa*) of January 1934 gave a new assignment to the economic political section (IIE 1), i.e. 'signs of subversion in the NSBO'; *GPSA Berlin*, Rep. 90 P, file 2/2. On the local and regional levels the disputes dragged on until the fall of 1934.

were probably asking: Why are they doing this? Well, there were two ways to go. Either we could have smashed the unions completely at the time, outlawed them and left 12 million people without a home in our state; or we could have gone down the path that I did: following the Führer's orders. And let me tell you, gentlemen, nothing is more dangerous for a state than people without a home. Even the bowling league and the bridge club have a role to play here in preserving the state. The individual goes there in the evening and knows where he belongs. ... What was of inestimable importance here was that the Labour Front provide a place again in the state for these 12 million people. True, some of them were enemies, full of distrust and hate. But if the state had said: No, we can't use you; we don't want you; your children someday maybe, but not you; you're rejects – believe you me, that would've spelled trouble.

Pointing to the putative success of the Italian Fascist leisure time experiment *Dopolavoro*, Ley promised that the DAF and those organizations associated with it ('Strength through Joy', for example) – which were as yet nothing more than vague ideas – would 'in the not-too-distant future become pillars of support for the regime'. [31]

This prospect, however, did not allay the fears of industry, since Ley was at the same time forced to boost his image and that of the DAF in the eyes of the working class. The demagogic slogans with which Ley, Hitler and Goebbels inundated the country – 'Honour Work and Respect the Worker!', 'Reach Out to Your Men!', 'The Class Barriers Are Coming Down!', 'The Liberation of the German Worker', and so on – met with few objections from industrialist circles. At the same time, the press reports on the factory tours undertaken by Ley and his functionaries, describing how formerly Social Democratic and Communist workers were persuaded to relinquish their previous beliefs and how they were moved to tears as they embraced the new national-racial community (*Volksgemeinschaft*), surely aroused scepticism among any industrialists who read them.[32] But Ley did not fail to realize that even the increased use of terror and indoctrination would not be enough to banish forever the spectre of November 1918, which is why, time and again

31. Stenographic record: *BA Koblenz*, R43II, file 321/1. 'Twelve million' was a gross exaggeration; this figure represented the total number of people employed, not the number of union members. It is rather surprising that Ley formulated some of his ideas publicly; cf. his collected speeches, etc.: Robert Ley, *Durchbruch der sozialen Ehre*, Berlin, 1935, pp. 13f.
32. Propaganda slogans and speeches during these months from the DAF's organ *Arbeitertum*, June 1933 to March 1934. Hitler's address on National Labour Day (*Tag der nationalen Arbeit*, 1 May 1933): Max Domarus, *Hitler: Reden und Proklamationen 1932–1945*, 1st edn, Würzburg/Neustadt a.d. Aisch, 1962, vol. 1, pp. 259–64; Ley, *Durchbruch*, especially pp. 19, 55f.

after the dissolution of the unions, he issued warnings and assurances that under no circumstances would existing wage rates be lowered, and once even promised to raise the minimum wage.[33]

Against the background of the DAF's and NSBO's continuous and illegal meddling in wage policy at both the regional and local level, Ley's utterances sounded as if he were proclaiming an 'anti-business' social policy. Moreover, the DAF's deliberate attempts in the late summer and autumn of 1933 to bring the labour courts and social insurance under its control also aroused great distrust among the employer associations.[34]

The surviving documentary sources are not sufficient for a comprehensive analysis of the power struggle between the DAF and industry during October and November 1933. Leading industrialists were evidently pinning their hopes on the financial collapse of the DAF. A number of workers expressed their opposition to the Nazis by refusing to pay their union dues to the DAF. Added to this were the organizational deficiencies of the DAF and the corruptness of its functionaries, which further weakened its financial power. Ley himself reported that the monthly total of dues collected had plummeted from RM 17 million to RM 8 million during the summer of 1933. The employer associations suddenly became quite concerned about the living standards of their employees and registered their deep misgivings about the increase in automatic wage deductions following the Nazi seizure of power (deductions for the Party, the works programme, winter relief, as well as the DAF). In this context, the DAF's express desire to take over the social insurance system, with its potentially very large financial reserves, looked particularly menacing. Ley claimed that his 'enemies were telling Hitler that the Labour Front was bankrupt' (how it actually overcame this crisis remains an open question).[35]

At the same time leading representatives of industry were putting pressure on the government to give priority to their interests when mak-

33. See his pronouncement immediately after the dissolution of the unions: *DAZ Potsdam*, RMdI, file 26036, p. 82. Repetition of his warning: *Arbeitertum*, 15 May 1933. Wage increases promised to the Executive Committee of the DAF on 23 May 1933: *Der deutsche Metallarbeiter*, 3 June 1933. The Trustees of Labour also issued warnings: *DZA Potsdam*, RAM, files 235–8. It was the small businessmen in particular who sought to reduce wages, i.e. precisely the class that very strongly supported the NSDAP.

34. Letter from Karl Raabe to Ernst Poensgen and Ludwig Grauert during the first half of October 1933: *GPSA Berlin*, Rep. 320, file 16. The negotiations on social insurance were very complicated and would be worthy of a special study; we cannot pursue them any further here. Documents: *DZA Potsdam*, RWM, vols 10327, 10328, 10367.

35. Ley, *Parteitag der Arbeit*, pp. 268, 267; his version of overcoming the crisis (he said he had immediately built up secret reserves in May; op. cit.) is patently untrue. See also Ley, *Durchbruch*, p. 16. Concerning deductions: Raabe-Poensgen-Grauert correspondence, (see Note 34 above); additional petitions from industry in this matter: *DZA Potsdam*, RWM, file 10327. Further details, see pp. 156–8 below.

ing decisions about new socio-political institutions. Karl Raabe of Düsseldorf appears to have been the spokesman of western German heavy industry within this lobby, and his ideas, even though framed partly in the language of corporatism, coincided in all important respects with those of Carl Goerdeler: the fundamental defect of the Weimar system had been the separation of economic and social policy at the governmental and non-governmental (*Verbände*) levels; non-governmental institutions should in future be subordinated to the government; and therefore the DAF – if there were any role for it at all – should be limited to propaganda tasks. An economic and social policy capable of solving the crisis could be formulated only as a result of close and uninterrupted co-operation between government and industry. Worker representatives, the industrialists asserted, could be tolerated only at the factory level and, if worse came to worst, in each branch of industry within a district (*Bezirk*); and even then they would only be permitted to advise and recommend, not to decide. Workers, they said, were meant to work: and that was that. In these and other memoranda on the new social order that came from conservative and industrial circles there was not even a hint of uneasiness about the fact that such a system could only be maintained through permanent police suppression of any trade unionist or socialist aspirations on the part of the working class. [36]

The new regime, by contrast, took a brutally and frankly realistic position here. In 1933 only the Nazi regime, with its still indispensable corps of aggressive followers, was willing and able to carry out such acts of repression. Conservative forces lacked the requisite political base. Their notions about the authoritarian state never really crystallized into practical ideas about ways and means to maintain authority. With a kind of haughty disdain, they left the dirty work to the street brawlers whom they otherwise distrusted. Industry could be quite certain that its petitions would be looked upon with favour by the government: the bureaucracy and the military were also troubled by the interventions and individual acts of violence carried out by the mass Nazi organizations, and the idea of establishing a new and bigger organization did not mesh with their deeply-rooted ideas about the state's monopoly of responsi-

---

36. Raabe-Poensgen-Grauert correspondence (see Note 34 above); Goerdeler's memorandum of 7 September 1933. *DZA Potsdam*, RWM, file 9931, pp. 119–34. Cf. also similar ideas of Thyssen on restructuring social relations within the factory: Schweitzer, *Big Business*, p. 361. On the Chambers of Industry and Commerce (*Industrie- und Handelskammer*), see Schulz, in Karl Dietrich Bracher, Wolfgang Sauer and Gerhard Schulz, *Die nationalsozialistische Machtergreifung. Studien zur Errichtung des totalitären Herrschaftsystems in Deutschland 1933–4*, Cologne/Opladen, 1960, pp. 643–7.

bility for maintaining public order. During the summer of 1933 all positions in the bureaucracy responsible for these questions were filled by men from the ranks of industry. [37]

Ley obviously did not want to have the DAF's freedom of action diminished in this radical fashion. If we disregard for a moment the crude sociological reasoning he used in his address to the industrialists on 20 September, justifying his call for expanded responsibilities for the DAF, we can see that, given the basic dynamism of Nazism, no organization within the Party could resign itself to a sharp and permanent division of power that threatened to undermine its own position. Thus the draft of a law on the German Labour Front, which the DAF independently submitted to the government in September 1933, stated, 'The German Labour Front has endowed itself with a constitution that defines its responsibilities and tasks'.[38] This kind of dynamism was utterly characteristic: it stemmed not only from an ideologically determined project of indoctrination, but also from the closely related struggle for political power, for ever more attempts to usurp the responsibilities and authority of the old regime. In his initial struggle with industry, however, Ley was forced to recognize the superior strength of his opponent. For while he and Hitler had envisaged a DAF that needed the employers, the employers never felt that they needed the DAF. After the destruction of the unions and working-class parties, Hitler's first priority in social and economic policy was to forbid any interference with private ownership that might upset his already shaky relations with the old governmental and social power structure or endanger the beginning stages of the economic recovery. The DAF was thus compelled to distance itself from the NSBO by inviting employers to join its organization; it was obliged to mirror the class harmony of the *Volksgemeinschaft*, thereby making itself acceptable to the employers.[39] Two other alternatives were never even an issue – on the one hand, evolution into a trade union, since that might have upset the civil truce that had been achieved with such brutal

37. Cf. Schweitzer, *Big Business*, p. 360. Sauer in Bracher, Sauer and Schulz, *Machtergreifung*, pp. 862–77. In 1933 Schmitt, Seldte and Grauert came directly from industry to politics or government service, as did Werner Mansfeld, an employers' federation attorney in the Ruhr who took over the department in the Ministry of Labour responsible for wage and social policy and drafted the Law on the Organization of Labour (*Arbeitsordnungsgesetz*).

38. *BA Koblenz*, R43II, file 531.

39. The industry associations which were reorganized between 1933 and 1935 and combined into a new 'Federation of Trade and Industry' (*Organisation der gewerblichen Wirtschaft*) remained outside the DAF. As early as 20 May 1933 Hitler was aware of its basic principle of organization: Address upon the Occasion of the Founding of the DAF (*Rede zur Gründung der DAF*) – complete text: Paul Nassen, *Kapital und Arbeit im Dritten Reich*, Berlin, 1933, ch. VIII.

force and, on the other, abandonment of the project of this kind of mass organization, since that would have meant the end of the Nazis' efforts to control policy in this crucial arena.

Ley, a sworn enemy of 'Marxism' who had worked for I. G. Farben for several years, immediately appropriated this strategy, adhered to it tenaciously in the face of all opposition and adjusted easily to situations in which he was obliged to put aside his ambitious plans for the DAF in the interests of the grand design.[40] The translation of this design into practical policy illuminated the conjunction of two important points: that the interest of the employers in ensuring their absolute hegemony inside the factory coincided nicely with the notion of a hierarchical *Volksgemeinschaft*, which was fashionable in conservative circles. The Nazis were committed to the idea of a *Volksgemeinschaft*, but in 1933 they had no concrete plans for actually making it part of the structure of government. The DAF therefore had to moderate its own plans for organizing workers in the factories.[41] This set-back, which resulted from the vagueness of their communitarian ideology, had the same effect as the second, or strategic, factor: from the outset the social heterogeneity of the Nazi followers prompted Party leaders to try to neutralize serious differences by creating elaborately structured organizations, something which as early as 1933 had become an ingenious technique for manipulation. Only when all employers, as well as all workers, had become members of the DAF could it play an autonomous role within the regime, ostensibly impartial to the selfish interests of hostile classes. It remained an open question whether this impartiality would repose merely in the fact of the organization's autonomy, or rather in a more active social policy that aimed to veil class antagonisms. Already by 1933, however, the Party leadership seemed to consider the one conditional upon the other. This became evident on those rare occasions in 1933 when Hitler, Ley and Goebbels dropped their bombastic slogans about the reconstitution of society and instead sought to conceal the Nazi movement's actual drive for power behind an unctuous 'common sense' approach to governing. As Hitler said at the founding congress of the DAF on 10 May, 'Thus destiny has perhaps chosen me more than anybody else to be the honest broker – I have the right to apply this word to myself – the honest broker for all sides. I have no personal interests; I am dependent neither on the state nor on public office, nor am I behold-

40. In the DAF's very first, short-lived organizational plan, industry was well represented on all important advisory bodies, in both the Executive and Pilot Committees (*Grosser und Kleiner Konvent*).

41. The mechanical precision of bourgeois ideas pointed up their limitations with regard to the overall political situation.

en to business or industry or any union. I am impartial'.[42] In this role as political broker Hitler believed he could influence both sides; but first he needed two parties who were willing to negotiate.

However, to Ley and his functionaries the price that industry and the state were asking was much too high. The DAF considered that the compromise agreement on its functions, which was worked out in the middle of November 1933, was tantamount to a defeat, a defeat that had to be redressed immediately.[43] This agreement – one of the first examples of the domestic political 'pacts' between opposing groups striving for 'sovereignty' within the regime, a trend that became the hallmark of the system – was signed by Ley, Seldte (Minister of Labour), Schmitt (Economics Minister) and Keppler (Hitler's economic advisor):

> The German Labour Front is the union of all working people, irrespective of financial or social standing. In the German Labour Front workers shall stand side by side with employers; no longer will they be separated according to groups or associations dedicated to the protection of particular economic or social classes.
>
> Of prime importance to the German Labour Front is the worth of the individual, regardless of whether he is a worker or an employer. Trust can be built up only between one individual and another, not between one association and another. According to the wishes of our Führer, Adolf Hitler, the German Labour Front is not the place to decide the material questions of workday life or to harmonize the naturally different interests of individual working people. Procedures *governing conditions of employment* will soon be worked out, according to which leaders [*Führer*] and followers [*Gefolgschaft*] will be assigned those positions which National Socialist ideology has prescribed for them.
>
> The lofty goal of the Labour Front is to instil in all German working people the National Socialist way of thinking.
>
> The German Labour Front assumes special responsibility for the *training of individuals* who are called upon to play a critical role in business or in our social service institutions, labour courts or social insurance system.
>
> The German Labour Front will ensure that the social honour [*soziale Ehre*] of the factory leader [*Betriebsführer*] and his followers becomes the driving force behind our new social and economic order.
>
> In this spirit we call on all German workers of head and hand to enter the German Labour Front in order to gather our energies for the success of our great enterprise.

---

42. Text according to Domarus, *Reden*, vol. 1, p. 267. During this period Hitler was in fact extremely dependent on industry for many things, but was struggling to achieve his political independence. Ley later took up the honest broker theme again; see below, p.167.

43. Cf. pp. 166ff. below. Ley indicated his displeasure and spoke of 'tough, protracted negotiations'; he interpreted the results as a simultaneous victory for the NSDAP, businessmen and the working class but with a different emphasis from that of the government and industry: Ley, *Durchbruch*, pp. 45–55.

Only now was the Reich Estate of German Industry (*Reichsstand der deutschen Industrie*) prepared to encourage employers to enter the DAF (as individual members). As a sop to the DAF, it was permitted to introduce the public to its new leisure time organization, 'Strength through Joy' (*Kraft durch Freude*). Significantly, the agreement defining the functions of the DAF was first made public at the meeting called to announce the founding of Strength through Joy. The skilful coupling of the two announcements was designed to conceal as best as possible the DAF's defeat in the debate over fundamental principles, while not detracting from the political significance of the outcome.[44] At the Cabinet meeting of 1 December 1933 the Economics Minister reported on these principles and then added another: 'Nor shall the Labour Front own business enterprises, lest such an expansion of its economic apparatus stifle the rest of the economy'.[45] Schmitt also touched on the restructuring of industrial relations, which was shortly to be worked out on the basis of the agreement. The outcome was the Law on the Organization of National Labour (*Gesetz zur Ordnung der nationalen Arbeit*) of 20 January 1934, one of the most comprehensive and thoroughgoing examples of Nazi legislation, but one that was virtually devoid of the influence of Party organizations.

In terms of labour law, social policy, and ideology, the 'factory community' (*Betriebsgemeinschaft*) was the heart of the New Order, not associations or classes or mass organizations or even any political philosophy. [46] The top position in the factory community was occupied by the entrepreneur in the capacity of 'factory leader' (*Betriebsführer*); his workers, called 'followers' (*Gefolgschaft*), were obliged to pledge him their fealty. 'In all matters pertaining to the factory the factory leader shall decide on behalf of his followers. ... He shall see to the welfare of his followers.' In order 'to increase mutual trust within the factory community', the leader was assigned a Council of Trust (*Vertrauensrat*);

44. Text of speeches by Ley, Schmitt and Goebbels, 27 November 1933 (W.T.B. Report): *BA Koblenz*, R43II, file 557.

45. Agreement and minutes: *BA Koblenz*, R43II, file 531; the original minutes were written in indirect speech. More on the economic enterprises of the DAF, see below pp. 217f.

46. *RGBl.* I, p. 45. All quotations in this section have been taken from the text of the statute. The statute can be best be studied today using the official commentaries, which contain the numerous executive orders as well as the decisions of the Reich Labour Court on individual paragraphs: Werner Mansfeld, *Die Ordnung der nationalen Arbeit: Handausgabe mit Erläuterungen*, Berlin, 1941. More details in Alfred Hueck, Hans Carl Nipperdey and Rolf Dietz, *Gesetz zur Ordnung der nationalen Arbeit*, 3rd edn, Berlin, 1939. On the origin of the law, see Timothy Mason, 'Zur Entstehung des Gesetzes zur Ordnung der nationalen Arbeit vom 20. Januar 1934', in Hans Mommsen, Dietmar Petzina and Bernd Weisbrod (eds.), *Industrielles System und politische Entwicklung in der Weimarer Republik*, Düsseldorf, 1974, pp. 322–51.

this council was to advise on 'all measures concerned with improving production, working out and implementing the general conditions of employment ..., strengthening the ties connecting factory members with one another, with the factory itself, and with the welfare of all members of the community.' The Council was 'elected' by secret ballot, but the list of candidates was prepared by the factory leader and the local DAF overseer (*Obmann*).[47] The Council of Trust could only act in collaboration with the factory leader; it was thus deprived of any legal right to represent interests. The control of every aspect of industrial relations not already covered by statute (working hours, minimum wage, health protection, and so on) was to be covered by a 'factory code of rules' (*Betriebsordnung*). Although they had to be discussed in the Council of Trust and approved by the Trustee of Labour (*Treuhänder der Arbeit*), the factory leader alone could make the final decision as to their content; the establishment of pay rates beyond the minimum wage was included in the factory code.

The government's provisional administrative arrangement for balancing the various economic interests, which had begun in May 1933 with the appointment of the Trustees of Labour, was confirmed and amplified in the Organization of Labour Law. The Trustees were civil servants under the supervision of the Minister of Labour, who together with the Economics Minister set guidelines for them. The Trustees had responsibility 'for the maintenance of industrial peace', first in specified areas of the economy and later in entire branches of industry. In the spirit of the Organization of Labour Law, however, the Trustees were to exercise deliberate restraint and not carry out any police or enforcement functions, for a genuine and permanent end to the class struggle – and to the Nazis this meant nothing more than a change in *attitude* – could be achieved only if the individual cells of the social organism were given responsibility for the solution of everyday problems. Behind this model of society, which Hitler described as a 'process of the coming together' of the 'artificial classes' in the nation,[48] stood the persistent demand by German industry once and for all to be 'master in its own house' again. The job of the Trustees was to safeguard the interests of the state by wisely managing this huge socio-political superstructure so as not to ignite class warfare from above through brutal economic repression. Other authorities were responsible for dealing with subversive (*klassenkämpferisch*) acts by the workers – namely, the Gestapo and the concentration camps. Thus the Trustees were to refrain as much as possible (and the DAF entirely) from interfering in the internal affairs of the

---

47. For further details, see below pp. 166, 177f., 218f.
48. Speech of 1 May 1933, quoted in Domarus, *Reden*, vol. 1, p. 260.

factory community. The Office of the Reich Trustee was conceived of as a kind of socio-political court of last resort whose only legally sanctioned authority consisted in the following: evaluating the necessity for mass layoffs; checking for adherence to the minimal conditions of employment as laid down in existing wage agreements (*Tarifverträge*) recognized by the new regime; gradually revising the agreements and re-enacting them as 'wage codes' (*Tarifordnungen*); overseeing the establishment and management of the Councils of Trust; and keeping the government informed of the socio-political climate.

The legislators realized that the abolition of the class struggle in the factory through a process of closer contact between 'leaders' and 'followers', ideological training, increased trust and the like, would take considerable time. However, instead of explicitly instructing the DAF to force the pace, they established a new system of 'courts of honour' for the unregenerate: 'Gross violations of the social responsibilities established by the factory community shall be considered by the courts of honour as offences against social honour.' In this context, it was an offence for employers or others to maliciously exploit the labour power of their followers, or for followers to endanger the peace of an enterprise by maliciously inciting their comrades. Only the Trustee was allowed to institute proceedings. Since the courts of honour had originally been conceived as an educational experiment, the penalties were mild.[49]

The DAF was barely mentioned in the statute. Not until the issuance of the second executive order was it given a few unimportant and strictly limited responsibilities under the new system of labour law. The Trustees were permitted to summon a board of experts to advise them on general questions affecting their particular areas of the economy; the DAF was given the right of nomination to this board from among members of the Councils of Trust and works leaders.[50] Beyond that, the DAF managed to acquire only one more position of power within the formal hierarchy of the system, through the expansion of compulsory arbitration as a kind of 'antechamber' to the labour courts, designed to mediate disputes and thereby reduce the number of court cases.[51] All committees or councils set up in the Weimar Republic to advise the social insurance authorities, labour exchanges and so on, which had consisted of an equal

49. The largest group of defendants were the owners of small businesses.
50. Second Executive Order (DVO) to the Labour Organization Law, 10 March 1934: *RGBl.* I, p. 187.
51. Law on the Labour Courts Assessors and Arbitration Authorities (*Gesetz über die Beisitzer der Arbeitsgerichts- und Schlichtungsbehörden*), 18 May 1933 (*RGBl.* I, p. 276), according to which the DAF initially acquired only the right to nominate Assessors. Consolidation and expansion of the provisions: Labour Organization Law, para. 66. Detailed treatment of the subject: Frieda Wunderlich and Ernst Fraenkel, *German Labor Courts*, Chapel Hill, 1948.

number of representatives from the unions and the employer associations, were summarily dissolved as the 'leadership principle' (*Führerprinzip*) was introduced; the DAF acquired no authority in these areas. Apart from its role in preparing the lists for elections to the Councils of Trust, the DAF had no statutory functions in the factories. If there were serious differences in a Council, the Trustee and not the DAF was to be called upon for advice. In the expanded struggle for power, of which the Labour Organization Law was the provisional outcome, the DAF won only a single, very uncertain victory: the employer associations dissolved themselves and the newly organized economic associations agreed to renounce all activity in the area of social policy (an agreement which, however, they honoured only in the breach).[52]

A thorough investigation of the historical, ideological, economic and immediate political context of this radical restructuring of the norms of social organization would require a separate study. The various component parts were not only heterogeneous in origin, but were also to a great extent inconsistent with one another. For example, the emphasis on the shop or factory as the primary and self-governing unit for dealing with class conflict reflected two contradictory impulses: on the one hand, it derived from the need of small businesses and non-competitive or labour-intensive industries to reduce their wage costs (for which the elimination of the unions and the whole Weimar system of collective bargaining was indispensable); on the other, it stemmed from the newest theories in industrial engineering and industrial psychology, associated with the wave of industrial rationalization, which were actually being tested in the economically healthiest and technologically most advanced firms and branches of industry. This brings to light another paradox: collective bargaining was particularly appealing to the progressive segments of German industry and corresponded closely with the wider tendency towards economic concentration that was geared to uniform wages and prices at the national and industry level.[53] It was irrelevant whether a factory community was to be established in a small business through the personal influence of a factory leader, or in a big company by the application of the costly techniques of personnel management –

52. There were heated arguments about this between the DAF and industry in 1934; the DAF – with some success – called on the Gestapo to dissolve these associations: *DZA Potsdam*, RWM, file 9073, pp. 16, 30, 32–5. Decree of *Gestapa* II E, 24 February 1934, in the *Nachrichtenblatt des Gestapa*, 1934, no. 6: *GPSA Berlin*, Rep. 90 P, file 2/1. The leading economic associations continued to maintain 'socio-economic sections' (*Sozialwirtschaftliche Referate*).

53. Cf. Robert A. Brady, *The Rationalization Movement in German Industry*, Berkeley, 1933; idem., *The Spirit and Structure of German Fascism*, London, 1937, ch. IV/2; Ludwig Preller, *Sozialpolitik in der Weimarer Republik*, Stuttgart, 1949, pp. 416f. There is still no comprehensive social history of industrial relations during the Weimar period.

both instances presupposed the dominant position of the boss as 'master in his own house'. Though this idea was not entirely negative, it was still mostly so. 'Obstacles and obstructions' in the form of labour unions, factory councils and working-class parties had to be eliminated. However, even the potential translation of the theory of the works community into the practice of 'industrial relations' offered no guarantee to its proponents that their over-arching economic, social and political goals could be achieved on this particular basis.

To disenfranchise the working class and deprive it completely of power while pursuing a programme of rearmament and territorial expansion[54] that imposed great burdens and hardships on the workers – a programme that depended on the absence of any resistance on the part of labour – was ambitious, to say the least. To the industrialist, in particular, it was essential to push for the linking of the two goals of the factory community and rearmament: the unions and the working-class parties would have obstructed the rearmament process, or even rendered it impossible. On the other side, this linkage could be achieved only through the use of force, that is, through the state and the Nazi Party. At the beginning of 1934 the industrialists had good reason to assume that both were under their control. Whether the political leadership would be compelled in the future to maintain industrial peace by other means less favourable to industry had to be left undecided for the time being. It would soon become apparent that the foreign-policy successes which the domestic political programme was originally designed to support were bound to sustain the division of power worked out in 1933/4, and in a form that was increasingly disadvantageous to German industry.[55]

Thus the economic and social origins of the factory community as the nucleus of the new social order were contradictory, and their relationship to the dynamism of the Nazi regime – a dynamism that had been revealed in outline to the old power elite as early as 1933[56] – was at best problematical. The only reason the concept of the Labour Organization Law seemed viable at all was because of the Depression. Behind the ideological and sociological factors (which were anything but trivial) that were involved in the emergence of the Labour Organization Law loomed the critical question of who would control the labour market. Before 1930 the unions, with the support of government authorities, had

54. This is not to say that industry agreed from the outset with the actual goals of Nazi foreign policy; however, the reinstatement of Germany as a great power was a goal pursued by all the leaders of the German economy since 1919. For further details, see Henry Ashby Turner, Jr, *Stresemann and the Politics of the Weimar Republic*, Princeton, NJ, 1963, ch. 7.
55. Cf. chapter 6 below.
56. Hitler's remarks to the generals on 3 February 1933 (Meinck, *Aufrüstung*, pp. 17 f.) and leading industrialists in the General Council on the Economy on 20 September 1933 (*BA Koblenz*, R43II, file 321/1) left no room for doubt.

repeatedly managed to push through wage increases in spite of continuing high levels of unemployment.[57] Together with the working-class parties and the factory councils, the unions forced employers to share control of the labour market. With 1 million unemployed this arrangement was still tenable; with 7 million it had become an impossibility. Having wrested back temporary control of the labour market because of mass unemployment, the employers were not about to relinquish it. As early as March 1933 some of the employer associations were asking the government whether it made any sense to enter into collective bargaining with the unions since the lifespan of the wage agreements might exceed that of the unions.[58] It was also mass unemployment that made it impossible for the unions to fend off the political attacks of the employers – attacks that seemed to assure the latter permanent and unimpeded control of the labour market. The totalitarian factory community had the best chances of survival wherever workers lived in constant fear of layoffs or where they viewed their job as a liberation from years of misery, hunger and distress.

The new regime, however, had called for rearmament and a 'battle of labour'; it had granted credits for this and announced grandiose plans. 'Give me four years!' shouted Hitler, knowing full well that his regime could not survive continued mass unemployment.

57. Schweitzer, *Big Business*, pp. 364–99, correctly puts great emphasis on this point. The average real hourly wage in industry rose from 82 (1924) to 115 (1929) (index: 1913 = 100); Gerhard Bry, *Wages in Germany 1871–1945*, Princeton, NJ, 1960, p. 71.

58. Working Committee of Nationalist Industrialists (*Arbeitsausschuss der deutschnationalen Industrieller*) to the RAM, 10 March 1933: *DZA Potsdam*, RAM, file 2185, pp. 90–3. Other petitions in the same vein from smaller associations: ibid., file 6577, pp. 41–54. On the similar position of the Leverkusen office of I.G. Farben: *GPSA Berlin*, Rep. 335, file 204. The attitude of the major companies and associations on this point still calls for detailed study.

4

The Condition of the Working Class in Germany, 1933–1936

4. 1. Employment Creation Programmes

The employment creation programmes of the Nazi regime have already been studied from a number of different perspectives, but all historians seem to agree that they were a success for the new regime in two respects. First, they enabled it to pursue an accelerated and covert programme of rearmament, and second, they helped it to produce a rapid solution to the problem of mass unemployment. 'Hitler eliminated unemployment' – this widely-held belief calls for careful examination; however, this is less a matter of questioning Hitler's role than of analysing the condition of the working class during this period and clarifying the origins and methods of Nazi economic and social policy.

Considering the political importance of solving the economic crisis, the government's job-creation policy can only be described as timid, overly conservative in its choice of methods and severely limited in scope. No new steps worth mentioning were taken until June 1933; when the employment programmes were terminated in the spring of 1935, approximately RM 5-6 billion had been expended on measures to overcome the economic crisis and create jobs. Not quite half this sum had already been appropriated by the two previous governments, under the Weimar Republic. Public investment, though now bearing the title 'employment creation', constituted an even smaller, albeit indispensable proportion of the total. During the same period spending on armaments rose to about RM 4.4 billion, further increasing the demand for labour. Taken together, the totals for 1933/4 averaged about one-third of total government expenditure, increasing the national debt by 30 per cent. In contrast to the previous year, the indexes of industrial production rose dramatically, whereas the GNP and consumer spending continued to stagnate. Though there was a slight upward movement in 1934, the growth rates lagged behind those that were to be achieved in later years when unemployment was declining even more slowly.[1]

There were several reasons for the delays in overcoming the economic crisis, one of the most important being the continuing decline in the balance of payments, which throttled imports and made it seem imperative to hold down prices so that the competitiveness of German exports would not be hampered in the process. In addition, there was the unfounded but deep-seated fear in Germany that renewed inflation would be the inevitable result of any 'experimentation with the currency'. This attitude was not without influence on the scope and methods of the regime's financial policies.[2] Third, mention must be made of the heated arguments that flared up in industry and inside the regime over the focus and methods of the government's measures to stimulate the economy. The disagreements centred mainly on the question of priorities – public works, contracts to the private sector, or a general increase in real wages.[3] Lastly, rearmament, the financing of which took precedence over everything else,[4] was not exactly conducive to an economic upturn, especially in the light of the limits imposed by the secrecy sur-

1. Cf. Table 4.2 and the sources cited there. The figures used to calculate the increase in armaments expenditures are based on outlays for 1931/2. Expenditures for employment procurement are based on Gerhard Kroll, *Von der Weltwirtschaftskrise zur Staatskonjunktur*, Berlin, 1958, pp. 410f.; René Erbe, *Die nationalsozialistische Wirtschaftspolitik im Lichte der modernen Theorie*, Zürich, 1958, pp. 31, 183. Dietmar Petzina's figure – RM 3.8 billion by the beginning of 1935 – seems to take no account of tax remissions: 'Hauptprobleme der deutschen Wirtschaftspolitik 1932/33', *Vierteljahrshefte für Zeitgeschichte*, vol. 15/1, 1967, p. 49. For comparison, cf. Erbe, *Wirtschaftspolitik*, p. 32. Debt: ibid., p. 54. There is still no detailed study of these questions based on primary sources; all figures are estimates.

2. This fear was encouraged by conservative circles before January 1933 in order to discredit the employment procurement programmes which they found unacceptable. After 1933, however, these same circles quickly dropped their earlier objections. Partly out of a concern for public opinion the new regime disguised most of its methods for creating credit (tax vouchers, Mefo bills, etc.). Hoarding and a persistent trend towards the accumulation of tangible goods gave the regime cause for concern in 1933–4

3. See Eberhard Czichon, *Wer verhalf Hitler zur Macht?*, Cologne, 1967, pp. 24–56; Kurt Gossweiler, 'Der Übergang von der Weltwirtschaftskrise zur Rüstungskonjunktur in Deutschland 1933 bis 1934', *Jahrbuch für Wirtschaftsgeschichte*, 1968, part II, especially pp. 71–98.

4. There is some controversy about the degree to which Nazi economic and financial policy was directed to rearmament during the first eighteen months after the seizure of power; cf. Sauer, in Karl Dietrich Bracher, Wolfgang Sauer and Gerhard Schulz, *Die nationalsozialistische Machtergreifung. Studien zur Errichtung des totalitären Herrschaftsystems in Deutschland 1933–1934*, Cologne/Opladen, 1960, pp. 795–803, whose heavy emphasis on the regime's fixation on rearmament from its inception is not entirely convincing. He is surely correct in saying that there was no clear civilian phase in the process of stimulating the economy, but his estimate of armaments expenditures for 1933 at beween RM 2 billion and RM 3 billion seems too high. Cf. the more cautious treatment by Petzina, 'Hauptprobleme', pp. 44f.

rounding the programme during the first two years of the Nazi regime.[5] Moreover, in contrast to other possible ways of moving the economy forward, rearmament required enormous organizational and technical efforts preparatory to actual production – efforts which would necessarily delay any benefits to the general economy. These benefits would, in any case, be minimal, since goods manufactured for the military are normally of no use to the general economy; once they have been produced, they do not tend to stimulate further demand or create markets.[6]

The fact that the lag in the economic upswing was not fully reflected in the unemployment statistics was due in no small measure to a change, initiated in 1933, in the way in which the figures were compiled: occasional workers were no longer considered unemployed. Young farm workers and members of the Labour Service, who had previously (and understandably) been counted among the jobless, now disappeared from the official unemployment statistics altogether. Even those hired on a strictly temporary basis to do relief work for the municipalities and labour exchanges were no longer listed as jobless. Thus the highly touted decline in general unemployment was to a large extent nothing more than a propaganda ploy. Among the 3.5 million persons who had supposedly found jobs by the middle of 1934, approximately 400,000 were young people sent to work for a pittance as farm hands, while over 600,000 were relief workers who, in part because they feared having their unemployment benefits cut, were forced to perform heavy labour in mines, on reclamation projects and so on for wages that were hardly better than their unemployment benefits had been.[7]

True, steady employment had been found for approximately 2 million unemployed workers and another 500,000 people who had never

5. First England (1939–40) and then the USA (1941) showed how quickly an economy can be shifted to armaments production (they, of course, began the changeover in much more favourable political circumstances). As significant as the desire for rearmament was in 1933–5, it still seems relatively modest. Occasionally, industry complained about the limited scope of rearmament and the slowness in awarding contracts.

6. Cf. the analysis by Erbe, *Wirtschaftspolitik*, pp. 151f., 161–8, who stresses the clearly negligible secondary effects of public investment after 1933 (multiplier 1.5). This does not of course entail any judgement about another economic purpose of rearmament, i.e. economic imperialism.

7. See the detailed contribution by Fritz Petrick, 'Eine Untersuchung zur Beseitigung der Arbeitslosigkeit unter der deutschen Jugend in den Jahren von 1933 bis 1935', *Jahrbuch für Wirtschaftsgeschichte*, 1967, part 1, pp. 287–300. According to Petrick the number of relief workers peaked in the spring of 1934 at 630,000. All told, there were over 1.5 million people performing relief work at any one time in 1934 alone: *Statistisches Jahrbuch für Deutschland*, 1936, p. 336. The extremely hard working conditions led to numerous complaints, strikes and walkouts: cf., for example, Bernhard Vollmer, *Volksopposition im Polizeistaat*, Stuttgart, 1957, pp. 96f.; *DZA Potsdam*, RAM, file 2185, pp. 323–6; file 2186, pp. 41–5.

had a job before. Many of the relief workers, farm hands and Labour Service 'comrades' viewed any kind of work as freeing them from the tedium, inactivity and hopelessness that characterized the worst years of the crisis. Yet, as we shall show in greater detail below, it was impossible to speak of a government-planned employment creation programme established *in the interests of the working class*.[8] To Hitler and to heavy industry, rearmament always took first priority.

It was the job of propaganda to bridge the gap between an attitude that was basically indifferent to social issues and a realization that only a rapid recovery from the economic crisis would legitimize the new regime. In this context 'propaganda' means not only the use of the written and spoken word or the manipulation of attitudes by the state. Under National Socialism, political actions and decisions – and the social processes set in motion by them – very often turned into propaganda themselves, offering bogus or pseudo-solutions to real problems, or instantly transmogrifying real problems into pseudo-problems. This presupposed, of course, the existence of a political dictatorship that was able to eliminate public control of its methods of domination. Employment creation therefore became not so much a question of economics as of political psychology.[9] The scene was set for a garish war fought with unemployment statistics – a noisy attempt to convince people that the economy was on the mend without actually confronting the misery which the majority of Germans were still suffering. To be sure, Germany's unfavourable balance of trade and lack of foreign currency, as well as the protectionist policies of the other capitalist countries, placed obstacles in the path of a rigorous assault on economic hardship. However, the measures adopted to deal with mass unemployment in 1933/4 show that stop-gap solutions enabled the government to weather the difficult period before armaments production began to run at full capacity.

The rapid absorption of the unemployed into industry was not easy to accomplish, nor was it desired by the political leadership if it in any way impeded rearmament. But people had to be got off the streets.[10] The heavily propagandistic character of the employment creation policy was a product of these factors. In the middle of March 1933 Hitler called on the government 'to direct people's activities to strictly political affairs, since decisions on the economy had yet to be taken'.[11] However, even

8. Additional material on this in section 2 of this chapter.

9. Petzina, 'Hauptprobleme', considers the emphasis put on this aspect to be one of the regime's special achievements; he does not go into detail about the consequences for the workers. One can easily imagine a very different job creation policy that takes into consideration the material interests of the people, thereby promoting political 'trust' without being so dependent on propaganda.

10. Cf. Sauer, in Bracher, Sauer and Schulz, *Machtergreifung*, p. 799.

11. Petzina, 'Hauptprobleme', p. 45.

when these decisions were finally taken, they did not eliminate the need to distract the people politically, precisely because the economic plans were themselves a 'diversion' from the real problems.

The number of relief projects increased sevenfold during the winter of 1933/4 as compared to the same period in 1932. The chief beneficiaries, however, were not the relief workers or the general economy, but the statisticians. It was also questionable whether the work of the Labour Service or of farm assistants was of any appreciable benefit to the economy. The tax measures designed to stimulate consumption were likewise kept within modest bounds for the reasons mentioned above; their only significant impact was on the home-building and home repair industries and – if we factor in the marriage loans – on the furniture and home appliance industries. The company tax laws, on the other hand, were much more generous; to a degree that is difficult to determine precisely, they specifically benefited the armaments industry.[12] Another set of laws was designed to increase direct public investment, for instance in transportation and communications. Although these laws helped increase military preparedness as well as improve the infrastructure, they were – with the exception of highway construction – one-time expenditures of limited duration. Again, this was not a carefully planned policy which envisaged employment creation as an opportunity to satisfy pent-up demand or to expand facilities to benefit the public.[13]

Given the current state of research, it is not possible to be more exact in breaking down the data on employment creation expenditures into specific categories. Until now scholarly research has focused mainly on financing methods, and even here the raw data have been handled rather sloppily. It is impossible to determine precisely the total value of the tax vouchers and long-term labour bonds (*Arbeitsschatzanweisungen*) in circulation,[14] not to mention their impact on the economy. Thus we are only able to produce a crude breakdown of the distribution of revenue according to socio-economic categories (e.g. relief work, stimulation of consumption, promotion of production) and a rough estimate of the effects of the various methods used to stimulate the economy. In general, the employment creation policy was designed to meet the demands of big industry for government contracts (armaments, railways), tax reductions and tax waivers. It paid scant attention to increasing the consumer

12. On tax policy, see Erbe, *Wirtschaftspolitik*, pp. 28–32; Sauer, in Bracher, Sauer and Schulz, *Machtergreifung*, p. 800.

13. Thus investment in the national railway system (*Reichsbahn*), for example – one of the most important vehicles for job creation – was far less than required: Erbe, *Wirtschaftspolitik*, p. 26; the same was true for housing construction; see below pp.149f.

14. Kroll, *Weltwirtschaftskrise*, pp. 472, 580ff., is contradictory on this point. Erbe's figures are also not consistent: *Wirtschaftspolitik*, pp. 42, 45.

purchasing power of the majority of the population. Only between June 1933 and June 1934 did the government release any sizeable amounts to fund the public works projects to which industry took exception. After that period government contracts to industry far and away exceeded all other types of economic stimulation. Unfortunately, the results of historical research do not allow us to break down job creation expenditures even for those branches of industry favoured by the government. If we disregard tax vouchers for a moment, it is clear that the building industry was the chief beneficiary. Taken together, the additional investments in rural areas (housing developments, reclamation projects) and the tax benefits granted to agriculture probably exceeded RM 1 billion.[15]

The diversity of these various measures mirrors both the origins of the policy and its ultimate advantage, that is, the search for an economical way of satisfying the greatest number of interest groups quickly and efficiently.[16] Deprived of its own representatives, the working class was unique in not benefiting from this policy. The 'social conscience' of National Socialism now represented labour's interests. By 'social' the Nazis meant initiatives and institutions that were supposedly neutral with regard to the class struggle, as reflected in the concepts of 'reason' and 'justice' embodied in the catchword *Volksgemeinschaft* (national-racial community). What was important about this aspect of social policy was that it addressed itself directly to the individual and seemed to align his personal interests with those of the entire community. Thus, extra-governmental organs of the Nazi movement undertook a number of initiatives – paralleling the government's own employment creation policy – to redistribute existing jobs according to 'social' principles. The Nazis' claims to have co-ordinated the energies of the German people to combat this aspect of the nation's plight had a certain pseudo-practical (i.e. propagandistic) effect. Although there are no figures to substantiate this, the sources suggest that, as a result of the new regime's hostile policy towards labour, employers were actually more likely to grant workers certain social concessions than they had been during the previous era of confrontation with the trade unions. In any event, the factory inspectors frequently reported on intensive efforts to divide work among the greatest number of people by reducing individual

15. The beginnings of this kind of analysis in Petzina, 'Hauptprobleme', p. 47, note 91; Erbe, *Wirtschaftspolitik*, pp. 28–32; also in the contemporary study by Leo Grebler, 'Work Creation Policy in Germany 1932–1935', *International Labour Review* (cited below as *ILR*), Geneva, vol. 35, nos. 3 and 4 (March–April 1937). The whole problem of job creation calls for a broad study grounded in social and economic history and using the now accessible official documents.

16. Only the textile and clothing industries were almost completely unaffected by the economic upswing, mainly because of the restrictions imposed on importing raw materials in the middle of 1934.

working hours.[17] The same trend is reflected in a law that remained in force until the autumn of 1934, limiting relief work to no more than 40 hours per week.[18]

More striking than the indirect influences on employers and their authority were the initiatives that originated at the lower echelons of the Party, which allowed unemployed labourers to co-opt positions already occupied by other workers. Young people and women in particular were urged to leave the workforce so as to free up jobs for unemployed heads of families. These initiatives touched on an issue of great importance to many unemployed adult males. During the years of crisis a number of worker households had only been kept above water because of the income earned by a wife or a daughter; however, these arrangements had also often led to a decline in the standard of living and to psychological tensions within families.[19] It was ironic that as a result of the economic crisis the NSDAP's principles for once actually coincided with real-life problems. Many people found themselves in agreement with the Party's efforts to limit the role of women to the 'three Ks' (*Kinder, Küche, Kirche*), if it meant that additional jobs would be made available for men.[20] In the case of young workers, the problem was that at the beginning of the economic recovery employers had hired them in preference to older workers. Whereas in June 1933, 26.1 per cent of the unemployed were under the age of 25, a year later they constituted only 18.8 per cent; during the same period the proportion of 40- to 60-year-olds among the unemployed rose from 26.4 per cent to 31.6 per cent.[21]

17. Cf. the *Jahresberichte der Gewerbeaufsichtsbeamten und Bergbehörden 1933–34*: 'Preussen' (Prussia), pp. 33f., 63f., 70f., 169, 307–11, 329–32, 380f.; 'Bayern' (Bavaria), p. 20. The report titled 'The Reduction of the Working Week in Germany', *ILR*, vol. 32, no. 6 (June 1934), pp. 166–82 gives an overview of the problem. In spite of these efforts, the length of the average workday increased in the wake of the economic upswing (see Table 4.1); still, its importance, especially in 1933, should not be underestimated.

18. Law on Reducing Unemployment (*Gesetz zur Verminderung der Arbeitslosigkeit*), 1 June 1933: *RGBl. I*, 1933, p. 323. A relief worker earned about RM 20 for a forty-hour week.

19. See J. Grünfeld, 'Rationalisation and the Employment and Wages of Women in Germany', *ILR*, vol. 29, no. 5 (May 1934), p. 609. The reason for this development lay, first, in the heavy concentration of women in the consumer goods industries, which were less severely affected by the crisis and, second, in the fact that they were paid less. Female unemployment is not a proper measure by which to evaluate this question, since many more unemployed women than men dropped out of the labour force entirely. Thus, in January 1933, not even 20 per cent of the unemployed were women; whereas they constituted 36 per cent of all those holding a job. Figures in *Stat. Jahrbuch*, 1930, p. 374 and *Stat. Jahrbuch*, 1939/40, p. 312. For further details, see Timothy W. Mason 'Women in Germany, 1925–1940: Family, Welfare and Work', part 1, *History Workshop Journal*, no. 1, 1976, pp. 91ff.

20. The crisis also gave impetus to the idea of the rural settlement (*Siedlungsideologie*); unemployed people with large gardens found it easier to weather the crisis, as was noted for example in southern Germany.

21. *Stat. Jahrbuch*, 1936, p. 338.

The unofficial measures taken by the Party with regard to the preferential hiring of unemployed adult males were largely supported by the government and anchored in legislation. Among the most effective instruments were the marriage loans given to women workers to encourage them to marry and give up their jobs.[22] The economic crisis had forced many young couples temporarily to postpone marrying and setting up a household; the number of marriages had declined from 597,000 in 1929 to 516,000 in 1932. Following the award by the state of 366,000 marriage loans in 1933/4, the number of marriages jumped to 638,600 in 1933 and 740,200 in 1934, falling back to 650,000 by 1935 (when only 157,000 loans were awarded). Loans averaged RM 600. The measure achieved two objectives. It certainly earned the Party the gratitude of those for whom marriage had been made easier at a time of grave economic hardship, and it helped free jobs for others, often adult males. Also, since the law provided for reducing the amount of the loan to be repaid by one-third for every child born, it fitted in well with the regime's policy of encouraging population growth.[23] The government also made other attempts to replace women industrial workers with men. However, even though the number of home assistant jobs increased as a result of the elimination of taxes and insurance contributions,[24] the proportion of women employed in 1936 – 5.5 million out of a total labour force of 17.7 million – was still below that of the 1920s. The call to give priority to men in hiring, which had been issued purely for propaganda reasons, seemed to have had the desired effect. Of course, the fact that the majority of newly-created jobs were in industries that employed mostly men in any case turned out to be even more effective than direct state intervention in the labour market.[25]

By contrast, government attempts to cut down on the hiring of young people in favour of older workers moved ahead much more slowly, since the general population and even employers had much less sympathy for such measures. It was not until the directive of 28 August 1934 that works leaders were legally obligated and the labour exchanges empowered to examine the age make-up of a company's workforce and replace single workers under the age of 25 with unemployed heads of

22. Law on Reducing Unemployment, 1 June 1933, *RGBl.* I, p. 323.

23. *Stat. Jahrbuch,*1936, p. 35; Petrick, 'Jugend', p. 290, note 15; *Deutsche Sozialpolitik. Bericht der Deutschen Arbeitsfront, Zentralbüro, Sozialamt, 30. 6. 1936 bis 31. 8. 1937*, p. 59 f. The families thus favoured had on average twice as many children as other families. Cf. also Mason, 'Women', pp. 95ff.

24. Cf. the Law of 12 May 1933 and the executive order of 16 May 1933; *RGBl. I*, pp. 265, 283 (Social Insurance); Erbe, *Wirschaftspolitik*, p. 32.

25. Figures for June 1936: *Stat. Jahrbuch*, 1937, p. 324. As early as this year success proved to be two-edged, for it was not easy to attract women back to work in industry, as became increasingly necessary in the future. Cf. pp. 235–8 below.

families, as long as 'undue hardship' was not imposed.[26] The approximately 130,000 young people who subsequently lost their jobs could not, of course, be allowed to stay unemployed; they were sent off to farm-work or to the Labour Service. More effective than simply removing one worker and replacing him with another was the mechanism provided by a clause in the same directive, by which workers under the age of 25 required the prior approval of a labour exchange to get hired. This allowed the labour exchanges to enjoin employers to hire older workers. It is impossible to measure the success of this directive statistically; however, even though the number of cases in which one worker directly replaced another probably exceeded 130,000,[27] the success of the whole campaign was quite limited. Despite the large number of school-leavers in 1934 and 1935 – the result of the post-First-World-War baby boom – the proportion of youth and young workers among the jobless by November 1935 had increased only slightly, to 22.2 per cent (1934: 18.8 per cent). This development was due in part to the manipulation of statistics mentioned above and partly to the growing expansion of the armed forces.[28] Last but not least, it reflected the interests of the employers in profiting from the labour of younger workers who were physically stronger, cost less to pay (until they reached 21), and tended to bring fewer trade union or socialist ideas to the workplace.[29]

However, another drive, supported mainly by Party organizations, to redistribute existing jobs on a 'social' basis was opposed by the government, at least so far as it was carried out forcibly. The aim here was to eliminate the multi-income family. Even the last governments under the Weimar Republic had appealed to households with two or more wage-earners to give up their additional sources of income in order to help families in which no one had a job. But the Nazi movement did not limit itself to mere appeals, and in November 1933 the government was forced to take action against the uncontrolled activities of Party members. The reasons for this can be deduced from Cabinet documents reporting that not only was the concept of the double wage-earner difficult to define but that the Nazis' actions often penalized 'the best and

26. Directive on Manpower Distribution (*Anordnung über die Verteilung von Arbeitskräften*), 28 August 1934: *DRA*, no. 202, paras. II and III. Informative discussion of the problems in Friedrich Syrup, *Hundert Jahre staatlicher Sozialpolitik*, ed. Otto Neuloh, Stuttgart, 1957, pp. 419f. Details below from Syrup.

27. Especially because of the large number of 'voluntary' exchanges that took place before the enactment of this law, usually under pressure from one of the Party organizations. The expansion of the Labour Service played an important role here.

28. Cf. Petrick, 'Jugend'.

29. The articles on 'Preussen' in *Jahresberichte der Gewerbeaufsichtsbeamten ...1933–34*, p. 14; and on 'Sachsen', pp. 33ff., 65.

most productive people'. Moreover, the 'authority of the state' was being threatened and an atmosphere conducive to 'denunciations of the worst kind' fostered. The campaign against double wage-earners was being carried on 'with particular fury of late'. A number of agencies had become involved in this question and 'special commissions' set up to 'force employers – sometimes by threatening them with the severest measures (concentration camp) – to fire employees who were deemed double wage-earners'. In 1933 the government itself had taken up the struggle against double wage-earners, maintaining that propaganda alone was the best means to solve the problem. It therefore announced that 'in the future' these uncontrolled activities 'would be prosecuted to the full extent of the law'.[30]

As inadequate as the the social-policy initiatives of the Nazi movement were – measured against the misery of the times and the lost opportunities for a government-controlled economic policy – they must not be viewed as strictly diversionary actions. However, the social idealism stressed by the new regime lost much of its persuasiveness when it became obvious that the Nazis were primarily interested in creating jobs for themselves. Finding employment for veteran Party members (*alte Kämpfer*) was doubtless the most successful aspect of the Nazis' employment creation policy. From the outset there was far-reaching agreement between the government and the Party on the urgency of finding regular employment for Nazis. A 'Special Initiative' (*Sonderaktion*) undertaken for this purpose was so successful by October 1933 that in every district at least 40 per cent – and in some cases as many as 70 per cent – of formerly unemployed 'members of nationalist military formations' had found a job; in Saxony the proportion was no less than 96 per cent by May 1934. In October 1933 the Special Initiative was re-examined and streamlined, in the process of which the individuals who were to receive preferential treatment from the labour exchanges were more precisely defined. These included the following: members of the SA, the SS and the *Stahlhelm*, provided they had belonged to these organizations prior to 30 January 1933; Nazi Party members with a membership number below 300,000; all func-

30. Reports to the Cabinet by the Ministers of Labour and Economics, 26 October 1933: *BA Koblenz*, R43II, file 537/2. These principles were approved by the government and published in amended form in *R.Arb.Bl.*, 1933, part II, no. 33. In the case of the civil service, the government went beyond appeals, prohibiting civil servants from having supplemental incomes and forbidding the hiring of married women in a civil service capacity: Law on the Amendment of Regulations Pertaining to the General Civil Service Pay and Pension Law, 30 June 1933 (*Gesetz zur Änderung von Vorschriften auf dem Gebiete des allgemeinen Beamten-, des Besoldungs- und des Versorgungsrechts*): *RGBl.* I, p. 433. Additional details in the appendix to the report, ibid. Cf. also the discussion of the problem in Syruph, *Hundert Jahre*, pp. 421f. I was unable to find material on the results of the government's policy or on the continuation of the campaign by Party authorities.

tionaries (*Amtswalter*) of the Party and its affiliated organizations, provided they had occupied their positions for at least a year. The labour exchanges were obliged to give preference to these groups over all others seeking employment (except disabled veterans of First World War).[31] Thus under the new regime jobs that were already being hotly competed for were parcelled out according to *political* criteria, as a result of which trade union members and members of working-class parties – their organizations having already been destroyed – were now dealt yet another and, in light of the desperate economic situation, harder blow.[32] Purely political arbitrariness was now added to the uncontrolled and random forces of the labour market to which they had already been exposed. The social and political power of the German working class had probably never been at a lower ebb than in 1933/4.

The Special Initiative went considerably beyond its officially sanctioned limits, of course; largely on their own, the lower echelons of the SA and the Party expanded the definition of those who were to receive preference in job allocation, going so far as to establish their own labour exchanges. Not only were they interested in the new jobs that had been created in the wake of the economic recovery, but they frequently sought to arrange for the firing of whatever 'Marxists' had been able to keep their jobs during the crisis, replacing them with the Nazis' own nominees. But no matter how willing the new regime was at first to accede to the wishes of its supporters, it was unwilling to keep covering up these kinds of 'uncontrolled' activities. Even political favouritism had to be regulated and controlled from above. So when the SA leadership and Party authorities subsequently refused to adhere to previous agreements and refused to abandon their own independent labour exchanges, the government, on 10 August 1934, formally granted the Reich Institute for Labour Exchange (Reichsanstalt für Arbeitsvermittlung) exclusive authority in questions of employment.[33]

31. Order of the Führer's Deputy of 24 July, 1933: *BA Koblenz*, R43II, file 417; decree of the President of the Reich Institute for Labour Exchange (Reichsanstalt für Arbeitsvermittlung) to the presidents of the *Land* employment exchanges (*Landesarbeitsämter*, or LAA), 18 October 1933; ibid., file 534; 'Sachsen' in *Jahresberichte der Gewerbeaufsichtsbeamten...1933–34*, p. 26. A number of employers accepted advice on their hiring policies from the NSBO and the DAF; complaints from the Self-Defence Organization (*Selbsthilfe*) of the *Stahlhelm* to Seldte in June/July 1933: *DZA Potsdam*, RAM, file 6463, pp. 193f., 237ff., 246, 257f., 307.

32. Cf. above, pp. 86f.

33. The agreements had been negotiated in October 1933; decree of the President of the Reichsanstalt (see note 31 above) and his report to the Minister of Labour, 4 December 1933: *BA Koblenz*, R43II, file 534. Thus almost a year passed before the government took any legal action to curb uncontrolled actions; in the meantime most of the veterans of the Party had probably found employment. Decree on Manpower Distribution (*VO über die Verteilung von Arbeitskräften*), 10 August 1934: *RGBl. I*, p. 786. For background information: Syrup, *Hundert Jahre*, p. 407.

In 1934 a few more measures were introduced which, it was hoped, would reduce unemployment in the hardest hit areas, primarily the big cities and the industrial centres. But the President of the Reichsanstalt made only limited use of the authority given him in May 1934 to ban industrial migration to these areas. Only in the cases of Berlin, Hamburg, Bremen and, after March 1935, the Saarland did the government require workers from outside to obtain special permission to take jobs in these areas, even though other major cities, particularly in central Germany, had a higher rate of unemployment and had specifically requested a ban on immigration. But as was the case for so many measures taken by the Nazis, the regime was pursuing several goals at once. The choice of the port cities of Hamburg and Bremen, for example, was motivated by the desire to prevent large-scale overseas emigration, since that was considered to be incompatible with the Nazis' demographic and racial policies (in fact, the number of emigrants did decline by 25 per cent as compared to the 1920s).[34] In the meantime, other big cities and industrial centres benefited from the effects of another set of new laws. Several ordinances passed between May 1934 and March 1935, for example, made it more difficult to leave farm-work and easier to return former farm-workers from their jobs in industry to their previous work on the land.[35]

As we conclude this survey of Nazi employment creation policy, we should mention the attempt by the labour exchanges to fill the enforced leisure time of the unemployed with continuing education courses. Given the radical reduction in the number of apprenticeship positions and opportunities for on-the-job training between 1930 and 1933, these courses could have been much more than a mere tactical 'act of charity'; they could have been a way to supply industry with sufficient numbers of skilled workers in the future. But probably for financial reasons the courses never developed beyond their modest beginnings. In 1933 they were attended by only 116,000 salaried employees and 169,000 industrial workers.[36]

The fact that the successes of employment creation policy were more apparent than real becomes clearer when we realize that the govern-

34. Law on Regulating the Deployment of Labour (*Gesetz zur Regelung des Arbeitseinsatzes*), 15 May 1934: *RGBl. I*, p. 381 (para. 1). The ban on immigration was an effective remedial measure, especially in Berlin, where there were 650,000 unemployed in January 1933. However, in the eyes of the authorities it too often hindered individuals' career prospects to be of use in Breslau, Chemnitz, Dresden, Plauen and several cities in the Ruhr, where the number of unemployed as a proportion of the population was in some cases higher than in Berlin. See Syrup, *Hundert Jahre*, pp. 412, 415f., *Stat. Jahrbuch*, 1934, p. 310.

35. For details, see pp. 147f. below.

36. Syrup, *Hundert Jahre*, p. 410. For more information on the training of skilled workers, see pp. 232ff. below.

ment-sponsored work projects were ordered to use the least possible amount of mechanical equipment, so that the state could inflate its employment statistics. As a rule, the mining and reclamation projects in 1933/4 were supposed to be carried out by manual labour alone; productivity was not an issue. For similar reasons the government in July 1933 forbade the installation of new machines in cigar factories and ordered the scrapping of all production machinery, the replacement of which had been encouraged by the new tax-relief measures.[37] In the government's political calculations, the winter of 1933/4 figured as a possible flashpoint in 'the battle of labour' (the new term for what had previously been called employment creation). All its measures were therefore directed at maintaining the level of employment that had been achieved in the fall of 1933. From the above description of the limited scope of these measures, it should be obvious, however, that the government was less concerned with the benefits of production to the economy or with improving the lives of workers than it was with churning out numbers for the statisticians. According to official statistics, the government had largely achieved this political aim. Unemployment rose only slightly – by 344,000 (9.3 per cent) – from its low point in November 1933. On the other hand, as the government consolidated the power it felt it had gained as a result of creating jobs, it cut relief work by half, and seasonal unemployment grew considerably. The difference between the low and the high points in unemployment in 1934/5 was 705,900 (31.1 per cent); in 1935/6 the gap widened to 814,300 (47.7 per cent). In January 1935 there were still nearly 3 million people officially listed as jobless, and in December of that year 2.5 million.[38] These figures underscore once again the predominantly propagandistic nature of 'the battle of labour' in 1933/4.

Given the formulation of the problem presented here, it might seem possible to begin drawing conclusions about Nazi social and economic policy on the basis of subsequent changes in unemployment and level of employment. However, the fact that the only available employment statistics broken down according to branch of industry are for 1933 and

37. Cf. Kroll, *Weltwirtschaftskrise*, pp. 466f. The unemployed, who were often undernourished, naturally found physical labour on construction and reclamation projects to be extremely hard.

38. *Stat. Jahrbuch*, 1936, pp. 334f. In December 1934 the number of relief workers fell to 270,000, and a year later it was down to 120,000 (ibid., p. 325), concentrated mostly in depressed areas. Among other things, this policy was based on the assumption of those in power that many unemployed persons simply did not want to work; Ministerial Conference (*Chefbesprechung*), 10 January 1935: *BA Koblenz*, R41, file 24, pp. 2–7.

1938 makes this extremely difficult.[39] The decline in unemployment can be traced fairly accurately using the occupational data on the unemployed. But that decline was by no means related to changes in the level of employment, for when a jobless person was rehired, he was often placed in a position different from the one he had occupied before entering the ranks of the unemployed. Newly hired employees have to be factored into the equation, too. To a certain degree, the gap in the statistics can be filled by industry reports on levels of employment, utilization of capacity, and so on. However, these data represent only a cross-section and, unlike the unemployment statistics, they are not a comprehensive employment census. In general, we can say that the numbers of those employed rose much more quickly than the corresponding unemployment statistics would indicate. Yet any detailed comparison is doomed to failure because of the variation in the assignation of firms to different branches of industry in the two sets of data.[40]

The overall changes in the level of employment and unemployment for 1933–6 were as follows (according to the official statistics):

Table 4.1 Highest and lowest figures for employment and unemployment (in 000s).

	1933		1934		1935		1936	
Employed[a] (*Beschäftigte*)	12 078	14 458	13 984	16 072	15 042	17 124	16 001[c]	18 364
Registered unemployed (*Gemeldete Arbeitslose*)	6 014	3 715	3 773	2 268	2 974	1 706	2 508[c]	1 035
Available labour force[b] (*Vorhandene Arbeitskräfte*)	18 083	18 587[d]	17 757	18 418	18 016	18 933	18 694	19 471

[a]Employed: according to health insurance (*Krankenkassen*) membership statistics.

[b]Available labour force = employed + unemployed; does not add up exactly, since the high and low points in the numbers of employed and unemployed persons do not always coincide in the same month.

[c]December 1935

[d]According to the occupational census of 25 June 1933: 20,247,000.

Source: *Stat. Jahrbuch*, 1939–40, pp. 371, 389

39. See *Stat. Anhang*, Doc. I d.

40. Thus, for example, it is not very useful to juxtapose the tables on pp. 340f. and p. 350 in *Stat. Jahrbuch*, 1937. In the unemployment statistics all the branches of the iron and metal industry are combined; whereas in the industry reports they are listed separately. The statistics in the industry reports do not comprise even half of all those employed in industry and handicrafts; they are based on a large representative cross-section of firms: cf. *Stat. Handbuch*, p. 480. The figures given there are indexed. Cf. *Stat Anhang*, Doc. I b.

Thus between the beginning of 1933 and the autumn of 1936 the number of employed persons increased by 6.3 million, while the number of unemployed decreased by about 4.9 million; the total available workers in the whole economy thus increased by about 1.4 million.[41] What is striking, however, is that this increase in the workforce, according to the official statistics, did not begin until the spring of 1935, after the number of employed had shrunk temporarily by almost another 350,000 between January 1933 and January 1934. This is another indication of the degree to which casual workers were not counted in the 1933 statistics. The fact that the subsequent increase in the employment figures continued even beyond the middle of 1934, when the decrease in the number of jobless had already slowed, resulted from the simultaneous entry (in 1934 and 1935) into the job market of large numbers of young people leaving school or university (the latest members of the post-First-World-War baby boom generation). The expiration of measures aimed solely at employment creation was also reflected in the unemployment statistics after 1934.[42]

The different developments in the separate branches of industry were determined mainly by the government's economic policy. The fact that the same few branches of industry were the invariable beneficiaries of job creation and the rearmament programme (which was becoming increasingly important to the economy) was in keeping with Hitler's intentions and the interests of the army and the industrialists. In 1936 the level of employment throughout industry was almost equal to that of 1929. But while the 1929 level had already been exceeded by 5-6 per cent in the production and capital goods sector, it was still a good 15 per cent lower in the consumer industries sector. The fastest and most far-reaching upturn was recorded in the building industry, which boasted the most important employment creation projects while at the same time being a major beneficiary of the rearmament programme (highways, barracks, airfields, armaments factories, etc.). Thus the number of people employed in the building and natural resources sector (*Bau/Steine/Erden*) between 1932 and 1934 had doubled, and in 1936 was significantly above 1929 levels. The growth in the building industry itself was even greater; the number of employed increased fivefold between 1932 and 1936, thereby exceeding

---

41. This figure only indicates the trend: on the one hand, it does not take casual labour into account; and on the other it is seasonal, i.e. it disregards the disparity between the low point in 1933 and the high point in 1936. The two factors should somewhat cancel each other out. Cf. *Stat. Anhang, Doc. I a.*

42. The slowdown in the decline of unemployment was also caused by a recession in the late summer of 1935. By the end of August the number of unemployed was already starting to rise again. Possibly this was the result of problems in foreign trade.

the 1929 level by more than 30 per cent.[43] While unemployment in general dropped by an average of 68.5 per cent, it decreased by 74.3 per cent in the building industry,[44] and by 77.6 per cent in the building materials industry. The number of jobless in all branches of the iron and steel industry dropped by as much as 80.5 per cent, even though the increase in the number of employed was somewhat less than that in the building industry. Nevertheless, the number of employed in all branches of the building industry approximately doubled between 1932 and 1935, thereby surpassing the 1929 level by between 12 per cent and 18 per cent. No other branch of industry even came close to achieving such positive results. Only two other branches of industry had reached the 1929 level of employment by 1936,[45] and in only two non-industrial occupations (housekeeping and farming) was the decline in unemployment comparable to that in the occupations that had benefited as a result of the recovery. In mining and transportation, in the foodstuffs and luxury food industry as well as in the hotel industry and among unskilled workers, salespeople and office workers, the decline in unemployment was between 6 per cent and 17 per cent below the national average. In other branches of industry (for example, textiles, leather goods, clothing) unemployment decreased at the same rate, but the level of employment still remained far below that of 1929.

This is not the place to go into greater detail about about the economic and political causes of these developments in the labour market and in the composition of the labour force. The crucial factors were, first, the state's steadily rising demand for certain goods and services and, sec-

43. All data on the level of employment come from industry report statistics. part of the numerical data has been included in *Stat. Anhang, Doc. I b*. Comparing these statistics with the official numbers for 1933 and 1938 (*Anhang, Doc. I d*), we can see they are somewhat higher, especially in the case of the industries profiting from the recovery; this is probably due to the nature of the sample.

44. Not including temporary workers, in whose case the decrease was 63.1 per cent. The strong recovery in the construction industry in 1933–5 attracted a number of unemployed unskilled workers into the field. All data on unemployed based on *Stat. Jahrbuch*, 1936, p. 340.

45. The lumber industry and the foodstuffs and luxury food industry: ibid. Both sets of numbers on the foodstuffs and luxury food industry point up the limited value of statistical sources. According to the employment statistics, developments in this branch were about average, but the decline in unemployment (54.5 per cent) was well below average. Since this industry was not among the most attractive to workers, the explanation can only lie in the way the statistics were compiled. The data on the textile and clothing industry are exactly the opposite: a decline in unemployment that matched the average, together with an employment level which in 1936 was below that of 1929. The reason for these discrepancies was partly an exodus from these branches of industry. It is important to note that the government did not at first consider it necessary to establish a better basis for collecting data. The problem was not corrected until the labour pass (*Arbeitsbuch*) census of June 1938. Cf. also *Stat. Anhang, Doc. I d*.

ond, the government's partially successful attempts through direct intervention (in particular by limiting wage increases) to make the economy's unexploited reserves available exclusively to those branches of
industry critical to the war economy.

The signficance of this statistical data for social policy calls for explanation. First, it should be noted that the branches of industry which most
profited from the recovery of 1936 were those that had been most severely affected by the Depression. In January 1933 the building and building
materials industry plus the iron and steel industry accounted for more than
one-third of all the unemployed in Germany; in March 1936 they still
accounted for one-quarter. Even at that time, however, it was already clear
that these 480,000 people represented a kind of residual class of unemployed that would – barring a new global trade war or radical changes in
the state's economic policy – soon be absorbed by industry. On the other
hand, unemployment in the consumer goods industries had been relatively low during the economic crisis and their recovery was correspondingly
weaker after 1933.[46] The fact that the capital goods industries are the most
susceptible to economic crises but also the fastest to recover is characteristic of major downturns in the business cycle in capitalist economies. In
any event, both trends were particularly pronounced in Germany from
1929 to 1936. Measured in purely statistical terms, these branches of
industry had not only rehired 80 per cent of their former employees by
1936, but had also absorbed into newly-created positions a large share of
the new job seekers and the unemployed coming from other occupations.

The proof that these figures corresponded to reality is reflected both in
the statistics on the occupational preferences of young people leaving
school,[47] and in the data on the occupational and age distribution of the
German labour force in June 1938.[48] Clearly, the real process of social
change was much more complex than is indicated by the sources. Thus,
besides the industries that were benefiting from the recovery, the public
sector was also growing in importance as a source of employment, especially after the reintroduction of conscription in March 1935. Furthermore,
the Labour Service, the SS, the police, and a host of other new organs of
the state and the Party had a considerable – albeit a virtually unquantifiable

46. *Stat. Jahrbuch*, 1936, p. 340.

47. From July 1935 to June 1936 a third of all men who asked the labour exchanges for
advice and help in locating apprenticeships were looking for training in the iron and steel
industry. No more than about one-ninth of those seeking job counselling were interested in
all the other branches of industry put together: *Stat. Jahrbuch*, 1937, p. 361. Cf. also *Doc.
3, part II 6*.

48. *Stat. Jahrbuch*, 1939–40, p. 376. On average, 54.2 per cent of all male workers
were under the age of 35; in the iron and steel industry the proportion was 58.4 per cent.
Transportation, the printing and textile industries as well as the salaried employees group
were considered 'superannuated'.

– impact on developments in the labour market.[49] Although there are no precise data on the degree to which people changed occupations between 1933 and 1936, it is quite likely that there were a number of cases in which skilled workers were hired as unskilled labourers to fill positions for which they had no training, particularly in 1933/4.[50] During the period before 1936 we can also see a definite tendency to move away from industries which, as result of the one-sidedness of the economic recovery, offered poor career and earnings prospects. This was particularly true of the mining, textile and clothing industries, as well as agriculture.

A second change, which would become of fundamental importance to the labour market, was related to the nature of the unemployment that still existed in 1936. The rationalization movement from the mid-1920s – combined with the lack of liquid capital which had prevailed in this period, and the cutbacks in production by the cartels – had resulted in predominantly *structural* unemployment in German industry. Even with a booming economy, the number of jobless between 1926 and 1929 had rarely dropped below 1 million, and during most months it was higher. This structural unemployment primarily affected the metal, textile and clothing industries, followed by white-collar employees and unskilled workers.[51] Industry's rationalization efforts were apparently not significantly interrupted for any great length of time by the new regime;[52] but

49. The data from the labour pass census bore absolutely no relation to actual conditions in the public service; cf. *Stat. Anhang, Doc. I d* and accompanying explanation. It remains unclear whether this was a deliberate cover-up or whether it was part of the statistical methodology not to count members of the armed forces and the Labour Service. The only other published statistics on the number of people in government service list twice as many: 4.46 million (1939); see John P. Cullity, 'The Growth of Governmental Employment in Germany 1882–1950', *Zeitschrift für die gesamte Staatswissenschaft*, vol. 123, no. 2, April 1967, p. 202. This question is important not only in terms of social history, for the building of a system of total domination presupposed a broad expansion of state power, the actual scope of which, however, cannot be determined.

50. The problem was repeatedly mentioned by factory inspection officials (*Jahresberichte...1933–34*). There were also a few retraining courses for workers who because of this or on account of an extended period of unemployment were no longer qualified to do their job. The statistics of 1938 on the employed who had 'unlearned' their job (*Stat. Anhang, Doc. I c*) probably underestimated the extent of the problem.

51. *Stat. Jahrbuch*, 1931, pp. 301, 312.

52. Caution is warranted here, since the problem has yet to be studied in detail. Little weight need be given to the frequent hostile utterances from Party officials concerning rationalization. Of more importance were statements by the Nazis on the scientific management of work. There were practically no measures carried out in 1933–5 to save on wage costs. On the other hand, the increases in production in the 1930s as well as the statistics on investment clearly indicate a strong trend in the direction of technological improvement; cf. Kroll, *Weltwirtschaftskrise*, ch. 9 (production), and Berenice A. Carroll, *Design for Total War: Arms and Economics in the Third Reich*, The Hague/Paris, 1968, pp. 187 f. (investment). Carroll's criticism of Burton H. Klein, *Germany's Economic Preparations for War*, Cambridge, Mass., 1959, seems perfectly justified on this point.

the tendency towards structural unemployment slowed down as a result of the boom in the armaments industry and the increased exploitation of capacity in heavy industry. Thus, only a tiny minority of the 1,937,00 jobless in March 1936 were actually long-term unemployed. Their absorption into the production process was not impeded by the interaction between technological progress and limited markets. Unemployment in the production and capital goods sectors was caused in part by the lack of raw materials, but, with the exception of coal-mining, it was clearly abating. There were obvious economic and political reasons for the unemployment in the consumer goods industries, but again because of the boom in armaments from 1936/7, this too was waning. Another type of unemployment that was extremely important during the period 1934/7 was seasonal joblessness, the extent of which was a result of over-expansion in the building industry. But only a few tens of thousands – mostly older white-collar workers, miners and textile workers – were still 'redundant' in the true sense of the word.[53] By 1936 it could already have been predicted that finding jobs for the largest group of the unemployed – temporary workers without a permanent occupation,[54] would not be hampered because of the economy's lack of ability to absorb them.

In conclusion, it should be stressed once again that Nazi employment creation policy in the narrower sense of the term (excluding rearmament policy) was characterized by relatively minor expenditures and distinguished more by propagandistic than by politico-economic considerations. Even though it is not totally valid to say that the solution to the Depression in Germany was linked to rearmament as early as 1933, it is true that in its effort to stimulate the economy, the government did its utmost to avoid anything that might be detrimental to a future rearmament programme. By not promoting consumption more forcefully and not supporting large-scale long-term public works projects at the beginning of the crisis, the government's claim to have reduced unemployment by the spring of 1934 was a sham – a politically necessary sham, which was accompanied and cloaked by a host of 'social' initiatives for redistributing existing jobs. Where conditions truly did improve, the improvements derived from a revival of those branches of industry

53. After the increase in the demand for coal in the Four-Year Plan, this no longer applied to the mining industry, though it came as a complete surprise: see *Docs. 85–93*; explanatory text preceding *Doc. 125*. The situation of older employees was already desperate at the beginning of the drive to increase efficiency. At the end of 1934 insignificant subsidies were paid to businesses that employed older as well as younger workers. Cf. Syrup, *Hundert Jahre*, pp. 429 f.; Directive on Manpower Distribution, 28 August 1934, *DRA*, no. 202, p. 16; for further developments: *Doc. 10*.

54. In March 1936: 573,000 (excluding temporary construction workers).

which would be important in the future to the rearmament programme. After the spring of 1934, the continuing economic recovery was increasingly a spin-off of the upturn in the armaments industry, which received RM 11 billion in 1936 (1933: RM 1.5 billion).[55] Rearmament planning now determined the character and pace of employment policy; it was responsible for the rapid growth in jobs in the capital goods sector, the faltering developments in other branches of industry and the relatively slow solution to the problem of mass unemployment, considering what actually might have been possible. If, during the period between 1933 and 1936, national expenditures and government credits had been used on the same scale as they had been to promote the rearmament programme, unemployment would likely have been eliminated more quickly, more vigorously and more equitably.

4. 2. Wages, Living Standards and State Social Policy

A rigorous employment creation policy aimed at eliminating poverty and despair would at the same time have increased real wages and thereby helped to revive the general economy. The policy actually pursued was quite different. Its effects on the living standards of the working class will be examined in the following section. As in the case of most questions dealing with the economic and social history of Nazi Germany, there is a lack of reliable numerical data. However, as fragmentary and questionable as the following pieces of information may be individually, together they offer us the picture of a war economy which took priority over all other claims on the nation's economic resources. The most striking features of this picture were clear at the beginning of the economic recovery, when it had become obvious that the government did not need to concern itself with invalidating those other claims, since the Depression had already prepared the ground for this. At the beginning of the recovery, the start-up was necessarily slow, since much of the capacity in the armaments sector was idle in 1933. The government's basic economic decisions were straightforward and fully in line with the interests of the main factor behind the recovery, the capital goods industry. Both sides were interested in stabilizing prices and money-wage rates at the level of January 1933.[56] To do so required, above all, the dissolution

55. According to Carroll, *Design*, pp. 74 (note 3), 184, 263.
56. Prices in this sector, which were largely controlled by the cartels, declined only slightly during the economic crisis. The fall in prices of consumer goods and foreign raw materials was much greater: cf. Kroll, *Weltwirtschaftskrise*, p. 92. The branches concerned were interested in perpetuating the resulting cost benefits as well as those deriving from wage developments.

Table 4.2: Data on the development of the economy, 1928/9–37

		1928	1929	1932	1933	1934	1935	1936	1937
1.	Gross National Product (in billion RM)	–	89.0	58.0	59.0	67.0	74.0	83.0	93.0
2.	Military expenditure (% of GNP)	–	1.0	1.0	3.0	6.0	8.0	13.0	13.0
3.	Private consumption (% of GNP)	–	72.0	81.0	78.0	75.0	72.0	65.0	64.0
4.	Employment (in millions; annual averages)	–	18.4	12.9	13.4	15.5	16.4	17.6	18.9
5.	Average weekly work hours in industry	–	46.04	41.47	42.94	44.56	44.44	45.56	46.06
6.	Total wages and salaries (in billion RM)	44.9	–	27.4	27.7	31.2	35.4	37.7	41.5
7.	Earned and unearned income *plus* total undistributed profits (in billion RM)	25.6	–	15.6	16.7	19.4	22.1	25.2	28.6
8.	Average hourly earnings of workers in industry; index 1932 = 100	–	–	100.0	96.9	99.3	100.8	102.5	104.6
9.	Weekly earnings of workers; index 1932 = 100	–	132.7	100.0	102.2	109.7	112.3	116.6	120.6
10.	Official cost of living index; 1932 = 100	–	127.7	100.0	97.8	100.4	102.0	103.2	103.7
11.	Total industrial production; index 1928 = 100	–	100.9	58.7	65.5	83.3	95.8	106.7	116.7
12.	Producer goods; index 1928 = 100	–	103.2	45.7	53.7	–	99.4	112.9	126.0
13.	Consumer goods; index 1928 = 100	–	98.5	78.1	82.9	–	91.0	97.5	102.8

Sources:
1–3. In current prices: Carroll, *Design*, pp. 184, 186.
4–5. *Stat. Jahrbuch*, 1939–40, pp. 374, 384.
6–7. Erbe, *Wirtschaftspolitik*, p. 101. In current prices.
8–10. Bry, *Wages*, pp. 239–264. Actual gross earnings.
11–13. Kroll, *Weltwirtschaftskrise*, p. 610; *Stat. Jahrbuch*, 1936, p. 52.*

of the trade unions. In this way, wage demands could largely be ignored, thereby maximizing the profit that could be reinvested in the economy and keeping one of the most important cost factors relatively stable.[57] In the same way, the expansion of the consumer goods industries could be held in check, so that capital, hard currency and raw materials could be channelled primarily into heavy industry.

Table 4.2 illustrates the government's remarkable success in achieving the major goals of its programme in the period between 1933 and 1936/7. (I will return later to a discussion of the reasons for this success.) A 5 per cent rise in GNP between 1929 and 1937 contrasted with a 16 per cent increase in industrial production. Most of the growth in earnings from wages and salaries between 1933 and 1936 was due to increased employment opportunities, and most of the increase in average weekly earnings was a result of extending hours of work beyond the low point reached during the Depression.[58]

The wages and standard of living of industrial workers are the most important issues for the present study. For a proper analysis the figures presented above need to be modified and expanded. Even before 1936 the government's official cost-of-living index was subject to sharp criticism by the Ministry of Labour, which was responsible for wage policy. Measures taken by the Reichsnährstand, the new Nazi organiza-

57. Cf. Table 4.2, items 6 and 7. These statistics do not represent absolute values. They have been taken from summary data on the economy and since the figures, viewed arithmetically, always agree with each other, their tidiness makes them somewhat suspect. There is, of course, a reason for this, since their source (Erbe, *Wirtschaftspolitik*) is more concerned with economic theory than empirical history; but his numbers undoubtedly do give a correct picture of the main developmental tendencies and probably suffice for producing a general interpretation. However, the fact that every economist who deals with these problems uses his own numbers, which seldom agree with those of others, leaves the non-specialist rather at a loss, especially since relatively small differences in the statistics on certain questions can be of great significance, for example in comparing the distribution of national income in the 1920s with that of the 1930s. For the latest discussion, cf. Carroll, *Design*, ch. 10 and pp. 262–7, which does not, however, completely dispel the confusion. The entries under *Government expenditures* and *Investments* are especially troublesome. The numbers in Süphan Andic and Jindrich Veverka, 'The Growth of Government Expenditure in Germany since Unification,' *Finanzarchiv*, new series, vol. 23, no. 2 (January 1964), do not seem too reliable for the 1930s. Wolfram Fischer, *Die Deutsche Wirtschaftspolitik 1918–1945*, 2nd edn, Stuttgart, 1968, is based in part on Andic and Veverka.

58. A more precise formulation would be misleading. The following calculations are typical of the problems involved in statistical analysis: given the approximately 10 per cent increase in working hours and the 4 per cent growth in average hourly earnings (1932–7), one would expect total earned income to rise more quickly than the number of employed persons. However, both categories show a nearly identical rate of increase: approx. 50 per cent. Even lower figures for earned income in Kroll, *Weltwirtschaftskrise*, p. 607.

tion for agriculture, to improve agriculture led to a steep rise in food prices between 1933 and 1935.[59] Critics charged, however, that some of these increases had not been included in the official price indexes. Shortages in the supply of meat, vegetables, lard and dairy products were so great that in many cases price rises in 1935 exceeded plannned ceilings. Given these market conditions, the Reichsnährstand's efforts to stabilize consumer prices by cutting back on profit margins were doomed to fail. These problems were so formidable that they gave rise to serious disputes between the two authorities concerned, in the course of which the Minister of Labour complained about a 'major decline' in 'the purchasing power of real wages ... since 1934' and spoke of the 'ominous effects' of price increases 'in the social and political spheres'.[60] These issues, however, were barely reflected in the government's index, which recorded an increase in food prices of just under 10 per cent between January 1933 and January 1936, most of which had occurred during the first twelve months of the Nazi dictatorship. According to this calculation, food prices had risen by only 1 per cent between July 1934 and January 1936 and, despite a simultaneous jump in the price of clothing, the overall price index had moved up just 2 per cent.[61]

Although he tended to exaggerate problems when his own ministry was involved, the Minister of Labour's view of the situation is largely

---

59. See the very well documented dissertation by J. E. Farquharson, 'The NSDAP and Agriculture in Germany 1928–1938', Ph.D. thesis, University of Kent, 1972. These problems are treated cursorily in Bracher, Sauer and Schulz, *Machtergreifung*, pp. 570–8 and in Dietmar Petzina, *Autarkiepolitik im Dritten Reich. Der nationalsozialistische Vierjahresplan*, Stuttgart, 1968; David Schoenbaum, *Die braune Revolution*, Cologne/Berlin, 1968, ch. 5 contains somewhat more detail. The dissertation by Horst Gies, 'R. Walther Darré und die nationalsozialistische Bauernpolitik in den Jahren 1930 bis 1933', Frankfurt am Main 1966, is a valuable source. For a detailed analysis of the published sources, see Frieda Wunderlich, *Farm Labor in Germany, 1820–1945*, Princeton, NJ, 1961, pp. 222–91.

60. Letters of the Minister of Labour to the Minister of Food and Agriculture, 17 August and 3 September 1935: *BA Koblenz*, R43II, file 318; Seldte to Lammers, 30 October 1935: ibid., file 311. The problem was considered of major importance, the correspondence was passed on to all Reich ministers concerned, and both Lammers and Krohn (State Secretary in the Ministry of Labour) had a meeting with Hitler about the matter; see 'Aufzeichnung über die Einkommensverhältnisse' (Note on the Earnings Situation), 4 September 1935, *BA Koblenz*, R43II, file 318; *DZA Potsdam*, RWM, file 10296, p. 252. Not until the beginning of February 1936 did the Reich Trustees of Labour report a major improvement in the stability of food prices: ibid., pp. 305–323. On foreign trade, see Arthur Schweitzer, 'The Foreign Exchange Crisis of 1936', *Zeitschrift für die gesamte Staatswissenschaft*, vol. 118, no. 2 (April 1962); Petzina, *Autarkiepolitik*, pp. 30–45.

61. *Stat. Jahrbuch*, 1936, pp. 294f.

borne out by independent sources.[62] The evidence is in the form of the statistics on per capita consumption of basic food commodities, according to which the average consumption of meat, lard, cheese and eggs declined in comparison with the previous year. Consumption of milk, butter, and margarine increased only slightly, despite the rise in the number of employed and the increase in weekly earnings. Even in 1936, per capita consumption of the major food commodities – with the exception of fish, which consumers were increasingly using as a substitute for meat – was below the level of 1929, lower at least than the figures on average real wages would suggest.[63] To go back and revise the official statistics would, of course, be extremely difficult. Estimates in a recent study showing that food prices rose overall by 9 per cent in 1935 seem to coincide with actual conditions.[64] (In interpreting the numbers cited here, one must remember that worker households spent 45–55 per cent of their earnings on food.)

An additional drain on worker earnings, in comparison with 1929, were the salary and wage deductions not included in the offical statistics. These consisted of the increased contributions for social insurance mandated by the Emergency Decrees of the Brüning government and the added deductions for the Labour Front, Winter Relief Aid (*Winterhilfe*), and other Nazi organizations, not to mention numerous 'voluntary' donations. Both government and industry took a dim view of these added burdens, as emerged during their discussions on the new structure of social policy and on the measures to stimulate the economy; their reservations

62. The most important confirmations are the reservations about the index expressed by the State Secretary in the Ministry of Food and Agriculture at a special meeting of the Reich Trustees on 27 August 1935 as well as the markdowns on potatoes and certain categories of meat and cheese that he ordered the next day (Minister of Labour to the Minister of Food and Agriculture, 3 September 1935: *BA Koblenz*, R43II, file 318). The Minister of the Interior held the same view as the Minister of Labour; petition to the Reich Chancellery in July 1935: ibid. The Reich Trustees were extremely critical of the official index; report on the meeting of 14 August 1935: *DZA Potsdam*, RWM, file 10296, pp. 34 f. Even the Reich Chamber of Industry (Reichswirtschaftskammer) considered the index's figures too low: report by K. Reichhold, 'Einkommen, Verbrauch und Sparung in Deutschland 1929–1932–1936' (pp. 19 f.), *BA Koblenz*, R43II, file 311. Contemporary description of statistical methods in Alfred Jacobs, 'Statistik der Preise und Lebenshaltungskosten', in Friedrich Burgdörfer (ed.), *Die Statistik in Deutschland nach ihrem heutigen Stand*, vol. 2, Berlin, 1940. Critique of statistical methods in Bry, *Wages*, p. 260. Cf. *Stat. Anhang, Doc. IIa.*

63. According to this index: 1929 = 117, 1932 = 100, 1935 = 111, 1936 = 144. The statistics on consumption were constantly being corrected, in most cases upward; the reason for this is not clear. But even the higher figures in *Stat. Jahrbuch*, 1939/40, pp. 398 f. change little in the picture sketched above. Cf. *Stat Jahrbuch*, 1936, pp. 350f.; *Stat. Jahrbuch*, 1937, pp. 362f.

64. Petzina, *Autarkiepolitik*, p. 33, note 41. The revisions by Bry, *Wages*, p. 264 do not begin until 1937 and then suddenly turn out to be 5 points higher than the official index, producing a rather skewed picture.

derived largely from their shared distrust of the Labour Front. Yet in the light of the decision to stabilize wage scales, cutbacks in these deductions were the only available means by which to increase real wages. However, government and industry were not particularly successful in this regard; they achieved only negligible reductions in March 1934.[65] The government, though, was able to impose legal restrictions on the number of fund-raising campaigns allowed to the various Party organizations after these had got out of hand in 1933, and to exempt certain occupations in agriculture, inland shipping and domestic work from obligatory contributions to unemployment insurance. On the other side, the exemption for workers in the hard-coal-mining industry was rescinded as early as July 1933.[66] It was not until December 1936 that formerly unemployed welfare recipients who had found a job were no longer liable to reimburse the welfare offices and municipalities for the support they had received, at least not for that portion received up to 1 January 1935.[67] All told, added deductions after 1929 constituted approximately 2–4 per cent of earnings, depending on wage level, family status, and so on.[68]

On the basis of these data and considerations, we can attempt a rough revision of the official picture of workers' living standards from 1933 to 1936/7. The impression given by the official statistics that the increase in average hourly earnings generally kept pace with the rising cost of living is no longer tenable.[69] Nor is the claim that *real* wages had almost reached 1929 levels in 1936.[70] According to the above calculations, the actual cost of living in 1935/6 was about 6–7 per cent higher than that indicated in the government's index. From this I derive the following index for real wages: 1929: 118; 1932: 100; 1936: 107/8. The overall rise since 1932 was due exclusively to the lengthening of working hours.

65. Kurt Gossweiler, 'Der Übergang von der Weltwirtschaftskrise zur Rüstungskonjunktur in Deutschland 1933/1934', *Jahrbuch für Wirtschaftsgeschichte*, 1968, part II, pp. 86–97.

66. On compulsory contributions, see the various directives and laws: *RGBl. I*, 1933, pp. 148, 265, 311, 519. In 1935 over 4 million workers had been exempted from compulsory contributions: *Stat. Jahrbuch*, 1936, p. 324. The repeal of the exemption in the coal-mining industry was hotly contested and led to violent protests: *BA Koblenz*, R43II, file 534.

67. Syrup, *Hundert Jahre*, p. 532.

68. Deductions thus constituted between 13 per cent and 20 per cent of gross income after 1933; see 'Aufzeichnung über Einkommensverhältnisse', 9 September 1935: *BA Koblenz*, R43II, file 318. Bry, *Wages*, p. 264, seems to underestimate this factor in his calculation of real wages, citing them as 1 per cent of earnings up to and including 1935, and as 2 per cent thereafter. Cf. also Erbe, *Wirtschaftspolitik*, p. 93.

69. Cf. Table 4.2.

70. Cf. note 62 above. The observations by Kroll, *Weltwirtschaftskrise*, pp. 622–5, which barely jibe with his own statements about the development of wages (see pp. 606f.), tend in the same direction. Erbe's comparison of statistics on real wages with retail business sales (*Wirtschaftspolitik*, pp. 94f.) helps to confirm the revisions carried out above. Cf. also the rather diffuse discussion of this problem in *Stat. Anhang, Doc. II a*.

These averages and aggregate statistics are really only useful for identifying general trends and tendencies. From the Ministry of Labour table reprinted in *Arbeiterklasse und Volksgemeinschaft*,[71] it is clear that the earnings and living standards of workers in different occupations varied greatly, and that these differentials became more pronounced between 1933 and 1936. As far as the Labour Front was concerned, industry falls into two groups. In the first group, to which mainly the capital goods sector belonged, the increase in nominal weekly earnings from September 1933 to September 1936 was between 10.6 per cent and 23.8 per cent;[72] whereas in the second, which consisted exclusively of consumer goods industries, weekly earnings fluctuated between +5.4 per cent and −1 per cent. Disregarding for the moment the printing and brewing industries, which were very adversely affected by the political and economic situation,[73] we see that the industries in the first group were also those with the highest wages in 1933. The rise in weekly earnings in these industries derived from increases in hourly earnings which, with few exceptions,[74] exceeded corresponding increases in the consumer goods industries. Thus the rise in weekly earnings in the capital goods sector was due not simply to the extension of working hours; on the other hand, a number of companies in the consumer goods sector had cut back their hours slightly in September 1936, as compared to 1933, so that the small increase in hourly wages helped compensate for the loss in earnings.[75] Comparing these earnings statistics with the revised cost-of-living index, we see that the line separating these two sectors is equivalent to the differential separating occupations in which workers were able to improve their real wages (i. e. maintain their standard of living), from those in which they were clearly unable to do so.

Thus, on closer examination, it becomes clear that the regime's call for a wage freeze at 1933 levels was just an empty phrase, concealing two contradictory and potentially dangerous possibilities: first, a significant rise in earnings in the militarily important industries, which could

71. *Stat. Anhang, Doc. II a.*

72. This group also includes white-collar workers, whose salaries rose faster than workers' wages; cf. the report by K. Reichhold, cited above in note 62.

73. Workers in these industries were always paid relatively well. However, after 1933 Nazi press policy led to the closing of opposition newspapers and periodicals, causing persistent under-employment in the printing industry. The demand for beer was extremely elastic; sales continued to be hampered by restrictions on the planting of hops in favour of other crops.

74. Coal-mining and the clothing industry were exceptions: *Stat. Anhang, Doc. IIa.* All estimates in this section have been taken from this document.

75. According to the findings of industry reports the average daily work-day in most branches of the consumer goods sector had increased slightly from 1933 to 1936, and in all branches together it had gone up by a quarter-hour. By comparison, the increase in many branches of the capital goods sector was a good hour: *Stat. Jahrbuch*, 1937, pp. 342f. In his petition to Lammers of 30 October 1935 Seldte especially stressed this point: R43II, file 311.

eventually erode the state's purchasing power and, assuming no let-up in demand by the state, lead to inflation, and second, the immiseration of workers unable to find employment in the booming armaments industry.[76] A compromise solution in which pay hikes in prospering industries would have increased the demand for consumer goods, to the benefit of the consumer goods industry, was theoretically possible, but in actual practice it was bound to conflict with the one-sided economic strategy of rearmament.[77]

Because these problems were politically explosive, the regime was unable to come up with an effective solution. It is therefore misleading even to speak of a government wage policy in the period between 1933 and 1936. The intensity and acrimony of the propaganda battle waged against economic liberalism could not obscure the fact that the uncontrolled forces of the market – which put the individual worker directly at the mercy of the employer, unable even to establish his/her own market value – continued to govern wage policy. Actual state intervention during this period was limited to two very indiscriminate means of control: first, the use of police terror to prevent the formation of illegal union groups that might make wage demands in the factories; second, the fixing of minimum wage rates at the levels of May 1933, which could only be lowered further – and then strictly on a case-by-case basis – by the Trustees of Labour.[78]

Both of these forms of state intervention, however, were far from being a substitute for a wage policy; in fact, they were not even sufficient to carry out the government's proclaimed policy of stabilizing money-wage rates at their very lowest Depression levels. The Trustees were prohibited both from ordering pay hikes or cuts and from setting maximum wage rates. In practice this meant either that the collective bargaining agreements negotiated before 1933 remained in force without any changes, or that the wage provisions in those agreements were incorporated into the collective rules (*Tarifordnungen*) determined by the Trustees.[79] There were simply no new ideas or approaches to the

76. The government claimed to be very worried about this difference and the social tensions it was causing: cf. *Doc. 3, part I 2*.

77. That is exactly what happened in 1937–39. Cf. below, chapter 6, also *Doc. 132* and *Stat. Anhang, Doc. IIb*. The trend was heightened by the growing lack of manpower, which also forced the consumer goods industries to increase wages.

78. The 14th Executive Order to the Labour Organization Law, 15 October 1935 (*RGBl. I*, p. 1240, para. 2) authorized the Trustees to withdraw factories, departments within factories, and even individual workers from the official wage regulations, i.e. to permit payment below scale. The number of requests by industry to avail themselves of this authority wase so great that the Ministry of Labour ordered a thorough-going review: reports on the Trustee conference, 9 December 1935: *DZA Potsdam*, RWM, file 10296, pp. 254, 256.

79. Cf. *Stat. Anhang, Doc. IIa*.

problem. The reduction in average hourly wages in 1933 thus occurred as a result more of the fact that large numbers of workers took up poorly-paid jobs, than of the institution of further wage reductions after the Nazi seizure of power. The Ministry of Labour raised the wage rates in the old collective agreements only very rarely, for example in the case of home-workers or the lowest-paid categories of rural and construction workers. The result of this enormous inertia was that wage rates were largely determined by market forces. This tendency even manifested itself in the provisions of the Labour Organization Law, which left decisions on wage rates to the individual factory communities.[80]

From this perspective, the 'successes' of industry and the regime in ensuring an increased influx of manpower into the armaments industries while holding down consumption were not so much the result of the phased implementation of a well-conceived economic and social plan as they were the necessary consequence of conditions that were already in existence when the boom in the armaments sector began. These successes should therefore not be considered a unique political achievement; together with mass unemployment and the desperate economic condition of the population – both of which were the best possible preconditions for rearmament – they were a bonanza for the government. The only notable measures actually taken by the regime to exploit and maintain this uniquely favourable set of circumstances were the outlawing of the trade unions and the repression of the initially quite strong working-class resistance.

By the middle of 1936, however, even these measures were no longer effective. The time had passed when the unemployed would fight over any job that became available, when poorly-paid work in an unfamiliar occupation was welcome as a god-send, or when the newly employed would maintain the strictest 'labour discipline' or risk their health, already impaired by years of unemployment and malnutrition, simply to avoid being tossed out into the street again.[81] By constantly increasing the number of available positions, the booming war economy gradually ended the conditions in the job market that had initially favoured the employer. Faced with the opportunity of choosing his own job, the worker gained a certain freedom of movement, whereas the employer was becoming ever more hard-pressed. He now had once more to exert himself to secure a sufficient number of qualified workers. From the

80. Cf. above p. 104. Clearly, there was a different reason for this provision: the hope that workers' confidence in the works community would increase as a result of the acquisition of direct responsibility for fixing wages.

81. Anxious reports on workers' health, which had been seriously impaired as a result of long years of joblessness: 'Preussen' in *Jahresberichte der Gewerbeaufsichtsbeamten... 1933–34*, pp. 167f. and 434f. (emphasized by the occupational medicine committees). Cf. also developments in worker productivity in the coal-mining industry: *Docs. 85, 92.*

government's point of view, this change in the condition of the labour market, which had begun in the middle of 1936 (first in the iron and steel and building industries), was by no means a positive development. On the one hand, the wage increases resulting from the economic boom assured a continued influx of manpower into the armaments industries; and there was the hope that a rising standard of living would solidify the loyalty of workers employed in those industries. On the other hand, though, this development was incompatible with the other political and economic preconditions for an aggressive rearmament programme (e.g. the planning of the armaments budget) and with the maintenance of a stable currency, not to mention the preservation of 'social peace'.[82]

How little the government was prepared to deal with the structural problems described here and how perplexed and anxious it was in confronting them became clear during 1935. Conditions in the building industry provided the initial incentive to undertake a thorough examination of wage policy, for it was there, according to the Ministry of Labour, that the classification of wage scales by locality and the lack of skilled workers in some big cities and rural areas (already apparent since the spring of 1935) were beginning to have a negative impact on productivity. The Ministry concluded that the earnings differential between Hamburg, Berlin, Breslau, Leipzig and Königsberg on the one hand, and the rural areas surrounding them on the other, was too great – greater, indeed, than the actual differences in cost of living. Also, in comparison with cities in eastern Germany, wages in the Rhineland and the Ruhr were too low. This in turn meant that construction work in the disadvantaged cities, especially housing construction, would become more expensive, thereby hampering the expansion of the building industry. Furthermore, the possibility of maintaining a number of construction sites in rural areas (airfields, barracks, highways) would be threatened.

To remedy this situation, the Minister of Labour proposed a general adjustment of wages, a proposal that was approved by the other participating departments of government.[83] This arrangement, which was designed to equalize the various local differences and to raise the lowest wage rate

---

82. Cf. on strikes and wage negotiations, *Doc. 3*. In the long run this development was also incompatible with the existing division of power and authority within the system. In the discussions that took place between August 1935 and February 1936, the Trustees constantly came back to the point that the DAF was making social demands, interfering in their areas of responsibility, and so on. *DZA Potsdam*, RWM, file 10296, pp. 23–8, 32–42, 195f. See also chapters 5 and 6 below.

83. See Decree of the Ministry of Labour to the Special Trustees for the Construction Industry, 14 January 1935, containing extensive statistical appendices: *BA Koblenz*, R43II, file 552; Seldte to Lammers, 15 January 1935: ibid., file 542; Seldte to Lammers, 12 February 1935: ibid., file 552. At the beginning of March Seldte had a meeting with Hitler about the problem: Seldte to Hitler, 16 March 1935, with a new memorandum attached: ibid., file 552.

in the mining industry by 50 pfennigs per hour, failed as a result of resistance by influential Party organs, since it also included a provision for lowering the maximum wage rate. In a letter of 7 March 1935 to Hess (Hitler's Deputy), Kaufmann, the Gauleiter of Hamburg, expressed his objections as follows: 'As a result of my tireless efforts, I have succeeded in persuading the workers to trust the Party and the Labour Front. A reduction in wages such as this would do irreparable damage to everything that has been achieved.' Like the mayor of Hamburg, Krogmann, who also became involved in the controversy, Kaufmann pointed to the rising food prices, the forthcoming elections to the Councils of Trust in the factories, and the repeated public promises – by Hitler and Schacht, among others – that current wage scales would not be altered.

Kaufmann's objections, supported by other Gauleiters, soon attracted Hitler's attention. On 23 March Hitler ordered further discussions of the matter before the planned wage adjustment came into force.[84] In a letter to Seldte, Hess wrote that the interim result of these meetings was that all the Gauleiters were of the opinion that 'very important reasons' militated against any reduction in wages. He also pointed out that a number of employers in the building industry feared a decline in productivity if wages fell.[85] Finally, at a ministerial meeting on 2 May 1936, the government's incapacity to make any clear decisions on this issue was elevated to the status of a formal principle of the state's official wage policy. In general, existing wage rates were to remain in force without change. Ministerial circles felt that any extension of the state's influence on wage-setting beyond this would be inappropriate. Thus a decision of fundamental importance had finally been taken – one that had Hitler's express approval and that would be referred to time and again in the future: there would be no changes in agreed wage rates, but at the same time no restrictions on the payment of wages in excess of the collectively agreed scales. Fear of negative reactions on the part of the workers had thus rendered the omnipotent dictatorship incapable of taking any action.[86]

84 Kaufmann to Hess; Krogmann to Brückner, the Führer's Adjutant, 15 March 1935; memorandum of 27 March 1935 in the Reich Chancellery: *BA Koblenz*, R43II, file 552. Among the Gauleiters, Kaufmann always took special consideration of the mood in the working class; in November 1935, at his own initiative and against the objections of Darré, he announced the fixing of maximum prices in the wholesale food trade.

85. Hess to Seldte, 27 April 1935: *BA Koblenz*, R41, file 24, p. 42. A meeting of the Gauleiters took place on 11 April. I could not locate the minutes of that meeting.

86. Seldte to Hitler, 25 May 1935 together with transcript of the ministerial meeting; Lammers to Seldte, 13 June 1935: *BA Koblenz*, R41, file 25, pp. 48–57; R43II, file 542. The decision 'to adhere rigidly to current wage rates' was then announced to all higher authorities in the government, the Party and the Labour Front. Later in the summer, in reports on wage increases that had occurred without his involvement as well as on demands made by the Labour Front, the Minister of Labour tried in vain to convince the Reich Chancellery of the senselessness of this decision: ibid.

In the meantime, the conflicts over wage and social policy had not yet reached the point of crisis. The two overriding problems of 1935 could be either temporarily averted using half measures, or indefinitely postponed. Thus at the beginning of 1936 the minimum wage rates for unskilled construction workers, as well as travel allowances and severance pay for construction workers employed outside their home towns were increased, but only by a negligible amount.[87] For its own workers – the public employees who were then in desperate straits – the government could not even come up with half measures. State (Reich) employees generally received less pay than the labourers and white-collar workers employed by the municipalities; however, adopting an across-the-board salary increase as a way to equalize working conditions in the public sector was out of the question. Since the issue affected all public employees (except career civil servants), it was liable to develop into a question with major political implications; a desirable narrowing of wage differentials failed here for the same reasons it had in the building industry. Because of its inability to take action or make decisions, the government simply left the problem to market forces, as a result of which the public sector suffered from an increasing manpower shortage, until uniform working conditions were mandated in the spring of 1938.[88]

There was another similar case in which the plebiscitarian regard for discontented workers turned out to be less important than the development of a long-range plan to adjust labour relations to the long-term needs of the armaments economy. In the summer of 1936 the DAF became the spokesman for the extremely modest demands of workers in the Ruhr: reduced hours, an increase in the child-care allowance and a fair distribution of the risks of under-employment between employer and employee. However, after protracted negotiations, its request was turned down for general reasons of industrial and wage policy. Publicly, however, the reason given was the need to strive for an even more stringent organization of manpower and reserves in order to promote rearmament as outlined in the recently announced Four-Year Plan.[89] Ironically, the Four-Year Plan stipulated an increase in the German economy's requirements for coal just when the falling number of miners would soon be unable to meet the new demands. Although the average income in the mining industry was not bad compared to that in other branches of industry, the social insurance contributions required of the

87. Cf. the treatment of this question in the Trustee conference of 12 November 1935: *DZA Potsdam*, RWM, file 10296, pp. 191f.
88 Memoranda, draft proposals, etc. from May 1935 to December 1937: *BA Koblenz*, R43II, file 543; R41, file 24.
89. The decision-making process on wage policy at the government level can be followed quite precisely in this case: *DZA Potsdam*, RAM, file 106, pp. 53–138.

miners were considerably higher. Moreover, the lack of employment in mining after 1933 had led workers to leave the pits in large numbers, which an improvement in working conditions might have at least partially halted.[90] But what prevented a reasonable solution here was the emphasis put on the interests of employers and the fear that any move to improve conditions in the mining industry might too quickly be copied by other branches of industry.

Foresight and rational planning in the area of wage and labour policy seemed impossible within the National Socialist system. This was due not simply to the peculiarly National Socialist concept of politics which regarded 'merely' rational thinking as something alien; ultimately it was a result of the deep-seated social contradictions which the system was unable to resolve or eliminate. They were temporarily or partly papered over or deflected by political jockeying, or frequently concealed through the use of propaganda or, ultimately, suppressed by means of terror. If the regime's plans for aggressive expansion were to be realized, it was imperative to mobilize the greatest possible number of workers for the armament effort while at the same time lowering real wages and the standard of living. However, it was equally vital to ensure the political loyalty of the workers. The problem of providing a rationale for the workers' allegiance to the system in the face of the still largely unredeemed misery of the Depression and the subsequent brutal disenfranchisement of the working class by the very political forces that now demanded its loyalty presented a virtually insoluble task to the holders of power. The political leadership did not have a convincing programme with which to persuade workers to become active participants in a system whose goals were fundamentally opposed to their own political traditions and economic interests. In a superficial sense this problem was clear to everyone involved in the debates over wages and prices in 1935: lower wages and higher prices would only benefit the illegal Communist resistance movement. Gauleiter Kaufmann and Minister of Labour Seldte went one step further, stressing the close connection between the living standard of the broad masses and the political stability of the regime.[91]

It was difficult if not impossible to frame guidelines for social policy on the basis of such contradictions, which may explain why there were practically no measures taken to deal with the inevitable consequences of the boom in the armaments sector.[92] Disregarding the special prob-

90. For additional material on the situation in the coal-mining industry, see *Docs. 85–93*.

91. Cf. the documents cited in notes 60 and 84 above.

92. This inherent tendency towards inertia was further heightened because of the doubts harboured in the upper echelons of the civil service about the permanence of the economic boom: cf. note 42 above, and *Doc. 3, note 26*.

lems of agriculture (which will be discussed in more detail later), we see that the necessary measures to organize the 'deployment of labour' (*Arbeitseinsatz*), as it was now called, had not been prepared, let alone undertaken, by the government before November 1936. The most important exception with long-term implications was the introduction in the spring of 1935 of the compulsory labour pass (*Arbeitsbuch*).[93] In future no worker would be allowed to take a job without first having been issued a labour pass containing information on the bearer's vocational training, employment history, family status and so on. The labour exchanges kept copies of this information and thus gradually built up a card index that provided a complete survey of all working persons. After 1938 these data were of great help to the government when it needed to transfer workers into the armaments industry.[94] However, until the announcement of the second Four-Year Plan, the President of the Reichsanstalt made little use of his authority to limit the mobility in the labour market that had resulted from the growing demand for labour.[95] A number of regulations which had originally been designed to deal with unemployment (e.g. the need to get approval to hire younger workers) now had a potentially new application as the first bottlenecks in the economy became apparent; however, a future crisis had been anticipated only in the case of skilled metal workers. According to the Directive on the Employment of Skilled Metal Workers (*Anordnung über den Arbeitseinsatz von gelernten Metallarbeitern*) of 29 December 1934, metal workers had to obtain the approval of their labour exchange before accepting a position if their place of residence was located in a labour exchange district different from that of the job for which they were applying.[96] Since collective bargaining had been outlawed, changing jobs became more important to workers as a way of improving their working conditons. The purpose of this directive was to limit the anticipated mobility of the labour force and thereby assure the armaments

93. Law on the Introduction of the Labour Pass (*Gesetz über die Einführung eines Arbeitsbuches*), 26 February 1935: *RGBl. I.* p. 311. This registration of the working population was a very complex and costly administrative measure and was phased in. It was not considered completed until spring 1939; only civil servants, members of the liberal professions and certain groups of self-employed individuals remained unaffected (there was a special file, however, for artisans). Cf. the Executive Order on the Labour Pass, 22 April 1939: *RGBl. I*, p. 824. The initiative for the measure came from the Ministry of War, which bore most of the costs – a clear indication of the function of the labour pass: *BA/MA Freiburg*, WiIF 5, file 325/1.

94 On the use of the labour pass cf. *Doc. 12*; explanatory text preceding *Doc. 125* and *Doc. 125; Stat. Anhang, Doc. Id*; see also below p. 194.

95. Decree on Manpower Distribution (*VO über die Verteilung von Arbeitskräften*), 10 August 1934: *RGBl. I*, p. 786, para. 1; cf. above p. 120.

96. *DRA*, 1935, no. 2. One could still change jobs within a labour exchange district. It was a weak measure.

industry of a steady supply of skilled workers, but it never succeeded in doing so. Stricter, more unpopular measures were called for.[97]

Otherwise very little was done in the area of labour policy to prevent future bottlenecks. Thus, for example, it was not until 1936 that the number of apprenticeships exceeded 1929 levels, even though the estimated demand for apprentices was particularly high in the armaments sector, and the number of new apprentices had declined by almost a third in the period 1930/4. Extremely inadequate preparations had been made for the large number of secondary school-leavers (the classes of 1934 and 1935) entering the labour market; between June 1933 and June 1936 the labour exchanges were able to find apprentice positions for barely 40 per cent of the applicants.[98] The situation was similar in the administration of social policy. The number of personnel in the offices of the Trustees of Labour, which was wholly responsible for supervising wage policy and for implementing the Labour Organization Law, was totally inadequate. There were too few permanent positions for technical specialists, who were not even considered career civil servants until 1936. In such circumstances, it was difficult to attract qualified people. The Trustees continued to depend on the support and co-operation of the factory inspectors, who also had inadequate staffs and were always overworked.[99] The lack of qualified and experienced staff was also evident in the labour exchanges, especially after a number of Social Democratic and Liberal civil servants and technical specialists had been forced in 1933 to surrender their jobs to politically 'reliable workers', whose qualifications often consisted in nothing more than long years of

97. See *Docs. 8, 17–26*; and chapter 6 below.

98. This is a rough summary of a very complex question that deserves special study. For the total number of apprentices according to unemployment insurance statistics: *Stat. Jahrbuch*, 1930, p. 322: *Stat. Jahrbuch*, 1933, p. 296; *Stat. Jahrbuch*, 1937, p. 336. Number employed: Syrup, *Hundert Jahre*, pp. 444–7. Industry was aware of the seriousness of the situation; cf. *Wege zur Behebung des Facharbeitermangels (Veröffentlichungen des Reichsstandes der Deutschen Industrie*, no. 61), Berlin, May 1934. The statistics in Petzina, *Autarkiepolitik*, p. 159, note 15, appear to exaggerate the gap in the years prior to 1934; see *Stat. Jahrbuch*, 1934, p. 320. For additional information on this subject, see pp. 232ff. below and *Doc. 6*.

99. Continued complaints in this regard in the Trustee meetings 1935/6: *DZA Potsdam*, RWM, file 10296, pp. 37f., 41, 198, 200. 263, 313, 331–5. For these reasons the revision of the former wage agreements dragged on for years, and the position of the Trustees continued to remain weak with respect to other authorities, especially the law courts and the press. The Ministry of Finance, the Ministry of the Interior, and the Audit Bureau (Rechnungshof) were responsible for personnel questions. The DAF used the fact of the overworked staffs as an argument for expanding its own authority: cf. petition of the Social Office (Sozialamt) of the DAF to the Minister of Labour, 16 December 1936: ibid., file 10320, p. 15; cf. also below, chapter 6. At the end of 1936 the Minister of Labour lodged a complaint with the Reich Chancellery: *BA Koblenz*, R43II, file 529a; *Doc. 30 (Note 1)*. For further details on the organization of government social policy: 'Preussen' (Prussia), pp. 1, 5 ff. in *Jahresberichte der Gewerbeaufsichtsbeamten …1933–34*.

membership in the *Stahlhelm*.[100] It was not until the reorganization of 1939 that wage policy and labour deployment were given a status within the Ministry of Labour commensurate with their significance.[101]

For the reasons mentioned above, but in particular because of the self-imposed social contradictions within this system of domination, the Nazi regime had the worst imaginable resources to deal rigorously and effectively with the myriad problems of full employment.

Even though the remaining history of the Third Reich was to be dominated by the problems of rising wages and lack of manpower that emerged in the later 1930s, it would be inappropriate to end this survey of the social history of the period 1933/6 at this point. In 1936 the daily lives of most German workers were still characterized by poverty and deprivation, not to mention the added pressure of political terror. To give a rough picture of the material conditions of life that existed at the time, I will attempt to reconstruct a working-class family's household budget. According to the rather sketchy calculations of the economics specialist in the Reich Chancellery, the wages in 1934 of a low-paid municipal worker (RM 25 per week) with a family of five (wife and three school-aged children) can be divided into the following categories: deductions 11 per cent; food 54 per cent; rent, heating and utilities 30 per cent; clothing 2 per cent. Only 73 pfennigs were left for miscellaneous expenses. What is surprising is that expenditures for transportation, schooling, entertainment and the repayment of loans are totally absent from this listing. Moreover, the amount of food that could be purchased from these earnings was incredibly small – no more than 2 pounds of lard and 2 ½ pounds of meat per week for five people. Eggs, cheese, fruit and vegetables are not included in these statistics. The economics specialist gave no hint of how five people could clothe them-

100. Documents on a number of such cases in Seldte's reference file: *BA Koblenz*, R41, files 6, 7, 11. In Bavaria alone there was a shortfall of twenty technical specialists: ibid., file 221, p. 57.

101. Until then the main responsibility of Dept. IV of the Ministry of Labour had been the unemployment problem. In practice state supervision of the labour market was mainly the work of the Reichsanstalt and the labour exchanges subordinate to it. The appointment by Göring at the end of 1936 of the president of the Reichsanstalt and the director of Dept. III in the Ministry of Labour (responsible for Trustees of Labour, wage policy, labour law) to the Labour Deployment Task Force (*Geschäftsgruppe Arbeitseinsatz*) of the Four-Year Plan hardly changed the situation, for this was mainly an advisory group. According to a Decree of the Führer and Reich Chancellor of 21 December 1938, the Decree of the Ministry of Labour of 23 December 1938 and the Executive Order on Labour Deployment of 25 March 1939, the Reichsanstalt was incorporated into the Ministry of Labour; the president became director of the Dept. V, which was in charge of Labour Deployment. The centralization of the labour administration continued with the appointment of the directors of the industrial inspectorate and of the labour exchanges as deputies of the Trustees of Labour (1 August 1939). Cf. *RGBl. I*, 1938, p. 1892, *R.Arb.Bl. I*, 1939, p. 2; *RGBl. I*, 1939, p. 575; Syrup, *Hundert Jahre*, pp. 469f.

selves on RM 2 per month.[102] Even though the prices cited in this listing (and the figures were merely estimates) are too high, a careful study of household expenditures for families with an average income of RM 32 per week presents a similar picture: only 1.5 per cent of income was left for the purchase of beverages, 3.1 per cent for schooling, entertainment and relaxation. Practically all families at this income level were dependent from time to time on public and private assistance. It is impossible to calculate precisely the number of households that had to survive on RM 32 a week or less, but it was certainly not small.[103]

Another segment of the needy was the unemployed population, of whom there were still over 1 million in autumn 1936, plus an additional 800,000 jobless seasonal workers by the winter of that year. The proportion of welfare recipients who received support from the welfare associations on the basis of proven need, as well as those without any support at all, had indeed steadily declined; the reason for this, though, was that the rule disqualifying people from extended insurance benefits, which the Schleicher government had suspended, had not been reintroduced. Yet the benefit rates, which averaged 65 per cent of a worker's last pay-packet, had not been adjusted to the increased cost of living, so that the situation of the unemployed and their families remained quite deplorable.[104]

The living standards of short-time workers were not much better; because of the limitations imposed on the import of raw materials in 1934, they were mostly concentrated in the textile industry. The various types of government assistance benefited only workers who *regularly* worked less than 36 or 40 hours a week; on average this applied to about 100,000 people in 1935/6.[105] Although short-time workers were later

102. Memorandum of 4 September 1935: *BA Koblenz*, R43II, file 318. The memorandum was presented to Hitler. Although the calculation of the average factory wage is very problematical, we can say with certainty that RM 25 per week was *below* average. In contrast, the figures in the *Stat. Anhang, Doc. IIa, Tab. II* (September 1933: RM 30; September 1936: RM 35) are probably somewhat too high; see the comparative table in *Stat. Handbuch*, p. 469.

103. *Stat. Handbuch*, pp. 502 ff. Irregular sources of income have not been factored into the above analysis. The majority of male industrial workers in 1936 earned over RM 32 per week, and the households of workers who were either unskilled or employed in the consumer goods sector could probably often count on the income of other family members. Cf. ibid., pp. 470f.

104. The statistics are in *Stat. Jahrbuch*, 1937, pp. 350, 357–61. The desperate situation of the unemployed was somewhat eased by the added support of the DAF (if the unemployed person was a member), which constituted a maximum of 15 per cent of a worker's last pay-packet. One weakness in the statistics is that duration of unemployment cannot be more precisely calculated. There are figures here only for the recipients of emergency assistance, of whom 482,000 (= 61 per cent) had been unemployed for more than a year in August 1934; in August 1936 the number was still 297,000 (62 per cent); ibid., p. 360.

105. Review of the constantly changing rules: Wilhelm Wiedermann, 'Zur neuen Verordnung über die Kurzarbeiterunterstützung', *R.Arb. Bl.*, 1936, II, pp. 369–72. Statistics: *Stat. Jahrbuch*, 1937, p. 336.

able to make up for some of the severe loss in earnings that had occurred in the textile industry toward the end of 1934 and the beginning of 1935,[106] the compensation they received for lost earnings due to reduced hours was inadequate. In most branches of industry only a full-time weekly wage (over 45 hours per week) was adequate for even a barely tolerable standard of living. However, during the period 1934 to 1936 the hours of work in many occupations repeatedly fell below this full-time level, without any assistance being given to those workers affected. The main cause of these negative developments was the dearth in sales and raw materials; besides the textile industry, the industries hardest hit were coal-mining and metalworking. Mention should also be made of the building trade, where until 1937/8 lost working hours due to weather conditions had hit workers hardest.[107] Thus at the end of 1935 at least an additional 200,000 persons were significantly under-employed or underpaid.

With the upturn in the economy, poverty and unemployment were increasingly concentrated in particular areas. This development was due not only to the fact that certain regions were more dependent than others on the consumer goods industries. It might explain why in Saxony, for example, the decline in unemployment slowed down considerably after the autumn of 1934. But it does not provide a satisfactory explanation for similar developments in Silesia, Hesse and the Rhineland. At the beginning of 1933, approximately 40 per cent of all the unemployed lived in these four regions; by autumn 1935 the proportion had risen to more than 50 per cent.[108] In the case of the Rhineland, Hesse and Saxony, their location on the frontiers of the Reich was an important part of the reason. The economic recovery of the Rhineland, for instance, was much more sluggish than that in the rest of Germany. Until the entry of German troops into the Rhineland in March 1936, prohibitions against military-related construction work were still in force – work which in other areas had contributed significantly to a reduction in unemployment. In addition, industry was not inclined to make large investments in an undefended border region; the crisis of 1923 was still fresh in people's memories. The area around Aachen in the north, with its concentration of textile factories and barely-profitable mines, was

106. Cf. statistics in the industry reports, acccording to which the average monthly income reached the September 1933 level in only three months in the period July 1934 to December 1935: *Stat. Jahrbuch*, 1936, p. 332.

107. Statistical sources on this question are spotty and relatively unreliable. Klein, *Germany's Economic Preparations*, p. 70, and a DAF report on short-time work which was presented to Hitler in December 1935, are useful: *BA Koblenz*, R43II, file 553.

108. *Stat. Jahrbuch*,1936, p. 335.

particularly hard-hit.[109] The problems in the eastern frontier areas were even more critical. The generally low productivity of eastern German industry, caused by the inadequate infrastructure and poor market conditions as well as the migration of manpower to the western part of the country, continued to deteriorate after the redrawing of the frontier in 1919/20.[110] Both political and economic considerations argued against large investments, and the National Socialist system – despite all the propaganda about giving priority to the needs of the people in eastern Germany – was unable to do much to reverse this negative trend.

The issue of a 'disparity between east and west' runs like a red thread through all government discussions on questions of social and economic policy in the period 1933 to 1942. Even the aggressive programme of rearmament and later the war only magnified the problem, since most of the new armaments factories were being built – in part for political and military reasons – in central Germany. Thus in the middle of 1935 the average income in Hamburg was twice that of the border provinces of Posen and East Prussia, and miners' wages in Silesia were some 20 per cent below those of their counterparts in the Ruhr. Even the lower cost of living in the Ruhr could not make up for the difference.[111] Moreover, in the case of miners, working and living conditions were often incredibly primitive, and the authorities were usually unwilling or unable to improve them. In 1936, for example, miners in a Silesian pit saw no improvement in working conditions until the Gestapo reported that, because of their anger at the managers, the German miners would only speak Polish among themselves.[112] Lack of housing and uncertain food supplies were more prominent features of daily life in the eastern regions than in the rest of Germany. The regime tried to deal with the problem by giving preference to the border provinces in awarding gov-

109. See principally the memorandum of 5 February 1936 from the Provincial President (Oberpräsident) of the Rhineland to Schacht, 'Folgen aus der Entmilitarisierung für das linksrheinische Gebiet', *BA/MA Freiburg*, WiIF5, file 1282. Cf. the complaint by the Trustee of Labour for Hesse at the Trustees' meeting of 12 November 1935: *DZA Potsdam*, RWM, file 10296, p. 188. On the situation in the Aachen area, see Vollmer (ed.), *Volksopposition*, even though there is insufficient treatment of the economic problems in this collection of documents.

110. For general information on this subject, see the important essay by Hans Raupach, 'Der interregionale Wohlfahrtsausgleich als Problem der Politik des Deutschen Reiches', in Wolfgang Conze and Hans Raupach (eds.), *Die Staats- und Wirtschaftskrise des Deutschen Reichs 1929–1933*, Stuttgart, 1967, pp. 13–34, and the literature cited therein; further important information in a memorandum by the DAF's Arbeitswissenschaftliches Institut: 'Materialien zum sozialen Ost-West-Gefälle', *DZA Potsdam* .

111. Memorandum of 31 August 1935 from the Minister of Labour: *BA Koblenz*, R43II, file 311; *Stat. Jahrbuch*, 1936, p. 298.

112. This and similar cases from the period 1934–6: *DZA Potsdam*, RAM, file 105, pp. 114–69.

ernment contracts, but such measures were able only to delay somewhat the growing gap between the eastern and western parts of the country.[113]

In conclusion, mention should be made of another group of workers who were almost completely bypassed by the economic recovery: hired farm labourers. The continuing structural crisis in German agriculture and the inadequate unionization of farm labourers in the 1920s had only served to heighten the differences in the standard of living between the urban and rural population.[114] The new political proposals of the Reichsnährstand were directed primarily at improving the economic condition of the large landowners by promoting increased production; the idea of improving the living standards and working conditions of the rural population was no more than an after-thought. It was against this background that the capital goods industries, particularly the building trade, soon became very attractive to rural inhabitants, reviving the migration of farm-workers to the industrial centres. In fact, the flight from the land quickly became so massive that as early as 1934 farmers were having serious problems in harvesting their crops. A long-term programme to improve housing and working conditions in rural areas was inaugurated in August of that year,[115] but not until the authorities had tried to solve the problem through coercive measures directed at workers who had been employed in the agricultural sector for at least one out of the previous three years. After May 1934 these workers could be employed in certain industries only with the prior approval of the labour exchanges. If they already had a job in industry, the labour exchanges had the authority to request their employer to dismiss them. In the spring of 1935 this authority was extended to all industries, but in practice dismissal was limited to workers who had been employed in agriculture for two out of the pre-

113. There is no room here to enumerate even the most important sources on this subject; between 1934 and 1936 it was frequently the topic of ministerial meetings (cf. *BA Koblenz*, R43II, file 376; R41, file 24, pp. 2–6, 135 ff.), and was always on the agenda of the Trustee meetings (*DZA Potsdam*, RWM, file 10296, pp. 26, 189, 254. Regarding the absence of any substantial improvement of the situation, see the correspondence in September 1940 between the Minister of Labour and the Trustee for Silesia: *BA Koblenz*, R41, file 59, pp. 124–7.

114. Because of the great importance of payments in kind in rural areas, statistical comparisons are not possible. See *Stat. Jahrbuch*, 1936, pp. 136f. In January 1939 a Trustee of Labour estimated the gross real wages of a farm-hand at between 50 per cent and 70 per cent of the income of an unskilled industrial worker: *BA/MA Freiburg*, WiIF 5, file 1223. Cf. also Wunderlich, *Farm Labor*, pp. 235 ff., 253 ff.

115. Directive on Manpower Distribution, 28 August 1934: *DRA*, no. 202, para. 18; the programme was broadened by two directives of 10 and 18 March 1937: *RGBl. I*, p. 292; *DRA*, no. 67; in addition, Petzina, *Autarkiepolitik*, p. 93; memorandum titled 'Material zur Landarbeiterfrage', 14 December 1937: *BA/MA Freiburg*, WiIF5, file 1223.

vious three years.[116] However, the attempt to shackle the agricultural labourers to their poor living and working conditions failed almost totally, both because of the unpopularity of the measures and as a result of the growing demand for industrial manpower. Those responsible for the measures envisaged them mainly as a kind of psychological deterrent, but even they had to acknowledge the meagre success of their attempts. Since it was impossible to carry out these rules to the letter, they were quietly suspended at the end of 1936.[117] The farm-workers were indifferent to the propaganda of blood and soil, and as the economy worsened, the propaganda slogans also lost their power to persuade those whom they had originally been designed to influence – the farmers themselves.

A complete picture of the widespread misery that still existed in 1936 would have to include a number of other factors and segments of the population. One would, for example, have to consider the large number of small towns with technologically backward industries, which were also bypassed by the recovery. But such comprehensive treatment is impossible within the limits of this study. Still, two more questions must be addressed which, even though they did not affect large numbers of people, were to be of great political significance in the future.[118]

The words 'poverty' and 'suffering' might at first seem excessive to describe working conditions in the public sector (*öffentlicher Dienst*). But the conditions here were worse in every respect than those in the industries benefiting from the armaments-led boom. This applies not only to lower-level manual and clerical workers employed in the public service, but to career civil servants (*Beamte*) as well. For here the state

116. Law on the Organization of Labour Deployment (*Gesetz zur Regelung des Arbeitseinsatzes*), 15 May 1934: *RGBl. I*, p. 381. paras 2 and 3; also the Executive Order, 17 May 1934: *DRA*, no. 114. Law to Meet the Manpower Needs of Agriculture (*Gesetz zur Befriedigung des Bedarfs der Landwirtschaft an Arbeitskräften*), 26 February 1935: *RGBl. I*, p. 310; also the Executive Order, 29 March 1935: *DRA*, no. 76.

117. The formal lifting of these rules: Decree of 27 November 1936, *DRA*, no. 278; *R.Arb. Bl. I*, p. 302. More details on this in *Doc. 27 (Note 11); Doc. 33 (Note 25); Doc. 68.* At a meeting of the Lesser Ministerial Council (kleiner Ministerrat) Darré expressed his irritation at the uselessness of these measures: *BA Koblenz*, R43II, file 353a. Syrup's justification of his policy does not address the real problem: Syrup, *Hundert Jahre*, pp. 417 ff. The mass migration from the farm continued: *Doc. 102; Doc. 108, part 2; Doc. 147, part 2; Stat. Anhang, Doc. I d*; Darré's complaints and warnings in detail: *BA Koblenz*, R43II, file 213b. In March 1939 the requirement to obtain permission to leave farm employment was reintroduced as a means to solve the rural labour shortage: *Doc. 158.*

118. Precisely because nobody was interested in small businesses, the lack of primary sources is much more serious than, for example, in the case of the civil service. Moreover, in this study we have emphasized social policy, and except for a few attempts to improve conditions for those working at home, there was no government policy directed at these groups and localities. These questions would have an important place in a comprehensive social history of the period.

really did have the power to freeze wages at 1933 levels, equalizing tariff wages and current income, which had reached rock-bottom during the Depression. Moreover, this aspect of government wage policy was subject to the supervision of the Ministry of Finance and the Audit Bureau (Rechnungshof), both of which, having been deprived of responsibility for the most important component of national expenditure – military spending – had become that much more finicky and petty about overseeing the financially insignificant area of personnel expenditure. The shortage of staff in the public sector, which was the result of the wage freeze and the less-favourable legal status of public-sector employees, had not yet reached the critical stage in 1936; however, there was considerable discontent among those affected, and reforms were not implemented until shortly before the beginning of the war.[119]

The literature on living and working conditions in Germany during the 1930s constantly stresses the fact that the official statistics do not reflect the widespread decline in the quality of manufactured goods. Indeed, the statistical record is practically useless in studying this development, which is of such critical importance in the case of textiles. On the other hand, there are supplementary tables on the nation's housing which allow us to monitor how closely the statistics correspond to reality. Thanks to government controls, average rents remained unchanged, while the shortage of housing steadily rose, since the official policy of encouraging marriage by extending government loans to newly-weds conflicted with the increasing cutbacks in subsidies for residential building.[120] The estimated shortfall in housing rose from 1 million units in 1933 to 1.35 million within twenty-four months. The expansion in the building sector, which occurred within the framework of the employment creation programme, was primarily of benefit to the private home-owner; moreover, it was a

119. I could not find detailed statistical evidence on actual wages and salaries in the public-service sector or white-collar workers' salaries; the differences are not really reflected in the wage rates: *Stat. Jahrbuch*, 1937, pp. 327, 330–3. This description is based on a large number of individual complaints, e.g., about the salaries received by the Trustees of Labour: *BA Koblenz*, R43II, file 532; R41, file 24; *DZA Potsdam*, RAM, file 6635. For a detailed discussion of these problems, see Jane Caplan, 'The Civil Servant in the Third Reich', D.Phil. thesis, Oxford 1973. On the position of the Ministry of Finance, see H. Stuebel, 'Die Finanzierung der Aufrüstung im Dritten Reich', *Europa-Archiv*, June 1951, column 4131. For more information on general working conditions in the civil service, see below pp. 173f.; on the personnel shortage and its consequences, see below pp. 192ff. and *Doc. 100*.

120. Indices on housing costs: *Stat. Jahrbuch*, 1937, pp. 310 f. These figures too cannot be accepted without reservations, for it is improbable that, given the state of the housing market at that time, even the strictest controls could have prevented any rent increases. The index is based on the rental price for old buildings. Marriage loans: see above pp. 116f. State subsidies: Erbe, *Wirschaftspolitik*, pp. 27f. However Erbe's estimate of public funds as a percentage of gross investment in housing (13 per cent for 1933–1938 as opposed to almost 50 per cent in the late 1920s) seems somewhat too low. The whole question of policy in the housing market during this period warrants a special study.

one-time event. Thus although a net gain of 100,000 units over the previous year was registered in 1934, this figure fell to 40,000 units in 1935, and did not come close to the 1928/30 levels until 1936.[121] The housing crisis in the major cities increased noticeably, depressing living standards, hampering the population growth desired by the government and impairing the labour mobility that was critical to the armaments programme.[122] The unmarried itinerant worker or the itinerant worker separated from his family, living in barracks or at best in a rented room, became a typical phenomenon of industrial life in the 1930s.

Thus even if we factor in the significant increase in wages in the industries that profited from the economic recovery, we can still agree with the verdict delivered by the Trustee of Labour for Hesse when he evaluated the mood of the people after three years of Nazi rule: the apparent tranquillity among the workers was not in his view a 'real peace'; it was characterized more by 'resignation and surrender'. He then added: 'The prevailing opinion among the workers is that the employment creation programmes served only to save employers from economic disaster, but did nothing to benefit workers.'[123] Soon after this the Trustees finally began to recognize that discontent was not limited only to the most needy within the working class. In fact, it was those workers to whom the armaments boom had brought higher earnings and a certain degree of security who were proving to be increasingly undisciplined and who were unwilling to credit their modest gains to the efforts of the regime.[124] Both unemployment and full employment had hidden dangers. The development of the German Labour Front and its social policy contributed in no small measure to the widespread demoralization among the workers. This is the subject of the following chapter.

121. *Stat. Jahrbuch*, 1937, p. 181. The problem was often discussed at the ministerial level in 1935: *BA Koblenz*, R41, file 25, pp. 5f., 45f. (shortfall statistics).

122. *Cf. Docs. 84, 103, 151, Part VIII.* There are any number of documents such as these three in the files of the Reich Chancellery and the Ministry of Labour.

123. Trustee meeting, 7 February 1935: *DZA Potsdam*, RWM, file 10296, p. 305.

124. These problems as well as the incipient manpower shortage were discussed in detail at a special meeting of the Trustees on 19 August 1936. The minutes served as the basis for discussions on counter-measures (cf. *Doc. 3*): *BA/MA Freiburg*, WiIF5, file 203, pp. 349–61.

5

Social Policy and
Social Ideology, 1934–1936

The development of the DAF was sustained by a singular and complex dynamism in which class conflict, the political goals of the regime, and the interests of the organization itself in expanding its own power within the National Socialist system were inextricably intertwined. This dynamism was never the product of a viable social policy peculiar to National Socialism, which – once it had been universally acknowledged – would then give birth to a mass movement capable of translating that policy into reality. In actuality, the working masses were from the beginning either indifferent or hostile to the new regime. In fact, the functions of the DAF and the way in which it viewed itself were defined at first by its negative political tasks, by its efforts to weaken those structural elements of the social order which seemed to prevent the Nazis from achieving their overall objectives. There was never any agreement as to what would replace those elements, only about the need for their elimination.

In broad outline, these negative tasks may be postulated as follows: after the destruction of the trade unions, the working class was no longer to be left to its own devices or allowed to establish any independent organizations of its own, even if led by Nazis. The DAF was also not to be given any authority over economic questions. Class conflict was to disappear. The only positive imperative was to win the working class over to the new state.

These demands not only ran counter to the inevitable clash of interests in a class society, they were also self-contradictory. Consequently the original mission assigned to the DAF and approved by all those in charge was incompatible with its lack of power to deal with the material aspects of social policy. On the one hand, its propaganda mission forced the DAF to take a position in the conflict of interests between workers and employers; given the prevailing despair among the workers and in view of the DAF's political task, there was little doubt about whose side it would take. However, the scope and nature of the DAF's role in representing working-class interests could not be allowed to interfere with rearmament or the solidarity of the *Volksgemeinschaft*, the national-racial community. Because of these contradictions the DAF could probably never have been established without repressive political terror, and it certainly could not have continued to exist without the threat of terror. Yet in a political environment in which its existence was guaranteed by the power of the state, these internal contradictions – impossible to air publicly – helped propel it on the unique drive towards expansion that characterized its development.

These contradictions, present at its creation, obliged the DAF to create its own organizational identity. From the outset, organizational questions dominated the DAF's activities. Building the organization was both a substitute for and a cause of the Labour Front leadership's lack of practical political tasks. One responsibility it did have, however, was to educate or 'look after' (*betreuen*) the working class politically and ideologically, though it could not publicly claim this as the justification for its existence. Aside from this, its furious organizational activity turned out to be mainly an end in itself. The building of an enormous unified organization provided ambitious functionaries with a wealth of things to do. Moreover, there was always the hope of creating a political instrument which, even without having any clearly defined functions in the power structure, would be able, simply by virtue of its size, to influence social and economic decision-making. Eventually the DAF leadership was able by means of its organizational virtuosity to develop initiatives in so many different areas at once, that government officials and business associations could barely keep track of its various operations.[1] In 1934, of course, these future developments were scarcely discernible. Wedged as it was between the massive forces of industry and government, the DAF did not seem to have any tangible functions or a clearly delineated sphere of influence.

As intractable as the political situation of the DAF's leadership may have been at the beginning of 1934, it still had two decisive advantages in building an apparatus. First, it possessed the confiscated assets of the trade unions plus a portion of the employee associations' assets that had been transferred to it as trustee (though not as assignee);[2] this formed a firm financial foundation on which to build. Second, as the only

1. Reinhard Bollmus, *Das Amt Rosenberg und seine Gegner*, Stuttgart, 1970, is an excellent case study of this purely organizational factor in the domestic political history of the Third Reich.

2. Law on Granting Compensation for Seizure and Transfer of Assets (*Gesetz über die Gewährung von Entschädigungen bei der Einziehung und dem Übergang von Vermögen*), 9 December 1937: *RGBl. I*, p. 1333. It is not possible here to go into the extremely complex negotiations involved in the settlement of this problem: until the coming into force of this law it was treated as part of the overriding question of the legal status and legal capacity of the DAF, for which no legal formula could be found. The law simply legitimized the pillage of 1933. In juridical terms the DAF acquired new assets in December 1937.

National Socialist organization in the field of social policy, the DAF had a secure political base from which it could in effect question the political legitimacy of all the activities of the economic interest groups and government authorities. This, of course, was a far cry from assuring it pre-eminence in the power structure when it came to resolving issues of substance, but it gave the DAF leadership the opportunity to act as a kind of permanent ideological board of review for aspects of social policy and to provide the initial justification for its own actions.

In the course of the DAF's development, ideology and organization complemented each other without (as I shall explain in detail below) the former having any tangible content or the latter any clear function. The organization served primarily to propagate ideology and transform workers into politically reliable idealists; these missions in turn justified the expenditures on organization. Behind the DAF's imperial ambitions, which had become obvious as early as the end of 1934, was a desire to acquire real power and authority within the state, and not simply be content with its original mission.[3] Viewed from another perspective, this dynamism was triggered by the very disparity between its primary mission and the means placed at its disposal to achieve this. Given the brutal and oppressive goals of the regime and the contradictions within the social structure, the DAF was unable to carry out its educational tasks successfully and 'lead the working class into the National Socialist state'. Ultimately, there was no practical way to measure a political ideology that was rooted in an all-embracing ethic of struggle, no way conclusively to prove oneself in terms of problems limited in time and circumstance; since the contradictions and obstacles remained insuperable, the struggle never ceased. The more utopian the goal, the more frenzied the rhetoric became: 'The goal which National Socialism has set for the *Volksgemeinschaft* is open-ended; it can only be aspired to, attained and upheld through a continuous and constant process of education.'[4] Any genuine self-examination – and this was particularly true with regard to the question of class conflict – was bound to bring into even sharper forcus the growing disparity between the utopian goals and the actual attitudes of the people,[5] between the immensity of the educational work still to be done and the stubborn resistance of objective facts and the laws of social change. To use as yardstick a reality which had been

3. Ministerial Director Mansfeld of the Ministry of Labour stressed this point in a position paper on the question of the DAF's responsibilities, which was submitted to the Minister-President of Prussia (Göring) on 24 November 1936: *DZA Potsdam*, RWM, file 10321, pp. 5–12. See also below pp. 166ff., 210ff.

4. Hitler on 31 January 1939, quoted in Otto Marrenbach (ed.), *Fundamente des Sieges. Die Gesamtarbeit des Deutschen Arbeitsfront von 1933 bis 1940*, Berlin, 1940, p. 49.

5. See especially *Docs. 108* (covering letter) and *234*.

officially proscribed would be to acknowledge the degree of failure. Since the ideal could not be brought into line with reality, the regime had constantly and in every way to indoctrinate and preach on the factory floor, trumpeting the link between the factory leader and his retinue, the beauty of labour, the common bond between 'workers of the mind' and 'workers of the hand'. Most of this kind of activity degenerated into ritualized, carefully stage-managed propaganda events,[6] whose aim was always to serve the dominant economic interests. The dynamism of the propaganda was rooted in its open-endedness, its impracticability and above all its indispensability to the regime. The slogans became an essential part of the regime's effort to counteract what the workers were actually learning every day on the job, that is, a realistic sense of human social relations.

The proponents of the ideology, on the other hand, needed a measure by which to judge the success of their efforts, which is why the degree of organizational development of the DAF was of such importance to them; at least in this sphere the functionaries had a certain degree of latitude, after the violent elimination of their adversaries. The basic tendency of Nazism to balance the political power of different organizations was a direct consequence of the enormous disparity between the ideology and the social structure. Nowhere was this tendency more apparent than in the DAF. The meaningless interplay between organization and ideology in the DAF was brought into sharp focus by an event that signalled a temporary halt to the Labour Front's evolution: the promulgation of a decree in January 1936 establishing a code of honour and discipline. Members and officials who violated the code could be brought before a specially created court of honour. The creation of yet another administrative organ, one with quasi-judicial functions, formalized and strengthened purely bureaucratic control over the political leadership. Of particular note was the fact that the definitions of the violations listed in the code were framed in terms of ideology and attitude, ultimate punishment being expulsion from the DAF.[7] Thus the possibility of being expelled was used as a threat to deter anyone who might wish to dissent. Bureaucratic power and ideological conformity were now mutually interdependent.

The first step in ensuring a unified organization was to dissolve the employee and worker associations that had been co-ordinated in 1933

6. Cf. the informative report by the Reich broadcasting chief, Eugen Hadamovsky, on the use of high officials from the Ministry of Propaganda in industry to document a Goebbels propaganda initative on the end of 'class arrogance': *Hilfsarbeiter Nr. 50 000*, Munich, 1938.

7. *Amtliches Nachrichtenblatt der DAF*, series 2, 1936, pp. I–IV; *Fundamente des Sieges*, pp. 31f.

and still retained a modicum of independence as affiliated organizations of the DAF under NSBO direction. There had been, of course, no place in these associations for the employers who had now been invited to join the DAF. The reorganization at the top was completed by the turn of 1933/4; the process would take longer at the middle and lower echelons. The NSBO officials put up some resistance to the reform, since it was not in keeping with their populist ideas and threatened their power, not to mention their jobs. It was not until after the purge of the SA in June/July 1934 that Ley moved resolutely against these groups. There is no evidence of any politically significant ties between the SA and the NSBO. But those in power did not need any proof; they were only interested in eliminating any vestiges of political independence within the movement in order to establish the dictatorship in all areas of public life – in the economy and administration as well as in the military.[8]

The main feature of the reorganization was the strengthened position of the leadership, which was divided into defined areas of responsibility and ceased being merely an umbrella organization for a number of different economic interest groups. The centralization of the financial administration at the end of 1933 was of critical importance. The leadership's new central offices (*Führungsämter*) for press, education, organization, legal aid, and so on, were designed to assure authoritarian dominance over all DAF activities. They were filled mostly by younger Nazis who had not yet made a name for themselves (including several of Ley's colleagues from his days as Gauleiter of Cologne-Aachen). There was only a sprinkling of representatives from the old leadership of the NSBO and the former employer associations. However, at the same time, the incorporation of the DAF's leadership into the Political Organization of the Nazi Party, which was also under Ley's direction, underscored the *political* subordination of the DAF's *Führungsämter*.

In order to blanket the whole country as completely as possible, the DAF built up two parallel bureaucratic networks based on industry and geography. The regional network was patterned exactly on the NSDAP's division of the country into *Gaue*, each *Gau* in turn being divided and subdivided into districts (*Kreise*) and localities (*Orte*), with

8. On the problems discussed in this and the two following paragraphs, see Hans-Gerd Schumann, *Nationalsozialismus und Gewerkschaftsbewegung*, Hanover/Frankfurt am Main, 1958, ch. 4, as well as his graphic depiction of the organizational structure of the DAF (folded supplement); H.J. Reichhardt, 'Die Deutsche Arbeitsfront', Diss. Phil., Free University of Berlin, 1956, ch. 2. Because of the lack of primary documents, these two rigorous studies, based exclusively on printed sources, are still invaluable as sources on the structure of the DAF. Cf. I. Esenwein-Rothe, *Die Wirtschaftsverbände von 1933 bis 1945*, Berlin, 1965, Appendix on the DAF by D. v. Lolhöffel; Friedrich Syrup, *Hundert Jahre staatlicher Sozialpolitik 1839–1939*, ed. Julius Scheuble, revised Otto Neuloh, Stuttgart, 1957, pp. 407, 463.

the 'cell' and the 'block' as the smallest units; the DAF added a unit for each factory. The industrial network was based on the division of the economy into various branches of industry. These Reich Factory Communities (*Reichsbetriebsgemeinschaften*; later called *Fachämter*, or Branch Offices) were represented in the DAF's top echelon by their directors, and had their own departments for press, education, organization, and so on, as well as regional offices at *Gau*, *Kreis* and *Ort* levels. Thus the director of a *Gau* Factory Community was subordinate both to the head of the *Gau* industry network (*Gauwalter*) and to the chief of the Reich Factory Community; the director of the Education Division (*Schulungsamt*) of a Reich Factory Community was subordinate both to the head of the Reich Factory Community and to the DAF's *Führungsamt* for education. During the internecine struggles to which this complex organizational structure gave rise, the *Führungsämter* and the *Gauwalter* began to emerge as victors. This tendency towards institutional rivalry was heightened by constant reorganizations and renamings, and by the creation of new offices and departments. Furthermore, the leadership fought hard for new duties and responsibilities which were then represented by their own *Führungsämter*. In 1934 there were nine *Führungsämter*; by 1940 the number had risen to thirty-four.

Given the meagre responsibilities that were originally parcelled out to the DAF, its organizational structure was largely the effect of technical considerations. Chief among these was the need to increase membership as quickly as possible so as to boost the revenue from dues. This goal was met. According to its own account, the DAF had between 7 million and 8 million members by the middle of 1933; by March 1934 the number had risen to 14 million, and by 1935 to 16 million. It is still hard to know for certain how members were recruited. Former union members were promised the maintenance of their rights to additional unemployment and sickness benefits and so on. But apart from this and a guarantee of free legal aid, the DAF had little to offer workers in the way of concrete benefits. Political idealism and political opportunism – both went hand in hand in 1933/4 – surely caused a number of people to join the DAF, but neither these motives nor the effects of the DAF's big propaganda campaign in the winter of 1933/4 are sufficient to account for the huge jump in membership during this period. Membership dues, after all, averaged between RM 1.50 and RM 2 per month, an outlay which very few workers could easily afford during this period.[9] Moreover, membership in the DAF was not particularly attractive to anyone hoping for the independent and responsible work on behalf of

---

9. Figures according to Reichhardt, 'Deutsche Arbeitsfront', pp. 62, 64. The amount of dues was based on income; on average they were lower than union dues before 1933.

his workmates which this kind of association offered in theory. For one thing, official positions were filled largely by veteran Party members. For another, after the reorganization of the DAF in 1934, an applicant could only become a member of a single integrated mass organization, that is, he belonged neither to a local group with its own areas of responsibility nor to an occupational association. Thus members were deprived of any direct influence on DAF policy. It was the factory leader, not the street or factory cells, who had the sole power. Ley described the leader as the factory's 'sergeant major'.[10] As the number of members grew, direct and indirect sanctions against non-members (political persecution, unemployment) probably played a much more important role than any positive incentives to join.

The number of requests by the DAF for a law to compel everyone working in commerce or industry to join up is clear proof that recruitment was a problem for the leadership. Their requests, however, were turned down by the government, and the principle of choice was safeguarded, at least formally. Ley made a propagandistic virtue out of necessity; the recruitment of new members became a large and politically innocuous form of activity for his officials.[11] In actuality, of course, conditions were such that by the end of 1935 membership in the DAF had *de facto* become compulsory. To coerce workers the DAF needed stronger support from other institutions – mainly the employers, the labour exchanges and the Gestapo – than it had received during the first twelve months of its existence. Even though there was no reason in 1933–4 to assume that the labour exchanges and the employers would make membership in the DAF a formal requirement for new or continuing employment, the DAF kept pushing for just such a rule. Given the state of the labour market at the time, the mere threat of being denied a job would, as we have already suggested, have the intended effect. Moreover, anyone who stubbornly refused to join would probably have to use arguments that would make him appear an enemy of the regime, since the DAF was considered the official guardian of the *Volksgemeinschaft*.

Political calculations were not the only reason why compulsory membership seemed imperative. At the end of 1933 the DAF was facing a grave financial crisis. The recruitment of new dues-paying members was a question of survival, for without a broad and secure financial base a costly organization like the DAF could not survive. The collection of

10. Decree 45/35 of the Reich Leader of the DAF: *Amtl. Nachrichtenblatt der DAF*, 1936, p. 150.
11. Reichhardt, 'Deutsche Arbeitsfront', p. 58. The leadership was still pushing for compulsory membership at the factory level in the second half of 1935: *DZA Potsdam*, RWM, file 10288, pp. 184–213; file 10296, p. 124.

dues by the DAF's overseers or neighbourhood block captains (*Blockwalter*) turned out to be unprofitable, and supervision of the collectors and the DAF members proved unreliable. What finally led to the absorption of all workers into the DAF and secured its financial base was the willingness of employers to deduct dues from workers' earnings along with taxes, and in some cases to insist that all their employees join the Labour Front. So far as the latter demand was incorporated in factory codes as a condition of employment, it was resisted by the Ministry of Labour and the Ministry of Economics, though they both approved direct wage deductions in October 1934 (in 1939 approximately 70 per cent of factories were collecting dues for the DAF).[12] With this the DAF had become the richest and largest of the National Socialist organizations, and its position was further enhanced as a result of the constant increase in the number of members and the increased income from dues. At RM 539 million in 1939, the revenue of the DAF was more than triple that of the Party itself, supporting among other things a cadre of functionaries that comprised nearly 44,500 persons. [13]

The direction in which the DAF wanted to steer this huge organization became obvious at the end of 1933 with the founding of its most successful contribution to industrial relations: 'Strength through Joy' (*Kraft durch Freude*, or KdF). The very name of this leisure-time organization summed up one of the most important components of Nazi social ideology.[14] Its stated aim was to raise productivity in the armaments sector by encouraging workers to identify personally with the goal of rearmament. That this would not happen automatically under existing political and social conditions was clear to the Party leadership. However, since there appeared to be no way to change these conditions of class antagonism and low wage levels, the search began to find other means with which to secure social tranquillity and increase productivity, using propaganda and the resources of the organization to tout them. Not much could be expected from pressure alone; the solution had to be sought in areas where there was a demonstrable community of interests among all involved. In the broad political arena a community of interests had been created by ceaselessly invoking the differences between the Germans and other nationalities, countries and political systems;

12. In 1940 income from DAF members whose dues were collected by functionaries averaged about half the targeted amount; this and other points are based on Reichhardt, 'Deutsche Arbeitsfront', pp. 65f. The initiative for the direct deduction of dues from wages originated with the Saxon Reichsstatthalter Mutschmann: *DZA Potsdam*, RWM, file 10287, pp. 187–191.

13. Figures based on Reichhardt, 'Deutsche Arbeitsfront', pp. 64, 56.

14. It first bore the vacuous name, 'After Work' (*Nach der Arbeit*): *W.T.B.* Report on the Founding Meeting, 27 November 1933, *BA Koblenz*, R43II, file 557. Cf. also Robert Ley, *Durchbruch der sozialen Ehre*, Munich, 1935, pp. 19–33.

now the DAF had to substantiate this so-called community through ideological education and social policy. The consequent social solidarity – 'trust', as it was constantly called – would gradually overshadow class differences and cushion the burdens imposed by rearmament and war.

The question of paid holidays exemplified the programme. An extension of paid leave had never been among the most important demands of the trade unions; consequently the issue carried no political overtones. Before 1933, tourism in the modern sense barely existed; for financial reasons travel was almost exclusively the province of the bourgeoisie. But a survey among Siemens workers in Berlin conducted jointly by management and the functionaries of 'Strength through Joy' showed that there was a latent demand for it. Of the 42,000 workers polled, 28,500 had never taken a vacation outside the Berlin area, and other leisure-time activities were correspondingly modest.[15] Most important, the campaign to promote holiday leave was in keeping with the call to boost productivity, its slogans being simplistic versions of concepts culled from the fields of industrial psychology and ergonomics. Free time and leisure were not individual rights; they were instruments to strengthen mental and physical capabilities, and thereby increase productivity. It is uncertain whether employers were impressed by these arguments. It must nevertheless have been a novel experience for them to see this kind of demand justified on the basis of their own and the economy's interests. Even the sceptics among them must have been impressed by the argument that granting additional paid holidays was a small price to pay for the elimination of the trade unions and the working-class parties. Moreover, the granting of longer holiday time was not imposed globally, but was phased into the new factory codes (*Betriebs- und Tarifordnungen*). In each individual case the strength of the local DAF and the attitude of the particular employer played a decisive role, thus helping to keep the scale of the reform within bounds. On average, minimum annual holidays were increased from three to six days; young workers and those who participated in holiday courses sponsored by Nazi organizations received a few additional days.[16] To the workers this represented only a slight improvement, and one that they themselves had not demanded or pushed through; but to the employers the government was offering an opportunity to demonstrate their social conscience.

This was the foundation on which 'Strength through Joy' built its mass tourism organization and entertainment industry. It seemed to be guided by three main considerations: achieving the highest possible organizational efficiency, the broadest possible base, and a cost-benefit ratio

15. *Siemens-Mitteilungen*, February and July 1934.
16. See Syrup, *Hundert Jahre*, p. 489, for a summary.

in keeping with workers' earnings.[17] Moreover, the KdF sought constantly to emphasize that leisure activities were one of the new regime's
unique achievements – one that it hoped would receive appropriate political recognition. Organized leisure time, of course, also offered an opportunity for increased political supervision and indoctrination.[18]
Developments proceeded apace, and soon 'Strength through Joy' was
organizing all sorts of leisure acitivities, ranging from symphony con-
certs in the factory to cruises to Madeira, from variety programmes to
theatre visits and athletic events. Large open-air seaside swimming pools
were built, and only the war prevented the 'Kdf-Wagen', or Volkswagen,
from being mass-produced. An enormous organizational effort transformed the countryside and the nation's culture into commodities, making them accessible to everyone and translating them into tools for
boosting political *joie de vivre* and industrial productivity. According to
official statistics the number of people taking holiday cruises jumped
from 2.3 million in 1934 to 10.3 million in 1938, and the number taking
part in other leisure activities during the same period sky-rocketed from
from 9.1 million to 54.6 million. In 1939 the annual turnover of 'Strength
through Joy' was RM 2.5 billion.[19] As suspect as these numbers may be,
there is no doubt about the popularity of 'Strength through Joy'.

It is of course another question whether this popularity had anything
to do with the ostensible goals of the organization. In popular parlance it
was said that people had lost their strength because of too much joy, and
in July 1938 Ley himself had occasion to warn the passengers on a plea-
sure boat against regarding KdF as simply an institution for having fun;
letting onself go, he said, had little to with real joy.[20] The organization

17. There is still a need for a detailed study of KdF and comparable developments in
Western Europe; it would well repay the effort. One of the most important questions
would be the social background of participants in the KdF cruises and so on. Many of
these tourist groups were spied upon by the Gestapo; a number of their reports indicate
that, in comparison to the bourgeoisie, the *alte Kämpfer* and Nazi Party officials, wage-
earners were under-represented, especially on long cruises: *BA Koblenz*, R58, files 943–9.

18. Cf. Ley's statement to the General Council on the Economy, pp. 96f. above. Resistance
fighters often tried to hide their political activities behind the façade of athletic clubs.

19. Statistics and a brief survey of the KdF's many activities in Marrenbach (ed.),
Fundamente des Sieges, pp. 331–70, especially pp. 334f., 355. On finances: report from
Ley to Funk in May 1941: *BA Koblenz*, R43II, file 352b. Cf. also Schumann,
Gewerkschaftsbewegung, pp. 137–43; David Schoenbaum, *Die braune Revolution*,
Cologne/ Berlin, 1968, pp. 143ff.

20. *BA Koblenz*, R58, file 944: Ley's words lost some their impact because of his reputation as the 'Reich boozer'. The great need of leading officials to let themselves go in
this way is an interesting commentary on the political morality of National Socialism and
the demands the system imposed on individuals, the rulers as well as the ruled: thus the
Gestapo uncovered two prostitutes among the passengers on a KdF cruise for Gauleiters,
and the Nuremberg Party rallies were only too well known for their nocturnal
debaucheries.

was so bent on promoting itself that it demanded that every participant regard every event as the fulfilment of the ideals of the National Socialist world-view, as a service to the economic requirements of the national community. Ironically, it was precisely for the opposite reason that 'Strength through Joy' was popular: it was indeed one of the few opportunities offered by the system to escape the constant pressure of politics and the economy and 'to let oneself go'. As I will show below, the pressures of daily life under Nazism made impotent resignation and escapism the only avenues for people to deal with a system that sought to submerge them totally in a hideous, irrational world of illusion.[21] In principle, the system did not object to this attitude – initially it spurred the organization to ever greater efforts – but the popular tendency to indulge in these kinds of 'joy' was potentially incompatible with the system's drive for armed 'strength'. The KdF was totally unsuitable as a spur to increase productivity, and it was of only questionable value as an outlet for pent-up discontent.

In time even the architects of the organization realized this. In the summer of 1941 Ley increased his criticism of the low educational and cultural level of the events staged by the KdF. Even Goebbels, notoriously indifferent to ideology and cynically manipulative towards anything to do with popular morale, was concerned that 'Strength through Joy' might degenerate into nothing more than a 'movement for amusement'.[22] These opinions gain in significance when one considers that self-criticism was a rarity among the Nazi leaders. They corroborate the theory that the KdF's popularity had absolutely nothing to do with spreading the nation's cultural wealth among the masses or reinvigorating the *Volk*.[23] Rather, it was rooted in the desperate need for fun and diversion, a need which was continually being created by the regime itself. Though organized to death, the KdF entertainment industry continued to flourish, largely because of pervasive fear, repression and alienation. The much-lamented vulgarity and superficiality of its various spectacles was a perfect reflection of the day-to-day life imposed on its consumers. After the novelty had worn off, the KdF became both a symptom and a cause of wide-ranging demoralization.[24]

Since no other organization laid claim to the sphere of leisure-time activity, it was an area in which the DAF could readily expand its own

21. Cf. the repeated complaints by the authorities on the morale of the workers in 1938/39: Timothy W. Mason, *Arbeiterklasse und Volksgemeinschaft*, Opladen, 1975, documents section, chs. 11, 12, 15, 17, 21.

22. Cf. Bollmus, *Amt Rosenberg*, p. 108; Willi A. Boelcke, *Kriegspropaganda 1939–1941*, Stuttgart, 1966, p. 308.

23. Ley made this claim in November 1939: *Doc. 299*.

24. Cf., however, the less critical opinions of Schumann, *Gewerkschaftsbewegung*, pp. 140f.; Ludwig Preller, *Sozialpolitik: Kernfrage des Aufbaues*, 2nd edn Stuttgart, 1947, p. 60.

power. Hence there were very few conflicts with industry, the state or the Party, and the KdF did not really violate the DAF's negotiated agreement not to involve itself in the 'day-to-day material questions of workers' lives'. Its second area of responsibility, social policy within the factory, did touch on these questions, however. Daily life on the job was supposed to reflect the cohesion of the factory community; workers and employers were supposed to discover their common interests on the shop floor, by narrowing their vision of social relations to a concentration on the labour process alone. According to DAF propaganda, increased outlays for lighting and ventilation in the factories, for the building or improvement of canteens, lounges, and washing and changing rooms would not simply benefit employers and employees materially, by boosting productivity for the employer and through higher wages (*Leistungslöhne*, or incentive pay) and better working conditions for employees. More importantly, they would bear witness to the solicitude for workers' welfare and thereby increase 'trust' on the shop floor.

This was not a novel idea. It had been foreshadowed in the patriarchal views of the first and second generation of German industrial magnates, and was revived in the 1920s as industrialists used scientific management to study the psychological effect on productivity of worker attitudes and the working environment.[25] However, as a result of the Depression many innovative plants and facilities had fallen into disuse. Even though a number of individuals before 1933 had advocated the improvement of working conditions as a possible way of eliminating class conflict, it was the Nazis, with their systematic approach, their fervour, and their ability to suppress any criticism, who introduced a new element, namely a political doctrine of social salvation. This doctrine was reflected in the very name of the office within the DAF and KdF responsible for social policy: 'Beauty of Labour' (*Schönheit der Arbeit*).

The 'Beauty of Labour' office sparked a great deal of activity in the form of exhibitions, publications, designs for new facilities, propaganda campaigns on specific topics ('Clean men in a clean factory', 'Join the fight against noise', 'Good lighting means good work') and, above all, factory inspections. It even had a certain resonance among groups of employers. It is difficult to generalize about the extent of the reforms

25. This subject also awaits its historian: informative approaches in Preller, *Sozialpolitik in der Weimarer Republik*; Syrup, *Hundert Jahre*; Robert A. Brady, *The Rationalization Movement in German Industry*, Berkeley, 1933; idem., *The Spirit and Structure of German Fascism*, London, 1937. In the 1920s German industry got a number of ideas on management from the United States; see, e.g., Fritz Tänzler, *Aus dem Arbeitsleben Amerikas*, Berlin, 1927. The general study by Ernst Michel, *Sozialgeschichte der industriellen Arbeitswelt, ihrer Krisenformen und Gestaltungsversuche*, Frankfurt am Main, 1948, is essayistic in approach and therefore finds it easy simply to ignore the period 1933–45. Cf. also below, note 49.

actually implemented or to separate those that would not have happened without pressure from the DAF from those that would have resulted anyway as a result of the extension of the principles of scientific management. A number of employers were evidently pleased to have the chance to present themselves to their workers as benevolent father figures without having been pressured to do so by hostile forces from below. The elimination of the trade unions gave them the assurance that by acknowledging their obligation to provide welfare services they would be perceived not as weak or as inviting additional demands from labour, but rather as rendering a service to the national community that would win the praise of the nation's only labour organization. In any event, the still largely independent factory inspectorate reported on major investments of this kind as early as 1933/4, even before 'Beauty of Labour' had got off the ground.[26]

According to its own statistics, 'Beauty of Labour' found a growing audience among employer groups, and by the end of 1936 it had inspected some 38,000 places of business, in half of which the proposals it had made for improving working conditions were carried out, at a total cost of over RM 200 million.[27] Furthermore, the work of this office probably gave an indirect boost to the plans of the various Councillors of Trust (*Vertrauensräte*) and factory overseers (*Betriebsobmänner*) in the DAF. Of course, the funds expended were nothing compared to the rising profits in industries benefiting from the armaments-led boom, which were in a good position to finance these proposals.[28]

Without a detailed study of business archives, it is practically impossible to gauge the effect of these measures on worker morale and productivity. There are some indications that they were negligible. First, it does not seem very plausible that workers trained in trade-union or Communist principles could have been easily persuaded to swallow the line that new recreation rooms, open-air facilities and better ventilation in the workplace would improve their situation more than a reduction in hours, increased wages and the guarantee of expanded rights. Even the most generous factory improvements could not alter the fact that employers were adamantly opposed to these fundamental demands. Second, it is very doubtful whether the heavily propagandized 'Beauty of Labour' or the often-invoked deepening of trust on the shop floor

26. Cf. the chapters 'Miscellaneous' (*Sonstiges*) at the end of the individual reports on the *Länder* in *Jahresberichte der Gewerbeaufsichtsbeamten...1933–34*.

27. Marrenbach (ed.), *Fundamente des Sieges*, p. 324. For additional statistics on social expenditures by business: *Jahrbuch des Arbeitswissenschaftlichen Instituts der DAF*, 1938, vol. 2, pp. 576ff.

28. On industry profits, see Table 4.2, p. 129 above; on the differences in working conditions between the industries that benefited from the boom and the other sectors of the economy, pp. 134f. above; *Doc. 3*. Expenditures for social welfare were tax-free.

really could have increased productivity.[29] These steps were taken with politics and ideology in mind rather than with a scientific view to the problems of labour organization; significantly, in the pronouncements of the DAF and in the propaganda literature there is not a shred of scientific proof to back up its claims. Not only were many other factors more important in affecting productivity – technological developments, for example, or as happened after 1942, political challenges – but the economic plight of the working class itself was probably the best assurance of high productivity in Germany. After full employment had been achieved, employers never ceased to complain about their workers' diminishing 'joy in work'.[30] Further improvements in factory social policy after 1936 evidently failed to have the desired effect on workers; once aroused, their expectations only grew. After years of deprivation, they grabbed at anything offered them. When one Reich Trustee insisted that authoritarian reforms, concessions and bribery would have no effect on industrial harmony or worker morale, he was merely drawing a conclusion which a number of other observers of industry had alluded to but not expressed outright.[31] Measured against these realities, 'Beauty of Labour' was a total failure.

It is clear from these two examples of the DAF's activities that Nazi social policy was focused on the humanization of class and labour relations.[32] In accordance with the *Führerprinzip*, however, this meant that primary responsibility rested with the employer, the so-called factory leader, who was obliged to change his attitude completely compared with the years of organized class struggle: he had to understand, or be made to understand, that the preservation of social peace called for the sympathetic exercise of economic and social authority. But as far as the workers were concerned, they were not asked to do anything for themselves; they were merely expected to accept unquestioningly their 'comradely' treatment by the factory leader or the DAF functionary, and to respond with the appropriate degree of loyalty. In the language of the time, the workers were to have the feeling that they were being 'looked

29. Post-war studies indicate that such improvements produced at most a short-term rise in productivity. On the methodological problems of judging these questions, see Horst Buhl, *Ausgangspunkte und Entwicklungslinien der freiwilligen sozialen Leistungen in industriellen Unternehmungen*, Inaugural-Diss., Free University of Berlin, Economic and Social Science Dept., 1965, pp. 47–69. The factory inspectorate often complained about the neglect of facilities, e.g., damage caused to new canteens by workers, among others. Even genuine, timely welfare measures hád totalitarian characteristics: 'Preussen' (Prussia) in *Jahresberichte der Gewerbeaufsichtsbeamten...1933–34*, pp. 328, 332. Cf. also *Doc. 97*.

30. Cf. especially *Docs. 85, 92, 145, 147, 150, 156*.

31. Cf. *Doc. 96 Part 2e, 3d*. On the background, see below pp. 222ff.

32. Cf. below pp. 211–6.

after' (*betreut*). The DAF did look after the workers directly to some extent, but mainly it had to exert its influence indirectly, by educating the factory leaders. To this end, the DAF organized a steadily increasing number of obligatory industrial relations courses for factory leaders, which they took alongside the Councillors of Trust and the DAF functionaries from their factories. In DAF training camps the factory community was 'drilled'[33] in the same sealed quarters in which they lived, took their meals and exercised together. The DAF press published a number of 'confessions' by factory leaders, describing how they had first come to understand their workers 'as human beings' and to share their concerns during these courses. Issued in many editions, these confessions had a wide readership.[34] To translate the spirit of the courses into the reality of daily work, the DAF established 'industrial brigades' or 'ideological militias' (*Werkscharen*) in 1935. These uniformed political assault troops, stationed in the factory and composed mostly of Labour Service veterans, devoted themselves mainly to propaganda work and indoctrination; they were even supposed to try and induct factory leaders into their rank and file. But even with these methods the DAF was unable to influence as many employers as it deemed necessary: in 1938 there were *Werkscharen* in approximately 9,000 factories and about 30,000 factory leaders took part in DAF indoctrination courses. Because it lacked effective sanctions, the DAF was not able to exercise real control over individual employers, despite their compulsory membership. Warning about the implications of a possible failure in this area, Ley gave an accurate description of communitarian ideology in practice. Without the *Werkscharen*, he said at Nuremberg in 1937, 'It would all simply be a lot of fine words meaning nothing but beer evenings and cigarette handouts.'[35]

The question of how much influence the DAF should be allowed to have on economic and social policy in the industrial sector had been the subject of serious discussion early on. The areas in which the DAF could actually demonstrate a community of class interests were too few and far between, the pressures it could exert on industry were too unreliable, and the rejection of the system by the workers was too widespread for it to be able to fulfil its educational role in circumstances as

---

33. The word is Speer's; see Reichhardt, 'Deutsche Arbeitsfront', p. 112. For general information on DAF training: ibid., pp. 111ff.

34. Cf. the report by J.B. Ring on the DAF's factory community school near Hamburg (*Arbeitertum*, 1 June 1935), where the groups were called 'factory families'.

35. Robert Ley, in *Der Parteitag der Arbeit vom 6. bis. 13 September 1937. Offizieller Bericht über den Verlauf des Reichsparteitages mit sämtlichen Kongressreden*, Munich, 1938, p. 270. Statistics: Marrenbach (ed.), *Fundamente des Sieges*, pp. 60, 64, 69; Reichhardt, 'Deutsche Arbeitsfront', pp. 125–32. In the compilation of these statistics the concept of factory leader was probably very generously interpreted.

they existed in 1934. In addition, there were the initial problems of building the organization, the lack of personnel trained in the field of social policy and industrial relations, and the conflict with political forces in the NSBO. The dimension of the problems that confronted them in the realm of education was clearly reflected in the results of the first elections to the Councils of Trust in the spring of 1934: approximately 60 per cent of those eligible to vote stayed away from the polls. We will probably never know how many of the remaining 40 per cent rejected the list of candidates put up by the employers and the DAF overseers (*Betriebsobmänner*). The DAF had not won the respect of the workers; in fact, it was probably less respected than the regime as a whole.[36] The experience of the elections was probably what caused Ley to try and get Hitler to expand the DAF's authority to the entire field of social policy.

This, however, would required new legislative measures, and was not in keeping with Hitler's initial ideas about the DAF's mission. Instead he said that the DAF should aim to create a kind of 'customary law' (*Gewohnheitsrecht*) which would secure the observance of National Socialist norms in areas of social relations beyond the reach of statutory law.[37] Gradually, however, Ley managed to convince Hitler that an organization responsible for such an undertaking needed more power in its dealings with other govermental institutions. Ley's plans probably benefited from the growing criticism of the DAF among conservative groups. As early as June 1934 the Minister of Defence complained to Hitler about the expectations the DAF was creating for an improved standard of living, which could only hamper rearmament.[38]

During the summer the Economics Minister and the Minister of Transportation complained about interference by high DAF officials in the work of the Trustees of Labour, and about the DAF's wage demands.[39] At the end of October 1934 the Deputy Leader of the

36. Theodor Eschenburg's sources on this in 'Streiflichter zur Geschichte der Wahlen im Dritten Reich', *Vierteljahrshefte für Zeitgeschichte*, vol. 3/3, 1955, pp. 314ff. are confirmed in a confidential memorandum of May 1935 in the Reich Chancellery: *BA Koblenz*, R43II, file 550. The factory inspectorate was apparently already using falsified figures: 'Preussen' (Prussia) in *Jahresberichte...1933–34*, pp. 43–9. On the background of the elections, see Schumann, *Gewerkschaftsbewegung*, pp. 128f.; Günther Gross, *Der gewerkschaftliche Widerstandskampf der deutschen Arbeiterklasse während der faschistischen Vertrauensrätewahlen 1934*, E. Berlin, 1962.

37. Cf. Ley's own report of these discussions in his speech at the Nuremberg Party rally of 1937, which – including his silence on the decree of 10 October 1934 (see below) – is quite plausible.

38. Berenice A. Carroll, *Design for Total War: Arms and Economics in the Third Reich*, The Hague, 1968, pp. 88f.

39. Economics Minister to Ley, 9 June 1934; Transportation Minister to the DAF, 3 September 1934: *DZA Potsdam*, RWM, file 10287, pp. 39, 157–61.

Economy, on the basis of detailed observation, warned of the dangers of 'a union possessed of such enormous dynamism'.[40] Hitler did not like to hear criticism of Party organs from these groups; in the event, he backed the DAF. On 24 October he signed a Decree on the Nature and Goals of the German Labour Front (*Verordnung über das Wesen und Ziel der Deutschen Arbeitsfront*), which was totally in conflict with the Labour Organization Law. It stipulated that:

> 2. The goal of the German Labour Front is to build a true performance-oriented national community embracing all Germans. Its responsibility is to see that each individual assumes a place in the economic life of the nation in a mental and physical condition that will allow him to do his utmost and thus to be of optimal use to the national-racial community.

> 7. ... The German Labour Front has the task of mutually reconciling the legitimate interests of all parties in a manner which is consistent with the principles of National Socialism and which will reduce the number of cases which, under the Law of 20 January, are to be decided solely by the authorized state bodies.[41]

The other Reich ministers first read about the decree in press reports, and discovered that its elastic clauses legitimized all manner of DAF interventions in social policy. Probably in a bid to avoid such direct confrontations with the DAF, the Economics Minister and the Minister of Labour had left the formal supervision of the DAF to Hitler's deputy, Rudolf Hess, who should therefore have been shown the decree in draft form. However, he was in no position to control the DAF, especially since Ley had direct access to Hitler.[42] Although the available sources do not permit us to reconstruct the subsequent controversy, it is obvious that the Reich ministers and the Party agreed among themselves to regard Hitler's decree as a dead letter, and to continue instead to observe the terms of the earlier Labour Organization Law. That they were able to do this was in part because Hitler's interest in these questions had been waning for some time, and Ley was not in a position to carry on an open struggle for power with all government departments. In the next two

40. Petition from von der Goltz to Lammers, 26 October 1934; *BA Koblenz*, R43II, file 530; quoted in detail in T.W. Mason, 'Labour in the Third Reich 1933–1939', *Past and Present*, no. 33, April 1966, and Martin Broszat, *Der Staat Hitlers*, Munich, 1969, pp. 199–202.

41. The decree was not included in most of the labour law compendia. It was published in, among other places: *Oranisationsbuch der NSDAP*, Munich, 1938; *Amtl. Nachrichtenblatt der DAF*, 1936, pp.146–50; Schumann, *Gewerkschaftsbewegung*, pp. 143ff.

42. Bormann to Lammers, 5 March 1938; *BA Koblenz*, R43II, file 530a. Cf. Peter Diehl-Thiele, *Partei und Staat im Dritten Reich*, Munich, 1969, pp. 209–16, especially p. 211. On the continuation of these conflicts in the spring of 1938, see below pp. 220ff.

years the DAF only referred to the decree a few times as a back-up in defending its position.

Although the DAF did not undertake any systematic action to increase its general influence on the state's social and economic policy or on industry, Reich Economics Minister Schacht considered its aggressive ambitions and its legally confused status as threats to the economy and rearmament.[43] The DAF had been conceived as a communitarian organization of workers and employers; yet within a year and a half it had become a representative of workers' concerns and an independent organization with its own special interests – so much so that Schacht decided that it was imperative to redefine the DAF's role in organizing industry. Any formal recognition, however, delighted the DAF and was interpreted as a sign of progress in overcoming its lack of power. Clearly, the Nazis did not limit themselves to foreign policy in concluding agreements with the idea of undermining them.

In the light of their very different assumptions, it was inevitable that the so-called Leipzig Agreement, concluded by Schacht, Ley and Seldte in March 1935, would provoke more conflicts than it would resolve. Schacht sought to bring all the DAF's activities in the area of economic policy under the control of the corporative organization of the economy, the Chambers of the Economy (*Wirtschaftskammer*). National and regional committees, to be called Labour and Industry Councils, with equal representation of labour and employers, were to consult on all common problems. To ensure a uniform direction in social and economic policy the Business Bureau of the Reich Chamber of the Economy was at the same time to function as an economic department (*Wirtschaftsamt*) in the central office of the DAF, while the Business Bureaus of the regional chambers would have the same role at the *Gau* level of the DAF. The Trustees of Labour, however, would continue to be solely responsible for resolving individual disputes in social policy.[44] For Ley this agreement represented a valuable opportunity to increase his influence over industry. Thus he saw the new dual status of the Business Bureaus of the Chambers of the Economy as the first stage in a

43. The tensions between the Ministry of Labour and the DAF in 1934/35 were greatest in the areas of trade and handicrafts; cf. Arthur Schweitzer, *Big Business in the Third Reich,* Bloomington, IN, 1964, pp. 41f., 137–49; for the numerous sources: *DZA Potsdam,* file 9029. Schacht's initiative, however, stemmed from fundamental considerations which were sparked by the confrontations of October 1934.

44. Printed excerpts from and analysis of the agreement: Syrup, *Hundert Jahre,* pp. 499f. Cf. also Schweitzer, *Big Business,* pp. 148f., 363f.; Marrenbach (ed.), *Fundamente des Sieges,* pp. 98–101. Detailed report on the DAF Conference in Leipzig, where the agreement was made public: *Arbeitertum,* 15 April 1935. A few brief references to the negotiation of the agreement plus the text of Schacht's Leipzig address, in which he claimed to have been the initiator: *DZA Potsdam,* RWM, file 10287, pp. 302–8, 337.

DAF takeover of all economic organizations. He drafted a constitution for the Reich Labour and Industry Council which would have made it an organ of the DAF, and in the name of 'social self-reliance' he attempted to set up local and occupational labour committees, in which employers and DAF functionaries could discuss global questions of social policy. Parallel to the Chambers of the Economy, the DAF also established Chambers of Labour (*Arbeitskämmer*) at the *Gau* and national levels. In the course of the heated arguments that inevitably ensued, Schacht pulled the representatives of industry out of the Reich Labour and Industry Council, prohibited members of the Chambers of the Economy from working in the Chambers of Labour, and asked Ley to put a stop to his propaganda campaign announcing the imminent absorption of the economic interest groups into the DAF.[45]

Schacht could not, of course, prevent the establishment of the labour committees; within twelve months 1,300 committees, all under the direction of the DAF, began operation. They became increasingly important as a vehicle for the DAF to apply its version of 'National Socialist customary law' to industrial social policy. Violating the assurances given to the Ministry of Labour that they would deal only with ideological matters and would co-ordinate their activities with the Trustees of Labour, these committees gradually involved themselves in every aspect of industrial relations: maternity rights, holiday entitlements and pay, sickness benefits, supplemental pension insurance, reimbursement for hours lost as a result of registration for the draft or participation in military manoeuvres, and so on. The labour committees, some of whose members were also members of the Trustees' panels of experts, advised on the drafting of new wage codes, with the DAF representatives on the committees often arguing for wage increases.[46] By 1939 the number of these committees had mushroomed to between 3,000 and 4,000. Since they mainly sought to bring their influence to bear at the level of customary law and practice in industrial social policy, it is extremely difficult to generalize about their real impact on employers and working conditions in industry. The

45. The fight over the interpretation of the agreement broke out immediately, in the summer of 1935; as early as 8 August Schacht bitterly reproached the DAF leadership: *DZA Potsdam*, RWM, file 10288, p. 82. More correspondence in subsequent months: ibid., pp. 130ff.: RWM, file 9819, pp. 300ff., 394ff.; file 10312, pp. 340–64, 408–24; file 10314, pp. 60–3, 67. On the founding of the Chamber of Labour in December 1935: *BA/MA Freiburg*, WiIF 5, file 1260.

46. Marrenbach (ed.), *Fundamente des Sieges*, pp. 103–7. Basic complaints by Mansfeld on 24 November 1936 about the lack of real responsibility and the encroachments of the labour committees into the Reich Trustees' area of responsibility: *DZA Potsdam*, RWM, file 10321, p. 8; additional complaints during the summer of 1937: ibid., file 10311, pp. 11–99; more complaints at the beginning of 1938: *Doc. 130*. Minutes of the meetings of 11 November 1935 and 7 February 1936 of the Trustees regarding the labour committees (in the presence of leading DAF officials): ibid., file 10296, pp. 121ff., 311ff.

direction of their efforts was, however, transparent, that is, the realization of 'the German Labour Front's minimum social policy requirements for maintaining productivity'.[47] Their activities were so wide-ranging that the state authorities were unable to keep track of them. All their demands were extravagant; as early as 1936 it was doubtful whether they were of any real value in maintaining worker productivity. The crude tactics used by the DAF to press its demands on industry barely concealed the fact that it was emphasizing the interests of the workers in order to maintain the stability of the regime.

These tactics, which were a means to broaden its power base, also helped to conceal the DAF's aggressive expansionism. This drive to expand was clearly reflected in Ley's interpretation of the Leipzig Agreement, for which he received a stern rebuke from Schacht. Then in 1936 the DAF began to test the waters and assert itself against the authority of other economic interest groups. Its first move was directed against the system of commercial and vocational education; this had long been an object of criticism, partly because it was less well organized than other segments of industry, and partly because of the growing shortage of skilled workers.[48] The craft and artisanal sector was extremely important because of its contributions to the training of skilled workers; and the DAF had always been interested in vocational education.[49] The relationship between craft and industrial skills was

47. Marrenbach (ed.), *Fundamente des Sieges*, p. 104.

48. The first reason was more important in the beginning: cf. note 43 above. After the Nazi Kampfbund des gewerblichen Mittelstandes had brought the regime into increasing conflict with industrial and consumer interests during the first half of 1933, it was incorporated (under the new name NS-Hago) into the DAF, only to be split into the Reichsbetriebsgemeinschaft Handel (for commerce) and Das Deutsche Handwerk (for crafts), and renamed. Given their historical background, these DAF Central Offices were much more interested in purely economic matters than the other Central Offices of the DAF and regarded the comparable Reich Groups for commerce and crafts established by the Economics Ministry from the outset as competitors. On the background of these conflicts: Schumann, *Gewerkschaftsbewegung*, pp. 84–7.

49. The German Institute for Practical Skills Training (Deutsches Institut für technische Arbeitsschulung, or Dinta) founded by the German Ironworkers Association (Verein Deutscher Eisenhüttenleute) and run by Karl Arnhold was among the most important and interesting institutions of social policy during these years. In July 1933 the word 'National Socialist' was added to its name, and shortly thereafter it was incorporated into the DAF under the name Office of Vocational Education and Industrial Organization (Amt für Berufserziehung und Betriebsführung), still under Arnhold's direction. Until 1934 the Institute specialized mainly in the technical and political training of apprentices in the factory, primarily in heavy industry. Arnhold strove for military obedience and loyalty in the day-to-day life of industry. The subject warrants its own study. Brief surveys in: Robert A. Brady, *The Spirit and Structure of German Fascism*, London, 1937, pp. 153–64; Marrenbach (ed.), *Fundamente des Sieges*, pp. 243–65; Willy Müller, *Das soziale Leben im Neuen Deutschland – unter besonderer Berücksichtigung der DAF*, Berlin, 1938, pp. 159–65; Timothy W. Mason, 'Gesetz zur Ordnung der nationalen Arbeit', in Hans Mommsen, Dietmar Petzina and Bernd Weisbrod (eds.), *Industrielles System und politische Entwicklung in der Weimarer Republik*, Düsseldorf, 1974.

extremely close. The DAF's Reich Organization for German Crafts (Reichbetriebsgemeinschaft Deutsches Handwerk) sought to absorb the state's Reich Group Crafts (Reichsgruppe Handwerk), and its Office of Vocational Education and Industrial Management (Amt für Berufserziehung und Betriebsführung) began a protracted struggle with the Chambers of Commerce and Industry (Industrie- und Handelskammer) for control of vocational training. Although the DAF's attempts to inter-vene in the affairs of the economic interest groups had been sharply rebuffed by Schacht with Hess's support,[50] it redoubled its efforts to take over vocational training on both the local and national levels. It was through the education of young people, after all, that the Nazis hoped to anchor their ideology in society, and the DAF regularly stressed ideolo-gy in its training courses. By the end of 1936 the Office of Vocational Education and Industrial Management had over 400 training workshops, with 150 more in the pipeline, and over 25,000 vocational teachers; DAF courses had been attended by 2.5 million workers. The establish-ment of the Reich Vocational Competition (*Reichsberufswettkampf*), which was conducted jointly with the Hitler Youth, gave a fillip to this aspect of the DAF's work. Vocational certification, though, remained the province of the Chambers of Commerce and Industry.[51]

By the time of the announcement of the Four-Year Plan in September 1936 the lines in the struggle over economic and social policy had been drawn. Under the banner of overcoming class conflict – that is, solving it according to Nazi principles – and of an ostensible increase in productiv-ity, the DAF had become the advocate of improved working and living conditions for the industrial worker. Acceptable improvements were those that corresponded to Nazi goals, as defined by the hideous com-pound term *Leistungsgemeinschaft* – the performance-oriented communi-ty. The focus was on communal facilities, especially those provided by the factories themselves. The DAF never became a trade union in the tra-ditional sense of the term. Its role in social policy and industrial relations was largely determined by the need to satisfy the material interests of the working class and to represent them effectively. Neither terror nor the ceaseless Nazi social rhetoric affected the way in which the working class prioritized its concerns: shorter hours, higher pay, a better standard of liv-ing. As early as 1936 workers had a chance to assert their claims in those

50. Detailed responses and complaints by Schacht to Ley, 26 June 1936: *DZA Potsdam*, RWM, file 10314, pp. 60–3; and to Göring, 12 December 1936: ibid., file 10321, pp. 2f. Further sources on these power struggles: ibid., files 9029, 10312. Cf. also Schweitzer, *Big Business*, p. 149; also *Doc. 1, Note 2*.

51. For more details: Müller, *Soziales Leben*, pp. 164–169; Marrenbach (ed.), *Fundamente des Sieges*, pp. 278–292; Schoenbaum, *Braune Revolution*, pp. 133ff. (including references). On the further development of the struggle over authority, see below pp. 216f., 220f.

branches of industry and geographic regions which were suffering from manpower shortages. At the lowest level of the production process – on the shop floor, at the construction site, in factory departments – individual groups of workers found they could make their demands felt if they maintained group solidarity.[52] The DAF was ill-prepared to deal with the situation. The ideological principles underlying its social policy did not provide any guidance in meeting the challenge. Since the organization was not trusted by most workers, it lacked the support to stem the tide, overtly or covertly. The functionaries, concerned about their own popularity, were forced to adopt or at least back some of the workers' demands. At a meeting on social policy in February 1936, the gloomy representative of the War Ministry summed up the situation succinctly: 'The managers will not be able to hold out against the pressure from their men'.[53] The pressure from below, however, gave the DAF the impetus to continue expanding its empire and to press ahead at the government level with its demands for building more facilities for the workers.[54] Gradually, the government bureaucracy and the industrial interest groups closed ranks against the DAF's demands and proposals, in part to protect their own authority and position, but mainly to assure themselves the economic resources to sustain rearmament and prepare for war. By the spring of 1936 they had largely succeeded, especially in areas where the judicial authority of the government and the bureaucracy was firmly established.

The government's social-policy reforms during the period 1933 to 1936 were pathetic. The revision of the rules on working hours in July 1934 did not produce any substantive improvements,[55] and the efforts to co-ordinate and improve safety regulations for workers were stalled.[56] The only area in which some minor improvements were carried out was in protecting young people and women employed in mining and in the iron, metal and glass industries in March 1935.[57] The Minister of Labour

52. Cf. especially *Doc. 3*. The monthly reports of the Trustees attest, among other things, the inexorable spread of this attitude throughout industry in the period 1937/8: *Docs. 52, 96, 104*.

53. Trustees' meeting, 7 February 1936: DZA Potsdam, RWM, file 10296, pp. 305f.

54. For some examples in 1937: *Docs. 53–65*; see mainly the comments below on the productivity competition in German industry and on the power struggle at the beginning of 1938, pp. 211ff.

55. Decree on the Revision of the Rules Governing Working Hours (*VO über die neue Fassung der Arbeitszeitordnung*), 26 July 1934: *RGBl. I*, p. 803. Subsequently, however, protective legislation was made stricter for occupations in which very long working hours were the norm (butchers, barbers, truck drivers, restaurant workers): Syrup, *Hundert Jahre*, pp. 485f.; *DZA Potsdam*, RWM, file 10296, pp. 108ff., 136.

56. For a summary: Syrup, *Hundert Jahre*, pp. 501f., 510ff. The resumption of negotiations in the summer of 1938 produced results only for the protection of young people.

57. Decree on the Protection of Young Men and Women Workers (*VO über den Schutz der jugendlichen Arbeiter und Arbeiterinnen...*), 12 March 1935: *RGBl. I*, p. 387.

gave in to the DAF on only two minor points. At the end of 1934 industrial inspectors were enjoined to use stricter guidelines, mainly with regard to showers, recreation rooms, washrooms and so on, and to keep a more systematic record of workers' complaints.[58] At the same time, the provisions of the Labour Organization Law dealing with workers' protection against summary dismissal were amended, increasing maximum compensation to the equivalent of one year's salary (previously it had been one-third). Rules protecting workers against unlawful dismissal had been substantially weakened by the abolition of the old factory councils, and the subsequent wave of dismissals raised an outcry among industrial workers, and probably among DAF representatives as well.[59] But beyond this, the DAF had little opportunity to assert itself at the government level. Its calls for a major expansion of the rules against unlawful dismissal were turned down and its demands for an extension of various provisions of the Labour Organization Law to small businesses, where employers still exercised virtually unlimited authority, were also rejected.[60] Similar conditions obtained in the civil service, which had been exempted from the provisions of the Labour Organization Law at the beginning of 1934, against the advice of the Labour Minister. In the years that followed, the other ministries continued to reject his pleas to set up consultative councils with jurisdictional authority inside the civil service.[61] It seems that there was no place within the political

58. The Labour Ministry's decrees in November 1934 were preceded by attacks on the factory inspectors in the *Völkischer Beobachter*, in which the newspaper made itself the spokesman for 'Beauty of Labour'; another reason was the arrest of the director of a large rolling mill who had ignored his responsibility for industrial welfare. This kind of pressure was extremely rare and was clearly used to produce glaring examples of misconduct for propaganda purposes. All relevant documents: *DZA Potsdam*, RAM, file 2804, no. 9, pp. 161–221.

59. Law on the Extension of Protection against Summary Dismissal (*Gesetz zur Erweiterung des Kündigungsschutzes*), 30 November 1934: *RGBl. I*, p. 1193 (an amendment of para. 58 AOG). An explanation of the background: Syrup, *Hundert Jahre*, pp. 486–9.

60. On the first point: *Doc. 13*. It is significant that the government relented only after changes in the condition of the labour market made an extended notice of dismissal seem desirable for quite different reasons. On the second point: *BA Koblenz*, R43II, file 548 (the DAF's draft decree of May 1935); R 41, file 24, p. 101. The problem of codes of practice in small businesses was taken up again in February 1937 and January 1938, but no reforms were adopted: ibid., R43II, file 528; *DZA Potsdam*, RWM, file 10285, pp. 38, 41. According to para. 7 of the Labour Organization Law only businesses with more than twenty employees had a Council of Trust to which a dismissed employee could turn for help and which was authorized to request mediation from the Trustees of Labour.

61. The deliberations on the Labour Organization Law had been almost concluded when on 14 December 1933 the Ministers of Transportation and of the Interior requested that civil service employees be exempted from coverage by the law. Their request was approved (cf. para. 63 AOG). Law on the Organization of Labour in Public Administration and Enterprises (*Gesetz zur Ordnung der Arbeit in öffentlichen Verwaltungen und Betrieben*), 23 March 1934: *RGBl. I*, p. 220. Sources on this subject for the period 1933–9: BA Koblenz, R43II, files 547, 548, 555; R41, file 24, pp. 116–19, 131ff.; *DZA Potsdam*, RWM, file 10286, pp. 30f.; file 10296, pp. 38ff.

order's 'sphere of command' (*Direktionssphäre* – Otto Kirchheimer's term) for even the appearance of participatory management (*Mitbestimmung*); all that counted here was authority, undivided responsibility, and obedience.[62] Although it often noted the restiveness of civil service employees,[63] the DAF, like the NSDAP and its associated organizations, consistently avoided using the labour laws to remedy the problems of its own employees or enterprises, a fact which speaks volumes about the importance the Party attached to its own rhetoric.[64]

The attempts by the DAF from 1934 to 1936 to gain prominence by influencing the Trustees of Labour also proved unproductive. Since the Trustees were obliged to follow governmental wage guidelines, the DAF's right to nominate members to the panel of experts that issued wage and factory codes was meaningless. Thus from the outset the DAF *Führungsämter* preferred to deal directly with the Labour Minister. Even so, their recommendations for wage increases in the petroleum, lignite and potash mining industries were all rejected.[65] In these circumstances, clashes between the Trustees and the DAF at the regional level were inevitable. At issue was not only wage policy, but industrial peace within the factory. With its much larger organization the DAF was better placed than the Trustees to intervene in factory labour disputes. The DAF called upon its officials to report routinely on any incidents, even though the Labour Organization Law specified that incidents which could not be settled by the Councils of Trust were to come under the purview of the Trustees of Labour. At a meeting with Hauptamtsleiter Selzner of the DAF, for instance, 'various Trustees of Labour' complained 'about the lack of understanding for the work of the Trustees on the part of German Labour Front officials, which had resulted in the Trustees and their senior aides being threatened with law-suits, expul-

62. Cf. the position of the Reich ministers on the participation of their departments in German industry's productivity competition (*Leistungskampf*). Aside from the question of the Councils of Trust, conditions in the civil service were more authoritarian, in that administrative officials and shop stewards – both subject to disciplinary jurisdiction in their capacity as civil servants – had no recourse to the 'courts of honour'; and the Special Trustee of Labour for the Civil Service was subject not only to the Minister of Labour and the Minister of Economics, but to the Minister of Finance as well: see *Gesetz zur Ordnung der Arbeit in öffentlichen Verwaltungen und Betrieben*, paras 3, 18, 20.

63. For example at the Trustees' meeting on 7 February 1936: *DZA Potsdam*, RWM, file 10296, pp. 308f.

64. Cf. the Trustees' criticism of the Eher publishing house, which refused to establish a Council of Trust in a number of its offices: ibid., p. 39; also Hess's demand at the ministerial meeting in October 1936 that Party employees and their associations not be subject to the protection of the labour laws: *BA Koblenz*, R41, file 24, p. 132. Party-owned businesses and Party administrators were among the most ruthless employers.

65. *DZA Potsdam*, RAM, file 92, pp. 85–167; file 178, pp. 339–47; file 206, pp. 72–6.

sion from the Party, and the filing of complaints against their conduct with the Ministry of Labour'.[66] However, in 1935/6 these differences were insigificant compared with those in subsequent years.[67]

It was very important that the DAF could generally count on the support of the Party in these confrontations. It must be remembered, of course, that 'the Party' had a variety of different institutional incarnations. Hess's Office of the Führer's Deputy, for example, had good reason to view the DAF as a competitor and did its utmost to oppose any formal increase in the power of the DAF at the governmental level.[68] Be that as it may, the attitude of the Gauleiters, Reich Commissioners (*Reichsstatthalter*), and the Party press were of much greater importance with regard to changes in the direction of social policy. So far as the Propaganda Ministry and the Gauleiters were concerned, popular morale took precedence, and, as the Gestapo continually emphasized in its reports, this depended to a large extent on living standards. The Gauleiters and the *Reichsstatthalter*, on whose views the DAF's *Gauwalter* certainly had more influence, occupied key positions in the power structure – positions which they consistently used to thwart any attempt to impose additional burdens on the people. Gauleiter Kaufmann's intervention in the deliberations over miners' wages and food prices may have been unusual in its radicalism, but not in its spirit;[69] and he had a ready ally in the person of Bürckel, the Gauleiter of the Saarland. In the middle of 1936 Bürckel had personally ordered an across-the-board increase in wages for his hard-hit region. He was among the most fervent representatives of the populist wing in the Nazi Party and did not shrink from open confrontation with Schacht and Seldte over this issue.[70] The Reich ministers, the armed forces and

66. *DZA Potsdam*, RWM, file 10296, p. 123. Similar complaints were also aired in meetngs on 14 August and 23 December 1935 as well as on 7 February 1936; ibid., pp. 26, 204f., 306f. By the end of 1936 things had reached the point where the DAF had instituted 'honour court' proceedings against members of its own organization who had had direct contact with the Trustees: Mansfeld to the Prussian Ministry of State, 24 November 1936, ibid., file 10321, p. 5.

67. Cf. below pp. 218f., 249f.; *Docs. 42, 99, 130.*

68. See Reichhardt, 'Deutsche Arbeitsfront', p. 81; cf. also above pp. 167f. and below pp. 221f. In January 1937 Hess ordered, probably not for the first time, that correspondence between Party officials and the Reich ministers pass through his office: *BA Koblenz*, R41, vol. 22, p. 1; more in *Doc. 60*. Cf. Peter Diehl-Thiele, *Partei und Staat im Dritten Reich*, Munich, 1969, ch. 6a. For background material, Dietrich Orlow, *The History of the Nazi Party*, vol. 2: 1933–1945, Newton Abbott, 1973, chs. 1–4.

69. See above p. 138. On the background: Peter Hüttenberger, *Die Gauleiter. Studie zum Wandel des Machtgefüges in der NSDAP*, Stuttgart, 1969.

70. *DZA Potsdam*, RWM, file 10300, pp. 43–59. Cf. Bürckel's position in the disputes over paying workers for legal holidays: *Docs. 53–5.* Hüttenberger cites another example in *Die Gauleiter*, p. 140.

industry received little support from the press for their policy of cutting back on consumption in favour of capital investments and rearmament. The Trustees of Labour complained constantly about the heedless pursuit of popularity by the mass-circulation dailies which, they felt, were raising unrealistic hopes about social policy and doing nothing to hammer home the need for restraint and sacrifice. Their own measures, which attempted to enforce the wage-freeze with inadequate powers, were decried in the press, if they were mentioned at all.[71]

The opinions of those who held power in the Nazi regime were divided on this fundamental question. As emerged at at the meeting of the Reich Labour Chamber in November 1936, one group considered expansionism and the economic means required to achieve it as the most important goal, whereas the other put the regime's popularity first in order of priority.[72] In a certain sense, the two groups complemented each other, and their conflict over an issue of such vital importance to the state, carried out behind the scenes as it was, actually helped to ensure the stability of the whole regime: a one-sided 'resolution' of that conflict in favour of either the military and the state on the one hand, or the populist forces within the Nazi movement on the other would have threatened the very existence of the system. In 1936, however, a sea change took place: full employment had come to the capital-goods sector at nearly the same time as the DAF had completed the structuring of its organization and had learned how to fashion a social policy. The growing labour shortage was a political boon to the DAF, for it was now responsible for 'looking after' a scarce commodity.

An even-handed, non-confrontational report on DAF policy, written in November 1936 by Werner Mansfeld, the most influential official in the Labour Ministry, unintentionally revealed the split within the regime, and its causes. This authoritarian legalist found it difficult to understand why the framework for industrial relations he had envisaged in the Labour Organization Law was in any need of amendment. He was both concerned and baffled as he observed the seemingly endless and often obscure charges traded between the ministerial bureaucracy and the economic interest groups and the DAF. These increasingly danger-

71. There were six such complaints at Trustee meetings in August, October and November 1935: *DZA Potsdam*, RWM file 10296. This problem became especially acute at the beginning of the war: *Docs. 193, 229–31*. A detailed study of press policy on the question of living standards would be most useful. The tentative findings of this study point to a total failure of the Propaganda Ministry, which sought to divert attention from these problems by cooking up sensational reports rather than providing a rational explanation of the need to make sacrifices. At the same time, however, it should also be noted that the DAF had a huge press empire.

72. Cf. *Doc. 1*; above pp. 19f.

ous confrontations seemed totally capricious to him. He did concede that in those few areas in which the DAF had a definite political responsibility – advice on labour law, the KdF – it had accomplished some useful things.[73] In terms of its main responsibility in the area of popular education, however, he judged the DAF to be a failure. In Mansfeld's view, this was where it should concentrate its energies – not in destructive struggles to co-opt the authority of other legitimate and efficient institutions. Mansfeld's prognoses were without exception pessimistic, although he never explicitly identified the reasons for his gloom. Clearly, however, it derived from the continuing class conflict in industry and the impetus this gave to the DAF's imperial ambitions. For its part, the DAF was willing to grant first priority to the goal of rearmament, but only rhetorically, not in practical terms. This apparently superficial misunderstanding is an outstanding illustration of the deep rifts in the social order and in National Socialist policy. Indeed, the significance of the first three years of the Nazi regime was that, after the initial period of confusion in 1933, these 'misunderstandings' only became deeper and more widespread.

The object of these conflicts – the workers – were put in a confusing position. At one moment, they were called upon sternly to do without, to sacrifice, to maintain discipline; then they became an object of solicitude, wooed by welfare and ideological slogans; while in their own eyes, they were simply underpaid labourers. The main point, though, was that the workers were still regarded as politically unreliable. After their clear rejection of National Socialism in the first elections to the Councils of Trust, the vote was rigged in the spring of 1935. Even Bormann did not believe in the accuracy of the results announced by the DAF: 90 per cent voter participation, 83 per cent of the ballots cast for the list prepared jointly by the factory leaders and overseers. A reporter for the Party feared that these numbers would 'simply appear ridiculous to the workers'.[74] Hitler shared this view, for he cancelled the elections the following year, shortly before election day. The results would most likely have been a less ringing endorsement of the regime than the pending plebiscite on the recently completed reoccupation of the Rhineland.[75] Council elections were never again held. In a controversial

73. Mansfeld expressly indicated that he did *not* want this acknowledgement to be interpreted as an endorsement for giving the DAF additional responsibilities. Petition to the Prussian Ministry of State, 24 November 1936: *DZA Potsdam*, RWM, file 10321, pp. 5–12.

74. Cf. note 36 above.

75. I would like to thank Dr Kurt Gossweiler of the Academy of Sciences of the GDR for this convincing explanation of the cancellation of the elections. The elections were not actually abolished until 1938; until then, Hitler would simply cancel them every year. The documents on this decision are in *BA Koblenz*, R43II, file 547b.

move, the members were simply appointed by the factory leader, the overseer and the Trustees of Labour. The Councils of Trust subsequently withered away, and the role of the overseer, who in the larger factories supervised a staff of aides, grew in importance.[76]

During a meeting with the Trustees of Labour in February 1935, the Reich Labour Minister pondered these problems. The public image of the Trustees was not enhanced, he felt, when they appeared alongside the Gestapo during walkouts and similar protests. Too much use had been made of 'preventive arrest'; there was a need to deepen the sense of trust in the factories. This, he said, was the most important task of the Trustees.[77] In 1936 an average of 1,000 Communist resistance fighters per month had been arrested by the Gestapo.[78] The reason Seldte was able to prattle on about 'trust', of course, was that the workers who could have challenged his use of the word, had been systematically terrorized: under National Socialism trust took root in the soil of fear.

76. On the controversy between the DAF and the Labour Ministry over this method of selection, see below pp. 218f.; on the position of the overseer: Reichhardt, 'Deutsche Arbeitsfront', pp. 113ff. In general, the Trustees had bad relations with the overseers, whom they once described as a 'shadow administration' (*Nebenregierung*) inside the factory: *DZA Potsdam*, RWM, file 10296, pp. 309ff.

77. Ibid., pp. 313f.

78. Cf. Walter Ulbricht *et al.* (eds.), *Geschichte der deutschen Arbeiterbewegung*, vol. 5, E. Berlin, 1966, p. 142; *Institut für Marxismus-Leninismus, Zentrales Parteiarchiv*, St. 3, vol. 106, pp. 143 ff; Martin Broszat, 'Nationalsozialistische Konzentrationslager 1933–1945', in Hans Buchheim et al., *Anatomie des SS-Staates*, vol. 2, Olten/Freiburg i. B., 1965, p. 47.

6

Social Policy, Rearmament and War, September 1936 to December 1939

The people, you see, will be the decisive factor. They must believe in us with such unquestioning trust that, even if an obvious mistake were actually made, they would never dream of the consequences; rather they would swallow defeat like a well-trained army and say, 'Let's have another go at them and this time pay them back with interest'. That is the attitude we need in order to get out of a dreadful situation. Otherwise we would be stuck there forever.

A people has to be taught to march through thick and thin with its government and to feel totally at one with its government; it must be instantly susceptible to every psychological factor, able to be whipped into a frenzy, and be inspired and roused. If this is not possible, then all our efforts will be in vain, we will be forced to surrender.

Hitler addressing the General Council on the Economy, 30 September 1933[1]

6.1. Social Consequences of Rearmament

The situation was hopeless, but there was no surrender. After Stalingrad the German people did 'swallow' defeats 'like a well-trained army'. However, it could not be whipped into a frenzy, let alone be inspired to fight on to final victory. The 'victory within', which Hitler had once called the indispensable condition for breaking 'the iron shackles of the enemy without', was incomplete.[2] Hitler himself had repeatedly referred to the yardstick against which the incompleteness of the 'victory within' had to be measured: the total subordination of domestic policy to the needs of military expansion. The goal and *raison d'être* of Nazi rule were the transformation of the entire country into a powerful armed

1. *BA Koblenz*, R43II, file 321/1.
2. Hitler, 'Warum musste ein 8. November kommen?', *Deutschlands Erneuerung*, 1924, p. 207.

camp, in which all activity could be funnelled into a programme of aggressive territorial expansion and racial hegemony. 'No revolution on the home front', Hitler promised his assembled commanders at the end of November 1939, in order to make the prospects for the imminent invasion of France appear more favourable.[3] For the moment he was correct, thanks to the Gestapo. However, the legitimate assumption that there was no reason to fear a revolution at home did not mean that the German people were enthusiastic about the war; this assumption could therefore not be used as proof of the solidarity of the domestic front. But solidarity was precisely what was needed, a fact that Hitler acknowledged as early as 22 August to the same audience:

> In the final analysis it is not machines that fight one another, but people. And we have the best people. It is not true that we lost in 1918 because of a shortage of *matériel*; in 1918 we were actually in better shape materially than in 1915 or 1916. What we lacked were the essential moral prerequisites to be able to hold out.[4]

The message these words conveyed did not derive from a conviction backed by hard political facts, but from the speaker's wish to convince himself and his audience at all costs of the solidarity of the 'home front'. Even though the generals who were present may have agreed with Hitler's version of the stab-in-the-back legend,[5] they apparently did not see its relevance to the situation in the autumn of 1939. Moreover, they were unable to work up much enthusiasm for the coming war, precisely because they were so well informed about the strengths and weaknesses of Germany's military preparations and were better able than Hitler to make a realistic appraisal of the strategic situation.[6] From their standpoint, machines were indeed important. Furthermore, there was a big difference between waging an ongoing war that had started despite shortages of *matériel* and starting a new war without a strong war economy.

The three years following the announcement of the second Four-Year Plan in September 1936 were marked by an intensification of the rearmament programme and of strategic preparations. At first glance, the social

---

3. *IMGH*, vol. 26, pp. 327–35, Doc. 789–PS; reprinted in Hans-Adolf Jacobsen, *Der Zweite Weltkrieg. Grundzüge der Politik und Strategie in Dokumenten*, Frankfurt am Main, 1965, p. 71: 'Besprechung beim Führer', 23 November 1939.

4. Notes of General Admiral Boehm, *IMGH*, vol. 41, pp. 24f., Doc. Raeder-27. For the sources of Hitler's address, see Winfried Baumgart, 'Zur Ansprache Hitlers vor den Führern der Wehrmacht am 22. August 1939', *Vierteljahrshefte für Zeitgeschichte*, vol. 16/2, 1968, pp. 120–49.

5. Cf. above, chapter 1.

6. Except for Keitel and Jodl. Cf. Harold Deutsch, *The Conspiracy against Hitler in the Twilight War*, Minneapolis, 1968, chs. 1–3; Berenice A. Carroll, *Design for Total War. Arms and Economics in the Third Reich*, The Hague, 1968, chs. 9, 11.

history of this period seems incidental to economic and military policy. However, manpower shortages, soaring wages, poor work discipline, hidden inflation, economic bottlenecks and the resultant rivalries and power struggles in the state, the bureaucracy, industry and the Party, were the direct results of the hectic preparations for war. Thus before we can analyse the interplay between social policy, the armaments sector and foreign policy, we must first take a brief look at the scope and structure of rearmament.

The achievements in this area were considerable. In terms of numbers, national spending on armaments quintupled from RM 6 billion in 1935 to approximately RM 30 billion in 1939. This was the main reason that the gross national product rose from RM 74 billion to RM 130 billion; the percentage expended on armaments was 8 per cent in 1935 and about 23 per cent at the beginning of the war. Only about two-thirds of the enormous increase in these and other government expenditures were covered by tax increases. From 1935 to 1938 the national debt doubled to almost RM 42 billion. As a result of the Four-Year Plan, a growing proportion of government investment was channelled into industry. Between 1935 and 1939 investments in the capital goods sector increased fourfold, and after the autumn of 1936 nearly half of all fixed investments were in the militarily-important branches of industry that came within the purview of the Four-Year Plan. It is therefore not surprising that the consumer sector's share of GNP fell from 72 per cent (1935) to 54 per cent (1939).[7] In terms of 'production', the German armed forces at the beginning of the war had over 103 army divisions, including five fully mechanized and four light Panzer divisions (3,200 tanks), more than 3,646 combat-ready aircraft, and a Navy consisting of fifty-seven U-boats, twenty-two destroyers, nine cruisers and six battle cruisers. The build-up of this force, which was stronger than that of any other nation at the outbreak of war (with the exception of the Royal Navy),[8] took place mainly between 1935 and

7. The figures are according to Carroll, *Design*, pp. 184–7; René Erbe, *Die nationalsozialistische Wirtschaftspolitik 1933–1939 im Lichte der modernen Theorie*, Zürich, 1958, pp. 48–55. Petzina's statistics on investment have been used above; Carroll's figures (p. 188) differ markedly from Petzina's. There is an urgent need for a detailed study of government investment during the 1930s. Petzina's numbers are probably too low: Dietmar Petzina, *Autarkiepolitik im Dritten Reich*, Stuttgart, 1968, p. 184.

8. The figures are according to B. Mueller-Hillebrand, *Das Heer 1935–1945*, vol. 1, Darmstadt, 1954, pp. 68–71; K.-H. Völker, *Die deutsche Luftwaffe 1933–1939*, Stuttgart, 1967, p. 189; Carl-Axell Gemzell, *Raeder, Hitler und Skandinavien*, Lund/Frankfurt am Main, 1965, pp. 197f.; Hans-Adolf Jacobsen, *Fall 'Gelb'*, Wiesbaden, 1957, pp. 1–8, 139, 197ff.; Andreas Hillgruber, *Hitlers Strategie*, Frankfurt am Main, 1965, pp. 33–40. See also the contributions by Chilston and Hillmann in *Survey of International Affairs*, 1938 (vol. III) and 1939 ('The World in March 1939'), as well as R.H.S. Stolfi, 'Equipment for Victory in France 1940', in *History*, vol. 55, no. 183, 1970, pp. 1–20. A numerical comparison of the military power of the various countries does not make much sense, since technology and tactics were what counted most; what is significant in this context is that the German army and air force had caught up with those of the other military powers within six years.

1939 and was made possible by the enormous expansion of industrial plant and the manufacture within Germany of all strategically-important raw materials. These questions cannot all be discussed individually here, and the existence of a number of detailed economic histories makes this unnecessary in any case.[9]

Despite the fact that the economic and social history of these years was characterized by the frantic pace of rearmament, there is no now doubt that Germany's arsenal in the last few months of 1939 was not up to the strategic demands placed on it. This finding differs from the views of Hitler's contemporary critics, who foresaw the inevitability of a world war but assumed that this rested on adequate economic preparations.[10] For although the basic idea behind the blitzkrieg strategy was to concentrate on specific aspects of economic and military policy, the requisite *scale* of rearmament had not been worked out in detail. Germany's war industries did not have the resources even for this limited-war strategy, a fact reflected as much in the Wehrmacht's glaring lack of equipment as in the often very low stocks of some essential raw materials. After the quick and relatively easy subjugation of Poland, the shortages of ammunition and military vehicles had become so massive that the next campaign had to be postponed for months. In October 1939, when Hitler called for an immediate invasion of France in order to repair the damage done by his miscalculation of the French and British reaction to the invasion of Poland, the generals opposed him chiefly because the lack of sufficient armaments made his plans unrealistic. On 8 October 1939 the Quartermaster-General announced that the army had barely enough ammunition to supply one-third of its divisions for a maximum of four weeks of fighting; the Luftwaffe had a minimal number of bombs; it was extremely difficult to procure replacements or spare parts for the tanks, trucks and aircraft damaged or destroyed during the Polish campaign; motorized units were only restored to full strength in the middle of April 1940 as a result of siphoning off 16,000 trucks from industry and confiscating 10,000 trucks in the Protectorate of Bohemia and Moravia. In addition, there were still major shortages of fuel and rubber for the divisions, yet on 3 February 1940 the expansion of facilities for the manufacture of synthetic rubber and petroleum was cut back in order to free all available capacity for the production of munitions. For all these reasons Halder, Jodl and almost all the other generals were in agreement both then and later that a German attack on

9. See especially Petzina, *Autarkiepolitik*, and Carroll, *Design*.
10. Cf. Carroll, *Design*, especially chs. 2, 9.

France before Christmas 1939 – as Hitler wanted – would lead to military disaster.[11]

If Hitler could have realized his dream of a neutral Britain, Germany's military strength might have coincided more closely with his policy. Although this dream was shattered on 3 September, it still seemed to the countries involved that Germany was in a very favourable strategic position in the winter of 1939/40. In reality, however, her economic preparations for war were inadequate to carry out Hitler's own strategic plan.[12] The reason for Germany's success during the first two years is to be found not in the ostensible superiority of her war economy, but in the military and political weaknesses of the other Great Powers, in superior German tactics and, even more important, in Hitler's willingness to go for broke: to risk the whole Nazi system and the lives and well-being of the German people without giving them a second thought.[13]

Although these findings have been accepted by most historians,[14] there is still no systematic study of the background to these developments. The simplistic argument that Hitler's strategy did not call for any additional expenditure of the economy's resources on rearmament is no longer tenable.[15] Not only is it contradicted by the existence of shortages in the military sector, but government documents covering the period 1938–9 demonstrate that the greatest possible efforts – in the circumstances – were being undertaken to strengthen the military machine.[16]

---

11. Jacobsen, *Fall 'Gelb'*, pp. 19ff., 131–7, 187ff., 192–7; Hillgruber, *Hitlers Strategie*, pp. 34f., 38, 445; Georg Thomas, *Geschichte der deutschen Wehr- und Rüstungswirtschaft (1918–1943/45)*, ed. Wolfgang Birkenfeld, Boppard am Rhein, 1966, chs. 17–19, also Appendix 3, Doc. 2; Elisabeth Wagner, *Der Generalquartiermeister. Briefe und Tagebuchaufzeichnungen des Generalquartiermeisters des Heeres, General der Infanterie EduardWagner*, Munich, 1963, p. 142. Deutsch, *Conspiracy*, does not attach enough importance to this factor in his analysis of the military resistance.

12. It is noteworthy that Hitler refused to acknowledge the weaknesses of the wartime economy. Only because of unfavourable weather reports was Hitler persuaded to order three crucial postponements of the attack on France, on 7, 9 and 13 November 1939: Jacobsen, *Fall 'Gelb'*, pp. 49ff., 141. For more on the chronology, see below pp. 252f.

13. On the gambler in Hitler, see the illuminating observations by Alan Bullock, 'Hitler and the Origins of the Second World War', *Proceedings of the British Academy*, vol. 53, pp. 259–87 (reprinted in E.M. Robertson (ed.), *The Origins of the Second World War*, London, 1971).

14. Cf. Carroll, *Design*; Petzina, *Autarkiepolitik*; Hillgruber, *Strategie*, pp. 33–40.

15. For example, Burton H. Klein, *Germany's Economic Preparations for War*, Cambridge, Mass., 1959, p. 25, on the 'fundamental reason' for the limited character of rearmament; Alan S. Milward, *Die deutsche Kriegswirtschaft 1939–1945*, Stuttgart, 1966, makes the same argument; also some observations by Hillgruber point in this direction, e.g., *Hitlers Strategie*, p. 45, note 82.

16. See for example Göring's address to the Reich Defence Council, 18 November 1938: *Doc. 152*. All the meetings of the Reich Defence Committee during the period 1936–9 give the same impression: *BA/MA Freiburg*, WilF 5, files 560, 560/1, 560/2.

There was no deliberate neglect of the war economy just because the strategic situation made further measures seem superfluous. On the contrary, by the middle of 1938 government and industry seemed to be overwhelmed by the magnitude of the rearmament programme. Even this still inadequate level of rearmament had been achieved only by drawing on all the economy's reserves. This was not simply a crisis of the kind that the Nazi preference for frenetic activity tended to provoke in all areas of public life. This was a genuine political, social and economic crisis.

First and foremost among the 'circumstances' hindering the chance for an armaments-led economy to succeed was the incomplete domestic victory of National Socialism. As the records of the ministries concerned show, social conditions between 1937 and 1939 were not simply the effect of the hectic pace of rearmament; they were the single most important barrier to an increase in armaments production. Full employment and its consequences jeopardized a victory on the domestic front by making it much more difficult to channel the requisite share of GNP, raw material reserves, industrial capacity, and manpower into the armaments sector. In fact, it was the rearmament programme itself, in so far as it determined economic and social policy, that threatened to undermine the subordination of domestic policy to foreign policy and military strategy. Measures to remove this threat by limiting consumption and controlling the workers were contradicted by the efforts of those in power to secure the goodwill of the people. The whole process was a spiralling crisis without end, for in the atmosphere of open international confrontation that existed after March 1938, the mobilization of Germany's economic and military resources increased the economy's and the Wehrmacht's demands for manpower, thereby magnifying the problem of the working class's political reliability.

Since the crisis was not exclusively economic, but rather a crisis of the entire regime and its policies, numbers alone cannot give us a sense of its dimensions. The main weakness of most works on this subject is that they ignore this basic fact, implying that the government could have solved the crisis by better evaluating its needs and its resources or by using modern production planning techniques – as if the redistribution of the social product could have been accomplished by a mere administrative decision.[17] For example, even though the statistics on the labour

---

17. Petzina, *Autarkiepolitik*, pp. 158–68, 190–5, is a strong proponent of this view; the secondary sources cited by him fetishize numbers in a similarly apolitical way that is reminiscent of Speer's views: Albert Speer, *Erinnerungen*, Frankfurt am Main, 1969, p. 546, note 1. In contrast, see Sauer, in Karl Dietrich Bracher, Wolfgang Sauer and Gerhard Schulz, *Die nationalsozialistische Machtergreifung. Studien zur Errichtung des totalitären Herrschaftsytems in Deutschland 1933–1934*, Cologne/Opladen, 1960, p. 755.

market from 1937 to 1939 provide us with information on an important aspect of the crisis, they only partially convey the scale of the problem as a whole. The number of employed rose from 19.66 million to 21.65 million between August 1937 and August 1939, while unemployment dropped from half a million to 34,000.[18] By the autumn of 1938 the number of employed had reached a new high, despite the call-up of nearly a million young men.[19] By May 1938 there were no longer any manpower reserves among the registered unemployed; those counted either may have been in the process of changing jobs on the day statistics were collected, or they were not fully fit for work. In fields suffering critical shortages, such as the building industry, agriculture and the metal industry, there were simply no more unemployed. Although there was an untapped reserve of labour among unemployed women and in branches of industry which, to use the bureaucratic jargon of the time, were not vital or critical to the war effort, the regime could not bring itself to introduce the necessary coercive measures. In November 1938 the Labour Minister estimated the unmet demand for workers in the economy at around a million.[20]

Bottlenecks in production were the first serious consequences of the regime's strategy of expansion, and in the diplomatic and strategic context of these years they assumed crisis proportions. As the government directed the course of international politics towards war, industry found it could not fully meet the constantly increasing demands of the Wehrmacht.[21] The crisis did not portend imminent economic collapse; rather it manifested itself as a rapidly growing disproportion between urgent ends (military expansion) and available means (reserve factors of production). All that many observers, even informed ones, could see was Germany's prosperity (a unique phenomenon in German history), the high rates of investment, the well-filled order books, and so on.[22] So far as we can judge, uninformed opinion in Germany held similar views. Only those who were able to make economic forecasts, who knew or suspected that there was no room for compromise in international rela-

18. *Stat. Jahrbuch*, 1939/40, pp. 347, 389 (according to health insurance plan statistics).

19. Klein, *Preparations*, pp. 67ff.; *Statistisches Handbuch von Deutschland,* Munich, 1949, p. 474; *Doc. 146* (Seldte's statistics are imprecise: explanatory text preceding *Doc. 2*).

20. *Docs. 107, 146*. On the *political* problem of manpower reserves among able-bodied workers and on the measures to increase the number of wage-earners, see below pp. 230ff.

21. This is a generalization about the economic history of the period based on the source material. Later we will discuss the question of the kind of war being aimed at, and the question of the relationship between rearmament and Hitler's projection of the strategic situation in the event of war; see below pp. 255–66.

22. For example, the English economist C.W. Guillebaud, *The Economic Recovery of Germany*, London, 1939, ch. 6; idem, *The Social Policy of Nazi Germany*, London, 1941.

tions based on German policies, recognized the crisis in the economy for what it was. Thus the following analysis will emphasize the discrepancy between what was desired or considered essential in the sphere of production, and what was actually accomplished. My aim is to uncover the causes of the missed opportunities and explain why, despite the sharp rise in production in all branches of industry during these years, output was insufficient to meet the needs of the military or to fulfil strategic planning.[23]

The best example of production bottlenecks due to the labour shortage is the hard-coal-mining industry, where production exceeded planned targets but was still unable to meet sky-rocketing demand. This resulted in a decline in exports in 1939 (when the scarcity of foreign currency threatened to become critical), a reduction in supplies to the *Reichsbahn* (whose reserves were far below what was required in wartime) and, starting in the winter of 1938/9, repeated shortages of coal for home heating.[24] The other causes of the bottlenecks were comparatively insignificant: for example, the shortage of iron and steel for demolition equipment, repairs, railway cars, steel pit-props for the mines and so on. To boost the output of hard coal the government concentrated on obtaining more manpower, but without any notable success. With continued full employment, not only was it difficult to attract workers to this demanding and unglamorous occupation, but those who were already working there were becoming increasingly demoralized. Per-capita production had slipped by 10–15 per cent in the last years before the war; even the introduction of longer shifts, with incentive pay for the additional hours, resulted in only a partial and short-term improvement in output.[25]

The causes of bottlenecks in other sectors of industry were somewhat more complex, for in only a few of them was the work as labour-intensive and as little dependent on subcontractors as coal-mining. In the other, more technologically advanced industries and in all those dependent on sub-contractors for parts, shortages in two other major areas – liquid capital and imported raw materials – played a critical role. So far as the specific importance of the manpower shortage is concerned, we can at least agree with Petzina's judgement in his study of the Four-Year

23. Cf. the excellent table of statistics in Petzina, *Autarkiepolitik*, p. 182, which compares plan targets with actual production figures.
24. The latter was partly the result of transportation problems (a shortage of railway wagons).
25. For the pertinent sources: *Docs. 85–93*; also *Doc. 125*; for more information, Petzina, *Autarkiepolitik*, pp. 101f.

Plan that this was no less important than any of the other shortages in the German armaments economy.[26] The fact that only six of twenty-six production targets for products critical to the war effort had been met was due in large part to the manpower shortage.[27] The Plenipotentiary-General for Special Problems in Chemical Production, Krauch, who held what was probably the most important position in the armaments sector after the reorganization of the Four-Year Plan in the summer of 1938, complained constantly about the lack of manpower in the plants and construction sites for which he was responsible. Thus top-priority munitions plants in central Germany had a total shortage of 3,000 workers; even the 'combing-out' (*Auskämmung*) of workers from factories with important export contracts, together with the conscription of other workers under the civil conscription law (*Dienstpflichtverordnung*),[28] netted only 2,000 men. In August 1939 Krauch reported an unmet need for 13,000 construction workers, which he revised upward to 40,000 during the first week of the war. In April 1940, 4,000 positions for technical specialists and skilled workers in the chemical industry went unfilled.[29] Caution should be exercised in evaluating these reports and requests, for the government procurement authorities and big industry had learned long before the beginning of the war that by overstating their needs they were more likely to get what they actually required – that, in fact, it was necessary to exaggerate one's requirements. This does not, however, alter our historical interpretation of the situation. The shortages were real and acute. An example from the aircraft industry may help to illustrate the problem. Shortly before the outbreak of war, the Luftwaffe reported a shortage of 2,600 engineers; to the Labour Ministry this figure seemed too high, and after a careful investigation the number of vacant engineer positions was revised downwards to 1,500. By May 1940 153 engineers had been transferred to the Luftwaffe by the Ministry of Labour.[30]

---

26. Petzina, *Autarkiepolitik*, p. 102. Klein, *Preparations*, overestimates by far the ostensibly deep-seated fear of inflation on the part of the government that supposedly led to unnecessary timidity in the awarding of public contracts; see T.W. Mason, 'Some Origins of the Second World War', *Past and Present*, no. 29 (December 1964), pp. 83–7. Much more important was the hard currency situation, which steadily worsened at the end of 1937 because of the recession in the USA; cf. Göring's position: *Doc. 152*; Petzina, *Autarkiepolitik*, pp. 109–14; Bernd-Jürgen Wendt, *Appeasement 1938. Wirtschaftliche Rezession und Mitteleuropa*, Frankfurt am Main, 1966; Hans-Erich Volkmann, 'Aussenhandel und Aufrüstung in Deutschland 1933 bis 1939', in F. Forstmeier and H.-E. Volkmann (eds.), *Wirtschaft und Rüstung am Vorabend des Zweiten Weltkrieges*, Düsseldorf, 1975.

27. Petzina, *Autarkiepolitik*, p. 182.

28. Cf. below pp. 245ff.; *Docs. 110–127*.

29. Petzina, *Autarkiepolitik*, p. 131; *BA Koblenz*, R41, file 188, pp. 137–40, 146ff.; file 278, p. 127; file 189, pp. 152–60.

30. Ibid., file 25, pp. 8–80.

As is clear from the documentary sources printed in *Arbeiterklasse und Volksgemeinschaft* and elsewhere, similar conditions obtained in all sectors of the economy. In the building industry, however, they were particularly acute.[31] Because of the resultant shortages in manpower and building materials, the frantic construction work on the Siegfried Line during the second half of 1938 caused a general halt in housing construction, which in turn made it more difficult to find lodging for workers at the new manufacturing sites mandated by the Four-Year Plan and the Wehrmacht.[32] In the labour exchange district of Hanover alone, where some of the Four-Year Plan's most important projects were under construction, there was a shortage of 100,000 workers in April 1939, half of them in the building industry alone. Hitler's personal programme for the renovation of Germany's cities, which was supposed to be carried out at the same time as the building of the Siegfried Line and the construction of new factories for the production of synthetic rubber and petroleum, caused enormous strain and many conflicts of interest. Thus, for example, it was not until June 1939 that the chief city planner of Munich succeeded in getting even a third of the 30,000 construction workers he had requested (the documentary record breaks off abruptly at the point at which he lodged a personal complaint with Hitler through the Ministry of Labour).[33] The building industry also found itself in the ridiculous position of having to hire a number of additional workers away from the building materials industries at higher wages, the inevitable consequences of which were more delays in the delivery of bricks, cement and lumber to construction sites.[34] Bottlenecks often caused such chain reactions. Increasing the use of the Danube waterway, for instance, to facilitate Germany's access to Romanian oil seemed to be an urgent necessity during the winter of 1939/40 in order to relieve a critical fuel shortage; however, there were not enough shipyard workers or raw materials available for building the tugboats.[35]

Companies producing mainly for foreign markets were particularly hard hit by the manpower shortage, since the necessity of remaining competitive significantly limited their freedom of action in the area of

31. On general developments, see esp. *Docs. 96, 104, 108, 147, 150, 156*. On the building industry in particular, see *Docs. 66–84*. The address by Oberregierungsrat Luyken at the meeting of the Oberregierungspräsidenten and Regierungspräsidenten in June 1938 is particularly informative: *BA Koblenz*, R41, file 283, pp. 3–39.

32. Cf. especially *Doc. 84*.

33. *BA Koblenz*, R41, file 190, p. 28; R43II, file 1021: letter from Generalbaurat Giesler to Seldte, 2 June 1939.

34. Cf. *Doc. 151, Section 14: Doc. 108, part I*. Karl-Heinz Ludwig, *Technik und Ingenieure im Dritten Reich*, Düsseldorf, 1974, pp. 184–9, gives a very good over-view of the labour market in the building industry.

35. *BA Koblenz* R41, file 152, pp. 76–129.

wage and social policy. Unlike the armaments and construction industries, they were unable to pass on to the state the costs incurred as a result of enticing workers away from other jobs. Even though keeping the export trade afloat was an indispensable condition for rearmament,[36] the government was unable to defend successfully the interests of export firms in the labour market. Since the summer of 1938 there had been a steady rise in the number of complaints by individual industrialists about the threat that the manpower shortage and the resulting wage increases posed to exchange-yielding exports. The Economics Ministry repeatedly drew the attention of the Ministry of Labour to the problem, but the latter was unable to come up with any effective countermeasures.[37]

The reports of the Reich Trustees give the impression that the manpower shortage was not particularly severe in the iron and steel sector as a whole until the middle of 1938.[38] But this picture calls for correction, for there were special conditions in this sector. In evaluating the sources it is important to remember that there was a large and steady supply of workers entering the iron and steel industry. While manpower reserves were shrinking in agriculture and mining, employers and government officials could rely on the fact that better working conditions and higher pay throughout the iron and steel industry would guarantee an increase in the number of workers over the long term.[39] To be sure, there were also serious and regular local bottlenecks in the labour market here beginning in 1935, which caused delays in industrial expansion and in meeting delivery deadlines, but these were solved by market forces. Not until the autumn of 1938 was the point reached where the demand for metalworkers universally and consistently began to exceed supply. Thus the imbalance between supply and demand finally made itself felt in this sector of the economy. Moreover, it should be noted that, in contrast to most other branches of industry, the supply of raw materials in the metal industries remained shaky until 1938. Since production bottlenecks and short-time work became the norm, the attention of employers and government officials was to some extent diverted from the situation in the labour market and the problems were somewhat played down.[40]

36. Cf. Göring's statements: *Doc. 152.*
37. See explanatory text preceding *Doc. 118*; explanatory text preceding *Doc. 125.* The Reich Trustees give numerous examples of the difficulties experienced by export firms: *Docs. 27, 41, 47, 96, 156*; also *Doc. 151.* Correspondence between the Economics Minister and various businessmen and with the Minister of Labour: *DZA Potsdam*, RWM, file 10410. (It is somewhat misleading to speak of 'export firms' or the 'export industry', for most large companies produced for both the domestic and the foreign market.)
38. See the relevant sections of *Docs. 47, 52, 96, 104, 108.*
39. Cf. the statistics in *Stat. Anhang, Doc. 1 d.* The increase in the entire sector was approximately 30 per cent between June 1933 and June 1938.
40. Cf. above pp. 145f. and *Docs. 3, 27, 30, 33, 36.* In places the recovery and employment seemed threatened.

The importance of a third factor here is not as easy to measure. Since the advanced production methods in various branches of the iron and steel industry required that as many as 60 per cent of the workers be fully trained, the labour shortage in this sector was mainly a shortage of skilled workers. This situation became apparent at the very beginning of the economic recovery, making iron and steel an exception in this respect too, but it was largely viewed as an atypical problem and treated accordingly. Thus in the late 1930s the shortages in this sector were not new. The situation was no longer a novelty, and some steps had been taken to alleviate it.[41] In reports on the condition of the labour market, this subject did not rank among those most often discussed.[42]

It would be misleading, however, to think that the iron and steel industry was running smoothly and was firmly under state control. When in the summer of 1938 the government began to push simultaneously for the expansion of all three branches of the armed services,[43] the number of local bottlenecks increased alarmingly, for armaments were a large and constantly growing component of the iron and steel industry.[44] By August 1939 the situation had become so serious that in Berlin alone there were 25,000 unfilled jobs in this sector, and this at a time when only 55,000 of the 405,000 metalworkers in the entire labour exchange district were not already employed in the armaments industry.[45] Here as in other parts of Germany armaments firms actually had to turn down orders from the armed forces because of the lack of manpower.[46] Among these firms were such well-known companies as Rheinmetall-Borsig, which was unable to utilize all of its expanded production capacity even after hiring Austrian women and illegal Polish immigrants. Management was living more or less from hand to mouth. Just in

41. On the subject of vocational education, see above p. 142 and below pp. 232ff. Cf. also *Doc. 6*. On the deployment of labour, see *Docs. 7, 17–26*.

42. Another reason for the low-key treatment of these problems is the fact that the manpower shortage in the metal industry did not have the same kind of ripple effect as that in the building industry, where swings were usually much greater.

43. Strictly speaking, the rapid expansion of the navy did not begin until early 1939: Jost Dülffer, *Weimar, Hitler und die Marine. Reichspolitik und Flottenbau 1920–1939*, Düsseldorf, 1973, pp. 471–512.

44. Cf. *Doc. 145*. The files of the War Economy Staff contain extensive sources on these developments in the form of correspondence with the various firms and of general reports: see especially *BA/MA Freiburg*, WiIF 5, files 176, 1215; cf. also *Docs. 147, 150, 156*. It is particularly regrettable in this connection that the reports of the Reich Trustees for the period after March 1939 are missing.

45. Monthly report of the War Economy Inspector, Berlin, August 1939: *BA/MA Freiburg*, WiIF 5, file 176 (excerpt); letter of the Armaments Inspector, Berlin, to the War Economy Staff, 7 December 1939: ibid., WO 8, file 103/12.

46. There were three such cases in Berlin in May 1939, three in Dresden between May and August, one in Stuttgart in June: *BA/MA Freiburg*, WO 1–8, files 282, 283; ibid., WiIF 5, file 176.

order to keep production going, skilled workers were obliged to do the work of unskilled labourers. In such circumstances it is not surprising that production costs sky-rocketed and deadlines for delivering *matériel* to the armed forces were no longer being met.[47]

The situation in Berlin may have been especially serious, but it was far from untypical.[48] It clearly illustrates the problems that made strategic planning in this sector of the economy unreal in two important respects. First, metalworkers were supposed to be trained to take over the jobs of armaments workers drafted in the event of war. Second, it was generally recognized that provision needed to be made for adding an extra shift to the armaments industry after the beginning of hostilities. Both these plans, however, presupposed a manpower reserve that was non-existent before September 1939 and could only have been created by draconian measures.[49] In the first few weeks of the war there were replacements for only two-thirds of the conscripted armaments workers. At the same time manpower needs in the aircraft, naval shipbuilding and munitions industries increased unexpectedly, forcing the authorities to 'comb out' workers from the metal industries in order to force an optimal use of available manpower. Even as a result of this drastic move, industry was able to meet only the military's minimum requirements.[50]

Even before the beginning of the war, government authorities were unable to plan either for the long term or for emergencies. They were forced to concentrate on finding quick solutions for only the most pressing problems. On those rare occasions when the top bureaucrats took a long-term view of the crisis, they came up with barbaric and utopian solutions, for example the idea of forcibly conscripting several million women.[51] They also made the macabre suggestion of using the skills of the approximately 8,000 metalworkers who were serving time in prison, and perhaps even pardoning them.[52]

---

47. One of the company's chief clerks was an agent of the Berlin War Economy Inspector whose monthly reports described the company's problems in great detail: *BA/MA Freiburg*, WO 1–8, file 282.

48. Cf. explanatory text preceding *Doc. 151.*

49. On these plans, see below pp. 253ff. During a two-day meeeting, on 8–9 January 1940, Thomas examined in detail the consequences of not carrying out these plans: *BA/MA Freiburg*, WiIF 5, file 384.

50. Undated memorandum of the Labour Minister (end of September 1939): *BA Koblenz*, R41, file 278, p. 1. For extensive material on the 'combing out' of armaments firms: ibid., files 244, 278, 285; *BA/MA Freiburg*, WO 8, files 103/12, 106/17, 110/3.

51. Syrup, for example, on June 23, 1939: *IMGH*, vol. 333, pp. 144–60, Doc. 3787-PS. Cf. the War Economy Staff report 'Status of the Economic Situation' ('Stand der wirtschaftlichen Lage'), 1 July 1939: *BA/MA Freiburg*, WiIF 5, file 176.

52. Cf. the decree of 18 May 1938: *R.Arb.Bl. I*, p. 207. For additional correspondence on this subject: *BA/MA Freiburg*, WiIF 5, file 1215. Mention must also be made here of the reduction of the duration of apprenticeships: see below p. 234.

The authorities had to deal daily with a flood of conflicting requests. The labour exchanges were forced constantly to shift workers from one armaments plant to another, giving rise to protests on the part of the firms forced to surrender workers that they could no longer carry on production critical to the war effort. After the president of the Brandenburg district labour exchange had confirmed that a large number of construction workers had found jobs in the metal industry, he realized that he was caught in a vicious circle, for these workers were urgently needed by both industries. Some firms took radical measures to help themselves. When they failed in their efforts to get their skilled workers released early from duty in the armed forces or the Labour Service, they literally tried bribery in a desperate attempt to ensure that these workers would return to their old jobs.[53]

The Economics Minister dealt with the impending chaos in the only way he knew how, by refusing in July 1939 to accept individual firms' requests for the allocation of workers. The bureaucrats could no longer cope with the spate of requests and complaints from the private sector; government procurement agencies were instructed to review all such requests themselves; from now on ministry officials were supposed to deal only with the procurement agencies, not with the suppliers.[54] However, the assumption that the government's own contractors would handle these problems more efficiently than their private counterparts proved illusory. As early as November 1938, General Thomas of the Reich Defence Committee had to issue a warning to public authorities to be more restrained and co-operative, but to no avail. In April 1939 the army and the navy had become embroiled in a bitter dispute in Wilhelmshaven as to which of several engineers belonged to which branch of service. In this case the navy was judged to have been at fault, yet four months later the navy was charging the Ministry of Transportation with poaching its engineers.[55] One reason the various ministries and the bureaucracy were not able to deal with the problem is that they themselves suffered from severe manpower shortages. Although the number of people employed in the public sector increased rapidly after 1933, the increases could not keep pace with the enormous growth in responsibilities that resulted from the expansion of the dictatorship. By the end of the 1930s, for every category of job in the public sector – from chauffeur to secretary to technical expert – the private sec-

---

53. Monthly reports of the War Economy Inspector, Berlin, during the first half of 1939: *BA/MA Freiburg*, WO 1-8, file 282.

54. *BA/MA Freiburg*, WiIF 5, file 1215, p. 391. Starting in September 1939, the War Economy Inspectors were no longer allowed to ask companies about their manpower needs, because their answers had always been misleading: *BA Koblenz*, R41, file 278, p. 5.

55. Note by Thomas, 27 October 1938: *BA/MA Freiburg*, WiIF 5, file 560/1.

tor offered better pay. Raises came late and were minimal; vacant positions were not being filled. In 1939, after several conventional but unsuccessful attempts to contact the Minister of Labour, the Postal Minister sent him a telegramme to make him aware of the deficiencies in the telephone system, a system whose efficient operation would be critical in time of war.[56] A dictatorship founded on terror was forced to prepare for the reduction of the regular police from 170,000 to 100,000. It is unlikely, however, that Hitler's decree to this effect (18 May 1939) was ever carried out, for all such efforts to streamline the administrative apparatus by reducing staff were doomed to failure before the beginning of the war. The ministries were too overworked to spare experienced civil servants to examine the administrative structure.[57]

The effectiveness of the government's wage policy also suffered, as a result of the shortage of personnel in the offices of the Trustees of Labour after June 1938.[58] The fate of city governments in these circumstances was even worse than that of the national government. In 1940, for example, the city of Rostock no longer had enough staff to supervise the rent control laws. In Kiel productivity in the shipyards was falling because there were not enough conductors to operate the trams and the shipyard workers were forced to walk to work.[59] Over all government offices loomed the Wehrmacht with its insatiable hunger for manpower. Within a period of twelve days at the beginning of the war, 640,000 workers were conscripted just from plants deemed critical to the war effort and vital human services. In March 1940, when industry needed 500,000 workers just to fulfil urgent arms contracts, the army increased its requests for manpower by 750,000 for the next six months.[60] Even the long overworked Labour Ministry, which had the thankless task of reconciling all the conflicting and impossible demands, was not spared by the Wehrmacht. According to a tabulation of October 1938 the central office (at that time the Reichsanstalt, and after 23 December 1938 the new Department V in the Labour Ministry) was told to be ready to surrender sixty-eight career civil servants to the Wehrmacht. When the war began several heads of the regional labour exchanges were trans-

56. Correspondence from the period March to August 1939: *BA Koblenz*, R41, file 158, pp. 3–24.
57. Report of the Reich Defence Committee, 5 June 1939 on the 'Status of Reich Defence Measures' ('Stand der RV-Massnahmen'): *BA/MA Freiburg*, WiIF 5, file 560/1.
58. *Docs. 210, 212*.
59. *BA Koblenz*, R41, file 153, pp. 72, 101. Cf. *Doc. 151, part 14*; there were similar conditions in Braunschweig, starting in September 1938: *DZA Potsdam*, RWM, file 10410, pp. 191ff.
60. *BA Koblenz*, R41, file 278, p. 1. Labour Minister to the Reich Chancellery, 21 March 1940: ibid., file 144, p. 44ff. Exact listing of industry requirements in March 1940: ibid., file 285, p. 144.

ferred to the Ministry to help out.[61] However, the ratio of workload to number of personnel in the labour exchanges was still more acceptable than in the case of the Gestapo and the Security Service (*Sicherheitsdienst*), which because of the increasing number of acts of 'sabotage' had to check everyone employed in armaments plants for political reliability. Because of the shortage of personnel, however, these background checks never really got off the ground.[62]

As early as 1938 the government had to deal with a serious crisis in the agricultural sector. Although the harvest was extremely good that year, the friendly weather was heavily outweighed by the burden of the strained labour situation in agricultural production. Far more public attention was directed to the record harvest than to the reality that annual production in practically all labour-intensive areas of agriculture had declined or at best only reached the levels of the previous year. In private communications between government agencies, however, the problem was frequently mentioned. Although the government was happy to have plentiful reserves of grain for the event of war, it was very concerned about bottlenecks in the dairy industry, in the distribution of fruit and vegetables, and in the import of foodstuffs that had to be paid in hard currency.[63] Even though an epidemic of foot-and-mouth disease had contributed to the bad situation, the decline in production and the increase in imports in 1938 were mainly due to the manpower shortage. For various reasons it is difficult to find precise statistics on migration from the land during the 1930s. When the results of the labour pass survey and the occupational census were published, it was clear that the initial estimates by the Labour Ministry had been much too optimistic. Of particular significance was the migration of male farm wage-workers (i.e. not members of a farm family), whose numbers had declined from 2.5 million to 2.1 million, or by 16 per cent. This was the group that the agricultural sector could least afford to do without. The downward trend becomes even clearer when we take into account the fact that the number of people employed in agriculture had fallen by 1.4 million to 12.26 million.[64]

Neither prohibitions on leaving the farm nor propaganda campaigns proved successful. The attractiveness of industry to rural workers increased as wages in industry rose and as the price scissors between

61. *BA Koblenz*, R41, file 124, p. 52: file 23, pp. 1–10.

62. Comprehensive documention on this question: ibid., files 217–220.

63. Production statistics: *Stat. Handbuch*, pp. 124 f., 190–3, 215; imports: pp. 414ff.

64. Seldte's estimates: *Doc. 154*. The number of family assistants (*mithelfende Familienangehörigen*) rose slightly during this period, the number of self-employed fell slightly: *Stat. Handbuch*, pp. 31f.; cf. *Stat. Anhang, Doc. I d*; also Timothy W. Mason, 'Women in Germany, 1925–1940: Family, Welfare and Work' (part 2), *History Workshop Journal*, no. 2, 1976, pp. 17f.

agriculture and industry began to reopen. All the authorities concerned realized that the flight from the farm was primarily due to the difference in living standards between the city and the countryside.[65] Although there are no statistics to prove this, there can be no doubt that the differential had increased between 1936 and 1939. Following the debates of 1935,[66] the government forbade price increases on agricultural products. Reich Minister Darré failed to convince Hitler of the necessity for a modest increase in the price of milk and lard and a hefty surcharge (25 per cent) on the price of butter. With only a few exceptions (probaby the most important being artificial fertilizers), the prices of the industrial products needed by agriculture had risen sharply. Farm indebtedness was threatening to get out of hand again.[67] For all these reasons farmers were unable to offer wages and working conditions competitive with industry. Darré left nothing undone to convince the government of the seriousness of the problem. There was a steady increase in the number of detailed reports submitted to the Reich Chancellery which described farmers forced to sell their dairy cows to the butcher and farmers' wives collapsing under the weight of their work while their sons and farm hands struggled to get jobs in industry. The problem was not denied by the other ministries either. The Labour Minister himself estimated the number of unfilled jobs in agriculture in April 1938 at 250,000, but the only solution he envisaged was making it obligatory again, and harder, for farm-workers to get official approval before changing jobs (15 March 1938).[68] This coercive measure had already proved a failure in 1936.

Darré's own diagnosis of the problem was as reasonable as his solution was impractical: the number of public contracts (Darré meant armaments contracts but he was afraid to use the word) should be drastically reduced in order to cool inflation in the industrial sector and to take the pressure off the labour market, so that the number of jobs corresponded

65. Cf. here the relevant passages in the reports of the Trustees of Labour (note 31 above) and *Doc. 102*. The detailed petition of 21 January 1939 from Darré on which the following remarks are based is in *BA Koblenz*, R43II, file 213b, along with similar petitions and complaints, 27 February 1935, 2 December 1937 and 21 December 1938, as well as the memorandum of 4 April 1938 of the Minister of Labour and descriptions of conditions in the *Gau* of East Hanover (February 1939) and Hesse-Nassau (March 1939). Cf. also Darré's petitions of 9 February and 21 December 1939 to Göring: ibid., file 611. For background on agricultural policy, see Petzina, *Autarkiepolitik*, pp. 91–6; David Schoenbaum, *Die braune Revolution*, Cologne/Berlin, 1968, ch. 5; Frieda Wunderlich, *Farm Labor in Germany 1810–1945*, Princeton, NJ, 1961; J.E. Farquharson, 'The NSDAP and Agriculture in Germany 1928–1938', PhD thesis, Univ. of Kent, Canterbury, 1972.

66. See above pp. 130ff.

67. Cf. Schoenbaum, *Braune Revolution*, pp. 210f.

68. *Doc. 158, para. 8*. The directive of 1 March 1938 (*Doc.101*) was apparently also used to prevent the flight from agriculture: Friderich Syrup, *Hundert Jahre staatlicher Sozialpolitik 1839–1939*, ed. Julius Scheuble, revised Otto Neuloh, Stuttgart, 1957, p. 431. For 'solving' the problem through the use of foreign workers before September 1939, see below pp. 238f.

to the number of available workers. If price increases for industrial products were impossible, then wages and prices in industry should be reduced by at least a quarter. Significantly, Hitler found no time to discuss the problem with Darré. When the the companies building the Siegfried Line began to advertise for workers in the autumn of 1938, conditions in the Rhineland, the Palatinate and Hesse-Nassau suddenly got worse.[69] Industry was now dependent on migration from the farm, and agriculture had to wait for the arrival of hundreds of thousands of slave labourers and prisoners of war – in other words, for the war itself – in order to solve its manpower shortage.[70] After the end of the campaign in Poland, the government planned to have German school children bring in the harvest. In the end, several army divisions, fortunately not needed elsewhere on the front for those few weeks, were detailed to do the job, along with prisoners of war.[71]

The manpower shortage was thus a major factor hampering the aggressive rearmament programme envisaged in the Four-Year Plan. Many of the impasses, unsolved problems, hasty preparations and insufficient supplies that were hallmarks of the Wehrmacht's rearmament until the middle of 1940 and beyond could be traced directly to German industry's lack of manpower reserves. It is clear from the sources that this was the case; whether it had to be is another question. Furthermore, the sources confirm the impression that certain effects of over-employment had the effect of worsening the situation. These included above all the wage increases that resulted partly from improvised collective action by the workers and partly from concessions by the employers, who could find no other way to deal with the labour shortage. These developments, it should be emphasized once again, were inextricably tied to the manpower shortage that had the whole economy in its grip up to 1938. Until that year the regime had suppressed the workers as a class, neglected their interests, and sought to eradicate their traditions. The workers used all their energies to exploit the one thing the system of domination had bequeathed them: their status as a scarce commodity. Employers were baffled by the situation, as was the government. Since the armaments industry paid the highest wages, the state and the armed forces had to bear the brunt of very rapid price increases on public contracts, which curtailed the Wehrmacht's purchasing power.

69. Cf. the sources cited in note 65 above.

70. This is not entirely true, in that production in the labour-intensive sectors increased slightly in 1939 for unexplained reasons; cf. the statistics in note 63 above.

71. The Decree on the Deployment of Older School-Age Children (*Verordnung über den Einsatz der älteren Schuljugend*), 22 September 1939 was printed in the *RGBl.* (I, p. 1867), but because of objections by Schirach it was never enforced: *BA Koblenz*, R43II, vol. 652; see also *Docs. 218, 221 (note 2), 225*. If France had been invaded immediately, it would have been impossible to use soldiers.

Between December 1935, when regular wage surveys were begun, and June 1939 gross average *hourly* earnings in industry increased by 10.9 per cent; the increases in the capital-goods sector (11.3 per cent) and among skilled and semi-skilled workers (11.7 per cent) were somewhat higher; for all other workers they were somewhat lower. Part of the increase in earnings was due to longer hours, because overtime was added to regular wages in calculating average hourly earnings. This becomes clearer when we consider *weekly* earnings. The rise in weekly earnings during the same period averaged 17.4 per cent; significantly, it was higher in the consumer industries than in the capital goods sector (20.7 per cent vs 16.8 per cent).[72] On average, a German working-man received RM 5.80 more per week in 1939 than in 1936, a working woman RM 2.50 more.[73] This factor alone boosted the consumer spending power of the working population (except for the self-employed) by approximately RM 85 million per week, which jumped by an additional RM 115–20 million per week as a result of the steady increase in the number of employed.

The more stringent price controls under the Four-Year Plan were most successful where they most directly affected the daily lives of workers, especially in food prices. Unfortunately, the unreliability of the statistical sources precludes any detailed or thorough examination of this problem for the period under study. The official government figure of 1.4 per cent for the rise in the cost of living between 1936 and 1939 is clearly misleading, though less so than the corresponding figures for 1933 to 1936.[74] In the light of the large number of impressionistic reports on this subject that supplement the statistical data,[75] it seems correct to assume that the price increases for textiles were greater than those cited in the official index and that after 1936 rents and food prices were tending to rise. We may estimate the actual increase in the cost of living from 1936 to 1939 at approximately 4 per cent. Taking the similarly adjusted figures for the preceding years, we can conclude that the base figure for the cost of living index at the beginning of the war was around 113/114, or about 10 per cent higher than that given by the government. More important in the present context is the fact that these numbers were still a good 12 per cent below the levels of 1929.[76]

72. Gerhard Bry, *Wages in Germany 1871–1945*, Princeton, NJ, 1960, p. 242; cf. *Stat. Anhang, Doc. IIb*. The extremely low wage level in 1935 played a crucial role in the development of the consumer goods industries: see above pp. 134f.

73. *Stat. Handbuch*, p. 469.

74. Cf. Bry, *Wages*, p. 264. Bry's adjustment of these numbers is questionable: see above p. 133.

75. See, for example, *Docs. 156 part 2, 159*.

76. Cf. above pp. 128ff.; Bry, *Wages*, pp. 264, 426f.

According to Bry's calculations, which probably somewhat understate the wage increases of the 1930s, average nominal weekly earnings in German industry in 1939 were likewise 12 per cent below 1929 levels.[77]

This problem can be approached from a different angle. Despite the decline in prices, total consumer spending (within the German borders of 1937) was almost as high in 1938 as in the year before the beginning of the Depression.[78] Of course, we have to take into account the fact that the population had increased by 3.8 million (nearly 6 per cent), so that consumer spending was spread over a larger number of people. But even so, the demographic change did not alter the fact of the real growth in prosperity.[79]

These aggregate figures, of course, conceal a multitude of different trends. First, almost all segments of the middle class shared in this unprecedented prosperity.[80] The radical variations up to 1936 in workers' standards of living in different occupations became less pronounced during the years immediately before the outbreak of war, but they were not reversed: the real weekly earnings of many men and women employed in the consumer-goods sector in 1939 were probably below the levels of 1929.[81] However, in all branches of the iron and steel industry, in building, mining and in several smaller branches of industry, average weekly real earnings had risen sharply, and before the beginning of the war had considerably outstripped the previous highest levels; the lengthening of working hours by three to four hours per week was, of course, a significant contributing factor.[82] The regime's propaganda, which boasted of the unparalleled prosperity, especially with regard to the working class, clearly presented a distorted picture of the facts.[83] Nevertheless, the majority of Germans, including most industrial workers, were no worse off in material terms in 1939 than they had been at the end of 1920s.

77. Ibid., p. 239. Bry cites the results of the official compilations as annual averages, and thus includes the September wage cuts in the figures for 1939. Additional sources of error are: (a) the weekly earnings figures for the building industry, which could only be estimated and not determined precisely (the estimate was very likely too low); (b) the large number of bonuses and premiums of all kinds, which were largely ignored in the wage statistics; cf. the 8 January 1939 report by Trustee of Labour Wiesel to Thomas: *BA/MA Freiburg*, WiIF 5, file 1223. Also, *Stat. Anhang, Docs. IIb, IIc, IId.*

78. It definitely increased in 1939, but because of the territorial acquisitions in 1938 and 1939, it is impossible to calculate the increase precisely.

79. Carroll, *Design*, p. 186; *Stat. Handbuch*, p. 18. We must also point out here the huge increase in savings deposited in the savings banks: ibid., p. 517.

80. This is perfectly clear from the following analysis of sales statistics.

81. On wage differentials by industry 1936–9, see Bry,*Wages*, p. 250f.

82. Cf. *Doc. 132*; see also below pp. 239f.

83. Thus, e. g., *Wirtschaft und Statistik*, 1940, p. 433, claimed that average weekly real earnings in 1939 were 6 per cent higher than in 1929.

The historian's assessment of this state of affairs is much more dependent on his frame of reference than is normally the case. Three different perspectives come to mind immediately. The absolute numbers above, which describe actual levels of earnings and consumption, can only tell us so much. We must also take account of relative values, and according to that measure, there was a precipitous drop in wage rates and consumer spending as a percentage of GNP.[84] Finally, it is necessary to put the level of earnings and consumption in the context of the regime's political and military objectives. The improvement in the standard of living was miniscule when compared to the increase in GNP, the growth of which was increasingly driven by the rise in capital investments and armaments expenditures. Given the state of the labour market, free and independent trade unions would surely have been able to obtain even greater wage increases. Thus the Nazi regime clearly succeeded in raising the level of economic exploitation to a point where there was nothing elsewhere with which to compare it in the 1930s.[85] However, that was small comfort to the Nazi government prior to the beginning of the war, for it was becoming increasingly obvious in the years 1937–9 that the curbing of consumption that had been achieved so far was not sufficient to ensure the realization of the strategically important armaments programme. The growth in real wages led ineluctably to a demand for consumer goods that increasingly threatened to hamper rearmament: 'We shall never defeat England with radio sets, vacuum cleaners and cooking utensils', General Thomas pointed out bitterly to the country's leading industrialists in November 1939.[86]

Analysing the statistics on consumer expenditure in the 1930s and comparing them to the armaments programme, we can easily see the reasons for Thomas's unease. The per-capita consumption of foodstuffs and luxury food items in 1938/9 was almost without exception higher than in 1930.[87] Only in the consumption of poultry, eggs, milk, margarine, citrus fruits and beer were the levels of 1930 not quite equalled. Consumption of tobacco and alcohol (wines and spirits) had risen sharply. The impression of a burgeoning consumer economy is bolstered by the data on sales. In virtually every branch of the retail and

84. Petzina, *Autarkiepolitik*, p. 167; Erbe, *Wirtschaftspolitik*, p. 101.

85. There is no basis for comparison with the Soviet economy of the 1930s. Cf. the brilliant introduction by Alec Nove, *An Economic History of the USSR*, London, 1969.

86. Thomas, *Geschichte*, p. 501. He could just as well have said 'France' as 'England'.

87. *Stat. Jahrbuch* 1939/40, pp. 398–401; *Stat. Handbuch*, pp. 488f. 1929 would have been a better year for comparison, but the corresponding figures are unavailable: *Stat. Jahrbuch*, 1931, pp. 319–24. Comparison is also complicated by the fact that the methods for calculating the figures were changed slightly in 1937, thereby producing somewhat higher numbers: *Vierteljahreshefte zur Statistik des deutschen Reiches*, 1937, no. 1; 1938, no. 4.

wholesale trade, sales in 1938/9 were considerably above 1929/30 levels. The overall average in retail sales was somewhat lower due to the shortage of dairy products and the price freeze on foodstuffs, but businesses that sold household goods, confectionery, shoes, stationery and business machines had a significantly higher turnover than before the Depression. Conditions in the wholesale trade (consumer co-operatives) were similar. The restaurant business, in particular, prospered greatly after 1937. Goods with an elastic demand enjoyed sharply rising sales in the years preceding the war. Overall the total taxable sales of German business had outstripped the previous highest levels as early as 1937 and continued to rise until the beginning of the war.[88]

From the point of view of the armed forces and industry this was an unwelcome burden on the already low reserves of foreign currency, which were urgently needed to pay for imports of strategic raw materials. Although neither the volume nor the value of food imports reached 1928/9 levels, the upward tendency after 1935 was unmistakable. The actual value of these imports (in current prices) was somewhere around RM 1.44 billion in 1935, rising to RM 2.39 billion by 1938. As a percentage of total imports, foods increased from 34.5 per cent to 39.5 per cent during the same period. Among them were such semi-luxuries as leaf tobacco, coffee and cocoa; in 1938/39 these items were considerably above Depression levels both in terms of absolute quantities and as a proportion of total imports.[89] The import programmes of industry were better positioned to meet the needs of the armaments programme. Yet in 1938 clothing still constituted 30 per cent of total imported industrial goods, and the proportion was declining slowly, since the rising standard of living had not yet made the new synthetics an attractive alternative. Imports of wool, yarn and woollen goods started to increase again between 1936 and 1938. In general, the list of imported manufactured goods for the years 1938 and 1939 contained a considerable proportion of luxury items and consumer goods.[90]

The consumer industries competed with the military not only for foreign currency, but for manpower as well. The rising standard of living

88. The different statistical methods as well as uncertainty about changes in retail prices make it difficult to use these figures as evidence for the standard of living. We are more concerned here with the turnover of goods, i.e., with the 'overburdening' of reserves and capacities as a result of consumer goods production. Erbe, *Wirtschaftspolitik*, pp. 93ff., comes to similar conclusions. Statistical tables: *Stat. Jahrbuch*, 1934, pp. 332–5: 1936, pp. 361f.; 1939/40, pp. 402–13; *Stat. Handbuch*, pp. 576f. Because of the lower price levels in 1938–9 the number of sales was considerably higher than the value of goods sold as compared to 1928–30; in order to study this in greater detail, we would need complete production statistics, which the *Stat. Handbuch*, ch. 5c, only has for certain selected items.

89. *Stat. Handbuch*, pp. 395, 402.

90. Statistics: ibid., pp. 395, 404, 405, 408. 'Clothing needs' = raw materials, semi-fin-

was a stimulus to many branches of the consumer sector. We have already mentioned the above-average increases in weekly earnings. Although increased consumer demand did not begin to compensate for the gap between the military and the consumer industries, it did result in the extension of hours in the consumer sector, setting limits to the armaments industry's ability to attract workers. Although the results of the occupational census of June 1933 are not completely comparable to the labour-pass survey of June 1938, a juxtaposition of the two sets of data provides us with a reliable picture of occupational changes among workers. While the machine-building and construction industries and public administration were attracting large numbers of workers, agriculture and the foodstuffs and luxury-food industries were losing a substantial number of employees (500,000 and 250,000 respectively). By contrast, mining, the texile and clothing industries, the toy and wood industries, commerce and transportation and the hotel industry lost only in the tens of thousands of workers.[91] Thus the armaments sector with its endemic labour shortages stood in stark contrast to a consumer goods industry with a surprisingly stable proportion of available manpower. By 1938 manpower shortages had become so widespread that they were having an adverse effect in textiles, as well as in the building and chemical industries. In 1938, therefore, workers in textiles were themselves able to make demands, something which had been common in heavy industry since the autumn of 1936. Even occupations that had no particular tradition of trade-union militancy, such as barbers and salespersons, were asserting their right to demand changes in social policy. A large, spontaneous movement to demand earlier shop closings on Saturday was causing major headaches for shop-owners, the Labour Front and the government.[92] Even though young people leaving school preferred jobs in the booming armaments sector, the situation of employees in the consumer-goods industries had become much more tolerable as a result of increased earnings and more freedom in the factory, for they too had become irreplaceable.[93] To put it in the simplest terms, the armaments industry was getting its additional workers from agriculture – the sector that could least afford to spare them. Although its share of the labour market had shrunk between 1930 and 1936, the consumer-goods industry was still able to hold onto that share from 1936 to 1939.

91. *Stat. Jahrbuch*, 1939/40, p. 379; details in: *Stat. Anhang, Doc. Id.*

92. See *Doc. 108, no. 7.* Starting in the autumn of 1937, the campaign to close shops dragged on for over two years. Initially the DAF supported the demand, but was forced to change its line bcause of a Labour Ministry directive; some shop-owners used the reform to recruit workers: *DZA Potsdam*, RWM, files 10280, 10352, 10353.

93. Choice of an occupation: *Stat. Jahrbuch*, 1936, p. 361; 'Tenth Report of the Reichsanstalt', Supplement to the *R.Arb.Bl.*, 1939, I, p. 25. There were still isolated instances in 1938 of what could be termed brutal exploitation, e.g., in the textile industry: *Doc. 180, no. 5.*

The nature of the armaments boom affected another aspect of the economic preparations for war. The burdens placed on the economic reserves and capacity that were mobilized at the beginning of the war, happened so quickly and so drastically that there was practically no chance to adapt the economic structure to carry out its existing and impending tasks. Except for the rationing of raw materials in the iron and steel industry, which had a negative effect on small businesses and the handicrafts industry, economic conditions after 1936 were so favourable that all manner of business and production methods continued to be practised without any thought to the future. True, there was a significant process of concentration: the number of businesses with over 200 employees doubled between 1933 and 1939 and – even more remarkable – large-scale enterprises had twice as many workers in 1939 as they had had in 1933 (5.4 million). In some sectors the very smallest businesses had problems keeping their key employees and getting credit in 1938. Yet in 1939 there were as many workers in businesses with fewer than eleven employees as there had been in 1933 (3.7 million). Those employing between eleven and fifty workers burgeoned in the 1930s, increasing their total number of employees from 1.28 million to 2.05 milllion. This development was as marked in strategic war industries as in other branches. In May 1939 more than a quarter of all workers were employed in very small businesses (fewer than eleven employees); for the iron and steel sector and the clothing industry, the proportion was more than one-third. The number of artisanal workshops had slowly been declining, but despite the state's effort to shut them down, there were as many at the beginning of the war as there had been before the Depression. The situation in the retail trade was similar – a barely perceptible decline in the number of businesses and employees. The available statistics do not allow us to draw any definitive conclusions, but it is clear that in May 1939 some 30 per cent of all permanently employed persons (including the self-employed) had jobs in the service sector, in the retail trade or in small businesses with fewer than six employees. Their activities were at best only indirectly of benefit to the rearmament programme. These kinds of businesses had mushroomed during the Depression years, since they were the only possibility of survival for broad sections of the population; in 1939 they still had not fallen victim to the scientific management methods that were a necessary concomitant of the boom in the armaments sector.

To be sure, the very smallest businesses had come under increasing economic and government pressure since 1938/9. But changes were not likely to happen quickly, since these enterprises owed their existence not only to the rugged individualism of their owners, but also to the boom conditions created by the armaments programme. There was a genuine demand for their goods and services. In the conditions of 1939 this example of the working of the laws of supply and demand set limits to any further increases in strategic goods production.[94]

Thus in the twelve months before the beginning of the war, the structure of the German economy was very peculiar: its war industries were extremely productive yet unequal to the probable demands of a strategy of aggressive expansion. The economic recovery between 1933 and 1936 rested on the massive exploitation of the Depression and of its effects on the labour market and on the German people's standard of living. Yet by reversing this favourable starting position, the armaments-led boom in the economy had created a civilian sector that diverted enough manpower, raw materials and purchasing power to produce the signs of a real crisis in the summer of 1938. The armaments industry had doubtless set the pace in this process, and in the summer of 1938 it was simply unable to find the economic resources to meet its needs. This predicament was due to the increase in demand after the annexation of Austria (armaments expenditures: 1937, 13 per cent of GNP; 1938, 17 per cent of GNP) and to the fact that for the first time there were simply no more extra reserves and virtually no more unemployed persons. The armaments sector had for quite some time been at a point where increased capacity could only be achieved at the expense of other branches of the economy – branches that had themselves profited from the armaments-led boom. It was high time for a planned redistribution of resources to replace an economic policy that had been basically interested in maximizing productivity in all sectors simultaneously. The alternative was territorial expansion, which meant solving the problem at the expense of other countries and peoples.

To describe the paradoxical situation of the German economy from 1938 to 1941, it has been variously called a 'war economy in peacetime' and a 'peace economy in wartime'. Since these descriptions imply a planned transition, I prefer another label: it was both a war and a peace economy. Government, armed forces and heavy industry let the rest of the nation carry on a desperate struggle over the distribution of the national product. The system as a whole had never been able to come down clearly in favour of either a war or a peace economy. In other words, it wanted to have its cake and eat it too. These inconsistencies also help to explain the frenzied tone of the debates on these questions. Behind the tidy-looking decisions on individual issues loomed the major unresolved political questions.

---

94. On the state's efforts to divert manpower from this sector to the armaments industry, see below p. 234. In the building industry there were almost 235,000 construction sites, but just 1,300 firms employing more than 200 workers each. Statistics from *Stat. Jahrbuch*, 1936, pp. 128f.; 1939/40, p. 379; *Stat. Handbuch*, pp. 238–43. Supplementary statistics in Schoenbaum, *Braune Revolution*, pp. 173f., 185.

6.2. The Regime's Reaction to the Impending Crisis

The government's social and economic policy responses to the crisis situation described above were wholly reactive and unplanned, as were those of industry and the DAF. This is all the more remarkable when we consider that the basic outlines of the crisis were clearly visible early on. By September 1936 at the latest it must have been evident that the growth rate in the armaments sector would inevitably lead to bottlenecks throughout the economy. It was easy enough to calculate, and the first warning signs were there for anybody to read.[95] There was no lack of Cassandras. As early as the end of 1934 the signs of the coming crisis were noted and discussed in some detail at a conference of state secretaries; in January 1937 the Institute for Research on the Economy (Institut für Konjunkturforschung) published a statistical forecast that warned of the dangers of full employment; and the government departments most directly affected by the crisis – the Ministry of Labour, the Ministry of Food and Agriculture, and the Reich Price Commissar – reported their own particular concerns about developments to the appropriate authorities.[96] However, compared to the dimensions of the problem these voices were neither very numerous nor especially strong, and they tended to emphasize only specific issues. So soon after the end of the Depression, over-employment was not exactly considered a major cause for concern or government planning. On the contrary, until the spring of 1936 attention was centred on the unemployment statistics, and the actions of the various ministries were understandably conditioned by their experiences with the crisis just ending. On the other hand, until the end of 1936 and the beginning of 1937 there was good reason to fear that the recovery would not last.[97] However, with time this fear gave way to another, namely that an accurate diagnosis of Germany's economic potential would reveal the insanity of the Nazi drive for imperial expansion. Thus, discussions of economic and social policy in 1937/8 were conducted in cautious, self-deluding language. No one mentioned the compelling reasons for slowing down the preparations for war; instead they talked about such things as the need to control government contracts or the advisability of accommodating total

95. Cf. *Doc. 3*; see above pp. 136–43, 150.
96. Meeting of 6 December 1934: *BA Koblenz*, R43II, file 376. *Vierteljahreshefte für Konjunkturforschung*, part A, vol. 11, no. 3, pp. 274–97. Revision of these figures by the Reich Chamber of the Economy in April 1938: *BA Koblenz*, R43II, file 311; cf. also *Docs. 2, 27, 35, 128*, as well as the references in note 65 above. Thomas also had no illusions about the limits of the economy's reserves.
97. Cf. *Doc. 3 (Note 26)*.

economic activity to available manpower or to the threat of inflation, and so on.[98]

Concern over inflation was indeed well-founded, for the main characteristic of the Four-Year Plan was the total neglect of the input side without which economic planning is barely distinguishable from wishful thinking. True, the amount of available capacity was carefully calculated, and to some extent estimates were made of the need for raw materials and strategically vital products. However, there was no systematic examination of whether there were enough reserves of manpower, money and hard currency to meet the demands. The question of whether the various military aims were compatible with one another or how they could be reconciled with the needs of the civilian sector was never asked.[99] These omissions cannot simply be explained away as the result of a poor understanding of economics. Even Göring, who boasted publicly of his incompetence in this area, was well aware that the crucial weakness of the Four-Year Plan was its failure to determine and to allocate available resources.[100] But this was above all a question of politics rather than economics. After November 1937 (the date of the so-called Hossbach Conference), any meticulous economic calculations would have been branded as defeatism. This is not, however, the only reason why the plan's targets for 1936 were not met, nor why they were fundamentally revised in 1938; the policy of aggressive expansion during this period necessitated constant short-term shifts in the economy, making systematic control virtually impossible. Even if Hitler had achieved his unrealistic goals with respect to the timing and strategic preparations for the beginning of the European war ('peace' until 1942/3), his plans were doomed to fail because of the general economic and political conditions of the Nazi dictatorship.

To be sure, this is an opinion based on a hypothetical scenario, and cannot be proven beyond a doubt. But the events and problems during the eighteen months preceding the outbreak of war make it difficult to draw any other conclusion than that the regime had over-extended itself as a result of the crisis. Under the pressures of both a potential and then an actual war, the regime was incapable of making fundamental changes in its economic and social policy. Its policies in this area were piece-

---

98. Cf. above p. 195; *Docs. 2, 14, 16, 35, 40, 49, 94, 105, 107, 128, 131.* Schacht was an exception in this respect; he cited the danger of inflation caused by armaments expenditures as the reason for his resignation.

99. Petzina, *Autarkiepolitik*, pp. 90f.; he probably attaches too little importance to this feature of the planning process.

100. Göring's address at the annual meeting of the DAF in Nuremberg, September 1938 (*Der Parteitag Grossdeutschlands*, Munich, 1939, pp. 251f.) and his speech shortly afterwards to the Reich Defence Council: *Doc. 158.*

meal, timid and very inconsistent. It could not make the decisive break-through in the armaments sector or curb the rising standard of living.[101] In light of these facts, Hitler's optimal strategy of beginning the war after 1942 was utterly unrealistic from the point of view of domestic social policy; it is simply inconceivable that the measures that were required to carry out the plans and meet the armed forces' needs in the period 1938 to 1941 could have been implemented without the pretext provided by the pressures of war. The level of armament which Hitler's plan presupposed could not have been achieved – partly because of Germany's insufficient economic reserves, but mainly because the government never succeeded in carrying out the necessary redistribution of the national product. The ability to continue the policy of operating a simultaneous 'war-and-peace economy' during the period 1939–41 presupposed not only the continuation of the 'phony war', but also the seizure of slave labourers, war *matériel* and raw materials from occupied territories, and the resumption of broad-based trade relations with the Soviet Union after the signing of the Non-Aggression Pact.[102] Without these additional reserves, there would have been serious economic bottlenecks or political disturbances. Then draconian measures would have been needed to depress real wages and redistribute available manpower; otherwise the labour-intensive industries in the agricultural sector would have quickly broken down and entire branches of industry – not just individual firms – would have had to turn down armaments contracts. These kinds of draconian measures in their turn would have encountered the silent, bitter and very effective resistance of the workers, such as had happened in October and November 1939 in spite of the war. (We shall return to the forms and circumstances of this passive resistance in the last section of this chapter.)

In brief, this was the predicament of the Nazi leadership, and we shall illuminate the particular causes of this situation. Unfortunately it is not possible within the framework of this study to discuss in detail what were described above as the objective limits of Germany's economic resources. This assumes a background in economics and technology that the author does not possess, as well as preliminary studies on industrial management, production methods, trade and fiscal policy that have not yet been undertaken. But this much is certain: the objective obstacles to pressing ahead

101. These subjects are documented in detail in *Docs. 110–43, 174–244*. It would repay studying in depth the regime's tax and finance policy from this perspective. On consumption and the standard of living in 1940/41: Milward, *Kriegswirtschaft*, pp. 31ff.

102. Cf. Hillgruber, *Strategie*, p. 257, note; Alan S. Milward, *The New Order and the French Economy*, Oxford, 1970, chs. 2–4; Ferdinand Friedensburg, 'Die sowjetischen Kriegslieferungen an das Hitlerreich', *Vierteljahreshefte für Wirtschaftsforschung*, 1962, no. 4, p. 331; Carroll, *Design*, p. 199; Thomas, *Geschichte*, pp. 228ff.; Eva Seeber, *Zwangsarbeiter in der faschistischen Kriegswirtschaft*, East Berlin, 1964.

with the military build-up were considerable – obstacles which Hitler himself referred to repeatedly and used as a rationale for his blitzkrieg strategy. Small conquests would have to create the economic foundations for major conquests. Hitler was doubtless thinking of Germany's limited reserves of food and raw materials and their inhibitory effect on the production of critical war *matériel*, which was heightened as a result of the decline in world trade between 1930 and 1936.[103] A variety of means were used to deal with this critical and pressing problem: currency controls, which under Schacht quickly degenerated into state control of all foreign trade; subsidies for exports; bilateral 'barter agreements'; and finally the Four-Year Plan's expansion of facilities for the production of synthetic raw materials. However, there were no quick fixes; the situation continued to be critical, because rearmament was automatically pushing the demand for imported raw materials and goods to the limits of the country's foreign currency reserves. Only an unexpected upturn in world trade in 1937, which increased German imports by 30 per cent and its exports by 25 per cent, made it possible to accelerate the rearmament programme under the Four-Year Plan. The very sober economic forecast of 1937 had not predicted this recovery in international trade and therefore painted an even gloomier picture of the future. The upturn was short-lived, however; the American recession at the end of 1937 hindered German exports, and following the laws of economics, the subsequent international boom in armaments led to an increase in the price of Germany's imports.

After the spring of 1938 the situation had once again become critical.[104] Thus there was very little room for manoeuvre in trade and raw materials policies. However, this was only one side of the problem; the distribution of foreign currency and raw material reserves to the various sectors of the economy was even less efficient and less conducive to rearmament than trade policy itself. When Göring assumed responsibility for this area in the spring of 1936, virtually no priorities had been set. Decisions were made on the basis of the political and economic power struggles in which the military almost almost always came out the winner but was still unable to push through its demands. In the beginning, planning techniques were extremely crude, especially in the rationing of raw materials.[105] Most crucial was the fact that the shortages as well as

103. This element in Hitler's thinking is stressed by Carroll, *Design*, pp. 101–6. Cf. also Milward, *Kriegswirtschaft*, ch. 1.

104. Cf. Petzina, *Autarkiepolitik*, pp. 30–6, 40–8, 109–14, who, however, does not sufficiently stress the gradual transition to plunder, beginning with the annexation of Austria, as an alternative to trade. See Volkmann, 'Aussenhandel', in Forstmeier and Volkmann (eds.), *Wirtschaft und Rüstung*, pp. 106ff.

105. Cf. the analysis of the allocation of iron and steel by Johann Sebastian Geer, *Der Markt der geschlossenen Nachfrage*, Berlin, 1961. For general information on this question: Carroll, *Design*, p. 172, note 27, pp. 193–203; Petzina, *Autarkiepolitik*, pp. 153–8.

the number of urgent economic tasks had become so enormous that, as Göring admitted publicly in November 1938, prioritization was a virtual impossibility. As always, the most important principle of order in these circumstances was struggle: the 'struggle among all who needed manpower, raw materials, and money' (Keitel).[106] After 1936 there was a move towards a centralized economy, but up to the beginning of the war and beyond, it did not eliminate the competition for the scarce factors of production that was characteristic of a market economy. It should not surprise us that investment in the consumer-goods sector in 1938–9 – at a time when there was a lack of capital, building materials and workers for the munitions plants – surpassed the previous highest level. Hitler's continuing plans for renovating the cities were a more egregious though economically less obvious example, depriving the war economy of valuable iron and lumber and diverting these commodities for use in the tourist and entertainment industries. Privately owned vehicles were consuming more and more petroleum and rubber, both of which were urgently needed by the armed forces. But both Hitler and Funk refused to curtail private transportation, since they felt that would have been 'intolerable domestically'.[107]

There is almost no end to the number of these examples. The magnitude of the reserves wasted in this way alone – reserves that could have been of immediate use to the armaments industry – cannot be expressed in terms of numbers. It is impossible even to estimate the indirect effects of tighter armaments-related rationing. However, one conclusion is obvious: as strained as German trade and currency policy was, there was still a considerable margin of free reserves that could have been channelled to the armed forces. Otherwise there was no other area of economic policy in which the Third Reich had reached the limits of its capacities and reserves before the onset of war. A few senior officials sometimes acted as if this were so in the area of public finance. A 'shortage of capital' did indeed lead to some delays in the Four-Year Plan's investment projects; this was the reason a reduction was ordered in the armed forces' budget, although it was never carried out.[108] But these dif-

106. Göring: *Doc. 152*. Keitel before the Reich Defence Committee, 15 December 1938: *BA/MA Freiburg*, WiIF 5, file 560/2. Even a year later Thomas considered the statement à propos: Carroll, *Design*, pp. 210f.

107. Petzina, *Autarkiepolitik*, pp. 185f. Numerous sources on the subject of the renovation of the cities, for example, on the building of a gigantic hotel in Danzig, May 1941: *BA Koblenz*, R43II, file 1015; on the start of the prgram in 1936/7, including the rebuilding of the Schiller Theatre in Berlin: ibid., file 355. Cf. also *Doc. 151 part 8*. Thomas's statements at a meeting of the War Economy Inspectorate (W-In.) on 21 August 1939 regarding private transportation: *BA/MA Freiburg*, WiIF 5, file 384.

108. Klein, *Preparations*, pp. 24ff., however, greatly exaggerates the importance of this factor. Documents on the ministries' discussions of finance policy from January to May 1939: *BA/MA Freiburg*, WiIF 5, file 420/3

ficulties resulted more from a total misunderstanding of the problems involved in financing a war, compounded by the fact that no one considered the possibility of a hefty increase in taxes.[109] So far as the working population was concerned, its limits, as will be shown, had nowhere near been reached.

The aim of the final part of this study, therefore, will not be to examine these suggested weaknesses in Germany's economic and strategic situation between 1937 and 1939, but to investigate the origins and nature of the domestic constellation of forces and of government policies, both of which seriously exacerbated those weaknesses. We will be concerned primarily with the political aspect of class relations, in other words with the relationship between the regime and the working class. The imperative to ration all resources systematically was bound to be accomplished mainly at the expense of the workers. Extended hours of work, reductions in living standards, intensified labour discipline, workers' willingness to accept hardships such as separation from their families or the obligation to stay in a particular job: these were the preconditions for a successful acceleration of the pace of war preparations. The power of industry to dispose freely over its capacities, workers and markets ought also to have been curtailed. The extant documentary sources do not indicate that strict economic planning would have encountered significant resistance on the part of employers. By the time of the establishment of the Hermann Göring Works at the latest, industry was tied, for better or for worse, to the Nazi regime. Nor did it seem to mind the relationship.[110]

On the other hand, relations between the regime and the workers were extremely strained. The degree and effect of these tensions are clearly reflected in the changes in the German Labour Front's responsibilities after the achievement of full employment. Even before this point it had seemed very doubtful whether the DAF would be able to carry out its task of political indoctrination. In the mid-1930s the attitude of industrial workers was characterized by anxiety, resignation and bitter-

109. The only notable tax increases during the 1930s were the tax on additional income in the New Finance Plan of 20 March 1939 (*RGBl. I*, p. 561), the new military service exemption tax of 20 July 1937 (*RGBl.* I, p. 821), and the increase in corporation tax from 25 per cent to 40 per cent. They had no effect on dampening purchasing power. The great difficulties caused by these questions are clearly reflected in *Docs. 160–73*.

110. On this see Dietrich Eichholtz, *Geschichte der deutschen Kriegswirtschaft 1939–1945*, vol. 1, 2nd edn, East Berlin, 1971; T. W. Mason, 'The Primacy of Politics', in S. J. Woolf (ed.), *The Nature of Fascism*, London, 1968, originally published in *Das Argument*, no. 41 and critiqued in no. 47 by Eberhard Czichon, Dietrich Eichholtz and Kurt Gossweiler. Louis P. Lochner, *Die Mächtigen und der Tyrann*, Darmstadt, 1955, cites some examples of uneasiness in heavy industry in 1940 (pp. 221ff.). The logical conclusion to draw from these doubts about the sufficiency of the economic reserves was to plan more carefully, something which was actually called for by groups in industry, for example, in talks with Thomas during the first weeks of the war: *BA/MA Freiburg*, WiIF 5, file 412.

ness and then, as a result of the economic recovery, by apathy and an indifference to politics as well. Only the person of Hitler and occasional gestures in the direction of national self-assertion seemed to meet with the approval of the workers. The DAF itself was viewed mostly with scepticism. Active Communist and Social Democratic resistance began to subside only after the Gestapo had perfected its methods of surveillance and record-keeping and the number of annual arrests rose to 15,000 (1936).[111] The DAF collaborated reluctantly with the police, because every act of resistance in the factory on the part of the working class merely served to confirm its own political shortcomings. The only thing important to the Third Reich and its various organizations was success – swift, conspicuous success. After 1936 the DAF no longer had any hopes for success in the area of popular indoctrination. The old slogans about community spirit and the dignity of work were repeated endlessly in the constantly growing number of DAF publications; in addition, some new slogans were invented and new 'campaigns' initiated.[112] But aside from a virtually unquantifiable effect of wearing down workers through the continuous and noisy repetition of slogans, the costly propaganda campaigns were a flop. There was hardly anything new to say and little prospect of noticeably changing workers' opinions.

The shift to full employment, however, proved beneficial to this huge organization with its impossible tasks, disembarrassing it of the burden of having to come up with a well-formulated practical programme. The new conditions in the labour market after 1936 enabled workers to set some of the conditions of their own political subjugation. Since the DAF was responsible for securing that subjugation, it assimilated a good deal of the working class's demands, at minimum its demand for a share in the growing prosperity. However, this inevitably led to an increase in the number and intensity of conflicts between the DAF and those authorities and interest groups opposed to any wage increases, paid holidays, the expansion of factory welfare facilities, and so on. Industrial conflicts offered the DAF the possibility of achieving two concrete successes: triumphing over the bureaucracy and industry by achieving the implementation of its policies; and winning the loyalty of the working class by wresting certain limited material concessions from employers and the government. Thus the transition from an unemployment crisis to a manpower shortage enabled the DAF for the first time to develop a

111. *IML/ZPA*, St. 3, vol. 106, St. 3, file 106, pp. 143f. Cf. Walter Ulbricht *et al.*, *Geschichte der deutschen Arbeiterbewegung,* East Berlin, 1966, vol. 5, p. 142.

112. For example, the Reich 'Appeal to Industry', when a radio address by Ley would be piped into all the factories in a particular branch of industry – during working hours. Employers and the Economics Ministry had some success in opposing these appeals: *DZA Potsdam*, RWM, file 10312, pp. 146–76, 217f.

programme that appeared both practical and practicable, because it now had hard facts – the laws of supply and demand – on its side. It hardly needs to be emphasized that that the programme was never articulated in this way, and neither did Ley and his cohorts ever seek to advertise their social policy as a contribution to the fulfilment of the regime's expansionist goals.[113] They had not become covert trade unionists; rather they swam with the tide of socio-economic change, for taking the course of least resistance seemed to promise a surer prospect of enhancing their own power and influence. If the DAF had actually opted for a policy of material sacrifice, of 'blood, sweat, toil, and tears', the employers, the bureaucracy and the military would surely have supported its efforts to limit consumption, but then it would quickly have lost its usefulness to the regime as a mass organization. Given the continuing concern of those in power to legitimize their rule, the passive aggressiveness of the working class proved strong enough to have made this a moot point from the outset. The workers' favour had to be courted in *la plébiscite de tous le jours*.

The announcement of the Four-Year Plan in September 1936 offered an opportunity to tighten up social policy in order to press ahead with the military build-up. Indeed, the real aim of the Four-Year Plan – preparing industry and the armed forces for war within four years – virtually demanded changes in social policy. This was clearly underlined in the various ministries' initial drafts of measures required to fulfil the Plan.[114] The content and organization of the Plan were still open; it had not even been formally presented to the government. Yet having just finished writing his memorandum on the Plan, Hitler signed on 29 August Ley's decree establishing a prize for the 'Model National Socialist Factory', to be 'awarded upon the recommendation of the German Labour Front'. Factories 'in which the National Socialist concept of the factory community has been most completely realized by the works leader and his retinue in the spirit of the Law on the Organization of Labour and in the spirit of the German Labour Front' would have the right 'to display the Golden Flag of the Labour Front'.[115] It is possible that Hitler was pursuing a deliberate policy: that he realized the necessary but dangerous socio-political consequences of the Four-Year Plan, and that this gesture to the DAF was a warning against excessively repressive measures against the workers while the Plan was being accomplished. It is safe to assume, however, that he had no idea of the uses to which the DAF would put the the decree he had just signed. His

---

113. Cf. the rhetorical similarities and the differences in principle between Ley and Thomas on this point: *Doc. 1*; also above pp. 19ff.

114. See *Doc. 3*.

115. *Amtliches Nachrichtenblatt der DAF*, vol. 2, no. 23, 2 September 1936.

decision was probably just another case of his typical indulgence towards the Party's leadership clique.

Ley's position, however, is quite easy to reconstruct, despite the paucity of documentary sources. Basically, the factor that had caused the manpower shortage was the same one that reinforced the DAF's position within the Nazi system and suggested the necessity for a new approach to economic policy, that is, the accelerating armaments-led boom. Since the beginning of 1936 it had been an open secret that a possible new course in economic policy would involve a diminution of Schacht's authority and an expansion of Göring's economic responsibilities.[116] Schacht was Ley's fiercest opponent and the most consistent critic of the DAF's efforts to have a voice in the direction of economic and social policy. Göring, on the other hand, was a Party man, whose increased influence in the economic sphere gave new hope to many Party members that economic life could be co-ordinated (*gleichgeschaltet*) and permeated with the spirit of National Socialism. How these hopes could be realized remained unclear to them, but Ley now saw his oportunity. Even before Hitler had publicly announced the Four-Year Plan and Göring's appointment as Plenipotentiary-General (on 9 September in Nuremberg), Ley revealed his own plans. The same issue of the *Amtliches Nachrichtenblatt* (Official News Bulletin) of the DAF in which Hitler's decree on National Socialist model enterprises had been published also contained a reprint of the Führer's decrees of 24 October and 11 November 1934 on the essence and goals of the DAF, with a new commentary by Ley.[117] Basing himself on this decree, Ley came up with a new 'summary demand', arguing that the economic interest groups and the state's social administration be placed under the DAF. The provisions of the decree were so vague that in his commentary Ley did not feel obliged to discuss in detail the new division of authority. The DAF alone, he wrote, was responsible for 'the building of a broad-based national-racial community [*Volksgemeinschaft*] and a performance-oriented community [*Leistungsgemeinschaft*] to embrace all Germans'. This was an unmistakable challenge both to the state authorities and to the Federation of Trade and Industry (Organisation der gewerblichen Wirtschaft). His commentary, under the title 'Basic Rules' ('Grundsätzliche Anweisungen'), became a kind of charter for the DAF's cadres in future negotiations and conflicts.

---

116. Arthur Schweitzer, 'The Foreign Exchange Crisis of 1936', *Zeitschrift für die gesamte Staatswissenschaft*, vol. 118, no. 2, 1962; Petzina, *Autarkie-politik*, pp. 30–47.
117. Cf. above p. 167.

Although the results of Ley's challenge were long-term and cumulative in nature,[118] Hitler's decree on the National Socialist model enterprise soon provoked an angry confrontation between the various ministries and the DAF. The DAF had been charged with the responsibility for working out the criteria and rules for awarding the prize. To this end Ley announced a 'German industry efficiency contest', which would take place annually and call for detailed examination by the DAF of every aspect of factory life. He made no secret of what he expected to gain from this competition: 'Thus we shall make the factories come up to our standards, creating new and effective means to implement the German Labour Front's claim of total responsibility, and inculcating every factory with the spirit of National Socialism. The Führer has given us a powerful weapon of social policy – and we know how to use it!'[119] Clearly, 'community spirit' would be difficult to gauge and compare among the various factories, and in practice selection would be based on the degree to which factories complied with the specific criteria of the DAF's social policy. The contest was thus an ideal means for the DAF to combine two of its main aims: the drive to make gains at the expense of industry and the government bureaucracy, and the desire to improve the condition of the workers within the framework of industrial social policy. They also fitted nicely into Ley's plan to take the efficiency of management into account in his choice of winners. This was an area from which the DAF had so far been totally excluded and which would give it access to all aspects of economic policy in the strictest sense of the term (resource allocation, investment decisions, dividends, the welfare budget, and the like).

The Reich ministers did not learn about the efficiency contest until reports appeared in the press. They then voiced grave misgivings about the whole project, misgivings that addressed precisely that aspect of the plan from which the DAF had expected the greatest dividends – the desire on the part of factories suffering from manpower shortages to prove that their social amenities were exemplary and thus to be able to attract more workers. However, most of the outstanding factories were in the armaments sector, which was heavily dependent on government contracts and in which working conditions were better than in other industries. The Reich ministers rightly feared that an increase in welfare expenditures in the armaments sector, especially at state expense, would threaten price stability. They were also afraid that widening the gap in living and working conditions between the military and civilian sectors

118. Cf. below pp. 219ff.
119. *Der Angriff*, 7 September 1936.

of industry would inevitably lead to great unrest.[120] On top of this, the efficiency contest appeared to be fundamentally incompatible with the demands of the Four-Year Plan: it was an unnecessary additional burden on government officials and factory managers; an arbitrary provocation to government authorities which would only produce more conflicts; and an undesirable diversion of public funds. In the event that the contest could not be cancelled, the Reich ministers set conditions that would have effectively crippled it: they insisted that the Federation of Trade and Industry and the Reich Trustees of Labour have a determining role in the selection of a winner and that all public enterprises, armaments factories, and businesses receiving government subsidies be barred from participating.[121] In his capacity as Plenipotentiary-General for the Four-Year Plan, Göring was supposed to resolve the conflict. He vacillated for several months, but then, on 4 April 1937, called upon all factories to take part in the contest.[122] The Reich ministers did not actually find out about the contest for 1936/7 until just after Hitler had personally scheduled the presentation of the Golden Flags to the 'National Socialist Model Enterprise' for the 30 April meeting of the Reich Chamber of Labour. Among the winners were armaments factories and government offices. Schacht refused to participate in the awards ceremony.[123] Subsequently the dispute over whether to continue to hold the contest erupted with renewed vehemence. Without Göring's backing the Reich ministers were clearly the underdogs in the struggle with the DAF. After the imposition of an interim ban on participation by all enterprises, the Economics and Labour Ministers won some minor concessions in autumn 1937: the Chambers of Commerce and Trade obtained the authority to judge management efficiency, and the adherence of an enterprise to the government's wage and price guidelines became a prerequisite for eligibility.[124] The DAF acquiesced, and managed to silence the reservations of some industry groups through a combination of political pressure and persuasion. (Participation, however,

120. Comments by the Ministers of Labour and of Economics from October 1936 to February 1937: *DZA Potsdam*, RWM, file 10316, pp. 310–5. Later correspondence shows that the Ministers of Finance and of War agreed with this position: ibid.. Cf. also *Doc. 64.*

121. Ministers of Economics and of Finance to Ley, 8 February 1937: *GPSA Berlin*, Rep. 318, file 841. I was unable to locate other relevant documents; however, they are referred to in letters of 7 April and 5 May 1937 from the Economics Minister to Göring: *DZA Potsdam*, RWM, file 10316, pp. 347f., 385f., 470.

122. *Völkischer Beobachter*, 4 April 1937 (Berlin edn).

123. Ibid. Memorandum, 27 April 1937: *DZA Potsdam*, RWM, file 10316, p. 370.

124. Decree of 5 August 1937 from the Minister of Economics to the Reich Chamber of the Economy; decrees issued on 30 August 1937 by the commissioner responsible for conducting the productivity competition (Hupfauer) and by the director of the Reich Chamber of the Economy: *DZA Potsdam*, RWM, file 10316, pp. 509, 526–9.

remained largely 'voluntary', in the sense in which the Nazis usually misused this term.)[125]

As a result, the efficiency contest was significantly expanded. At the *Gau* level the DAF instituted a series of rounds preliminary to the final competition, thereby increasing the demands placed on the various enterprises in the area of social and industrial policy. These included such 'educational' exercises as enrolling the factory leader in a work crew and replacing the time clock by a system of morning roll calls, as well as offering material inducements to workers, for example, more generous Christmas bonuses or a share in the profits of supplemental pension funds. The DAF issued a whole series of badges for outstanding achievements in industrial welfare, including such areas as vocational education, industrial safety, worker housing, and the encouragement of workers to take 'Strength through Joy' cruises. The earning of these badges was a prerequisite for admission to the final round of the performance competition for the Golden Flags.[126] The number of participating enterprises rose from 81,000 in the 1937/8 contest to 273,000 in 1939/40.[127] As the Reich ministers had feared, the idealistic aspects of the factory community took a back seat to material factors; the degree of 'trust', or of commitment to the works community, was now to be measured by the amount spent for social welfare.[128] The value of the additional fringe benefits offered by industry as a result of the contest is impossible to calculate; however, the increase in expenditures which resulted from suggestions made by the 'Beauty of Labour' office, from RM 80 million (1936) to over RM 200 million (1938), gives some indication of the magnitude of the changes implemented. One Trustee of Labour estimated that the total number of fringe benefits during this period, including paid holidays, was tantamount to a pay increase of around 6.5 per cent. The DAF did not draw up a financial balance sheet, but assembled a pedantically detailed list of benefits that covered two whole printed pages and mentioned every conceivable aspect of industrial social policy. Thus, for example, from 1937 to 1939 participating

125. For an example of the art of persuasion as practised by DAF functionaries, see *Doc. 65*. At least one large firm, the Gutehoffnungshütte in Oberhausen, refused to participate. (I am indebted to Mr Bodo Herzog for this information.)

126. Some of these requirements came through in Hupfauer's speech (*Doc. 65*). The list developed by the DAF's *Gauobmann* in Franconia in July 1937 was more comprehensive: no reduction in piecework pay scales, increased protection against summary dismissal, etc.: *DZA Potsdam*, RWM, file 10316, p. 483.

127. Hans J. Reichhardt, 'Die Deutsche Arbeitsfront', Ph.D. thesis, FU Berlin, 1956, pp. 146–9.

128. The Arbeitswissenschaftliches Institut (AwI) of the DAF studied company ledgers from this perspective, but the numbers were too unreliable to draw any definite conclusions: AwI, *Jahrbuch*, 1939, vol. 2.

enterprises supposedly built 622 sports grounds, 111,000 factory hous-ing units and 4,600 company canteens, hired 3,400 company physicians, arranged for 160,000 workers and Council of Trust members to go through ideological training, and granted over 460,000 workers an allowance for KdF trips.[129]

Although there is legitimate doubt as to the accuracy of these figures, and even though the efficiency contest became ritualized and the Golden Flag was sometimes awarded for reasons not covered by the official rules, the event was clearly a success. By organizing the competition on a broad basis, the DAF established its claim to have a determining voice in social policy on a level beyond the direct control of state authorities. It had significantly modified the employers' position of dominance in industrial affairs, as envisaged in the Labour Organization Law, and suc-cessfully challenged the Labour Ministry's exclusive responsibility for social policy. In the context of the manpower shortage, the efficiency contest allowed the DAF to give practical expression to its ideas about the role of customary law in social policy. Politically, the DAF had acted in conformity with the Nazi system: it was defending itself against other interests and organizations and could claim it was contributing to the pacification of the working class. However, since there was an urgent need to channel the greatest quantity of economic reserves into the arma-ments sector, it was difficult to decide what exactly constituted confor-mity with the system, which is why Göring soon regretted having indulged the DAF. During a meeting with armed forces representatives in July 1938 he noted laconically, 'The Labour Front should create more strength and less joy', and in October he threatened to proceed 'ruthless-ly' against the DAF and block the allocation of raw materials or man-power for social welfare purposes, if the DAF did not put a stop to the building of sports grounds, canteens and the like on its own.[130]

However, so long as the manpower shortage persisted, and the 'deployment of labour' and wage policy remained unregulated, the con-ditions that had led to the establishment of the efficiency contest in its original form persisted. This same constellation of circumstances gave the DAF in 1937 enough confidence in its own strength to intensify the struggle with state officials and economic interest groups over the con-

---

129. Wiesel to Thomas, 8 January 1939: *BA/MA Freiburg*, WiIF 5, file 1223; Otto Marrenbach (ed.), *Fundamente des Sieges. Die Gesamtarbeit der Deutschen Arbeitsfront 1933–1940*, Berlin, 1940, pp. 325–30; for details, see the DAF series *National-sozialistische Musterbetriebe*.

130. Notes of a meeting on 16 July 1938: *BA/MA Freiburg*, WiIF 5, file 412. Klein, *Preparations*, p. 25. As a result, Hupfauer warned that the building of marble swimming pools on factory grounds should not be considered a qualification for the gold flag: *Völkischer Beobachter*, 16 August 1939.

trol of all contested areas of responsibility. At the end of 1936 the DAF had gone so far as to set up its own system of certifying examinations for vocational education courses in a number of *Gaue*, forcing education authorities to co-operate under threat of disciplinary action by the newly established courts of social honour. The bitter confrontation dragged on for more than a year, and Schacht felt compelled to make sure that the legally required examinations be administered by the Chambers of Commerce and Industry. Even Göring's intervention against the DAF in December 1937 did not clarify the situation completely, since government reform of vocational education, which all sides considered urgently necessary, had never been carried out.[131]

Constantly in search of new responsibilities and driven by its imperial ambitions, the DAF recognized no clear boundaries in the spheres of labour or social policy. At least in the area of vocational education the DAF had some plausible explanations for its encroachments: the need to increase the number of students attending vocational school, the technical qualifications of its Office of Management Training and the need to co-ordinate the professional and political education of young people.[132] But the DAF's other expansionist goals in the late 1930s had no connection whatsoever with its original responsibilities. When the DAF embarked on a campaign to take over the state's responsibilities for housing policy towards the end of 1937, relations between the Ministry of Labour and the DAF soured perceptibly. When Gauleiter Bürckel supported the DAF in what seemed at first like a minor conflict, Seldte responded by cutting off state subsidies for housing construction in the Saarland; only after receiving instructions from Hitler did Seldte rescind his order. The dispute over the question of authority continued to escalate, the DAF's 'campaigns' became more far-reaching, and its claims against the Labour Ministry more insistent, until Hitler finally transferred all responsibility for housing policy to the DAF in November 1942.[133] To the surprise of government authorities and the economic interest groups, the DAF had even managed by 1939 to increase its direct involvement in banking and insurance. When the cornerstone of the Wolfsburg Works was laid on 26 May 1938, it also got its foot in the door of the automotive

131. Schacht's complaint to Göring, 23 December 1936: *DZA Potsdam*, RWM, file 10321, pp. 2f.; Schacht's decree of 3 March 1937: ibid., file 9030, p. 2; Göring's decree of 21 December 1937, file 10257, pp. 305f. These three files contain further extensive correspondence regarding this question. Cf. also below pp. 232ff. The Directive on the Training of Skilled Workers' (*VO über die Ausbildung von Fachkräften*), 15 December 1939, confirmed the authority of the Minister of Economics: *RGBl.*, I, p. 2425.

132. Cf. above pp. 170f.

133. *GPSA Berlin*, Rep. 318, file 910 (Saar). On the continuation of the dispute: *BA Koblenz*, R43II, files 1007–7b, 1009–9b. Housing construction occupied a central place in the regime's peace planning for the period after 'final victory'.

industry. Then it began eyeing the retirement insurance programme, which Hitler made into a pensions department within the DAF in February 1940. In February 1941 the DAF was also assigned responsibility for the consumer co-operatives.[134] Clearly, the DAF was aiming to carry out its long-term task of balancing 'the legitimate interests' of all Germans in accordance with 'National Socialist principles'[135] by extending its organizational authority over all aspects of social life. All the DAF's important initiatives after 1937 were directed at achieving this organizational goal and were thus only indirectly connected to its original task of responsibility for the political education of the working class – a task that did not offer similar prospects for 'success'.

Before the war broke out, the DAF had yet to reach the apex of its power. The political crisis triggered by the DAF and the Labour Ministry in early 1938 revolved partly around the question of responsibility for the workers' welfare, the issue which had provided the original justification for the DAF's existence. Relations between the DAF and the Labour Ministry began deteriorating rapidly after Ley broached the subject in September 1936. The conflict, represented as a struggle over authority, actually concealed deep-seated differences of opinion regarding the most important questions of wage and social policy. In the summer of 1937 there was a public confrontation between Ley and Seldte over the growing influence of DAF functionaries who acted as mediators in the settlement of disputes within factories. The Minister of Labour insisted that such cases were the exclusive province of the Council of Trust and the Trustee of Labour, as provided in the Labour Organization Law. The DAF, however, repeatedly ordered its functionaries to refer these cases directly to their superiors for mediation, under threat of disciplinary action.[136] The issue was never resolved, and heated exchanges continued over the years. Housing and vocational policy have already been mentioned. The DAF and the Labour Ministry also locked horns over the future composition and function of the Councils of Trust and their relationship to the DAF. In May 1938 Hitler pronounced himself in favour of abolishing all future elections to the Councils of Trust. A new arrangement would probably have been to the detriment of the DAF; the weaker the Councils of Trust, the greater the

134. Banking: Funk's letter, June 1941, *BA Koblenz*, R43II, file 352b. Insurance: Seldte's complaint, 5 November 1937, ibid., file 206. Wolfsburg, ibid., file 1204. Pension insurance: *Doc. 131;* Marrenbach (ed.), *Fundamente des Sieges*, p. 20. Consumer co-operatives: Decree of 18 February 1941 and ensuing differences of opinion between Ley and Funk, R43II, file 352b.

135. Cf. above p. 167.

136. See *Doc. 42*. Also Mansfeld to Göring, 24 November 1936: *DZA Potsdam*, RWM, file 10321, p. 5 (disciplinary proceedings). Additional correspondence: ibid., file 10319, and *BA Koblenz*, R43II, file 530.

influence of the factory overseer (*Betriebsobmann*), who reported directly to the DAF.[137] In the negotiations that began in 1937 on reducing miners' contributions to their insurance fund and increasing legal protection for young workers, major differences emerged between the position of the Labour Ministry and that of the DAF, for in both cases the DAF argued in favour of major concessions to the workers.[138] In addition, a protracted controversy ensued over the system of regional wage differentials, as well as an obscure conflict over the role of the Labour Committees (*Arbeitsausschüsse*), whose number had grown to 3,000 by 1939.[139]

This was the political background to the first tentative discussions by the government of possible measures to limit consumer spending, measures that had now become an urgent necessity. In December 1937 the Reich Price Commissar presented detailed draft proposals for safeguarding the armaments programme through improved contract management and tighter wage and price controls. The reaction of the Labour Minister was basically positive; he made it perfectly clear, however, that cutbacks in consumer spending in favour of armaments expenditures would be possible only if the DAF's influence on the shop floor could be curbed at the same time. The state alone possessed the requisite power and prestige to accomplish this, but now needed to establish the institutional structure necessary to assert its authority.[140] The DAF had always regarded all questions involving wages as sensitive. On the one hand, DAF functionaries were subject to pressure from the workers, who constantly demanded higher wages. On the other, the DAF was sufficiently enmeshed in the Nazis' *Volksgemeinschaft* ideology that such demands seemed all too reminiscent of the class struggle; moreover, they were bound to Hitler's decision of 2 May 1935.[141] However, the two most important catchwords used by the Nazis to describe their concept of society – 'performance' and 'community' (combined into the single concept 'performance-oriented community' or *Leistungsgemeinschaft* after 1936) – were vague enough to allow a fair amount of latitude in

137. Drafts of a bill by the Minister of Labour, with position papers by the Economics Minister, Hitler's Deputy (Hess), the Reich Industry Group, the DAF, etc.: *BA Koblenz*, R43II, file 547b; *DZA Potsdam*, RWM, file 10290, pp. 130–93; file 10286, pp. 24–56. A new law was not passed.

138. See explanatory text preceding *Doc. 87* (miners' insurance); *DZA Potsdam*, RWM, file 10349; Syrup, *Hundert Jahre*, p. 508 (protection of young people).

139. See *Docs. 62–3;* Marrenbach (ed.), *Fundamente des Sieges*, p. 104.

140. *Docs. 99, 128–31.*

141. Wage differentials were to remain unchanged; see above pp. 137f.; cf. *Doc. 60*. This did not prevent the DAF from suggesting individual wage increases to the Ministry of Labour, for example, in March 1938 for employees of the consumer co-operatives: *DZA Potsdam*, RWM, file 10293, p. 280; and in May/June 1938 for dairy workers: ibid., file 10280, pp. 3f.; file 10332, p. 491. Cf. also below pp. 236f. (equal pay for women).

wage policy, which the DAF exploited to the hilt, at least in its propaganda. Thus, although as an organization it did not call publicly for a general increase in wages, from 1936 onwards it came out in favour of various guaranteed bonuses, a cut in some taxes and social insurance contributions, profit-sharing, the elimination of piecework ceilings, payment for days off due to military service, and so on.[142] Of course, after 1936 the manpower shortage was a more decisive factor in the rising standard of living of the workers than all the campaigns and speeches of all the DAF functionaries. By the end of 1937 it had become clear to the DAF that its success as a mass organization was inextricably bound up with a continuous rise in the standard of living. First, this was in line with the interests and wishes of its members; and second, the DAF's power within the system depended to a large extent on its ability to help assert these interests individually against competing claims. It was precisely because the bureaucracy, the armed forces, agriculture and, to some degree, industry were all interested in stabilizing wages that the DAF was able to defend its position in the unbridled struggle for power simply by representing the opposite point of view. This helps to explain the DAF's violent reaction to the continuing discussions among government officials, for it seemed as if they were threatening to curtail the DAF's right to develop customary law (*Gewohnheitsrecht*) in industrial policy.

At the beginning of February 1938 the DAF introduced four detailed bills, the purpose of which was to make the Labour Front the most important organization in the entire political system.[143] The draft Law on the DAF required that all gainfully employed Germans (not just those employed in industry and commerce, as previously) become members of the DAF, that the DAF *Reichsleiter* be placed directly under Hitler, and that its central offices (*Führungsämter*) have a direct part in shaping legislation. It defined its sphere of responsibility as 'the intellectual, physical and professional training [*Ertüchtigung*] of all working Germans' – a definition which would allow it to claim a share of responsibility in every area of domestic policy. Its draft Law on Self-administration in Labour Policy (*Gesetz über die arbeitspolitische Selbstverwaltung*) aimed to raise the status of the DAF's Chambers of Labour and Labour Committees, thereby transforming the DAF into a partly advisory, partly regulatory organization paralleling the Labour Ministry and the Trustees of Labour. The draft of a 'Law on Chambers of the Economy' (*Wirtschaftskammergesetz*) was

---

142. For this and many more examples, see *Deutsche Sozialpolitik*,1938.
143. *BA Koblenz* R43II, file 530a; *BA/MA Freiburg* WiIF 5, file 1260. On the background and the rivalry betweeen Hess and Ley, see Dietrich Orlow, *The History of the Nazi Party*, vol. 2: 1933–1945, Newton Abbott, 1973, ch. 4.

designed to streamline the organization of industry, in such a way as to enhance the importance of the proposed *Gau* economic chambers (*Gauwirtschaftskammer*). While the DAF wanted a seat on the board of the Reich Chamber, it was not prepared to grant the Chamber reciprocal membership in the plenum of the Chamber of Labour. In vocational education the DAF envisaged 'a consultative and guiding role' for itself; the draft acknowledged the 'leadership of the state', but proposed that the Economics Ministry be required to seek the consent of the DAF for all decrees and guidelines bearing on vocational education. What is striking in these drafts is the vagueness of their language, which betrayed the DAF's intention to add to the ambiguity surrounding all questions of authority and responsibility and thus to create conditions favourable to new attempts to acquire ultimate control of the state and the economy. Apart from the subordination of the DAF *Reichsleiter* to Hitler, there was not a word in these drafts about the DAF's responsibilities to any other state authorities.

For weeks, discussions of domestic policy were dominated by these demands. The various departments of government put their deliberations on important social-policy measures on the back burner. Talks on the drafts lasted well into the summer, but then gradually died down without any real decisions having been made. For once there was general agreement among offices that were usually at variance with one another. Himmler and Hess both saw in the DAF's move an attempt to usurp the position of the Nazi Party itself. Darré, who had long been under pressure by the DAF to improve working and living conditions in agriculture, was concerned about the future role of the Reich Food Estate *(Reichsnährstand)* if all farm-workers were forced into membership of the DAF. The Reich Chamber of the Economy was worried about the position of industry within the power structure. The armed forces emphasized their interest in having the state maintain tight control of social policy. The Ministers of Justice and the Interior emphasized that the DAF had no intention of reporting to any ministry.[144] Only Funk, the Economics Minister, gave any consideration to the draft bills. His position paper had been prepared by a department chief who had once been Ley's deputy in the DAF and had been transferred to the Ministry of Economics following Schacht's resignation. Moreover, Funk, newly appointed to his ministry, was interested in restoring – at the expense of the Labour Ministry – some of the authority he had lost

144. Most position papers are in *BA Koblenz*, R43II, file 530a; the Labour Ministry's: ibid., R41, file 22, pp. 26ff.; the Economic Ministry's: ibid., R43II, file 584b; the Armed Forces Supreme Command: *BA/MA Freiburg*, WiIF 5, file 320. I could not locate a report on the ministerial meeting of 4 March 1938.

as a result of the Four-Year Plan, and therefore saw the DAF as a wel-come ally.[145] The only tangible result of the crisis was another order from Hess to Ley to pass all communications with the government through the office of the Führer's Deputy. No solutions could be found to issues of substance; they had to wait on further developments in domestic and foreign policy, that is, they were to be decided in the course of the political power struggles.

Only three of the ministerial responses contained counter-proposals aimed at limiting the activities of the DAF in in the interests of strategic planning.[146] Not one department of government dared to criticize these activities publicly, even though it had meanwhile become obvious that the efficiency contest, the KdF and so on, had contributed nothing to raising productivity or maintaining labour discipline, and that the increase in fringe benefits at the factory level only helped firms to retain workers or poach them from someone else.[147] The position papers, memoranda and debates barely mentioned this aspect of the problem. Nor did they touch on the tension between social policy and war prepa-rations – the real cause of the crisis, as the earlier discussions among state authorities suggested. The reason for this silence is probably not to be found in the power of the DAF itself, nor in its 'popularity' among the workers, but rather in the fact that this conflict exemplified the extremely problematical relationship between people's living and work-ing conditions on the one hand, and the legitimacy of the regime on the other. A year before, when the question of paid holidays had been at issue, the state secretary in the Labour Ministry hit the nail on the head when he asked whether the Reich Price Commissar was willing and able to prohibit all wage increases absolutely.[148] He received no answer. By the spring of 1938 nobody was even asking the question. Apparently, from the standpoint of the government and the economic interest groups, it was less important, and more risky, to address the real prob-lems than to understand the implications of the DAF's bills for the divi-sion of power and authority within the system.

As influential as the DAF was, its changing role during the period 1936 to 1938 has not been studied here simply for its own sake. More than this, it typifies the many other forces in domestic and economic

145. These events were later the subject of detailed study in the ministry: *DZA Potsdam*, RWM, file 10311, pp. 143–60. Thomas was under the impression that Funk had made an agreement with Ley ahead of time: letter to Körner, 14 January 1938: *BA/MA Freiburg*, WiIF 5, file 203.

146. The position papers of the Labour Ministry, the Reich Chamber of the Economy (both of which were more concerned about their departmental interests than about rearma-ment), and the Armed Forces Supreme Command (OKW).

147. Cf. *Docs. 150, 151, 156.*

148. *Doc. 54.*

policy that were in latent contradiction with the rearmament programme. The serious tension between Ley and Hess should not blind us
to the fact that the DAF and the important organs of the Party, above all
at the *Gau* level, found much to agree about here. The DAF's willingness to make concessions to the working class, dressed up as a kind of
aggressive populism, also received steady support from the propaganda
apparatus and the Party press. Thus the Nazi power structure had deep
fissures within it that severely impaired the domestic policy-making
process. True, Ley, Goebbels and the Gauleiters were far from actually
undermining the power of the bureaucracy, industry and the armed
forces; however, their policies did have a restraining and unsettling
effect on these authorities – an effect which became more profound as
their efforts to wrest material concessions coincided more closely with
the growing discontent among the workers.[149]

These dynamic and conflict-ridden developments in the structure of
political relations within the Nazi system had absolutely nothing to do
with the DAF's original responsibilities, as these had been envisaged in
1933–4. The hope that the organization would be able to halt the rise in
the standard of living and make palatable a policy of sacrifice for the sake
of military expansion proved completely illusory. As Thomas had told
the political leadership in November 1936,[150] the DAF, instead of constantly calling on the people to make sacrifices, forged the hackneyed
slogans of National Socialism into an instrument with which it was able
to represent many of the traditional interests of the working class.
Nevertheless, the DAF never became a trade union in the real sense of the
term, for its leaders were too wedded to the goals and methods of the
regime. What this meant was that the battles over the workers' interests,
the DAF's popularity and the power of the old elite within the state and in
the economy could not be fought openly. As soon as these elites managed
to agree (a rare enough occurrence) on a definite line in domestic policy
that also had the backing of Hitler or Göring, the DAF was left only with
the option of obstructing the implementation of measures that had
already been adopted.[151] Thus its role within the system was ultimately
more functional than constructive. Without the protagonists fully realizing it, as they became mired in the endless and complex trench war over
the question of authority, the DAF's main role now was to prevent the
exploitation and repression of the working class becoming totally unen-

149. On Hitler's evaluation of his own role in domestic policy, see Edward N.
Peterson, *The Limits of Hitler's Power*, Princeton, NJ, 1969, pp. 4–18.
    150. Cf. *Doc. 1*.
    151. It is significant that the DAF was not represented in the deliberations that took
place between 1936 and 1939 on social policy legislation in the event of war: *Docs.
160–73.*

durable.[152] It acted as a kind of buffer between the rulers and the ruled; yet the DAF was far from satisfied with this thankless task. In light of its dynamic development from 1936 onwards, it is not difficult to understand why the power elites never realized that the trench war with the DAF was becoming a permanent condition, a means of giving expression to the class struggle in a form compatible with the system. In the spring of 1938 it definitely seemed as though winners and losers would emerge from these conflicts. However, it was not the organizational aspect of the confrontations that turned out to be decisive, but rather the content of the debates and their implications for military policy.

The Labour Ministry and the central office of the Four-Year Plan agreed that the continued drive for rearmament would only be successful if sacrifices were made in the area of social policy; but they were still unwilling to advocate this approach with any enthusiasm in governmental deliberations, for to do so would have been too unpopular and too difficult. The foreign-policy situation, however, was making it urgently necessary, as well as possible, to push forward with rapid rearmament. There is no doubt that the suppression of the conflict over the DAF's function was primarily a result of the exacerbation of tensions in Europe that were triggered by the German invasion of Austria on 12 March; it was not until 'total war' had been proclaimed, however, that these conflicts lost their explosive potential.

But here I am anticipating one of my central hypotheses, which will be discussed in the final part of this study. The documentary sources tend to direct historians' attention to the reasons why Germany's economic preparations for war were so inadequate, and why there was such a blatant failure to adopt corrective measures. But no unequivocal answers can be given to these questions, because the sources only provide clues; they do not give us the kind of uninterrupted view of the decision-making process at the apex of the political structure which is essential for a definitive historical interpretation. This is not only due to the well-known fact that Hitler was slovenly in his approach to governing and preferred to issue verbal orders, which, as far as domestic policy was concerned, were seldom detailed or written down. In this case, the main reason for the paucity of primary sources is the fact that the leadership (Hitler, Göring, Funk, Goebbels, Ley) was reluctant to admit that the problem even existed. This is what drove the proponents of a planned economy (Darré, Wagner, Thomas, later also certain industrial-

152. The DAF's leadership never realized this either: see Ley's reply to Thomas, *Doc. 1*. Parenthetically it might be noted that another function of the DAF was to organize a kind of spurious social mobility: some of the 1.4 million honorary functionaries were probably workers who had thereby satisfied their craving for status: Marrenbach (ed.), *Fundamente des Sieges*, p. 46.

ists) to distraction. This blindness on the part of the leaders was not simply ideological or psychological in nature. Hitler insisted that overcoming economic bottlenecks was purely a 'question of will',[153] and refused to understand that a modern economic policy demands continuous decisions about the most rational allocation and best possible utilization of scarce resources. Whether his attitude was a reflection of some deeper psychological cause is a moot question; what is more important in this context is that it clearly reflected the actual state of the economy in its relation to strategic goals. The fundamental choice with which the imperialist aims of National Socialism confronted Hitler and his regime was one between impossibilities. Regardless of which choice was made, the political system would inevitably be imperilled. Thus the reason for the paucity of the sources is that these were not the kinds of problems people in the Third Reich cared to discuss. Here, then, we will begin with an analytical rather than empirical approach to the problem.

If for a moment we separate the general problem from the actual flow of events, we see that there were two conceivable approaches to planning German rearmament and strategy during the late 1930s, both of which were mentioned as possible alternatives in governmental correspondence, though infrequently and in vague terms. One view, for which Labour Minister Seldte was a weak spokesman and which necessarily reflected the day-to-day practice of many government agencies, was to allow the scale of armaments production to be determined by the quantity of *available* economic reserves, manpower, and so on.[154] This did not mean that rearmament was to be neglected; rather, that the ministries were reconciled to the fact (and were able to convince the military) that in light of existing shortages certain military projects were either unfeasible or would have to be delayed for a considerable time. These kinds of *ad hoc* calculations (of which the negotiations over military construction work in Brandenburg at the end of 1937 provide an excellent example),[155] were based on the assumption that the military sector would have to compete for the required production capacity and reserves, and that in the case of most bottlenecks it was neither possible nor desirable to secure the necessary supplies through either indirect economic controls or direct state intervention in the civilian sector. This

---

153. Wilhelm Treue (ed.), 'Hitlers Denkschrift zum Vierjahresplan 1936', *Vierteljahrshefte für Zeitgeschichte*, vol. 3/3, 1955.

154. *Docs. 2, 3, 49, 68*. Cf. also above p. 204. The position of Finance Minister Krosigk as revealed to Göring on 5 November 1936 was similar: *BA/MA Freiburg*, WiIF 5, file 420/1.

155. Cf. *Docs. 69–70*. The building plans of the various military contractors had to be drastically reduced, since they were either incompatible with one another or interfered with on-going civilian projects. On the other hand, these were projects of the highest military importance.

attitude was largely in line with existing economic and social-policy legislation, which had not provided the legal basis for a more active policy by the summer of 1938.[156] When the growing number of military contracts threatened to overtax the entire economy and to cause the bottlenecks and inflation mentioned above, government authorities sought to apply a lesson from their previous experience by calling on the military to adopt contract planning – that is, to prioritize their needs. Once again the building sector provides an excellent example of the problem.[157] In practice, this procedure would have been tantamount to adapting the rearmament programme to available reserves and capacity, so that, at least in the form proposed for the building industry, the size of the civilian sector was taken as a given. This approach would mean allowing the scope and pace of rearmament to be determined mainly by economic factors that were accepted as more or less given. For this purpose, available reserves needed to be assessed and then allocated according to a list of priorities, in order to build up the greatest military strength possible within these limitations, and at the same time avoid sudden jolts to the economy. But this alternative, in the form of draft plans for the organization of the building industry, was flatly rejected by Hitler in February 1938.[158] Though the relevant records do not contain any explicit reason for his decision, we can reconstruct his motivations with a fair degree of certainty.

The plan would have imposed a clear limitation on Hitler's freedom to decide issues of strategy and foreign policy – not so much in the sense that armaments production would have been hampered by such an approach to planning, but more because the results of any thorough inventory of reserves and resources would have revealed the weaknesses in the economy's capacity to support an expansionist foreign policy. A general and systematic management of procurements in the armaments sector would have inevitably led (at the end of 1937) to a sober assessment of what could and could not be accomplished, and thus to the establishment of a more realistic balance between foreign and domestic policy. This would have considerably enhanced the power of the bureaucracy and of industry, by necessitating a process of planning and continuous decision-making – a process that would have been difficult to monitor and that would at the same time have directly affected foreign policy. Hitler could hardly have been interested in such an arrangement.

156. Göring's original mandate as Plenipotentiary for the Four-Year Plan would have sufficed to provide a legal basis, if he had wanted to use it: Petzina, *Autarkiepoltik*, p. 57. Cf. *Doc. 76.*

157. Cf. *Docs. 71–3.*

158. *Doc. 78.* With regard to Schacht's finance policy requests, Hitler was just as unsympathetic and inflexible.

There are quite a few indications that he was extremely fearful of the kind of economic consolidation often suggested to him by Schacht and Seldte, among others, precisely because it would have inevitably shifted power back to the 'old elites'. Equally, it would have made it more diffi-cult for him to intervene instantly in European politics with his 'world-historical decisions', as occasion or intuition dictated.[159] From the perspective of domestic and power politics, there is no doubt that Hitler's position – indeed that of the Nazi movement generally – was greatly strengthened in all spheres, albeit for only a short time, by the policy of 'flight forwards' (*Flucht nach vorn*). There was a strong element of deliberate political manipulation in the constant overloading of the state apparatus, the military and industry. It was precisely because of the enor-mous dynamism in military and foreign policy, of the challenges created by ever new and more difficult tasks, that these groups never had the respite they needed in order to assert their own claims to power. During this period it was not just in the sphere of foreign policy, but within the structure of the regime as a whole that the principles of 'the movement' and of order proved to be fundamentally incompatible (and this, even though the Nazi 'movement' itself had long been relegated to a position of secondary importance as a political factor in the system).[160]

There are two other related elements behind this rejection of a prag-matic plan for the war economy. In terms of the 'psychology' of rule as it was understood by the holders of power, any attempt to adjust arma-ments policy to existing conditions would have been tantamount to a retreat. It was one of the few firm principles of Nazi policy that the very act of striving for the impossible would assure the achievement of the possible. This is not a complete explanation of the 'utopian' element in Nazi ideology and in the goal of imperialist expansion, yet the behav-iour of the Nazi leadership towards the bureaucracy and the top military was characterized by the cynical exploitation of its own utopian rhetoric to exhort these groups to carry out specific concrete actions. (There is no need here to dwell on Hitler's well-known contempt for the bureaucra-

159. It would perhaps be profitable to study the year 1937 from this perspective. Thus, for example, it is striking that armaments expenditures grew somewhat more slowly than before or after, and that Schacht was apparently able to win the support of some generals for his policy; see E. M. Robertson, *Hitler's Pre-War Policy and Military Plans*, London, 1963, pp. 84ff. There were also some first, tentative efforts at a consolidation of conserva-tive groups in these sectors, e. g., in the iron industry.

160. The following works provide clues as to what an 'orderly', systematic develop-ment of Germany's power might have looked like in 1938–9: Hermann Graml, in W. Schmitthenner and H. Buchheim (eds.), *Der deutsche Widerstand gegen Hitler*, Cologne, 1966, and Bernd-Jürgen Wendt, *München 1938*, Frankfurt am Main, 1965. As the military resistance movement in the autumn of 1938 showed, Hitler's policy created its own neme-sis; however, conservative groups were unable successfully to challenge the power of the political leadership.

cy.) A remark made by Hitler to Himmler, in which he said that it would very likely take six years to fulfil the Four-Year Plan, may suffice as an example.[161] Any strategy of compromise in economic or armaments policy would have run totally counter to this trait in Nazi thinking, since it implied that some of the military's economic plans were in fact unfeasible. Hitler always bristled at what he saw as a self-defeating attitude in such calculations. To him the only path to ultimate success, and even to interim successes, was to press on incessantly along every front simultaneously. Closely bound up with this was the 'institutional Darwinism' of the Nazi leadership,[162] according to which unbridled struggle among the interlocking organizations and interest groups within the power structure would strengthen all those involved and ensure the survival of the politically fittest. Translated into economic terms, this meant that in the period 1937–8 the armed forces would have to aim to meet their needs on their own initiative and through their own efforts. There was always an implied threat that the non-fulfilment of responsibilities would have unpleasant personal and organizational consequences for the leaders.[163]

Even though the experience of the preceding years gave little cause for hope that the various military and government officials were willing or able to co-operate constructively with the economic interest groups in developing a global approach to rearmament planning, adherence to the principles of Darwinism at least provided a rationale to evade responsibility in the economic circumstances of 1937–8. The political leadership was basically unwilling to take on the difficult and unpopular task of deciding how to allocate scarce resources among the competing branches of the armed forces and of industry. Quite apart from the ideological sources of this attitude, it was simply easier to let nature make the decision in the course of the struggle among the various competitors.[164] 'Führer wants to make as few decisions as possible', noted Göring. At least in this respect Hitler was consistent: after the disputes between the army and the air force in the autumn of 1937, he did in fact avoid making these kinds of decisions. He displayed the very same attitude that had marked his behaviour during the conflicts over the functions and

161. Petzina, *Autarkiepolitik*, p. 125. His ulterior motive was probably to induce those responsible to exert themselves to the maximum.

162. Schoenbaum, *Braune Revolution*, p. 249; cf. also Carroll, *Design*, pp. 121, 171.

163. This was also reflected in the ambiguities inherent in the division of power within the wartime economy. Even in this sector there was no effective central planning authority that could have lobbied for the needs of the armed forces as a whole: Petzina, *Autarkiepolitik*, pp. 67–8; Carroll, *Design*, chs. 8, 9. Cf. the confusion caused by unrealizable demands, which Göring enlarged upon in a speech in November 1938: *Doc. 152*.

164. Cf. note 106 above.

policies of the DAF.[165] The reasons outlined above thus appear to have been decisive in the rejection of this option in economic strategy.

This device of abstracting from the events as such allows us to postulate a second possible direction that economic policy could have taken and that also promised a way out of the impending crisis. The outlines of this second plan are evident in a speech delivered by Colonel (later General) Thomas to the Reich Chamber of Labour in November 1936.[166] In subsequent years Thomas consistently maintained his line in the name of the armed forces, and was supported, if for different reasons, by the authorities responsible for price regulation and agriculture.[167] By dint of its origins his plan was more oriented towards military than economic policy, but as a result of growing shortages and spiralling inflation in 1937, it also became directly applicable to economic policy. To Thomas the conditions for strategic success became synonymous with the possible means for forestalling the latent economic and political crisis, that is, safeguarding and increasing armaments production by imposing severe limitations on all other sectors. Thomas was fully aware that this approach would inevitably demand the introduction of strict controls in the labour market and in the regulation of wages and prices, cutbacks in consumption, tax increases and a much more effective policy for rationing available capacity and raw materials.[168] Successful measures such as these might have dampened inflationary pressures and helped check the growing disparity between the military's demand for armaments and the productive capacity of industry. In fact, the very economic consequences of the armaments-led boom called for the immediate transition to a full war economy (as envisaged by Thomas), simply in order to continue the rearmament programme, regardless of whether the strategic position of the Reich or the strategic objectives of the leadership had changed. These were the problems that gave rise to the Four-Year Plan in 1936; as implemented, however, the Plan did little to solve them. Aside from expanding capacity in those sectors of the economy critical to the war effort, virtually nothing was

165. Göring made this remark during a meeting with high-ranking officers on 16 July 1938: *BA/MA Freiburg*, WiIF 5, file 412. Cf. Hermann Gackenholz, 'Reichskanzlei 5. November 1937', in *Forschungen zu Staat und Verwaltung. Festgabe für Fritz Hartung*, Berlin, 1958. On the priority given to the navy according to Hitler's decree of 27 January 1939, see Thomas, *Geschichte*, p. 132. On the partial shift in priority from the navy to the air force during the summer of 1939: *BA Koblenz*, R41, file 190, pp. 25–37. Hitler took no position in the dispute over the DAF in the spring of 1938.

166. Cf. *Doc. 1.*

167. See Carroll, *Design*, ch. 2, esp. pp. 47ff. The support Thomas received from Wagner and Darré, however, was not the subject of an agreement. The parallels necessarily resulted from the economic situation. Cf. *Docs. 57–8, 128, 187*, as well as Darré's petitions cited above in note 65.

168. Carroll, *Design*, p. 43. Cf. note 107 above.

done. To boost the rearmament programme the government relied mainly on its purchasing power, yet without devoting much attention to the
conditions required to sustain it.

The second economic policy option, like the first, never had a chance
before the summer of 1938. Only in a few cases, and then with a conspicuous lack of success, did the government make any attempt to come
to the aid of the armaments sector in its struggle for means of production, manpower and so on. The methods of intervention which are pertinent here can be divided into three categories: measures to directly
control job changing; general measures to 'ration' able-bodied workers;
and measures to reallocate capacity throughout the economy. The relevant documentary sources on the first method have been made available,[169] so that we need only comment briefly here. The attempt to
control the labour market made it obligatory for a worker to get permission before taking a new job. It is interesting, however, that both the
government and the Reichsanstalt sought to reduce to a minimum the
number of persons affected by the new restrictions and to be as gentle as
possible in enforcing them. Until June 1938 these restrictions basically
applied only to young workers and to particular jobs in the metal industry and in the building sector; only in the metal industry did this measure
affect entire groups of workers after February 1937.

The documentary record is insufficient to permit an assessment of
how this attempt to restrict the freedom to change jobs affected the individual worker, but all the facts indicate that it did nothing to solve the
real problems of the economy. It also failed to keep wages down; pay
increases for those hit by the regulations were no lower than for those
who were not affected.[170] In the first place, the procedures for process-
ing applications to change jobs were extremely cumbersome, since in
each individual case the worker's application had to be checked for a
number of factors that were very difficult to assess – and the numbers of
individual cases in the metal industry in 1937 were in the hundreds of
thousands.[171] Second, most workers probably wished to change jobs in
order to increase their earnings, and the armaments sector offered them
the best prospects in any case. We may therefore conclude that the
labour exchanges rarely turned down such applications, a conclusion
bolstered by the fact that the labour exchanges were instructed not to

169. *Docs. 7, 11, 12, 17–26, 38, 66, 81, 101.*

170. Cf. above p. 197. See also *Doc. 104, part I 3; Doc. 132; Stat. Anhang, Doc. II b,
d.* Wage stability was really the prerequisite for dealing with the problem of job changing;
cf. Syrup, *Hundert Jahre*, p. 470.

171. Some 447,000 job applications were processed by the labour exchanges in this
branch of industry: *Stat. Jahrbuch*, 1938, p. 373.

obstruct workers' attempts at occupational self-betterment.[172] It is still unclear how requests to change jobs were handled within the armaments sector. Moreover, regulations such as these encouraged a kind of short-term collusion between the worker who wanted to change his job and his potential new employer, which must have made it extremely difficult to apply the regulations strictly. This state of affairs was acknowledged by the authorities in the explanatory introduction to the Decree on Regulating the Changing of Jobs in Selected Firms, issued in March 1938, which referred to repeated violations of existing regulations by employers.[173] There is no mention in the surviving files of the Ministry or the Reichsanstalt of any punitive action having been taken on the basis of these regulations. Workers who were determined to change jobs knew full well how to subvert the system through uncooperative behaviour and make their employer glad to part with them.[174] The Decree on Implementing the Four-Year Plan by Prosecuting the Illegal Dissolution of Labour Contracts showed similar weaknesses.[175]

This bid to restrict freedom of movement amounted to the serious violation of people's civil rights, though the intent of the new decrees – to prevent the employment of skilled workers outside the armaments sector – was purely negative and their effectiveness extremely limited. In any event, they were totally inadequate to cope with the problems in the labour market that were being reported by government officials in the period 1936–7.[176] The fact that the system of leaving certificates (*Freigabescheine*) was dismantled by these measures shows how mindful the legislators were of their popularity among the workers. The leaving certificates were part of a system of agreements among local employers that bound the signatories not to poach workers from each other, and even though the system had the partial approval of industry and the military authorities, government officials considered it highly unpopular. They remembered that it was among the most bitterly resented economic measures of the First World War.[177] As was the case in the

172. The president of the Rhineland Labour Exchange is supposed to have approved 80 per cent of such applications: memorandum of 10 October 1938, *Betriebsarchiv des VEB ORWO-Wolfen*, file A3717, p. 407.

173. *Anordnung zur Regelung des Arbeitsplatzwechsels in einzelnen Betrieben*, 1 March 1938; Syrup, *Hundert Jahre*, p. 431; *Doc. 101*. Cf. Seldte's perceptive assessment of the effectiveness of these regulations: *Doc. 68*; likewise his unwillingess to broaden them: *Doc. 105*.

174. Cf. *Docs 145; 150; 156*.

175. *Anordnung zur Durchführung des Vierjahresplans über Strafmassnahmen bei rechtswidriger Lösung von Arbeitsverhältnissen: Doc. 12. Cf. Doc. 36, part I 5; Doc. 41, part I 6; Doc. 156*.

176. See *Docs. 2, 3, 30, 36*.

177. Cf. *Docs. 17–28*.

previous (and soon abandoned) use of such methods to prevent the migration of agricultural labour, the authorities were gambling on the 'psychological' (i.e. deterrent) effect of the regulations. However, judging by the situation in Saxony in the spring of 1938, we are driven to conclude that its effects were minimal.[178]

Measures to reinforce and redistribute the working population were more promising, since they did not run counter to entrenched interests. But what is immediately striking is the government's laxity in actually testing the usefulness of the state's power to influence events. For example, pressure put on employers to hire older unemployed office workers was a vestige of the employment creation policy, and had little relevance to the manpower shortage.[179] A more important problem was addressed by the Third Decree on Implementing the Four-Year Plan, issued in the autumn of 1936, namely the numerous workers employed in jobs for which they were not qualified.[180] The obligation imposed on employers to report the names of metal and construction workers who were in jobs other than those for which they had been trained should have given the measure some bite; however, it was never strictly enforced, as we can see from the fact that in the middle of 1938 stonemasons were still, as before, the occupation with the largest number of workers employed outside their field. The documentary records offer no other clues by which to judge the success of the decree, but it is important to note that a number of other occupations in which this problem soon became acute were never even covered by the decree.[181]

The government made an effort to expand vocational education in order to help alleviate the dangerous shortage of skilled workers, an effort that likewise met with little opposition from special interest groups. Industry and handicrafts were apparently easily persuaded that the government's action was in their own interest, and after the issue of the First Decree on Implementing the Four-Year Plan they worked closely with the labour exchanges to promote the government's plan.[182] For school-leavers in 1938/9 there were twice as many apprenticeships available as in 1935/6.[183] However, this great expansion in vocational education, in which practically all branches of industry and handicrafts

---

178. On Darré's scepticism, see above p. 148; on the effects of restricting freedom of movement in Saxony: *Docs. 37–9*.

179. *Doc. 10*.

180. *Doc. 8*.

181. See *Stat. Anhang, Doc. I c*. In June 1938 there were over a million workers employed outside their own occupation.

182. *Doc. 6*.

183. *Stat. Handbuch*, p. 483.

participated,[184] created its own problems. Because of the slight but steady decline in the number of school-leavers, it was becoming increasingly difficult to utilize newly created capacity. In the period 1938–9 the labour exchanges had apprenticeships for 807,000 persons, but the majority of the 871,000 school-leavers who consulted them were either unsuitable or found other employment.[185] Older youths who were already doing unskilled work apparently moved into the unfilled apprentice positions, but this solution had some disadvantages. While adult skilled workers constituted only a third of all industrial workers in 1938, apprentices made up over half of all the young workers employed in industry during the same period.[186] The changes this signalled in the composition of the workforce seemed so far-reaching that the statisticians of the Reich Industry Group forecast a shortage of *unskilled* workers. They noted in this connection that migrants from agriculture would become a vital source of manpower. Every success in this area seemed to lead directly to the next bottleneck.

Meanwhile, there was still a severe shortage of skilled workers in industry. The accumulation of crises in this area led to another intervention by the state at the beginning of March 1938, when school-leavers were obliged to register with the labour exchanges and submit to a kind of enforced job counselling.[187] While this innovation came too late (measured against the seriousness of the situation in the labour market), a general reform of vocational education – the second precondition for a significant increase in productivity – never took place at all. Until the very beginning of the war there was a general lack of clarity about examination requirements and who was responsible for testing. Moreover, in many cases apprentices were so exploited that there was no assurance they were being properly trained. A large part of the reason for this deplorable state of affairs was that almost two-thirds of all apprentices were being trained in the handicrafts sector, many more

184. The expansion was not just limited to the armaments sector; in fact, it was below average in the big metal concerns. For more on this, see the results of a detailed statistical study by the Reich Industry Group covering 1936–8: 'Die Facharbeiter- und Nachwuchsfrage' ('The Skilled Worker and the Need for New Trainees'), *BA/MA Freiburg*, WiIF 5, file 1917.

185. Statistics in Syrup, *Hundert Jahre*, pp. 444f., slightly different figures: *Stat. Handbuch*, p. 483.

186. These figures refer to industry in the narrower sense, i. e., to those firms included within the subdivisions of the Reich Industry Group, except for handicrafts: 'Die Facharbeiter- und Nachwuchsfrage'; see note 184 above.

187. Decree on the Registration of School Leavers (*Anordnung über die Meldung Schulentlassener*), 1 March 1938: *DRA*, no. 51, 2 March 1938. Decree Amending the Decree on Manpower Distribution (*Anordnung zur Änderung der Anordnung über die Verteilung von Arbeitskräften*), 1 March 1938: *R. Arb. Bl. I*, p. 69; with Executive Order, 15 May 1938: ibid., p. 206.

than would eventually find employment as journeymen. A good number of these skilled workers went into industry. But no matter how much industry profited from the training done in craft workshops, industry spokesmen increasingly questioned the dominant role of small business in vocational education, for the gap between the skills acquired there and industry's need for technical expertise continued to widen.[188] There was an urgent need for a complete reorganization of vocational education, but negotiations over a new law stalled. The extravagant 'Reich Vocational Competition', jointly sponsored by the DAF and the Hitler Youth, aimed more at propaganda effect than at a solution to the problem.[189]

When the plans for reform failed to materialize, the state, as so often in the history of National Socialism, reverted to the use of force. At the end of 1938, against the violent opposition of the Reich Estate of German Crafts (*Reichsstand des deutschen Handwerks*), it unilaterally ordered a reduction in the regulation length of apprenticeships,[190] though only after the crisis in international affairs had already come to a head. Measures to reduce the number of workers who, from the perspective of the armaments sector, were unproductively employed proceeded at a similar pace. The search for such workers in the handicrafts sector and in the retail trade did not begin until the spring of 1939.[191] The subsequent 19 per cent drop in employment in the handicrafts sector during the second half of 1939 was largely a result of the military draft, an indication of the size of the unused reserves.[192] Until the spring of 1939 there had been practically no such intervention by the state. The partial elimination of unemployment benefits for temporary workers in the textile and clothing industries in June 1937 was a first modest step; soon, however, even these sectors would be suffering from a shortage of

188. 'Die Facharbeiter- und Nachwuchsfrage', see note 184 above.

189. Cf. above p. 217. The records that have turned up so far on the negotiations over reforms in this area are very fragmentary.

190. Decree of the Minister of Economics, 22 October 1938 and reply from the *Reichsstand des deutschen Handwerks*, 9 November 1938: *BA Koblenz*, R22, file 2070. The same trend characterized the reduction in the required number of years of compulsory secondary school education and in the length of university study.

191. Decree on Implementing the Four-Year Plan in the Handicraft Sector together with Executive Order (*VO über die Durchführung des Vierjahresplans auf dem Gebiet der Handwerkswirtschaft nebst Durchführungsanordnung*), 22 February 1939: *RGBl, I*, pp. 237f.; Decree on the Elimination of Overstaffing in the Retail Trade together with Executive Order (*VO zur Beseitigung der Überbesetzung im Einzelhandel nebst Durchführungsanordnung*), 16 March 1939: *RGBl. I*, pp. 498f.

192. The estimate of 19 per cent comes from an analysis of labour allocation completed by the Labour Ministry in August 1940: *BA Koblenz*, R41, file 144, p. 201. It is probably too high: cf. *Stat. Handbuch*, p. 481, where the decline between May 1939 and May 1940 was estimated at 20 per cent.

workers.[193] The only other government intervention was one which affected the numerically insignficant group of peddlers and itinerant workers, who were prohibited from exercising their occupations in December 1937.[194]

Two other possible ways of eliminating the manpower shortage got nowhere until the beginning of the war: enlisting the labour power of German women and of foreign workers. Although the number of permanently employed women had increased by 2 million between 1933 and 1939, it was still approximately 400,000 below the level of 1928.[195] The government responded passively to this situation. It did repeal the regulation tying the award of a marriage loan to the married woman's leaving her job.[196] But other measures to force or entice women into taking jobs in industry were either slow in coming or never adopted.

Given the Nazis' ideological reservations about employing women in industry, which partly explain the omissions in this area,[197] it is significant that the only compulsory measure that was adopted in the pre-war period was the establishment of a Reich Labour Service designed specifically for young women. The so-called 'duty year for girls' was introduced on 15 February 1938 and amended ten months later in order to increase the number of women obligated to serve; to fulfil their commitment the girls were obliged to work on a farm or in domestic service.[198] The crisis in agriculture was an undeniable fact, but it was not going to be solved by untrained young women; at the same time industry, which had a shortage of women workers, was being denied the use of this labour force. The measure was unpopular, it contained a number of loopholes that could be used to evade service, and it was beset by serious organizational problems. Numerically the one-year service obligation made absolutely no significant contribution to overcoming the labour shortage.[199] No other measures to conscript able-bodied women were adopted, not even in the spring of 1940 when all

193. See *Doc. 41 (Note 14)*. Manpower shortage: *Doc. 96, part I 6; Doc. 156, part IV 5*.

194. Decree of 14 December 1937: *DRA*, no. 289, 15 December 1937.

195. According to health insurance statistics: *Stat. Handbuch*, p. 474.

196. Exceptions were allowed at first, but the regulations were definitively repealed on 1 October 1937: *Deutsche Sozialpolitik 1938*, p. 181.

197. For background information, see Schoenbaum, *Braune Revolution*, ch. 6.

198. Decree on Implementing the Four-Year Plan with Regard to the Increased Use of Female Labour Power in Agriculture and Domestic Work (*Anordnung zur Durchführung des Vierjahresplan über den verstärkten Einsatz von weiblichen Arbeitskräften in der Land- und Hauswirtschaft*), 15 February 1938, together with Executive Order, 16 February 1938: *DRA*, no. 43, 21 February 1938. A further Executive Order, 23 December 1938: *DRA*, no. 305, 31 December 1938.

199. Syrup, *Hundert Jahre*, pp. 450f.; Schoenbaum, *Braune Revolution*, p. 232, calculated that in 1940 some 200,000 girls were doing their one-year service. Cf. also *DZA Potsdam, RAM*, file 9400, p. 46. On the effects in the textile industry, see *Doc. 104, part II 2*. See also Wunderlich, *Farm Labor*, pp. 329ff.; Jill Stephenson, *Women in Nazi Society*, London, 1975, pp. 103ff.

sides, especially the military leadership, agreed that such measures were desperately needed.[200] Monetary inducements were another possibility for solving the problem, but the government hesitated to use them. The DAF strongly backed reforms in the rules protecting pregnant women in factories and plants. New maternity legislation was planned but never adopted, and the changes made during this period to the industrial safety provisions pertaining to women were insignificant.[201]

With regard to equal pay, the most important question, only a few concessions were made to working women, and nothing was done to make work financially attractive to the great number of unoccupied women.[202] The crux of the problem was that the general increase in wages had freed many married women from the necessity of working outside the home, and considerable financial incentives would have been required to reverse this trend, for many of the women whose family circumstances would have allowed them to take a regular job were only prepared to do so if they desperately needed the additional income. The fact that the number of working women actually declined by over 400,000 during the first six months of the war was due in good measure to the relatively generous allowances given to soldiers' wives in an effort to maintain morale among the troops.[203] The government was caught in a vicious circle: conscription was unpopular and therefore out of the question; but so also was any scheme to adjust wages, because of the effects on consumer spending and inflation. Industry was apparently not ready to undertake any systematic attempts at introducing half-day shifts and so on.[204]

200. For a summary of this situation, see Dietrich Eichholtz, 'Zur Lage der deutschen Werktätigen im ersten Kriegsjahr 1939/40', *Jahrbuch für Wirtschaftsgeschichte*, 1967, part 1, pp. 163–9. Additional material: *BA Koblenz*, R41, files 144, 244; R43II, file 652. Deportations from the occupied areas were the preferred method to relieve the manpower shortage. Cf. also above p. 193, as well as the disjointed and poorly edited sources in Ursula von Gersdorff (ed.), *Frauen im Kriegsdienst 1914–1945*, Stuttgart,1969, nos. 115–8, 121, 130.

201. *Deutsche Sozialpolitik 1938*, pp. 49ff., 118–24.

202. Women's wages (actual earnings) were on average 25 per cent to 40 per cent below those of men's. Detailed statistics in Bry, *Wages*, p. 248. The DAF strongly backed equal pay for women and during the first year of the war the Labour Ministry made some concessions: *BA Koblenz*, R41, file 69, especially pp. 6f. (Decree of 15 June 1940).

203. On the readiness of married women to work: *Docs. 150, 156*. Employment statistics: *Stat. Handbuch*, p. 474; the decline was partly seasonal in nature. Separation allowances were as much as 85 per cent of a family's previous income: Eichholtz, 'Werktätige', p. 167. The rates were adopted in the spring of 1939, after the absence of any such support had led to considerable unrest at the time of the partial mobilization in September 1938. Because of the predictable effect of these measures on the employment picture, the Labour Ministry raised objections even at that time, but without success: *BA Koblenz*, R41, file 161, pp. 65–255. It is not surprising that the number of marriages skyrocketed in 1939: *Stat. Handbuch*, p. 47. For further details on this topic and an attempt at interpretation, see Mason, 'Women in Germany', part 2, *History Workshop*, no. 2, 1976.

204. Cf. *Doc. 233*.

There was a further dimension to this question. The kind of work women tend to do under industrial capitalism does not generally represent an attractive alternative to housework. In this respect almost nothing had changed in Germany during the 1930s. The fact that women were only offered undemanding, dull jobs was in keeping with the view that they should leave the workforce after starting a family. The labour situation only served to reinforce and confirm this traditional outlook. The fact that the work performed by women gave them no incentive to stay on the job seemed to prove that money spent to train them would be wasted. According to a survey by the Reich Industry Group in October 1936, only 6.1 per cent of women who were able to work were employed in industry. The proportion among 18 to 20 year-olds was 17.4 per cent. It is probably correct to assume that there is a correlation between this surprising finding and the fact that no more than 4.8 per cent of all female workers in industry had completed a vocational training course. (The average for the industrial workforce as a whole was 28.7 per cent.)[205] In the entire iron and steel industry there were only 13,300 female skilled workers. The remaining 95 per cent of female industrial workers was fairly even divided between unskilled and semi-skilled. The number of semi-skilled workers was relatively large – greater than among male workers and due largely to the nature of the work in the textile and clothing industries.[206] Finally, at 45 per cent the proportion of unskilled workers among the female workforce was also significantly higher than that among male workers. Thus women had only minimal career prospects in industry,[207] and in this regard too their productive capacity was being wasted.

Important economic interests were so enmeshed with deep-seated attitudes and expectations that there was no hope for radical change in this area. Yet the government agencies concerned were apparently unaware of the problem, for the two identifiable directions in government social policy were mutually contradictory. On the one hand, they encouraged large families through a campaign of propaganda, reinforcing the factors that largely determined the life cycle of a working woman – school, a few years in an unskilled trade, marriage, starting a family, leaving the workforce. On the other hand, the dual pressures produced by legislation and the labour shortage created a situation in

205. 'Die Facharbeiter- und Nachwuchsfrage': see note 184 above. There is no explanation in the report about the correlation between age and level of training.

206. There was also a growing, albeit tiny number of skilled female workers in the metal-working industry (114,000), i.e. in a branch in which female labour would be of critical importance to armaments production. The omissions of pre-war policy are especially obvious in this particular case.

207. The low pay for women was, of course, closely related to this.

which the number of apprenticeship positions for young women work-ers had nearly doubled between 1935/6 and 1938/9.[208] Neither of the two directions in social policy produced any notable successes. Until very late in the war the number of women workers in industry remained negligible; at 1.48 million out of a total of 11.6 million in October 1936, they constituted barely 13 per cent of all employed women. The over-whelming majority of working women were concentrated in agriculture, commerce and the service sector.[209] The provisional guidelines for the employment of women in wartime offer a fitting commentary on this aspect of Nazi social policy: '3. Women should not be employed in positions requiring particular mental alertness, initiative or efficiency. 4. In general, women should not be entrusted with work requiring special technical knowledge or technical expertise'.[210]

Despite the conclusion of agreements with Poland and Italy, the number of foreign workers in Germany remained small until the begin-ning of the war. In the middle of 1939 there were approximately 525,000, representing an increase of about 140,000 over previous years.[211] The continuing shortage of foreign exchange put limits on solving the crisis in this way, since foreign workers insisted on exercis-ing their right to send a portion of their earnings home. In addition, a number of employers had become dissatisfied with their foreign work-ers, who had a difficult time adjusting to the repressive aspects of German labour law.[212] German employers were therefore all the more eager to utilize the new reserves that seemed to have become available as a result of the annexation of Austria and the Sudetenland. However, their wish to recruit German-speaking, including nationalist, workers in these areas collided head-on with the racist imperialism of the Nazis, who were intent on establishing a German elite throughout Central and Eastern Europe. For this reason the government prohibited such recruit-ing on principle, allowing exceptions in only a few special cases (the prohibition was often ignored and had to be repeated frequently).[213] This was an early indication of one of the basic internal contradictions inher-

---

208. Cf. *Stat. Handbuch*, p. 483. The number in 1935 was very low and in 1938 consti-tuted slightly over a quarter of all apprentice positions. Most of them were sales jobs.

209. 'Die Facharbeiter- und Nachwuchsfrage': see note 184 above.

210. Von Gersdorff, *Frauen*, no. 111, appendix: Decree of the Minister of Labour, 16 September 1938. See also Mason, 'Women in Germany', part 2.

211. Syrup, *Hundert Jahre*, pp. 411f.; *Stat. Jahrbuch*, 1938, p. 362.

212. Cf. e.g, *Doc. 180, part 2; Doc. 147*. Complaint of 3 August 1938 from the Construction Company of the Niedersächsisches Handwerk to the Hermann Göring Works regarding Dutch bricklayers: *BA/MA Freiburg* WiIF 5, file 1215.

213. Extensive correspondence on this subject in *BA Koblenz*, R41, file 221; *BA/MA Freiburg*, WiIF 5, file 1215; *DZA Potsdam*, RWM, files 10280, 10410. Cf. *Doc. 144*. Austrian workers were not always more industrious or more disciplined than Poles or Italians: Cf. *Doc. 108, Part I*.

ent in the Nazi policy of acquiring additional *Lebensraum*: the economic preparation for conquest often ran counter to the basic intent of this
goal, at least so far as its policy of encouraging Germans to settle in the
East was concerned. The booming armaments sector, in desperate need
of manpower, began to attract workers from all parts of Germany, from
the 'Greater German Reich', ultimately from all the lands of occupied
Europe, into the industrial centres of western and central Germany,
where the workers' standards of living were generally much higher than
in West Prussia, Silesia, the Sudetenland or Austria.[214]

In the absence of radical measures to 'ration people' (*Menschen-
bewirtschaftung*, as it was called) before the middle of 1938, and failing
the possibility of using foreign reserves, an extension of working hours
remained the only viable way to overcome the bottlenecks in production
caused by the manpower shortage. The inadequacies in the official statistics do not permit a precise analysis of this phenomenon, but evidently hours were considerably lengthened. As compared to the official
average of 46 to 47 hours per week in 1938, a 60-hour work week in the
aircraft industry, for example, was no longer a rarity in October of the
same year. A survey done six months later revealed that over half the
workers in three other branches of industry (machine-building, the automotive and the building industries) were working over 48 hours per
week.[215] Even a decree issued in the spring of 1938 to amend the law
regulating hours of work left intact the legal principle of the eight-hour
day; up to two hours of overtime could be specially negotiated but they
had to be paid at the legal overtime rate.[216]

The contribution of longer working hours to an increase in armaments production before the beginning of the war should not be underestimated, yet the consequences, limitations and disadvantages of this
became increasingly evident. The first consequence was the inflationary
effect of bonus rates for overtime, which raised production costs and
increased workers' purchasing power. It is more difficult to judge the
psychological and health effects of longer working hours. What is certain is that the Labour Ministry, the Reichsanstalt, the War Economy
Inspectors and some workers rejected a regular 10-hour day because of
the consequent decline in productivity,[217] and that after the middle of
1938 complaints from various groups about absenteeism, poor work dis-

214. See chapter 4, note 110 above.

215. Bry, *Wages*, p. 48; *BA/MA Freiburg*, WiIF 5, file 1215; *Stat. Anhang, Doc. II c.*
Cf. also *Docs. 145, 150.*

216. Decree of 30 April 1938: *RGBl. I*, p. 447.

217. Cf. Syrup, *Hundert Jahre*, p. 486; *BA/MA Freiburg*, WiIF 5, file 176. According
to Syrup it was primarily the political leadership that called for the extension of the length
of the working day. On the longer shifts in the coal mines: *Doc. 87*; this measure too was
hotly debated.

cipline and the overworking of industrial workers became more frequent and more insistent.[218] For two reasons, however, we must be cautious in drawing the obvious conclusion that these reactions were due mainly to the extension of working hours. First, the final years of the war show that it was clearly possible to increase workloads enormously even under incomparably harder conditions. Second, the agencies that kept complaining about the overburdening of workers were those that had found in extended hours at least one good reason for the failure of their own policies that was beyond their control.[219] Even so, one must conclude that the marginal utility of extending working hours in 1938–9 was negligible and was, in fact, declining during this period.[220] In this connection we must also mention German industry's extremely slow adoption of shift work, in which the individual worker's hours can be kept low while production facilities are exploited to the maximum. This involved night shift work and was unpopular, though the failure to introduce it was probably due more to the shortage of available workers or the unwillingness of the government to let the armaments industry have any additional workers.[221]

The impact of the preparations for war on the labour force can also be represented statistically, in crude figures. Despite the manpower shortage of 1939, the number of people actually working, as a proportion of those of employable age, was no higher than in 1925, that is, somewhere between 67 and 68 per cent. The natural increase in population within the employable age category (by 1.5 million between 1933 and 1939) was just enough to meet the increased demands of the armed forces and the Labour Service, so that the absolute number of workers available to

218. Cf. Docs. *145, 147, 150, 156, 221, 223*. See also below pp. 266–74.

219. The Labour Ministry in particular used this argument in situations in which the bureaucrats were obliged to justify their actions: see e.g. *Doc. 224* (comments by Mansfeld).

220. This raises the extremely difficult problem of worker productivity during the 1930s. A thorough study of this subject would call for several kinds of expertise, which the author of this study does not possess. Rough estimates, however, do make current theories seem very questionable. Both Bry, *Wages*, pp. 22, 71, 362, and David S. Landes, *The Unbound Prometheus*, Cambridge, 1969, pp. 409–20, describe an impressive rise in the productivity of labour. However, if we compare production statistics, first with prices, and secondly with total labour input (number of workers times number of man-hours worked), we see that per-capita productivity stagnated during the period 1935–9; we are led to the same conclusion by the fact that the gross national product grew significantly faster than industrial production; the slowdown in the rate of growth in industrial production in 1937–8 is also noteworthy. These very rough calculations reinforce the impression of many contemporary observers that the level of productivity was quite low. The question remains unresolved. The statistical data in Walter G. Hoffmann, *Das Wachstum der deutschen Wirtschaft*, Berlin, 1965 are indispensable but obscure.

221. Thus in April 1942 90 per cent of Germany's armaments industry was still working only one shift: Milward, *Kriegswirtschaft*, pp. 85, 37, 46. Cf. also Thomas, *Geschichte*, p. 195.

industry and handicrafts during the same period rose by only 5 per cent. In purely arithmetical terms, this increase of around 600,000 workers was achieved at the expense of agriculture which, as shown above, was also suffering from a serious shortage of manpower.[222] The bloated administrative apparatus of Party and state, indispensable as it was for the maintenance of the system of domination, siphoned off hundreds of thousands of workers from industry.[223] Thus in 1939 the newly created armed forces were dependent on an industrial labour force that was scarcely larger and that worked only somewhat longer hours than that of the 1920s. Neither the most rapid advances in technology nor the most scientific management of the means of production could rectify the situation.[224] Grand designs and coercive measures in themselves were not likely to solve the crisis, at least not within Germany's pre-Second World War borders: production capacity was simply not large enough to cope with the demands placed on it. On the other hand, the failure of the government to do anything to 'ration' the workforce was a significant contribution to the crisis in 1939, that is, to its relatively early emergence.

The third group of measures envisaged a redistribution of overall economic capacity for the benefit of rearmament, but they were even less effective.[225] This is not the place to discuss in detail the attempts at a planned economy that become evident after 1936. Experiments with the rationing of raw materials (quotas for the various users), with measures to ensure the husbanding of scarce raw materials (e.g. limitations on the use of structural steel) and with the use of substitute materials (e.g. in the textile industry) were all more or less meant to benefit the rearmament programme. But before the middle of 1938 they were insufficient to provide any effective support to the armaments sector in the competition for the factors of production, and even after this date they were only of very limited value.[226] In the present context, however, the opportunities to limit consumption are of primary importance. A restrictive wage policy was not introduced until the late summer of 1938, and then was administered rather loosely, as we shall see. What is more striking is the absence

222. Klein, *Preparations,* p. 69; *Stat. Anhang, Doc. I d.* See above pp. 194f.

223. The official statistics on this point are unreliable, often contradictory; the lowest estimate of the increase in the number of those employed in administration and so on is 500,000. For a discussion of the problem: *Stat. Anhang, Doc. I d.*

224. There is still no study of this aspect of the economic history of the 1930s. Klein, *Preparations*, pp. 71f., believes that the application of scientific management to industrial production was minimal after 1933; however, he deals with the subject only in passing. The fact that the military leadership constantly felt obliged to complain about the diversity of armaments, which suggests that they had been produced by a variety of individual craftsmen, argues for Klein's hypothesis. Cf. now Ludwig, *Technik.*

225. Cf. above pp. 196–203.

226. Cf. above all Petzina, *Autarkiepolitik,* passim.

of any attempt to increase sales or income taxes or to increase the price of food and so on. Such increases would have had a dual effect: the improvement of the Reich's and/or agriculture's financial situation (both of which were in urgent need of help), and the reduction of purchasing power in such a way as to free capacity in the consumer-goods industry. But they were never implemented. By the time the military-service exemption tax (*Wehrsteuer*) was introduced in July 1937, it was largely irrelevant, and in any case it yielded minimal revenue. The majority of the workers were unaffected by the tax increases included in the 'New Financial Plan' of March 1939, since the 30 per cent tax on supplementary income applied only to annual earnings in excess of RM 3,000.[227] Although this measure, along with the increase in corporation tax from 20 per cent to 40 per cent which was phased in from 1936 to 1939, helped to alleviate the disastrous state of the government's finances, it was not an effective barrier against the expansion of the civilian sector of the economy. So long as consumer purchasing power was not curtailed, the other methods of reallocating GNP for the benefit of rearmament would come to naught. In these circumstances, a move such as the selective shutting down of businesses in the consumer sector might result in inflation, which would erode public confidence in the currency and the economic system. Moreover, such a step would have been 'psychologically intolerable'. Shutdowns of this sort were therefore not initiated until the spring of 1940, and then only timidly.[228]

Most of the Nazi leadership's attempts to develop an economic strategy were utterly unrealistic. The regime was dedicated to aggressive territorial expansion; it would stand or fall on the outcome of that issue. For this reason a modest rearmament programme, geared to available reserves, was unthinkable. Expansionism would then become the hostage of economic conditions that were not exactly favourable to it. On the other side, for domestic policy reasons it was impossible before the war to force the workers to make the material sacrifices that were the indispensable prerequisite for building up the country's military strength to a level adequate to the strategic risks of aggressive military expansion. Armaments

227. Law on a Tax for Individuals Exempted from Two-Year Active Military Service (*Gesetz über eine Steuer der Personen, die nicht zur Erfüllung der zweijährigen aktiven Dienstpflicht einberufen werden*), 20 July 1937: *RGBl. I*, p. 821; Law on the Financing of the Reich's National-Political Tasks (*Gesetz über die Finanzierung nationalpolitischer Aufgaben des Reichs*), 20 March 1939; *RGBl. I*, p. 561.

228. Address by Göring: *Doc. 152*. Cf. the reports of the Regional Economic Offices (*Bezirkswirtschaftsämter*) of April 1940; *BA Koblenz*, R41, file 285. Carroll, *Design*, pp. 204f. Labour policy aspects of the shutdowns in February 1940 along with complaints by Göring on the slowness of carrying them out: *BA Koblenz*, R41, file 64, pp. 5–17; file 244, pp. 99–103. Opposition by the NSDAP and criticism by Thomas: meeting of the War Economy Inspectors on 8 January 1940, *BA/MA Freiburg*, WiIF 5, file 384; Thomas, *Geschichte*, p. 160.

spending and other public expenditures as well as investments in the armaments industry rose steadily (somewhat more slowly in 1937); however, they were becoming an increasing strain on economic reserves – a strain that was jeopardizing the success of these expenditures. The government lacked the authority – objectively as well as according to its own estimations – to implement the draconian social and economic measures that might have reduced or eliminated this strain. The major Nazi organizations contributed absolutely nothing to the solution of this problem; on the contrary, their efforts tended in the opposite direction. The NSDAP, for example, succeeded in having legal holidays made into paid holidays,[229] and there was increasing pressure from its ranks and from the DAF to improve living and working conditions, pressure that was reflected in all Party publications.[230] There were no limits to the desire for prosperity and a lighter working day.[231] The government was incapable of setting a deadline by which its bid to satisfy these desires could be considered as accomplished, and then proceeding on that basis to harness policy to the attainment of its imperialist goals. Even highly-paid groups of workers did not seem to show much sympathy for the goals and problems of the regime or to be any more prepared to exert themselves or subordinate their wishes on its behalf.[232] The material advantages that resulted from full employment did *not* create any new basis for political trust; at best, they helped to reduce some of the distrust. The hatred of National Socialism among workers was surely less marked than it had been before 1933, but the awareness of certain collective interests that were opposed to those of the groups in control remained largely intact and was expressed in innumerable expressions of solidarity on the shop floor. One War Economy Inspector, who sought to get an undistorted sense of the mood of the workers by making a trip around the arms factories and mines of the Ruhr, summed up their opinions and complaints at the end of his report; with one exception, they amounted to a fundamental rejection of National Socialism. Aside from demands for freedom of movement, higher wages, reduced hours, lower prices and so on, he encountered strong anti-war sentiment and the desire for free speech and a free press.[233]

229. *Docs. 53–5.*

230. The DAF's official annual report, *Deutsche Sozialpolitik 1938*, consists almost exclusively of reports on its success in improving social conditions. Cf. *Docs. 97–9*, and above pp. 215f.

231. Cf. the 'illegal' lengthening of legal holidays, even after they had become paid holidays: *Docs. 56, 150, 156.*

232. There are numerous examples of this unwillingness to repay the regime for the improved standard of living: *Docs. 51, 145; 147, 150.*

233. War Economy Inspector, Münster, to W. Stab, 3 September 1938: BA/MA, WiIF5, file 187. The exception was the person of Hitler, who seemed to meet with much approval. Apart from full employment, it was the use of police terror that was primarily responsible for defusing open political frustration.

The domestic political situation could give the government no cause for comfort or hope. The subordination of domestic to foreign policy had to stop abruptly at the point where the regime became concerned about the material bases of its popularity on the home front. That point was already clearly visible in autumn 1936, and had certainly been reached by the end of 1937. The government was passive and indecisive until the growing tensions in Europe finally roused it to take action on behalf of its expansionist goals.

Hitler's decision of 28 May 1938 (following the partial mobilization of the Czech army) to smash Czechoslovakia by autumn was followed in quick succession by the introduction of civilian conscription, the empowerment of the Trustees of Labour to set maximum wages,[234] the working out of a prioritized programme for rearmament within the framework of the Four-Year Plan, and the coming into force of a new system to calculate prices for public contracts in order to keep inflation down.[235]

It is clear from the discussions that took place at the end of 1937 on wage and price policy and on the regulation of the building industry that the necessity for these and other measures had been apparent for quite some time.[236] The decision to use military force to expand the Reich obviously heightened the necessity; and it also seems to have created the circumstances in which the government for the first time felt confident enough to take the necessary measures. The regime apparently needed a foreign-policy crisis before it felt able to take preventive measures against potential threats on the domestic front. Nazi foreign policy, imperialist and racist in its aims, always had a general domestic-policy component, in that it sought to contribute to the unity of the German people on the home front, and to eliminate political, religious, regional and especially class differences. In realizing its objectives it would elevate the German people to the status of Europe's political, economic and racial elite, an elite which would come together to preserve its advantages, even if not out of any genuine feeling of racial superiority. In the history of National Socialism, it was the initial success of its foreign

---

234. Compulsory service: *Doc. 110*; Wage policy: *Doc. 133*.

235. New Production Plan for the Wartime Economy (*Wehrwirtschaftlicher Neuer Erzeugungsplan*), 12 July 1938, often called the 'Karinhall Plan': Petzina, *Autarkiepolitik*, pp. 124–33. Prices: Decree for Public Contracting Agencies on Setting Prices Based on the Original Cost of Production, 15 November, 1938 (*VO über die Preisermittlung auf Grund der Selbstkosten bei Leistungen für öffentliche Auftraggeber*), together with Executive Orders, *RGBl., I*, pp. 1623–30. We cannot go here into any further detail on these problems. The price policy of the public procurement agencies was doubtless one of the main sources of inflation, but it was the only way they could safeguard their interests in the marketplace: Cf. *Doc. 47 (notes 7 and 8); Docs. 66–78; Doc. 96 part I, 3d; Doc. 108 (note 11); Doc. 131, appendix 3; Doc. 151 parts 3, 4.*

236. Cf. *Docs. 72–8, 128–31.*

policy, more than any other factor, that won popular support within Germany and helped to strengthen the regime during the 1930s. Beginning in May/June 1938, however, a subtle but important change was taking place in the relation between foreign and domestic policy. From the documentary sources we get the impression that the problems facing the social and economic policy-makers had become so over-whelming that the only way the government could envisage bringing them under control or 'solving' them was by finding an occasion to incite nationalist sentiment – in other words, by threatening war.[237]

Judging by the appearance of the measures adopted in the summer of 1938, we would conclude that the government had indeed fully exploit-ed this occasion. The list of the new powers to regulate the economy was comprehensive and apparently uncompromising. In its 'New War Economy Production Plan' the government seemed finally to have acknowledged the necessity of setting priorities within the armaments programme. By introducing powers for civilian conscription, it created the means to channel additional manpower to factories producing high-priority items. With this new authority, the Reich Trustees of Labour were empowered to deal with the negative effects of wage increases on prices and on labour allocation by 'taking all necessary measures to pre-vent any adverse effects on combat capability or on the implementation of the Four-Year Plan due to changes in wage rates or other working conditions'.[238] To reinforce this measure and ease the burden on the state's finances, the government revised the method for calculating prices in awarding public contracts. All previously free sectors of the economy were now ostensibly brought under state control, so that the way was clear to subordinating all industrial production to the war effort. The social-policy measures in particular seemed at first glance to attest to a brutal resolve to force the working class into playing the part of a mere factor of production, with which industry and the state could do whatever they pleased.

This intent was unmistakably reflected in the texts of the decrees. Far from being arbitrary, it was perfectly adapted to the new situation. The reduction of the worker to a cog in the machinery of war was a neces-sary consequence of rearmament, and a necessary precondition for its continued expansion. But government action was confined to recogniz-ing problems, planning to meet them and drafting decrees. It never got as far as embarking on a really new course in social and industrial poli-cy. Up to the beginning of the war and beyond, the crisis in the labour market, in wage regulation, in labour discipline and productivity contin-

---

237. See Concluding Remarks below, pp. 255ff.
238. *Doc.133.*

ued with little change, for the working class did not readily or quickly accept the role assigned to it. Because of the political instability of the regime, the result of the measures adopted in summer 1938 was a general unwillingness on the part of industrial workers to make any sacrifices to prepare for war. Accordingly, the government made relatively little use of its new powers to regulate the lives of industrial workers – 'little', that is, considering the seriousness of the problems in the middle of 1938 and the existence of a political leadership that was rushing head-long into war.[239] The room to manoeuvre that had resulted from the international crisis and the new legislation was in reality very restricted, and it allowed mainly tactical, not strategic, mobility. Just as propaganda concentrated its efforts on exploiting individual political events and avoided any openness with the people about the inevitability of hardships and personal sacrifices,[240] so the new powers to shape social policy were only used to deal with short-term problems or tasks; they were never adequate to tackle the major structural challenge of the manpower shortage and all its attendant problems. The vacillation and omissions that characterized the social context of war preparations are fully documented in the last five chapters of *Arbeiterklasse und Volksgemeinschaft*. It is neither possible nor necessary within the scope of this brief analysis to describe in detail the hectic and confused decision-making process. The following brief overview is therefore limited to three major problem areas: civilian conscription, by which workers were compelled to take 'jobs of particular political importance'; the state's initial attempts to intervene directly in the area of wage policy; and the failure of further compulsory measures during the first ten weeks of the war.

The introduction of civilian conscription had become necessary because the armaments sector could find no other way to get additional workers. There were serious fiscal dangers in a continued reliance on high wages as a way to attract workers, and there were other reasons why this would not have been likely to help. First, workers could only have been lured from sectors that were also suffering from manpower shortages and were of equal economic importance (e.g. agriculture, the building-materials industry, export firms). Second, additional wage increases in the armaments sector would probably have encouraged job changing within this sector, with employers competing more intensely

---

239. By any other standards of judgement, government actions were barbaric enough; here, however, only the objective implications of these developments are our concern.

240. See *Docs. 136, 137, 156*. The problems of social policy played an astonishingly minor role in the deliberations of the Labour Ministry during the first months of the war: cf. Willi A. Boelcke, *Kriegspropaganda 1939–1941*, Stuttgart, 1966. Cf. also *Docs. 221, 229*. The Reich Chancellery was also fully aware of propaganda's weakness in this respect; memorandum of 21 December, 1939: *BA Koblenz*, R43II, file 468, p. 26.

than before for workers and with no assurance that the armaments industry would end up with a larger proportion of the labour force.[241] The
restrictions imposed on freedom of movement for workers in the metal
and building industries, which had come into force before the summer
of 1938,[242] were practically useless in these circumstances, for it was no
longer a matter of preventing workers from job changes that were harm-
ful to rearmament, but of positive measures to compel them to take a
particular opening.[243] The immediate occasion for the civil conscription
decree of 22 June 1938 – the crisis that made state intervention possible
– was the rapid expansion of the fortifications in the West, which called
for approximately 400,000 additional workers. The government naturally had no intention of limiting the application of the decree to this high-
priority project. There was a general need for more such measures, and
legislation took increasing account of it.[244]

Yet civilian conscription did not lead to concerted resistance. The
Gestapo was too efficient to allow that to happen, and the illegal organizations of the working class had for too long been exposed to systematic
persecution and destruction. What the measure could not do, however,
was win the sympathy and understanding that a conscription system
depended on for its success, given the inevitable hardships it imposed on
individual workers, and the enormous complexity of its implementation.
As sporadic and ineffective as the actual manifestations of workers'
anger were,[245] they were enough to make the government hesitant to rely
on the 'blind trust' of the obligation itself. It is clear that the overwhelming unpopularity of civilian conscription was the decisive reason why it
was in fact rarely used – though it is unclear when and on the basis of
what evidence this decision was reached,[246] or whether there was any formal decision at all. There were no more than two episodes of mass conscription in 1938–9, when the government saw no alternative but hoped
that the conscripts might just concede that the significance of the projects
justified the action. Of the approximately 1.3 million workers conscript-

241. *Docs. 96, 104, 108, 145, 174, 150* offer numerous examples of these two directions.
242. *Docs. 17, 66, 80.*
243. Further restrictions on freedom of movement were also necessary so that other
branches of industry could meet their needs, and so that permanent employees would not
leave factories in which non-permanent workers from the outside had been forced to take
on jobs. Cf. the decree of 10 March 1939: *Doc. 158.*
244. Cf. explanatory text preceding *Doc. 119*, and the amendment to the decree of 13
February 1939: *Docs. 119–21.*
245. Cf. *Doc. 114, note 6; Docs. 116, 117, 123, 127.* Individual refusals to be conscripted: *Docs. 147, 156.*
246. Though this cannot be proven conclusively in this case, the criticism of the decree
by Party and DAF officials probably played an important part. *Docs. 112, 113,127* indicate this, and during the years 1939–42 a number of Gauleiters opposed the transfer of
workers from one *Gau* to another. See also below pp. 253f.

ed by the end of 1939, nearly 400,000 were sent to work on the Siegfried Line, and over 500,000 were dispatched to factories retooling for war. Most were short-term conscripts; in March 1940, for example, only 208,000 were liable for longer terms of service.[247]

Although it was significant that the regime was able to quash these isolated sources of danger with bureaucratic power, and although both these projects were colossal feats of organization, the basic structural problems deriving from the manpower shortage remained as insoluble as ever. In domestic as well as in military affairs, the regime was only capable of conducting 'blitzkrieg' campaigns. Attempts to use conscription as a permanent solution to the manpower shortage in the armaments industry do not seem to have got beyond the earliest stages. By the end of 1939 only some 400,000 workers had been conscripted into service, a number that was far less than the actual demand. The executive order to the amended conscription decree of 14 March 1939 established strict procedures to review applications from business and industry for conscript workers and to turn down those that were not adequately supported. At the same time the Ministry of Labour admitted openly that 'for economic and social reasons' it could no longer issue conscription orders 'in sufficient numbers to meet all manpower needs'.[248] Even so, Göring felt obliged in July 1939 to pressure all agencies concerned to reduce the number of conscription notices.[249] Many employers evidently shared the concerns of the political leadership, for although their armaments contracts were acknowledged by the decree to be of 'particular significance to the state', they preferred to make do without conscripted labour.[250] Yet there were conspicuous shortages of manpower throughout the armaments sector in the year preceding the onset of war, shortages that led directly to delays and breakdowns in production and even to orders from the military being turned away.[251] Thus the regime's hands were tied; it was unable to make systematic use of the potentially most effective means for meeting the manpower needs of the armaments industry. Of course, the situation would have been easier if the economic policy-makers had first freed up reserves by closing down businesses in the consumer sector. But it is typical of the Nazis' preference for

247. Cf. *Doc. 127.* Additional statistical data: *DZA Potsdam*, RAM, file 9400, p. 46; *BA Koblenz*, R41, file 279, p. 96. The total number of short-term conscripts at the beginning of the war was probably above the numbers given in *Doc. 127*, which refer only to the first twelve days of war. By the end of November the labour exchanges, using the data in their labour pass files, had transferred 1.8 million workers to new jobs, most of whom, however, were not conscripts: *BA Koblenz*, R43II, file 529b.

248. *Doc. 121, part 2; Doc. 158.*

249. *Doc. 124.*

250. See explanatory text preceding *Doc. 125.*

251. Cf. above pp. 190f.; also Ludwig, *Technik*, pp. 184f., 348ff. (especially p. 350, note 19).

coercive solutions that they introduced civilian conscription before considering closures; it was their tendency to appease and their anxieties that made closures seem impractical and at the same time kept conscriptions to a minimum. As well, only a limited number of people were affected by civil conscription, whereas a reduction in the output of consumer goods would have caused the whole nation to suffer.[252]

The same vacillation that characterized the exercise of the government's plenary powers also determined the treatment of those workers who had actually been conscripted. The initially quite generous wage settlement, especially for those drafted to work on the Siegfried Line, gave way in February 1939 to a system that made only minimal provisions for lost wages, increased cost of living, and so on. Then because of the increased unpopularity of civil conscription that followed, separation allowances and various other kinds of assistance were introduced during the summer, only to be cancelled at the beginning of the war, and then reintroduced a few weeks later.[253] These confused and confusing changes epitomised the great insecurity felt by the regime itself; no one knew how much the workers would take. That sweeping changes were needed was acknowledged, but then accompanied every step of the way by fear of potential social and political turmoil. The example of civilian conscription, important as it is on its own, also showed clearly the extent to which relations between the regime and the working class had deteriorated by the beginning of the war. In these circumstances, there were really only two contradictory courses of action possible for those in power: a policy of force or a policy of concession. The government floundered between the two extremes. The Nazi regime itself had destroyed any possible basis for co-operation between the government and the working class; and the DAF had long ceased to be an effective or even dangerous intermediary – unlike the trade unions during the First World War.[254]

Clearly, the intent of the Decree on Wage Structure issued on 24 June 1938 was not just to make further wage increases impossible.[255] By keeping its enabling provisions sufficiently broad, the framers were able to put almost all aspects of industrial relations under the authority of the Trustees of Labour, in effect transforming a large part of labour law into criminal law. The basic aim of the decree was to tighten up

---

252. In this respect the institution of civil conscription was typical of the repressive methods of the Nazis; in their most radical form they were selective, in order to preserve the appearance of normality for the majority: cf. below pp. 250, 272f.

253. Cf. *Doc. 111, para 13; Doc. 120, para 17–18; Doc. 121, part 5; Docs. 122, 124, 183–4, 241.*

254. Cf. Feldman, *Army, Industry and Labor*, ch. 4.

255. *VO über die Lohngestaltung; Doc. 133.*

labour discipline; given the numerous complaints from industry at the time, this was hardly insignificant for production.[256] Unlike the situation immediately after the seizure of power in 1933, it was no longer possible to continue expanding economic capacity indefinitely; it was now crucial to cut consumer purchasing power and to use wage controls to prevent further increases in the cost of industrial production, with their adverse implications for state finances. The June decree gave the government the formal legal authority to carry out these measures, but the regime was simply not politically or administratively capable of doing this: wage policy was precisely the arena in which the long-term structural contradictions made one-off actions by the state incapable of producing solutions. The new wage policy ran counter to the laws of the market, the interests of those involved and the patterns of behaviour of both worker and employer – patterns which could not simply be changed by fiat.

For these reasons the measure was unpopular, and not just among workers. The press, which had long been accustomed to presenting its readers with nothing but reports of success, showed little interest in a policy that was focused not just on the rhetoric of sacrifice, but that actually called on people to bear real privations and hardships.[257] Only with the greatest reluctance did the leadership of the DAF acquiesce in a new policy that threatened to deprive it of a large measure of its freedom of action at the factory level.[258] Most of the DAF press withheld reports of the decree, and the organization's annual report commented on it in such a way as to directly encourage its provisions to be disregarded and circumvented.[259] (A dispute between Schmeer, Ley's deputy, and State Secretary Krohn at the Nuremberg Party Congress gives us an insight into the unusual tensions that disagreements about wage policy provoked between the DAF leadership and the Labour Ministry: Schmeer charged that the DAF had never been invited to participate in the drafting of the decree; Krohn denied the charge, and when Schmeer kept insisting he was right, Krohn challenged him to a duel.) [260] On the other side, more than a few employers viewed higher wages as the only practical inducement to prevent workers from leaving jobs and to maintain production

256. Cf. *Docs. 138–140*, as well as the explanatory text preceding *Doc. 138*; see also *Docs. 145, 147, 150, 156*; and cf. also below pp. 267ff.

257. Cf. *Doc. 137* (especially note 5); *Docs. 150, 156*.

258. Cf. *Docs. 137, 156*. The regulations in *Doc. 140*, in particular, tended to set limits to the DAF's demands for better fringe benefits for workers.

259. *Deutsche Sozialpolitik 1938*, pp. 92f; *Doc. 137 (note 5)*.

260. *Berlin Document Center*, Supreme Court of the Party (*Oberster Parteigerichtshof*), Krohn file. A few weeks later, people were relieved to discover that Hitler had forbidden duels between party members.

and work discipline; to the extent that they were producing for public contractors, higher wages would cost them nothing anyway.[261]

Of crucial importance in gauging the impact of the decree was the assumption that the stabilization of maximum wage rates and the reduction of existing rates (high as a result of the economic boom) would not be the kind of cause which the various power elites would come together to support.[262] The executive authorities found it hard to swim against a tide in which the laws of economics converged with the short-term political interest of the ruling circles and the Nazi movement in maintaining their own popularity. In addition, they found it hard to organize the effective implementation of a wage policy that called for a large number of experienced personnel, who simply did not exist. The power of the bureaucracy was not massive enough simply to force adherence to the new guidelines, and the Trustees of Labour were obliged to rely partly on the deterrent effect of spot checks and punishing violators to set examples, and partly on getting the co-operation of employers.[263] It is not surprising in these circumstances that wage increases in the twelve months after the decree came into effect were higher than those during the preceding twelve months. On average, hourly earnings in industry went up by about 5 per cent and weekly earnings by nearly 9 per cent between June 1938 and June 1939.[264] The increase might have been higher without the decree. But that was small comfort to the agencies responsible for price stabilization and the expansion of the armaments sector.[265]

One tangible effect of the new wage policy was that the Labour Ministry was now confronted with the realities of class conflict. The experience with government wage controls came just in time to influence the preparations for wartime social-policy legislation, and it made the authorities realize that the planned general reduction in wages would be next to impossible to implement – absolutely impossible if there were no simultaneous and proportionately greater tax increase on all other sources of income. Since there was still no draft legislation to this effect

261. Cf. *Docs. 136, 137, 156, 274.* See also note 148 above. This is in contrast to the impression of the Trustees of Labour that employers would willingly go along with the move to reduce wages: *Doc. 136.*

262. Among the Gauleiters, Sauckel seemed to have been an exception; cf. *Doc. 141.*

263. Extension of the administrative responsibilities of the Trustees in 1939: explanatory text preceding *Doc. 138.* This did not lead to complete control either; cf. *Doc. 212.* Problems in implementing wage controls: *Docs. 150, 151, 156.* Examples of reductions in wages: *Docs. 136, 137.* Punishments to set an example: explanatory text preceding *Doc. 138; Doc. 220.* Public service: explanatory text preceding *Doc. 138,* especially note 9.

264. Bry, *Wages,* pp. 242f.

265. Besides *Doc. 187,* see also the bitter retrospective observations on this question by Wagner in a letter of 21 December 1939 to the Ministry of Finance: *BA Koblenz,* R2, file 24251. On the same day Darré also wrote to Göring in the same tone: ibid., R43II, file 611.

by the beginning of 1939, the Labour Ministry withdrew its consent to the reduction of wages to the official levels (i.e. by an average of about 13 per cent, a higher percentage in the case of the armaments industry), and called instead for a simple wage freeze in the event of war.[266] It is difficult to determine the extent to which the Labour Ministry was seeking to evade its responsibilities by pointing to the unwillingness of other agencies to tax the middle class in proportion to the demands made on the working class; its implied argument, that the kind of class discrimination the other ministries were still trying to push through would lead to bitterness and perhaps to unrest, was certainly plausible. Beyond this, there was the fear that any reduction in wages would necessarily lead to a decline in productivity.[267] These doubts, nourished by the reaction to rather trivial measures after June 1938, proved to be totally justified at the beginning of the war. The compromise settlement on wage and tax policy that was worked out by the ministries during the final days of August 1939 and that was embodied in the War Economy Decree of 4 September proved a failure in practice. Despite the state of war and a 50 per cent increase in the income tax for the middle class, workers were not ready to resign themselves to even a limited reduction in wages, to the elimination of overtime pay or to the suspension of industrial safety regulations.[268] The NSDAP, worried because of the plebiscitary foundations of the regime, quickly made itself the proponent of a moderate wage policy, and within a month everything had returned to normal, that is, a wage freeze with wage reductions only in cases of higher-than-average earnings.[269] The dissatisfaction and passive resistance continued, however, until mid-November 1939, when the government saw itself forced to make further concessions in social policy. Bonus pay (except for the ninth and tenth hours of work) and holiday leave were restored, and this was quickly followed by the re-enactment of most of the industrial safety regulations.[270]

The shift in October and November did not, as might appear at first, signal the synchronization of social and economic policy with the strategic situation; there was no attempt to exploit the 'phony war', the passivity of England and France, to defer unpopular measures because they were not yet inevitable. When the wage policy was revised in early October 1939 the course of the war was still a totally open question, and when the ministries saw themselves obliged to complete a second with-

266. *Docs. 164–9, 173.*
267. *Docs. 171, 172.*
268. Taxation: *Doc. 185, section 2*; wages: *Doc. 191*; bonuses: *Docs 185, para. 18*; industrial safety legislation: *Doc. 176*. On other repressive measures: *Docs. 177, 178, 185.*
269. *Docs. 201–3, 206.*
270. *Docs. 227, 228, 235.* Cf. also *Docs. 237, 241.*

drawal in the area of social policy on 10 November, the invasion of France was scheduled to begin nine days later.[271] Thus the preparations in domestic policy for the extension of the war to all of Western Europe involved the surrender of important positions in the war economy. The proponents of a hard line tried in vain to oppose the heavy pressure from below and the political leadership's readiness to make concessions: 'It is not possible to wage war if we wrap one section of the population, the workers, in cotton wool'.[272]

This decisive retreat was of much greater significance than the published sources on social policy indicate, for during this same period the organizational principles underlying policy for the war effort, indeed the entire structure of German industry, were under discussion. In planning for mobilization it had been assumed that a war against the Western powers, which came to pass on 3 September, could only be fought by radically transforming the German armaments industry. The plans involved the ruthless concentration of all production within the large concerns and the transfer of men and machinery from smaller and less efficient firms to big industry. These smaller companies as well as many firms in the consumer-goods sector were to be closed down at once. It was quite obvious that civilian conscription would be an important instrument in carrying out this colossal intervention by the state; not only would the 'freed' workers be forced to live apart from their families, but their employment would have to be centrally controlled in order to meet the changing needs of the big concerns. It is still an open question whether these plans had been worked out in precise detail in autumn 1939; in any event, they were now being discussed in earnest and had an influential spokesman in the person of General Thomas.[273]

It was Thomas, indeed, who was ordered to disclose the final and complete version of the plans on 13 November 1939, just before the scheduled invasion of France. To a gathering of generals and state secretaries he reported on Hitler's instructions to Keitel the day before. Hitler had said that it was 'out of the question' to separate workers from their families because of conscription; smaller firms should be 'retooled' to make them useful to the armaments industry; there should be a ban on the further expansion of large concerns, and on the formation of new conglomerates; if at all possible, workers should be

271. Jacobsen, *Fall 'Gelb'*, p. 141. By this time, the invasion had already been postponed twice.

272. *Doc. 224*. On this see Eichholtz, *Kriegswirtschaft*, ch. 2/1.

273. Until now I have only been able to find scattered sources on this topic. The above sketch is based primarily on notes taken at meetings on 21 August (Thomas) and 30 October 1939 (Posse): *BA/MA Freiburg*, WiIF, files 384, 412. Cf. Thomas *Geschichte*, chs. 17–19, especially pp. 167ff. and pp. 402–5, 498–511. Thomas's description, however, seems somewhat restrained.

employed in their home towns. Thomas's listeners received this news with undisguised relief, emphasizing that the discarded plans would have established two potential 'danger zones' – the inevitable unemployment in the transition period, and the concentration of large numbers of embittered workers in the immediate vicinity of the large armaments plants. To Thomas himself this reaction seemed inappropriate; while the majority of those present approved the new decision 'for political and social reasons', he gave priority to the strategic dimension, that is, its effect on the war effort. The manpower shortage in the armaments sector was becoming increasingly dangerous and was reflected in the inability to supply the armed forces with essential war *matériel*. By Christmas Paris was supposed to be in German hands. Thomas concluded with the telling observation that spreading armaments contracts over the large number of firms in the metal industry was no doubt the proper policy – for a *short* war.[274]

The decision to limit the number of civilian conscripts to a minimum and to give up the idea of concentrating armaments production was approved by the Ministerial Council (*Ministerrat*) on 15 November and made public by the Labour Minister on 24 November.[275] It was then the grounds for Göring's important decree of 29 November.[276] In contrast to the retreat on the issue of working conditions, where every change in policy was open to public view, the history of contradictory decisions in this case and the existence of an alternative to the policy of dispersing contracts were largely concealed from the people.

This confrontation, which profoundly influenced all aspects of economic and social policy, had a number of important repercussions. The general tendency in the development of class relations since 1936 was finally confirmed during the crisis. National Socialism had not succeeded in transforming the working class into a willing tool of its expansionist policy. In superficial terms, events showed that even in wartime it would not be possible to correct the omissions of previous years through social policy and propaganda. For too long the regime had allowed anxiety and inertia to continue unchecked in this area. For too long it had been unable to deal with the consequences of an armaments boom that was of its own making, and it could not now make the necessary transi-

274. Detailed record of this meeting: *BA/MA Freiburg*, WiIF 5, file 412. On 12 November the invasion of France was scheduled for 19 November 1939.

275. See *Doc. 240*. On the approval of the Ministerial Council, see the unofficial notes of the War Economy Staff's representative: *BA/MA Freiburg*, file 384; the subject was not mentioned in the official minutes.

276. Guidelines for Combining All Efforts to Boost Armaments (*Richtlinien zur Zusammenfassung aller Kräfte zur Steigerung der Rüstung*): *BA/MA Freiburg*, WiIF 5, file 3142. Cf. Carroll, *Design*, p. 204. In the months that followed, this was considered a fundamental decision which was not to be questioned.

tion from a peace-and-war economy to a pure war economy. The regime's powerlessness, however, was not primarily the result of miscalculations and omissions; rather, its misjudgements and mistakes were the symptoms of the insoluble class antagonisms which ultimately determined the regime's inability to act domestically. The policy of expansion eventually intensified the basic contradictions in the social order to the point where the government was left with nothing more than an assortment of mistakes among which to choose. That this did not have grave consequences for the conduct of the war itself was due purely to chance and external factors.

6.3. Concluding Remarks

The Blitzkrieg Strategy and Domestic Policy

Until now scholarly discussion of the Nazis' economic mobilization for war has been dominated by the conflict between Hitler's strategic concepts and those of the armed forces. There is a largely tacit assumption in this discussion that a different rearmament policy might have been possible and that the policy actually pursued was mainly the result of deliberate decisions made by Hitler in the areas of strategy and economic policy.[277] This view seems to be based on an untenable overestimation of the real power of the political leadership, and on an unrealistic exaggeration of its ability to control the social and economic system. An analysis of Nazi social policy after 1933 suggests that the level of war preparations was determined chiefly by domestic political factors: on the one hand, by the reluctance of the entire population, particularly the working class, to acquiesce in the economic preparations for war after 1936; and on the other, by the inability of the political leadership to withstand the pressures from below for improved living and working conditions. This situation derived mainly from full employment, which in turn was the inevitable result of rearmament. As the problem got worse, it became important for powerful organizations within the power structure, primarily the DAF and the NSDAP, to represent the desire of the workers to better their lot – even if they did this unsystematically, with minimal determination, and for selfish political reasons that had little to do with the welfare of the workers. But the decisive factor was the

---

277. Cf. Klein, *Preparations*; Milward, *Kriegswirtschaft*; Carroll, *Design*.

government's anxiety about the solidity of its political authority. After the obvious failure to indoctrinate the workers in the philosophy of National Socialism, the only way to allay this anxiety was for the government to take account of the working class's stubborn desire for improved living conditions. The domestic crisis at the beginning of the war showed how well-founded and profound these concerns were and how patently impossible it would be to implement a social policy that sought to adjust living and working conditions to the demands of war. The government was therefore forced to yield. It was this constellation of forces that described the limits within which economic mobilization for war was possible. The overriding importance of these factors was openly acknowledged during the 'war games' played by the ministries responsible for social policy. In the course of these games, Hitler's political and strategic calculations – that a blitzkrieg would, because of its speed, preclude any need for radical domestic policies – took second place to the fundamental questions of class relations, political stability, increasing armaments production and maintaining labour discipline.[278] The claim that Hitler's strategy did not require more concentration of the nation's economic strength on rearmament is contradicted by the efforts that were in fact undertaken in that direction – efforts which ultimately showed just how inept the regime really was. The strategic situation following Britain's declaration of war made it absolutely imperative to impose wage cuts and cancel bonuses and holiday claims,[279] but by then the state had reached the limits of its effective power.

There are other powerful reasons to question the assumption that, against the background of Hitler's political and strategic calculations, the social and economic situation was appropriate to military needs. Since the beginning of negotiations for wartime legislation it had been clear that the government would have to pursue a hard line in social policy.[280] As early as the beginning of 1938 the situation there left no doubt that even short blitzkrieg campaigns would require far-reaching economic controls. The acute shortages of reserves in all the important factors of production ruled out any possibility of doing without such controls. The continued delays in their implementation at least had the advantage of ensuring domestic tranquillity and avoiding the social and political tensions which would undoubtedly have been provoked by coercive measures to reduce consumer spending and allocate manpow-

278. *Docs. 160–73.*
279. Of all the social policy measures introduced at the beginning of the war, only the War Economy Decree (*Kriegswirtschaftsverordnung*) was *not* issued on the day Poland was attacked: *Doc. 185.*
280. Cf. *Docs. 160–3.*

er.[281] But otherwise procrastination brought disadvantages and only made problems worse. In 1936, for example, it was still possible to think about bringing wages down to tariff rates in the event of war, but by 1939 the gap between tariff rates and actual earnings had become so great in most branches of industry that such a move could only have been contemplated at the risk of serious civil unrest. The plans to control wages and prices and to 'ration' manpower, necessary as they were, were quite as important and complex as any social measures. An administrative apparatus capable of dealing with these issues could not be created by magic,[282] and the planning techniques and mechanisms for co-operation between the many agencies involved could not be learned overnight. Wage and price control policy, contract management and direct control of the employment of labour were all closely interrelated.[283] In practice, one control gave rise to another, the first then becoming dependent on the next one. Given the shortages in the economy, it was impossible to conceive of a solution that lay midway between the largely indirect controls of 1933–8 and the developing centralized administrative controls, at least so far as the power and responsibilities of government authorities were concerned. If administrative controls were going to be more than mere words on a printed page, they needed more time to take effect than they were given. However, regardless of whether the war was going to be short or long – in fact, regardless of whether there was going to be a war at all in 1939 – they had to be intro-

281. Hitler occasionally mentioned another possible advantage, namely that the decision not to issue wartime laws prematurely was a way of maintaining the element of surprise before launching an attack. The generals would have preferred to publish a wartime constitution (*Wehrverfassung*) ahead of time in order to let the people become familiar with its provisions. This did not happen; even in 1939 economic mobilization did not take place publicly. Publicity was a negligible issue, however, in the case of social policy, since the the measures that were necessary in wartime differed neither in content nor in spirit from those that had been issued before the war. See the explanatory text preceding *Doc. 110*.

282. Cf. Göring's criticisms of the labour exchanges: *Doc. 152*. His remarks were based on Thomas's statements regarding the course of the crises in this area in 1938: *BA/MA Freiburg* WiIF 5, file 560/1, pp. 197–203. Wide-ranging criticism by the Gauleiters, the *Oberpräsidenten*, and the *Regierungspräsidenten* of the lack of co-operation between the domestic administration and the labour exchanges in spring 1940: *GPSA Berlin*, Rep. 320, file 365, pp. 257–68. The relation between wage policy and labour allocation was improved as a result of the appointment of the Labour Office director (*Arbeitsamtsleiter*) to the position of deputy to the Reich Trustees of Labour on 1 August 1939: Syrup, *Hundert Jahre*, pp. 469f. The Trustees were still very overworked and had fallen far behind in issuing wage codes: *Doc. 163*. Cf. also the slow implementation of wage reduction measures: *Doc. 212*.

283. This interdependence also affected the sequence of state interventions in the second half of 1938; see above, pp. 244ff. For example, a more stringent price policy for public contracts would have hampered the rearmament programme only until the introduction of wage controls and the imposition of limits on workers' freedom of movement.

duced immediately.[284] Yet the controls did not become effective or comprehensive until sometime in 1942. After the Depression had been fully exploited as a launching pad for economic recovery and the expansion of indigenous sources of raw materials had been ordered during the second year of the Four-Year Plan, the social and economic preparations for war continued to lag behind developments in foreign and strategic policy. These delays in coming to grips with social and economic policy call for an explanation. In this case, Hitler's blitzkrieg strategy will not suffice as an answer, for it too was in dire peril as a result of the inadequacies of the war economy.

Hitler's Foreign Policy

It may be possible to clarify these issues further by approaching the problem from the other side and looking at the reasons for the dynamism in the development of Nazi foreign policy after 1937. I do not intend in the following brief survey to question the foundations of previous research on this subject. There can be no doubt that the development of international relations during this period was propelled by its own inner logic, or that the position of Great Britain and France up to the occupation of Prague and beyond encouraged Hitler's aggressive actions. However, the impact of Hitler's foreign policy on domestic policy during this period has not received the attention it deserves. One aspect of this subject has been pointed out above: the interrelationship between crises in foreign policy and coercive measures taken in social policy. The steps taken to militarize the lives of workers, which we are concerned with here, can be divided into three clearly distinct phases: November 1936, June 1938 and September 1939. Between these three dates no laws or decrees of importance were issued.[285] Only the first set of decrees can be described as preventive measures. Yet even the controls introduced in November 1936 were weak – weaker in fact than they had been in draft form.[286] The difference between the first and the later periods was due not only to the fact that the problems in social policy had not yet come to a head, but to the more tranquil atmosphere in international affairs in November 1936. No excuse could be found in the international situation to warrant making massive and radical changes in working and living conditions. With

284. Thus wartime legislation consisted, in part, of measures which had already been in the preparation stage in summer 1939; see below p. 259.
285. The decrees issued in February and March 1939 (*Docs. 119–21,158*) are only a partial exception; they are basically amendments to the decree on civil conscription issued in June 1938.
286. *Docs. 3, 6–12.*

regard to the actions taken in June 1938 and September 1939, it is proper to conclude that the government was fully aware of the difficulties and dangers inherent in an assault on the living standard of the working class and was simply waiting for an international crisis to erupt before it dared to tackle domestic problems. The adverse effects of the upward spiral in wage rates and of the workers' new freedom of movement in the labour market were evident even before the frenzied work on the Siegfried Line had begun; they had been the subject of constant discussions among all the ministries concerned at least since autumn 1936, and wage policy had been the subject of a detailed but still-born plan for state intervention since at least December 1937.[287]

Similar conditions existed as the war began. In several areas of social and economic policy firmer measures were necessary, but had not yet come into force. The specialist in the Labour Ministry responsible for wage policy thus saw the beginning of the war as a welcome opportunity to push more vigorously for a total reform of the wage structure.[288] Even before the beginning of the war, officials in the Labour Ministry had considered giving the Trustees of Labour the power to impose penalties so that they could effectively implement their guidelines on wage policy and labour discipline without first having to go though the cumbersome and time-consuming process of taking matters to court.[289] In another department of the Ministry a decree was being drafted which would have required anyone wishing to change jobs to get prior approval.[290] The Reich Price Commissar, whose unhappiness over the increase in prices was growing by leaps and bounds, had already circulated the draft of a decree which would authorize him to combat rising inflation more effectively.[291] All the proposals seem indeed to have been necessary and appropriate to existing circumstances. Yet none was implemented until the beginning of the war; they were all adopted in the body of decrees issued during the first days of the war.[292]

287. *Docs. 128–31.* Strictly speaking, the limitation on the freedom of movement of construction workers of 30 May 1938 (*Doc. 80*) must be considered one of the measures taken without regard to the international situation. The fact that the decree coincided chronologically with Hitler's decision to build the Siegfried Line was most probably pure coincidence. Of all agencies, the Reichsanstalt and the labour exchanges subordinate to it were the ones most prepared to act without always thinking about public reactions; however, the head of the Reichsanstalt only had negative power, i. e, to limit freedom of movement. Cf. *Docs. 17, 66, 101.*

288. *Doc. 193.*

289. *DZA Potsdam*, RWM, file 10401, p. 55.

290. See *Doc. 172.*

291. See *Docs. 187* and *159.*

292. Wages: *Doc. 185, para. 18; Docs. 190–1.* Legal penalties: *Doc. 185, para. 21.* Changing jobs: *Doc. 177.* Price-setting: *Doc. 185, section 4*; cf., however, *Docs. 189–90.*

Even though the sources do not conclusively prove that the political leadership *deliberately* used the tactic of deferring the expansion of its dictatorial powers on the home front until some event in the international arena offered a propagandistically useful pretext, the opposite conclusion – that the government intervened in domestic affairs only when it was truly necessary to do so – is clearly untenable. The expansionist goals of the regime dictated the use of pre-emptive action in order to secure the greatest possible concentration of economic resources in the armaments sector. However, it generally failed to carry out such measures when they affected the workers in their capacity as producers or consumers. The main reason for this is that the government's goals were never recognized by the workers as sufficient justification for their subjugation, their material sacrifices or the additional burdens imposed on them. This fact was recognized by the regime in so far as it only attempted to impose sacrifices and discipline on the working class through the use of force after it had begun its war of aggression.

But even this tactic failed miserably. At best, the period between June 1938 and September 1939 brought some improvement in supplies to the armed forces, but no readjustment of social policy to the needs of an intended war. It was impossible to win the working class over, and this remained true even after the European war had actually begun. There was no enthusiasm at the outbreak of the war. It is difficult to say on the basis of the extant documents whether the government had anticipated the failure of its attempt to link the increased repression of the working class with the unleashing of a war. The only evidence I find is the anxiety expressed in Labour Ministry and OKW documents that were written at the eleventh hour. Considering their experience with wage policy and civil conscription since the middle of 1938 and the value they placed on domestic tranquillity, the political leadership must have had a deep sense of unease.[293] Nevertheless, there was a systematic move towards war in 1939. This question leads us to consider another dimension of the relationship between foreign and domestic policy during the years 1937 to 1939: the problem of the domestic political causes of the war.

The pragmatic view of the relationship between ends and means, which never bulked large in National Socialism, disappeared entirely from the perspective of the regime's policy-makers after the middle of

293. Even State Secretary Posse of the Economics Ministry doubted in May 1939 whether the planned reduction in wages was advisable: *BA/MA Freiburg*, WiIF 5, file 420/3. Cf. also Hitler's dissatisfaction with the 'defeatist' attitude of the people: Wilhelm Treue (ed.), 'Rede Hitlers vor der deutschen Presse (10 November 1938)', *Vierteljahrshefte für Zeitgeschichte,* vol. 6/2, 1958, pp. 175–91.

1938. Policy was totally caught up in the maelstrom of the impending war. Yet it was not as though public life had been systematically adjusted to future armed conflict; what emerged was an impenetrable tangle of linkages between the military requirements to prepare for war and the political preconditions for waging war: between strategic goals on the one hand and the crisis-laden effects of any attempt to realize those goals on the other. It was less a matter of the phased implementation of plans and measures to prepare for a war with concrete (i.e. limited) objectives, than of rearming and waging war in order to be able to go on rearming and waging war. In terms of economic and domestic policy, the conduct of war had become the precondition for continuing to prepare for war. After the middle of 1938 all Nazi policy was increasingly becoming an end in itself; to the holders of power, ends and means – cause and effect to the historian – had become hopelessly confused. Aside from the long-term goals – *Lebensraum*, the total reorganization of Europe on the basis of race – which the political leadership pursued with fanatic zeal and from which foreign policy derived much of its dynamism in 1938–9, serious problems were emerging that required instant, short-term solutions: problems which intensified this dynamism and determined its practical consequences. Thus the various phases in the expansion of the Reich until October 1939 have a Janus-like quality: they were at the same time stepping-stones to the long-desired conquest of 'the East', and annexations indispensable to the economic support of the drive to expand. Eventually, the expansion of the German currency zone, the seizure of production facilities, reserves and sources of raw materials in the occupied territories,[294] and the employment of Polish slave labourers all helped to overcome the bottlenecks in the armaments sector during the war years.

I do not mean to say that the regime had speeded things up before the war simply in order to solve these problems; the situation was not that simple. There is no easy answer to the question of what would have happened in economic and social policy if there had been no material or political gains from the annexations. All I can say is that the continuation of the war-and-peace economy would have led to greater and greater economic problems. It must be emphasized, incidentally, that this was also clear to the leaders of the country. Göring's programmatic address to the Reich Defence Council in November 1938 left no doubt as to the crisis situation in economic and social policy. Referring to his own, anything but inflated list of emergency measures that were indis-

---

294. See Jörg-Johannes Jäger, *Die wirtschaftliche Abhängigkeit des Dritten Reiches vom Ausland, dargestellt am Beispiel der Stahlindustrie*, Berlin, 1969, ch. 3A; also cf. above, pp. 200f.

pensable to the maintenance of the armaments programme, Göring said, 'it all really seems impossible'; his own 'proposals to solve the problems' did not go much beyond calls for more discipline, tightening up on organization, and so on.[295]

Hitler was informed about the situation regularly and in great detail.[296] Although the sources on which to base an interpretation of his view of the problem are skimpy, a certain theme recurs in Hitler's few recorded statements on the relationship between economic and social policy and the strategy of expansion – the idea of a 'flight forwards' (*Flucht nach vorn*). This meant not taking a position on or analysing problems in domestic policy, but bypassing them by concentrating single-mindedly on the achievement of foreign-policy goals. The story behind the so-called Hossbach Conference, quite as much as the minutes of the meeting itself, exemplifies this point. The meeting had originally been called to settle serious differences between the army and the air-force, but Hitler sought to circumvent the issue by revealing his wide-ranging plans for aggressive expansion.[297] The same escapist mode of thought runs throughout Hitler's statements at the conference:

> If, in territorial terms, there existed no political outcome corresponding to this German racial core...the greatest danger to the preservation of the German race at its present peak would lie in the continuance of these political conditions. To arrest the decline of Germanism [*Deutschtum*] in Austria and Czechoslovakia was as little possible as to maintain the present situation in Germany itself. Instead of increase, sterility was setting in and in its train disorders of a social character must arise in course of time, since political and ideological ideas remain effective only so long as they furnish the basis for the realization of the essential vital demands of a people...
>
> It was not possible, in a continent sharing more or less the same standard of living, to meet food supply difficulties over the long run by lowering that standard or by rationalization.[298]

One function of the war, therefore, was to prevent domestic threats. The very weaknesses of the regime – its dependence on a political ideology

295. *Doc. 152*. To what extent Göring's wavering attitude towards Hitler's foreign policy in 1938–9 was caused by his awareness of these problems has not yet been clarified.

296. We can assume that Göring reported verbally to Hitler. Thomas tried several times to make Hitler aware of the weaknesses in the war economy: Carroll, *Design*, pp. 48f.; Thomas, *Geschichte*, pp. 508ff. Until the beginning of 1938 Lammers frequently presented Seldte's and the Trustees' reports to Hitler: *Docs. 52, 68*.

297. Hermann Gackenholz, 'Reichskanzlei 5 November 1937', *Forschungen zu Staat und Verwaltung. Festgabe für Fritz Hartung*, Berlin, 1958.

298. Minutes of the meeting in the Reich Chancellery on 11 November 1937: *Akten zur deutschen auswärtigen Politik, 1918–1945*, series D, Baden-Baden, 1950ff., vol. 1, pp. 26f. (hereafter referred to as ADAP).

that could paper over internal contradictions only so long as it was validated by outward successes; the possibility of a 'decline in Germanism', of stagnation and sterility; the political impossibility of lowering the standard of living – were trotted out as reasons for military expansion. The same peculiar logic underlay Hitler's description of Germany's economic situation in May 1939. It was precisely the problems in this area that made war a necessity:

> The ideological problems have been solved by the mass of 80,000,000 people. The economic problems must also be solved. To create the economic conditions necessary for this is a task no German can disregard. The solution to the problems demands courage. We must not allow the principle to prevail that one can accommodate oneself to the circumstances and thus shirk the solution of problems. The circumstances must rather be adapted to suit the demands. This is not possible without breaking into other countries or attacking other people's property.[299]

This latter idea had become a reality during the previous March at the latest, after the occupation of the rump of Czechoslovakia. As a top officer on the staff of the Quartermaster-General of the army noted:

> Considerable quantities of military equipment of all kinds ... already on their way to Germany, an enormous increase in strength. ... Up to now thousands of serviceable aircraft...The Führer is glowing. ... Very large supplies of raw materials...Up to six weeks' worth of fuel supplies, coal sufficient. ... Lots of money and foreign currency...The Führer can hardly wait to get a summary of the war *matériel* and is constantly pressing us.

The '500 trainloads of war *matériel*' were indeed sufficient to outfit five new German divisions.[300] But this was still not enough to meet the military's needs. On 22 August 1939 Hitler tried to convince the generals of the necessity of attacking Poland. In so doing he used a line of reasoning which sounds as though he were seeking to defuse the warnings he had received in the preceding months from the military and economic agencies, or, more specifically, to turn them to his advantage: 'We have nothing to lose; we have everything to gain. Because of our limitations our economic situation is such that we can only hold out for a few more years. Göring can confirm this. We have no other choice, we must act'.

---

299. Ibid., vol. 6, pp. 477ff. In this statement Hitler is thinking in terms of a shorter period of time than in his general remarks about the necessity of territorial expansion in Europe for securing the economic wherewithal to expand the war. This latter component of Hitler's strategic thinking is stressed in Carroll, *Design*, ch. 5.

300. Wagner, *Generalquartiermeister*, pp. 82f. (17–18 March 1939; my emphasis); on the captured equipment from Poland cf. also pp. 124f., 139; Jacobsen, *Fall 'Gelb'*, p. 20.

According to a second version, Hitler is supposed to have said: 'Göring has pointed out [that the] Four-Year Plan [is] a failure and [that] we are finished if we do not win [the] coming war'. On this occasion and later during a speech to a similar group on 23 November 1939, Hitler returned to the general problem of the relation between war and domestic stability, which he had touched on as early as the end of 1937. The contradictions in his remarks reveal a discomfiture that was propelling him into a kind of arbitrary decisionism (*Dezisionismus*).[301] On the one hand, he considered the German people to be in danger of losing their fitness because of the 'long period of peace', while on the other, he regarded them as the guarantee of victory, despite their having become unaccustomed to 'hardships and burdens': 'our people are the best'. Hitler emphasized the 'moral [*seelische*] foundations of perseverance', which are 'the essential thing'.[302] On 9 October the conquest and exploitation of France was called an urgent task, failing which there was the fear that the 'moral position' of the German people might be harmed.[303] On 23 November 1939 Hitler again delivered himself of a delphic remark: 'Behind me stands the German people, its morale can only get worse'. Apparently, he revealed his fears in this regard only to his closest confidants. In justifying the need to design the new government headquarters like a fortress, Hitler told Speer in 1939, 'It is not inconceivable, after all, that I may be forced to take some unpopular measures. Perhaps there will be a revolt then'.[304] To keep up morale on the home front, thousands upon thousands of Polish farm-workers and prisoners of war were in the process of being dragooned into taking the lowest-paying and worst jobs in the German economy. On this subject there was also a programmatic utterance by Hitler: Poland must remain a poor country, so that Germany can use it as a manpower reserve. Here was a precarious way to avoid 'unpopular measures'.[305]

---

301. Cf. the analysis of political decisionism by Wolfgang Sauer in Bracher, Sauer and Schulz, *Machtergreifung*, pp. 859f. Sauer considers the salient characteristic of decisionism to be the 'evasion of real decisions'. Cf. also Sauer's view of war as economic armed robbery, ibid., pp. 760–4.

302. Hitler's address to the commanders-in-chief, 22 August 1939: *ADAP*, series D, vol. 7, pp. 168–71. Different opinion on the problem of the economy in the notes of Admiral Boehm: *IMGH*, Doc. Raeder-27, vol. 41, p. 18. On the value of the various notes as sources for Hitler's address, see Winfried Baumgart, 'Zur Ansprache Hitlers vor den Führern der Wehrmacht am 22. August 1939', *Vierteljahrshefte für Zeitgeschichte*, vol. 16/2, April 1968. Hitler's speech to the commanders in chief, 23 November 1939: *IMGH*, Doc. 789-PS, vol. 26, p. 336. Cf. also Carroll, *Design*, p. 104.

303. Memorandum justifying the invasion of France: Hans-Adolf Jacobsen, (ed.), *Dokumente zur Vorgeschichte des Westfeldzuges 1939–1940*, Göttingen, 1956, p. 9.

304. Speer, *Erinnerungen*, p. 173.

305. Note by Keitel on the meeting of 17 October 1939: *IMGH*, Doc. 864-PS, vol. 26, pp. 378ff.

Without the 1.5 million foreign workers and the 1.3 million prisoners of war who worked in German industry and agriculture for low wages or none at all in June 1941,[306] the Germans would have either suffered military defeat or been obliged to take draconian measures to force German workers to bear the full brunt of the war economy. Even at the time it was clear that the German war economy would have collapsed in 1939/40 if the occupied areas had not been looted of raw materials, foodstuffs, war *matériel* and production capacity, or if the Soviet Union had not delivered vital supplies.[307] These facts plus Hitler's amply justified pessimism with regard to the situation in social and economic policy warrant the heavy emphasis I have placed on the statements quoted above. Although his speeches and memoranda during this period were generally characterized by a plain disregard for logic, Hitler consistently referred to the necessity of a 'flight forwards'. This theme runs like a subterranean stream through the wild speculations on foreign affairs and the ideological platitudes that dominate the written record of his reflections on the beginning of the war. Indeed, these observations were grounded in reality in a way that few of his other utterances were.[308]

They referred to a genuine crisis in domestic and economic policy, a crisis that was in fact a consequence of the underlying causes of the war. These causes may be grouped under two headings: first, the incontestable racist and anti-Communist goals of the Nazi leadership; and second, the economic imperialism of German industry.[309] However, the preparations for this expansionist war created domestic conditions that

306. *BA Koblenz*, R41, file 146, pp. 115–20; file 147, p. 35. Cf. Seeber, *Zwangsarbeiter*; H. Pfahlmann, *Fremdarbeiter und Kriegsgefangene in der deutschen Kriegswirtschaft*, Darmstadt, 1968.

307. Thomas in 1945, quoted in Louis P. Lochner, *Tycoons and Tyrants*, Chicago, 1954, p. 210. For a basic source on this issue, see Milward, *New Order*, chs. 1–4, especially pp. 80f.

308. This interpretation is strongly supported by the contemporary views of the British Foreign Office and of the leading representatives of the conservative resistance within Germany: cf. C. A. MacDonald, 'Economic Appeasement and the German "Moderates" 1937–1939', *Past and Present*, no. 56 (August 1972); Bernd-Jürgen Wendt, *Economic Appeasement. Handel und Finanz in der britischen Deutschland-Politik 1933–1939*, Düsseldorf, 1971; Gerhard Ritter, *Carl Goerdeler und die deutsche Widerstandsbewegung*, Munich, 1964, pp. 218f., 224, 231f.; Hjalmar Schacht, *My First Seventy-Six Years*, London, 1955, ch. 51; A. P. Young, *The 'X' Documents*, London, 1974; Ulrich von Hassel, *Vom anderen Deutschland*, 3rd edn, Zürich, 1947, pp. 19, 24f., 36, 42f., 45–8, 51f., 66, 72, 98, 107–10, 122. A 'flight forwards' was fully expected by these groups.

309. The interrelationship between these two dynamic factors has still not been sufficiently explained: cf. T. W. Mason, 'Der Primat der Politik', *Das Argument*, no. 41 (December 1966); I have expanded and revised that contribution in several places. Eichholtz, *Kriegswirtschaft*, vol. 1, offers a detailed and stimulating critique. Cf. also Klaus Hildebrand, *Deutsche Aussenpolitik 1933–1945: Kalkül oder Dogma?* Stuttgart, 1971.

severely limited Hitler's freedom of movement in foreign policy and forced him to gamble. His original foreign-policy plans simply could not withstand the pressure from below. As the war dragged on, therefore, the programme for a short war of plunder, which had been forced upon him, merged with the ambitious long-range, almost epochal goals of the system. But under the pressure of war both became so muddled up that they were useless as a strategy for power politics.

Hitler himself once alluded to this constellation of problems: 'The conflicts today are different from what they were a hundred years ago. Today we can speak of race conflict. Today we are fighting over oil-fields, rubber, minerals, etc.'[310] No compelling reason can be found as to why race conflict should be escalated into all-out war in the year 1939. On the other hand, a war over mineral resources and manpower could not be postponed indefinitely.

Terror, Capitalism and War

The war intensified the elements of terror within the Nazi system. Until the end of 1938 undisguised police terror was directed mostly against the real or imagined enemies of the regime – Communists, Social Democrats, trade unionists, religious Christians, and German Jews. Organized terror also served to intimidate other groups, which were not actually directly threatened. Even at this time there was hardly a social group, hardly a sphere of public life, that was spared from this cycle of intimidation and fear, which gradually became more extreme and affected every aspect of life in this demagogic dictatorship.[311] Whether seen from the perspective of the functional preservation of the regime, or from the subjective situation of any of the repressed groups, the difference between this form of induced fear and the systematic use of police terror was at best a matter of degree.

As fluid as the boundaries were, they must nevertheless be emphasized in any analysis of Nazi policy. On closer examination, the assumption that the targets of terror were arbitrary and that the extension of terror was primarily a result of the Gestapo's drive to extend its own power within the bureaucracy is unfounded. The intensification of terror during the winter of 1938/9 was a reaction on the part of all those in power to events which, taken together, raised the spectre of social disintegration. This danger was a product of the system itself. The extreme political and economic conditions of 1939/40 – intensified propaganda barrages, the con-

---

310. Speech of 23 November 1939: *IMGH*, Doc. 789-PS, vol. 26, pp. 329f.
311. It was not this cycle as such that was peculiar to the Nazi state, but its intensity.

stant threat of war, actual war, ruthless economic competition, the extreme demands on physical and mental energies, the omnipresent state intervention in all areas of social life and the growing uncertainty – were rooted in the interdependence of the capitalist economy and the political dictatorship, giving rise to widespread demoralization which the regime was able to control only through the use of terror. And *only* through terror, since it had exhausted all other possibilities. The NSDAP had long ago squandered its meagre ideological resources. The drive to prepare for war had not generated any zeal; demonstrations of enthusiasm were limited in space and time to the Party congresses – short-lived, stage-managed events isolated from everyday life.[312] Even anti-Semitism was clearly losing its popularity, and in the social and economic struggle of all against all the cohesive effect of lofty ideals was nil.[313]

What was of much greater significance was the fact that the population had become used to the level of coercion employed so far, thereby making it less effective. In the decisive arena of the labour market the regime itself had been forced to moderate its tactics after the armaments-led boom in the economy had eroded the fear of unemployment and poverty that used to help keep workers in line. Moreover, there were many people who were just basically indifferent to the 'Third Reich'; they did not obey any of the rules and sought their advantage wherever they could find it, without any regard for authority. This attitude was particularly widespread among the young people who grew up after 1933: every system produces its own 'anti-social' elements. Below we shall discuss this in somewhat greater detail in order to illustrate the importance of terror in the fully developed National Socialist system.

The groups holding power tended to apply the label of 'declining work discipline' to a number of different modes of behaviour which had only one thing in common, in that they reduced productivity and industrial profits. Although the growing indifference and insubordination of the workers in the factory becomes clearer against the backdrop of the new security generated by full employment, this development needs to be examined more closely. First, it is important to emphasize that political factors played a small part here. Although the Gestapo sought to track down Communist and trade-union 'wire pullers' and although exile groups called for work slow-downs,[314] the growing demoralization in

312. Cf. *Doc. 106.*
313. See especially *Doc. 151.*
314. Thus, for example, the 'ten commandments' of the German Communist Party were widely known to many groups in the Ruhr. They called upon workers to exploit to the full all legal means of interrupting the flow of production, by taking sick leave, overwhelming management with trivial requests, and so on: address by the War Economy Inspector, Münster, at a conference on 21 August 1939, *BA/MA Freiburg*, WiIF 5, file 384. It is in any case highly improbable that the workers needed such encouragement to behave in this way.

industry apparently had little to do with organized resistance on the part of the working class.[315] Moreover, it is obvious that the state's wage and labour policy had a powerful influence on the attitude of industrial workers. Although demoralization was a long-term process that obeyed social laws – in other words, it was the only possible reaction of repressed and exploited people – it was also more than that. Every time the state tampered with the rights or living standards of the working class, it provoked a wave of resentment, which really represented a kind of passive, prepolitical opposition. Whether it was civil conscription or the attempt to limit wages in 1938–9 or the massive, concerted assault by the government along the entire front of social policy at the beginning of the war, the occasions and causes of discontent were clear and specific. Absenteeism, loafing on the job, carelessness, taking sick leave and insubordination assumed the character of a collective protest in this context. In many individual instances as well, workers would react in a hostile fashion when they were denied permission to change jobs, or else they would try to provoke their dismissal in order to accept a better position.[316]

Another important feature of this general development is not as open to clear interpretation: the statistics on sick leave, which rose sharply in industry between 1937 and 1939. At first glance, this is not surprising, since employers during this period were anxious to increase the pace of work and lengthen hours. The very long journeys to work, which were a result of the housing shortage in most industrial areas, also played a role. So far as the question can be measured objectively, we may assume with some confidence that the health of the German working class had deteriorated prior to the beginning of the war.[317] A number of observers, including employers and military officers, spoke of the havoc that the hectic pace of rearmament was playing with the physical strength of the population. Still, it is probably true that a considerable proportion of the absenteeism reportedly due to illness had no identifiable physical cause.[318] Included in this category were workers who were simply overtired or overstrained, as well as others who just wanted a few days off without losing any pay. Finally, in many borderline cases the decision to

315. Larger acts of opposition were necessarily public and would have revealed the existence of conspiratorial groups.
316. *Docs. 136, 137, 145, 147, 150, 156, 216–25* offer numerous examples. Cf. also the reports of the War Economy Inspectors: *BA/MA Freiburg*, WiIF 5, file 176 (excerpts). I analyse this aspect of class conflict in Nazi Germany in detail in ch. 7 of my dissertation.
317. This subject would be worthy of special study. The contemporary study by Martin Gumpert, *Heil Hunger! Health under Hitler*, New York, 1940, especially ch. 8, is still the most informative treatment. Cf. also C. W. Guillebaud, *The Social Policy of Nazi Germany*, Cambridge, 1942; Syrup, *Hundert Jahre*, p. 522.
318. Cf. *Docs. 147, 150, 156, 223*. The War Economy Inspectors also dealt with this question in great detail: *BA/MA Freiburg*, WiIF 5, file 176 (excerpts).

call in sick was, and is, a function of the social situation; people who would previously have toughed things out now went to the doctor. The doctors, who had just expended their energies on expelling their many Jewish colleagues from the medical profession, found it impossible to cope with the increased case loads and were very generous in writing notes to excuse workers from the job. This annoyed employers and the state authorities, put a number of industrial health insurance companies into the red and confronted the recently expanded medical examiner service of the social insurance programme with an overwhelming amount of work.[319]

The decline in work morale was much more than merely the sum of its individual manifestations. The abundant source material suggests a broad and stubborn, albeit subliminal denial of co-operation in all areas. In the summer of 1939 the War Economy Inspector for Berlin spoke of 'passive resistance' by the working class. A few armaments firms reported that their workers had expressed their resentment by sabotaging the scheduled completion of orders. There were complaints from all sectors of the economy about declining productivity. The owner of a tannery in Dresden was probably speaking for many employers when he called the actions of his workers a 'disguised strike'. When he asked them why they did not give their real reasons for wanting to change jobs, the workers answered that everything was disguised nowadays and they had to behave accordingly. It was also the War Economy Inspector for the Dresden area who encouraged the armaments firms during these months to call the Gestapo into their factories as a way of ruthlessly combating loafing on the job.[320]

It was when these manifestations of silent opposition assumed the character of 'sabotage' that it became impossible to ignore the fact that the process of disintegration had become a primitive form of the class struggle. It continued to expand, was class-specific and was marked by an increasing economic class consciousness. Employers and the authorities did not hesitate for a moment to show the workers the effects of their stubborn opposition on rearmament and the war effort; and they did not shrink from threatening workers with serious penalties. But nothing worked. Resentment was indeed 'deep-seated'.[321] It represented

319. Ibid.; Monthly report of the War Economy Inspector, Münster, for June 1939: *BA/MA Freiburg*, WO I–8, file 285. On the medical examiner service, see Syrup, *Hundert Jahre*, p. 375; *Stat. Handbuch*, p. 533.

320. Monthly report of the War Economy Inspector, Berlin, for July 1939: *BA/MA Freiburg*, WO I-8, file 282; the War Economy Inspector, Wiesbaden, made similar observations in August: ibid., file 291. Report of the War Economy Inspector, Dresden, to the War Economy Staff, 17 August 1939: ibid., file 283.

321. War Economy Staff, summary overview of the reports of the War Economy Inspectors, 10 June 1939: *BA/MA Freiburg*, WiIF 5, file 176.

the last opportunity to take action, without directly risking their lives, for the exploited and the dispossessed who were not willing to become the tools of ruthless capitalist interests or Nazi policies.

All observers were struck early on by the fact that it was precisely the young people who were least disciplined and least able to withstand the routine of hard work. Employers in industry ascribed this to the fact that young workers had never known what it meant to be unemployed;[322] but such crude explanations could not account for the scope and the manifestations of this 'dissolute behaviour', as it soon came to be called. The phenomenon had spread so quickly throughout the industrial and agricultural sectors that a War Economy Inspector thought he detected the beginnings of a general 'breakdown' among young workers.[323] In the navy's North Sea shipyards it was concluded that workers between the ages of 25 and 30 years were working at a rate of only '50 per cent of normal productivity'.[324] The Labour Service also had to deal with demonstrations of discontent and passive resistance.[325]

The fact that the behaviour of young people was more than just a particularly conspicuous example of the manifestations of class opposition, that in general it reflected a new generational problem, becomes clear when we examine a another series of events, which we can only touch on very briefly here. First, young people were committing crimes and forming gangs to such a degree that the Ministerial Council for the Defence of the Reich (*Ministerrat für die Reichsverteidigung*) decided shortly after the beginning of the war to increase criminal penalties for juvenile delinquents.[326] No less suspicious in the eyes of those in power were other forms of dissolute behaviour, notably the formation of groups among middle-class youth who had completely turned their back on National Socialism and only wanted to lead a comfortable, 'modern' life.[327] These young people did not seem to feel that they were bound by any higher social obligations. Whether this process of demoralization ceased when some of these young men were conscripted into military service has not been adequately investigated. General von Brauchitsch's readiness during his infamous meeting with Hitler on 5 November 1939

322. *Doc. 30, Part II 2*.

323. Cf. *Docs. 85, 96, 156*. Report of the War Economy Inspector, Münster, to the War Economy Staff, 3 September 1938: *BA/MA Freiburg*, WiIF 5, file 187.

324. Naval Division of the War Economy Inspectorate, Hamburg, memorandum on the mobilization of the economy up to the end of February 1940: ibid., WO 8, file 110/4. Conditions in Wilhelmshaven were identical: ibid.

325. See *Doc. 156*.

326. Cf. *Doc. 226*. Decree on Protection against Youthful Criminals, 4 October 1939 (*VO zum Schutz gegen jugendliche Schwerverbrecher*): *RGBl. I*, p. 2000.

327. See Werner Klose, *Generation im Gleichschritt*, Oldenburg/Hamburg, 1964, pp. 222 ff.

to cite the poor discipline of his men as a reason to postpone the invasion of France is revealing in this regard. In any event, he considered it a plausible argument.[328]

To complete the picture, however, it has to be pointed out that young people were often and not without reason considered to be among those whom the regime could count on to be most fanatically loyal to the system. Both of these contradictory tendencies are, in fact, clearly evident. How they related to each other, whether one was merely the reverse of the other,[329] has not been sufficiently studied. The signs of decadence among the youth are important not only because they have often been overlooked or because they preoccupied the holders of power. They are significant precisely because they were exhibited by people whose conscious experience of public life began after 1933. They as well as their fanatical contemporaries were products of one and the same system. The behaviour of gang members, of work-shy anti-social elements and young middle-class hedonists alike was a reflection of the basic characteristics of the public order, primarily of that destructive desire for cheap short-term successes that had become an integral component of the economic life and of the foreign policy of the 'Third Reich'. Only the young people, however, directed this tendency against the regime, rather than in conformity with the system's own ostensible norms. Their corruption, their violent behaviour, their laxness and their selfishness threatened rearmament and the war effort and laid bare the bogus slogans of the official ideology. Beyond that, the lack of a sense of commitment for which they were repeatedly criticized cast doubt on the system's ability to reproduce itself. All the leading groups relied heavily on the enduring influence on the population of traditional moral values; but the combination of political dictatorship and a ruthless, Darwinian struggle for selfish social and economic advantage tended in practice to undermine the commitment to these values.[330] The tightly integrated but fragile system of social rewards and punishments that made the hard alienating work under industrial capitalism seem bearable for long periods of time was in the process of disintegration. To oversimplify, it seemed at the beginning of the war as though the older generation was still motivated by habits and

328. Von Brauchitsch could not prove his point, but what divisional commander likes to admit such problems? It would be valuable to study the morale of the army in greater detail. See Jacobsen, *Fall 'Gelb'*, pp. 44–8.

329. The figure of Baldur Persicke in Hans Fallada's novel *Jeder stirbt für sich allein*, Frankfurt, 1964, is an illustration of this hypothesis: a Hitler Youth leader who was dissolute, corrupt *and* fanatical.

330. Similar to this development was the 'parasitic disintegration of the traditional authoritarian state' (Hans Mommsen's phrase), on whose gradually reduced effectiveness the regime was to a large extent dependent; cf. Hans Mommsen, *Beamtentum im Dritten Reich*, Stuttgart, 1966. The decline in morals and discipline was a subject to which conservative resistance groups devoted a great deal of attention.

mores that had been developed in previous decades – habits that often led to a partial rejection of National Socialism but that were indispensable for the continued existence of the social order.[331] But where were the younger generation supposed to learn the values of common decency, conscientiousness, respect for authority, sacrifice and especially self-restraint – values on whose practice the continued existence of this type of class society was based? To oversimplify the problem again, the youth were either good for nothing or useful only for the criminal adventures of an expansionist war.[332]

The only instrument the regime had to oppose the constant threat posed by the lack of discipline in the working class and among the youth was undisguised terror. Administrative decrees and fear of the Gestapo increasingly took the place of crumbling social norms and indirect means of control. There are several reasons for this development. The risk that the lack of discipline would ultimately lead to disintegration and collapse on the home front was too great for these phenomena simply to be ignored. In the strained economic circumstances after the middle of 1938 there was little room for the use of material incentives; moreover, the experience with 'Strength through Joy' cast doubt on their effectiveness. The various methods of 'enlightenment' had been completely exhausted. Still, the problem was pressing and becoming more important, for bad work discipline in the industrial sector would ultimately disrupt armaments production. Quick solutions were called for, but neither the government nor industry had the personnel needed to build up an inspection system; so it was decided to use police terror as the most expedient means to repress and deter. To the ruling groups the logic of the situation was a not unwelcome spur to action. Even before 1938 the Gestapo had shown a lively interest in the disturbances and work stoppages in industry; it already had some experience with 'slackers', 'anti-social elements', and so on. Although this new responsibility involved difficult and time-consuming tasks, it was no *terra incognita*. The employers and Trustees of Labour for their part were so worn down that they were grateful for any kind of help.[333]

---

331. As a report on mobilization in the shipyards of Wilhelmshaven stated, 'old people loyal and unflagging': *BA/MA Freiburg*, WO 8, file 110/4. A number of these older people were probably still Social Democrats and Communists.

332. The many young people active in political resistance groups were, of course, an important exception. On the social history of the preceding generation as well as on the question of generation in general, see the outstanding essay by Peter Loewenberg, 'The Psychosocial Origins of the Nazi Youth Cohort', *American Historical Review*, vol. 76/5 (Dec. 1971). A similar analysis of the generations of 1919–24 would be most interesting.

333. See Martin Broszat, 'Nationalsozialistische Konzentrationslager', in Hans Buchheim *et al.*, *Anatomie des SS-Staates*, Olten/Freiburg im Breisgau, 1965, vol. 2, pp. 91–3.

The turning-point in the area of labour discipline came, as was pointed out above, with the wage-policy measures introduced in the second half of 1938, which virtually transformed the entire body of labour law into criminal law.[334] However, co-operation between the Trustees of Labour and the judicial administration remained unsatisfactory; the effect of the few penalties actually imposed was limited in terms of both place and time. Thus after the beginning of the war the Trustees were empowered to impose administrative penalties (*Ordnungsstrafen*), which exempted them from having to prosecute offenders in the courts, and gave them the power to levy on-the-spot fines; but fines, as many employers already knew, were no longer a sufficient sanction, and the number of court cases continued to mount. In the Ruhr alone more than 1,000 workers were on trial at the end of November 1939 for loafing on the job, refusing to work, and the like.[335] The court system was collapsing under the weight of the case load and sought to help itself by intensifying the use of arbitrary terror as a means of repression: the district courts (*Amtsgerichte*) were therefore ordered to administer summary justice to alleviate the situation.[336]

As unlikely as it was that in 1939 German courts were handing down verdicts to German workers based on something that deserved to be called law, the position of those prosecuted by the legal system was enviable when compared to the alternatives. The most important changes in this area, in fact, were taking place outside the judicial system. Developments in the I. G. Farben film factory in Wolfen may serve as an example. Three workers were sentenced to prison in December 1938 for violating an order of the Reich Trustee; a few months later the courts handed down four more sentences for violations of the rules on smoking.[337] Labour discipline continued to slip, however, and in May 1939 nine 'slackers' were hauled before the Council of Trust by the works leader to receive a warning directly from the Reich Trustee's deputy. Yet calling in sick, drinking on the job, breach of contract and above all absenteeism did not decrease. Neither the closing of the beer parlour nor the extension of the deadline for giving notice, neither fines nor repeated official warnings were able to restore order. After an official visit by the Reich Trustee and the *Gauobmann* of the DAF in August 1939 had also failed to produce any results, Gajewski, the works leader, distributed a notice to all workers in which he regretted to inform them that in future all slackers would be handed over to the Gestapo and their names posted on the bulletin board.[338]

334. Cf. *Docs. 133–40, 156, 216.*
335. Report of the War Economy Inspector, Münster, 22 November 1939: *BA/MA Freiburg*,WO-I 8, file 106/17.
336. See *Doc. 244.*
337. Files of the Social Office of the Agfa-Wolfen Film Factory: *Betriebsarchiv Wolfen*, file A3714, pp. 167–247.
338. Ibid., file A3717, pp. 474, 616f.

The example of the film factory was far from untypical. As early as April 1939 four firms in Nuremberg called in the Gestapo, and one employer introduced a regular system of co-operation between his personnel office and the Gestapo.[339] At the beginning of the war the Gestapo took the initiative by declaring itself responsible for all instances involving a refusal to work, and on 8 September the terror reached a high point with the announcement of the execution of a Communist for supposedly declining to work.[340] This was evidently intended more as a demonstrative propaganda gesture than as the beginning of a new policy, for in the first few months of the war the authorities and the employers made do with a more intensive level of co-operation.[341] At the end of November 1939, for example, a special five-man Gestapo team was permanently stationed at the Wolff Munitions Works in Bomlitz; work discipline improved and productivity started to rise again.[342] That same month the Deutsche Waffen- und Munitions-AG in Berlin began reporting to the Gestapo the names of workers who repeatedly failed to show up for work.[343] After the Naval Shipyard in Wilhelmshaven had experimented with sending 'troublemakers' to a Gestapo prison for various terms of incarceration (ten to thirty days), the Wesermünde labour exchange built its own concentration camp for those who were unwilling to work; it had seventy inmates by June 1940.[344] A special concentration camp for juvenile delinquents (in Neuwied) soon followed.

Terror had thus become an indispensable means of 'education' in the daily lives of workers, the ultimate and most important guarantee of the survival of the economic and political system of domination. It was a straight line from the factory community to the factory-as-concentration-camp. The various intervening steps were a necessary consequence of the dissolution of the trade unions and the precondition for conducting a war of expansion. Only one further step could follow after the workers had been totally reified: the destruction of human beings in the production process for the sake of production. This fate was reserved for the foreign slave labourers.

---

339. War Economy Staff, summary overview of the reports of the War Economy Inspectors, 20 April 1939: *BA/MA Freiburg*, WilF 5, file 176.

340. William L. Shirer, *Berlin Diary*, London, 1941, p. 166.

341. Cf. *Docs. 180–2.*

342. Notes by the War Economy Inspector, Hamburg, 8 November 1939: *BA/MA Freiburg*, WO 8, file 110/3.

343. Report of the War Economy Inspector, Berlin, 9 November 1939: ibid., WO I-8, file 282. Cf. *Docs. 214, 215, 217, 219.*

344. Decree of the OKW (*Oberkommando der Wehrmacht*), 20 November 1939: *BA/MA Freiburg*, WO 8, file 110/6. Notes of the War Economy Inspector, Hamburg, 13 July 1940: ibid., file 110/26. Cf. *Doc. 243.*

Epilogue

1. Introduction

This epilogue, written at a distance of twelve or thirteen years from the original book, attempts to discuss a variety of themes and questions. It is an unusual literary form, and the choice of it derives, as indicated above in the Introduction, precisely from this long delay between the German and the English publication. The delay has arisen from what I have perceived as severe inadequacies in my approach to the study of Nazism, and from my failure to resolve these in the form of a different, new and much more wide-ranging book on the subject, which was the book that I really wanted to offer to English readers. These inadequacies and unsolved problems form the main underlying theme of the following epilogue, and it is best to start by making some explicit comments upon them.

Social Policy in the Third Reich remained in essence a monograph; it is largely limited to the making and implementation of German labour policies between 1933 and 1940, in the context of class conflict. I did not want to stop there, and to present, even temporarily, so relatively narrow a piece to work to a broad, non-specialist readership. The monograph appeared, illusorily, to be the cornerstone on which I could construct a much more comprehensive analysis of the Third Reich, extending the work a lot both chronologically and thematically. In a methodological sense the monographical cornerstone did not seem to require fundamental revision. The work to be done appeared to be, above all, a work of extension – extension into the war years, into the history of women, and above all into the study of general policy-making in Nazi Germany, into those reasons for its defeat which were internal to the regime. This project of an overall, coherent analytical history was not only overambitious in a general sense, but it became increasingly clear that it was an intellectually flawed ambition. The big book which I wanted to write could not be written because it is not possible to move outwards from the 'core area' of class relations towards a potentially all-inclusive political social history of Nazism and the Third Reich. Such a book would have to have a different starting-point – the regime itself – a different structure of interpretation; and a complete reordering both of the materials presented above and of the areas of research into which I wanted to extend my analysis. I could not resolve these problems, and remained stuck with abortive drafts and with essays which never advanced from being suggestive or critical towards building a new, substantive framework of interpretation.[1] Meanwhile other historians, especially Martin Broszat, Ian Kershaw, Hans Mommsen, Detlev Peukert, Jane Caplan and Lutz Niethammer, were opening up vital new questions on the basis of new sources, which suggested quite different avenues towards possible synthetic interpretations.

The book that I wanted to write slipped further and further from my intellectual grasp, and I gradually came to realize that if I had a contribution to make to the study of Nazism it was the original monograph on labour policies and class relations, which had to be taken for what it was: a limited piece of work on a particular theme, marked by very definite boundaries, and not the first step towards a general reinterpretation of the Third Reich. Hence the long delay, and I count myself very fortunate in having the opportunity to present the monograph to English readers after so long a time.[2]

There were two main problems that prevented me from developing the work further, and they call for discussion here since they represent the concrete limitations and inadequacies of the monograph itself. The work does not touch upon two of the great historical facts about Nazism: the fact that the regime held itself and the German people together until the bitter end in 1945; and the fact that the Third Reich enacted policies of genocide. These are fundamental issues.

On the first point, the behaviour of the German population, civilian and military, from early 1943 to May 1945 remains to me in the end incomprehensible. In circumstances in which the war was obviously lost and the 'Hitler-Myth' was crumbling, there was also no longer much room for that give-and-take between the regime and the people, for those small concessions to carefully expressed opposition and grievances, to which I attach so much importance in accounting for the stability of the regime up to 1940. In particular my reading of the late 1930s suggested that there should have been more acts of resistance, especially by workers, than there in fact were. The clear lesson of the last year of the war is that quite other factors were at work in mediating the relationship between the regime and the people than those to which I

1. Among these essays: 'Open questions on Nazism', in Raphael Samuel (ed.), *People's History and Socialist Theory*, London, 1981, pp. 205ff.; 'Intention and Explanation: A Current Controversy about the Interpretation of National Socialism', in G. Hirschfeld and L. Kettenacker (eds.), *Der "Führerstaat": Mythos und Realität*, Stuttgart, 1981, pp. 23ff.; 'Die Bändigung der Arbeiterklasse im nationalsozialistischen Deutschland', in Carola Sachse et al., *Angst, Belohnung, Zucht und Ordnung*, Opladen, 1982, pp. 11ff.

2. The only substantive advance that I made beyond the themes of the monograph is represented by two articles, 'Women in Germany, 1925–1940: Family, Welfare and Work', *History Workshop Journal*, nos. 1 and 2, 1976.

have given especial importance.[3] I shall argue below that the whole experience of the war did indeed drastically alter the position and the perspectives of the German working class, but it cannot be argued that the way in which the German people held out until the bitter end was due mainly to factors which only came into play after July 1944 – intensified police terror, fear of the Red Army, the apathetic confusion of those bombed out of their homes, and so on. These were not secondary matters, but they pale into insignificance beside the fact that the last year of the war was also the last year of twelve years of Nazi rule: crucial longer-term forces must have been in play, forces which I have not been able to grasp properly and which lie beyond the boundaries of the way in which I have tried to explore the problem.

Thus my history is, and has remained, a story quite without an appropriate ending. It ends in the winter of 1939/40, which was a turning-point in Nazi labour policies, but which also marked a point at which the sheer volume of original documentation threatened to escape my control. It is in no way an historical conclusion, and if the ending of the story is arbitrary, wrong or just missing, this means that there must also be something wrong with the very beginning of the story too, with my starting-point: class relations, rather than the story of the regime. This choice does not represent a contradiction, but is a complex question of priorities in the analysis: class relations are an integral part of the history of the regime, but in my interpretation the balance is askew. Fear of a repetition of the revolution of November 1918 was indeed one consistent motive force in Nazi policies, but there were quite different motive forces which with time became more and more powerful. These demand a place at the start of the story, and make it easier to understand the actual historical end of it.

The difficulty of understanding the last year of the Nazi war is only made greater when one compares this German experience with the insurgency of the Italian working class between March and September 1943 and after. I have argued elsewhere that the crucial difference lay in the capillary character and the much greater executive power of the various German administrative machines.[4] As an answer it is far from complete, but it immediately points to the need to place the regime and the state at the beginning and end of the story, of which class relations

3. Among reviewers, only Klaus Wernecke pointed firmly to this central unresolved problem, in *Das Argument*, no. 117, 1979, p. 782.
4. See my 'Massenwiderstand ohne Organisation. Streiks im faschistischen Italien und im NS-Deutschland', in Ernst Breit (ed.), *Aufstieg des Nationalsozialismus, Untergang der Republik, Zerschlagung der Gewerkschaften*, Cologne, 1984; 'Gli scioperi di Torino marzo 1943', in Francesca Ferratini Tosi, Gaetano Grassi and Massimo Legnani (eds.), *L'Italia nella Seconda Guerra Mondiale e nella Resistenza*, Milan, 1988.

were only an important part. My book has little to say about Nazi administration; more to the point it catches Nazi social administration at the moment of its greatest weakness, the years 1936–9. Consideration of the war years makes it clear that this emphasis is wrong, as I shall show below. But there is a difference between emphasis and perspective in historical writing: one can get the emphasis wrong and yet get the overall perspective right. The fact that my story has no place for the very real ending of April/May 1945 – defiance to the better end – means that the perspective is incorrect for the larger book that I wanted to write.

Biological racism and genocide pose a similar problem of basic interpretations. Anti-Semitism appeared to me to be a matter of insignificance to the German working class, and the space given to it in this book faithfully reproduces the space given to it in the sources which I used. These (mostly) internal governmental documents certainly understate the emphasis on anti-Semitism in the media ('The Jewish War', etc.), but they leave absolutely no doubt about the fact that the holders of power regarded living standards and working conditions as massively more important than 'the Jew' in the decisive matter of ensuring social and political cohesion. I do not believe that this impression is wrong. But no broader study of the Third Reich could possibly leave this issue there. Nor was it just a matter of tracing the actual complicity of some groups of workers and soldiers in genocidal policies, of trying to estimate the extent of knowledge of these policies in the working class, or the diffusion of racist sentiments among wage-earners. At stake is the central question of what the Nazi regime was really all about, what its main aims were.

On this aspect of the problem of Nazism I remained basically silent. I confined myself to investigating some of the conditions for the war of social and racial imperialism. I came to understand more and more strongly that in the large book, as I had conceived it, there was no real place for the actual facts of biological politics and genocidal extermination. The main elements of my enquiry into Nazi dominion were ultimately secondary to those actions of the regime which demand our predominant moral and historical attention, and thus belong at the start and at the conclusion of any work which aspires to be comprehensive. Class and race are not blankly incompatible points of departure for an analysis of Nazism; they connect with each other in a wide variety of concrete ways. But I failed to open a door on biological racism, such a massive part of the historical reality, and I cannot now see how to weave it together with the social, economic and political themes of this book.

Recent research has made this omission appear even more fundamental, for biological racism informed Nazi social policies in ways
which are not at all apparent in my study of these policies. It is becoming increasingly clear that the regime set out violently to reconstitute
'German' society on a biological basis.[5] So numerous and so ruthless
were the eugenic interventions and propaganda in this respect that Nazi
social policy needs to be understood as 'social racism' (in Gisela Bock's
phrase). In its implications, this project transcended (though it included)
my emphasis on the abolition of class conflict. The creation of an organic 'purified' *Volk* called for an increasingly radical and comprehensive
discrimination between the 'fit' and the 'unfit', which soon led from the
persecution to the physical elimination of many of the latter, especially
of the mentally ill. These were measures of everyday life, openly discussed and, euthanasia excepted, openly enacted. They must have resonated through all classes of German society. Beginning with the
decisive step of the compulsory sterilization of those suffering from
supposedly hereditary diseases in 1933,[6] the regime proceeded to stig-
matize and persecute a vast assortment of so-called 'anti-social elements and parasites' on the grounds that their economic costs, their
disutility and their 'racial' danger to the community were biologically
determined and thus irredeemable. Charity, except towards the deserv-
ing poor, was perniciously sentimental and unscientific. Tramps and
vagabonds, alcoholics (as long as they were not leading Nazis), homosexuals, the 'work-shy' and habitual law-breakers were all under the
arbitrary jurisdiction of the Gestapo and the camps by the late 1930s;
mulattoes were sterilized; especially vicious was the stigmatization,
sterilization and then extermination of the Gypsies, who were designated as hereditarily criminal. Doctors and health administrators were especially fervent advocates of this pseudo-scientific eugenic cleansing, the
culmination of which came with the euthanasia actions of the early war
years. But even all this was not clear and rigorous enough. During the
war the identity of the person who was 'alien-to-the-community'
(*gemeinschaftsfremd*) was being worked out as a comprehensive politi-
cal-eugenic *legal* category: this piece of quasi-constitutional legislation
would have defined systematically all the people to be excluded from

5. For an excellent introduction to this theme see Jeremy Noakes, 'Nazism and
Eugenics: The Background to the Nazi Sterilization Law of 14 July 1933', in R. J. Bullen,
H. Pogge von Strandmann and A. B. Polonsky (eds.), *Ideas into Politics*, London, 1984.
6. See Gisela Bock, *Zwangssterilisation im Nationalsozialismus. Studien zur
Rassenpolitik und Frauenpolitik*, Opladen, 1986. For an excellent extended discussion of
this important work in English, see Paul Weindling, 'Compulsory Sterilisation in National
Socialist Germany', in *German History*, no. 5, 1987, pp. 10ff.

the 'national community', discriminated against, persecuted.[7] All of this was vigorously and publicly advocated in the 1930s by the Nazi Welfare Organization (NSV), which demanded that 'degenerates' should not be assisted at all, 'worthless' lives should be liquidated, and that the goal of all policy should be to help the fit to become fitter and more numerous.[8] This was not mere rhetoric; it filtered down well before the war into specific acts of eugenic persecution against individuals and families in relatively isolated industrial towns.[9]

This dimension of biologically based social racism is of vital importance for two reasons. First it shows the deep and broad political, ideological and administrative roots of what became the genocidal 'New Order' in Europe. There were competing schools of racist eugenics, but together they made up an irreducible core and a central continuity of Nazi politics. Race-thinking and racial policies in the widest sense were to be the foundation, or goal, of a new social order on a national and continental scale.[10] This belongs in the foreground of any overall analysis; and I could not find a proper place for it. Second, Nazi eugenics erected a positive stereotype of the useful, worthy member of the community, which carried powerful pseudo-moral overtones. The physically and mentally fit not only possessed an intrinsic biological value (of which the propagandists were certainly more conscious than the people themselves), but they were productive, diligent and dutiful, and thus good potential political material if they could be made aware of their superior worth. Only they, it was incessantly suggested, could contribute – by their work, by their fecundity in the case of healthy women – to the creation of a race/society which was efficient and organically harmonious; efficient on account of its organic harmony. 'The Jew' was from the outset the absolute antithesis, the implacable enemy of this

7. This approach to the study of Nazi social policies was pioneered by Detlev Peukert in his incisive study *Inside Nazi Germany: Conformity, Opposition and Racism in Everyday Life*, New Haven, 1987. Peukert has refined and developed his arguments in a series of important essays: 'Arbeitslager und Jugend-KZ: die "Behandlung Gemeinschaftsfremder" im Dritten Reich', in Detlev Peukert and Jürgen Reulecke (eds.), *Die Reihen fast geschlossen*, Wuppertal, 1981; 'Das "Dritte Reich" aus der "Alltags"-Perspektive', in *Archiv für Sozialgeschichte*, vol. 26, 1986; 'Alltag und Barbarei. Zur Normalität des Dritten Reiches', in Dan Diner (ed.), *Ist der Nationalsozialismus Geschichte?*, Frankfurt am Main, 1987.
8. See Herwart Vorländer, 'NS-Volkswohlfahrt und Winterhilfswerk des deutschen Volkes', *Vierteljahrshefte für Zeitgeschichte*, vol. 34/3, 1986; Adelheid Gräfin zu Castell Rüdenhausen, '"Nicht mitzuleiden, mitzukämpfen sind wir da!" Nationalsozialistische Volkswohlfahrt im Gau Westfalen-Nord', in Peukert and Reulecke (eds.), *Die Reihen*.
9. See Klaus Tenfelde, 'Proletarische Provinz. Radikalisierung und Widerstand in Penzberg/Oberbayern', in Martin Broszat et al. (eds.), *Bayern in der NS-Zeit*, vol. 4, Munich/Vienna, 1981.
10. This point is forcefully argued by Michale Geyer in the course of a brilliant bibliographical essay, 'Krieg als Gesellschaftspolitik', *Archiv für Sozialgeschichte*, vol. 26, 1986.

positive stereotype, parasitic, genetically and ideologically subversive.[11] But from 1933 on increasing groups of 'Germans' were excluded and persecuted with basically the same kind of pseudo-scientific and pseudo-moral justification. The annihilation of Nazism's political opponents, above all the organizations of the working class on which I have concentrated, was the essential prelude to this social-racial project. The groups singled out for persecution, whether the mentally ill, the 'work-shy', law breakers, homosexuals, and others, were almost certainly socially isolated anyway, objects of widespread fears and prejudices in all classes of society.[12] Nazism not only massively reinforced this isolation, but probably thereby also conferred confirmation, a sense of security, perhaps flattery, on the mass of healthy and hard-working, 'decent' people in all walks of life. This is a hypothesis only, which calls for a lot of difficult further research. But two preliminary comments are perhaps in order. First, the traditional strong work ethic of the German labour movement, collective pride in hard, skilled, productive labour, was persistently appealed to in the Nazi eugenics campaigns and was endowed with a social-moral worth of its own, fractured from its historical context of class ideology and politics. How well this rhetorical trick worked we do not know.[13] It seems more certain, second, that the biologically based social racism of the 1930s decisively prepared the ground for the acceptance of (or indifference to) the genocides and the programmes of racial enslavement in the war years – for that murderous finale of Nazi politics of which I did not begin to give an account.

Murderous biological politics of all kinds remain the great legacy of National Socialism. I tried to deal with some of their preconditions: with the social counter-revolution, the political terror, the preparation of war, the increasingly dynamic and aggressive instability of the economy and the regime, and with that specific war of social and racial imperialism which followed from this instability. But the central legacy of the regime cannot be extrapolated from, or drawn out of these considera-

11. For a lucid analysis, see Fred Weinstein, *The Dynamics of Nazism*, New York/London, 1980, ch. 4.

12. For Hitler's capacity to play on prejudices of this kind (*das gesunde Volksempfinden*), see especially Lothar Kettenacker, 'Sozialpsychologische Aspekte der Führer-Herrschaft', in Hirschfeld and Kettenacker (eds.), *Führerstaat*.

13. There are many hints in the oral and documentary evidence that groups of older workers did preserve their strong work ethic, without being seduced by Nazi politics. For one example see Gerhard Hetzer, 'Die Industriestadt Augsburg. Eine Sozialgeschichte der Arbeiteropposition', in Broszat et al. (eds.), *Bayern in der NS-Zeit*, vol. 3, pp. 123–30. On workers' responses to incentive wages (*Leistungslohn*), see Rüdiger Hachtmann, *Industriearbeit im 'Dritten Reich'. Untersuchungen zu den Lohn- und Arbeitsbedingungen in Deutschland 1933–1945,* Göttingen, 1989. The whole complex of questions remains, however, wide open, especially as far as moments of crisis such as the autumn of 1939 are concerned.

tions: it remains an absence. This absence made it in the end impossible to use this book as the basis and framework for the general study which I wanted to write.

The absence of biological politics and genocide from the perspective of this book is not just a matter of a faulty approach or a defective theory. Approaches and theories have their emotional foundations, and I have always remained emotionally, and thus intellectually, paralysed in front of what the Nazis actually did and what their victims suffered. The enormity of these actions and these sufferings both imperatively demanded description and analysis, and at the same time totally defied them. I could neither face the facts of genocide, nor walk away from them and study a less demanding subject. I find it almost impossible to read the sources, or the studies and testimonies which have been written on the subject. I know that many historians of Nazism have had a similar experience. This is one of the main reasons why the literature on the preconditions of Nazism, on the movement's rise to power, on the structure of the regime and on its foreign policies has been until recently so much larger and richer than the literature on its crimes against humanity. The horrifying scale and character of the latter seem to constrain historians to adopt an indirect, or explanatory, approach in which what requires an account remains in the background, presumed to be known and familiar, but undescribed and unanalysed on its own terms. This unsatisfactory way of writing history has to be understood as the outcome of an unrelenting dilemma and of an uncompleted struggle on the part of historians who are faced with an awesome piece of emotional, moral and intellectual work. I do not in the least wish to imply that the only books worth reading about Nazism are those which deal in detail with sterilization, euthanasia, the death squads and the extermination camps, but unless these latter are placed explicitly at a central point of the enquiry, the perspective of a work is wrong.

This is the second reason why this book, contrary to my aspirations, has remained as it is, a part-study, a confined contribution. The limitation does not only concern the extermination of the European Jews, but also those basic policies of the regime, usually summed up as *Lebensraum*, as they unfolded during the years 1939–43. The murderous biological-political component in these policies went far beyond what I have called social and racial imperialism. The immense destruction of human life, both casual and deliberate, and the massive movements of populations have to be related in some way or another to the cardinal issue of the evolving vision and practice of a new German racial empire.[14] I have not been able

14. Geyer, 'Krieg als Gesellschaftspolitik'. On the mass killing of potentially useful workers, see Ulrich Herbert, 'Arbeit und Vernichtung. Ökonomisches Interesse und Primat der "Weltanschauung" im Nationalsozialismus', in Diner (ed.), *Ist der Nationalsozialismus Geschichte?*.

to integrate these race policies into an analysis of what the war was really about. I emphasize strongly the need for the plunder of resources and of people, and argue that this had quite a lot to do with the timing, and with the failure, of the Nazi war. But why the regime set out on a war of racial-imperial conquest/annihilation in the first place, and how it was conducted, I do not discuss. There are no simple answers, but the acts of genocide against the Slav peoples form an integral part of the story. Here too my historical imagination kept on failing me: facts which I could not face, and therefore could not understand and not give a proper place to.[15]

It might be fruitful to pursue this line of self-critical reflection further. The identity of the historian is seldom related in open discussion to his/her work, and with respect to no subject is this more necessary than to Nazism, which assaults the deepest roots of the student's identity. Such a discussion, however, is now a matter for careful collective reflection on the part of all those who face the bitter difficulties involved. Energies would surely be better spent in this direction than in the acrid and violent polemics on inter-war German history, which have been so much a feature of the 1980s; in some of these polemics, the violence of the past appears to be re-enacted rhetorically, often at a tangent to the real historical events, rather than being confronted and analysed.

These introductory remarks are intended to explain the delay in the publication of this book, and the unusual form which it has now taken. I shall not write the larger book which might remedy some of its deficiencies, a book which begins and ends with the Nazi regime and not with the politics of social conflict. This perspective would be necessary in order to account for the two phenomena which I do not account for: genocides and the fact that Nazi Germany held out until the bitter end in 1945. On the other hand, those general studies of the regime that do exist, tend to concentrate overmuch on politics and ideology and to leave the regime acting in a social and economic vacuum. Thus, as far as overall interpretations are concerned, this book may act as a kind of partial corrective, or as a contribution to an on-going discussion, in which I begin to try to tell the end of one part of the story.

The main part of this epilogue is made up of a series of essays which attempt to respond to some of the debates which the book originally

15. Among the historians who in different ways have succeeded in resolving this kind of problem are Hannah Arendt, *The Origins of Totalitarianism*, New York, 1951; Alexander Dallin, *German Rule in Russia, 1941–1945*, London, 1957; Raoul Hilberg, *The Destruction of the European Jews*, London, 1961; Martin Broszat, *Nationalsozialistische Polenpolitik 1939–1945*, Frankfurt am Main, 1965; Herbert Jäger, *Verbrechen unter totalitärer Herrschaft*, Olten, 1967; Norman Rich, *Hitler's War Aims*, 2 vols., New York/ London, 1973, 1974; and (despite some misinterpretations) Arno J. Mayer, *Why Did the Heavens not Darken? The 'Final Solution' in History*, New York, 1989.

generated, to draw some lessons from the new original research in social history which has been carried out in the intervening years, and to summarize the history of Nazi labour policies and of class relations in the war years.

2. Class

Many critics objected to the strong emphasis that this book gives to class and to class conflict. I did not try to develop this emphasis into an articulated Marxian theory of capitalist reproduction and state monopoly capitalism under Nazism. I was working empirically towards a political social history of the regime, and the materials that I used did not lend themselves to the construction of this kind of theoretical history. Nor have I found this kind of writing especially useful in understanding Nazism.[16] Given the absence of such explicit theorizing about class relations, given my insistence (following E. P. Thompson) on class as lived experience, some critics questioned whether it was worthwhile, or possible, to write about class at all: the problems of the making and implementation of social policy in the Third Reich could, they tended to suggest, be dissolved into matters of industrial relations on the one hand, and the needs of the regime to maintain 'popular' support in general on the other. On this count 'class' is an obscure abstraction. Many liberal German historians deliberately and consistently use the term *Arbeiterschaft* (loosely, 'working people') instead of *Arbeiterklasse* ('working class') precisely because it appears to be descriptively neutral and conceptually unburdened, as though workers were just another group in society, like farmers, shopkeepers, clerks and so on. The distinction is crucial, because to speak about class immediately invokes class conflict, class antagonism, as something fundamental to the capitalist social order. For the period under discussion (which was different from the 1980s) it seems essential to do this. At a very simple but fundamental level Nazism was part of an epoch of general and acute class conflict throughout Western Europe, when relations between capital and labour, left and right, were the axis of public affairs. These conflicts

16. Franz Neumann, *Behemoth: The Structure and Practice of National Socialism*, London, 1942, remains invaluable precisely because it is theoretically modest. Alfred Sohn-Rethel, *The Economy and Class Structure of German Fascism*, London, 1987, is rescued from obscure notions only by Jane Caplan's 'Afterword'. For some overstrained but suggestive comments which link concepts of Marx and Engels to the destruction of the working class in 1945, see Lutz Niethammer, Ulrich Borsdorf and Peter Brandt (eds.), *Arbeiterinitiative 1945*, Wuppertal, 1976, ch. 3 (by Hajo Dröll). On Marxism-Leninism, see the concluding remarks in this section.

encompassed the distribution of power at the workplace, all aspects of local and national social and economic policy and, especially in Germany, foreign policy and the constitution itself, to say nothing of the vast world of political culture. It was one of the main aims of Nazism to abolish this class society precisely because it was conflictual. These are powerful reasons for insisting upon the vocabulary of class.

Nevertheless, one major criticism does now seem to me to be fully warranted. In the original PrefaceI wrote that 'class relations are *the* constitutive element in the history of industrialized capitalist states'. This is an overstatement which led to too narrow a perspective. While the evidence does show that class conflict remained much more important in the Third Reich than has commonly been accepted, and influenced some policy-making at the highest levels, there is no clear path that can be traced from class conflict to the fundamental projects of the Third Reich. These projects presupposed the successful abolition of class conflict (never fully achieved), but they reached far beyond this negative goal. Thus 'the constitutive element', as argued above, was the regime.

Otherwise, I tend to stand by my original positions. To begin with the situation as seen 'from below', class conflict remained endemic in Nazi Germany. It was qualitatively different, on account of its actual economic and its potential political importance ('the legacy of 1918'), from other types of social and economic antagonism. Class, under a system of rule which denied the working class its own organizations, can only be understood as a diffuse, dynamic, relational phenomenon (lived experience), and cannot be encompassed in clear sociological or organizational categories. This leads to a sustained and self-conscious vagueness in the definition of the 'working class' (and of class in general) throughout the book, which reinforced the basic doubts of some critics. There is nothing to be done about this, because in the Third Reich the working class made itself felt in the most diffuse variety of conflicts, either actual or anticipated by the holders of power. It is the conflicts, which involved some workers for most of the period and most workers at a whole series of critical junctures, which give content to the notion of class.[17] I concentrated for pragmatic reasons upon industrial wage-earners (who clearly did not make up the whole working class). I took for granted the elementary fact of their quite distinctive, antagonistic and mass experience of extreme subordination, discipline, alienation and exploitation at the workplace, an observation common to expert stu-

17. I am indebted for this precise formulation to Stephen Salter, 'Structures of Consensus and Coercion: Workers' Morale and the Maintenance of Work Discipline, 1939–1945', in David Welch (ed.), *Nazi Propaganda*, London, 1983, p. 101.

dents of factory organization who propose the most diverse theoretical points of view.[18] I clearly should have spelt this out in more detail. What gave these conflicts their crucial significance was the involvement (actual or potential) of *masses* of workers, acting either in deliberate concert with each other,[19] or acting spontaneously in large numbers in the same way, in opposition to employers and/or the state. Informal, seemingly individual protests on the part of large numbers of workers point, as has been rightly emphasized, to 'a common awareness of common interests' in class terms, even when such protests were not collectively articulated.[20] I believed that this mass quality of class conflict, whether actual or feared by the regime, was too obvious to need underlining. I was wrong, for a particularly dedicated critic has argued that individual film-stars and industrial managers exploited their own scarcity value to demand higher remuneration in the late 1930s and early 1940s, and so look in class terms like workers.[21] Superficially similar behaviour has, however, a totally different meaning, depending upon the social and political context. The wage demands, passive resistance and indiscipline of large sectors of the German working class in 1939 carried a totally different significance from the vigorous self-advancement of individual professionals: the former challenged the state at the very centre of its economic and military policies at a time of international and economic crisis, because theirs were the actions of masses, undertaken at the vital and vulnerable point of production.[22]

This silly and polemical invocation of go-getting professionals does, however, raise a larger question. It has been pointed out that the book works throughout with a rough-and-ready *two-class* model of German

---

18. Among the quite different works which have informed my perspective are Barrington Moore, Jr, *Injustice. The Social Bases of Obedience and Revolt*, London/Basingstoke, 1978, chs. 6 and 7; Stanley B. Mathewson, *Restriction of Output among Unorganized Workers*, Carbondale, 1969, with an introduction by Donald F. Roy (the original edition of this classic was published in 1931); Huw Beynon, *Working for Ford*, Harmondsworth, 1973. The latter's analysis of 'factory consciousness' and 'factory politics' is a brilliant discussion of themes which I have only been able to suggest.

19. For the case of strike actions in the 1930s, see now the excellent research of Günter Morsch, 'Streik im "Dritten Reich"', *Vierteljahrshefte für Zeitgeschichte*, vol. 36/4, 1988; and in greater detail, idem, 'Arbeitsniederlegungen im "Dritten Reich". Eine quellenkritische Dokumentation der Jahre 1936 und 1937', in Hasso Spode, Heinrich Volkmann, Günter Morsch and Rainer Hudemann, *Statistik der Streiks und Aussperrungen in Deutschland* (forthcoming).

20. See Salter, 'Structures of Consensus and Coercion', p. 101.

21. Wolfgang Franz Werner, *'Bleib übrig!' Deutsche Arbeiter in der nationalsozialistischen Kriegswirtschaft*, Düsseldorf, 1983, pp. 14, 108.

22. Werner goes to excessive lengths to dissociate his own work from mine. In fact his fine research, and not a few of his formulations, are much more consonant with my interpretation of the domestic crisis of 1939 than he suggests. See, e.g., ibid., pp. 33–8, 58, 69, 71ff.

society, which is nowhere elaborated or justified.[23] This is true, and calls for belated elucidation. I am concerned throughout with the dynamic of the changing social basis of politics, not with the differentiations of social structure. In these terms the Nazi seizure of power initiated a radical distinction between dominators and dominated. The vast mass of the dominated possessed only their labour power, whereas most owners of the means of production, professional people, public officials and the like were clearly among the dominators, at least well into the 1930s. The abolition of the rule of law and the destruction of the labour movement created a huge body of powerless and largely rightless 'citizens', who were confronted by a coalition of property owners with the new political and administrative elite, a coalition which was relatively quick in settling its main internal differences (June–August 1934). This coalition of the dominators calls for separate discussion below. Important here is the fact that the sector of the dominated grew steadily in size in various ways: white-collar workers tended to lose their higher social status and privileges;[24] small farmers became state-controlled producers under increasingly disadvantageous conditions;[25] artisans and shopkeepers came under growing pressure to give up their independent economic existence.[26] The basic distinction was that between those who gave orders, economic and political, and those whose duty was to obey. This distinction was blurred less by processes of social and economic differentiation, than by the existence of the large Nazi organizations that conferred growing political powers on their officials, powers which were increasingly independent of their (sometimes lower) social status. With this very important exception of political-social mobility, I still incline to stand by a rough-and-ready two-class model of German political society under Nazism (at least for the period before the massive importation of foreign labourers during the war). As far as the dominated are concerned it is a rough-and-ready model. My aim has not been to draw a refined sociological map of German society: the great value of an enterprise of this kind is demonstrated by, among other works, the six volumes on *Bayern in der NS-Zeit*.[27] But I was searching for the

23. See the constructive criticism in the review by Jürgen Kocka, *Journal of Modern History*, Sept. 1978, and the aggressive questioning of the whole approach by Peter Hüttenberger, *Vierteljahrschrift für Sozial-und Wirtschaftsgeschichte*, 1977, no. 1.

24. See Michael Prinz, *Vom neuen Mittelstand zum Volksgenossen*, Munich, 1986, chs. 3 and 4; also Marie-Luise Recker, *Nationalsozialistische Sozialpolitik im Zweiten Weltkrieg*, Munich, 1985, especially p. 300.

25. Gustavo Corni, *Hitler and the Peasants. Agrarian Policy of the Third Reich, 1930–1939*, New York/Oxford/Munich, 1990.

26. Heinrich August Winkler, 'Der entbehrliche Stand. Zur Mittelstandspolitik im "Dritten Reich"', *Archiv für Sozialgeschichte*, vol. 17, 1977.

27. Broszat et al. (eds.), *Bayern in der NS-Zeit*, 6 vols., 1977–83.

right basic categories for a political social history, which would encompass 'high politics'. For all their crudity, the 'us-them' categories seem to serve this purpose best. (This is, of course, not to deny for a moment that at various times there were many among the dominated who regarded the regime with great favour.) They involve an attempt to locate and describe the most constant and recurrent, the most intractable and most dangerous lines of conflict in German society after 1933. The largest and most homogeneous group among the dominated was the working class, wage-earners in industry, transport, services, and so on, and this group itself tended to grow in size. These comprise one set of reasons for simplifying the picture in terms of conflict within a two-class society.

There are, however, other reasons. Conflict is a matter of two sides. I have stressed in the Preface that this book is in the first instance a study of class conflict from above: a study of the perceptions, motives, techniques and policies of the dominators. In the reception of the book this emphasis was overshadowed by discussion of the new evidence which I put forward concerning the forms and extent of the opposition of the dominated, evidence which came as a surprise both to me and to many readers, and the significance of which has been the subject of debates to which I shall return later in this epilogue. At this point, however, it is essential to restore the original emphasis on the forms and measures of domination. This is the main theme of the book. We are much better informed about this side of the conflict. The overwhelming majority of the documentation upon which this study could draw was written by members of the dominating groups. With the exception of one important source, which did not become readily available until 1980,[28] the dominated were systematically deprived of their voice, deprived of the possibility of registering their experiences and opinions for posterity. The narrative and the analysis thus revolve heavily around the perceptions of the economic and political rulers of Nazi Germany. These perceptions strongly bear out the notion of a two-class society, of the existence of a clear, continuous and potentially dangerous gulf between dominators and dominated. For this reason, some of the most striking proofs of the intractability of class conflict come not from open acts of defiance from below, but from the pervasive uncertainties of those in power about just how many sacrifices, just what degree of exploitation, what measures of compulsion they could impose upon the dominated,

---

28. *Deutschland-Berichte der Sozialdemokratischen Partei Deutschlands (Sopade), 1934–1940,* 7 vols., Salzhausen/Frankfurt am Main, 1980. For a sensitive analysis of these smuggled reports in so far as they concern industrial conflicts see Michael Voges, 'Klassenkampf in der "Betriebsgemeinschaft". Die Deutschland-Berichte der Sopade (1934–1940) als Quelle zum Widerstand im Dritten Reich', in *Archiv für Sozialgeschichte,* vol. 21, 1981.

without conflict exploding into mass opposition. In the absence of independent negotiating machinery for determining issues of this kind, decision-making was left to the (often cautious or pessimistic) intuitions of those in power. The dialectic of conflict, repression or concession, was thus in a significant sense transplanted from the realm of social reality to that of the erratic estimates and guesswork of those who formulated and enforced (or not!) policies towards the dominated.[29] This fact calls for some further discussion (see below). What I wish to emphasize at this point is that their confidential perceptions of the social order, expressed in memoranda and reports and so on, corresponded consistently and closely to that of a two-class society; they evoked a situation in which they were called upon to control – until perhaps 1942 – an increasingly refractory class of dominated persons. In this sense my whole approach to the problems of class and power is in fact highly conventional in historiographical terms: theory and analysis are subordinate to, or grow out of, an effort to explicate what the ruling groups *thought* they were seeing and doing, how they discussed these problems among themselves, and what practical conclusions they drew. It is in the last instance an immanent approach, which is indebted to Marx for questions, not for a mode of analysis nor for answers.

It has been argued by way of criticism that the authors of the sources upon which I have drawn misperceived and misunderstood the political society which they presided over and about which they wrote. I shall take up this interesting discussion at a later point. Here it is sufficient to insist that, however mistaken they may have been, their perceptions were what actually counted in the making of Nazi policies during the crucial years between 1936 and 1939; and I am concerned mainly with

---

29. The dilemmas and hesitations of the civilian ministries, the Four-Year Plan were due mainly to the extreme delicacy of the decisions that they had to take. But it is also not clear that they were informed in a systematic and comprehensive manner about changes in working-class attitudes, behaviour and expectations. The individual monthly reports of the regional Trustees of Labour (now lost) were certainly more detailed than the summaries which I published in *Arbeiterklasse und Volksgemeinschaft*; but Morsch, 'Arbeitsniederlegungen', points out how badly informed all the authorities were about strikes. This had something to do with the profusion and confusion of reporting agencies and their addressees. The surviving reports on industrial workers by the War Economy Staff of the OKW for 1938 and 1939 are often more detailed than the papers of the Ministries of Economics and Labour, which is why I draw upon them frequently in chapter 6, but this information was not regularly shared with the civilian authorities. It was to meet the need for better assessments of people's attitudes as an integral part of policy-making that the 'Meldungen aus dem Reich' were introduced at the end of 1939: see Heinz Boberach (ed.), *Meldungen aus dem Reich, 1938–1945: die geheimen Lageberichte des Sicherheitsdienstes des SS*, Herrsching, 1984. For an exemplary analysis of the various flows of information from the bottom to the top of the adminstrative pyramids, and of the erratic use made of it, see Ian Kershaw, *Popular Opinion and Political Dissent in the Third Reich. Bavaria 1933–1945*, Oxford, 1983.

these policies. This is a simple but fundamental point for a study which aspires to be a political social history, rather than a study of class composition or, as one historian has persistently misconstrued it, 'a view' of Nazi politics 'from below'.[30]

However, given the emphasis upon class conflict from above, my identification of the ruling class(es), the dominators, does indeed remain indefensibly vague. The narrative moves silently back and forward between big capital, state authorities, Nazi agencies and Hitler, creating a needless uncertainty and imprecision.[31] As in the case of the 'working class', a degree of vagueness is inevitable and justified, but I should have been more explicit. To resolve this problem properly would require a separate large book on a subject on which several detailed and serious studies have already been made.[32] The best that can be done at this point is to try to dispel some unnecessary confusions, and to remedy a culpable silence.

First, although the Third Reich retained to the end a capitalist economy of a singular kind, real economic power passed at the latest in 1936 (Four-Year Plan) from big business to the regime itself; after then the regime became the predominant active co-ordinator of social and economic policies in a way which had not been true of the years 1933–4, when big business at first set its stamp upon the new order (see chapter 3 above). This is the reason why, in the course of the narrative, the regime, understood in the widest sense, becomes the main protagonist in class conflict with the working class.[33] Second, over and beyond some continuing conflicts between some business interests and certain agencies of the regime, the regime itself was indeed riven by conflicts over the policies to be adopted towards the working class. I have pointed especially to three of these: the military demand for guns before butter; the endless disputes over the powers of the DAF; and the conflicts

30. Thus Richard J. Overy in his 'Reply' to the debate on 'Germany, "Domestic Crisis" and War in 1939', *Past and Present*, no. 122, 1989, pp. 230, 233.

31. The demand for clearer, more articulated definitions is a central part of Ludolf Herbst's extensive critique, 'Die Krise des nationalsozialistischen Regimes am Vorabend des Zweiten Weltkrieges und die forcierte Aufrüstung. Eine Kritik', *Vierteljahrshefte für Zeitgeschichte*, vol. 26/3, 1978, pp. 356, 362, 373.

32. Neumann, *Behemoth,* remains in my view the best balanced treatment of the relationships between regime and capital. For a variety of diverse interpretations with a wealth of new research see Arthur Schweitzer, *Big Business in the Third Reich*, Bloomington, IN, 1964; Dietmar Petzina, *Autarkiepolitik im Dritten Reich*, Stuttgart, 1968; Ludolf Herbst, *Der Totale Krieg und die Ordnung der Wirtschaft*, Stuttgart, 1982; Dietrich Eichholtz, *Geschichte der deutschen Kriegswirtschaft 1939–1945*, E. Berlin, vol. 1, 1971, vol. 2, 1985; Lotte Zumpe, *Wirtschaft und Staat in Deutschland 1933 bis 1945*, E. Berlin, 1980.

33. I sketched out this argument in an essay, 'The Primacy of Politics – Politics and Economics in National Socialist Germany', in S. J. Woolf (ed.), *The Nature of Fascism*, London, 1968, but I failed to develop either this or the issues from a consequent debate in *Das Argument*, no. 47, 1968, into the body of the book. The argument and the debate in fact required further development.

over war priorities before and after the invasion of Poland. There were others, and not even in the Speer years did Nazi war capitalism develop into a harmonious symbiosis of the various regime agencies and entrepreneurial interests.[34]

Such divisions were often very bitter and led to dismissals and radical changes in policy, but they do not, however, make it impossible to speak of *a* ruling class or classes. The dynamics of the development and crises of twentieth-century capitalism everywhere led to economic, social, ideological and political divisions within the ruling class/state. No capitalist state before 1945 produced a single, coherent long-term strategy for the conduct of class conflict. The internal tensions and dynamics of the system precluded any such thing.[35] The divisions within the ruling bloc in Nazi Germany were perhaps especially acute on account, first, of the extreme speed of the economic and social changes engendered by forced rearmament, and second, of the fissiparous, quite uncoordinated nature of the dictatorship's political institutions. But it remained in the end a ruling bloc, changing in character all the time, but never broken asunder.[36]

Thus, to take the most relevant example, the sharp objection that the profound and vitriolic conflicts between Schacht and Ley make it meaningless to consider both as representatives of 'a ruling class' is without real substance.[37] Not only did the two men and their institutions work out a series of (admittedly unstable) compromises over a vital period of four years. More important, their differences concerned alternative strategies which the dominant groups could adopt towards the working class. The ultimate goals of the DAF had nothing to do with the supercession of the capitalist order, but rather with its comprehensive socioeconomic rationalization and modernization – with a view to making it more popular, and to be carried out in such a way that the DAF itself would become a key component of a reconstituted ruling class (see below). On these issues Schacht was a convinced conservative, the political spokesman of those business and administrative interests which were hostile less to the dictatorship as such than to a Nazi moderniza-

34. See Herbst, *Der Totale Krieg*; Gregor Janssen, *Das Ministerium Speer. Deutschlands Rüstung im Krieg*, Berlin, 1968.

35. The clearest example is Roosevelt's New Deal, in which the divisions and conflicts were conducted in public; they led to the change, not the breakdown, of the ruling order.

36. I emphasize this point in contrast to the economic, military and political fractures which broke the ruling bloc in fascist Italy in the first half of 1943.

37. This is the pointed, polemical manner in which Hüttenberger formulated his general objections in his review; see note 23 above. Whether 'class' is used in the singular or the plural in this context is not, contrary to Hüttenberger, a fundamental theoretical issue: the plural form is intended merely to point to the plurality of interests and functions within the formation.

tion and reconstitution of the ruling class. The differences between them were great, but they concerned different visions of how a *class society* should function.[38] This is why it does in the last resort make sense to consider both the adversaries as exponents of an overall ruling class in a dynamic two-class model of the politico-economic system. (It is not irrelevant that Schacht and then Ley shared the common fate of being losers in the never-ending conflicts among the dominant groups.)

This same basic argument applies to the relative importance of all such conflicts and divisions as the system of domination developed towards that of a total war economy. None of them threatened to question the necessity of what I have called the two-class order.[39] On this fundamental negative point all the dominant groups did maintain a notable homogeneity. (On a political level, the economically dominant groups were heavily underrepresented in the conspiracy to overthrow Hitler and the regime in July 1944.) But both in the economy and in the regime, and in relations between the two spheres, there was a continuous conflictual process of recomposition, of redefinition both of powers and policies, processes of concentration and amalgamation (the Speer era), but also processes of fragmentation (the SS). The ruling class, as I intended it to be understood, was far from stable or homogeneous, without thereby ceasing to function overall as a ruling class, a dynamic coalition of interdependent dominators.

The above schematic comments cannot make good an important omission in the argument of the book. They aspire to diminish a justly criticized lack of clarity and to furnish a slightly more precise element for future discussions. Greater definitional precision, however, is I believe excluded by the historical facts. In developing a general argument as a framework for this specialized investigation it is necessary to blur the boundaries between politics and economics precisely because the two spheres became increasingly intermeshed. (A monograph on raw materials allocation or capital investment would need to make distinctions which lie beyond the scope of this enquiry.) Thus the notion of a ruling class remains essential to the analysis, but the notion must remain highly elastic in order to take account of divisions and mutations.[40]

38. Schacht, of course, had other and for him more important differences with the political leadership over economic and financial policy; those over financial policy led to his dismissal in 1939.

39. Goebbels did make some purely demagogic threats in this direction during the last stages of the war.

40. This fact was perhaps reflected in the diversity and the changes in working-class perceptions of the ruling classes. The source materials on this subject are not good, but many workers clearly came to understand that they could play on divisions among the dominating groups, at least within certain limits. This tended to diffuse antagonism and to confuse images of conflict, especially during the war years: see section 4, '1939–45', below.

Marxist-Leninist interpretations of the ruling class tend in my view, in their effort to be more stringent, both to underestimate the dynamic pluralism of the dominating groups and agencies, and to overstate the autonomous power of capital. Writing from this vantage point, one sympathetic critic argued that I could have resolved my confusion by assigning primacy, as the 'real' enemy of the working class, to big business and finance capital, of which the Nazi regime was an 'instrument' or 'organ'.[41] I have found very little evidence to sustain this conception of the ruling class for the years after 1934; many industrial archives have become accessible since I completed my original research, but while they shed a great deal of new light on economic affairs and on workplace relations, they do not seem to underpin this theoretical approach. If there is no evidence of heavy, continuous and successful pressure on the regime from the side of big business and finance capital in matters of labour and social policy, the question becomes one of meta-theory, rather than of history. Large employers were, of course, interested in the details of Nazi labour policies, and especially in the war years there were intense and continuous interchanges between them, state and Party authorities, the Gestapo, and so on, on the question of labour discipline (see below). But my concern is with the overall relationship between class antagonism on the one hand and high-level policy formation on the other. Here it remains a striking and important fact that the documentation with which I am familiar does *not* demonstrate effective business interventions in policies towards the working class at any of the turning points in these policies with which my book is concerned – the autumn of 1936, June 1938, and September 1939 – although these policies were of vital interest to business.[42] The decisive initiatives here seem to have come from the bureaucracy, the military and above all from the political leadership.[43] On a host of lesser issues, such as workers' rights to change jobs, special bonuses for coal-miners and wage levels in general, employers were repeatedly overruled in the 1930s by the state authorities. Then, the singular economic and social crisis of 1938–9 was the specific crisis of a militarized Nazi-dominated capitalist system, not a typical crisis of systems of imperialist finance capitalism (see below). As for the general policies of conquest and racial imperial-

41. See Lotte Zumpe, 'Ein Beitrag zur Wirtschafts-und Sozialgeschichte des deutschen Faschismus', *Jahrbuch für Wirtschaftsgeschichte*, 1979, part 4, pp. 169–71.

42. Business may have exerted greater effective influence during the war, especially over slave labour policies: see section 4, '1939–45', below.

43. At the very least it cannot be proved that big business constituted 'the real wire-pullers', as Zumpe puts it; 'Ein Beitrag', p. 171. See the documentation in *Arbeiterklasse und Volksgemeinschaft*, documentary part, chs. 2, 13, 14, 17–20. Recker, *Sozialpolitik*, p. 45, has discovered one intervention by the head of the Reich Industry Group *against* wage reductions at the start of the war.

ism, German finance and monopoly capital was a willing, often inventive junior partner of the regime, not the major historical agent.

It is for reasons of this order that I have tended to portray the Nazi regime, rather than German capitalism, as the principal protagonist in the class conflict. It is not a radical distinction, but a matter of emphasis which must take account of shifts in power over time.[44] There remains a vast amount more to be said about the complex relations between big business and the regime. But I believe, finally, that the above remarks have the merit of corresponding roughly to the perceptions and actions of many German workers, who objected much more strongly and in greater numbers to political interventions against their interests, than to the habitual everyday experience of exploitative employment (although overt opposition to the latter grew in the late 1930s and during the war years). All of these points run counter to an 'objective' economistic definition of the ruling class. It is the fluctuating, often disguised conflicts that open up the question of class to investigation and analysis. German workers were confronted by a unique coalition of authoritarian employers and a new type of dictatorship, under economic conditions in which they could still make their weight felt.

3. Domestic Crisis and War, 1939[45]

That part of the book which has aroused the most extensive discussion is the concluding section in which I suggest that there was a causal connection between the social and economic crisis in Germany and the acceleration of military expansionist policies towards war in 1938–9. This discussion has modified my original hypotheses, and it calls here for a critical review and re-elaboration. Such a review must start from first principles.

There is widespread agreement that the war which began in September 1939 was a disaster for Nazi Germany. This was Hitler's own view, clearly expressed at the time: 'My whole work is now falling to pieces. My book was written for nothing'.[46] Contrary to the foreign-policy axioms laid out in *Mein Kampf* and frequently repeated thereafter, the Third Reich found itself at war with Great Britain and the

---

44. One of the most important of these shifts was the delegation of powers to industrialists by the Speer Ministry in 1942/3. This should be seen as a partial fusion of state and capital, on the former's terms, rather than as a restoration of a capitalist ruling class.

45. This section is a substantially revised version of a paper first published in Thomas Childers and Jane Caplan (eds.), *Reevaluating the Third Reich*, New York, 1992.

46. See Joachim C. Fest, *Hitler. Eine Biographie*, Frankfurt am Main/Berlin/Vienna, 1973, p. 827 and note 295.

British Empire. Contrary to the 'timetable' for military expansion which Hitler elaborated as late as November 1937, and kept on repeating to Mussolini, the Third Reich found itself involved in a major European war already in 1939, rather than in the years around 1943, the time which Hitler seemed to believe would be optimal for large-scale conflict and conquests. Hitler's own erratic, confused and increasingly unrealistic conduct of policy in the ten weeks which followed the British and French declarations of war is but one important proof of the extreme seriousness of the new international situation brought about by the German invasion of Poland. The Nazi-Soviet Pact was an expedient which, having failed as a deterrent to Britain and France, did little to make good this damage. The major long-term damage lay in the possibility of Britain drawing the power of the United States into the war against Germany.

What went wrong? I think it is important to put the question in this way because it is quite conceivable that Nazi domination of Europe and of adjacent subcontinents could easily have been wider, longer and even more destructive than it actually was. The Third Reich's opportunities to consolidate and extend its empire in the late 1930s were very great. These opportunities were put at extreme risk, and soon (in December 1941) destroyed, by the war which Hitler had wanted in 1938 and actually began in September 1939. Why did Hitler force the pace in this way, disregard his own 'timetable', undermine his own continental and world strategy with respect to the British Empire? Since my argument is much concerned with the timing of events and decisions, it is important to note that he already wanted to take this huge risk in September 1938 and would clearly have preferred a war to the Munich settlement.[47]

In the preceding pages, also in a separate synthetic article,[48] I put forward the hypothesis that the accelerating dynamic of Nazi aggression in 1938 and 1939 was strongly conditioned by the internal problems of the regime, problems which progressively narrowed the margins for foreign policy choices and made it increasingly difficult for the regime to wait for the right moments to launch its wars of conquest. These internal problems appeared as consequences of forced rearmament after 1936 – of a rearmament drive which required resources far in excess of those available in (or to) Germany; and the excess of requirements over supplies was magnified by the way in which the regime and the markets

---

47. The evidence is well summarized by Fest, *Hitler*, pp. 763ff., 776.
48. This was written with the title 'Zur Funktion des Angriffskrieges' for Gilbert Ziebura (ed.), *Grundfragen der deutschen Aussenpolitik seit 1871*, Darmstadt, 1975; also published as 'Innere Krise und Angriffskrieg 1938/1939', in Friedrich Forstmeier and Hans-Erich Volkmann (eds.), *Wirtschaft und Rüstung am Vorabend des Zweiten Weltkrieges*, Düsseldorf, 1975.

distributed economic resources. (By 1939 the rearmament targets were in excess of all imaginable supplies, but that is a slightly different argument.) In this context I concentrate especial attention on the labour market and the working class. The basic new fact of the late 1930s was the large and rapidly growing shortage of labour, which raised a host of intractable economic, social, administrative and political problems. These problems imperilled the stability of the economy and impeded the progress of rearmament. To what precise degree they impeded rearmament is a contentious issue.[49]

At the same time, in June 1938 and again in the winter of 1938/9, the regime vastly expanded its armaments programmes, thus making much more acute all of the contradictions inherent in the situation. These were real politico-economic contradictions, not just technical problems which could be resolved by more sophisticated organizational and administrative interventions (though there were some of these too). In their essence they raised a fundamental problem of the dichotomy between means (the regimentation of people and resources) and ends (further rearmament), and thus tended to develop into a deep crisis of the power and legitimacy of the whole regime which necessarily spilled over into the sphere of foreign policy.

It must be repeated that the labour market and relations between the regime and the working class were not the only area in which signs of acute economic overstrain appeared during 1938 and 1939. Budgetary problems and the threat of inflation became drastic for a time at the end of 1939. Foreign trade and agriculture also came under heavy pressure, the former as a result of the world-wide recession of late 1937 which restricted Germany's capacity to export (and thus to import vital raw materials), agriculture as a result of a massive labour shortage and of strict price controls on foodstuffs. As in the labour market, in these sectors the government did not intervene early and in a consistent and rigorous manner in order to allocate resources to the armaments industries and to the farmers. In both cases such interventions would have meant heavy sacrifices for the mass of the urban consumers. It is vital to observe that all of these four acute new social and economic problems came to a head at the same time: during 1938.[50] They posed a major

49. It is not possible to give numerical values to the impediments that arose from these problems. My impression is that they were considerable. Herbst, 'Krise', p. 390, simply denies this, without giving evidence or arguments. Impediments also arose from other sources: Michael Geyer has pointed out that during 1937 German heavy industry was limiting output to optimum levels in terms of plant economics and was giving priority to the temporarily flourishing export market for iron and steel; see 'Rüstungsbeschleunigung und Inflation. Zur Inflationsdenkschrift des Oberkommandos der Wehrmacht vom November 1938', *Militärgeschichtliche Mitteilungen*, 1981, no. 2, p. 135 and note 105.

50. See Mason, 'Angriffskrieg'; Geyer, 'Rüstungsbeschleunigung'.

new set of simultaneous challenges to a regime which, in political, economic and administrative terms, was not well prepared to meet them.

Hitler, I have argued, concluded that if the economic and social-political situation in Germany really was so strained, this was in fact a strong reason for launching military aggression sooner rather than later.[51] There is a striking correspondence between his utterances in this sense and the actual situation in the country. This reading of Hitler's reasoning also fits in well with the generally accepted picture of him as a politician for whom sheer defiance and risk-taking were ultimate virtues. The documentation is neither ample nor unequivocal, but Hitler seems to have come to see the need for plunder through military conquest as a means of breaking the chains of pressing immediate bottlenecks and dangerous policy choices. His celebration of the booty gained through the occupation of Prague marks the point in time when this calculation became quite open.[52] There is a vital difference between this kind of short-term logic and the long-term goal of racial-economic imperialism, *Lebensraum*, to which Hitler was primarily committed.

There was in Hitler's mind a second connection between the urgency of war and the state of domestic affairs, a connection which I did not emphasize enough. He was constantly worried by the fear that the German people would lose what he imagined to be their sense of aggressive discipline, militarism and ideological fervour if the period of peace and relative prosperity of the later 1930s continued for too long. People could easily forget, he feared, what the true heroic goals of Nazism were and how many sacrifices they entailed; and once the war was started this became for him a reason for making one military campaign follow another in swift succession.[53] As we have seen, ministers, generals and senior civil servants gave concrete meaning to this piece of Hitlerian logic in that they saw the beginning of the war as the

---

51. Relevant quotations from Hitler are given above, pp. 262f. See also Herbst, *Der Totale Krieg*, p. 72.

52. See above, p. 263; for greater detail, see Wilhelm Deist, *The Wehrmacht and German Rearmament*, London/Basingstoke, 1981, pp. 88f.

53. Fest rightly emphasizes this point: *Hitler*, pp. 738ff., 831f., 840, 924f. Andreas Hillgruber quotes two striking examples of Hitler's worries on the same account in *Hitlers Strategie. Politik und Kriegführung 1940–1941*, Frankfurt am Main, 1965, pp. 219, 365. This central consideration casts much doubt on the validity of the argument that the Nazi leaders saw a close link between their race thinking and their social policies, in the sense that a degree of prosperity, good nutrition and working conditions and so on, would raise the quality of the 'racial stock'. If they really did think along these lines, as Herbst suggests (*Der Totale Krieg*, pp. 71, 89, 150, 163), we are faced with a fundamental contradiction in their ideas, which is quite possible. But there is no evidence that the regime as a whole (with the exception of the DAF/KdF) deliberately sought higher living standards in the later 1930s for eugenic reasons. The housing conditions of the working class, a key factor in 'racial progress', were badly neglected throughout, and the war economy measures of September 1939 showed a total disregard for eugenic or health considerations.

crucial opportunity to put the whole economy 'in order': to cut wages, lengthen working hours, extend civil conscription and so on. They hoped that the emergency of war would make acceptable to the German people a mass of repressive measures which had long been necessary anyway; that it would restore discipline, sacrifice and the Nazi sense of communal struggle (for which Hitler yearned, but which in this sphere he feared to impose) to the everyday conduct of economic life. This historic mission of the 'Thousand-Year Reich' required the pre-eminence of austere martial values in all walks of life, and an actual state of war was the only guarantee of this; non-war was a threat to it.

To summarize the argument very roughly, in 1938–9 only either peace or war could stabilize, or temporarily strengthen the politico-economic system. Indefinite further forced rearmament within Germany's existing boundaries, even after March 1939, was not a practical policy option. Further aggression entailed a wild gamble concerning the response of the United Kingdom and France. This is a domestic, social and economic argument about the timing, and thus about the international constellation, of the start of the Second World War which assigns a crucial role to Hitler personally. In this sense it differs both from neo-Marxist interpretations which minimize Hitler's personal power and leave no space for biography, and from Marxist-Leninist interpretations which attach great weight to the economic imperialism of big financial and industrial combines. In my view it was rather the perceived possible breakdown of the whole system of Nazified, militarized capitalism which precipitated events.

Most other historians working in this field have more or less rejected my hypotheses.[54] Direct, or more usually indirect, support for the line of enquiry which I have pursued has come from the research and interpre-

54. For a clear summary with a full bibliography of the first stages of the discussion, see Andreas Hillgruber, 'Forschungsstand und Literatur zum Ausbruch des Zweiten Weltkrieges', in Wolfgang Benz and Hermann Graml (eds.), *Sommer 1939. Die Grossmächte und der europäische Krieg*, Stuttgart, 1979, pp. 340ff. For other negative judgements (I am sure the list is incomplete), see Heinrich August Winkler, 'Vom Mythos der Volksgemeinschaft', *Archiv für Sozialgeschichte*, vol. 17, 1977; Alan S. Milward, *War, Economy and Society 1939–1945*, London, 1977, p. 14; Fritz Blaich, 'Wirtschaft und Rüstung in Deutschland', in Benz and Graml (eds.), *Sommer 1939*; Klaus Hildebrand, 'Monokratie oder Polykratie? Hitlers Herrschaft und das Dritte Reich', in Hirschfeld and Kettenacker (eds.), *Führerstaat*; Recker, *Sozialpolitik*, p. 24; Ian Kershaw, *The Nazi Dictatorship*, London, 1985, pp. 78ff. (with many useful references); and, above all, Herbst, 'Krise'. Since I believe that Richard Overy's critique, 'Germany, "Domestic Crisis" and War in 1939', in *Past & Present*, no. 116, 1987, rests upon a fundamental misunderstanding of what constitutes evidence for the existence of a crisis, I shall make few references here to his original arguments. I have replied separately to Overy in *Past and Present*, no. 122, 1989.

tations of Hans-Erich Volkmann, David E. Kaiser, Wilhelm Deist and, with a decisive modification, Michael Geyer.[55]

One part of my argument revolves around the connections between what was going in in German society and what was going on in Hitler's mind, and the importance of these connections for the acceleration of Nazi foreign policy towards war. It must be stressed (and I should have stressed it more) that it is extremely difficult to reconstruct Hitler's thinking, until his *Table Talk* began to be recorded. This is not due only to his antipathy to paperwork and the consequent dearth of good documentation. Military leaders who conversed daily with him during the war found it very difficult to understand how his mind worked, to comprehend the real meaning of what he said, to distinguish between his tactical rhetoric and his serious intentions; Jodl summed him up as 'a book with seven seals'.[56] To give one additional illustration, it is not easy to interpret, or to give the right weight to, Hitler's emphatic statement to a relatively disinterested listener on 11 August 1939 that Germany faced acute food shortages: 'I cannot accept that my people suffer hunger . . . We know what it is to die of hunger'. Better to have two million men die on the battlefield than for even more to die of hunger...[57] On the one hand, the problem that he named was indeed beginning to become real and his chosen solution was unambiguous; a straightforward interpretation thus tends to sustain my line of enquiry. On the other hand, it could have been a promiscuous argument which, coupled with his assertion that his whole policy was in fact directed against Russia, was intended to be relayed by his interlocutor to the Western powers in order to seek their acceptance of the invasion of Poland. I incline towards a straightforward reading of the text, but caution and doubts are in place with respect to all such sources. Much attention has been focused upon Hitler's concerns and calculations, and most historians have argued that quite other things were at the forefront of his mind in these two years than agricultural problems, shortages of human and material resources, and the risks of mass discontent. Three such interpretations call for brief discussion at this point.

55. Hans-Erich Volkmann, 'Die NS-Wirtschaft in Vorbereitung des Krieges', in Wilhelm Deist, Manfred Messerschmidt, Hans-Erich Volkmann and Wolfram Wette, *Ursachen und Voraussetzungen der Deutschen Kriegspolitik*, vol. 1: Das deutsche Reich und der Zweite Weltkrieg, Stuttgart, 1979, especially pp. 327ff., 364ff.; David E. Kaiser, *Economic Diplomacy and the Origins of the Second World War*, Princeton, 1980, especially pp. 268, 282. See further Kaiser's 'Comment' on Overy's intervention in *Past and Present*, no. 122; Deist, *The Wehrmacht*, esp. chs. 6 and 7; Michael Geyer, 'Rüstungsbeschleunigung' and 'Krieg als Gesellschaftspolitik'.

56. See Hillgruber, *Hitlers Strategie*, p. 24.

57. Hitler was addressing the League of Nations High Commissioner for Danzig. For this passage see Fest, *Hitler*, p. 804. Rich, *War Aims*, vol. 1, p. 126, gives a strongly diplomatic emphasis to Hitler's statements on this occasion.

First, I cannot accept the terms of reference of that school of historiography which sees Hitler as immersed in the relationship between the week-by-week tactics of diplomacy and his longer-term goals, and which thus tends to suggest that the 'wrong' war of September 1939 was in some sense the outcome of a series of diplomatic errors. I simply do not believe that the foreign policy of the major powers, least of all that Nazi Germany, was 'foreign' policy of this older kind. As Michael Geyer insists, the regime was setting out violently to recast the whole order of social domination in Germany and across the continent, and this meant that domestic, foreign and strategic policies were inextricably linked.[58]

Much more persuasive is the elementary strategic argument that Hitler *never* understood Britain and the British Empire, that his idea of some kind of division of world power between a Germanized continent of Europe and a sea-based British Empire grew out of a total misconception of British interests, and that any British government (even that of Chamberlain) was bound to become involved in war with Nazi Germany as soon as the latter threw itself into military expansion. This line of argument emphasizes not the faulty application in the 1930s of the ideas which Hitler had elaborated so clearly in *Mein Kampf*, but the fact that that strategy itself was founded upon a deep misunderstanding of the basic British need for some kind of balance of power in Europe. This did not rule out the semi-peaceful revision of some of Germany's frontiers, but it did rule out expansionist wars, all and any of which threatened the independence of France and manifestly implied that Germany was aiming at continental hegemony.

The case that Hitler fundamentally misconceived British interests seems to be a strong one. What remains very difficult to explain, however, is his failure to read the increasingly clear signs from late 1938 on (from March 1939 at the very latest) that he was in fact heading for an immediate war with Britain and the Empire. He had after all interpreted Chamberlain's interventions in the Munich crisis as a latently hostile act. Decisively, the British Parliament ratified the military guarantee to Poland immediately after the signing of the Nazi-Soviet Pact. For reasons which remain open to further discussion and analysis, Hitler was quite unable to recognize and to adjust to very clear evidence of the impending collapse of one of the central axioms of his strategy. This blindness or inflexibility in the summer of 1939 are hard to account for. Although he sometimes said as much, it is very difficult to accept that he believed the Chamberlain government to be too weak to go to war: at

58. For his thorough critique of the diplomatic approach, see 'Krieg als Gesellschafts-politik', pp. 560f, 565.

least, any such belief on his part requires a lot of careful examination and explanation, given all of the evidence to the contrary which was so easily available.[59] Explanation really is essential on this point. My suggestion, and also that of Manfred Messerschmidt, is that Hitler's concern with the urgency of domestic and economic problems played some part in producing his blindness and his groundless hopes with respect to British and French policy.[60] Here it is necessary briefly to set the record straight. It has never been any part of my argument that Hitler actually sought a European war in 1939 in order to extricate his regime from its domestic crises. R. J. Overy has repeatedly misrepresented my central point in this sense by ascribing to me, without any foundation, the view that a major war in 1939 was a German 'intention'; that economic crisis prompted 'Hitler to launch a general war in the west'; that 'war with Poland was designed to ensure that' the Western powers would fight; that the war of September 1939 'obligingly gave Hitler the escape route he wanted'.[61] This is a none-too-subtle travesty of the real question, for there has never been any debate about the fact that the Anglo-French declaration of war was a very severe blow to Hitler's strategy. The question at issue, which remains open, is why he took this insensate risk. This, it should be obvious enough, is one of the matters that I am attempting to account for.

Two further alternative interpretations of what was on Hitler's mind in 1938–9 both stress his sense that the factor time was turning against him. For his biographer, Fest, this had the quality of an existential change in Hitler: the collapse within him of the controlled, calculating politician who was capable of holding back and compromising in order to wait for the right opportunity, and a regression to the impatient, millenarian and, above all, violent mob leader of before 1923. The description is sensitive and convincing on its own terms. It leads Fest to formulate precisely the crucial question: 'why did he, who almost exclusively determined the course of events, get involved, contrary to all his plans, in *this* war at *this* point in time?' Fest has no doubt that Hitler did see the 'difficulties and risks', but disregarded them.[62] However, no reasons are given why this personality change should have occurred in 1938, not earlier, not later; the biography is personal rather than political. Dülffer's critique of my

59. Overy rests most of his interpretation of September 1939 on Hitler's mistaken belief that Britain and France would not intervene, without, however, subjecting this huge error of judgement to any critical scrutiny or analysis. See 'Germany, "Domestic Crisis" and War', pp. 161–6, and, with renewed emphasis, his 'Reply', pp. 221, 235–7.

60. See Manfred Messerschmidt, 'Aussenpolitik und Kriegsvorbereitung', in Deist et al., *Das Deutsche Reich und der Zweite Weltkrieg*, vol. 1.

61. Overy, 'Reply', pp. 228, 234, 236, 238; also p. 223.

62. Fest, *Hitler*, pp. 788, 832–42; quotations from pp. 833, 841.

work does offer a military-political reason for Hitler's new haste. Hitler, he argues, was increasingly concerned that Nazi Germany was losing its lead in the international arms race, losing its advantage (especially from late 1938 on) to Britain and the Soviet Union; and he was already casting an eye towards the United States.[63] This trend, it follows, strongly induced Hitler to take great diplomatic and military risks in 1939, to launch a war of conquest before the other powers were rearming at full speed, to win this real race against time. (This argument, it should be noted, has less purchase for mid-1938, when Hitler was already set on war.) That Hitler was preoccupied by the problem is beyond doubt, but the arms race, as he saw it, brings us back to the question posed at the outset: why was Nazi Germany unable to accelerate further the pace of its own rearmament after 1936 and thus maintain its relative advantage? Part of the answer lay clearly in the regime's inability to allocate resources consistently and effectively in favour of the armaments sector of the economy, in its inability to co-ordinate economically its various rearmament projects, in its continued prosecution of giant civilian projects, above all in the necessity that it attempt both to produce the strongest army in the world and at the same time to placate its working population with high real wages. These basic components of Nazi politics had become incompatible by 1938–9.[64] If this is correct, the regime needed war and conquest *in order to* go on rearming at a high rate.[65] Ministries, for example, were always pressing for tough economic measures, which then could not be enacted except in conjunction with an international crisis.[66] Thus the international arms race cannot be dissociated from the basic conditions of production inside Germany, from the limits on German rearmament. Dülffer's point therefore adds an important dimension to my interpretation, but does not contradict it.

A broader criticism calls for extended consideration: this is that my documentary sources tend to exaggerate the acuteness of the social and economic crisis in 1938–9. It has been said that I take the sources that describe the details and symptoms of this crisis too much at face value, and that the real situation on the domestic front was less tense, less fragile than I have portrayed it.[67] This is not one single criticism, but an

63. Jost Dülffer, 'Der Beginn des Krieges 1939: Hitler, die innere Krise und das Mächtesystem', in *Geschichte und Gesellschaft*, vol. 2/4, 1976, especially pp. 461ff.

64. Dülffer, ibid., p. 469, allows that they would have become incompatible in time, but his own full evidence of the massive state civilian and military projects of 1938/9 shows that that time was coming sooner rather than later.

65. Deist, *The Wehrmacht*, p. 111, agrees with this conclusion.

66. See above, pp. 258f.

67. Herbst, 'Krise', pp. 351f., develops these points in a serious and articulated manner, and what follows is an attempt to respond mainly to his arguments, which are in marked contrast to Overy's superficial and dismissive remarks in 'Germany, "Domestic Crisis" and War', p. 148.

argument that contains a series of different points which require to be discussed in sequence.

The first such point is easy to identify but less easy to assess in quantitative terms. It was always obvious that some employers and some procurement agencies deliberately overstated their needs for resources, in the hope that, by then 'making concessions', they would finally end up with roughly the amounts of raw materials and workers that they could actually use. This was a transparent technique in the struggles over shortages, and the decision-making bodies frequently recognized it as such. But it has been sufficiently demonstrated (and further examples follow below) that many real problems of insoluble shortages remained, and indeed grew as the armaments projects were extended, when such inflated demands are discounted.

The problems of interpreting the regular situation reports and the legislative proposals emanating from the higher civil service and the military-economic administration cannot be dealt with so swiftly. First, it has been argued that the authors of these documents were mainly of traditional conservative/authoritarian formation, and that they were disturbed above all by the *disorder* which Nazi policies produced in the social and economic processes and for this reason magnified the problems which they observed and sought to control.[68] While there may be much in this argument as far as the law and the interior administration is concerned, I think it strikes a quite wrong emphasis in respect of social and economic affairs. Most of the top officials of the Ministries of Labour and Economics and of the War Economy Staff emerge rather as technocrats who very much wanted to make their vital contribution to the regime's military preparedness. They were concerned with 'order', but in the sense of persistently striving, often in vain, to impose a more austere, dictatorial order in their spheres of competence, precisely in order to make the Third Reich more powerful.[69] Efficiency and output were their overriding concerns. On this count their documents contain much evidence of frustration and of growing and well-founded doubts about whether the regime had the political resources, whether the country had the human resources, necessary to achieve success.[70]

68. Herbst, 'Krise', p. 354.

69. The one clear exception to this group portrait was the great reluctance of Friedrich Syrup (President of the national system of labour exchanges and State Secretary in the Ministry of Labour) to introduce civil conscription for workers in June 1938; see Mason, *Arbeiterklasse und Volksgemeinschaft*, p. 666.

70. These doubts got through to Göring and were amply reflected in his exceptionally explicit, aggressive and pessimistic speech to the first meeting of the Reich Defence Council on 18 November 1938, to which many references have been made in chapter 6 above; see especially pp. 262f. above.

This is closely related to a second problem in interpreting these sources: that of identifying particular political goals or institutional interests which may have led the authors to distort in some measure (but in a consistent manner) the situations that they were describing; in this case, to magnify the economic and social problems as a means of pressing for solutions which would augment their influence over policy, give their own institutions greater weight. Herbst argues that I have underestimated the difficulties in eliminating such biases from an accurate reading of the documentation.[71] The difficulty certainly exists, but in my view it definitely does not call for a rereading of the evidence which would alter the overall picture of 1938–39. The most important sources at issue here are the regular report materials of the top-level administration.[72] These documents certainly did give special emphasis to unresolved or growing problems, in the hope of drawing the attention of ministers, of Göring, if possible of Hitler, to the need for more incisive policies. The Ministry of Labour was quite explicit about the purpose of this emphasis in its summaries of the reports of the Trustees of Labour.[73] But the overwhelming general reason for the mostly pessimistic tone of all such sources lay in the reporting officials' sense of duty to the cause of rearmament and economic stability, rather than in the indirect prosecution of the interests of their own institutions. They saw their task as trying to influence the overall policies of the Reich towards greater efficiency by being clear and frank about all the various weaknesses, shortages, discontent, and so on. If they had not had this general sense of their duty, the top-level civilian and military administrations would not have been such a source of strength for the regime in this period of crisis. For these reasons I believe that the documentation on which chapter 6 of this book is based possesses a relatively high and straightforward descriptive validity; as far as it goes, it does not make matters look worse than they actually were.

A further question remains, however. Do these sources (and my account) understate the actual progress which was made with rearmament and war preparations in 1938 and 1939? If this is so, it would be

71. Herbst, 'Krise', p. 352; he gives no telling examples of the problem.
72. I have tried to rely less on the descriptive materials in memoranda which arose out of open institutional and political conflicts; institutional rivalries permeate such documents, and special pleading is easily identifiable, if not always easy to assess precisely. None the less, some such documents *are* valuable for their factual contents, which are sometimes corroborated by other sources. See for example the heavy incursion by the Reich Price Commissar into wage policies, 12 December 1937, *BA Koblenz* R43II/355 (*Doc. 128*), and Darré's insistent pleas for changes in agricultural and economic policy referred to in chapter 6 above – here special pleading is justified by evidence, which is in large part valid.
73. See summary of reports for May and June 1938, *BA Koblenz* R43II/528 (*Doc. 108*).

true that my portrayal overstates the 'reactive' character of the regime's policies and understates its successful war-economy interventions; to see the regime mainly reacting to shortages, confusions and crises raises a wrong perspective – it was also pursuing some effective policies.[74] This is a delicate matter of emphasis, in which I think the criticism is partly justified.[75] I put the accent upon obstacles and difficulties for a number of reasons, the last of which is explicit in the report materials. First, the actual military-economic achievements of the regime in these years were isolated projects which remained quite uncoordinated in strategic terms.[76] This led me to underestimate them. (Their cumulative effectiveness in terms of fighting power was not realized in practice until after the enforced period of consolidation between October 1939 and May 1940, as we will see below.) Second, the social and economic preparations for war were always far behind the pressing needs of the armed forces. In the case of the army, if not of the air force and the navy, the military demands and programmes were realistic, well justified by the evolving strategic situation. This requires a continuous emphasis upon shortfalls in output and the reasons for them, as well as upon the partial successes achieved. Third and most important, every major advance in rearmament was impulsive and improvised, and left in its wake a host of unforeseen problems, to which the regime and industry had to react in an improvised manner. The severe dislocations caused by the sudden building of the West Wall have been outlined above. Scarcely less severe were the consequences of the simultaneous acceleration of naval and air-force construction in the early months of 1939. But the most fully documented example is the actual breakdown of the unrestrained armaments drive of June-October 1938. Michael Geyer's highly technical investigation of this episode shows in detail the shambles which ensued when limits upon armaments production were lifted at the end of May. Within five months there were insuperable shortages of iron, steel, non-ferrous metals, building materials, workers and funds for the new running contracts and programmes of the armed forces. Major cutbacks were then ordered and implemented with Hitler's assent.[77] These were truly *reactive* policies, as, in a different context, was the withdrawal of many war economy measures in October and November 1939. The reactive element in social and economic policies was always real and strong because each lurch forward towards war

---

74. See Herbst, 'Krise', p. 352; Overy, 'Reply', pp. 224, 229, repeats the point.
75. For my brief remarks on the goals achieved see above pp. 225ff. Deist, *The Wehrmacht*, chs. 6 and 7, strikes a better balance, emphasizing certain real military strengths and 'the grossly inadequate level of German rearmament in autumn 1939' (p. 102).
76. See ibid., pp. 91ff. for a succinct summary of this central argument.
77. Geyer, 'Rüstungsbeschleunigung'.

preparedness accentuated existing shortages, existing institutional confusions and existing popular discontent, and thus created new problems
to be solved, problems which normally had never been anticipated in
advance. To sum up, it is correct that the report materials understate the
progress made, but their pessimistic tone and their consequent implication that policies were mainly reactive accurately reflected a major part
of the reality.

No less complex is the argument that some ruling-class assessments
of the developing crisis were twisted by conservative fears and prejudices; that army officers, civil servants and industrialists were naturally
inclined always to blame the working class for economic problems, and
too often to go in fear of its possible subversive action. This may have
led to real misunderstandings of the problems that they actually faced.
Such was not always the case: officials of the Ministry of Labour and of
the War Economy Staff showed, already before the war, some verbal
sympathy for the (real) growing exhaustion of industrial workers. But
two critics have pointed to a good example of such a conservative ideological distortion. I gave some prominence to reports, among others to
one from the managing director of a large mining firm, that the per-
capita productivity of coal-miners was falling considerably in the later
1930s. This was attributed mainly to diminishing effort, declining work
morale, absenteeism, 'the human factor'; and I accepted this upper-class
interpretation of working-class behaviour.[78] It was to a considerable
degree wrong. One main cause of the fall in output in the mines was the
failure of employers to recruit young miners, the growing dependence
of the industry on older workers who were objectively less capable of
great physical exertion.[79]

Ruling-class misrepresentations, even panics, of this kind are not
easy to detect in a dictatorship. Wolfgang Franz Werner and Rüdiger
Hachtmann both suggest that such prejudices induced some employers
to exaggerate the sickness rates among workers in the late 1930s and to

78. Knepper to Oberberghauptmann Schlattmann, 16 November 1937, *GPSA,* Rep.
316/118 (*Docs. 85, 86*). See also the detailed memoranda and statistics on these problems
compiled by the Ministries of Labour and Economics from June 1939 on, in *BA Koblenz*
R41/174 and R22 Gr. 5/206 (*Docs. 89–93*).
79. Klaus Wisotzky, 'Der Ruhrbergbau am Vorabend des Zweiten Weltkrieges', in
Vierteljahrshefte für Zeitgeschichte, vol. 30/3, 1982, discusses this problem in a differentiated way. Werner, *'Bleib übrig!'*, pp. 25f., makes the point more bluntly, and attributes
to me deficiencies in the contemporary industrial and governmental statistics on productivity. On miners' sons, see Michael Zimmermann, 'Ausbruchshoffnung. Junge
Bergleute in den Dreissiger Jahren', in Lutz Niethammer (ed.), *'Die Jahre weiss man
nicht, wo man die heute hinsetzen soll.' Faschismuserfahrungen im Ruhrgebiet*,
Berlin/Bonn, 1983, pp. 97ff.

suppose that some sick workers were just taking time off.[80] This became a major issue during the war, as we shall see below. In the light of this unquestionable need for a sceptical reading of certain sources I have gone over the evidence again, but I have found no other systematic mis-representations of workers' behaviour. The descriptions by the labour administration of wage spirals, job-changing, breach of contract, declin-ing discipline and output, appear to be factually reliable; civil servants not only had a strong professional tradition of factual accuracy, but they had much less to gain than employers from making ideologically induced errors of judgement, and their reports could always be checked against those of other agencies.

In the political sphere the fears, repeatedly expressed by conserva-tives and Nazis, that there might be another 1917/18, another mass movement against exploitation and war, were clearly indelible memo-ries and ideological distortions that were not appropriate to the late 1930s.[81] The memories and invocations were surely persistent and dra-matic, and reached a public climax at the conclusion of Hitler's major speech at the height of the Munich crisis.[82] I never suggested that these fears reflected a real political possibility for the years after 1936, but the issue calls for more careful analysis than I actually gave it. There was obviously a great deal of resentment and economic ambition among the working population, but the leaders of the class had been killed, impris-oned or exiled, its organizations smashed. Thus the real danger was not insurgent strikes or open revolts, but rather (as I indicated, and as Ludolf Herbst argues at length) the steady disaggregation or disintegration of the social order and of the fascist disciplines on which it rested: obedi-ence, sacrifice, disciplined labour on behalf of a Greater Germany.[83] The real danger was that markets and grandiose projects would fall apart under the pressures of general economic overstrain, labour shortages and the manifold non-cooperation of the working population. Workers opposed dictatorial repressions in a multiplicity of ways, which, pru-

---

80. See Werner, *'Bleib übrig!'*, p. 26; also the materials quoted in note 78 above. Employers tended to measure the rising sickness rates against the exceptionally low fig-ures of the years of mass unemployment, a punitive and unrealistic yardstick. See also Rüdiger Hachtmann, 'Von der Klassenharmonie zum regulierten Klassenkampf', in *Soziale Bewegungen, Jahrbuch 1: Arbeiterbewegung und Faschismus*, Frankfurt am Main/New York, 1984, pp. 160f.; for a general argument concerning the exaggeration of sickness rates see now idem, *Industriearbeit im 'Dritten Reich'*, Göttingen, 1989, pp. 231ff.

81. See, for example, Werner, *'Bleib übrig!'* pp. 12, 31.

82. Fest, *Hitler*, p. 766. This theme runs like a red thread throughout Fest's biography; see also especially pp. 849, 924.

83. See above pp. 266f., 269f.; Herbst, 'Krise', pp. 365f., 373, 376. Herbst sees 'disin-tegration' as a possible prelude to open conflict within Germany, and seems to argue that only the latter would have constituted a real crisis.

dently, were least likely to provoke brutal persecution; they thus threatened the course of social and economic development, but only indirectly threatened the regime itself. This was a 'possible' form of mass opposition, not political resistance on the lines of the activity of the engineering shop-stewards in 1918.[84] Thus, in so far as they fixed their minds upon the November Revolution, the Nazi elite misrepresented to themselves the problems that they actually faced twenty years later.

This is surely a helpful clarification of the argument, which gives greater precision to an important issue. The fact remains, however, that the outcomes – in terms of tentative social and economic policies and inadequate rearmament – remained the same, whatever the reasons and motivations may have been. Indeed, fear of provoking mass discontent was incessantly and explicitly cited by the holders of power as a decisive reason for desisting from measures of austerity and coercion: these could not be implemented 'on political grounds'; or they were 'undesirable on political and social grounds'; or would cause 'politically undesirable unrest in the population';[85] they could have 'unfavourable psychological consequences';[86] or were 'not bearable for psychological reasons'; or could 'lead to a dangerous [*bedenklichen*] weakening of the domestic front'.[87] In this generic form anxiety about the consequences of the noncooperation of the working class permeated Nazi policies.

To redefine the issue of the legacy of the November Revolution in this way involves raising another major question for discussion. If it is true that the real danger facing the regime was that of a tendency towards a general disintegration of the social and economic order, then it must be asked: what was the position of other social groups and classes? Is it right to see the problem as, above all, that of the conflictual relationship between the regime and the working class?[88] Much research remains to be done on these questions, but it seems fairly clear that many sections of the middle class were also not called upon to make heavy sacrifices in the interests of the rearmament drive of the late 1930s.[89] Salaries in the private sector (not in the civil service) probably rose faster than wages at this time,[90] and there was a boom in middle-

84. I have drawn together (and thus perhaps implicitly overemphasized) evidence on this point in 'The Workers' Opposition in Nazi Germany', *History Workshop Journal*, no. 11, 1981. The distinction between opposition and resistance is crucial.

85. Quoted by Recker, *Sozialpolitik*, pp. 158f., 198, 270.

86. Quoted by Hachtmann, *Industriearbeit*, p. 128.

87. See Georg Thomas, *Geschichte der deutschen Wehr- und Rüstungswirtschaft*, Boppard, 1966, pp. 160, 503. Such quotations could be extended over pages.

88. See Herbst, 'Krise', p. 373.

89. It is evident here that my 'two-class model' of political society does not work for these questions of distribution; it was not intended to.

90. See Prinz, *Mittelstand*, pp. 165ff.; Werner, '*Bleib übrig!*', pp. 98, 108; Geyer, 'Rüstungsbeschleunigung', pp. 157; 183, note 204.

class consumption. On the fate of small entrepreneurs both before and after the beginning of the war the evaluations of the experts seem to diverge somewhat, but the government's attempts to close down small and inefficient workshops and retail units, in order to release capacities and workers for the big armaments firms, were something less than draconian.[91] The upper middle class's most important item of conspicuous consumption, petrol, remained unrationed before the war, although all the armed forces suffered from continuing and serious shortages of fuel. Well-to-do young ladies were effectively exempt from decrees which required working girls to perform a year of 'duty' in agriculture or domestic service, before entering regular employment or study.[92] It is true that income taxes for the middle classes were raised twice in 1939, and that the corporation tax was steadily increased; and it is true that Germany's farmers were squeezed very hard during 1938 and 1939. But overall it cannot be said that the regime paid a special regard to the economic interests of key sectors of the working class, trying to bribe them alone into passive acquiescence to the drive towards war. Rather, there was (with some regional and sectoral exceptions) a relatively flourishing civilian economy at most levels of society, which put limits to the expansion of rearmament in a wide variety of different ways.

In such an account the working class was a special case in an overall strategy of political pacification through the means of relative economic well-being. It was a special case because industrial wage-earners were so numerous, because they were in such desperately short supply, and because only they were well placed and likely to act disruptively on a large scale – no other socio-economic group had the means to cause the regime such anxiety. However, the basic problem was indeed a general one which encompassed the whole society in its relations with the regime, and I accept the need to redescribe the domestic situation in Germany in these wider terms. To do so has two diverse implications for my interpretation. On the one hand, it places class conflict in a broader context and attenuates the special significance which I gave to it in the dynamics of policy-making; on the other hand, it makes the regime appear even more tentative, in that it brings out its reluctance to intervene against many middle-class interests to the advantage of the armaments drive.

91. Two contributors to Benz and Graml (eds.), *Sommer 1939*, seem to differ a little in their assessments: Fritz Blaich, 'Wirtschaft und Rüstung in Deutschland', p. 41, and Ludolf Herbst, 'Die Mobilmachung der Wirtschaft 1938/39 als Problem des national-sozialistischen Herrschaftssystems', pp. 96ff. See also Herbst, *Der Totale Krieg*, pp. 120f., who points out that the trade sector got off more lightly than small producers (*Handwerk*). Winkler, 'Der entbehrliche Stand', pp. 32ff., argues that *Handwerk* was indeed being pushed to the wall. On the early war measures, see Werner, '*Bleib übrig!*', pp. 61f., 82ff.

92. See above p. 235; for further details, Dörte Winkler, *Frauenarbeit im 'Dritten Reich'*, Hamburg, 1977, pp. 57f.

Building upon this observation that the problems of administering the Nazi economy were indeed diffuse and heterogeneous, Herbst went on to challenge in a fundamental way the proposition that the Third Reich was in fact 'in crisis' in 1938–9. He threw the whole apparatus of systems theory at the question, demanding that the concept of crisis have a precise, theoretically and empirically verifiable definition, and he concluded that the position in Germany did not conform to any such definition, that my whole argument is thus mistaken.[93] The demand for precise definitions (which I did not furnish) clearly gives rise to a worthwhile discussion. I want to confine myself to four of the component arguments.

First, Herbst insists that the economy was just one of the 'sub-systems' of the whole system of power, and that it is necessary to examine all the other sub-systems in order to assess crisis-proneness. This point can be granted, but I wish to argue for the overriding importance of the economy at this juncture, and not in the first instance on theoretical grounds. A regime that was about to send its armed forces into war had to be able to equip them properly, and the Nazi regime was not in this position. (The conflict over strategy in October-November 1939 is discussed below.) This was the main economic fact. Furthermore, the economy was the area in which most Germans came into the most constant and conflictual contact with the regime in these years. But Herbst has in fact very little to say either about the real economy or about economic policies at this time.[94] He evades the vital question of whether the regime was unable, or rather chose not, to rearm more intensively, and he denies that the relevant problems were basically social and economic in origin.[95] The central fact in my analysis is the reality of the massive labour shortage and of its economic, social and political consequences. Herbst's approach reduces this, and all the other realities of extreme tensions in the economy, to very general problems of social justice and, above all, of politico-economic management of the system (*Steuerung*).[96] Systems management, however, must be measured against actual problems, as Geyer, Kaiser and I have tried to do.

To take an especially well documented example, Geyer leaves no doubt that the real economy was in immediate crisis late in 1938. Based upon a detailed analysis of the precipitous developments in industry and finance after the allocations to the armed forces were suddenly doubled in June 1938, he concludes that there arose an 'economic, armaments

93. See Herbst, 'Krise', pp. 365ff.
94. Herbst's book does not really remedy this defect in his article as far as 1939 is concerned.
95. Herbst, 'Krise', pp. 365, 388.
96. Ibid., pp. 375, 365ff.

and financial chaos'. It took the form of chronic shortages of all the factors of production and of rises in unit costs as the armed services competed with each other for non-existent industrial capacities. The Reich Treasury was temporarily empty. This then led to a sudden policy reversal in November which gave priority once more to exports and cut the armed forces' requirements for steel for 1939 by half; existing contracts were left hanging in the air.[97] Geyer is unambiguous that in May 1938 'the leadership of the Third Reich quite consciously risked a crisis'; 'the precarious armaments boom was transformed into an open economic and financial crisis'; there were no administrative solutions to 'the short-term and deliberate overburdening of German industry'.[98] This was especially acute in the building sector; I have emphasized the confusions which arose from the mad rush to construct the West Wall in these months, but as a result new munitions and armaments plants remained on the drawing board, and for 1939 the armed forces demanded for themselves more building capacities than existed in the whole German economy.[99] Geyer concludes his analysis thus: 'It was a reproduction crisis [of the capitalist economic system] under the conditions of Nazi rule. . . . [The] state was not capable of achieving the rearmament of the nation. . . . while at the same time guaranteeing private capital formation'.[100] There could be no structural solution to this crisis in peacetime. Temporary relief came from cuts in armaments output and fiscal reform, but industry remained heavily overstrained. Munitions production was heavily curtailed in February 1939 for lack of copper.[101] These and other cuts weakened the military at the time when Hitler was heading for the decision to invade Poland, but they did not take the pressure off industry.

It is to Geyer again that we are indebted for detailed evidence that by the summer of 1939 heavy industry in the Ruhr was faced with fast-rising production costs: these arose from the excessive (rather than optimum) use of capacities, from the lack of resources to continue with the modernization of plant, from shortages of labour, materials, machinery and transport facilities, from wage increases and from the slowness of the armed forces in paying for their contracts. The War Economy

---

97. Geyer, 'Rüstungsbeschleunigung', pp. 129f., 143f.

98. Ibid., pp. 136, 143, 146.

99. Ibid., p. 179.

100. Ibid., p. 146. Geyer (see also his 'Krieg als Gesellschaftspolitik', p. 563) is correct that I left it uncertain whether I thought it was a 'reproduction crisis' in a precise economic sense. I think he is right about the last two months of 1938, but I remain more interested in the larger politico-economic crisis, which continued.

101. See Wilhelm Deist, 'Die Aufrüstung der Wehrmacht', in Deist et al., *Das Deutsche Reich und der Zweite Weltkrieg*, vol. 1., p. 445, with other examples.

Inspector responsible for the area insisted in June 1939 that the situation was 'castastrophic', 'exceptionally serious'; he explicitly emphasized that he had not given a pessimistic tone to the picture – on the contrary, the detailed documentation gave cause for greater alarm, not less.[102] The repeated and precisely documented use of the term 'crisis', or analogues, in the above account is notable. On Herbst's own chosen ground of systems analysis this term seems wholly appropriate to the economic 'sub-system' of the Third Reich after May 1938.[103]

To take the second point, Herbst strongly advances the view that the regime in 1939 still had unused reserves of power to draw on: unused capacities to steer developments and manage problems, power to intervene with particular new measures or programmes in order to alleviate the most pressing difficulties and to stabilize the system. If such unused reserves of power existed, then it is premature to speak of 'crisis'.[104] There is a little evidence in favour of this hypothesis. Budgetary policies and credit creation could be largely reformed under the New Finance Plan of March 1939 so as to restore state purchasing power (though on a mostly unstable basis, which anticipated future revenues, or conquests).[105] Then, as Arthur Schweitzer has argued, the government did succeed in reimposing some rudiments of administrative order in parts of the economy during the first half of 1939.[106] Bureaucratic controls were far from generally effective, but the bureaucracy threw itself into a struggle to stabilize the system, and its authoritarian power, which could still be expanded and intensified, was an important resource for the regime.[107] The proliferating special economic agencies with their isolated, uncoordinated projects – the growing empires of Todt and Speer, the exceptional powers accorded to IG Farben, and so

102. Michael Geyer, 'Zum Einfluss der nationalsozialistischen Rüstungspolitik auf das Ruhrgebiet', *Rheinische Vierteljahrsblätter*, vol. 45, 1981, p. 252. This essay also adds new evidence in respect of the crisis of May-November 1938.

103. It is quite obscure why Overy in 'Germany, "Domestic Crisis" and War', p. 148, should see all these as 'frictional problems'. See my 'Comment', pp. 210ff.

104. Herbst, 'Krise', pp. 367ff., 388ff. Herbst does acknowledge, quite rightly, that particular instances of the actual use of such reserve powers tended in general only to postpone and to worsen the day of politico-economic reckoning.

105. See Fritz Federau, *Der Zweite Weltkrieg. Seine Finanzierung in Deutschland*, Tübingen, 1962. Richard J. Overy has recently added some important data on this question in '"Blitzkriegswirtschaft"?', *Vierteljahrshefte für Zeitgeschichte*, vol. 36/3, 1988, pp. 390f. The whole complex of the New Finance Plan deserves more detailed research.

106. See his 'Plans and Markets: Nazi Style', in *Kyklos. International Review for Social Sciences*, vol. 30, 1977, fasc. I, pp. 88ff. This is an exceptionally lucid article.

107. I agree with Herbst, 'Krise', p. 369, that the civil service played a very important role in holding the Third Reich together at this juncture, though as Hachtmann, *Industriearbeit*, pp. 95, 116ff., 349, points out, the labour administration was one of its least well-staffed and effective branches.

on – are a different matter. Their creation was the typically Nazi response to particular problems, and Herbst argues that in 1938–9 they performed a function of 'secondary stabilization' of the system. They appear to me on the contrary to have acted in a consistently destabilizing manner, because their absolute priority tasks were simply imposed upon the economy as a whole and not integrated into a practical conception of what was possible overall.[108] New special projects were a very doubtful source of untapped power for coping with the crisis.

What really matters in this argument is the general development of the real economy as a whole and the progress of rearmament. In the latter case the situation in 1939 was characterized by a combination of militarily dangerous restraints (procurement delays, no stockpiling), *and* the launching of new mythomaniac programmes for the air force and the navy which could only accentuate the basic problems. This deliberate creation of new contradictions does not look in the least like successful 'systems management' through the deployment of unused reserves of power. Although a detailed analysis of the economy in the months around Hitler's decision to invade Poland still has to be carried out, there is no doubt that the gap between strategic needs and mobilizable resources became greater as Germany's international position worsened. This is not to underestimate the regime's actual achievements in rearmament, but rather to point to the high degree of economic and political tension and instability which this effort generated. Hans-Erich Volkmann's overall picture of 1939 is that of an economy, and of the key economic agencies, working in highly straitened circumstances.[109] The one new measure of stabilizing management which could be deployed was the very important increase in trade with the Soviet Union. In internal policy there was less room for manoeuvre. With the exception of the reduction of piece-rates in Thuringia,[110] the wage controls of June 1938 were ineffective. In respect of social and labour policies the actual events which took place on the outbreak of war flatly contradict the view that the regime possessed hitherto unused reserves of power (see below). Finally, any attempt to assess the regime's capacity to draw on new powers every time the crisis worsened must come to terms with Göring's exasperated comment, that the 'Führer wants to

108. In *Der Totale Krieg*, pp. 112, 115, Herbst seems to take this view too; but see idem, 'Krise', pp. 369, 389.

109. See Deist et al., *Das Deutsche Reich und der Zweite Weltkrieg*, vol. 1, especially pp. 349ff.

110. For Sauckel's speech on this issue in April 1939 see *Doc. 141*. For the effects of this intervention by the Gauleiters and *Reichsstatthalter*, see Werner, '*Bleib übrig!*', pp. 36f.; Recker, *Sozialpolitik*, pp. 39, 42.

take as few decisions as possible'.[111] Hitler, the ultimate source of power to manage the system, was notoriously indecisive in social and economic matters; he usually preferred the soft, less unpopular options, while simultaneously demanding more and more weapons. On this central issue Hitler contradicted himself all the time, leaving his immediate subordinates in a state of permanent uncertainty.[112] This was a very important element of 'system destabilization'.

In sum, the argument, like many in systems theory, must to some degree remain hypothetical. Contrary to Herbst, I would maintain that by mid-1939 the regime had come very near to exhausting its capacities for self-stabilizing interventions, given the extreme pace of war preparations. It seems to me likely that the system needed war in order to create new sources of power for itself.

A third point concerning the definition of 'crisis' perhaps carries more weight. Is open confrontation an essential component of a true crisis? Herbst suggests that the real lines of confrontation in Germany on the eve of war were in fact not very clear-cut, that class conflict was too muffled to justify the use of the term crisis.[113] As examples of the blurring of these lines there can be quoted many cases of employers who gave in to wage pressure from below, improved fringe benefits and so on, and passed on the costs to the consumer (usually directly or indirectly the state); there were also many employers who engaged in open acts of piracy in the labour market, taking over workers from their competitors with offers of higher pay and better working conditions. Further, employers often put their own interests in plant efficiency before obedience to state regulations which were certain to disturb or disrupt their own labour forces. In such ways industrial conflict could be temporarily pre-empted. To this evidence of sporadic collusion between the two classes in industry Herbst adds the correct observation that sections of the Nazi Party and of the DAF were not at all happy about rigorous policies of reallocating resources from the civilian to the military sectors of the economy and imposing heavy sacrifices on the working population (though it is not clear how far these doubts, which were clearly expressed in internal memoranda, became public knowledge). Workers were thus faced with employers, some of whom might from time to time

111. In July 1938; quoted above, p. 228. Overy, 'Reply', p. 235, quite misunderstands the importance of Göring's frustration and of Hitler's equivocations and evasions in this illuminating confrontation. It does not prove that Hitler was uninterested in the economy, but that he did not want to take responsibility for such thorny problems.

112. In all his essays Overy persistently fails to see this contradiction, and gives unilateral emphasis to that Hitler who was always insisting on higher rates of rearmament. In practice he repeatedly denied to his subordinates the means to achieve such goals.

113. Herbst, 'Krise', pp. 376, 383.

appear as temporary allies on specific matters, and with a political regime of which different sections presented different attitudes on some matters of labour policy. Where was the real enemy? This was one important area in which the plurality of interests and strategies within the overall ruling class became manifest. Such complexity, or confusion, which was to become greater from September 1939 on,[114] acted, it is argued, as a kind of buffer between victims and oppressors, making the formers' sense of injustice less sharp, less well focused.

I believe this description is basically accurate in respect of part of the socio-economic developments in Nazi Germany; it is more subtly shaded than the picture which I sketched.[115] Open confrontations did take place, however, and always threatened to spiral. Concessions to workers, for example, did not always lead to satisfaction and greater co-operation; they sometimes made workers more aware of their market power and whetted their combative appetites for further concessions.[116] There were always quite clear lines of general conflictuality on every occasion that the regime did actually intervene against working-class interests. The formation of clear enemy camps may anyway be too pure a model of 'crisis'; much depends upon the precise kind of events which one imagines as being necessary for an actual crisis of 'the system' to break out. Given the intensity of surveillance and police terror, in the case of Nazi Germany one must clearly think first of a 'crisis' *within* the dominating groups, such as the acute policy conflicts of September–November 1939, rather than the type of strike movement which took place in Italy in March 1943. The crisis potential of popular unrest made itself felt in the perceptions, fears, uncertainties and contradictory needs of the elite. Then, at a more general level, not all historical crises worthy of the name manifest themselves in actual breakdown, revolts or the clear division of society into enemy camps: a crisis ultimately contained *in extremis* is not, for that, the less a crisis.[117] For all the elements of confusion, the processes of conflict and of social and economic disintegration which were taking place in Germany in 1938–9 constituted at least the solid preliminaries, the basic ingredients of a crisis in class relations. To put it in counter-factual terms, I believe that without war in

114. This is one of the main themes in the material collected by Werner, *'Bleib übrig!'*. See below for the summaries concerning late 1939, and 1940–5.

115. A good deal of relevant evidence for this more subtle description is contained in the documentation that I published in *Arbeiterklasse und Volksgemeinschaft*, but I did not give sufficient interpretive weight to it.

116. For examples that contradict Herbst's notion that concessions pacified class conflict, see Mason, 'Workers' Opposition', pp. 125f.

117. Italy in the later 1970s furnishes a good example of this point; by any definition the country was in crisis in these years.

1939 the regime would have been forced to make policy choices (severe austerity) which would have brought such a crisis nearer.

The above argument is incomplete in that it refers mainly to 'factory politics'. Did industrial discontent indicate a wide-scale, hidden political discontent? In this book I tend to imply that it did, thus reinforcing the notion of a general crisis. Although the unpopularity of the war in September 1939 is beyond doubt, I have since revised this view.[118] At bottom it rested on the unsustainable proposition that a passive, latent loyalty to the class organizations destroyed in 1933 was still widespread in 1938–9. I greatly underestimated the disillusionment and fatalism which the policies of the parties and the trade unions caused among their supporters in 1933, and the depoliticization that followed the crushing of the first waves of underground resistance. More recent local studies and oral history research underline the need for revision on this point, and on the degree to which some elements of Nazi attitudes made inroads into popular consciousness from the mid-1930s on. This subject is so important and so diffuse that I have drawn together some comments on it in a separate section, below, 'Attitudes and Experience'.[119] What matters in the immediate context is that rejection of Nazi social and economic policies where they hit people's immediate material interests did not *necessarily* imply a disguised rejection of the regime in general, even though such partial rejections were often resolute and sustained. This reconsideration magnifies the importance of the economic component in my notion of the interlocking crisis of domestic and foreign policies.

The final question about the precise meaning of the concept of 'crisis', and its applicability to pre-war Germany, concerns the degree of diffusion of the consciousness of crisis as such. There is no doubt that most people did *not* feel that they were living in the midst of a social, economic and domestic political crisis (as opposed to foreign-policy crises). Real crises, it is argued, are always and necessarily characterized by a widespread sense or understanding of the critical nature of developments. Herbst systematically develops an (all too casual) remark of my own, that real knowledge of this crisis, consciousness of it as such, was tightly restricted to the political, economic and military elite who were in possession of the facts about the social and economic problems as a whole; to those few who knew that the Nazi rulers were set upon vastly expanded armaments projects and upon war, and who knew that the regime had

118. See my introduction, 'Die Bändigung der Arbeiterklasse im nationalsozialistischen Deutschland', in Carola Sachse et al., *Angst, Belohnung, Zucht und Ordnung*, Opladen, 1982.
119. [Editor's note: this planned section does not exist; see 'Editor's Introduction', p. xvii, above.]

the greatest difficulty in finding the human and material resources for these projects.[120] Probably the lowest members of this group were the top-level administrators who drafted the strictly confidential documents on which I have based my interpretation. It included the narrow industrial, military and political elite who actually experienced the collapse of the armaments drive at the end of 1938; and the relatively large assembly of ministers, state secretaries, military and Party leaders who were permitted, at exactly this time, to listen to Göring's lengthy and desperate description of the economic situation at the first meeting of the Reich Defence Council on 18 November 1938. (This speech is the clearest evidence that Herbst is mistaken in believing that the top political leadership was not worried about the structural problems of the economy. Unlike Göring, Herbst quite ignores the elite's concern for future perspectives and trends.)[121] Their knowledge and understanding, above all their fears of an impossible future – Göring used the words 'that all seems impossible' – were of course top secret.[122] The regime had a monopoly of all relevant information and discussion. People working at lower levels of the economy and administration experienced and knew about only particular symptoms of the general problem: there were fears of inflation; managers had to deal with impossible bottlenecks and deadlines; workers found that they could exploit their scarcity value; train drivers were surely not the only ones to know that there was an acute shortage of railway wagons; some farmers found that they could not restock their farms fully – and so on. But they did not know much more. Certainly (unlike in 1928–33) the full dimensions of the economic problems, above all their future implications, were not common knowledge. In this sense the power of censorship in 'stabilizing the system' was very great. Can there be such a thing as a 'crisis' of which so few people were aware, a secret crisis of the system, so-to-speak? Herbst flatly denies this.[123] It is a serious and open argument. I think that it can indeed be true of a latent crisis in a dictatorship, of a crisis which had not yet reached an undisguisable breaking-point. This was narrowly averted at the end of 1938. September–November 1939 did mark such a breaking-point in so far as, faced with the punitive War Economy Decree, a sense of crisis among industrial workers was clear, widespread and politically effective.[124]

120. See Herbst, 'Krise', pp. 378f.
121. Ibid., p. 381.
122. *Doc. 152.*
123. See Herbst, 'Krise', p. 390. He also denies that elite consciousness of crisis is evidence of its real existence. Even as a general proposition I find this unacceptable; the point seems totally out of place in this particular context.
124. Herbst bypasses these crucial events in his discussion of the extent of the awareness of crisis.

To sum up, does this combination of ignorance and the confusion of political outlooks, which certainly was characteristic of the mass of the population, greatly attenuate or disqualify the concept of 'crisis'? I think it does only if we imagine 'crisis' to entail the incipient general breakdown of the whole system of rule. I now wish to argue a more restricted, perhaps more precise case: that the unwillingness of most of the population to co-operate *economically* in the preparation of the war, and the hesitancy or inability of the regime in coping with this non-cooperation, was by 1938 creating an *economic* crisis. The fact that the regime nevertheless continued with expansive armaments and foreign policies created a huge contradiction, which amounted to a fundamental crisis of policy choices, and thus to an (albeit hidden) crisis of the regime itself. That is to say, the economic crisis was in itself serious enough, and it had the widest range of ramifications. It brought in its tow political and then military problems of a basic kind which could only be disguised in peacetime, and narrowly and temporarily resolved in war.

This proposition needs to be illustrated in more detail, but first there is a final objection to my general picture that needs to be considered. It is argued that the yardstick against which I am measuring the equivocations and weaknesses or Nazi social and economic policy is a quite unrealistic, utopian one – that of a total war economy in peacetime.[125] This yardstick is said simply to have been taken over from the platform of the one general and economic expert, Georg Thomas, who did not share Hitler's view about the possibility of lightning wars against single smaller states, but thought that the priority should be to prepare Germany at once for a major war against France. My yardstick, my model for greater austerity and more comprehensive rearmament, does not in fact come mainly from this source; nor is it an abstract utopia; nor is it a *post hoc* model based upon the military deficiencies which became entirely apparent in October 1939. It is based rather upon a very large number of different proposals and demands for specific measures of austerity, which came from many different sources between 1936 and 1939: proposals by industrialists, the Price Commissar, the Minister of Agriculture, the Labour Administration, as well as the armed forces and many other agencies.[126] That is, it is an immanent model, composed of the kinds of legislation and intervention which were thought necessary at the time by most of those who held responsibility for labour, economic and armaments policies; most of these concrete proposals were put

125. See Herbst, 'Krise', pp. 385ff.; Overy, 'Germany, "Domestic Crisis" and War', p. 155.
126. I published a substantial number of such demands and proposals in *Arbeiterklasse*: see e.g. *Docs. 3, 71ff., 128, 151*; also for Darré's interventions on agriculture, see above pp. 195f.

into effect in part, with delay or not at all. An idea of what was objectively necessary in order to concentrate resources on rearmament must also take account of the huge new demands which were placed on the economy by the three massive additional programmes put into motion between June 1938 and January 1939: the building of the West Wall and the headlong rush for war with Czechoslovakia; and then the vastly expanded air force and naval programmes. Thus the yardstick by which the Nazi regime can be said to have held back the progress of rearmament is provided by the regime itself – both in its documented deliberate acts of omission and in the omnipotent targets for rearmament which it nevertheless set itself. No external, or superimposed utopian criteria are involved at all. It is a question of an empirically verifiable relationship between military ends and policy means. Clear projects for rigorous measures were implemented in part or not at all because of fear of unpopularity and discontent.

With the invasion of Poland and the British and French declarations of war, we move from the discussion of documentary evidence and of the concepts necessary to analyse it, to a series of dramatic events which I believe give weight to my general thesis about the crisis-ridden relationship between domestic affairs and war in 1938–9. The first of these, the War Economy Decree of 4 September 1939 and the speedy withdrawal of many of its clauses, I have already described in part above.[127] I want to reconsider these conflicts briefly in the next section, because later research has shown that they were both more bitter and more complex than they appear in my first presentation. But the basic fact was that right at the start of the war the government imposed a set of draconian sacrifices on the working class, harsher than those imposed on the rest of the population. This legislation met with such a degree of passive resistance and manifest hostility on the part of the workers that much of it had to be revised or repealed by the end of November 1939. On 12 November Hitler himself approved reducing the incidence of civil conscription (at precisely the same time as he was demanding the immediate invasion of France)[128] Even the real emergency of a major war

127. See in brief my 'Labour in the Third Reich 1933–1939', *Past and Present*, no. 33, 1966; in detail *Arbeiterklasse*, chs. 19–21. Werner, '*Bleib übrig!*', pp. 35–43, 48, 51–4, 66ff., 72–9, provides a much more comprehensive picture of this crisis, in that he covers fully the initial response to rationing measures; this response was especially hostile. For additional striking evidence of absenteeism, see Stephen Salter, 'The Mobilisation of German Labour, 1939–1945', D. Phil. thesis, Oxford, 1983, pp. 193f., 210. Werner, '*Bleib übrig!*', p. 80, is clearly mistaken in arguing that the core of regular industrial workers stood aside from these protests during these months. Later in the war it is true that women and young workers seem to have been more inclined to protest, take days off, and so on.

128. Minutes of ministerial meeting, 13 November 1939; *BA/MA Freiburg*, Wi F5, vol. 412.

would not induce the working class, dragooned and intimidated as it was, to accept repression and coercion of this kind. It will not do to present this retreat on the part of the regime merely as evidence of the shrewd psychological intuition of the leadership. This greatly understates the *conflictuality* of the situation, and overlooks the fact that the retreat formed a part of the wholesale dilution of the carefully prepared plans for full-scale economic mobilization in the event of war.[129]

These events shed a very clear light upon the pre-war situation. They prove that the regime could under no circumstances have imposed a policy of full austerity in peacetime. They show that those Nazi leaders had been *politically* correct – that is, Ley, Kaufmann and most of the Gauleiters, often Göring, usually Hitler himself – who had insisted that all sorts of material concessions be made to the working population in order to keep it quiet during the later 1930s. They show that the government never had much room for manoeuvre on these issues; that, contrary to what Herbst says, in this vast sector at least the regime did *not* possess unused capacities or reserves of power to intervene and accentuate the armaments drive, not even on the commencement of war. The events of September-November 1939 also show the most influential sections of the ruling classes putting the pacification of the working class before the overall (if not the shortest-term) demands of the war economy, even though Germany was at war with Britain and France, and was indeed about to invade France.

This domestic retreat was not accompanied by any deceleration in military strategy. On the contrary, at precisely the same time, Hitler, in a panic over the quite unexpected strategic situation, ordered the armed forces to prepare to invade France before Christmas 1939. Once again, contradictions were driven to an extreme point.[130] As late as 6 November 1939 the invasion of France was scheduled for 12 November, one week later. One of the main reasons why the whole military leadership opposed Hitler's demands on this point grew directly out of the long-term policy of guns *and* butter outlined above; that is, after the campaign against Poland the German armed forces lacked the munitions, the bombs, fuel, spare parts, trucks, cars and some raw materials and so on which were necessary to undertake any further military cam-

129. Herbst, 'Krise', p. 381, and *Der Totale Krieg*, pp. 109f., cites the retreat by the regime on the domestic front merely as evidence of the shrewd psychological intuition of the leadership. He greatly underplays the element of real conflict that was present in the situation. See also Overy, '"Blitzkriegswirtschaft"?'.

130. For summaries of these events, see Hillgruber, *Hitlers Strategie*, pp. 34–8, and Mason, 'Innere Krise', pp. 180f. Detailed accounts are furnished by Hans-Adolf Jacobsen (ed.), *Dokumente zur Vorgeschichte des Westfeldzuges 1939–1940*, Göttingen, 1956, vol. 1; and idem, *Fall 'Gelb'*, Wiesbaden, 1957. On the military opposition and resistance to Hitler, see Deutsch, *Conspiracy*.

paigns in the near future. As already noted, on one estimate the army had enough munitions to permit one-third of its divisions to fight for a further four weeks. The economic policies of the 1930s had left the Nazi Wehrmacht with sufficient resources only to defeat the weak Polish forces. Any immediate confrontation with France would, German generals were sure, have led to the Third Reich's defeat. This lack of military supplies thus produced one of the turning-points of the Second World War, and one of the major military-political crises in the history of the regime: on the agenda were either Germany's defeat on the battlefield, or a conservative military-civilian coup against Hitler.

In my original interpretation I did not give sufficient weight or sufficiently clear focus to this conjuncture, for the deep clash over the timing of the invasion of France, and its socio-economic background, encapsulate in a dramatic manner most of the elements of the argument: Hitler tried to make good the policy disaster of August-September 1939 by means of a still more adventurous, indeed quite desperate step, the invasion of France in November. The armed forces discovered that, because of past overall policies, they absolutely did not have the material resources for such a gamble (they also had no operational plans); as a result, a deeply serious threat arose to the unity and permanence of the regime; and while all this was going on, the government was dismantling many of its war-economy measures against the German population under the compulsion of domestic pressure and discontent.

The regime was splitting at the top and disintegrating openly at the base. This looks very much like a 'crisis', which meets virtually all the definitions required of 'crises' by the theorists.[131] In the event, an open internal confrontation and/or military defeat were averted, it appears, only because at the last minute Göring found a subtle way of persuading Hitler to back down: the risk of fog impeding the air attack over the Low Countries. The invasion of France was then postponed over thirty times until May 1940, by which time the German armed forces had been able to restock and retrain, thanks in part to supplies from the Soviet Union. Hitler remained throughout obsessed by the tension between strategic imperatives on the one hand and the war-economic and domestic weaknesses on the other: 'The Führer sees that we cannot hold out in a long war, the war must be ended quickly. . . . Everything must be gambled on this one card'.[132]

Because the invasion of France was then so overwhelmingly successful, I think the significance of the events of October-November

131. The element of publicity, and hence of public consciousness, was missing, for the conflict over the invasion of France remained top secret.
132. In December 1939; cf. Recker, *Sozialpolitik*, p. 76.

1939 has been widely underestimated. They shed a lot of light on the ways in which high policy (domestic and military) was made, not only in the critical weeks themselves but also in respect of war preparations in general. Contradictions led to politico-economic crises which helped to fuel military aggression; and when the first act of aggression created acute and long-term strategic danger, Hitler's immediate reaction was to try to launch a second one at once. Throughout, manifestly from 1938 on, the social and economic position was at odds with the strategic choices. Far from being co-ordinated, the two spheres were connected by an explosive conflictual relationship, in which economic overstrain was adduced as a powerful, wildly irrational argument for extreme strategic gambles; only early in November 1939 was such a disastrous gamble averted, and then by the narrowest of margins. In describing the drive towards war as a 'flight forwards' (*Flucht nach vorn*), I may have been seduced by the need to find a phrase which would put things in a nutshell. But the conflict over the invasion of France leaves no doubt that Hitler was capable of responding to crises in exactly this manner; and the particular instance was so important in itself that it is evidence of a basic disposition. The immediate disaster averted, this disposition revealed its own barbaric rationale, for the short-term gains from aggressive war were great, not least in economic terms.

Brief reference has already been made to the first and most important of these gains, the plunder of manpower. Hundreds of thousands of Polish prisoners of war were already performing essential labour in German agriculture in October and November 1939, thus providing immediate relief for what was probably the most severe of German economic difficulties. Hitler at once transformed this into a basic element of occupation policy: poverty should force Poles to migrate to work in Germany.[133] Ulrich Herbert has brought out well the novelty of this policy and its tensions with race policies.[134] One must also insist that it did match perfectly the most urgent needs of the German economy. It was the beginning of a whole new system of racial, social and economic domination on the continent. This was the great aim of the Nazi war, but also an essential condition for prosecuting it.

To sum up in an intermediate manner, my argument about the domestic components in the origins and timing of the war of 1939 needs to be refined, qualified and added to at many points. But Michael Geyer has recently proposed a basic modification. This concerns chronology,

133. See Ulrich Herbert, *Fremdarbeiter. Politik und Praxis des 'Ausländer-Einsatzes' in der Kriegswirtschaft des Dritten Reiches*, Berlin/Bonn, 1985, especially pp. 11, 36, 67 ff. This is among the most important of all recent studies of the history of Nazi Germany.

134. In addition to Herbert, see Kershaw, *Popular Opinion and Political Dissent*, chs. 1 and 7, for the position of farmers in Bavaria.

the temporal relationship between foreign and economic policy decisions, and thus the precise origins of the aggressive spiral which I have
tried to analyse. Geyer now argues that the regime's underlying choice
of war became a concrete reality on 28–30 May 1938 with Hitler's decision to 'smash Czechoslovakia by military action in the near future';
and that only after this date and in consequence of this fundamental
practical decision did the economic and social crises become so acute as
to reinforce the need for territorial expansion.[135]

It is true, as is clear from the above summary of Geyer's own
research, that the greatly accelerated rearmament drive of June-
November 1938 rapidly intensified all the phenomena of economic
overstrain and brought the economic crisis to a first climax. Geyer thus
assigns temporal and causal priority to a specific decision for war,
which he implies was relatively free from immediate internal constraints, since Nazism's true 'social policy' was from the 'very outset',
war: an ideologically determined programme to transform relations of
domination across the continent.[136] This war was set in motion in May
1938, a fact the significance of which has been disguised from historians by the postponement of actual hostilities until September 1939, but
which is of crucial importance in interpreting developments and policies in Germany in the intervening period. The power and persuasiveness of this very brief but incisive analysis lies in its capacity to suggest
a logical and empirical hierarchy of causes for the Nazi push towards
war: first came the overriding, non-negotiable long-term aim of war for
Lebensraum; second, the actuation of this drive, its transformation into
short-term military and economic policies, as a result of the May crisis
with Czechoslovakia in 1938; third, the crisis-ridden domestic consequences of these policies. Geyer persuades me that I underestimated
both the historic importance and the relative strategic autonomy of
Hitler's decision for war at the end of May 1938.[137] It was a decision to
turn the ideology of 'war as social policy' into reality which Hitler and
the armed forces never went back on, except temporarily in October-
November 1939.

Where does this leave the role of the 'domestic causes' of war which
I have emphasized and some of which Geyer himself explored so precisely without actually naming them as such?[138] It undoubtedly leaves
them diminished, by comparison with the deliberate, violent international competition of contrasting systems of domination which Geyer

135. Geyer, 'Krieg als Gesellschaftspolitik', pp. 563ff.; Rich, *War Aims*, vol. 1, p. 105.
136. Geyer, ibid., p. 558.
137. See above pp. 244ff., 258ff. The background to this decision is less than clear: it
was even more risky than that of August 1939.
138. Geyer, 'Rüstungsbeschleunigung'.

now rightly puts in the foreground of the history of the 1930s. But they do not vanish into insignificance, nor does this line of enquiry become, as Geyer suggests, basically misconceived. First, the problematic relationship between armaments programmes and economic resources was already clear before May 1938, though it became much more acute afterwards. At a general level the head of the General Army Office had already observed in August 1936 that the army's vast new rearmament plans (scheduled for completion in October 1939) would necessarily end either in war or in economic crisis.[139] Several specialist historians have concluded – maybe overstating their points – that the excessive armaments efforts had, on account of shortages of resources and funds, already led German policy into a 'dead-end street' in 1937–8.[140] In the face of an unpredictable foreign policy situation and an 'economically unsustainable volume of rearmament', in the summer of 1938 only a 'foreign-policy *va-banque* gamble, or a declaration of the bankruptcy of this foreign and military policy was conceivable'.[141] Manfred Messerschmidt argues that 'economic, financial and technological reasons' came together to create the imperative of the 'one-way-street' by the end of 1937 – an offensive strategy which in the end could take no account of British reactions.[142] He points to the 'decisive short-term war-economic motivations' for the annexation of Austria, going on to argue that 'in 1938 the war-economic and strategic importance of Czechoslovakia stood at the centre of German interests'.[143] All these judgements also stress the lags and delays in arms production from late 1936 to mid-1938, recurrent economic shortages and the lack of preparedness of the armed forces for anything more than a very swift campaign against Czechoslovakia alone. The need for plunder to make good these weaknesses was obviously not the principal reason behind Hitler's fundamental decision for war in May 1938: it was an ideological decision in the sense that there were many alternative ways of undermining and dismantling Czechoslovakia more gradually, and it was a foreign-policy decision in that it rested upon (very insecure) assessments of the probable responses of Britain, France and Italy. But the economic component cannot be disregarded, and must be seen in the context of the steadily worsening economic situation in Germany, where the wage spiral, the agricultural labour shortage, the confusion and overloading of the building industry, bottlenecks in the supply of some raw materials

139. Klaus-Jürgen Müller, 'Militärpolitik in der Krise', in Dirk Stegmann, Bernd-Jürgen Wendt and Peter-Christian Witt (eds.), *Deutscher Konservatismus im 19. und 20. Jahrhundert*, Bonn, 1983, p. 336; Deist, *The Wehrmacht*, pp. 46ff.
140. Müller, 'Militärpolitik', p. 337.
141. Ibid., p. 344.
142. Messerschmidt, 'Aussenpolitik und Kriegsvorbereitung', p. 624.
143. Ibid., pp. 637, 640.

and the intensifying foreign trade and foreign exchange problems had already for months been the subject of tense but quite fruitless top-level debate.[144] To point to the fact that it involved violently defying or breaking out of a wide variety of different policy constraints, external and internal, does not diminish the historic importance and qualitative novelty of Hitler's decision for war, which Geyer rightly emphasizes.

Then in domestic terms, the decision of May 1938 had the character of a self-fulfilling prophecy, in that the vastly accelerated and expanded armaments projects which followed immediately from it exacerbated the domestic causes of war as I have tried to define them: shortages of everything increased exponentially, economic disorder spread widely, some repressive controls were adopted, but they produced much discontent and few effects. It is right, however, to see these in the end as secondary factors. They were the feed-back effects of the decision for war; they confirmed the necessity of this decision and hastened its realization; and they determined the character of Nazi war social and economic policy in decisive ways. But their independent causal importance in bringing about the war was less than that which I attributed to them: the original decision for war produced a crisis which in turn made war more urgent and necessary in 1939, despite all the immense risks.

Geyer now seems inclined to disparage even this latter formulation of the issue because it still ascribes to the war an effective role in containing the domestic crisis, in producing an imperatively needed 'secondary integration' of the society, the economy and the institutions behind the regime's leadership, thus distracting our attention from the central fact that the purpose of war was war itself and the pursuit of vast war aims. This is not a simple question. On the one hand, the crisis, especially the economic crisis (as Geyer himself emphasizes), was severe and real from mid-1938 on, and there is no doubt that many ministers and high officials looked to the outbreak of hostilities as the occasion for drastic measures of crisis management: in this sense 'secondary integration' was on their agenda at the time. But their specific plans were nullified by the successful opposition to the economic mobilization programme in September-November 1939. In the short term, war produced something like the opposite of 'secondary integration', and it occasioned a major crisis over military strategy within the elite. In terms of both foreign and domestic policy the invasion of Poland was a huge risk which went badly wrong. For these reasons I have never suggested that 'secondary integration' in this narrow sense was a main purpose or

144. See documentation in Mason, *Arbeiterklasse und Volksgemeinschaft*, ch. 12; Kaiser, *Economic Diplomacy*; Volkmann, 'Die NS-Wirtschaft im Vorbereitung des Krieges'. The decision to redouble rearmament in June also solved the turnover problems of iron, steel and heavy engineering for a time: see Geyer, 'Rüstungsbeschleunigung'.

function of war, but have emphasized that in the short term war acutely intensified all these problems. They were resolved in part by economic concessions to the working class, but above all by cheap and sweeping military victories, by massive conquests and the economic exploitation of occupied territory. These produced a temporary propaganda consensus in 1939–41, and the main way out of the social and economic crises. War, in Geyer's overarching sense, was not least the conquest of human and material resources; and in my sense this was the main key to resolving the domestic impasses (it was more important than the mobilization measures in Germany before 1942). These two positions appear to be complementary rather than at odds with one another. I agree that war as 'crisis management' does not go to the heart of the question, but the problem of 'secondary integration' in the Third Reich in 1938–40 was a real one: the most important part of the solution to it was conquest and plunder – the constitution of a new order of domination, as Geyer puts it. Hitler, after all, was quite explicit about the economic need for conquest in his top-level address of May 1939, in the context of preparations for the invasion of Poland.[145]

I have tried to discuss the most important criticisms and modifications of my argument about the domestic origins and timing of the war; I cannot yet see the need to abandon the basic approach. Such debates are not well served by exaggerating the differences between the points of view at issue. I am in full agreement with Ludolf Herbst that the Third Reich tended to use its power and its violence to disguise and postpone the structural problems of Nazi rule; and that these problems tended therewith to become more acute, potentially more destructive in time. I also agree that 'in the interests of short-term efficiency, the system as a whole was subjected to processes of decay and dissolution'.[146] In its own programmed self-destruction the Third Reich took a substantial part of the world down in flames with it. The open question is when and why did these elements in the system actually become determinant of high policy. My own provisional answers remain: in 1938, and on account of internal contradictions which were located not only, but most importantly, in the economy.

A discussion of this kind, however, requires to be put into a longer historical perspective. Any specific interpretation of a particular turning-point or crisis in the history of the Third Reich has to stand the test of being an adequate or appropriate part of an overall interpretation. If the view put forward of a small part of the story does not fit in with any

145. See above p. 263.
146. Herbst, 'Krise', p. 391.

plausible picture of the whole, then that view of the part is likely to be wrong, however well documented it may appear to be. How do these vital criteria apply to my argument concerning the domestic component in the Nazi drive to war in 1938–9?

A variety of different long-term perspectives could be chosen with a view to testing the hypotheses in this sense (namely, class relations 1933–45, wartime changes in labour and social policy, war as an end in itself, and plunder). On the surface, my interpretation of 1938–9 does not fit in very well with what we know of the general development of class relations over the whole period between 1933 and 1945. Until 1936 mass unemployment continued to exercise the heaviest social and political discipline. In the picture that I have drawn the German working class, although deprived of its collective rights and independent organizations, reappears in the late 1930s as a fairly vigorous historical actor, able to cause the regime perplexity and weakness of purpose and able to secure changes in state policy. More recent research, which I discuss in detail in the following section, has shown that this did not continue to be the case to the same degree through the war years. The power of command of the regime over the industrial workers became greater not less, and even towards the end of the war movements of discontent and opposition tended to be isolated and exceptional. The years on which I concentrated, 1938–9, thus appear to be exceptional in respect of working-class behaviour and of relations between the class and the regime; they were novel but, on account of the war, they were not a portent of future conflicts or of future governmental weakness.

There are good reasons why these years were in fact exceptional. 1938/39 were the first years in which the number of jobs vastly exceeded the number of available workers, with all the new opportunities which this offered to workers, and with all the new challenges and disruptions which it caused to employers and to the state. For the same reason they were the first years in which the state had to try to regulate comprehensively the whole huge and complex area of the labour market, wages and working conditions; these were exceptionally difficult administrative tasks, which pitted a dictatorial machine lacking in personnel and experience against a most uncooperative population.[147] These were also the years of transition from peace to war, to a war which was not popular. For all these reasons the years 1938–9 formed a unique conjuncture, a special period of transition in which everything was at stake. In my original work I did not sufficiently emphasize their peculiarity as two critical years of transition. To call them such does

147. On the administrative weakness of the machinery of the Trustees of Labour, see Hachtmann, 'Klassenharmonie', pp. 163f. Schweitzer, 'Plans and Markets', contains hints in a similar direction for 1938.

not, I think, diminish the validity of the interpretation, but rather gives these problems their precise place in a long-term chronology.

On two other counts, however, the picture of a domestic crisis helping to propel Germany into war in 1939 does fit in more simply with long-term perspectives on the history of the Third Reich. I have argued that war became necessary in order for rearmament to be continued at a high level. Following from this, subsequently in time, war became in every sense an end in itself for the regime. This seems to me to be the overriding fact about the Nazi conduct of the Second World War, including resistance to the bitter end. It was not just a matter of Hitler extolling the virtues of martial combat. In a material sense, in the invasion of the Soviet Union the means (armed force) and the goal (living space) were collapsed into each other and, in the barbaric German policies of occupation, became indistinguishable from one another. It was clear in advance that the German armies would have to live off the land.[148] This war of racial destruction and economic imperialism became an end in itself, and that is one reason why Nazi Germany lost the war in Russia. If we try to imagine some kind of German victory, it was only to be a prelude to further military expansion in the Middle East and North Africa. And so on. If, for Nazism, wars basically served the prosecution of further wars, this decisive logic first broke through in Hitler's policy-making in 1938–9, when the limits of rearmament within Germany's existing boundaries and within her existing constitution were reached. Hitler's basic choice in 1938–9 was, perhaps, to get war started so that it could be continued – whatever the immediate strategic risks, and whatever basic strategic goals he may have had. It is not my intention in any way to belittle detailed investigations of the development of Hitler's strategy, but there may be some risk of overlooking the fact that this was based upon a categorical and continuing option for war *as such*, an option which made a perverse kind of sense in domestic and economic terms at the time at which it first became manifestly clear. After that, conquests were to provide the space and the resources for further conquests. To put it another way, a Third Reich 'at peace' is an unimaginable contradiction in terms.[149]

Plunder provides the last long-term perspective that tends to validate this approach to Nazi policy-making in 1938–9, above all the plunder of

148. See Hillgruber, *Hitlers Strategie*, pp. 264 ff.; Omer Bartov, *The Eastern Front, 1941–1945. German Troops and the Barbarization of Warfare*, London, 1985.

149. I do not wish with this argument to fall back towards earlier interpretations (e.g. by Hermann Rauschning and Alan Bullock) of Hitler as a cynical nihilist. It is possible to accept fully that he had an ideological commitment to the destruction of the Soviet Union and to the conquest of living space there, while maintaining the strongest possible doubts that the Nazi war would have ended, or even been greatly reduced in intensity, in the case of military victory in Russia.

people. This was not a long-nurtured goal of policy, rather an ineluctable necessity, given Nazi economic policy and aims. Some 8 million foreigners worked in Germany during the war, most of them as prisoners of war or deportees. This points to a basic fact which was already becoming visible in 1938: there were simply not enough German people to permit the fulfilment of Nazi ambitions, hence the need to conquer other people. But foreign workers were also used during the war in a very precise way: to keep to a minimum the sacrifices imposed upon German women. I discuss these questions in detail in the next section of this epilogue, but a few preliminary remarks are in order here. The protection of many German women from long hours in munitions factories was not only direct protection of the women themselves; quite as important, it was a protection of the regime's reputation among men, among the women's husbands and fathers, who were themselves mostly soldiers or armaments workers (and whose morale, or prejudices, the regime had to respect). The conscription of German women into industrial wage labour in large numbers would have been intensely unpopular among men; the regime knew this, and there is much evidence.[150] But on two occasions when this step had to be seriously considered the German armed forces conquered new populations who could be brought to work in Germany. This was the case with the French in the summer of 1940, and with the Russians in the winter of 1941–2. In each case the regime had been just about to take the bitter risk of conscripting German women, and then stopped because conquered labour could be used to fill the gaps. The level of mobilization of German women for war work remained low through to 1945.[151] In this vital sphere the policies of guns and butter, which were so distinctive of the later 1930s, were continued throughout the war by means of the conquest and plunder of foreign workers. War, that is, was essential to the maintenance of this very important piece of civilian economy in wartime Nazi Germany.

Finally, there is perhaps a basic dilemma of perception. At the level of one's deepest historical intuitions there must remain a great sense of incompatibility between the Third Reich which, on the one hand, we know to have mobilized such terrifying destructive energies, to have unfolded such sustained and violent bureaucratic and military power, to have resisted until the very end of the war, and, on the other hand, the Third Reich depicted above – a regime whose leadership was increasingly entrapped in economic and political contradictions largely of its

150. For some particularly striking evidence, see Niethammer, (ed.), *'Die Jahre weiss man nicht'*, pp. 126f., 267, 270.

151. See Mason, 'Women in Germany', part 2, especially p. 20; Herbert, *Fremdarbeiter*, pp. 96ff., 142, 175.

own making and which sought escape or resolution or maintenance of its distinctive identity through a series of sudden lurches in policy and through ever more explosive risk-taking. The crises and confessions, the desperate improvisations and the brutal irrationalities which so consistently characterized affairs at the apex of the politico-economic system seem to be instinctively out of key with the evidence of the sweeping march of conquest and genocide and with the tenacious defence of the Greater German Reich in 1944–5. How can the latter possibly have been the outcome of policy-making procedures which were demonstrably so incoherent and crisis-ridden, of a political and economic system so riven with conflict and contradiction? Something seems not to add up.

I believe that one must insist upon the truth and the compatibility of both of these faces of Nazi Germany. The historiographical problem is less that of reconciling the two realities, which may be attempted, for example, by emphasizing the manner in which Hitler himself personified both elements simultaneously. The problem is rather that of working out, in all spheres and at all levels, a set of dynamic and dialectical relationships between the strong centripetal pressures at work at the top of the regime and the efficacity of particular sections of it – the army, the police/SS, much of the civil administration and industry in the years 1942–4. These relationships may well have been positive rather than negative, at least in the short run. That is, crisis, violent irrationality and institutional decomposition at the top may in fact have furthered, for a time, the actual effectiveness of the component parts of the dictatorship. Competition among these component parts, their having to act perpetually under conditions of great pressure and often independently, drew out potentials of power which might otherwise have lain dormant. (The price of this was the growing fragmentation of the regime into a series of incompatible racial, economic and strategic projects, a process which was virtually complete by 1942.) These schematic remarks can do no more than suggest in a rough and ready manner how what I have called the basic dilemma of perception may be resolved; better, one possible approach to its resolution.

In one sense, the particular example which I have tried to analyse does not illustrate this general argument very well, for the preparation of and the mobilization for the war of 1939 was in many respects a failure: at every level (diplomatic, economic, domestic-political) the elements of overstrain were too great, and the Third Reich was saved in the crisis of October–November 1939 more by sheer good fortune than by anything else. But this was not true of earlier and later turning-points, from the Röhm Purge to the invasion of the Soviet Union, all of which illustrate the strict compatibility between crisis-ridden policy-making and the development and deployment of vast political and military power. The example of 1938–9 remains of value, however, not only because of its intrinsic historical importance, but also on account of the multiplicity and clarity of those elements in the situation which made Hitler's option for war such an explosive gamble. Violent lurches of this kind were no less essential parts of the history of Nazi Germany than such fluent manifestations of power as the extermination of the European Jews or the occupation of Italy in September 1943.

Analyses need to emphasize both elements in the system, and to explore their interdependence in a concrete manner. Versions that give exclusive emphasis to the Nazi regime's growing output of military and economic power inevitably create the impression that the steps that led in this direction were relatively smooth.[152] These steps were, on the contrary, highly discontinuous, decisionistic, risk-laden, increasingly violent. It is a central part of my argument that such policy-making was not only wilful, but emerged with a high degree of necessity from the economic and political system of Nazi Germany itself. It is no paradox, still less a contradiction, that policy-making of this kind could unleash phases, or sectoral blocs, of great power, especially of destructive power. In ways which still need to be understood in detail, the two in fact went hand in hand. What the system, and the policy-making which it engendered, could not do was to construct a coherent, imperial and stable Third Reich. That possibility already went badly awry in 1938–9 – an observation which in no way belittles the immense efforts necessary on the part of the Allied powers finally to defeat Nazi Germany.

4. 1939–45

Perhaps the first substantive part of this epilogue should consist in an attempt to furnish at least a part of the missing 'end' of the story. It can only be a part, for a full explanation of the capacity of the Nazi regime to resist until totally defeated would demand the coverage of many more themes than the history of its war time labour policies or even the history of class relations. Still, Hitler's repeated promise – whether nervous or triumphant – that there would never be another 'November 1918', that the war effort of the Third Reich would not be subverted from within, was in the end vindicated by the facts. The years 1944–5 saw no mass

---

152. This point constitutes my greatest disagreement with the recent work of Richard Overy on these questions. See Richard Overy, 'Hitler's War and the German Economy: A Reinterpretation', *Economic History Review*, 2nd series, vol. 3, 1982; 'Germany, "Domestic Crisis" and War'; and '"Blitzkriegswirtschaft"?'.

movements of discontent in the German working class. As long as they had factories to go to, most German workers continued to clock in and to perform whatever production tasks they could, in the midst of collapses in the supply of raw materials and power, which made the government's introduction of a 60-hour week coupled with a holiday ban in August 1944 a largely rhetorical gesture of total industrial mobilization.[153] There were few firms in a position to work a 60-hour week at this time. When their factories were bombed, many German workers were soon on the spot to clear up the rubble and to try to get production going again. There were some concrete bonds between worker and workplace which rein-forced this constancy: despite inflation and the rampant black market a money-wage still meant something in the last stages of the war; supple-mentary ration cards were distributed by employers, not by the food offices; and some employers did what they could to alleviate the distress of bombed-out workers in order to maintain at least the core of a skilled workforce for the time after the war. (Workers and employers often col-laborated to nullify the regime's scorched earth policies, and to save whatever plant and infrastructures could be saved.)

But Wolfgang Franz Werner is probably right in arguing that this con-stancy represented for most workers the only conceivable strategy of sur-vival by this time.[154] Amid the growing destruction and the nearing defeat, what else could they do, where else could they and their families go? To a class which by 1945 had been pulverized into a mass of suffering and insecure individuals, there seemed to be no alternative to carrying on as usual, as far as this was possible. Desertion of the workplace could lead to judicial murder, or conscription into the military front line. Real alterna-tives called for collective, at least for group, acts of defiance. But such collectivities found it very difficult to constitute themselves and to find appropriate fields of activity until after the unconditional surrender. Typical industrial workers, least of all those of middle age or older, were in no way attracted to the open gang warfare against the representatives of the regime, which was launched in the winter of 1944/5 by groups of young men and escaped foreign workers living a life of underground ille-gality.[155] Survival seemed to dictate a 'regression to the spheres of family and work'.[156] The terrible events of 1944–5 passed over a working class which had been very largely reduced to political and civic passivity.

Why did the war end this way, and not in any other? One would not have expected the sullen and unruly working class of 1938–9, firmly set

---

153. Werner, *'Bleib übrig!'*, pp. 335–8.
154. Ibid., pp. 356–8.
155. Detlev Peukert, *Die Edelweisspiraten. Protestbewegungen jugendlicher Arbeiter im Dritten Reich*, Cologne, 1980.
156. Werner, *'Bleib übrig!'*, p. 354.

upon self-betterment and resentfully aware of incursions into its rights, to have lived through the last year of the war as it did. If it is right to pose the question in this way, a large part of the answer, it can be argued, lies in the numerous drastic changes in the political, economic and social system which took place, or were imposed, during the war itself. While there were some important lines of continuity in the regime's policy towards the working class, the overall situation of the class was marked by increasingly radical discontinuities, which tended to wear down and undermine its powers of opposition and to demolish its capacity for collective action of any kind. These discontinuities grew out of the war situation as it developed, and out of the regime's wartime measures. The changes wrought in the lives of German workers during the war were immense, and whether they arose from circumstance or deliberate policy, most of them tended towards the (further) disaggregation of the class and the intensification of dictatorial controls.

With the exception of one important theme, most recent research suggests that this is the most realistic line of enquiry into the capacity of the Nazi regime to hold on into total defeat. This research has produced only sporadic evidence of a real popular solidarity with the regime among civilians during the second half of the war. German workers appear to have been positively impressed by the Nazi war effort only during the period of lightning victories up to late 1941, but these victories had the effect of making tighter industrial and economic disciplines seem less necessary. Hitler understood and pandered to this desire for a swift victorious peace, thereby tending to undermine the more intensive war production which he was simultaneously demanding. This was not the stuff of which a resilient 'home front' was made. Thereafter, the people on the home front suffered the war, stood up to its increasing strains, with greater or lesser degrees of tolerance.

The high levels of armaments output through the summer of 1944 are not in themselves evidence that this suffering was freely and fully accepted, still less that the war effort rested upon a broad consensus with Nazi politics. The regime frequently showed itself to be very insecure about the existence of such a consensus; it could reckon at best with a degree of fatalistic steadfastness. There is a mass of evidence concerning the resentment of workers with respect to the sacrifices forced upon them, and of the endless difficulties which the Nazi authorities had in mobilizing workers for war production both before and after Stalingrad. A good deal of this evidence was filtered upwards to the top policy-making bodies and fuelled their uncertainty in trying to decide what kind of coercive measures would prove to be acceptable or enforceable. It is true that the documentation concerning recalcitrance and discontent on the 'home front' was generated by field agencies of the regime, or by employers, whose task it was to solve such problems, and that their correspondence and reports thus concentrated upon the problems and difficulties rather than upon achievements.

Given the interminable and intractable problems actually posed by the 'home front', however, this fact does not raise a serious issue of bias within the sources themselves. The problems were real, and for the prosecution of the war, it was their resolution that mattered. The achievements of the war industries were never really adequate to military needs, after the end of 1941 never remotely so. There were many different reasons for this. Among them – though surely not the most important, compared, for example with the resistance of the Red Army – was the fact that the morale of wage-earners was never high, their active collaboration in the war effort restrained by a variety of limits. Extra effort, it seems, was not often freely volunteered in industry. Rather, the burdens of war economics were in general reluctantly accepted by the working class, when they could not be pre-empted or evaded.

The exception to this general picture of reluctance, of a regime involved in a constant uphill struggle, concerns not the home front but the behaviour of workers in military uniform. This vital question breaks the boundaries of my original enquiry and shows another of its limitations: it is not possible to discuss relations between the Nazi regime and the German working class without devoting attention to those 3–4 million industrial wage-earners who fought in the armed forces. In this context too, chronological completeness raises a major issue of substance and emphasis. Cutting off the story with the 'phony war' narrowed my perspective on the Nazi regime as a whole. It is not an omission which I am able now to make good in any detail. But the military history of the Second World War definitely suggests that morale in the German armed forces was consistently higher than on the home front, that German troops fought with an enthusiasm, commitment and discipline which was notably greater than that with which workers carried out their industrial duties, that military units and their leaders commanded greater respect than did employers and labour exchanges. Making war seems to have been experienced as a more positive activity than making munitions or mining coal. The regime and the armed forces had systematically prepared younger German males for this since the mid-1930s. The early sweeping victories marked a new high in the prestige of the military, and many young industrial workers volunteered for military service in 1940 and 1941.[157] Whether they enrolled out of a desire for

---

157. Werner, *'Bleib übrig!'*, pp. 58, 60f., 86–90; Salter, 'Structures of Consensus', p. 101. Conscription and volunteer enrolment alike played havoc with labour allocation policy.

adventure, a wish to escape from their narrow proletarian milieux or for any combination of other motives, this fact pointed towards significant changes in social and political attitudes.

However, the waves of conscription in the second half of the war brought under arms vast numbers of workers who had not been trained and indoctrinated to fight during their adolescence: industry lost at least 40 per cent of its male workforce to the armed services.[158] The latter, it appears, had little difficulty in integrating these men and in mobilizing their fighting powers; the rank-and-file of the military units seems to have fought with high levels of dedication right through to the hopeless end of the war. Field commanders and staff officers were far less worried by memories or images of 1918 than was the civilian leadership. This is a vast and complex subject, in which there are no obvious or simple explanations. It would be especially interesting to understand better how much the cohesion of the fighting troops owed to conventional patriotism or nationalism, how much to the organizational and professional spirit of the officer corps in the field, how much to a real approbation of the regime and its imperial projects,[159] and at the end, how much to the increasingly ferocious military discipline. But the only fact which really matters is that neither the early victories nor the later tenacious war of defence could have been achieved without the active co-operation of the troops, many of whom were workers in uniform. On any account, the armed forces were probably the most efficient of all institutions within the Third Reich, and this effectiveness in the fighting of war had an important social dimension. Making war was the essence of Nazism, armed struggle – according to Hitler – the basic condition of life. Although the armed forces were never fully Nazified even after July 1944, on these terms the actual conduct of the war constituted the regime's most terrible success. Working-class soldiers played their part in this success.

The recruitment of millions of workers to the battlefield certainly marked an enormous discontinuity, and not only in the lives of those who were called up. Given the acute labour shortage, their labour power had to be replaced and, at the same time, more and more workers had to be directed into war industries. This led, especially from 1942 on, to an ever more drastic recomposition of the remaining industrial labour force. The working class which had caused the regime such problems in 1938 and 1939 had been rather homogeneous: it had been overwhelmingly German, largely male, representative of all age groups, and still

158. Werner, '*Bleib übrig!*', pp. 274ff.

159. See Omer Bartov, *Hitler's Army. Soldiers, Nazis, and War in the Third Reich*, New York/Oxford, 1991.

had elements of a common collective biography (from 1933 on). The class which suffered on into military defeat in 1945 lacked all homogeneity, and was made up to a great extent of different people from that of 1939: it was mainly older skilled workers (45 and over) who escaped military conscription; other German males still in industry were either indispensable for weapons production, unfit for military service, or already among the war-wounded; mostly under the supervision of these two groups there laboured some 3.5 million foreign workers who were little better than slaves,[160] a slowly increasing number of German girls and women, and German boys who were still too young for the call-up. Big firms showed great aptitude in holding on to workers in the first of these groups (their so-called *Stammarbeiter*), but from 1942 on the remaining German workforce was increasingly reshuffled by administrative fiat, drafted from one firm to another in an effort to maximize war output. Between April and December 1942, 1.3 million German workers were pushed into new jobs in the armaments sector; the figure for the whole of 1944 was 1.7 million; beyond that, whole plants and factories were transferred to new locations, less exposed to Allied bombing.[161]

As these very large numbers of persons were forcibly moved around and scrambled up, old neighbourhood and workplace networks were smashed. These radical processes of ethnic differentiation, fragmentation and uprooting were surely conducive to industrial and civic passivity in the last stages of the war. Barrington Moore, Jr, has furnished some powerful general arguments, and some good examples, of why such experiences should lead to disorientation rather than to protest.[162] The only small question-mark which hangs over this general interpretation concerns those older groups of German skilled workers who were held together by their firms. They had had personal experience of free trade unionism and democracy in the 1920s; at a local or plant level they still formed fairly homogeneous groups, and they often acted independently as such after May 1945.[163] Probably they too did not see what else they could do towards the end of the war beyond trying to protect their homes, families and workplaces.

160. Comprehensive figures on the distribution of German workers, foreign labour, and prisoners of war are given in Herbert, *Fremdarbeiter*, pp. 270–3.

161. Werner, '*Bleib übrig!*', pp. 280ff., 285–92.

162. Moore, *Injustice*; and see Timothy W. Mason, 'Injustice and Resistance: Barrington Moore and the Reaction of German Workers to Nazism', R. J. Bullen et al. (eds.), *Ideas into Politics. Aspects of European History 1880–1950*, London, 1984, pp. 106–18.

163. See the two volumes of oral history edited by Lutz Niethammer, *Lebensgeschichte und Sozialkultur im Ruhrgebiet 1930 bis 1960*, vol. 1: '*Die Jahre weiss man nicht, wo man die hinsetzen soll': Faschismuserfahrungen im Ruhrgebiet*; vol. 2: '*Hinterher merkt man, dass es richtig war, dass es schiefgegangen ist.' Nachkriegserfahrungen im Ruhrgebiet*, Berlin/Bonn, 1983.

The skilled engineering workers who did so much to launch the revolution of 1918 were not burdened by such elementary anxieties, nor by fear of the revenge which might be exacted by millions of foreign deportees in the event of Germany's military collapse. But comparisons between the composition of the working class in 1917–8 and 1944–5 can only be of secondary interest, because above all the political context was so different. At the end of the First World War no overwhelming political defeat weighed upon all the organizations and traditions of the working class, as it did in 1945. Against the background of this comprehensive and sustained defeat from 1933 on, the ethnic and social fragmentation of 1944–5, the absence of the 20 to 40-year olds in uniform and the growing social confusion surely acted as elements of further weakness and disaggregation.

A further major discontinuity of the war years was the imposition of comprehensive measures of repression and terror in order to enforce discipline at the workplace. Obstinately recalcitrant workers had been liable to criminal prosecutions and gaol sentences since the summer of 1938,[164] and it was no novelty that the Gestapo should arbitrarily persecute strikers and 'anti-social elements'. But the blanket labour legislation at the outset of the war placed the whole working population under regulations concerning earnings and job-changing which amounted to a big extension of the criminal law.[165] More important, the regime used the war situation itself as an occasion to make much greater use of its repressive powers and to intensify them; this then appeared to be justified by the wave of passive resistance on the part of industrial workers during September-November 1939. While the regime gave way on many of the social and economic issues in this mute conflict, it became much more repressive against some of those who actually protested; this combination of approaches to the problem of labour discipline persisted through much of the war. On any account, policing the workplace swiftly became a central plank in the regime's wartime industrial policies. The threat of increasingly severe and frequent punishments was not only the essential condition for enforcing maximum wage levels, civil conscription and so on; the threat was also invoked – and this was a qualitative change – against all breaches of industrial discipline, especially against absenteeism, 'refusal to work'.[166]

Even when, in December 1939, the Trustees of Labour were empowered to fine 'slackers' on the spot, without recourse to the courts,[167] the

164. See above p. 249.
165. See above p. 273.
166. For a summary of the evolution of the legal basis for these measures, see Salter, 'Structures of Consensus', pp. 104–5.
167. See above p. 273; Werner, *'Bleib übrig!'*, p. 76.

procedures of repression were held to be too slow and cumbersome. The labour administration and the courts could not cope with the sheer numbers of 'offenders'. The crumbling of work morale seemed to many in positions of authority to call for swift and extreme measures of punishment and intimidation, and after some early hesitations the SS/Gestapo intervened regularly, adding a component of police terror to the conduct of everyday industrial relations. From the early months of the war on, some 'slackers' were sent straight into concentration camps. Then specially constructed 'Work Education Camps' were set up, and a whole network of them systematically organized under SS control in May 1941.[168] They were scarcely less brutal than the concentration camps themselves. In the early stages of the war it was by and large employers and the military authorities who favoured such terroristic interventions by the Gestapo; later Speer looked in this direction for a solution too.[169] Terrorism of this kind was supposed to be directed especially against those who were repeatedly absent from work, sometimes against the labour forces of factories where indiscipline was endemic. In fact its incidence was probably rather arbitrary. The main purpose seems to have been exemplary and intimidatory – to remove 'troublemakers' and to produce a propaganda effect on those who were not deported. There are fragments of evidence that it did indeed produce the desired effects, at least for a time.[170]

The statistics concerning the persecution of German workers in this manner are very fragmentary: they suggest that something like 2,000 were arrested by the police/Gestapo each month.[171] Compared with other punishments and official warnings this figure is relatively low. Terroristic labour discipline against German workers did not become a universal practice; rather, it remained a constant and real background threat. Meanwhile, the government issued a stream of new decrees and ordinances in June 1940, October-November 1940, May 1941, June 1941, November 1941, July 1942, October 1943 and September 1944, which steadily extended the range, severity and arbitrariness of lesser punishments for breaches of labour discipline.[172] Some of this legisla-

168. Salter, 'Mobilisation of German Labour', p. 222.

169. In May 1940 Ley instructed the DAF *Gau* overseers (*Obmänner*) to call in the Gestapo to enforce labour discipline where necessary: see Ronald Smelser, *Robert Ley: Hitler's Labor Front Leader*, Oxford/New York/ Hamburg, 1988, p. 266.

170. Such threats did have an effect in the mines. Both the threatened loss of bonus pay in cases of absenteeism following a Sunday shift (1941), and of supplementary payments for heavy work (1943) did reduce absenteeism; see Salter, 'Mobilisation of German Labour', pp. 270, 294, and 'Structures of Consensus', p. 102.

171. Salter , 'Mobilisation of German Labour', p. 229, and 'Structures of Consensus', p. 108.

172. Salter, 'Structures of Consensus', pp. 105ff.; Werner, '*Bleib übrig!*', passim; Recker, *Sozialpolitik*, passim.

Epilogue

tion empowered employers to penalize their workers on the spot. It was mainly to this large and refined machine of repression that the regime looked to maintain productivity and work morale; internment in the camps was firmly institutionalized, but has something of the character of an *ultima ratio*.

The reasons for this foreground emphasis upon repression rather than terror are much open to debate. The labour shortage surely played its part in this, for the available accounts suggest that at certain times and in certain places the sheer number of slackers was so great that their removal into the camps would have disrupted production much more than the absenteeism which such terror was intended to cure. This was probably a basic reason why many offenders got off with penalties which still left their unreliable labour power at the disposal of their employers.[173] More clearly documented is that fact that the resources of the Gestapo were overwhelmingly directed towards disciplining the growing numbers of foreign workers in Germany – against these people, the police proceeded with full autonomy, ruthlessly and on a massive scale;[174] indiscipline on their part was regarded at once as a political crime and, in the cases of Poles and Russians, a racial threat. A further consideration concerns the identity of the 'slackers'. It is clear that many among them were either young workers, or women, or men conscripted to jobs away from their homes. The regime did not normally regard these groups as suitable candidates for draconian measures of terror, and sought rather to intimidate or 'educate' them into more disciplined patterns of behaviour; a special system of brief imprisonment was instituted for young workers late in 1940.[175] More debatably it has been argued that intensive terror against adult male German workers was not really necessary because their levels of conformity to the demands of the war economy were relatively high.[176] This view is not really borne out by the high figures for formal warnings against 'slackers' (well over 20,000 in one administrative district in 1941),[177] nor by the incessant complaints of the employers. There were several deeply frustrated, even despairing reports on these problems from managers in the coal-mines and the aircraft industry, from sectors of employment, that is, in which there were not large numbers of adolescents or women.[178] Employers seemed to regard these problems with their workers as serious and

173. Werner, '*Bleib übrig!*', p. 320.

174. Herbert, *Fremdarbeiter*, passim, e.g. pp. 115–21; Salter, 'Structures of Consensus', p. 108.

175. Werner, '*Bleib übrig!*', p. 189; Salter, 'Structures of Consensus', pp. 106f.

176. Werner, '*Bleib übrig!*', pp. 192, 362.

177. Salter, 'Structures of Consensus', p. 108; see also Werner, '*Bleib übrig!*', pp. 179f.

178. Werner, '*Bleib übrig!*', pp. 186ff.; Salter, 'Mobilisation of German Labour', p. 208; Recker, *Sozialpolitik*, pp. 172f. (cases from the *Gutehoffnungshütte*).

endemic, though they never again reached crisis proportions after the last months of 1939.

This impression is confirmed by the stream of new punitive decrees and ordinances, which would not have been issued if the problems had been considered of secondary importance. It is also confirmed by the confusions and disputes among the repressive authorities concerning which of them should impose what kind of penalties. By the end of 1944 the punishments which could be inflicted upon workers were almost too numerous to list: wage deductions, loss of bonuses and of paid holidays, compulsory overtime, administrative fines by the Trustees of Labour, heavy ritual warnings either inside the factory or by public officials; after October 1943 employers could withhold the supplementary rations due to workers who performed especially heavy jobs, a penalty which was regarded as especially hard. On top of this there continued the steady flow of normal criminal prosecutions for absenteeism and breach of contract; gaol sentences (often up to six months) were enforced, or sometimes suspended as an extreme form of warning or threat which sent the worker back to his workplace, but such prosecutions often took months to come up because the courts were so clogged up with cases of this kind. The employers, the labour administration and the courts blamed each other for the fact that this enormous machine of repression failed to produce the desired results. Employers were reluctant to appear personally and visibly responsible for heavy-handed or mass punishments within the firm since they might lead to serious frictions and disruptions of production. The labour administration had enough problems in trying to find new workers, without the additional problem of finding replacements for large numbers of arrested workers. In this situation, workers were no doubt more aware than ever of their own scarcity value. It is, however, unlikely that the desire of the power-holding groups to pass the buck from the one to the other did much to diminish the massive pressure of threats, sanctions and penalties which weighed upon the German working class. 'Slacking' could result in a myriad of punishments, ranging from the loss of a Christmas box to immediate delivery into a concentration camp – something very close to a death sentence.

On one issue, many big employers did not hesitate to be ruthless. Workers often sought to justify their absences on medical grounds, but this justification was increasingly rejected as the war drew on. Workers' diets deteriorated, hours of work and travel increased, and exhaustion became more pronounced, but the methods of medical policing in the big plants became steadily tougher and more refined. Doctors, themselves hopelessly overburdened, collaborated with the health insurance institutions in declaring workers to be healthy in the most peremptory manner;

the latter not only stood to lose their insurance benefits, but if they continued to stay away from work they were committing a criminal offence. Employers exerted many different pressures and took many different initiatives to bring about this state of affairs. Many put doctors on their own payrolls for this purpose; and it was often claimed that sickness rates were lower in cases where the health insurance scheme was plant-based, rather than being a public institution. This widely deployed medical policing amounted to a very heavy machine of repression.[179]

To all these threats there was then added the threat of conscription to the Russian front. At the latest after Stalingrad civilian workers wanted to remain civilians. The only guarantee of this was a certificate of indispensability (uk – *unabkömmlich*) for purposes of war production. But the number and distribution of such certificates became the subject of increasingly difficult negotiations between the armed forces and employers. In the second half of the war the armaments industries too had to surrender men for military service, and they obviously released their least reliable or efficient workers first. The threat of having to fight the Red Army through the Russian winter appears to have had a strong disciplining effect upon German workers.[180] Not that the problems disappeared, but the monographic studies convey the impression that the 'work-morale' of adult German males did not worsen markedly in the last three years of the war.[181]

Repression, terror and fear were, of course, not the only reasons why the Third Reich remained so resilient through to May 1945. Precisely because they were omnipresent, their effects cannot be winnowed out from among the many other factors at work. They are perhaps best understood as a kind of universal and essential backcloth, in the foreground of which the regime was able to unfold its various wage and labour policies; as an increasingly oppressive context within which people had to live all the rest of their lives, make their choices both at the workplace and among friends. Certain more precise effects may be guessed at. First, much more than before 1939, the wartime repression and terror atomized the working class into individuals or tiny groups of people. To be sure, absentee/sickness rates of 15 per cent in a plant suggest a degree of tacit understanding among those concerned. But there seems to be less evidence in the war years of solidary collective action to defend, or to better, larger group interests. The odd instances of open

179. This topic is discussed by Werner, '*Bleib übrig!*', especially pp. 312–8, and Recker, *Sozialpolitik*, especially pp. 122–8.
180. See Herbert, *Fremdarbeiter*, p. 305; Salter, 'Mobilisation of German Labour'. Women were of course exempt from this threat.
181. See Werner, '*Bleib übrig!*', pp. 321–8; Speer and Sauckel give a different impression for late 1943: cf. Recker, *Sozialpolitik*, pp. 190–3.

riot were as remarkable for their rarity as for the uncertainty which the authorities showed in dealing with them.[182] The dominant reality was probably that reflected in the magnificent oral history research conducted in the Ruhr, where people seemed to become increasingly isolated from each other, increasingly dependent upon their relationships with immediate workplace superiors, increasingly concerned about their jobs and the survival of their families.[183] Repression and terror as forms of social discipline were directed pre-eminently at the individual, or at categories of persons, not at autonomous, well-cemented groups of people; such groups continued to exist at the workplace, but they served now much less as the focus or source of recalcitrant opposition to managerial norms. Second, it may be guessed that the wartime terror delayed and diminished the emergence of an anti-authoritarian, potentially anti-Nazi youth culture, not least among working-class youth. There was clearly ground here for the emergence of active dissidence and hostility to the regime on a wide scale. In the event, however, it was confined to a few remarkable instances of armed resistance, such as that sustained by the *Edelweisspiraten* in the Cologne area in the winter of 1944–5.[184] Further speculation is out of place, if only because it is virtually impossible to understand to what extent people were guided in their actions (and their acts of omission) by fear. To sum up on this point, repression and terror were the sine qua non of most other policies, but cannot be considered in isolation from them, nor from the other social, economic and political changes which took place in Nazi Germany during the war.

The basic points outlined above appear to me the most important in accounting for the fact that the 'industrial front' did not break down before May 1945. To these points, others of a more general order should be added: the diffuse, if declining, faith in Hitler as the great leader;[185] the growing certainty from 1943 on, unlike in 1918, that this war was a defensive war against a fearsome enemy, consciousness of which probably had a unifying effect upon the German people; the regime's almost complete monopoly of information; and the continued pitiless destruction of Communist and socialist clandestine cadres. In trying to explain why discontent in German industry never became more than discontent, these considerations are probably more important than the actual social and labour policies pursued by the regime during the war years.

182. Werner, *'Bleib übrig!'*, pp. 271f.
183. See the oral histories edited by Lutz Niethammer (note 163 above).
184. See Peukert, *Edelweisspiraten*; Reinhard Mann, *Protest und Kontrolle im Dritten Reich. Nationalsozialistiche Herrschaft im Alltag einer rheinischen Grossstadt*, Frankfurt/New York, 1987, ch. 5.
185. Cf. Ian Kershaw, *The Hitler Myth. Image and Reality in the Third Reich*, Oxford, 1987, part 2.

These policies none the less call for a brief analysis, a task which is made difficult by the complex, shifting and often contradictory character of the policies concerned. In the interests of clarity policies towards the working class can be broken down schematically into their main component parts, but this should not obscure the essential unity of the confusions and uncertainties to which most workers were subjected most of the time. As the war progressed they were on the receiving end of a wide variety of, in part, inconsistent initiatives at the same time, and it is to the simultaneous compound effects of all of them, taken together, that attention should be directed. In political terms, it may well emerge that the very inconsistencies of Nazi policies served in fact to stabilize the industrial front.

The approaches towards the organization of labour power for the war effort contained four principal elements:

(1)   The regime's need to exercise a light hand, to avoid the imposition of sacrifices which might cause mass unrest and falling output, and to offer some kind of minimal incentives to people to work hard.
(2)   The growing dependence of the whole economy upon massive imports of foreign labour.
(3)   The capacity of the regime to enforce some degree of real dictatorial control over growing sectors of the labour market.
(4)   The emergence of some specific common interests between employers and their workers which lessened conflictuality at the workplace and tended to put plants as a whole at odds with the new rationalizing agencies of the regime.

First, it must be noted that the last three of these elements were novelties and marked sharp discontinuities with the pre-war situation.[186] Second, there was no clear, incisive turning-point in Nazi wartime policies. The use of foreign labour, for example, proceeded piecemeal from the very start of the war and took a qualitative leap only with the decision to enslave Russians in November 1941. Third, the enforcement of capillary dictatorial controls over the labour market and earnings gathered pace only slowly in the years 1941–3, while here and in other spheres the light hand remained much in evidence until September 1944, and indeed to May 1945. The collusive bonds between employers and their core of skilled workers, so evident in the early years of the war, proved rather resistant to later administrative interventions.

---

186. This was not entirely the case with regard to collusive behaviour between employers and labour, which had already been evident before the war; cf. above pp. 250f.

By itself, the light hand could not furnish the central plank of new wartime policies. This would have entailed relying upon large-scale wage incentives to secure the redeployment of labour to war industries and to ensure maximum output there. While the regime had permitted some changes along these lines in the later 1930s, such a policy had already been fundamentally rejected in the summer of 1938: the German economy did not have the resources to cover the purchasing power which would have been unleashed by a basic reliance upon incentives, and civilian purchasing power was always considered to be excessive throughout the war.[187] This meant that the use of administrative force to mobilize workers and to direct them into war production was essential from the very outset,[188] but the early measures had only a slight impact and the shortages of armaments workers remained desperately acute until after the conquest of France. The measures of 1942–3 directed or redirected something like 3 million workers into war industries and services, but the economic effects of this notable increment in state power fell far short of the goals set. The opposition to this regimentation was great, and it can be argued that the degree of coercion used in the middle of the war struck a politically appropriate balance between draconian ruthlessness and business-as-usual; that is, the sudden imposition of more drastic and comprehensive regimentation might not have been accepted by workers (or indeed by some employers and some parts of the Nazi Party apparatus).

Both acts of omission at a governmental level and foot-dragging by field agencies and by employers could be justified in general terms (and also in very specific ways, as we shall see), by the huge imports of foreign labour during 1942–3. If foreign volunteers, conscripts and prisoners of war could fill the gaps, the case for massive forcible redeployments of German workers appeared a little less urgent. But this brutal complacency increasingly ran up against the armed forces' implacable demands for manpower from industry, and many of these workers could not easily be replaced by foreigners or by German women. This was the contradiction which finally destroyed all labour allocation policies in the autumn of 1944 – there were simply not enough adult German males.

Such were some of the main interconnections between the four basic elements in the situation identified above. Each of these elements in turn calls for a brief analysis. The policy of the light hand was not really a policy at all. It reflected, on the one hand, the view of Hitler and most

---

187. See Recker, *Sozialpolitik*, pp. 193–206.

188. See Decree on the Restriction of Job Changes (*VO über die Beschränkung des Arbeitsplatzwechsels*), 1 September 1939; cf. p. 259 above, and *Doc. 177.*

Party leaders that a call for major economic sacrifices could destabilize the regime, and this in turn reinforced Hitler's determination to bring the war to a swift victorious conclusion.[189] On the other hand, it grew out of the overwhelmingly negative response of most workers to the severe austerity measures of September 1939. The outcome was a policy of stabilizing wages at their existing levels, and not reducing them as planned. This in turn committed the government to maintaining a supply of basic essentials, especially foodstuffs, at fixed prices, on which workers' families could spend their earnings. Although money earnings tended to rise in the first 2–3 years of the war as both employers and workers found ways to circumvent the wage stop (and as hours were lengthened), the government was able to hold this line into 1942, thanks in part to the plunder of resources and of agricultural labour from occupied Europe. Thereafter, the quantity and quality of the basic foodstuffs available tended to decline slowly, and higher working-class incomes increasingly had to be spent on non-rationed goods, wherever these could be found and afforded. The light hand was also in evidence in the shelving of far-reaching plans swiftly to concentrate armaments production in the largest and most efficient plants. This meant that in the first two and a half years of the war the regime made diminishing use of that most unpopular measure of civil conscription, through which workers could be forcibly transferred from one factory or town to another. Thus, at least until 1942, efforts to 'comb out' (*auskämmern*) the workforce for superfluous labour and to close down consumer-goods factories were half-hearted and distinctly unsuccessful.[190] Such initiatives met not only with the opposition of the employers concerned and of local party bosses: it is important to note that the failure to 'comb out' or close plants exempted workers from the rigours of forcible redeployment and thus also represented a concession to their basic interests out of fear of arousing their discontent. To the disquiet of the military, increases in armaments output came to depend a lot on subcontracting, the retooling of existing plants, and a not very successful campaign to retrain workers on the job in the engineering sector.

These approaches to the problem of the labour shortage in the war industries imposed few additional sacrifices upon the workers concerned (they led indeed to some increases in earnings), and they did not bring swift and large increases in output. In one respect, the light hand also prevailed until the end of the war in the disputed matter of aggregate civilian purchasing power: despite repeated pressure from the Reich Finance Ministry and other agencies, income tax rates were never

189. Cf. Andreas Hillgruber, *Hitlers Strategie*; Fest, *Hitler*, pp. 615f.
190. See Herbst, *Der Totale Krieg*, pp. 120ff., 156f., 186, etc.

again raised after September 1939. Here too the regime feared for its popularity. As far as wage-earners were concerned, bonus payments for overtime, Sunday, holiday and night work were not only reintroduced late in 1939 and in 1940, but were exempted from taxation. This was one of the few small tangible incentives which the regime could offer to people to get them to work harder.[191]

Given the lack of resources for major material incentives in the present, the regime relied a lot during 1940–1 on promises of property, welfare and social justice in the near future, after victory had been won. Robert Ley and the Labour Front were licensed by Hitler to pledge the construction of a grandiose Nazi welfare state, which would concentrate above all upon the provision of much more generous pensions, also upon a major housing programme and improved health care. This was a major propaganda campaign to which the Labour Front was very seriously committed, and the future programmes and reforms were elaborated in some detail (despite the heavy opposition of the state agencies already responsible for welfare). These schemes were full of eugenic and politically discriminatory clauses, but they were intended to give wage-earners a real goal to toil for in the present, and the themes were skilfully chosen in that housing for low income groups and pensions were two areas in which the regime had in fact succeeded in enforcing austerity during the 1930s – there were great unfulfilled needs.[192] Not until December 1942 did Hitler finally forbid all further public discussion of these programmes (presumably on the grounds that such propaganda for the future made the present demands of the war seem less urgent).[193]

Behind the scenes of Ley's propaganda drive to give Nazism a 'social face' a totally different reality was being acted out. In the spring of 1940 ministers and top officials were engaged in the most difficult secret discussions about whether to conscript German women into war work. The number of women who were outside the labour market and whose family responsibilities were held to be light enough to permit them to take up paid labour was between 2 million and 3 million.[194] However, partly because of the high separation allowances paid to the wives of men in military service, the number of women actually in regular employment fell considerably during the first six months of the war. In this vital sphere the pressures on the regime to turn drastically towards a heavy-handed policy built up to a high level of intensity in the

191. Cf. Recker's valuable account, *Sozialpolitik*, pp. 51–8.
192. See Herbst, *Der Totale Krieg*, p. 163, and Karl Teppe, 'Zur Sozialpolitik des Dritten Reiches am Beispiel der Sozialversicherung', *Archiv für Sozialgeschichte*, vol. 17, 1977, pp. 195–250.
193. Recker, *Sozialpolitik*, pp. 217–8; Smelser, *Robert Ley*, pp. 275f.
194. Herbst, *Der Totale Krieg*, p. 119.

months before the invasion of France; but in the event, an alternative was discovered at the last moment, as we shall see.

This combination of half-measures, concessions and demagoguery was at best a negative and superficial political success in the first year and a half of the war, in that it minimized the occasions for popular discontent and opposition on the shop floor. Despite a lot of propaganda, it was not rewarded by a greater productive effort. It did almost nothing to meet the issue which, as early as October 1939, Göring had emphatically recognized as the key issue of the war: the ruthlessly efficient mobilization and allocation of labour power.[195] It was definitely not the case that the relative laxity of Germany's economic mobilization, either before or after the conquest of France, was tailored to, or justified by, the developing military situation. As Todt, the new Minister of Munitions, at once recognized in 1940, even Hitler's optimistic blitzkrieg strategy called at once for much more stringent economic measures in order to make adequate supplies available to the armed forces: a 60-hour week was imposed in armaments firms in June 1940,[196] and early in 1941 'bottleneck commissions' were sent into industry to enforce economies in the use of labour.[197] These and other policies initiated by Todt, to which we shall return, marked the beginning of the erection of an administrative iron cage around substantial sections of the German working class. But the short-term effects were slight when set against the needs of the armed forces: both against France and in the invasion of the USSR they operated on extremely narrow reserves of munitions, trucks, fuel, tires and so on, gambling, at first with extravagant success, upon their overwhelming battlefield superiority. This omnipotent gamble collapsed in the battle for Moscow at the end of 1941. That the margins of the armed forces' reserves of war *matériel* were too narrow was a direct result of the 'light hand' of the less-than-full economic mobilization between 1936 and 1941.

Hitler well understood the absolute urgency of gaining great victories quickly and on the cheap: 'The Führer sees that we cannot hold out in a long-term war, the war must be concluded quickly. . . . Everything must be gambled on this single card'. But Hitler was at this stage quite unwilling to insist upon the social and economic measures which followed necessarily from his own insight.[198] His sense of urgency derived not only from his fear of the superior war-economic potential of a world-wide anti-German alliance. As is shown by his own espousal of the light hand

195. Recker, *Sozialpolitik*, p. 58.
196. Werner, '*Bleib übrig!*', pp. 146–8; Todt's order was withdrawn on 27 September.
197. Recker, *Sozialpolitik*, pp. 157ff.
198. Hitler's comments to the War Economy Staff (*Wehrwirtschaftsstab*) in December 1939: ibid., p. 74.

at home and by his repeated promises to the German people of a swift and victorious peace, it was crucially determined by doubts about the popularity and resilience of the regime. His policies in the first two years of the war were deeply contradictory: he persisted with his ends of massive military expansion while shying off the means (comprehensive domestic mobilization) which were essential to pursue these ends. The historical problem is to understand how and why, after the gamble had failed, the regime was able to sell itself so dearly in defeat.

This leads to the second main strand in wartime labour and social policies. The Third Reich's resilience had a lot to do with its exploitation of conquered and dependent territories: fiscal levies together with cheap raw materials, foodstuffs and productive capacities all contributed greatly to the regime's economic resources.[199] For the domestic social and political history of the war, however, it was the (mostly forced) importation of foreign workers which was of outstanding significance. In schematic terms, this barbarous and almost wholly improvised policy had three vital dimensions. The first was numerical: Germany simply did not contain enough people to fight Nazism's wars and maintain the necessary production of goods and services. In the judgement of the most authoritative study of the subject, as early as mid-1941 the German economy was structurally dependent upon 3 million foreign workers (prisoners of war included), who were mostly doing heavy, poorly paid work in agriculture, construction, etc.[200] Without them, agriculture would have already collapsed in the autumn of 1940.[201] By 1945 the aggregate number of foreign labourers, including those who had died in the meantime, was probably well over 8 million; that was more than one-third of the pre-war insured German population. The mobilization of Germans for war work was still incomplete when the relevant policies fell into complete disarray in the autumn of 1944, but it is obvious that no conceivable measures of total mobilization could have come anywhere near to meeting a need of this magnitude.

The second dimension of the question was political, and it followed, albeit in a contradictory manner, from the immense numbers of foreigners involved. At times, especially in the latter half of 1940 and again in 1942–3, the potential supply of foreign labourers did in fact seem so abundant as to reduce the need for harsh mobilization measures against the German people. In particular, the conquest of labour repeatedly served to delay, and then to soften the application of, that one policy which was the most unpopular of all on the home front and which most

199. Alan Milward, *War, Economy and Society 1939–1945*, London, 1979, ch. 5.
200. Herbert, *Fremdarbeiter*, pp. 129–31.
201. Ibid., pp. 11, 36, 67ff.

threatened to undermine the legitimacy of the regime as a whole: the conscription of non-employed German women into factory labour. The hostility of the women concerned, and above all of their menfolk, to any schemes of this kind was massively documented and was fully familiar to the holders of power.[202] Since many of the men, the fates of whose female dependants were at stake, were fighting in the armed forces or held key positions in war production, the issue raised a deeply dangerous and general problem of political morale. Soldiers wanted to know that their wives were leading tolerable existences at home, and male workers wanted their wives to be there to look after themselves and their families; some of the latter went to extreme lengths to maintain this situation.[203] On the other hand, non-employed women who had no pressing responsibilities for small children represented, together with female domestic servants, by far the largest category of potential new German workers, and the need for their low paid, unskilled or semi-skilled labour in munitions plants and the like had already become critically acute in the winter of 1939–40.

These contradictory imperatives formed an agonizing dilemma for the leadership of the Third Reich. On at least three occasions its resolution was simply postponed by the sudden conquest of foreign workers. Comprehensive legislation for conscripting women into industry had been finalized in the spring of 1940, but as soon as German military victory in France seemed assured, Göring ordered that the decrees be shelved – French workers and prisoners of war would fill the gaps.[204] Minister Todt tried to force through the compulsory employment of women in January 1941, but was repudiated by Hitler 'for political reasons'.[205] In terms of racial policies the fundamental decision of November 1941 to employ Russian prisoners of war, and then civilians, inside Germany came as a problematic surprise to sections of the Nazi elite, but one of the arguments which Göring successfully used with Hitler was that the Russians would work instead of German women. He made the same point again forcefully in mid-1942.[206] It was, however, no solution, as the new Plenipotentiary for Labour, Sauckel, at once realized in the spring of 1942, and by the end of that year the labour supply problems

202. See Winkler, *Frauenarbeit*; also Carola Sachse, 'Hausarbeit im Betrieb. Betriebliche Sozialarbeit unter dem Nationalsozialismus', in Sachse et al., *Angst, Belohnung*, pp. 209–74, and 'Fabrik, Familie und kein Feierabend. Frauenarbeit im Nationalsozialismus', *Gewerkschaftliche Monatshefte*, vol. 9, 1984, pp. 566–79.

203. See Michael Zimmermann, 'Ausbruchshoffnung. Junge Bergleute in den Dreissiger Jahren', in Niethammer (ed.), *'Die Jahre weiss man nicht'*, p. 126.

204. That the regime's repeated reluctance to conscript women was not simply the effect of paternalist ideology is amply documented: see Mason, 'Women in Germany', part 2, pp. 14–22, and Recker, *Sozialpolitik*, pp. 72, 79, 159 etc.

205. Recker, *Sozialpolitik*, pp. 158f.

206. Herbert, *Fremdarbeiter*, pp. 142, 175.

had become so acute that a united political, economic and military leadership group could finally prevail upon Hitler to legislate for the registration and compulsory employment of certain categories of women in the course of 1943. This decree was enforced in an extremely circumspect manner, however, and by the end of the year no more than 500,000 women had been newly recruited into permanent jobs, by no means all of these in the armaments sector (and many in part-time work).[207] For this, the continuing stream of foreign conscript labour was as much responsible as the determined opposition of the German men and women concerned. Employers were quick to learn that they could inflict much more draconian work discipline, longer hours and other penalties on Russian conscripts (male and female) than on resentful, legally and socially protected German women. Some employers also began to learn that they could obtain quite high levels of production from the rapidly growing slave population, if the latter were given minimal standards of food and accommodation and the smallest monetary incentives.

The number of German women employed in the war work of the most various kinds did increase slowly, but certainly until the last winter of the war and the last desperate efforts at total mobilization, women as a whole constituted a relatively protected section of society (especially middle- and upper-class women). The exception was constituted by those women wage-earners who had been 'trapped' in industrial employment at the start of the war, and could not gain permission, or find a loophole, to leave it after 1939. In general the policy of the light hand remained in evidence, even if in a gradually diminishing degree. It did so because the regime was afraid of the extreme unpopularity which draconian measures could arouse; and it could indulge these realistic fears by giving priority to the ruthless exploitation of foreign labour.[208]

207. The basic measure was the Führer Decree on the Comprehensive Mobilization of Men and Women for Tasks of National Defence (*Führererlass über den umfassenden Einsatz von Männern und Frauen für Aufgaben der Reichsverteidigung*), 2 January 1943; see Herbst, *Der Totale Krieg*, pp. 207–18; Salter, 'Mobilisation of German Labour', pp. 77ff.; Recker, *Sozialpolitik*, pp. 180, 185, 266ff.; Winkler, *Frauenarbeit*, p. 141.

208. The question of levels of women's employment has recently become controversial and confused. Richard Overy has argued that the levels were in fact very high. He reaches this conclusion by including all 'economically active' women, especially the large numbers of wives and female dependants of farmers, craftsmen and shopkeepers called to the ranks, who tried to keep the small family enterprises going. He is right to insist upon the contribution of these women to the overall economic effort, but in his revisionist zeal he fails to see that the crucial issue for the regime was the drafting (or not) of women into *factory labour* in the war industries. This was where the most acute need was felt. It had already been seen before the war, and was confirmed in 1943, that between 2 million and 3 million women were in principle available for such work. Perhaps it was a slight overestimate, but if this basic fact is not placed at the centre of the interpretation, the endless tergiversations and conflicts at government level and the widespread social unrest during the war both remain quite inexplicable. See Overy, 'Reply', pp. 239f., and '"Blitzkriegswirtschaft"?'; Herbert, *Fremdarbeiter*, p. 419, note 6.

The third dimension of the mass enslavement of foreign labour is much more difficult to evaluate in summary form. It concerns the combined processes of social mobility and ethnic prejudice which were unleashed by the presence in German of between 7 million and 8 million foreign workers, most of whom were treated in a radically discriminatory manner. Most of them were treated as inferiors first in their employment, assigned to dirty, heavy, underpaid work, which Germans had already been reluctant to carry out before the war – agricultural and building labour, mining, heavy unskilled labour in mining and engineering.[209] Numerous groups in the German working population, especially foremen, skilled workers, farmers and lower-level management (public and private) suddenly became in effect a supervisory corps, organizing and controlling the labour of 'inferior' foreign workers; over the 'sub-human' and potentially 'subversive' Poles and Russians, their German superiors had informal auxiliary police powers.[210] This rapidly created a widely diffused sub-elite within Germany, which seems in general to have accepted happily its quite new status, even when this was not always accompanied by direct economic advantages, promotions at the workplace, and so on. It was a novel and apparently seductive form of social mobility.[211]

In particular, it was accompanied and given specific form by the massive official encouragement and enforcement of racial prejudice. The Germans were to become a master race in their own country, contentedly accustomed to seeing columns of sick and underfed Polish or Russian men and women marching backwards and forwards between their primitive barracks and their workplaces, proud to be exploiting and repressing this segregated 'inferior' human material, and accepting as axiomatic that Slav workers should be totally rightless, subject only to the terroristic dominion of the Gestapo and the SS. Did this practice and propaganda of extreme racial discrimination, which (unlike Auschwitz) was transparently visible across the whole country by 1943, strike positive chords in the German working population of a kind which helped to consolidate the regime itself? In his impeccably discriminating studies of these issues Ulrich Herbert concludes that there was at least a considerable degree of passive racism in all social classes: a general failure to perceive the origins and horrors of the new system of slavery, an uncritical acceptance of the new human hierarchies which were being constructed, and a universal tendency to think of foreign

<hr>

209. Herbert, *Fremdarbeiter*, pp. 270ff.; some prisoners of war and civilian workers from Western Europe did get jobs commensurate with their skills.
210. Ibid., pp. 212f.
211. See Ulrich Herbert, 'Apartheid nebenan. Erinnerungen an die Fremdarbeiter im Ruhrgebiet', in Niethammer (ed.), *'Die Jahre weiss man nicht'*, pp. 260f.

workers in terms of stereotypes (even when such stereotypes were not actually hostile).[212] If this was something short of active consent and approval, it was surely a potent new source of ideological confusion. There were also instances of racist sentiments outstripping official persecutions, or responding positively to them with great zeal. Thus Italian workers were very widely disliked, although their legal position was similar to that of Germans until September 1943; there were grotesque complaints during 1942 that foreign workers were being given too much to eat; the improvement of working conditions for French prisoners of war in the same year excited hostile criticism, as did the permission for some Polish workers to return home for brief holidays.[213] Resentment against bombing attacks on German cities was sometimes directed against foreign workers as representatives of 'the enemy'.[214] In some, not all, heavy industrial plants and coal-mines Polish and Russian workers were systematically subjected to extremes of gratuitous physical violence by their German overseers and foremen.[215] And from 1940 on a campaign of sexual-racial panic and intimidation was launched to outlaw intercourse between German women and foreign men, which led to a spate of denunciations and heavy punishments.[216] That Nazi racism of this type made some inroads into the consciousness and behaviour of most of the civilian population is thus beyond doubt.

The SS and the Party, however, did not think that this success was sufficient or secure. They viewed with great suspicion the efforts of Sauckel, Speer and Goebbels from 1942–3 on to give a bit more emphasis to the economic aspects of the 'foreign labour problem'. Elementary technocratic reasoning dictated a minimal attention to the dietary, health and housing needs of slave workers, and the provision of minimal incentives in cash or kind – these people would then produce more (and, in fact, they did, though this does not apply to the concentration camps). But this gradual and by no means great shift in policy put 'sub-humans' shoulder to shoulder with German workers, and tended to reveal them as able and diligent, as real persons, far removed from the vicious clichés of SS propaganda. Three and a half million of them were employed in industry, mining and transport in August 1944, and Herbert can illustrate the development of tentative and partial solidarities and mutual dependencies in some workplaces,[217] together with many cases of Germans who broke the law in order to give material and moral sup-

212. Ibid., pp. 247ff., and Herbert, *Fremdarbeiter*, pp. 356ff.
213. Ibid., pp. 170f., 183, 186.
214. Ibid., pp. 288ff.
215. Ibid., pp. 217, 225ff., 274ff., 284f.
216. Ibid., pp. 125ff., 178f.
217. Ibid., pp. 270, 210–13, 219f.

port to individual foreign workers. There were still farmers in the eastern parts of Germany who treated Polish labourers as normal migrant workers, rather than as slaves.

As things increasingly fell apart in the last year of the war, however, so there were ever more groups of homeless and workless foreign labourers drifting through the bombed cities and the countryside, stealing food and clothes to stay alive. The spectre arose that these groups and gangs could turn into the ferocious masses which might rise up and take a terrible revenge upon their German oppressors. Dramatizing these new racial fears, the SS further intensified its exclusive terroristic control over foreigners, shooting vagrants on sight or murdering those arrested, and encouraging brutal vigilantism among German civilians.[218] Thus at the end of the war some of the latter felt that they had a more immediate enemy than the regime which had oppressed them too, and had brought about the catastrophe of the war. Enslavement and racism of this kind were further reasons why the Nazi regime was able to hold out in defeat.

Alongside the light hand and the exploitation of foreign labour, the third component in the regime's wartime social policies was the incremental growth of effective dictatorial administrative controls over much of the German working population. This was a piecemeal and relatively slow process, the most important element in which was the actual power of the various administrative machines to move people into war-related work, to bind them there and to force them to work for relatively modest wages. It involved, that is, running the risk of provoking mass unpopularity, and a new determination to grind down all such opposition by means of force majeure. Before and immediately after the beginning of the war the regime possessed all these powers, but largely on paper only; it had neither the political will nor the capillary administrative capacity to translate them into incisive policies. Beyond the many examples from 1938–9 already cited, that of the failure to recruit more miners for the Ruhr in the first months of the war is very illuminating. Construction labourers discharged from the Siegfried Line and miners evacuated from the Saar were available and allocated for such work, but most of these men simply failed to turn up in the Ruhr.[219] By October 1944, when the number of German workers in the armaments industry reached it highest point, the situation was substantially different: it was very much more difficult for workers to defy or escape from directives and controls of this kind.

218. Ibid., pp. 327–39.
219. Werner, '*Bleib übrig!*', pp. 63ff.; Salter, 'Mobilisation of German Labour', p. 251.

One part of this story is fairly clear, that is, the growing power within the regime of agencies which considered such coercive policies to be essential. As Minister of Munitions, Todt initiated and substantially prefigured the whole programme during 1940–1. Speer and Sauckel tried to expand and press forward with such policies during 1942, and gained the very important political support of Goebbels, which facilitated the tougher measures of 1943 and 1944. The military authorities continually pressed for forcible interventions to redistribute labour and productive capacities in their own interests. This trend towards comprehensive dictatorial controls over German labour was, of course, reinforced by the steadily deteriorating military situation of the Reich. What is much less clear, however, is how the regime developed the administrative machinery which was at least in part able to implement and enforce these policies, although they aroused a great deal of opposition from the workers themselves, from many (especially smaller) employers and from many local agencies of the NSDAP.[220] Maybe the surviving evidence happens to give too much prominence to this opposition; but the reverse argument, that the coercive measures were more effective because they commanded a higher degree of consent during the war, seems impossible to sustain. The key seems to lie in administrative force. Mass coercion of this kind rested in the last resort upon the sanction of police terror, but for it to have been at all successful it demanded a high input of skilled and ruthless bureaucratic labour on the part of the Reich Trustees of Labour, regional and local labour exchanges, regional economic offices, the armaments inspectorates and the like. After the spring of 1942, when Sauckel took over labour policies, these offices appear to have worked with greater authoritarian efficiency than before. How and why this was the case cannot be said with certainty; perhaps they sensed stronger support and stricter imperatives from Berlin. It was definitely not a result of Sauckel having made the Gauleiters his regional deputies, for the Party as a whole, uneasy about its popularity and open to interest-group pressures, tended to slow down the transition to the total war economy.[221]

None the less, in the latter half of 1942, an increasing number of people were shifted into war production by administrative fiat; there was a new and more energetic campaign to close down inefficient plants and to cut back the production of consumer goods in order to release labour for the armaments sector. More efforts began to be made to ensure the most efficient use of labour in this sector. In addition, substantial groups

220. The number of civilian conscripts had fallen to 640,000 by April 1942: Salter, 'Structures of Consensus and Coercion', p. 100.
221. Recker, *Sozialpolitik*, pp. 165ff.; Herbst, *Der Totale Krieg*, pp. 225–31; Speer, *Memoiren*, pp. 229, 236, 325–7.

of men, women and children were temporarily drafted into agricultural labour.[222] Estimates of the number of people affected by the end of 1942 vary somewhat.[223] But the manpower budgets drawn up at this time for 1943 showed that measures of a totally different order were essential immediately: the German armies in Russia needed 700,000 more men at once, and the armed forces as a whole were claiming 2 million more conscripts; some of these men could only be taken out of the armaments industries, but this sector required 800,000 more workers by March 1943, and the whole economy 1.5 million more by June 1943.[224]

It was against this background of looming catastrophe that, as mentioned above, Hitler finally agreed to partial and circumspect mobilization of German women from January 1943 on. This measure lost a lot of its effectiveness in the course of the year as well over half a million women found ways and means to escape from their new employments.[225] It was accompanied by a new and, on paper, much more stringent policy for the closure of craft enterprises, firms in the retail and wholesale trades, restaurants, bars and so on. The closures provoked a storm of opposition, and were transformed into a more successful policy of again 'combing out' the civilian sector of the economy for workers who could be put into war employment. By the end of the year over half a million workers had been reallocated in this way, to whom must be added a similar number of women who had been unable to evade conscription. Again the figures are approximations, and industry was relatively slow to absorb these new, inexperienced workers.[226] But for all the exemptions granted, it did amount to a major new turn of the screw, a new stage in the militarization of labour. At the same time it was very far from meeting actual manpower needs – during the very same year, 1943, military conscription reduced the number of Germans in work by 1 million.[227] Not least in order to combat this endless labour shortage, in September 1943 Speer's ministry took control over much of manufacturing industry. The declared aim was the 'Concentration of the War Economy', the means involved more closures, more forcible movements of workers within the armaments sector, more controls on man-

222. Dietrich Eichholtz, *Geschichte der deutschen Kriegswirtschaft*, E. Berlin, 1985, vol. 2, p. 211.

223. Recker is sceptical about the effect of these efforts: *Sozialpolitik*, pp. 173–6; Werner, *'Bleib übrig!'*, p. 280, offers a higher estimate of the numbers.

224. Cf. Herbert, *Fremdarbeiter*, p. 237; Eichholtz, *Kriegswirtschaft*, vol. 2, pp. 193ff.

225. Herbst, *Der Totale Krieg*, pp. 210f.; Salter, 'Mobilisation of German Labour', pp. 77f.

226. For various computations, see Herbst, *Der Totale Krieg*, pp. 207–13, 222; Recker, *Sozialpolitik*, pp. 181–6, 266ff.; Werner, *'Bleib übrig!'*, p. 280.

227 Herbst, *Der Totale Krieg*, p. 213.

agement in the use of labour and the retooling of consumer goods plants for war production.[228]

Thus workers in production were increasingly enclosed in an implacable network of administrative constraints. Those inside the network were under quasi-military discipline, and the regime showed no signs of wavering or uncertainty towards them. Unpopular mass evacuations and relocations of plants were forced through in 1943 and 1944 against often vociferous opposition.[229] There still remained many outside of this network, and to some of them the regime turned its attention in a last paroxysm of total mobilization in the summer of 1944. A quarter-million more women were conscripted into industry, but ministers baulked at calling on children and soldiers' wives. Hitler, however, who had in the past so often protected the civilian population against the proposals of his direct subordinates, did agree in July 1944 to a drastic comb-out of white-collar workers in public and private employment, a 60-hour week, and a block on all holidays.[230] In fact, very soon labour allocation policies fell apart: 250,000 key armaments workers were called up for the last battles and hundreds of thousands more were conscripted for labour on improvised fortifications or for service in the *Volkssturm*.[231] But to the very last they were kept under strict regimentation and subjected to dictatorial orders, however useless and destructive. The bureaucratic, military and police machines of the regime enforced acquiescence; the space for non-suicidal defiance and opposition was minimal.

The earnings and living standards of industrial workers were also slowly drawn into an iron cage of administrative controls. Pressure for higher wages continued to be strong into 1942 and, despite the government wage stop of October 1939, the earnings of many groups of workers increased proportionately more in these years than their hours of work, though not by very wide margins.[232] Some of these increases derived from internal promotions and re-classifications of workers within the factories, but there were still many ways in which employers could circumvent the wage stop in order to keep their labour forces pacific and productive.[233] In June 1940 a senior official of the Ministry of Labour

228 Recker, *Sozialpolitik*, pp. 189–93; Herbst, *Der Totale Krieg*, pp. 179, 255f.; Werner, *'Bleib übrig!'*, pp. 282f.; Salter, 'Mobilisation of German Labour', pp. 91f., 97f.

229. Werner, *'Bleib übrig!'*, pp. 268–74, 285–92.

230. Goebbels's appointment as Plenipotentiary for Total War on 25 July was another plank in this platform; for these measures, see Recker, *Sozialpolitik*, p. 272; Werner, *'Bleib übrig!'*, pp. 335f.

231. Recker, *Sozialpolitik*, pp. 285ff.; Werner, *'Bleib übrig!'*, pp. 339–347.

232. Salter, 'Mobilisation of German Labour', pp. 122–9; Werner, *'Bleib übrig!'*, pp. 105ff., 120ff.; Recker, *Sozialpolitik*, p. 197.

233. See for example Gustav-Hermann Seebold, *Ein Stahlkonzern im Dritten Reich. Der Bochumer Verein 1927–1945*, Wuppertal, 1981, pp. 184f., 191, 195f., 198.

flatly told industrialists that the state could not reduce the high wages that employers were freely paying.[234] Any repetition, that is, of the calamitous direct attack on wage levels made in September 1939 was ruled out of court. However, beginning in 1940 and with gathering momentum through into 1942, the state began to attack the wage problem from the side of pricing policies. This was a complex economic-administrative reform of relations between the government, the armed forces and industry. The steady move to a system of fixed prices for public contracts increasingly forced employers to control their costs, especially labour costs, more strictly.[235] In June 1942 Sauckel still felt it necessary to launch a strong campaign against employers who were ignoring the wage stop, but the days when industrialists could give in to workers' pressure or recruit new workers by the offer of higher wage rates and then pass on the extra bill to the state, were steadily receding into the past. There remained only a variety of loopholes for more or less clandestine wage increases, and in 1943–4 average money earnings tended, with some differences between sectors, to level out, while the cost of living continued to rise.[236] On basic matters of wage policy the informal bargaining power of the working class had been largely ground down and the state had asserted some measure of primacy over the competitive interests of employers in the labour market. No other belligerent power was able to restrain earnings in this manner during the Second World War.[237] This considerable success of the dictatorship depended heavily upon the massive controls over the mobility of labour outlined above.

However, the interventions of the regime and some employers went beyond the enforcement of general wage controls. After the introduction of a pilot scheme in some shipbuilding yards in 1941, followed by a period of anxious hesitations and elite group conflicts, the whole basis of wage calculation in the engineering and armaments industries began to be changed in the latter part of 1942. The old system of piece-rates and bonuses, based in part on formal levels of skill qualification, was a rough-and-ready affair which allowed many abuses of the wage regulations; young semi-skilled men could make very high earnings, while highly skilled workers were tied to inflexible time-rates. The authorities, including the Labour Front, were convinced that the old system tended to put a variety of brakes on the workers' input of effort. The new scheme was based upon a detailed computation of time, work-processes and output for all specific production tasks, on the basis of which a wide range

234. Hachtmann, 'Klassenharmonie', pp. 181ff.
235. Salter, 'Mobilisation of German Labour', pp. 134ff.; Werner, *'Bleib übrig!'*, pp. 113ff.; Thomas, *Geschichte der deutschen Wehr- und Rüstungswirtschaft*, ch. 16.
236. Werner, *'Bleib übrig!'*, pp. 120ff., 239f.
237. Milward, *War, Economy and Society*, p. 237.

of incentive wages (*Leistungslöhne*) was calculated. This new 'scientific' version of piece-rates payment claimed greater equity, but its overriding purpose was to encourage (or force) people to work harder: there was a much wider differentiation of wage rates. While there were no upper limits on earnings, some established piece-rates were definitely cut. Only skilled men on time-rates were to be exempted, with guaranteed high earnings, from this Darwinistic wage system, which, it must be noted, surely tended to erode workplace solidarities: workers were now placed in one of eight different wage categories.[238]

There had already been a few local and not unsuccessful precedents for actions to cut piece-rates, and it is noteworthy that the regime delayed until it was losing the war before implementing a major scheme of this kind. (Here too, the enslavement of foreign workers probably made the urgency seem less pressing.) However, from October 1942 on, brigades of time-and-motion experts descended on the engineering and armaments plants, measuring everything that was measurable. It was an ambitious, complex and lengthy operation, even though, in the form finally adopted, it had the backing of most employers. The regime's claims of swift successes in the form of higher output have a distinct ring of propaganda, for there were not enough experts to impose the new system in anything like all the firms in the sector, and their interventions met with a wide variety of forms of non-cooperation and opposition on the part of the workers affected.[239] Still, even if the overall effects on productivity were not very great, the initiative demonstrated yet again the regime's determination to enforce capillary technocratic controls over the working class. To them and to the outside world it showed few doubts about its power to enforce its will. The dictatorship had developed greatly from its first confused and failed attempts to enforce wage limits in the latter half of 1938. It had become a much more formidable agency of class oppression.

This piece of the iron cage, intensified exploitation, was intimately related to another place, the lengthening of the working day/week. Many different attempts were made during the war to compensate for the labour shortage by extending working hours to a maximum of 60 hours per week or more. In general these attempts were not very successful. Many employers and the Labour Front were opposed to 10-hour shifts because the quantity and quality of the products diminished in the last two hours of work, and a working week of 60 hours or more led to

---

238. Tilla Siegel, *Leistung und Lohn in der nationalsozialistischen 'Ordnung der Arbeit'*, Opladen, 1989, especially ch. 5; Recker, *Sozialpolitik*, pp. 223–38; Werner, '*Bleib übrig!*', pp. 224–34.
239. Recker, *Sozialpolitik*, pp. 237–41.

exhaustion and higher rates of sickness. Intensification of labour effort was thus in one sense a practical alternative to the diminishing returns from the extension of hours. None the less, hours were considerably lengthened by comparison with the pre-war years. Legal restrictions were greatly relaxed, overtime became compulsory and average figures for a 54- to 56-hour week in 1941 already concealed longer hours in the armaments sector. The proven disadvantages of excessive hours were often ignored in crude efforts to force up output. This was another major element of administrative coercion and control over the whole working class, whose lives became more and more factory-centred. Hours were normally especially long in the iron and steel industries and in the air-craft industry. Special crash programmes to meet acute production bot-tlenecks repeatedly called for temporary extreme extensions of the working week. Another method used by the regime was to offer very large bonuses for the working of extra shifts. This was done to some effect in certain aircraft factories, and most conspicuously in the Ruhr coal-mines where, from mid-1941 on, miners gradually accepted more and more Sunday and holiday shifts in return for very substantial bonus-es in cash, food and tobacco – but attendance on normal shifts then tend-ed to be lower until new penalty clauses were enforced. In general workers had to be forced or seduced into working extra shifts; appeals for voluntary efforts of this kind met with very negative responses.[240] 'Working hours' too must not be understood literally: Allied bombing greatly increased the time which workers spent away from home, for commuting became much more difficult, air-raid protection duties were added to production work, nights were spent in cellars and air-raid shel-ters, and then there was the more and more frequent irregular labour of clearing up bombed factories and residential quarters. People simply became tired out, and this fact, together with the growing dislocation of transport and power supplies, meant that the final extensions of the working week in 1944 – to 72 hours in the aircraft industry, then 60 hours throughout the economy – remained for the most part brutal, impractical gestures. They demonstrated, however, the ultimate intran-sigence of the regime, its implacable determination to hold the working population in absolute subjection. There were no overt signs of govern-mental uncertainty or infirmity of purpose, which might have acted as catalysts for collective acts of resistance.[241] Many workers reacted to these endless and extreme physical and nervous pressures in a manner which Stephen Salter has accurately defined as common, though not

240. For responses to the so-called 'Stalingrad' or 'tank' shifts (*Panzerschichten*), see Werner, *'Bleib übrig!'*, pp. 251–6.
241. This judgement is based on the accounts by Werner, *'Bleib übrig!'*, pp. 151–9, 241–50, 255–9, and Recker, *Sozialpolitik,* pp. 272f.

collective – taking illegal rests from work, going absent, claiming sick leave: forms of defiance, which, as we have seen, were policed and persecuted with increasing intensity.

Before the discussion passes on to the fourth main element of wartime social policies, to the growing emergence of common interests between employers and workers on and around the shop floor, it is necessary to try to evaluate the crucial effects of the disciplinary iron cage into which German workers were thrust. This is a difficult and controversial matter. On balance my own impression is that administrative coercion served more to pre-empt and destroy the bases of possible class opposition than to secure dramatic increases in war output. These increases took place, but they had many other causes. One index most relevant to the argument concerns the average productivity of labour, figures which it is very hard to calculate precisely. The immediate postwar estimate put the average overall increase at 10 per cent to 12 per cent for the course of the war, a relatively low figure. Productivity increases in manufacturing industry were significantly higher, around 30 per cent, and in the armaments sector they reached 30 per cent in the single year between 1942 and 1943, and went on rising during the first half of 1944.[242] A part of these increases was due to the lengthening of hours; and the rise of armaments output after 1942 was much greater than the increase in the productivity of labour. These very rough calculations suggest that the notable strength of the German war economy rested less (it is a matter of degree) on an intensified, more scientific exploitation of German labour or on greater worker effort, than upon the major changes in the management of the whole economy initiated by Todt and Speer. These changes have been portrayed in detail elsewhere.[243] Here it is necessary only to emphasize that they took up an immense amount of slack which had existed in the spheres of military procurement programmes and contracts, the allocation and use of raw materials, the concentration of production in the best equipped plants and the standardization of production techniques, components and endproducts. The blitzkrieg strategy had, for example, not only required repeated, major, short-term and thus highly disruptive alterations in the priorities for the various weapon-types produced; it had also encouraged industrialists to think in terms of an early end to the war and thus left them reluctant to make big new investments in machinery or sharp economies in production techniques. From 1942 on, many of these very considerable sources of inefficiency and limitations on output were rad-

242. Milward, *War, Economy and Society*, p. 230; Eichholtz, *Kriegswirtschaft*, vol. 2, pp. 265f.
243. Milward, *War, Economy and Society*; Janssen, *Ministerium Speer*; Speer, *Memoiren*; Eichholtz, *Kriegswirtschaft*, vol 2.

ically diminished, together with numerous administrative frictions. Committees of major industrialists were made directly responsible for meeting production targets, and the result was an abrupt movement towards concentration and rationalization in the whole organization of industry through which the big modern firms gained greatly in economic power.

With the partial exception of Dietrich Eichholtz, there seems to be a consensus among expert historians that it was this new system of overall military-economic management which was the basic precondition of the high armaments outputs of 1943–4. Most of these measures, it is suggested (or implied), affected workers and the workplace indirectly; they were accompanied, it is true, by the more comprehensive general coercion of the working population outlined above, but such decisive shifts in policy as the turn to long production runs of staple weapons did not have great effects on work processes and wages and were not dependent for their success on high levels of morale on the factory floor, for which there is anyway little evidence.[244] On balance, the greater oppression of the working class in the form of the technical rationalization and subdivision of work processes, de-skilling and the dilution of labour seems to have played a secondary, though not trivial part in the big increases of armaments output in the second half of the war, certainly a much smaller part than Todt and Speer believed to be possible and necessary. Eichholtz does cite some important counter-examples of the introduction of production line methods and speed-ups, and so on, especially in production for the army, but his overall evaluation of the diverse sources of the big increase in weapons production after 1942 remains, at the end of his wide-ranging enquiry, rather ambivalent, and he perhaps tends to overstate the case for the hyper-exploitation of German workers.[245] On the other hand, for example, many manufacturers maintained a strong preference for universal machine tools (which were in plentiful supply), although they required a high proportion of scarce skilled workers to operate them. The transition to special machine tools and semi-skilled labour was very incomplete, despite the fact that it evidenced some isolated big increases in productivity.[246] One may conclude very provisionally that the enormous defensive economic effort of the Nazi regime

---

244. On the rationalization of armaments production processes, see Herbst, *Der Totale Krieg*, p. 174, Recker, *Sozialpolitik*, pp. 161f. (for the military and labour deployment context), and Seebold, *Stahlkonzern*, p. 306 (impact on one firm).

245. Eichholtz, *Kriegswirtschaft*, vol. 2, pp. 308ff., 302ff., 321f.

246. These last remarks apply especially to the aircraft industry; for a summary, see Salter, 'Mobilisation of German Labour', pp. 102–7, based on the pioneering work of Richard Overy; also Milward, *War, Economy and Society*, pp. 189f. Note the total failure to rationalize and retool for unskilled women: cf. Winkler, *Frauenarbeit*, p. 191.

rested upon the great mass of the workers performing much the same tasks as before, albeit under more and more difficult circumstances and under heavier coercion. The changes which mattered most were organizational and institutional, and their efforts in terms of output cannot safely be interpreted as evidence either of a new popular solidarity behind the Nazi war effort of 1942–4, or the widespread use of new, refined and unscrupulous techniques to extract the last ounce of effort. What mattered was that the working class was kept firmly in place.

That place, when the men were not called up, was at work. During the war many employers seem to have paid more attention to the problems of keeping people working pacifically. This is a complex and intricate topic which calls for more detailed research, but there are more than a few hints that the bonds of mutual dependence between employers and workers came more into the foreground in the war years than in the 1930s. To the underlying structure of informal class conflict were added new and/or more general elements of class collaboration on some specific issues. This was not the result of a sudden conversion of industrialists to the communitarian demands of the Labour Front, for the latter continued to be regarded with suspicion and irritation by most employers. Nor were the latter afflicted by a sudden flood of humanitarian or philanthropic insight into the acute strains under which the working class performed its onerous wartime duties – the calls for the ruthless punishment of absenteeists and the stringent medical policing of 'malingerers' show that no such change of heart took place. There was no 'war socialism'. It was rather that war conditions tended to modify management's perceptions of its own short- and long-term interests in the face of the fundamental fact of life: the increasingly oppressive labour shortage. After September 1939, obtaining and retaining workers, and keeping them basically co-operative, became much more difficult. Success in this sphere was absolutely essential for firms in the gaining and completion of contracts, and up until the end of 1941 it also seemed highly desirable in view of an imminent reconversion to a less war-centred economy. At the heart of this problem throughout the war remained the tenacious efforts of all larger companies to hold on to their basic core of long-serving, experienced skilled workers (*Stammarbeiter*), without whom they could not function at all.

Managerial interests dictated, as we have seen, limited illicit concessions on wages and fringe benefits, as long as these did not endanger profits, and as long as the regime did not persecute employers who paid excess wages.[247] Scope for pacifying or bribing workers in this way had

---

247. For an example of the many such circumventions and of a rare prosecution, see Seebold, *Stahlkonzern*, pp. 184f.

diminished considerably by the end of 1942, but was never entirely eliminated.[248] Workers were never fully reconciled to the war effort by such concessions, for they valued rest-time quite as highly as extra cash – even the removal of the ceiling on piece-rates in the coal-mines in September 1942 did not result in better work discipline[249] – but the new situation must have tended to shift some part of class antagonism from inside to outside the plant. Many employers presented themselves, hypocritically or not, as eager to pay higher wages, but prohibited from doing so by the regime.

The second similar issue which tended to put many workers and employers on the same side of the fence became more and more severe as the war drew on. The rationalizing agencies of Speer and Sauckel called it the 'hoarding of labour'. Even when the prospect of imminent victory had completely evaporated, management had a fundamental interest in not losing labour – either to other firms or to the armed forces. Such reallocations of workers could lead to partial or complete (possibly permanent) shut-downs, at least to diminished business activity. For their part, workers had a vital interest in not being moved away from their homes, in not being moved to less well paid or harder jobs, and in not being drafted to fight against the Red Army; this elementary concern put them under pressure to work in a reliable, disciplined manner, to appear indispensable to their present employers.[250] This particular community of interest at the plant level was the object of violent rhetorical attacks and threats on the part of the regime. In March and again in October 1942 Speer saw it as one of the first and most important problems for him to address publicly, and he had Hitler's verbal support.[251] Employers by and large failed to co-operate actively and freely, continued to claim more workers than they could use and so on, and in 1944–5 were repeatedly threatened with court martial if guilty of 'hoarding labour'.[252] Punishments in fact seem to have been few, but the whole issue, which assumed large dimensions, pointed towards a new relativization of class conflict at the workplace. The regime pushed at least some employers and some workers closer together. It is important to emphasize that in this context workers could rarely represent effectively their own collective interests (except occasionally through the mediation of anxious Labour Front or Party officials); the defence of

248. Werner, *'Bleib übrig!'*, pp. 97ff., 222ff.; Salter, 'Mobilisation of German Labour', pp. 67f.; Recker, *Sozialpolitik*, pp. 233f.
249. Werner, *'Bleib übrig!'*, pp. 235–9.
250. For a basic discussion of this, see Salter, 'Mobilisation of German Labour', pp. 93–7, and Werner, *'Bleib übrig!'*, pp. 275ff.
251. Herbst, *Der Totale Krieg*, pp. 176, 179.
252. Werner, *'Bleib übrig!'*, pp. 284f., 348.

their interests was secondary to and derivative of the interests of business. The two sides were then pushed even closer together in their common opposition (this time backed by Speer) to Hitler's scorched-earth policy at the end of the war.

While it is impossible to generalize accurately about the social welfare policies of firms towards their German workers during the war, there are numerous discrete hints that some employers were led, out of enlightened self-interest, towards a better treatment of the labour force in certain limited respects after 1939. Their widespread, if by no means always effective, scepticism about excessively long working hours is one case in point. The adequate feeding of workers, so that they remained fit enough to stand the strains, was another; firms could exercise a lot of pressure on the economic administration in order to obtain high and regular ration allocations, also adequate supplies of working clothes and boots, for their workers. There was an almost six-fold increase in the provision of canteen meals in industry.[253] Paternalism in German heavy industry had always been directed towards securing industrial peace and high productivity, and to this end some firm-based welfare policies were expanded during the war, though only to the benefit of the reliable and the diligent.[254] More notably, many employers in war industries made special new efforts to attend to the particular needs of new women workers, hiring female welfare officers especially for this purpose, installing kindergartens, and offering extra holidays and time off work. As a method of securing good labour discipline and high output from women workers these policies were not notably successful, but they demonstrated a practical concern for the relationship between (authoritarian) decent treatment and productivity.[255] Then in the emergency situation following Allied bombing raids big firms were often in a position to give practical assistance to their workers by procuring building materials and equipment for the repair of shattered homes, temporary accommodation, blankets, basic essentials, and so on. Thus workers could return more quickly to their jobs; but this economic and organizational power of private enterprise was the more important,

253. Ibid., pp. 209f. This was despite workers' preference for family meals over communal provision.

254. For paternalism at Krupps, see Ulrich Herbert, 'Vom Kruppianer zum Arbeitnehmer', in Niethammer (ed.) *'Hinterher merkt man'*, pp. 233–76; Seebold, *Stahlkonzern*, pp. 229ff. discusses the costs and profits involved.

255. See Sachse, 'Hausarbeit im Betrieb', pp. 254ff.; Seebold, *Stahlkonzern*, pp. 186f.; Ulrike Ludwig-Bühler, 'Im NS-Musterbetrieb. Frauen in einem Textilunternehmen an der Schweizer Grenze', in Niethammer (ed.), *'Wir kriegen jetzt andere Zeiten'*; Winkler, *Frauenarbeit*, pp. 77ff., 157ff. The DAF pushed for these policies; the women themselves were more interested in equal wages.

given the ineffectiveness of the government and Labour Front programmes to rehouse those who had been bombed out.[256]

All this may not have amounted to much more than straws in the wind, and such attempts to construct and document precise communities of interest were surely confined to the profitable war sectors of the economy. But they call for comment for two reasons. First, they were far removed from the harsh unyielding managerial policies of the mid-1930s – here too the war probably marked a considerable change in which employers found it necessary to take a bit more account of some of the immediate material interests of their German workers. Second, in some degree in contrast with employers, the regime itself had less and less space, as the war progressed, to make concessions designed to bribe and pacify the working class. This observation touches the central thesis of the book: that the domestic and military policies of the Third Reich were consistently influenced by the 'memories' and supposed lessons of the revolution of November 1918, by the fear that the war effort could be subverted from within if the working class were to be drastically alienated and overstrained. From 1942 on, the regime was compelled to begin running precisely such risks.

In the limited and concrete terms of labour policies this deep anxiety had always expressed itself more in acts of omission on the part of the government, failure to impose sacrifices, than in new initiatives designed to give plausible substance to the doctrine of class harmony. (The only major such initiative in the 1930s had been the extension of paid holidays and the organization of mass tourism.) There continued to be a stream of such acts of omission during the war, especially in taxation policies and the mobilization of women; the high separation allowances for soldiers' wives remained untouchable even in mid-1944. Proposed new impositions on the working population were repeatedly rejected with such formulas as 'for political and social reasons undesirable'.[257] Vetoes of this kind, remnants of the light hand, often derived from Hitler himself, as was openly stated at a vital top-level meeting in July 1944, in which Speer pressed for even more radical measures for the redistribution of the labour force: in the past 'in part . . . intended measures [had] not found the Führer's approval'.[258] In the second half of the war, however, these acts of omission diminished very considerably in scale and in political significance; they were anyway for the most part embarrassed secret policy choices, invisible, not trans-

---

256. Recker, *Sozialpolitik*, pp. 260 ff.; Werner, *'Bleib übrig!'*, pp. 259–68; Seebold, *Stahlkonzern*, pp. 272ff.

257. Recker, *Sozialpolitik*, p. 198.

258. Ibid., p. 271; cf. Herbst, *Der Totale Krieg*, pp. 213f.

formable into propaganda. Against this, as has been seen, from 1942 on key agencies of the regime were forced to find the courage to try to implement some hard and unpopular measures in respect of labour allocation, working conditions and wages, often without the support of employers. And they had very little to offer by way of material compensation compared with the immediate pre-war years. It is true that basic pensions were raised from their very low levels in 1941–2;[259] that a comprehensive law for the protection of working mothers of May 1942 introduced a variety of generous new benefits and controls in respect of pregnancy and child-birth;[260] that miners' pensions were substantially raised in January 1943 (though this was a purely instrumental measure to get older miners to continue working);[261] that the Labour Front continued to press with some success for the maintenance of paid holidays for short rest-cures for exhausted workers;[262] that there were some big bonuses for extra shifts worked. But that was about the sum of it.

More weighty were the gradually increasing hardships which the regime was now anxiously forced to impose upon the working class. These incremental hardships were not just absolute: in the last three years of the war they became relatively greater than the hardships enforced upon many sectors of the middle class. At the time of the collapse of the first package of austerity measures in November 1939 one high official had exclaimed, not without justification, that 'it is not possible to wage war if we wrap one section of the population, the workers, in cotton wool'.[263] During 1942–3 the balance of social forces and political pressures shifted somewhat to the advantage of the middle classes, parts of which were able to 'wrap themselves in cotton wool'. Speer and Sauckel seem to have been less haunted by the ghost of November 1918 than their predecessors, and than Hitler or Goebbels. In the crisis of the war many Party agencies and some of the ministerial bureaucracies alike came passively or actively to the defence of their natural social constituencies in the middle class. Although the latter posed no direct potential threat to the regime on the model of 1918, the state of their morale came to be taken seriously in policy-making, as came out for example in the fierce opposition to the closure of smaller enterprises in 1943.[264] Basic facts of property, wealth, income and networks of social and political connections came into their own, and the elementary structures of class society asserted their power.

259. See Karl Teppe, 'Zur Sozialpolitik des Dritten Reiches', p. 236.
260. Winkler, *Frauenarbeit*, pp. 154–7.
261. Werner, *'Bleib übrig!'*, pp. 297ff.; Salter, 'Mobilisation of German Labour'.
262. Werner, *'Bleib übrig!'*, pp. 143ff., 311.
263. See above, p. 253, and *Doc. 224.*
264. This is a major theme in Herbst, *Der Totale Krieg*; see especially part III, 2 and 3.

The first test case which brought this tendency fully into the open was the general reduction in food rations decreed in April 1942. Anxious reinvocations of the protests and strikes of the First World War accompanied this measure in the minds of Nazi leaders, and there was indeed a good deal of discontent and demoralization.[265] But the real and enduring problem was not a repetition of 'turnip winters' and near-starvation, so much as a growing and increasingly obvious gulf between the better-off and the mass of the working population in respect of access to food supplies. The former could afford to pay high prices for unrationed goods and enter actively into the expanding black markets, and the latter could not.[266] The regime did little to counter this growing inequality, neither extending and enforcing more rigorously the rationing system nor taxing higher incomes more severely. By the same token the steady and comprehensive reduction in the supply of consumer goods of all kinds fell earlier and more heavily on the working class than on the middle class. Social inequalities were also increasingly acutely perceived with respect to the mobilization and redistribution of labour. Middle- and upper-class women certainly found it easier than working-class women to circumvent the registration decree of January 1943 or to find themselves relatively undemanding occupations, and this was widely resented among wage-earners.[267]

The full burdens of economic mobilization also fell later and less heavily upon the burgeoning mass of white-collar and administrative workers in the public and private sectors. Middle- and upper-level administrators did very well out of the war, especially those with technical qualifications. The lower categories of salaried employees did not enjoy greatly higher living standards than armaments workers; they were, for example, not eligible for the extra food rations linked to heavy manual labour, and an increasing proportion of them were anyway lowly paid women. However, their working hours were normally lower than those of manual workers and they suffered less physical strain and sickness. More important, they seem to have enjoyed more security in their positions of employment than wage-earners: although various agencies of the regime realized early in the war that the swollen bureaucracies of the state, the military, commerce and business could be greatly streamlined in order to release manpower for more urgent tasks,[268] the combing-out and rationalization of these sectors remained very ineffective even after Goebbels and Speer ordered a desperate across-the-board cut of 30 per cent of all office workers in August 1944.

265. Werner, *'Bleib übrig!'*, pp. 194ff., 201–10.
266. Ibid., pp. 194–7, 201–10.
267. Winkler, *Frauenarbeit*, p. 136.
268. Recker, *Sozialpolitik*, pp. 177f.; Prinz, *Vom neuen Mittelstand*, p. 271.

Bureaucracies were centres of power and exercisers of power, and they were highly resistant to outside interventions in their procedures, however labour-intensive these were. In all spheres of life, from the wage offices to the Party organization to the police, they were the main instruments of control and repression. Who should control the controller? In addition, ministries with large and specialized regional and local agencies were reluctant to risk the disruptions associated with broad rationalizing reforms in the middle of a war.[269] As a result, salaried staff were forcibly shunted around from job to job much less than manual workers, and above all, very few were demoted to fill the gaps on the factory floor.[270] Finally, in this general context of class relations, it must be noted that the regime never adopted a policy for the comprehensive and compulsory reallocation of dwelling space in response to the Allied air-raids. People with large apartments and houses were not generally required to share their homes with those who had been bombed out.[271]

Of all the Nazi leaders Goebbels showed himself most sensitive to the political dangers which could arise from the emergence or manifestation of such new class inequalities.[272] Although his influence in all spheres of domestic politics grew from 1943 on, especially after his designation as Plenipotentiary for Total War in July 1944, there was little that he could do about the substantive policy choices. His distinctive contribution was a package of propaganda and declaratory legislation which made the Third Reich in its death-throes appear much more 'egalitarian' than it actually was. His exaltation of total war demanded and threatened the militarization of the whole social order, and to this end his rhetoric contained many attacks on the remaining privileges and exemptions of the middle classes.[273] There is no doubt that Goebbels wanted the regime to go much further in this direction in its practical policies than it actually did. In fact he achieved little more than to play upon the justified social envies and resentments of wage-earners and common soldiers, to suggest that the regime was in some way 'on their side' after all, and that they could identify with its aims and intentions if not with its still incomplete policies of levelling down German society. On the surface this seemed like the final demagogic effort to exorcise the ghost of November 1918. (In fact it was the nihilistic egalitarianism of total defeat and destruction.) It is important to say whether this socially radical propaganda had a positive resonance in the last year of the

---

269. See Recker, *Sozialpolitik*, pp. 273, 282–5.

270. This summarizes the more complex picture described by Prinz, *Vom neuen Mittelstand*, pp. 235–81, which shows that there was a degree of proletarianization.

271. Recker, *Sozialpolitik*, p. 265.

272. Herbst, *Der Totale Krieg*, pp. 198–202, 205f., 218f., 230.

273. See Prinz, *Vom neuen Mittelstand*, pp. 263ff., 271ff.

war; people were probably much too concerned with the basic problems of survival to pay much attention to this new rhetorical version of the 'national community', and they anyway had before their eyes daily evidence that it was all untrue, that wealth and status still carried advantages amid the growing chaos of defeat. It could not be otherwise. As Herbst has acutely pointed out, Goebbels's programme for the abolition of all socio-economic distinctions through total mobilization would have turned everyone into a rightless state employee. This could only have been brought about through the destruction of the economic bases of such inequalities, but the regime as a whole had neither the political will, nor the time, nor the necessary foundation of social support to collectivize German society in this manner.[274] The Third Reich remained very much a class society to the end, but there was no repetition of the working-class unrest of 1917–8.

The reasons for this were many and complex. I have emphasized in the above section the importance of those which derived from the great changes wrought by the Nazi conduct of the war, and have put in the foreground the social, administrative and political discontinuities of the war years as compared with the 1930s. It is necessary to stress once more, however, the effectiveness of one Nazi practice by which the leaders had set great store from the very outset – the elimination of all the leadership cadres of working-class resistance organizations of any kind. After 1941, the new Communist underground organizations were remorselessly smashed one after the other, and, as the case of fascist Italy suggests, such cadres were vital in stimulating mass protests.

274. Cf. Herbst, *Der Totale Krieg*, p. 240.

Appendix: List of Documents Reprinted in *Arbeiterklasse und Volksgemeinschaft*

Document numbers printed in italics in the footnotes above are references to these documents.

Kapitel I
Die beiden sozialpolitischen Richtungen im Nationalsozialismus 1936–1939

1 Wortprotokoll der 5. Tagung der Reichsarbeitskammer am 24. November 1936 in Berlin (Auszüge)

Kapitel II
Arbeitskräftemangel und Vierjahresplan 1936

2 Schreiben des Reichs- und Preussischen Arbeitsministers an den Chef der Reichskanzeil, Dr Lammers, vom 28. August 1936 **3** Entwurf eines Zweiten Gesetzes zur Regelung des Arbeitseinsatzes mit Begründung und Durchführungsbestimmugen vom 6. Oktober 1936 **4** Vermerk der Reichskanzlei über das Geset.z zur Regelung des Arbeitseinsatzes vom 30. Oktober 1936 **5** Rede Görings im Berliner Sportpalast am 28. Oktober 1936 (Auszug) **6** Erste Anordnung zur Durchführung des Vierjahresplans über die Sicherstellung des Facharbeiternachwuchses vom 7. November 1936 **7** Zweite Anordnung zur Durchführung des Vierjahresplans über die Sicherstellung des Bedarfs an Metallarbeitern für staats- und wirtschaftspolitisch bedeutsame Aufträge vom 7. November 1936 **8** Dritte Anordnumg zur Durchführung des Vierjahresplans über die Rückführung von Metallarbeitern und baufacharbeitern in ihren Beruf vom 7. November 1936 **9** Vierte Anordnung zur Durchführung des Vierjahresplans über die Sicherstellung der Arbeitskräfte und des Baustoffbedarfs für staats- und wirtschaftspolitisch bedeutsame Bauvorhaben vom 7. November 1936 **10** Fünfte Anordung zur Durchführung des Vierjahresplans über die

Beschäftigung älterer Angestellter vom 7. November 1936 **11** Sechste Anordung zur Durchführung des Vierjahresplans über das Verbot von Kennwortanzeigen für die Anwerbung oder Vermittlung von Metallarbeitern und Baufacharbeitern vom 7. Novenber 1936 **12** Siebente Anordnung zur Durchführung des Vierjahresplans über die Verhinderung rechtswidriger Lösungen von Arbeitsverhältnissen vom 22. Dezember 1936 **13** Erlass des Reichs- und Preussischen Arbeitsministers an die Treuhänder der Arbeit vom 30. Dezember 1936

Kapitel III
Arbeitsmarkt und Lohnstand um die Jahreswende 1936/37

14 Schreiben des Reichs- und Preussischen Arbeitsministers an den Chef der Reichskanzlei vom 2. Dezember 1936 **15** Bericht des Statistischen Reichsamts über die Entwicklung der tatsächlichen Arbeitsverdienste im Jahre 1936 **16** Schreiben des Reichs- und Preussischen Arbeitsministers an den Chef der Reichskanzlei vom 25. Januar 1937

Kapitel IV
Die Metallarbeiteranordnung vom 11. Februar 1937 und ihre Auswirkungen

17 Anordnung über den Arbeitseinsatz von Metallarbeitern vom 11. Februar 1937, mit Durchführungserlass **18** Erlass des Präsidenten der Reichsanstalt an die Landesarbeitsämter und Arbeitsämter vom 27. April 1937 **19** Erlass des Präsidenten der Reichsanstalt an den Präsidenten des Landesarbeitsamts Brandenburg vom 8. November 1937 **20** Bericht des Präsidenten des Landesarbeitsamts Brandenburg an den Präsidenten der Reichsanstalt vom 8. Januar 1938 **21** Bericht des Arbeitsamts Berlin an den Präsidenten des Landesarbeitsamts Brandenburg vom 20. Dezember 1937 **22** Schreiben des Reichs- und Preussischen Arbeitsministers an den Reichskriegsminister und den Reichsminister der Luftfahrt vom 17. Februar 1937 **23** Schreiben des Reichs- und Preussischen Wirtschaftsministers an die Geschäftsgruppe Arbeitseinsatz beim Beauftragten für den Vierjahresplan vom 12. Mai 1938 **24** Bericht des Prasidenten der Reichsanstalt an den Reichsarbeitsminister vom 6. August 1938 **25** Schreiben der Firma Rheinmetall-Borsig (Zentrale Verkauf Waffen, Berlin) an den Chef des Wehrwirtschaftsstabes vom 21. Juli 1938 **26** Bericht der Wehrwirtschafts-Inspektion VI (Münster) an den Wehrwirtschaftsstab vom 2. September 1938

Kapitel V
Die soziale und wirtschaftliche Entwicklung im Frühjahr 1937

27 Auszug aus den Monatsberichten der Treuhänder der Arbeit für den Monat Februar 1937 **28** Vermerk aus dem Geheimen Staatspolizeiamt II.A.2. vom 13. Februar 1937 **29** Monatsbericht des Sicherheitsdienstes II 1 2 1 über Linksbewegung im Februar 1937 (Auszug) **30** Auszug aus den Monatsberichten der Reichstreuhänder der Arbeit für den Monat März 1937 **31** Bericht des Statistischen Reichsamts über die Entwicklung der tatsächlichen Arbeitsverdienste im 1. Vierteljahr 1937 (Auszug)

Kapitel VI
Die soziale und wirtschaftliche Entwicklung April-Mai 1937

32 Bericht der Staatspolizeistelle Darmstadt an das Geheime Staatspolizeiamt vom 21. April 1937 **33** Auszug aus den Monatsberichten der Reichstreuhänder der Arbeit für den Monat April 1937 **34** Staatspolizeiliche Erlasse und Vermerke betreffs der Überwachung entlassener Schutzhäftlinge von August 1934 bis September 1937 **35** Schreiben des Reichs- und Preussischen Arbeitsministers an den Chef der Reichskanzlei vom 23. April 1937 **36** Auszug aus den Monatsberichten der Reichstreuhänder der Arbeit für den Monat Mai 1937 **37** Bericht des Treuhänders der Arbeit für das Wirtschaftsgebiet Mitteldeutschland an den Reichs- und Preussischen Arbeitsminister vom 20. Februar 1937 **38** Anordnung über den Arbeitseinstaz von Arbeitern der chemischen Industrie und des Baugewerbes in den Bezirken der Arbeitsämter Bitterfeld, Halle und Wittenberg vom 27. April 1937 **39** Wirtschaftlicher Lagebericht des Oberpräsidenten der Provinz Sachsen für die Monate Februar und März 1938 vom 25. April 1938

Kapitel VII
Die soziale und wirtschaftliche Entwicklung im Sommer 1937

40 Schreiben des Reichs- und Preussischen Arbeitsministers an den Chef der Reichskanzlei vom 26. Juni 1937 **41** Auszug aus den Monatsberichten der Reichstreuhänder der Arbeit für Juni [und Juli] 1937 **42** Artikel aus *Freies Deutschland - Organ der deutschen Opposition*, Nr. 23, vom 17. Juni 1937: "Neue Betriebskonflikte. Schattenkampf Seldte contra Ley" **43** Bericht des Statistischen

Reichsamts über die Entwicklung der tatsächlichen Arbeitsverdienste im 2. Vierteljahr 1937 (Auszug) **44** Lagebericht der Staatspolizeistelle Düsseldorf über die illegale marxistische und kommunistische Bewegung für das Jahr 1937 **45** Auszug aus den Monatsberichten der Reichstreuhänder der Arbeit für August [und September] 1937

Kapitel VIII
Die soziale und wirtschaftliche Entwicklung im letzten Vierteljahr 1937

46 Bericht des Statistischen Reichsamts über die Entwicklung der tatsächlichen Arbeitsverdienste im 3. Vierteljahr 1937 (Auszug) **47** Auszug aus den Monatsberichten der Reichstreuhänder der Arbeit für den Monat Oktober 1937 **48** Lagebericht der Staatspolizeistelle Lüneburg über die illegale marxistische und kommunistische Bewegung für das Jahr 1937 (Auszug) **49** Schreiben des Reichs- und Preussischen Arbeitsministers an den Chef der Reichskanzlei vom 20. Dezember 1937 **50** Bericht des Statistischen Reichsamts über die Entwicklung der tatsächlichen Arbeitsverdienste im 4. Vierteljahr 1937 **51** Lagebericht der Staatspolizei Dortmund über die illegale marxistische und kommunistische Bewegung für das Jahr 1937 **52** Auszug aus den Monatsberichten der Reichstreuhänder der Arbeit für die Monate November und Dezember 1937

Kapitel IX
NSDAP, DAF und die Sozialpolitik im Jahre 1937

A. Bezahlte Feiertage

53 Vermerk aus dem Reichs- und Preussischen Wirtschaftsministerium (undatiert: Anfang März 1937) **54** Aufzeichnung über die Besprechung im Reichsarbeitsministerium vom 5. März 1937 **55** Anordnung zur Durchführung des Vierjahresplans über die Lohnzahlung an Feiertagen vom 3. Dezember 1937 **56** Schreiben des Reichsarbeitsministers an den Beauftragten für den Vierjahresplan vom 22. Februar 1940

B. Löhne und Preise

57 Schreiben der Geschäftsgruppe Arbeitseinsatz beim Beauftragten für den Vierjahresplan an den Reichskommissar für die Preisbildung vom 24. April 1937 **58** Entwurf eines Schreibens des Reichs- und Preussischen Wirtschaftsministers an den Reichskommissar für die

Preisbildung (undatiert: Ende April 1937) **59** Runderlass des Reichskommissars für die Preisbildung an die Preisbildungsstellen vom 23. Mai 1937 **60** Anordnung des Stellvertreters des Führers der NSDAP vom 1. Oktober 1937

C. Das Ortsklassensystem

61 Vermerk aus dem Reichs- und Preussischen Wirtschaftsministerium vom 30. August 1937 **62** Schreiben des Hauptdienstleiters im Zentralbüro der DAF an den Reichskommissar für die Preisbildung vom 20. August 1937 **63** Schreiben der Geschäftsgruppe Arbeitseinsatz beim Beauftragten für den Vierjahresplan an den Reichskommissar für die Preisbildung vom 1. Oktober 1937

D. Der Leistungskampf der deutschen Betriebe

64 Schreiben des Reichs- und Preussischen Wirtschaftsministers an die Geschäftsgruppe Devisen beim Beauftragten für den Vierjahresplan vom 24. Februar 1937 **65** Referat des Leiters des Amtes Soziale Selbstverantwortung der DAF auf der Gauarbeitstagung der Arbeitskammer Sachsen am 23./24. Oktober 1937 (Auszug)

Kapitel X
Der Arbeitskräftemangel in der Bauwirtschaft 1937–1939

66 Anordung über den Arbeitseinsatz von Maurern und Zimmerern vom 6. Oktober 1937 **67** Erlass des Präsidenten der Reichsanstalt an die Landesarbeitsämter und Arbeitsämter vom 7. Oktober 1937 **68** Schreiben des Reichs- und Preussischen Arbeitsministers an den Chef der Reichskanzlei vom 22. Oktober 1937 **69** Bericht des Präsidenten des Landesarbeitsamts Brandenburg an den Präsidenten der Reichsanstalt vom 1. Oktober 1937 **70** Bericht des Präsidenten des Landesarbeitsamts Brandenburg an den Präsidenten der Reichsanstalt von 11. November 1937. Anlage: Niederschrift über die Besprechung vom 26. Oktober 1937 im Landesarbeitsamt **71** Schreiben der Geschäftsgruppe Arbeitseinsatz beim Beauftragten für den Vierjahresplan an den Reichskriegsminister u. a. vom 11. Dezember 1937 **72** Schreiben des Reichs- und Preussischen Wirtschaftsminister an den Reichskriegsminister u. a. vom 7. Dezember 1937 **73** Schreiben des Reichskommissars für die Preisbildung an den Reichs- und

Preussischen Wirtschaftsminister vom 4. Januar 1938 **74** Vermerk aus der Reichskanzlei vom 5. Januar 1938 **75** Schreiben der Geschäftsgruppe Arbeitseinsatz beim Beauftragten für den Vierjahresplan an den Reichs- und Preussischen Wirtschaftsminister vom 9. Januar 1938. **76** Vermerk aus der Reichskanzlei vom 4. Februar 1938 **77** Schreiben des Beauftragten für den Vierjahresplan an den Chef des Oberkommandos der Wehrmacht vom 19. Februar 1938 **78** Vermerk aus der Reichskanzlei vom 25. Februar/ 1. April 1938 **79** Erlass des Präsidenten der Reichsanstalt an die Landesarbeitsämter und Arbeitsämter vom 17. Mai 1938 **80** Anordung über den Arbeitseinsatz von Arbeitern und technischen Angestellten in der Bauwirtschaft vom 30. Mai 1938 **81** Erlass des Präsidenten der Reichsanstalt an die Landesarbeitsämter und Arbeitsämter vom 2. Juni 1938 **82** Erlass des Präsidenten der Reichsanstalt an die Landesarbeitsämter und Arbeitsämter vom 5. Dezember 1938 **83** Schreiben des Beauftragten für den Vierjahresplan an den Generalinspektor für das deutsche Strassenwesen vom 9. Dezember 1938 **84** Schreiben der Kriegsmarinewerft Kiel an das Oberkommando der Kriegsmarine vom 12. Oktober 1939

Kapitel XI
Die besonderen arbeitspolitischen Probleme des Bergbaus (November 1937 bis Juni 1939)

85 Schreiben des Vorsitzenden des Vorstandes der Gelsenkirchener Bergwerks-AG an Oberberghauptmann Schlattmann vom 16. November 1937 **86** Statistische Tabelle: Förderanteil je verfahrene Schicht bei der Gelsenkirchener Bergwerks-AG, 1931–1937 **87** Verordnung zur Erhöhung der Förderleistung und des Leistungslohnes im Bergbau vom 2. März 1939 **88** Schreiben der Geschäftsgruppe Arbeitseinsatz beim Beauftragten für den Vierjahresplan an den Beauftragten für den Vierjahresplan, z. H. Staatssekretärs Körner, vom 17. Mai 1939 **89** Vermerk, ohne Datum und Briefkopf (wahrscheinlich aus dem Reichs- und Preussischen Wirtschaftsministerium, Anfang Juni 1939) **90** Vermerk, ohne Datum und Briefkopf (wahrscheinlich aus dem Reichs- und Preussischen Arbeitsministerium, Anfang Juni 1939) **91** Vermerk, ohne Datum und Briefkopf (wahrscheinlich aus dem Reichs- und Preussischen Wirtschaftsministerium), über eine Besprechung am 19. Juni 1939 **92** Statistische Tabelle: Steinkohlenförderung 1913–1940 **93** Statistische Tabelle: Förderanteil und Verdienste je verfahrene Schicht in den Steinkohlenrevieren 1929–1940

Kapitel XII
Die soziale und wirtschaftliche Entwicklung im ersten Halbjahr 1938

94 Schreiben des Reichs- und Preussischen Arbeitsministers an den Chef der Reichskanzlei vom 12. Februar 1938 **95** Lagebericht des Geheimen Staatspolizeiamtes II A für den Monat Februar 1938 (Auszug) **96** Auszug aus den Monatsberichten der Reichstreuhänder der Arbeit für die Monate Januar und Februar 1938 **97** Schreiben des Reichs- und Preussischen Wirtschaftsministers an den Reichs- und Preussischen Arbeitsminister und an das Zentralbüro der DAF vom 6. Mai 1938 **98** Schreiben des Reichsarbeitsministers an den Reichswirtschaftsminister vom 7. Juni 1938 **99** Vermerk aus dem Reichsarbeitsministerium, ohne Datum (wahrscheinlich Januar 1938) **100** Bericht des Statistischen Reichsamtes über die Entwicklung der tatsächlichen Arbeitsverdienste in den ersten Monaten des Jahres 1938 (Auszug) **101** Anordnung zur Regelung des Arbeitseinsatzes in einzelnen Betrieben vom 1. März 1938 **102** Schreiben des Reichs- und Preussischen Arbeitsministers an den Chef der Reichskanzlei vom 16. März 1938 **103** Bericht der Geheimen Staatspolizeistelle Wihelmshaven an das Geheime Staatspolizeiamt vom 28. April 1938 **104** Auszug aus den Monatsberichten der Reichstreuhänder der Arbeit für die Monate März und April 1938 **105** Schreiben des Reichs- und Preussischen Arbeitsministers an den Chef der Reichskanzlei vom 23. Mai 1938 **106** Lagebericht der Geheimen Staatspolizeistelle Braunschweig an das Geheime Staatspolizeiamt für den Monat Mai 1938 **107** Schreiben des Reichsarbeitsministers an den Chef der Reichskanzlei vom 24. Juni 1938 **108** Auszug aus den Monatsberichten der Reichstreuhänder der Arbeit für die Monate Mai und Juni 1938 **109** Vermerk aus der Reichskanzlei vom 26. August 1938

Kapitel XIII
Dienstpflicht

110 Verordnung zur Sicherstellung des Kräftebedarfs für Aufgaben von besonderer staatspolitischer Bedeutung vom 22. Juni 1938 **111** Anordung zur Durchführung der Verordnung zur Sicherstellung des Kräftebedarfs für Aufgaben von besonderer staatspolitischer Bedeutung vom 27. Juni 1938 **112** Erlass der Geschäftsgruppe Arbeitseinsatz beim Beauftragten für den Vierjahresplan an die Präsidenten der Landesarbeitsämter vom 22. Juli 1938 **113** Schreiben des Präsidenten des

Appendix

Landesarbeitsamts Sachsen an den Generalstaatsanwalt beim Oberlandesgericht Dresden vom 5. August 1938 **114** Rede Görings auf der 6. Jahrestagung der DAF am 10. September 1938 (Auszug) **115** Die Lage der Dienstverpflichteten beim "Bauvorhaben West" **116** Bericht der Staatspolizeistelle Saarbrücken and das Geheime Staatspolizeiamt vom 29. November 1938 **117** Bericht der Staatspolizeistelle Aachen an das Geheime Staatspolizeiamt vom 3. Juni 1939 **118** Erlass des Reichswirtschaftsministers an die Wehrwirtschaftlichen Abteilungen vom 1. November 1938 **119** Verordung zur Sicherstellung des Kräftebedarfs für Aufgaben von besonderer staatspolitischer Bedeutung vom 13. Februar 1939 **120** Dienstpflicht-Durchführungsanordung vom 2. März 1939 **121** Erlass des Reichsarbeitsministers an die Landesarbeitsämter und Arbeitsämter vom 14. März 1939 **122** Erlass des Reichsarbeitsministers an die Landesarbeitsämter und Arbeitsämter vom 24. April 1939 **123** Bericht der Staatspolizeistelle Dresden an das Geheime Staatspolizeiamt vom 29. June 1939 **124** Erlass des Reichsarbeitsministers an die Landesarbeitsämter und Arbeitsämter vom 11. Juli 1939 **125** Erlass des Reichsarbeitsministers an die Landersarbeitsämter u. a. vom 9. Mai 1939 **126** Erlass des Reichsarbeitsministers an die Landesarbeitsämter und Arbeitsämter vom 30. April 1939 **127** Schreiben des Reichsarbeitsministers an den Reichsleiter der DAF vom 13. Januar 1940

Kapitel XIV
Die Anfänge der staatlichen Lohnpolitik

128 Schreiben des Reichskommissars für die Preisbildung and den Beauftragten für den Vierjahresplan vom 12. Dezember 1937. Anlage: Entwurf eines zweiten Gesetzes zur Durchführung des Vierjahresplans **129** Vermerk aus der Reichskanzlei vom 5. Januar 1938 **130** Vermerk aus dem Reichsarbeitsministerium, ohne Datum (wahrscheinlich Mitte Januar 1938) **131** Schreiben des Reichs- und Preussischen Arbeitsministers an den Beauftragten für den Vierjahresplan vom 21. Januar 1939. Anlage: vier Entwürfe **132** Bericht des Statistischen Reichsamts über die Entwicklung der tatsächlichen Arbeitsverdienste im 2. Vierteljahr 1938 **133** Verordnung über die Lohngestaltung vom 25. Juni 1938 **134** Proklamation des Führers auf dem Reichsparteitag der NSDAP am 6. September 1938 (Auszug) **135** Rede Görings auf der 6. Jahrestagung der DAF am 10. September 1938 (Auszug) **136** Auszug aus den Sozialberichten der Reichstreuhänder der Arbeit für das 3. Vierteljahr 1938

Kapitel XV
Die soziale und wirtschaftliche Entwicklung im zweiten Halbjahr 1938

Kapitel XVI
Der Stand der wirtschaftlichen und sozialen Kriegsvorbereitungen Ende 1938

Kapitel XVII

Die soziale und wirtschaftliche Entwicklung im ersten Vierteljahr 1939

154 Schreiben des Reichsarbeitsministers an den Chef der Reichskanzlei vom 4. Februar 1939 **155** Lagebericht der Staatspolizeistelle Lüneburg für das 1. Vierteljahr 1939 (Auszug) **156** Auszug aus den sozialpolitischen Berichten der Reichstreuhänder der Arbeit für das 1. Vierteljahr 1939 **157** Lagebericht der Staatspolizeistelle Berlin für das 1. Vierteljahr 1939 (Auszug) **158** Zweite Durchführungsanordung zur Verordnung zur Sicherstellung des Kräftebedarfs für Aufgaben von besonderer staatspolitischer Bedeutung (Beschränkung des Arbeitsplatzwechsels) vom 10. März 1939, mit Durchführungserlass vom 15. März 1939 **159** Schreiben des Reichsministers und Chefs der Reichskanzlei an den Reichskommissar für die Preisbildung vom 1. Juli 1939

Kapitel XVIII

Die 'Schubladengesetze' – sozialpolitische Vorbereitungen für den Kriegsfall 1936–1939

160 Protokoll über eine Besprechung am 14. August 1936 über Kriegssteuern **161** Schreiben des Reichs- und Preussischen Arbeitsministers an den Präsidenten des Reichsbankdirektoriums vom 29. August 1936 **162** Vermerk über eine Besprechung am 17. November 1936 über den Entwurf von Kriegssteuergesetzen **163** Schreiben des Reichs- und Preussischen Arbeitsministers an den Präsidenten des Reichsbankdirektoriums vom 3. Juli 1937 **164** Vermerk über die 4. Sitzung des Arbeitsausschusses I des Unterausschusses für den sozialen Ausgleich der Kriegsmassnahmen am 3. September 1938 **165** Bericht über die Arbeiten des Arbeitsausschusses I des Unterausschusses für den sozialen Ausgleich der Kriegsmassnahmen vom 4. November 1938 **166** Bericht von Major Gutscher (Wehrwirtschaftsstab) an den Chef der Amtsgruppe Wehrwirtschaftsstab vom 28. November 1938 **167** Schreiben des Reichsarbeitsministers an den Führungsstab des Generalbevollmächtigten für die Wirtschaft vom 19. Mai 1939 **168** Schreiben des Chefs des Oberkommandos der Wehrmacht an den Generalbevollmächtigten für die Wirtschaft vom 15. Juli 1939 **169** Schreiben des Vorsitzenden des Arbeitsausschusses I des Unterausschusses für den sozialen Ausgleich der Kriegsmassnahmen an die Mitglieder des Arbeitsausschusses vom 9. August 1939 **170** Schnellbrief des Generalbevollmächtigten für die Wirtschaft an die Mitglieder des Unterausschusses für den sozialen Ausgleich der Kriegsmassnahmen vom 22. August 1939 **171** Vortragsnotiz für den Chef der Amtsgruppe Wehrwirtschaftsstab vom 24. August 1939 **172** Vermerk des Reichswirtschaftsministers vom 23. August 1939 **173** Erlass des Reichsarbeitsministers an die Reichstreuhänder der Arbeit vom 23. August 1939

Kapitel XIX
Die wirtschafts- und sozialpolitische Gesetzgebung bei Kriegsbeginn

174 Rede Görings in den Rheinmetall-Borsig-Werken, Berlin, am 9. September 1939 (Auszug) **175** Dritte Verordnung zur Sicherstellung des Kräftebedarfs für Aufgaben von besonderer staatspolitischer Bedeutung (Notdienstverordnung) vom 15. Oktober 1938 **176** Verordnung zur Abänderung und Ergänzung von Vorschriften auf dem Gebiete des Arbeitsrechts vom 1. September 1939 **177** Verordnung über die Beschränkung des Arbeitsplatzwechsels vom 1. September 1939 **178** Erlass des Reichsarbeitsministers über die Neuregelung der Beschränkung des Arbeitsplatzwechsels vom 13. September 1939 **179** Verordnung zur Änderung von Vorschriften über Arbeitseinsatz und Arbeitslosenhilfe vom 1. September 1939 **180** Erlass des Chefs der Sicherheitspolizei an die Leiter aller Staatspolizei(leit)stellen vom 3. September 1939 **181** Tagesbericht der Staatspolizeileitstelle München vom 6. September 1939 **182** Erlass des Chefs der Sicherheitspolizei und des Sicherheitsdienstes an alle Staatspolizei(leit)stellen vom 20. September 1939 **183** Anordnung über Unterstützung für Dienstverpflichtete vom 4. September 1939 **184** Erlass des Reichsarbeitsministers zur Durchführung der Anordnung über Unterstützung für Dienstverpflichtete vom 30. September 1939 **185** Kriegswirtschaftsverordnung vom 4. September 1939 (Auszug) **186** Anordnung des Reichstreuhänders der Arbeit für das Wirtschaftsgebiet Brandenburg vom 2. Oktober 1939

Kapitel XX
Die Durchführung der Kriegswirtschaftsverordnung

A. Preise und Löhne

187 Erlass des Reichskommissars für die Preisbildung an den Leiter der Reichswirtschaftskammer vom 9. September 1939 **188** Schreiben des

Kapitel XXI
Der weiche Kurs (Oktober bis Dezember 1939)

Erlass des Reichsarbeitsministers an die Reichstreuhänder der Arbeit vom 21. November 1939 **211** Pressenotiz des Reichsarbeitsministers vom 21. November 1939 **212** Erlass des Reichsarbeitsministers an die Reichstreuhänder der Arbeit vom 2. März 1940. Anlage: Bericht and den Beauftragten für den Vierjahresplan **213** Vermerk aus dem Geheimen Staatspolizeiamt vom 4. Oktober 1939 **214** Schreiben des Chefs der Sicherheitspolizei an den Generalbauinspektor für die Neugestaltung der Reichshauptstadt vom 9. Oktober 1939 **215** Vermerk aus dem Reichssicherheitshauptamt vom 4. November 1939 **216** Bekanntmachung des Reichstreuhanders der Arbeit für das Wirtschaftsgebiet Brandenburg vom 2. November 1939 **217** Tagesbericht der Staatspolizeileitstelle München vom 18. Oktober 1939 **218** Bericht des Reichsverteidigungskommissars für den Wehrkreis III (Berlin) an den Generalbevollmächtigten für die Wirtschaft vom 27. Oktober 1939 **219** Tagesbericht der Staatspolizeileitstelle München vom 4. November 1939 **220** Bekanntmachung des Reichstreuhänders der Arbeit für das Wirtschaftsgebiet Brandenburg vom 25. Dezember 1939 **221** Lagebericht des Führungsstabes Wirtschaft in Dresden vom 10. November 1939 (Auszug) **222** Lagebericht des Führungsstabes Wirtschaft in Wiesbaden vom 10. November 1939 (Auszug) **223** Bericht zur innenpolitischen Lage vom 15. November 1939 (Auszug) **224** Niederschrift über eine Ressortbesprechung beim Generalbevollmächtigten für die Wirtschaft am 10. November 1939 **225** Vermerk über eine Besprechung beim Generalbevollmächtigten für die Wirtschaft am 10. November 1939 **226** Niederschrift über die Sitzung des Ministerrats für die Reichsverteidigung am 15. November 1939 (Auszug) **227** Verordnung zur Ergänzung des Abschnitts III der Kriegswirtschaftsverordnung vom 16. November 1939 **228** Anordnung über die Wiedereinführung von Urlaub vom 17. November 1939 **229** Aufruf des Reichsleiters der Deutschen Arbeitsfront an alle Schaffenden Grossdeutschlands vom 19. November 1939 **230** Bericht des Reichstreuhänders der Arbeit für das Wirtschaftsgebiet Sudetenland an den Reichsarbeitsminister vom 20. November 1939 **231** Erlass des Reichsarbeitsministers an den Reichstreuhänder der Arbeit für das Wirtschaftsgebiet Sudetenland vom 21. November 1939 **232** Lagebericht des Führungsstabes Wirtschaft in Dresden vom 24. November 1939 (Auszug) **233** Schreiben des Reichsministers des Innern an den Reichsarbeitsminister vom 28. November 1939 **234** Bericht zur innenpolitischen Lage vom 6. Dezember 1939 (Auszug) **235** Verordnung über den Arbeitsschutz vom 12. Dezember 1939 **236** Anordnung zur Durchführung der Verordnung über den Arbeitsschutz vom 14. Januar 1940 **237** Pressenotiz des Reichsfinanzministeriums vom 20. Dezember 1939 **238** Erlass des Reichsarbeitsministers an den

Reichstreuhänder der Arbeit für das Wirtschaftsgebiet Thüringen vom 18. Januar 1940 **239** Meldungen aus dem Reich (Bericht zur innenpolitischen Lage) vom 2. Februar 1940 (Auszug) **240** Erlass des Reichsarbeitsministers an die Präsidenten der Landesarbeitsämter vom 24. November 1939 **241** Zweiter Erlass zur Durchführung der Anordnung über Unterstützung für Dienstverpflichtete vom 12. Dezember 1939 **242** Meldungen aus dem Reich (Bericht zur innenpolitischen Lage) vom 8. Januar 1940 (Auszug) **243** Lagebericht des Generalstaatsanwalts in Stettin vom 30. März 1940 (Auszug) **244** Schreiben des Generalstaatsanwalts beim Kammergericht Berlin an den Reichsminister der Justiz vom 1. April 1940

Statistischer Anhang

Bibliography

[Editor's note: Archival records are listed according to their location at the time of the book's first publication in 1977, and do not reflect reorganizations that may have taken place since then. Books are listed in the editions cited in the original text; information on English translations or new editions is included where appropriate, in brackets following the main entry. The bibliography also includes all works cited in the new parts of the text.]

1. Unpublished Sources

Sources are listed here by archive and by file collection, not by the individual numbers of the files consulted for this study. A full list of the latter may be found in *Arbeiterklasse und Volksgemeinschaft*, but the following are the most important individual files used:

BA Koblenz, R 43 II, file 528: Extracts from the reports of the Trustees of Labour, 1936–9; file 533: Regular reports of the Reich Labour Ministry to the Reich Chancellery, 1936–9; file 542: Wage statistics, 1935–8.

BA/MA Freiburg, WiIF, file 176: Summaries of the reports of War Economy Inspectors, 1938–9; file 319: Economic and social contingency planning for mobilization, 1936–9; file 1917: Survey by the Reich Industry Group of the structure of the German industrial labour force, 1936–8.

DZA Potsdam, Reich Economic Ministry, file 10296: Detailed minutes of the monthly conferences of the Trustees of Labour, 1935–6; file 10401: Social policy measures in the first weeks of the war, 1939.

(1) Bundesarchiv Koblenz (BA):
R2 Reichsfinanzministerium
R 22 Reichsjustizministerium
R 26 Vierjahresplan
R 41 Reichsarbeitsministerium
R 43 II Reichskanzlei
R 58 Zentrale Polizeibehörden (Geheime Staatspolizei, etc.)
R 1010 Lokale Polizeibehörden

Bibliography

(2) Bundesarchiv/Militärarchiv Freiburg i. Br. (BA/MA):
WIF 5 Wehrwirtschaftsstab im Reichskriegsministerium/OKW
WO 1–8 Einzelne Wehrwirtschaftsinspektionen
WO 8 Kriegstagebücher der Wehrwirtschaftsinspektionen

(3) Deutsches Zentralarchiv Postdam (DZA):
RAM Reichsarbeitsministerium
RWM Reichswirtschaftsministerium
RMdI Reichsministerium des Innern
VJP Vierjahresplan
GIDS Generalinspektor für das deutsche Strassenwesen
RAB Reichsautobahndirektion
Reichsarbeitskammer
IG Farben

(4) Geheimes Preussiches Staatsarchiv (Stiftung Preussischer Kulturbesitz), Berlin-Dahlem (GPSA):
(The Reich records listed below have now been transferred to Koblenz.)
Rep. 77 Preussisches Ministerium des Innern
Rep. 90 Preussisches Staatsministerium
Rep. 316 Reichswirtschaftsministerium
Rep. 318 Reichsarbeitsministerium
Rep. 320 Reichsministerium des Innern
Rep. 335 Nürnberger Kriegsverbrecherprozesse: IG Farben

(5) Zentrales parteiarchiv im Institut für Marxismus-Leninismus beim Zentralkomitee der Sozialistischen Einheitspartei Deutschlands (IML/ZPA):
St. 3 Miscellaneous Gestapo files

(6) Berlin Document Center (BDC):
All extant personal files of the most important civil servants and DAF functionaries in the field of social policy.

(7) Deutsches Industrie-Institut Köln:
Minor collections from the archives of the Reichsverband/Reichsstand der deutschen Industrie and the Reichsgruppe Industrie.

(8) Gutehoffnungshütte Sterkrade AG (Oberhausen): Historisches Archiv (GHH/HA):
400 101

(9) VEB Filmfabrik ORWO- (ehem. Agfa) Wolfen: Betriebsarchiv Wolfen

2. Official Publications

Akten zur deutschen auswärtigen Politik 1918–1945, Series D: 1937–1945
  (Baden-Baden 1950ff.)
*Amtliches Mitteilungsblatt des Reichstreuhänders der Arbeit für das
  Wirtschaftsgebiet Brandenburg*, 1938–9
Amtliches Nachrichtenblatt der DAF, Berlin 1935ff.
Arbeitertum, Berlin 1931ff.
Der Arbeitseinsatz im Deutschen Reich, 1939ff. (Reichsanstalt)

Arbeitswissenschaftliches Institut der Deutschen Arbeitsfront, *Lohnpolitik: Ein
  Bestandteil der Gesamtpolitik* (Jan. 1936)
_____, *Die echte Rationalisierung* (Aug. 1936)
_____, *Lebenshaltung* (Mar. 1937)
_____, *Die Facharbeiterfrage im Vierjahresplan* (Sept. 1937)
_____, *Politische Maßstäbe der Lohnbildung* (Feb. 1938)
_____, *Die Landarbeiterfrage* (May 1938)
_____, *Das Anlernverhältnis* (June 1938)
_____, *Arbeit, Volk und Staat* (1st half-year, 1938)
_____, *Wandlungen in der wirtschaftlichen Dynamik seit 1933* (July 1938)
_____, *Die Regelung des Akkordrichtlohnes in Tarifordnungen* (July 1938)
_____, *Ermüdung, Arbeitsgestaltung, Leistungssteigerung* (Oct. 1938)
_____, *Arbeit, Volk und Staat* (2nd half-year, 1938)
_____, *Das Bedaux-System* (1939)
_____, *Die Ernährungslage im Winter 1938–1939* (mid-Jan. 1939)
_____, *Die Grundsätze der Gestaltung der Lohn- und Arbeitsbedingungen*
  (Jan. 1939)
_____, *Die Berücksichtigung des Stammestums bei der industriellen Um- und
  Neuansiedlung als gemeinschaftspsychologisches Problem* (June 1939)
_____, *Arbeit, Volk und Staat* (1st half-year, 1939)
_____, *Die Regelung der Arbeitsbedingungen in den Tarifordnungen* (July 1939)
_____, *Die Lohnpolitik im Weltkrieg 1914–1918* (Sept. 1939)
_____, *Betriebliche Sozialleistungen in der Kriegswirtschaft* (end Sept. 1939)
_____, *Zur lohnpolitische Lage* (Oct. 1939)
_____, *Wirtschafts- und Sozialberichte* (mid-Jan. 1940)
_____, *Zahlen zur gegenwärtigen reichsgesetzlichen Alters- und
  Invalidenversicherung* (June 1940)
_____, *Die Belastung des Arbeitsverdienstes durch Abgaben vom Einkommen*
  (end Aug. 1940)
_____, *Die Sozialstruktur des Gaues Württemberg-Hohenzollern* (Sept. 1940)
_____, *Materialien zum Ost-West Gefälle* (Oct. 1940)
_____, *Zur Problematik einer Reichslohnordnung* (Dec. 1940)
_____, *Wirtschafts- und Sozialberichte* (end Jan. 1941)
_____, *Kritische Bilanz der nationalsozialistischen Sozialpolitik* (Autumn 1943)
(All the above memoranda of the Arbeitswissenschaftliches Institut of the DAF
were published in manuscript, most designated as 'confidential/for official use

only'. Copies are held by, among others, the DZA Potsdam and the Institut für Zeitgeschichte, Munich.)

Arbeitswissenschaftliches Institut der DAF, *Jahrbücher* (Verlag der DAF, Berlin 1936–1940/1)

———, *Sozialpolitik zwischen zwei Kriegen in Deutschland, Frankreich und England* (Berlin 1940)

———, *Die Stellung der Sozialpolitik in der europäischen Ordnung* (Berlin 1943)

Das Archiv. Nachschlagewerk für Politik, Wirtschaft, Kultur, Bewegung, Staat, Volk (Berlin 1934ff.)

Ärtzeblatt für Berlin, 1937–1939

Berlin in Zahlen, ed. Statistisches Amt der Stadt Berlin, 1947

Deutsche Arbeitskorrespondenz (Sonderdienst der nationalsozialistischen Parteikorrespondenz; amtliche Korrespondenz der DAF, der NS-Gemeinschaft 'Kraft durch Freude' und der Reichsarbeitskammer)

Deutsche Sozialpolitik, Bericht der Deutschen Arbeitsfront, Zentralbüro, Sozialamt, 30.6 to 31.8.1937 (Berlin 1937)

Deutsche Sozialpolitik, Bericht der Deutschen Arbeitsfront, Zentralbüro, Sozialamt, 1.1 to 31.12. 1938 (Berlin 1939)

Documents on British Foreign Policy, 1919–1939, Third Series (London 1949ff.)

Fünf Jahre Arbeit an den Strassen Adolf Hitlers, pub. Generalinspektor für das deutsche Strassenwesen, ed. Waldemar Wucher (Berlin 1938)

History of the Second World War: Statistical Digest of the War, UK Civil Series (London 1951)

International Labour Office, *Studies and Reports*, series A, no. 33: Studies on International Relations I (Geneva 1930); series A, no. 35: Studies on International Relations II (Geneva 1932); series B, no. 18: The Social Aspects of Rationalization (Geneva 1931)

Internationaler Militärgerichtshof, Nürnberg: Index, Documents in Evidence, vols. 24–42 (Nuremberg 1949)

Jahresberichte der Gewerbeaufsichtsbeamten und Bergbehörden (Berlin 1932ff.)

Jahrbuch der deutschen Sozialversicherung, 1939

National Industrial Conference Board, *The Rationalization of German Industry* (New York 1931)

Organisation der Deutschen Arbeitsfront und der NS-Gemeinschaft 'Kraft durch Freude' (Berlin/Leipzig n.d. [1934])

Organisationsbuch der NSDAP (Munich 1938)

Der Parteitag der Arbeit vom 6. bis 13. September 1937. Offizieller Bericht über den Verlauf des Reichsparteitages mit sämtlichen Kongressreden (Munich 1938)

Der Parteitag Grossdeutschlands: offizieller Bericht (Munich 1939)

Reichsarbeitsblatt, parts I-V, 1932–41

Reichsarbeitsministerium, *Deutsche Sozialpolitik 1918–1928* (Berlin 1929)

Reichsgesetzblatt, part I, 1932–41

Reichsgesundheitsblatt, 1937–41

Reichskuratorium für Wirtschaftlichkeit, *Der Mensch und der Rationalisierung* (Jena 1931)

Reichsorganisationsleiter der NSDAP (ed.), *Die Berufserziehung in der Deutschen Arbeitsfront. Leistungsbericht des Amtes für Berufserziehung und Betriebsführung für das Jahr 1937* (Leipzig 1938)

'*Schönheit der Arbeit im Bergbau*', ed. Amt 'Schönheit der Arbeit' (Berlin 1941)

Schulthess' Europäischer Geschichtskalender, ed. Ulrich Thürauf (Munich 1933)

Statistisches Jahrbuch für das Deutsche Reich, 1931–39/40

Der Vierjahresplan. Zeitschrift für nationalsozialistische Wirtschaftspolitik (Berlin 1937–9)

Wege zur Behebung des Facharbeitermangels. Veröffentlichungen des Reichsstandes der Deutschen Industrie, no. 61 (Berlin 1934)

Wirtschaft und Statistik, ed. Statistisches Reichsamt (Berlin 1938–40)

'*Work and Joy*' – *World Congress: German Reports, Rome 1938 – XVI* (Berlin 1938)

3. Books

Abel, Karl-Dietrich, *Presselenkung im NS-Staat. Eine Studie zur Geschichte der Publizistik in der nationalsozialistischen Zeit*, Berlin, 1968.

Abel, Theodore, *The Nazi Movement: Why Hitler Came into Power*, New York, 1938. [Cambridge, Mass., 1986]

Abendroth, Wolfgang (ed.), O. Bauer, H. Marcuse, A. Rosenberg, *Faschismus und Kapitalismus. Theorien über die sozialen Ursprünge und die Funktion des Faschismus*, Frankfurt am Main, 1967. [1972]

Adorno, Theodor W. and Walter Dirks (eds.), *Betriebsklima. Eine industriesoziologische Untersuchung aus dem Ruhrgebiet (Frankfurter Beiträge zur Soziologie*, vol. 3), Frankfurt am Main, 1955

Allen, William Sheridan, '*Das haben wir nicht gewollt!' Die nationalsozialistische Machtergreifung in einer Kleinstadt 1930–1935*, Gütersloh, 1966. [*The Nazi Seizure of Power: The Experience of a Single Town*, New York, 1984]

Anderson, Evelyn, *Hammer or Anvil. The Story of the German Working-Class Movement*, London, 1945 [New York, 1973]

Andrexel, Ruth, *Staatsfinanzen, Rüstung, Krieg*, East Berlin, 1968

Arendt, Hannah, *Elemente und Ursprünge totaler Herrschaft*, Frankfurt am Main, 1962. [*The Origins of Totalitarianism*, New York, 1951]

———, *Eichmann in Jerusalem. Ein Bericht von der Banalität des Bösen*, Munich, 1964 [*Eichmann in Jerusalem*, Harmondsworth, 1977]

Armeson, Robert B., *Total Warfare and Compulsory Labour*, The Hague, 1965

Bibliography

Arndt, Heinz Wolfgang, *Economic Lessons of the 1930s*, rev. edn, London, 1970 [Royal Institute of International Affairs, 1986]

Arnhold, Karl, *Arbeitsdienstpolitik*, Düsseldorf, 1932

―――, *Das Ringen um die Arbeitsidee*, Berlin, 1938

―――, *Lerne, Leiste, Führe*, Dresden, 1942

Aronson, Shlomo, *Reinhard Heydrich und die Frühgeschichte von Gestapo und SD*, Stuttgart, 1971

Axmann, Artur, *Der Reichsberufswettkampf*, Berlin, 1938

Backhaus, H.-G., H.-D. Bahr, G. Brandt, F. Eberle, W. Euchner, C. Helberger, E. Hennig, J. Hirsch, E.T. Mohl, W. Müller, O. Negt, H. Reichelt, G. Schäfer and A. Schmidt (eds.), *Gesellschaft. Beiträge zur Marxschen Theorie*, vol. 6, Frankfurt am Main, 1976

Bakke, Edward Wight, *The Unemployed Man*, London, 1933 [New York, 1989]

Bartov, Omer, *The Eastern Front, 1941–1945. German Troops and the Barbarization of Warfare*, London, 1985

―――, *Hitler's Army. Soldiers, Nazis, and War in the Third Reich*, New York/Oxford, 1991

Bauer, Christian H., *Das Lied vom Westwall – Ein Zeitbild vom deutschen Frontarbeiter*, Stuttgart, n.d.

Bäumer, Peter C., *Das Deutsche Institut für technische Arbeitsschulung*, Munich, 1930

Bednarek, Horst, *Die Gewerkschaftspolitik der KPD 1935–1939*, East Berlin, 1969

Behrens, F., Walther Kolbe and Hans Marssloff (eds.), *Der Vierjahresplan: eine Sammlung der amtlichen Bestimmungen*, Berlin, 1937

Beier, Gerhard, *Das Lehrstück vom 1. und 2. Mai 1933*, Frankfurt am Main/Cologne, 1975

Beike, Heinz, *Betriebsarchive sagen aus: der Kampf der Arbeiter der Filmfabrik Agfa Wolfen*, Leuna/Merseburg, 1961

Bennecke, Heinrich, *Hitler und die SA*, Munich/Vienna, 1962

―――, *Wirtschaftliche Depression und politischer Radikalismus*, Munich/Vienna 1968; expanded edn, Munich/Vienna, 1970

Bennett, Edward W., *Germany and the Diplomacy of the Financial Crisis, 1931*, Cambridge, Mass., 1962

Bernhardt, Walter, *Die deutsche Aufrüstung 1934–1939. Militärische und politische Konzeptionen und ihre Einschätzung durch die Alliierten*, Frankfurt am Main, 1969

Beynon, Huw, *Working for Ford*, Harmondsworth, 1973

Bewley, Charles, *Hermann Göring*, Göttingen 1956/New York, 1962

Biallas, Hans and Gerhard Starcke (ed.), *Leipzig, das Nürnberg der Deutschen Arbeitsfront*, Munich, 1935

Biermann, Otto *et al.*, *Deutsche Gemeinschaftsarbeit. Geschichte, Idee und Bau des Westwalls*, ed. DAF, N.S.G. 'Kraft durch Freude' and Reichsamt Deutsches Volksbildungswerk, Stuttgart, n.d. [1940]

Bilanz des Zweiten Weltkrieges. Erkenntnisse und Verpflichtungen für die

Bibliography

Zukunft, Oldenburg/Hamburg, 1953

Birkenfeld, Wolfgang, *Der synthetische Treibstoff 1933–1945. Ein Beitrag zur nationalsozialistischen Wirtschafts- und Rüstungspolitik (Studien und Dokumente zur Geschichte des Zweiten Weltkrieges*, vol. 8), Göttingen/ Berlin/Frankfurt am Main, 1964

Blauner, Robert, *Alienation and Freedom. The Factory Worker and His Industry*, Chicago/London, 1964

Bloch, Charles, *Hitler und die europäischen Mächte 1933–1934. Kontinuität oder Bruch?*, Frankfurt am Main, 1966

_____, *Die SA und die Krise des NS-Regimes 1934*, Frankfurt am Main, 1970

Bludau, Kuno, *Nationalsozialismus und Genossenschaften*, Hanover, 1968

Boberach, Heinz (ed.), *Meldungen aus dem Reich. Auswahl aus den geheimen Lageberichten des Sicherheitsdienstes der SS 1939–1944*, Neuwied/ Berlin 1965 [*Meldungen aus dem Reich 1938–1945: die geheime Lageberichte des Sicherheitsdienstes der SS*, Herrsching, 1984]

Bock, Gisela, *Zwangssterilisation im Nationalsozialismus. Studien zur Rassenpolitik und Frauenpolitik*, Opladen, 1988

Böhnke, Wilfired, *Die NSDAP im Ruhrgebiet 1920–1933*, Bonn/Bad Godesberg, 1974

Boelcke, Willi A., ed., *Kriegspropaganda 1939–1941. Geheime Minister-konferenzen im Reichspropagandaministerium*, Stuttgart, 1966

_____, (ed.), *'Wollt Ihr den totalen Krieg?' Die geheimen Goebbels-Konferenzen 1939–1943*, Stuttgart, 1967

_____, (ed.), *Deutschlands Rüstung im Zweiten Weltkrieg. Hitlers Konferenzen mit Albert Speer 1942–1945*, Frankfurt am Main, 1969

Bohn, Willi, *Stuttgart Geheim! Ein dokumentarischer Bericht*, Frankfurt am Main, 1969

Bollmus, Reinhard, *Das Amt Rosenberg und seine Gegner. Studien zum Machtkampf im nationalsozialistischen Herrschaftssystem*, Stuttgart, 1970

Borkin, Joseph and Charles A. Welsh, *Germany's Master Plan*, New York, n.d

Born, Karl Erich, *Die deutsche Bankenkrise 1931. Finanzen und Politik*, Munich, 1967

Bottomore, Thomas Barton, *Classes in Modern Society*, London, 1965 [London, 1991]

Boveri, Margret, *Wir lügen alle. Eine Hauptstadtzeitung unter Hitler*, Olten/ Freiburg i. Br., 1965

Bracher, Karl Dietrich, *Die Auflösung der Weimarer Republik. Eine Studie zum Problem des Machtverfalls in der Demokratie*, 3rd edn, Villingen, 1960 [Düsseldorf, 1984]

_____, *Die deutsche Diktatur. Entstehung, Struktur, Folgen des Nationalsozialismus*, Cologne/Berlin 1969. [*The German Dictatorship: The Origins, Structure and Consequences of National Socialism*, New York, 1980]

_____, Wolfgang Sauer and Gerhard Schulz, *Die nationalsozialistische*

Machtergreifung. Studien zur Errichtung des totalitären Herrschafts-sytems in Deutschland 1933–1934, Cologne/Opladen, 1960 [Frankfurt am Main, 1983]

Brady, Robert Alexander, *The Rationalization Movement in German Industry. A Study in the Evolution of Economic Planning*, Berkeley, 1933 [New York, 1974]

———, *The Spirit and Structure of German Fascism*, London, 1937 [New York, 1971]

Braeutigam, Harald, *Das Wirtschaftssytem des Nationalsozialismus*, Berlin, 1932

Bramsted, Ernest K., *Goebbels and National Socialist Propaganda 1925–1945*, London, 1965

Brentano, Bernard von, *Der Beginn der Barberei in Deutschland*, Berlin, 1932

Bretschneider, Heike, *Der Widerstand gegen den Nationalsozialismus in München 1933–1945*, Munich, 1968

Briefs, Goetz, *The Proletariat, A Challenge to Western Civilization*, New York/London 1937, [New York, 1975]

Brockway, Fenner and Frederic Mullally, *Death Pays a Dividend*, London, 1944

Broszat, Martin, *Nationalsozialistische Polenpolitik 1939–1945*, Frankfurt am Main, 1965

———, *Der Staat Hitlers*, Munich, 1969 [*The Hitler State*, London, 1981]

———, (ed.), *Bayern in der NS-Zeit*, 6 vols., Munich/Vienna, 1977–83

Brown, A. J., *Applied Economics: Aspects of the World Economy in War and Peace*, London, 1947

Brügelmann, Hermann, *Politische Ökonomie in kritischen Jahren. Die Friedrich-List-Gesellschaft e. V. von 1925–1935*, Tübingen, 1956

Brüning, Heinrich, *Memoiren 1918–1934*, Stuttgart, 1970

Bry, Gerhard, *Wages in Germany 1871–1945*, Princeton, NJ, 1960

Buchheim, Hans, Martin Broszat, Hans-Adolf Jacobsen and Helmut Krausnick, *Anatomie des SS-Staates*, 2 vols., Olten/Freiburg i. Br., 1965 [*Anatomy of the SS State*, London, 1968]

Bühler, Theodor, *Von der Utopie zum Sozialstaat*, Berlin/Stuttgart, 1942

———, *Deutsche Sozialwirtschaft*, Berlin, 1943

Bullock, Alan, *Hitler: A Study in Tyranny*, Harmondsworth, 1962

———, *The Life and Times of Ernest Bevin: Minister of Labour 1940–1945*, vol. 2, London, 1967

Burden, Hamilton T., *Die programmierte Nation. Die Nürnberger Reichsparteitage*, Gütersloh, 1967 [*The Nuremberg Party Rallies 1923–39*, London, 1967]

Bürgdorfer, Friedrich (ed.), *Die Statistik in Deutschland nach ihrem heutigen Stand. Ehrengabe für Friedrich Zahn*, 2 vols., Berlin, 1940

Burhenne, Karl, *Werner Siemens als Sozialpolitiker*, Munich, 1932

Caplow, Theodore, *The Sociology of Work*, New York, 1954 [Westport, Conn., 1978]

Carr, William, *Arms, Autarky and Aggression: A Study of German Foreign*

Policy 1933–1939, London, 1972

Carroll, Berenice A., *Design for Total War: Arms and Economics in the Third Reich*, The Hague, 1968

Cohn, Norman, *Warrant for Genocide*, London, 1967 [Chico, Cal., 1981]

Cole, G. D. H., *A History of Socialist Thought*, vol. 5: *Socialism and Fascism 1931–1939*, London, 1961

Conway, J. S., *The Nazi Persecution of the Churches 1933–1945*, London, 1968

Conze, Werner and Hans Raupach (eds.), *Die Staats- und Wirtschaftskrise des Deutschen Reichs 1929–1933*, Stuttgart, 1967

Corni, Gustavo, *Hitler and the Peasants: Agrarian Policy of the Third Reich, 1930–1939*, New York/Oxford/Munich, 1990

Czichon, Eberhard, *Wer verhalf Hitler zur Macht? Zum Anteil der deutschen Industrie an der Zerstörung der Weimarer Republik*, Cologne, 1967 [Cologne, 1976]

———, *Hermann Josef Abs. Porträt eines Kreuzritters des Kapitals*, East Berlin, 1969

———, *Der Bankier und die Macht. Hermann Josef Abs in der deutschen Politik*, Cologne, 1970

Daeschner, L., *Die Deutsche Arbeitsfront*, Munich, 1934

Dahrendorf, Ralf, *Gesellschaft und Demokratie in Deutschland*, Munich, 1965 [*Society and Democracy in Germany*, Westport, Conn., 1980]

Dallin, Alexander, *Deutsche Herrschaft in Russland 1941–1945. Eine Studie über Besatzungspolitik*, Düsseldorf, 1958 [*German Rule in Russia, 1941–1945*, London 1961, 1981]

David, F. [pseud.?], *Ist der NSDAP eine sozialistische Partei?* Vienna/Zürich/Berlin, 1933

Deist, Wilhelm, *The Wehrmacht and German Rearmament*, London, 1981

———, Manfred Messerschmidt, Hans-Erich Volkmann and Wolfram Wette, *Das deutsche Reich und der Zweite Weltkrieg*, Stuttgart, 1979

vol. 1: *Ursachen und Voraussetzungen der Deutschen Kriegspolitik*

Dessauer, Friedrich, *Im Kampf mit der Wirtschaftskrise*, Frankfurt am Main, 1932

———, and Franz Fetzer, *Krisenwende?*, Frankfurt am Main, 1932

Deutsch, Harold C., *Verschwörung gegen den Krieg. Der Widerstand in den Jahren 1939–1940*, Munich, 1969 [*The Conspiracy against Hitler in the Twilight War*, Minneapolis, Minn., 1968]

Deutscher Textilarbeiterverband (ed.), *Mein Arbeitstag – Mein Wochenende. 150 Berichte von Textilarbeiterinnen*, Berlin, 1930

Deutschland-Berichte der Sozialdemokratischen Partei Deutschlands (Sopade), 1934–1940, 7 vols., Salzhausen/Frankfurt am Main, 1980

Devons, Ely, *Essays in Economics*, London, 1961 [Westport, Conn., 1981]

Didier, F., *Europa arbeitet in Deutschland*, Berlin, 1943

Diekmann, Hildemarie, *Johannes Popitz. Entwicklung und Wirksamkeit in der Zeit der Weimarer Republik*, Berlin, 1960

Diehl-Thiele, Peter, *Partei und Staat im Dritten Reich*, Munich, 1969

Diels, Rudolf, *Lucifer ante Portas. Zwischen Severing und Heydrich*, Zürich, n.d [1950]

Donay, Eduard, *Die Beziehung zwischen Herkunft und Beruf auf Grund einer statistischen Erhebung in der Dortmünder Bevölkerung*, Essen, 1941

Drechsler, Hermann, *Aktenstaub – Aus dem Tagebuch eines Wohlfahrtsdezernenten*, Berlin, 1932

Drechsler, Karl *et. al.*, (eds.), *Monopole und Staat in Deutschland 1917–1945*, East Berlin, 1966

Dröge, Franz, *Der zerredete Widerstand. Soziologie und Publizistik des Gerüchts im 2. Weltkrieg*, Düsseldorf, 1970

Drucker, Peter F., *The End of Economic Man: The Origins of Totalitarianism*, London, 1940 [New York, 1969]

Dülffer, Jost, *Weimar, Hitler und die Marine. Reichspolitik und Flottenbau 1920–1939*, Düsseldorf, 1973

Duhnke, Horst, *Die KPD von 1933–1945*, Cologne, 1972

Durkheim, Emile, *Suicide*, London, 1952 [London, 1979]

Edinger, Lewis J., *German Exile Politics. The Social Democratic Executive Committee in the Nazi Era*, Berkeley, Cal., 1956

Eichholtz, Dietrich, *Geschichte der deutschen Kriegswirtschaft 1939–1945*, 2 vols., East Berlin, 1971–85

―――, and Wolfgang Schumann (eds.), *Anatomie des Krieges. Neue Dokumente über die Rolle des deutschen Monopolkapitals bei der Vorbereitung und Durchführung des zweiten Weltkrieges*, East Berlin, 1969.

Einzig, Paul, *In the Centre of Things*, London, 1960

Engel, H. and J. Eckert (eds.), *Die Sozialversicherung im Dritten Reich*, Berlin, 1937

Engelmann, Horst, *Sie blieben standhaft – der antifaschistische Widerstandskampf in Dessau*, Dessau, 1965

Erbe, René, *Die nationalsozialistische Wirtschaftspolitik 1933–1939 im Lichte der modernen Theorie*, Zürich, 1958

Esenwein-Rothe, Ingeborg, *Die Wirtschaftsverbände von 1933 bis 1945*, Berlin, 1965

Esters, Helmut and Hans Pelger, *Gewerkschafter im Widerstand*, Hanover, 1967 [Bonn, 1983]

Facius, Friedrich, *Wirtschaft und Staat. Die Entwicklung der staatlichen Wirtschaftsverwaltung in Deutschland vom 17. Jahrhundert bis 1945*, Boppard, 1959

Fallada, Hans, *Jeder stirbt für sich allein*, Frankfurt am Main, 1964. [Reinbek bei Hamburg, 1989]

Fauvel-Rouif, D. (ed.), *Mouvements ouvriers et dépression économique de 1919 à 1939*, Assen/van Gorcum, 1966

Federau, Fritz, *Der Zweite Weltkrieg. Seine Finanzierung in Deutschland*, Tübingen, 1962

Feldman, Gerald, D., *Army, Industry and Labor in Germany 1914–1918*, Princeton, NJ, 1966, [Providence/Oxford, 1992]

Bibliography

Fest, Joachim C., *Das Gesicht des Dritten Reiches. Profile einer totalitären Herrschaft*, Munich, 1963 [*The Face of the Third Reich*, London, 1979]

Feuersenger, Marianne (ed.), *Gibt es noch ein Proletariat?* Frankfurt am Main, 1962

Fischer, Wolfram and Peter Czada, *Die Wirtschaftspolitik Deutschlands 1918–1945*, rev. edn, Cologne/Opladen, 1968

Flack, Werner, *Wir bauen am Westwall*, Oldenburg/Berlin, 1939

Flannery, Harry W., *Assignment to Berlin*, London, 1942

Flechtheim, Ossip K., *Die KPD in der Weimarer Republik*, rev. edn, Frankfurt am Main, 1969 [Hamburg, 1986]

Först, Walter, *Robert Lehr als Oberbürgermeister. Ein Kapitel deutscher Kommunalpolitik*, Düsseldorf/Vienna, 1962

Forstmeier, Friedrich and Hans-Erich Volkmann (eds.), *Wirtschaft und Rüstung am Vorabend des Zweiten Weltkrieges*, Düsseldorf, 1975

Fraenkel, Ernst, *The Dual State: A Contribution to the Theory of Dictatorship*, London/New York/Toronto, 1941 [New York, 1969]

Fried, Ferdinand, *Die soziale Revolution*, Leipzig, 1942

Friedrich-Ebert-Stiftung, (ed.), *Stand und Problematik der Erforschung des Widerstandes gegen des Nationalsozialismus* (Manuscript), Bad Godesberg, 1966.

Friedrichs, Heinz, *Marxismus und Nationalsozialismus in ihrer Bewertung der Arbeit*, Würzburg, 1940

Fritzsche, Rolf (ed.), *Jahrbuch der deutschen Wirtschaft 1937*, Leipzig, 1937

Funcke, L. von, *Der Deutsche Arbeitsdienst*, Munich, 1934

Gamm, Hans-Jochen, *Der Flüsterwitz im Dritten Reich*, Munich, 1963 [Munich, 1990]

Gedye, G. E. R., *Fallen Bastions*, London, 1939 [New York, 1972]

Geer, Johann Sebastian, *Der Markt der geschlossenen Nachfrage. Eine morphologische Studie über die Eisenkontingentierung in Deutschland 1937–1945*, Berlin, 1961

Gehl, Walther, *Der nationalsozialistische Staat*, Breslau, 1933

Geiger, Theodor, *Die soziale Schichtung des deutschen Volkes. Soziographischer Versuch auf statistischer Grundlage*, Stuttgart, 1932 [Stuttgart, 1967]

Geiss, Immanuel and Bernd Jürgen Wendt (eds.), *Deutschland in der Weltpolitik des 19. und 20. Jahrhunderts*, Düsseldorf, 1974

Gemzell, Carl-Axell, *Raeder, Hitler und Skandinavien. Der Kampf für einen maritimen Operationsplan*, Lund/Frankfurt am Main, 1965

Genschel, Helmut, *Die Verdrängung der Juden aus der Wirtschaft im Dritten Reich*, Göttingen, 1966

Georg, Enno, *Die wirtschaftlichen Unternehmungen der SS*, Stuttgart, 1963

Gereke, Günther, *Ich war königlich-preussischer Landrat*, East Berlin, 1970

Gerhardt, Johannes, *Deutsche Arbeits- und Sozialpolitik*, Berlin, 1939

Gerschenkron, Alexander, *Bread and Democracy in Germany*, London, 1944 [Ithaca, NY, 1989]

Bibliography

von Gersdorff, Ursula (ed.), *Frauen im Kriegsdienst 1914–1945*, Stuttgart, 1969

Gilbert, Bentley B., *British Social Policy 1914–1939*, London, 1970

Gilbert, G. M., *Nürnberger Tagebuch*, Frankfurt am Main, 1962 [*Nuremberg Diary*, London, 1948]

Goebbels, Joseph, *Vom Kaiserhof zur Reichskanzlei. Eine historische Darstellung in Tagebuchblättern*, 22nd edn, Munich 1937 [*My Part in Germany's Fight*, New York, 1979]

———, *Die Zeit ohne Beispiel. Reden und Aufsätze aus den Jahren 1939–1941*, Munich, 1941

———, *Diaries*, (ed.), Louis P. Lochner, London, 1948

von Gönner, R. (ed.), *Spaten und Ähre. Das Handbuch der deutschen Jugend im Reichsarbeitsdienst*, Heidelberg, 1937

Gossweiler, Kurt, *Grossbanken, Industriemonopole, Staat: Ökonomie und Politik des staatsmonopolistischen Kapitalismus in Deutschland 1914–1932*, East Berlin, 1971

Göring, Hermann, *Germany Reborn*, London, 1934

———, *Aus Görings Schreibtisch. Ein Dokumentenfund*, (ed.), T. R. Emessen, Berlin, 1947 [Berlin, 1990]

Goffmann, Erving, *Asylums*, New York, 1961 [New York, 1990]

Gritzbach, Erich, *Hermann Göring. Werk und Mensch*, 2nd edn, Munich, 1938 [*Hermann Goering: The Man and His Work*, Decatur, GA, 1980]

Groscurth, Helmuth, *Tagebücher eines Abwehroffiziers 1938–1940. Mit weiteren Dokumenten zur Militäropposition gegen Hitler*, (ed.), Helmut Krausnick and Harold C. Deutsch, Stuttgart, 1970

Gross, Babette, *Willi Münzenberg*, Stuttgart, 1967 [*Willi Münzenberg: A Political Biography*, East Lansing, Mich., 1974]

Gross, Günther, *Der gewerkschaftliche Widerstandskampf der deutschen Arbeiterklasse während der faschistischen Vertrauensräte-Wahlen 1934*, East Berlin, 1962

Grotkopp, Wilhelm, *Die grosse Krise. Lehren aus der Überwindung der Wirtschaftskrise 1929–1932*, Düsseldorf, 1954

Grunberger, Richard, *A Social History of the Third Reich*, London, 1971

Guillebaud, C. W., *The Economic Recovery of Germany: From 1933 to the Incorporation of Austria in March 1938*, London, 1939

———, *The Social Policy of Nazi Germany*, London, 1941 [New York, 1971]

Gumpert, Martin, *Heil Hunger!* New York, 1940

Haag, Lina, *How Long the Night*, London, 1948

Hachtmann, Rüdiger, *Industriearbeit im 'Dritten Reich'. Untersuchungen zu den Lohn- und Arbeitsbedingungen in Deutschland 1933–1945*, Göttingen, 1989

Hadamovsky, Eigen, *Hilfsarbeiter Nr. 50 000*, Munich, 1938

Hagemann, Walter, *Publizistik im Dritten Reich. Ein Beitrag zur Methodik der Massenführung*, Hamburg, 1948

Hale, Oron J., *Presse in der Zwangsjacke 1933–1945*, Düsseldorf, 1965 [*The Captive Press in the Third Reich*, Princeton, NJ, 1964]

Hallgarten, George, W. F., *Hitler, Reichswehr und Industrie*, Frankfurt am Main, 1962

Hamburger, Ludwig, *How Nazi Germany has Mobilized and Controlled Labor*, Washington DC, 1940

Hamel, Iris, *Völkischer Verband und nationale Gewerkschaft. Der Deutschnationale Handlungsgehilfen-Verband 1893–1933*, Frankfurt am Main, 1967

Hartwich, Hans-Hermann, *Arbeitsmarkt, Verbände und Staat 1918–1933. Die öffentliche Bindung unternehemerischer Funktionen in der Weimarer Republik*, Berlin, 1967

Harvey, Oliver, *The Diplomatic Diaries of Oliver Harvey 1937–1940*, ed. John Harvey, London, 1970

Hass, G. and W. Schumann (eds.), *Anatomie der Agression. Neue Dokumente zu den Kriegszielen des faschistischen deutschen Imperialismus*, East Berlin, 1972

Haug, Wolfgang Fritz, *Der hilflose Antifaschismus. Zur Kritik der Vorlesungsreihen über Wissenschaft und NS an den deutschen Universitäten*, Frankfurt am Main, 1967 [Cologne, 1977]

Heberle, Rudolph, *Landbevölkerung und Nationalsozialismus. Eine soziologische Untersuchung der politischen Willensbildung in Schleswig-Holstein 1918 bis 1932*, Stuttgart, 1963

Heer, Hannes, *Burgfrieden oder Klassenkampf. Zur Politik der sozialdemokratischen Gewerkschaften 1930–1933*, Neuwied/Berlin, 1971

Heiber, Helmut (ed.), *Reichsführer!... Briefe an und von Himmler*, Stuttgart, 1968

Heise, Wolfgang, *Aufbruch in die Illusion. Zur Kritik der bürgerlichen Philosophie in Deutschland*, Berlin, 1964

Henderson, Nevile, *Failure of a Mission*, London, 1940

Hennig, Eike, *Thesen zur deutschen Sozial- und Wirtschaftsgeschichte 1933–1938*, Frankfurt am Main, 1973

Herbert, Ulrich, *Fremdarbeiter. Politik und Praxis des 'Ausländer-Einsatzes' in der Kriegswirtschaft des Dritten Reiches*, Berlin/Bonn, 1985

Herbst, Ludolf, *Der Totale Krieg und die Ordnung der Wirtschaft*, Stuttgart, 1982

Hermens, Ferdinand A. and Theodor Schieder (eds.), *Staat, Wirtschaft und Politik in der Weimarer Republik. Festschrift für Heinrich Brüning*, Berlin, 1967

Hersey, Rexford B., *Seele und Gefühl des Arbeiters*, Leipzig, 1935

Herzfelde, Wieland, *John Heartfield. Leben und Werk*, Dresden, 1962, new edn, 1971 [Berlin, 1986]

Heyde, Ludwig, *Abriss der Sozialpolitik*, Leipzig, 1923

Heyen, Franz Josef, (ed.), *Nationalsozialismus im Alltag. Quellen zur Geschichte des Nationalsozialismus vornehmlich im Raum Main-Koblenz-Trier,* Boppard, 1967

Hilberg, Raul, *The Destruction of the European Jews*, London, 1961 [New York, 1985]

Hildebrand, Klaus, *Vom Reich zum Weltreich*, Munich, 1969
———, *Deutsche Aussenpolitik 1933–1945. Kalkül oder Dogma?* Stuttgart, 1971 [Stuttgart, 1990]
Hillgruber, Andreas, *Hitlers Strategie. Politik und Kriegführung 1940–1941*, Frankfurt am Main, 1965 [Munich, 1982]
———, *Staatsmänner und Diplomaten bei Hitler. Vertrauliche Aufzeichnungen über Unterredungen mit Vertretern des Auslandes 1939–1941*, Frankfurt am Main, 1967
———, *Kontinuität und Diskontinuität in der deutschen Aussenpolitik von Bismarck bis Hitler*, Düsseldorf, 1969
Hirschfeld, Gerhard and Lothar Kettenacker (eds.), *Der 'Führerstaat': Mythos und Realität*, Stuttgart, 1981
Hitler, Adolf, *Mein Kampf*, Munich, 1941 [*My Struggle*, London, 1981]
Hitlers Zweites Buch, ed. Gerhard L. Weinberg, Stuttgart, 1961 [*Hitler's Secret Book*, New York, 1983]
———, *Testament*, ed. François Genoud, London, 1961
———, *Reden des Führers*, ed. Erhard Klöss, Munich, 1967
———, *Reden und Proklamationen 1932–1945, kommentiert von einem deutschen Zeitgenossen*, ed. Max Domarus, Würzburg/Neustadt, 1967, [*Adolf Hitler: Speeches and Proclamations, 1932–1945*, vol. 1, Wauconda, Ill., 1990]
Hochmuth, Ursel and Gertrud Meyer, *Streiflichter aus dem Hamburger Widerstand 1933–1945. Berichte und Dokumente*, Frankfurt am Main, 1969 [Frankfurt am Main, 1980]
Hofer, Walther, *Die Entfesselung des Zweiten Weltkrieges. Eine Studie über die internationalen Beziehungen im Sommer 1939* (with documents), 3rd edn., Frankfurt am Main, 1964 [Düsseldorf, 1984].
Höhne, Heinz, *Der Orden unter dem Totenkopf*, Frankfurt am Main, 1969. [*The Order of the Death's Head*, London, 1981]
Hoffmann, Walter G., *Das Wachstum der deutschen Wirtschaft seit der Mitte des 19. Jahrhunderts*, Berlin/Heidelberg/New York, 1965
Hofstätter, R., *Die arbeitende Frau*, Vienna, 1929
Holborn, Hajo (ed.), *Republic to Reich: The Making of the Nazi Revolution*, New York, 1972
Holt, J. B., *German Agricultural Policy 1918–1934*, Chapel Hill, NC, 1936 [New York, 1975]
Holzapfel, Fritz, *Volkswagenwerk – Demagogie und Wahrheit*, Berlin, 1962
Homze, Edward L., *Foreign Labor in Nazi Germany*, Princeton, NJ, 1967
Hortleder, Gerd, *Das Gesellschaftsbild des Ingenieurs. Zum politischen Verhalten der technischen Intelligenz in Deutschland*, Frankfurt am Main, 1970
Huber, Ernst Rudolf, *Die Gestalt des deutschen Sozialismus*, Hamburg, 1931
Hueck, Alfred and Hans Carl Nipperdey, *Das Lehrbuch des Arbeitsrechts*, Mannheim, 1928
Hueck, Alfred, Hans Carl Nipperdey and Rolf Dietz, *Gesetz zur Ordnung der*

nationalen Arbeit, 3rd edn, Munich/Berlin, 1939

Hüttenberger, Peter, *Die Gauleiter. Studie zum Wandel des Machtgefüges in der NSDAP*, Stuttgart, 1969

Hughes, Everett C., *Men and their Work*, London, 1958 [Westport, Conn., 1981]

Hunt, Richard N., *German Democracy 1918–1933*, New Haven, Conn., 1964 [Chicago, Ill., 1970]

Ingham, Geoffrey K., *Size of Industrial Organization and Worker Behaviour*, Cambridge, 1970

Institut für Demoskopie (ed.), *Das Dritte Reich. Eine Studie über Nachwirkungen des Nationalsozialismus*, Allensbach, 1949

Irving, David, *The Rise and Fall of the Luftwaffe: The Life of Erhard Milch*, London, 1973

Jacobsen, Hans-Adolf (ed.), *Dokumente zur Vorgeschichte des Westfeldzuges 1939–1940*, vol. 1, Göttingen/Berlin/Frankfurt, 1956

———, *Fall 'Gelb'*, Wiesbaden, 1957

———, *Der Zweite Weltkrieg. Grundzüge der Politik und Strategie in Dokumenten*, Frankfurt am Main, 1965

———, *Nationalsozialistische Aussenpolitik 1933–1938*, Frankfurt am Main, 1968

Jäckel, Eberhard, *Hitlers Weltanschauung. Entwurf einer Herrschaft*, Tübingen, 1969 [*Hitler's Worldview: A Blueprint for Power*, Cambridge, Mass., 1981]

Jäger, Herbert, *Verbrechen unter totalitärer Herrschaft*, Olten, 1967

Jäger, Jörg-Johannes, *Die wirtschaftliche Abhängigkeit des Dritten Reiches vom Ausland, dargestellt am Beispiel der Stahlindustrie*, Berlin, 1969

Jahnke, Karl-Heinz, *Entscheidungen. Jugend im Widerstand 1933–1945*, Frankfurt am Main, 1970

Janssen, Gregor, *Das Ministerium Speer. Deutschlands Rüstung im Krieg*, Berlin/Frankfurt am Main/Vienna, 1968

Jochmann, Werner, *Nationalsozialismus und Revolution. Ursprung und Geschichte der NSDAP in Hamburg 1922–1933: Dokumente*, Frankfurt am Main, 1963

Jonas, Wolfgang, *Das Leben der Mansfeld-Arbeiter*, Berlin, 1957

Kaftan, K., *Der Kampf um die Autobahnen 1907–1935*, Berlin, 1936

Kahn-Freund, Otto, *Das soziale Ideal des Reichsarbeitsgerichts*, Mannheim, 1931

Kaiser, David, *Economic Diplomacy and the Origins of the Second World War*, Princeton, NJ, 1980

Kaskel, Walter, *Arbeitsrecht*, 3rd edn, Berlin, 1928

Keil, Wilhelm, *Erlebnisse eines Sozialdemokraten*, vol. 2, Stuttgart, 1948

Kele, Max H., *Nazis and Workers. National Socialist Appeals to German Labor 1919–1933*, Chapel Hill, NC, 1972

Kershaw, Ian, *Popular Opinion and Political Dissent in the Third Reich. Bavaria 1933–1945*, Oxford, 1983

———, *The Nazi Dictatorship*, London, 1985

Bibliography

_____, *The Hitler Myth: Image and Reality in the Third Reich*, Oxford, 1987

Kimche, Jon, *The Unfought Battle*, London, 1968

Kindleberger, Charles P., *The World in Depression 1929–1939*, London, 1973 [Harmondsworth, 1987]

Kirkpatrick, Clifford, *Nazi Germany: Its Women and Family Life*, New York, 1938

Klein, Burton H., *Germany's Economic Preparations for War*, Cambridge, Mass., 1959

Klemperer, Victor, *LTI (lingua tertii imperii): Notizbuch eines Philologen*, Darmstadt, 1966 [Leipzig, 1987]

Klose, Werner, *Generation in Gleichschritt. Ein Dokumentarbericht*, Oldenburg/Hamburg, 1964 [Oldenburg, 1982]

Klotzbach, Kurt, *Gegen den Nationalsozialismus. Widerstand und Verfolgung in Dortmund 1930–1945*, Hanover, 1969

Koch, H. W., *The Hitler Youth: Origins and Development, 1922–1945*, London, 1975

Koch, Max Jürgen, *Die Bergarbeiterbewegung im Ruhrgebiet zur Zeit Wilhelms II (1889 bis 1914)*, Düsseldorf, 1954

Kocka, Jürgen, *Klassengesellschaft im Krieg. Deutsche Sozialgeschichte 1914–1918*, Göttingen, 1973. [Frankfurt am Main, 1988; *Facing Total War: German Society 1914–1918*, Leamington Spa/Cambridge, Mass., 1984]

Köhler, Henning, *Arbeitsdienst in Deutschland. Pläne und Verwirklichungsformen bis zur Einführung der Arbeitsdienstpflicht im Jahre 1935*, Berlin, 1967

Kotze, Hildegard von and Helmut Krausnick (eds.), *'Es spricht der Führer'. Sieben exemplarische Hitler-Reden*, Gütersloh, 1966

Krebs, Albert, *Tendenzen und Gestalten der NSDAP. Erinnerungen an die Frühzeit der Partei*, Stuttgart, 1959 [*The Infancy of Nazism: the Memoirs of ex-Gauleiter Albert Krebs 1923–1933*, New York, 1976]

Krieger, Leonard and Fritz Stern (eds.), *The Responsibility of Power. Historical Essays in Honor of Hajo Holborn*, London, 1968

Kroll, Gerhard, *Von der Weltwirtschaftskrise zur Staatskonjunktur*, Berlin, 1958

Kuczynski, Jürgen, *Germany. Economic and Labor Conditions under Fascism*, New York, 1945 [New York, 1968]

_____, *Geschichte der Lage der Arbeiter unter dem Kapitalismus*, vol. 6: *Darstellung der Lage der Arbeiter in Deutschland von 1933 bis 1945*, East Berlin, 1964

Kühn, Erich, *Schafft anständige Kerle*, Berlin, 1939

Kühnl, Reinhard, *Der nationalsozialistische Linke 1925–1930*, Meisenheim am Glan, 1966

Kühr, Herbert, *Parteien und Wahlen im Stadt- und Landkreis Essen in der Zeit der Weimarer Republik*, Düsseldorf, 1973

Lärmer, Karl, *Vom Arbeitszwang zur Zwangsarbeit*, Berlin, 1961

_____, *Die Wahrheit über den Autobahnbau*, Berlin, 1963

Landes, David S., *The Unbound Prometheus: Technological Change and*

Industrial Development in Western Europe from 1759 to the Present,
Cambridge, 1969 [London, 1976]

Langhoff, Wolfgang, *Die Moorsoldaten. 13 Monate Konzentrationslager*,
Zürich, 1935 [Cologne, 1988]

Laum, Bernhard, *Die geschlossene Wirtschaft. Soziologische Grundlegung des
Autarkieproblems*, Tübingen, 1933

Larzarsfeld, Paul, Marie Jahoda and Hans Zeisl, *Die Arbeitslosen von
Marienthal*, Leipzig, 1933. [Frankfurt am Main, 1975; *Marienthal: The
Sociography of an Unemployed Community*, London, 1972]

Leach, Barry A., *German Strategy against Russia, 1939–1941*, Oxford, 1973.

Lebovics, Hermann, *Social Conservatism and the Middle Classes in Germany
1914–1933*, Princeton, NJ, 1969

Lederer, Emil, *Technischer Fortschritt und Arbeitslosigkeit*, Tübingen, 1931
[*Technical Progress and Unemployment: An Enquiry into the Obstacles
to Economic Expansion*, Geneva, International Labour Office, 1938]

Leithäuser, Joachim G., *Wilhelm Leuschner. Ein Leben für die Republik*,
Cologne, 1962

Lend, Evelyn, *The Underground Struggle in Germany*, London, 1938

Leppert-Fögen, Annette, *Die deklassierte Klasse. Studien zur Geschichte und
Ideologie des Kleinbürgertums*, Frankfurt am Main, 1974

Leuner, H. D., *When Compassion Was a Crime*, London, 1966 [London, 1978]

Levy, Hermann, *Industrial Germany: A Study of Its Monopoly Organizations
and Their Control by the State*, Cambridge, 1935 [New York, 1966]

Lewy, Guenter, *The Catholic Church and Nazi Germany*, New York, 1964

Ley, Robert, *Die Deutsche Arbeitsfront. Ihr Werden und ihre Aufgaben*,
Munich, 1934

_____, *Durchbruch der sozialen Ehre*, Berlin, 1935

_____, *Deutschland ist schöner geworden*, Berlin, 1936

_____, *Wir alle helfen dem Führer*, Munich, 1937

_____, *Soldaten der Arbeit*, Munich, 1938

Lindenlaub, Dieter, *Richtungskämpfe im Verein für Sozialpolitik*, 2 vols.,
Wiesbaden, 1967

Lingg, Anton, *Die Verwaltung der Nationalsozialistischen Deutschen
Arbeiterpartei*, 4th edn, Munich, 1941

Link, Werner, *Die amerikanische Stabilisierungspolitik in Deutschland
1921–1932*, Düsseldorf, 1970

Lochner, Louis P., *Die Mächtigen und der Tyrann. Die deutsche Industrie von
Hitler bis Adenauer*, Darmstadt, 1955 [*Tycoons and Tyrant: German
Industry from Hitler to Adenauer*, Chicago, Ill., 1954]

Ludwig, Karl-Heinz, *Technik und Ingenieure im Dritten Reich*, Düsseldorf,
1974 [Düsseldorf, 1981]

Lüdecke, Theodor, *Nationalsozialistische Menschenführung in den Betrieben.
Die Werkzeitung als Mittel der Wirtschaftsführung*, Hamburg, 1934

Lüke, Rolf E., *Von der Stabilisierung zur Krise*, Zürich, 1954

Lukács, Georg, *Von Nietzsche zu Hitler*, Hamburg, 1966

Luther, Hans, *Vor dem Abgrund 1930–1933*, Berlin, 1963

Maier, Charles S., *Recasting Bourgeois Europe: Stabilisation in France, Germany and Italy in the Decade after World World I*, Princeton, NJ, 1975 [Princeton, NJ, 1988]

de Man, Hendrik, *Der Kampf um die Arbeitsfreude. Eine Untersuchung auf Grund der Aussage von 78 Industriearbeitern*, Jena, 1927 [*Joy in Work*, New York, 1977]

Mann, Reinhard, *Protest und Kontrolle im Dritten Reich. Nationalsozialistische Herrschaft im Alltag einer rheinischen Großstadt*, Frankfurt am Main/ New York, 1987

Mannheim, Karl, *Diagnosis of our Time*, London, 1943 [New York, 1986]

Mansfeld, Werner, *Die Ordnung der nationalen Arbeit. Handausgabe mit Erläuterungen*, Berlin, 1941

Mansfeld, W., W. Pohl, G. Steinmann and A. B. Krause, *Die Ordnung der nationalen Arbeit. Kommentar*, Berlin/Leipzig/Mannheim/Munich, 1934

Marcuse, Herbert, *One-Dimensional Man*, Boston, Mass., 1966 [London, 1991]

Marrenbach, Otto (ed.), *Fundamente des Sieges. Die Gesamtarbeit der Deutschen Arbeitsfront von 1933 bis 1940*, 2nd edn, Berlin, 1940

Martin, James Stewart, *All Honorable Men*, Boston, Mass., 1950

Maschmann, Melita, *Fazit*, Stuttgart, 1963. [Munich, 1980; *Account Rendered*, London, 1965]

Mathewson, Stanley B., *Restriction of Output among Unorganized Workers*, Carbondale, Ill./Edwardsville/London/Amsterdam, 1969

Matthias, Erich and Rudolf Morsey (eds.), *Das Ende der Parteien 1933*, Düsseldorf, 1960 [Düsseldorf, 1984]

Mattick, Paul, *Arbeitslosigkeit und Arbeitsbewegung in den USA 1925–1935*, Frankfurt am Main, 1969

Matzerath, Horst, *Nationalsozialismus und kommunale Selbstverwaltung*, Stuttgart, 1970

Mauersberg, Hans, *Deutsche Industrien im Zeitgeschehen eines Jahrhunderts*, Stuttgart, 1966

Mayer, Arno, *Why did the Heavens Not Darken? The 'Final Solution' in History*, New York, 1989

Mayer, Milton, *They Thought They Were Free: The Germans 1933–1945*, Chicago, Ill., 1955 [Chicago, Ill., 1971]

Mayo, Elton, *The Human Problems of an Industrial Civilisation*, New York, 1960 [Salem, NH, 1986]

McCormick, B. J. and E. Owen Smith (eds.), *The Labour Market*, Harmondsworth, 1968

Meerwarth, Rudolf, Adolf Günther and Waldemar Zimmermann, *Die Einwirkung des Krieges auf Bevölkerungsbewegung, Einkommen und Lebenshaltung in Deutschland*, Stuttgart, 1932

Meichner, Fritz, *Wir hämmern den Sieg*, Heidelberg, 1943

Meinck, Gerhard, *Hitler und die deutsche Aufrüstung 1933–1937*, Wiesbaden, 1959

Merkl, Peter H., *Political Violence under the Swastika: 581 Early Nazis*, Princeton, NJ, 1975 [Berkeley, Cal., 1986]

Meystre, Fritz, *Allgemeine Sozialpolitik*, Munich, 1934

Michel, Ernst, *Sozialgeschichte der industriellen Arbeitswelt*, Frankfurt am Main, 1947 [Frankfurt am Main, 1960]

Milatz, Alfred, *Wähler und Wahlen in der Weimarer Republik*, Bonn, 1965

Milward, Alan S., *Die deutsche Kriegswirtschaft 1939–1945*, Stuttgart, 1966 [*The German Economy at War*, London, 1965]

———, *The New Order and the French Economy*, Oxford, 1970

———, *The Fascist Economy in Norway*, Oxford, 1972

———, *War, Economy and Society 1939–1945*, London, 1977

Mommsen, Hans, *Beamtentum im Dritten Reich. Mit ausgewählten Quellen zur nationalsozialistischen Beamtenpolitik*, Stuttgart, 1966

———, Dietmar Petzina and Bernd Weisbrod (eds.), *Industrielles System und politische Entwicklung in der Weimarer Republik*, Düsseldorf, 1974

Moore, Jr, Barrington, *Injustice: The Social Bases of Obedience and Revolt*, London, 1979

Mosse, George L., *The Crisis of German Ideology. Intellectual Origins of the Third Reich*, New York, 1964 [New York, 1981]

Müller, J. Heinz, *Nivellierung und Differenzierung der Arbeitseinkommen in Deutschland seit 1925*, Berlin, 1954

Müller, Oscar (ed.), *Krisis: ein politisches Manifest*, Weimar, 1932

Müller, Willy, *Das soziale Leben im neuen Deutschland unter besonderer Berücksichtigung der Deutschen Arbeitsfront*, Berlin, 1938

Mueller-Hillebrand, Burkhart, *Das Heer 1933–1945*, vol. 1, Darmstadt, 1954; vol. 2, Frankfurt am Main, 1956

Münz, Ludwig (ed.), *Jahrbuch für Sozialpolitik 1937*, Leipzig, 1937

———, and Carl Lehmann, *Führer durch die Behörden und Organisationen*, Berlin, 1934

Münzenberg, Willi, *Braunbuch über Reichstagsbrand und Hitler-Terror*, Basel, 1933 [Frankfurt am Main, 1983]

Nassen, Paul, *Kapital und Arbeit im Dritten Reich*, Berlin, 1933

Nathan, Otto, *The Nazi Economic System. Germany's Mobilization for War*, Durham, NC, 1944 [New York, 1971]

Neuloh, Otto, *Die deutsche Betriebsverfassung und ihre Sozialformen bis zur Mitbestimmung*, Tübingen, 1956

Neumann, Franz, *Behemoth: The Structure and Practice of National Socialism*, New York, 1942 [New York, 1972]

———, *The Democratic and the Authoritarian State*, ed. Herbert Marcuse, Glencoe, Ill., 1957

Neumann, Sigmund, *Permanent Revolution. Totalitarianism in the Age of International Civil War*, 2nd edn, New York, 1965

Nicholls, Anthony and Erich Matthias (ed.), *German Democracy and the Triumph of Hitler*, London, 1971

Niedhart, Gottfried (ed.), *Kriegsbeginn 1939. Entfesselung oder Ausbruch des*

Zweiten Weltkriegs? Darmstadt, 1976

Niethammer, Lutz (ed.), *Lebensgeschichte und Sozialkultur im Ruhrgebiet 1930 bis 1960*, vol.1: *'Die Jahre weiss man nicht, wo man die heute hinsetzen soll.' Faschismuserfahrungen im Ruhrgebiet*; vol. 2: *'Hinterher merkt man, daß es richtig war, daß es schiefgegangen ist. Nachkriegserfahrungen im Ruhrgebiet*; vol. 3: *'Wir kriegen jetzt andere Zeiten'. Auf der Suche nach der Erfahrung des Volkes in nachfaschistischen Ländern*, Berlin/Bonn, 1983–5

――――, Ulrich Borsdorf and Peter Brandt (eds.), *Arbeiterinitiative*, Wuppertal, 1976

Niewyk, Donald L., *Socialist, Anti-Semite, and Jew: German Social Democracy Confronts the Problems of Anti-Semitism, 1918–1933*, Baton Rouge, LA, 1971

Noakes, Jeremy, *The Nazi Party in Lower Saxony 1921–1933*, Oxford, 1971

Nolte, Ernst, *Der Faschismus in seiner Epoche*, Munich, 1963 [Munich, 1979; *Three Faces of Fascism*, London, 1965]

――――, (ed.), *Theorien über den Faschismus*, Cologne, 1967 [Königstein, 1984]

――――, *Der Nationalsozialismus*, Frankfurt am Main Berlin/Vienna, 1970

Nonnenbruch, Fritz, *Die dynamische Wirtschaft*, Munich, 1939

Nove, Alec, *An Economic History of the USSR*, Harmondsworth, 1969 [Harmondsworth, 1989]

Nyomarkay, Joseph, *Charisma and Factionalism in the Nazi Party*, Minneapolis, 1967 [Ann Arbor, Mich., 1990]

Oermann, Joseph and Hans Meuschel, *Die Kriegssteuern (Bücherei des Steuerrechts*, vol. 22), Berlin/Vienna, 1939

Oppenheimer, Max, *Der Fall Vorbote. Zeugnisse des Mannheimer Widerstandes*, Frankfurt am Main, 1969

Orlow, Dietrich, *The History of the Nazi Party*, vol. 1: *1919–1933*; vol. 2: *1933–1945*, Newton Abbott, 1973

Parkin, Frank, *Class Inequality and Political Order*, London, 1971

Paterna, Erich, *et al.*, *Deutschland von 1933 bis 1939*, East Berlin, 1969

Peterson, Edward N., *Hjalmar Schacht. For and Against Hitler*, Boston, Mass., 1954

――――, *The Limits of Hitler's Power*, Princeton, NJ, 1969

Petrick, Fritz, *Zur Sozialen Lage der Arbeiterjugend in Deutschland 1933 bis 1939*, East Berlin, 1974

Petzina, Dietmar, *Autarkiepolitik im Dritten Reich. Der nationalsozialistische Vierjahresplan*, Stuttgart, 1968

Peukert, Detlev, *Die Edelweisspiraten. Protestbewegungen jugendlicher Arbeiter im Dritten Reich*, Cologne, 1980.

――――, *Inside Nazi Germany: Conformity, Opposition and Racism in Everyday Life*, New Haven, Conn., 1987

Pfahlmann, Hans, *Fremdarbeiter und Kriegsgefangene in der deutschen Kriegswirtschaft 1939 bis 1945*, Darmstadt, 1968

Picker, Henry and Percy Ernst Schramm, (eds.), *Hitlers Tischgespräche im*

Bibliography

Führerhauptquartier 1941–1942, Stuttgart, 1963, [Frankfurt am Main, 1989]

Pieper, Josef, *Thesen zur sozialen Politik: Die Grundgedanken des Rundschreibens Quadragesimo Anno*, Freiburg, 1933

The Pilgrim Trust, *Men Without Work*, Cambridge, 1938 [New York, 1968]

Pirker, Theo (ed.), *Komintern und Faschismus 1920–1940. Dokumente zur Geschichte und Theorie des Faschismus*, Stuttgart, 1965

Pius XI, *Rundschreiben über den atheistischen Kommunismus vom 19. März 1937*, Recklingshausen, 1951

Poole, K. E., *German Financial Policies 1932–1939*, Cambridge, Mass., 1939 [New York, 1969]

Postan, M. M., *British War Production. History of the Second World War*, UK, Civil Series, London, 1952

Predöhl, Andreas, *Das Ende der Weltwirtschaftskrise*, Hamburg, 1962

Preller, Ludwig, *Sozialpolitik: Kernfrage des Aufbaues*, 2 vols., Stuttgart, 1947
_____, *Sozialpolitik in der Weimarer Republik*, Stuttgart, 1949 [Düsseldorf, 1978]

Pridham, Geoffrey, *Hitler's Rise to Power: The Nazi Movement in Bavaria, 1923–1933*, London, 1973

Prinz, Michael, *Vom neuen Mittelstand zum Volksgenossen*, Munich, 1986

Pross, Helge, *Manager und Aktionäre in Deutschland*, Frankfurt am Main, 1965

Ramm, Thilo (ed.), *Arbeitsrecht und Politik. Quellentexte 1918–1933*, Neuwied, 1966

Rauschning, Hermann, *Germany's Revolution of Destruction*, London, 1939
_____, *Hitler Speaks*, London, 1939 [London, 1981]
_____, *The Beast from the Abyss*, London, 1941
_____, *Makers of Destruction*, London, 1942

Recker, Marie-Luise, *Nationalsozialistische Sozialpolitik im Zweiten Weltkrieg*, Munich, 1985

Rehberger, Horst, *Die Gleichschaltung des Landes Baden 1932/1933*, Heidelberg, 1966

Reich, Nathan, *Labor Relations in Republican Germany*, London/New York, 1938

Reich, Wilhelm, *What is Class Consciousness?* Copenhagen/Prague/Zürich 1933; new edn, London, 1971
_____, *The Mass Psychology of Fascism*, New York, 1946 [Harmondsworth, 1983]

Reimann, Guenter, *Patents for Hitler*, London, 1945

Reinhardt, Fritz, *Die Arbeitsschlacht der Reichsregierung*, Berlin, 1934

Reinisch, Leonhard (ed.), *Die Zeit ohne Eigenschaften. Eine Bilanz der zwanziger Jahre*, Stuttgart, 1961

Reulecke, Jürgen (ed.), *Arbeiterbewegung an Rhein und Ruhr. Beiträge zur Geschichte der Arbeiterbewegung in Rhe-Westfalen*, Wuppertal, 1974

Reupke, Hans, *Das Wirtschaftssystem des Faschismus*, Berlin, 1930

Rich, Norman, *Hitler's War Aims*. vol. 1: *Ideology, the Nazi State and the*

Course of Expansion, vol. 2: *The Establishment of the New Order*, New York/London, 1974

Richter, Lutz, *Treuhänder der Arbeit*, 2nd edn, Munich, 1934

Riedel, Matthias, *Eisen und Kohle für das Dritte Reich: Paul Pleigers Stellung in der NS-Wirtschaft*, Göttingen, 1973

Riedler, Anton, *Politische Arbeitslehre*, Berlin, 1937

Ringer, Fritz K. (ed.), *The German Inflation of 1923*, New York, 1969

Ritter, Gerhard, *Carl Goerdeler und die deutsche Widerstandsbewegung*, Munich, 1964 [*The German Resistance: Carl Goerdeler's Struggle Against Tyranny*, Freeport, NY, 1970]

Ritter, Gerhard A. (ed.), *Entstehung und Wandel der modernen Gesellschaft. Festschrift für Hans Rosenberg zum 65. Geburtstag*, Berlin, 1970

Roberts, Stephen H., *The House that Hitler Built*, London, 1937 [New York, 1975]

Robertson, E. M., *Hitler's Pre-war Policy and Military Plans 1933–1939*, London, 1969

——, (ed.), *The Origins of the Second World War*, London, 1971 [Basingstoke, 1984]

Rohe, Karl, *Das Reichsbanner Schwarz-Rot-Gold*, Düsseldorf, 1966

Rowney, D. K. and J. Q. Graham (eds.), *Quantitative History*, Homewood, Ill., 1969

Rühle, Gerd, *Das Dritte Reich. Dokumentarische Darstellung des Aufbaus der Nation*, vol. 1, Berlin, 1934

Rupprecht, Adolf, *Wie die Nazis das Eigentum der S.P.D. raubten und zerstörten*, East Berlin, 1960

Sachse, Carola, Tilla Siegel, Hasso Spode and Wolfgang Spohn, *Angst, Belohnung, Zucht und Ordnung*, Opladen, 1982

Saitzew, Manuel (ed.), *Die Arbeitslosigkeit der Gegenwart*, parts 1–3, Munich/Leipzig, 1932–1933

Samhaber, Ernst, *Die neuen Wirtschaftsformen 1914–1920*, Berlin, 1940

Samuel, Raphael (ed.), *People's History and Socialist Theory*, London, 1981

Sarti, Roland, *Fascism and the Industrial Leadership in Italy, 1919–1940: A Study in the Expansion of Private Power under Fascism*, Berkeley, Cal. 1971.

Sauvy, Alfred, *Histoire économique de la France entre les deux guerres,* 3 vols., Paris, 1967 [Paris, 1984]

Schabrod, Karl, *Widerstand an Rhein und Ruhr 1933–1945*, ed. VVN-Landesverband Nordheim-Westfalen, Düsseldorf, 1969

Schacht, Hjalmar, *Abrechnung mit Hitler*, Hamburg, 1949

——, *76 Jahre meines Leben*, Bad Wörishofen, 1953. [*Confessions of 'The Old Wizard': The Autobiography of Hjalmar Horace Greeley Schacht*, Westport, Conn., 1974]

Schäffle, A., *Die Quintessenz des Sozialismus*, Gotha, 1919 [*The Quintessence of Socialism*, London, 1922]

Bibliography

Schauff, Johannes, *Das Wahlverhalten der deutschen Katholiken im Kaiserreich und in der Weimarer Republik*, ed. Rudolf Morsey, Mainz, 1975

Scheffler, Wolfgang, *Judenverfolgung im Dritten Reich*, Frankfurt am Main, 1961

Schieder, Theodor, *Hermann Rauschings 'Gespräche mit Hitler' als Geschichtsquelle*, Opladen, 1972

Schlotterbeck, Friedrich, *The Darker the Night, the Brighter the Stars*, London, 1947

Schmelzer, Janis, *Der Faschismus muss sterben, der Sozialismus wird leben! Der antifaschistisch-demokratische Widerstandskampf der ausländischen Kriegsgefangenen und Deportierten in der Filmfabrik Wolfen 1939–1945*, Wolfen, 1964

Schmelzer, Janis, *Dies war ein Staatsgeheimnis*, Wolfen, n.d

———, *Die Braune Box: Zu den Anfängen der Zusammenarbeit Monopole-Nazismus-Neonazismus*, Wolfen, 1967

Schmidt, Karl T., *German Business Cycles 1924–1933*, New York, 1934 [New York, 1971]

Schmitt, Kurt, *Die Wirtschaft im neuen Reich*, Munich, 1934

Schmitthenner, Walter and Hans Buchheim (eds.), *Der deutsche Widerstand gegen Hitler*, Cologne/Berlin, 1966 [*The German Resistance to Hitler*, London, 1970]

Schoenbaum, David, *Die braune Revolution*, Cologne/Berlin, 1968 [*Hitler's Social Revolution*, New York, 1980]

Schorr, Helmut J., *Adam Stegerwald: Gewerkschaftler und Politiker der ersten deutschen Republik. Ein Beitrag zur Geschichte der christlich-sozialen Bewegung in Deutschland*, Recklingshausen, 1966

Schroeder, Hans-Jürgen, *Deutschland und die Vereinigten Staaten 1933–1939. Wirtschaft und Politik in der Entwicklung des deutsch-amerikanischen Gegensatzes*, Wiesbaden, 1970

Schroeder, Max, *Handbuch des Tarif- und Dienstrechts der Angestellten und Arbeiter im öffentlichen Dienst*, Berlin, 1938

Schüddekopf, Otto-Ernst, *Linke Leute von rechts*, Stuttgart, 1960 [Berlin, 1973]

Schüler, Felix, *Das deutsche Handwerk in der Kriegswirtschaft*, Stuttgart/Berlin, 1941

———, *Das Handwerk im Dritten Reich. Die Gleichschaltung und was danach folgt*, Bad Wörishofen, 1951

Schulz, F. O. H., *Komödie der Freiheit. Die Sozialpolitik der grossen Demokratien*, Vienna, 1940

Schulz, Gerhard, *Aufstieg des Nationalsozialismus. Krise und Revolution in Deutschland*, Frankfurt am Main/Berlin/Vienna, 1975

Schuhmann, Walter and Ludwig Brucker, *Sozialpolitik im neuen Staat*, Berlin, 1934

Schumann, Hans-Gerd, *Nationalsozialismus und Gewerkschaftsbewegung. Die Vernichtung der deutschen Gewerkschaften und der Aufbau der*

Bibliography

'*Deutschen Arbeitsfront*', Hanover/Frankfurt am Main, 1958

Schwarzbart, André, *The Last of the Just*, New York, 1960 [Harmondsworth, 1984]

Schwarzwälder, Herbert, *Die Machtergreifung der NSDAP in Bremen 1933*, Bremen, 1966

Schweitzer, Arthur, *Big Business in the Third Reich*, Bloomington, Ind., 1964.

_____, *Die Nazifierung des Mittelstandes*, Stuttgart, 1970

Schwenger, Rudolf, *Die betriebliche Sozialpolitik im Ruhrkohlenbergbau*, Munich, 1932

_____, *Die betriebliche Sozialpolitik in der westdeutschen Grosseisenindustrie*, Munich, 1934

Seeber, Eva, *Zwangsarbeiter in der faschistischen Kriegswirtschaft*, Berlin, 1964

Seelbach, Hermann, *Das Ende der Gewerkschaften. Aufzeichnungen über den geistigen Zusammenbruch eines Systems*, Berlin, 1934

SED Kreisleitung Eisleben, *Sie trugen das Banner der Nation. Beiträge zum antifachistischen Widerstandskampf im Mansfelder Land*, Eisleben, 1965

SED Kreisleitung VEB Leuna-Werke 'Walter Ulbricht', *Kämpfendes Leuna*, part 1: 1933 bis 1945 (*Geschichte der Fabriken und Werke*, vol. 3), East Berlin, 1961

Seebold, Gustav-Hermann, *Ein Stahlkonzern im Dritten Reich. Der Bochumer Verein 1927–1945*, Wuppertal, 1981

Seldte, Franz, *Sozialpolitik im Dritten Reich*, Berlin, 1935

_____, *Sozialpolitik im Dritten Reich. Neue Beiträge 1936*, Berlin, 1937

_____, *Sozialpolitik im Dritten Reich 1933–1938*, Munich/Berlin, 1939

Sell, Karl, *Der Vertrauensrat*, Munich, 1934

_____, (ed.), *Adolf Hitler und Staatsrat Dr. Ley zum Recht der Arbeit*, Munich, 1933

Sering, Paul [= Richard Löwenthal], *Jenseits des Kapitalismus*, Vienna, 1948 [Berlin, 1977]

Seydewitz, Max, *Civil Life in Wartime Germany*, New York, 1945

Shirer, William L., *Berlin Diary*, London, 1941 [Boston, Mass., 1988]

_____, *The Rise and Fall of the Third Reich: A History of Nazi Germany*, New York, 1960 [London, 1991]

Siebert, Wolfgang (ed.), *Das Recht der Arbeit*, Berlin, 1941

Siegel, Tilla, *Leistung und Lohn in der nationalsozialistischen 'Ordnung der Arbeit'*, Opladen, 1988

Siemering, Hertha, *Deutschlands Jugend in Bevölkerung und Wirtschaft. Eine statistische Untersuchung*, Berlin, 1937

Simpson, Amos E., *Hjalmar Schacht in Perspective*, The Hague/Paris, 1969

Sinzheimer, Hugo and Ernst Fraenkel, *Die Justiz in der Weimarer Republik*, Neuwied/Berlin, 1968

Smelser, Ronald, *Robert Ley. Hitler's Labor Front Leader*, Oxford/New York/Hamburg, 1988

Smith, Howard K., *Last Train from Berlin*, London, 1942 [Berlin/New York, 1962]

Bibliography

Sörgel, Werner, *Metallindustrie und Nationalsozialismus*, Frankfurt am Main, 1965

Sohn-Rethel, Alfred, *Ökonomie und Klassenstruktur des deutschen Faschismus. Aufzeichnungen und Analysen*, Frankfurt am Main, 1973. [*The Economy and Class Structure of German Fascism*, London, 1987]

Sombart, Werner, *Die Zukunft des Kapitalismus*, Berlin, 1932

Sommer, Willi (ed.), *Die Praxis des Arbeitsamtes. Ein Gemeinschaftsarbeit von Angehörigen der Reichsanstalt für Arbeitsvermittlung und Arbeitslosenversicherung*, Berlin/Vienna, 1939

Sonnenberg, L. von and A. Kääb, *Die Volkskartei. Ein Handbuch*, Munich, 1939

Speer, Albert, *Die neue Reichskanzlei*, Munich, n.d. [1939?]

———, *Erinnerungen*, Frankfurt am Main, 1969 [*Inside the Third Reich: Memoirs*, London, 1970]

Spengler, Oswald, *Preussentum und Sozialismus*, Munich, 1921

———, *Jahre der Entscheidung: Deutschland und die weltgeschichtliche Entwicklung*, Munich, 1933 [Munich, 1961]

Starcke, Gerhard, *NSBO und Deutsche Arbeitsfront*, Berlin, 1934

———, *Die Deutsche Arbeitsfront. Eine Darstellung über Zweck, Leistungen und Ziele*, Berlin, 1940

Steinert, Marlis G., *Die 23 Tage der Regierung Dönitz*, Düsseldorf/Vienna, 1967

———, *Hitlers Krieg und die Deutschen. Stimmung und Haltung der deutschen Bevölkerung im Zweiten Weltkrieg*, Düsseldorf/Vienna, 1970. [*Hitlers War and the Germans: Public Mood and Attitude during the Second World War*, Athens, Ohio, 1977]

Stenbock-Fermor, Alexander, *Meine Erlebnisse als Bergarbeiter*, Stuttgart, 1929 [*My Experiences as a Miner*, New York, 1930]

———, Alexander, *Deutschland von unten – Reise durch die proletarische Provinz*, Stuttgart, 1931 [Frankfurt am Main, 1980]

Stephenson, Jill, *Women in Nazi Society*, London, 1975

Stern, J. P., *Ernst Jünger: A Writer of Our Time*, Cambridge, 1975

Sternberg, Fritz, *Germany and a Lightning War*, London, 1938

Sturmthal, Adolf, *Die grosse Krise*, Zürich, 1937

Sturmthal, Adolf, *The Tragedy of European Labour 1918–1939*, London, 1944. [New York, 1970]

Swatek, Dieter, *Unternehmenskonzentration als Ergebnis und Mittel nationalsozialistischer Wirtschaftspolitik*, Berlin, 1972

Sweezy, Maxine Y., *The Structure of the Nazi Economy*, Cambridge, Mass., 1941 [New York, 1968]

Syrup, Friedrich, *Hundert Jahre staatlicher Sozialpolitik 1839–1939*, ed. Julius Scheuble; revised Otto Neuloh, Stuttgart, 1957

———, *Sicherstellung des Kräftebedarfs für Aufgaben von besonderer staatspolitischer Bedeutung*, Berlin/Leipzig/Vienna, 1939

———, *Der Arbeitseinsatz und die Arbeitslosenhilfe in Deutschland*, Berlin, 1936

Tänzler, Fritz, *Aus dem Arbeitsleben Amerikas*, Berlin, 1927

Bibliography

Taylor, A. J. P., *The Origins of the Second World War*, rev. edn, London, 1963 [London, 1985]

Teichova, Alice, *An Economic Background to Munich: International Business and Czechoslovakia 1918–1938*, London, 1974

Textor, Hermann, *Völkische Arbeitseignung und Wirtschaftsstruktur*, Berlin, 1939

Thier, Erich, *Gestaltwandel des Arbeiters im Spiegel seiner Lektüre*, Leipzig, 1939

Thies, Jochen, *Architekt der Weltherrschaft. Die 'Endziele' Hitlers*, Düsseldorf, 1976

Thomas, Georg, *Geschichte der deutschen Wehr- und Rüstungswirtschaft*, ed. Wolfgang Birkenfeld, Boppard, 1966

Thomas, Katherine, *Women in Nazi Germany*, London, 1943

Thöne, Karin, *Entwicklungsstadien und Zweiter Weltkrieg. Ein wirtschaftswissenschaftlicher Beitrag zur Frage der Kriegsursachen*, Berlin, 1974

Thyssen, Fritz, *I Paid Hitler*, London, 1941 [New York, 1972]

Tillich, Paul, *Protestantisches Prinzip und proletarische Situation*, Bonn, 1931

Timpke, Henning (ed.), *Dokumente zur Gleichschaltung des Landes Hamburg 1923*, Frankfurt am Main, 1964

Titmuss, Richard M., *Problems of Social Policy: History of the Second World War*, UK, Civil Series, London, 1950

Todt, Fritz, *Drei Jahre Arbeit an den Straßen Adolf Hitlers*, n.p., 1935

Trevor-Roper, Hugh R. (ed.), *Hitler's Secret Conversations 1941–1944*, New York, 1961 [New York, 1981]

_____, *The Last Days of Hitler*, 2nd edn, London, 1962 [London, 1987]

Trotsky, Leo, *Schriften über Deutschland*, vol. 2, ed. Helmut Dahmer, introd. Ernest Mandel, Frankfurt am Main, 1971

_____, *The Struggle Against Fascism in Germany*, introd. Ernest Mandel, New York, 1971 [Harmondsworth, 1975]

Turner, Henry A., Jr (ed.), *Nazism and the Third Reich*, New York, 1972

_____, *Faschismus and Kapitalismus in Deutschland*, Göttingen, 1972

_____, *Stresemann – Republikaner aus Vernunft*, Berlin/Frankfurt am Main, 1968. [*Stresemann and the Politics of the Weimar Republic*, Princeton, NJ, 1963]

Tyrell, Albrecht (ed.), *Führer befiel ... Selbstzeugnisse aus der 'Kampfzeit' der NSDAP*, Düsseldorf, 1969

Uhlig, Heinrich, *Die Warenhäuser im Dritten Reich*, Cologne/Opladen, 1956

Uhlig, Otto, *Arbeit – amtlich angeboten. Der Mensch auf seinem Markt*, Stuttgart, 1970

Ulbricht, Walter, *et al.*, (eds.), *Geschichte der deutschen Arbeiterbewegung*, vols. 4 and 5, East Berlin, 1966

Unger, Aryeh L., *The Totalitarian Party: Party and People in Nazi Germany and Soviet Russia*, London, 1974

Unterseher, Lutz, *Arbeitsvertrag und innerbetriebliche Herrschaft. Eine historische Untersuchung*, Frankfurt am Main, 1969

Bibliography

Van der Wee, Hermann (ed.), *The Great Depression Revisited: Essays on the Economics of the Thirties*, The Hague, 1972

Varga, Eugen, *Die Krise des Kapitalismus und ihre politischen Folgen*, ed. Elmar Altvater, Frankfurt am Main, 1969

VEB Hydrierwerk Zeitz. Betriebsgeschichte, part 1: 1937–1962, Zeitz, n.d. [1963?]

Vetter, Heinz Oskar (ed.), *Vom Sozialistengesetz zur Mitbestimmung. Zum 100. Geburtstag von Hans Böckler*, Cologne, 1975

Völker, Karl-Heinz, *Die deutsche Luftwaffe 1933–1939. Aufbau, Führung und Rüstung der Luftwaffe sowie die Entwicklung der deutschen Luftkriegstheorie*, Stuttgart, 1967

Vogelsang, Reinhard, *Der Freundeskreis Himmler*, Göttingen/Zürich/Frankfurt am Main, 1972

Vollmer, Bernhard (ed.), *Volksopposition im Polizeistaat. Gestapo- und Regierungsberichte 1934–1936*, Stuttgart, 1957

Wagenführ, Rolf, *Die deutsche Industrie im Kriege 1939–1945*, Berlin, 1955

Wagner, Elisabeth (ed.), *Der Generalquartiermeister. Briefe und Tagebuchaufzeichnungen des Generalquartiermeisters des Heeres, General der Infanterie Eduard Wagner*, Munich/Vienna, 1963

Wehler, Hans-Ulrich (ed.), *Sozialgeschichte Heute. Festschrift für Hans Rosenberg zum 70. Geburtstag*, Göttingen, 1974

Weingartner, Thomas, *Stalin und der Aufstieg Hitlers. Die Deutschlandpolitik der Sowjetunion und der Kommunistischen Internationale 1929–1934*, Berlin, 1970

Weisenborn, *Günther, Der lautlose Aufstand. Bericht über die Widerstandsbewegung des deutschen Volkes 1933–1945*, Hamburg, 1962 [Frankfurt am Main, 1981]

Welter, Erich, *Falsch und richtig planen. Eine kritische Studie über die deutsche Wirtschaftslenkung im 2. Weltkrieg*, Heidelberg, 1954

Wendt, Bernd-Jürgen, *München 1938: England zwischen Hitler und Preussen*, Frankfurt am Main, 1965

———, *Appeasement 1938. Wirtschaftliche Rezession und Mitteleuropa*, Frankfurt am Main, 1966

———, *Economic Appeasement. Handel und Finanz in der britischen Deutschland-Politik 1933–1939*, Düsseldorf, 1971

Werner, Wolfgang Franz, '*Bleib Übrig!' Deutsche Arbeiter in der nationalsozialistischen Kriegswirtschaft*, Düsseldorf, 1983

Werth, Alexander, *The Destiny of France*, London, 1937

Weinstein, Fred, *The Dynamics of Nazism*, New York/London, 1980

Wheaton, Eliot B., *The Nazi Revolution 1933–1935. Prelude to Calamity*, New York, 1968

Wiedemann, Fritz, *Der Mann, der Feldherr werden wollte*, Velbert/Kettwig, 1964

Winkler, Dörte, *Frauenarbeit im 'Dritten Reich'*, Hamburg, 1977

Winkler, Hans-Joachim, *Legenden um Hitler (Zur Politik und Zeitgeschichte, no. 7)*, Berlin, 1961

Winkler, Heinrich August, *Mittelstand, Demokratie und Nationalsozialismus. Die politische Entwicklung von Handwerk und Kleinhandel in der Weimarer Republik*, Cologne, 1972
―――, (ed.), *Organisierter Kapitalismus. Voraussetzungen und Anfänge*, Göttingen, 1974
Winnig, August, *Vom Proletariat zum Arbeitertum*, Hamburg, 1930
―――, *Der weite Weg*, Hamburg, 1932 [Hamburg, 1959]
―――, *Rund um Hitler. Aus zwanzig Jahren – Erfahrungen und Erinnerungen*, London, n.d. [1947?]
―――, *Aus 20 Jahren*, Hamburg, 1951
Winschuh, Josef, *Männer, Traditionen, Signale*, Berlin, 1940
Witt, Friedrich-Wilhelm, *Die Hamburger Sozialdemokratie in der Weimarer Republik*, Hanover, 1971
Wolkersdörfer, Hans (ed.), *Sozialpolitisches Lexikon*, Berlin, 1938
Woolf, S. J. (ed.), *European Fascism*, London, 1968 [London, 1981]
―――, (ed.), *The Nature of Fascism*, London, 1968 [London, 1981]
Woytinski, Wladimir, *Der deutsche Arbeitsmarkt – Ergebnisse der gewerkschaftlichen Arbeitslosenstatistik 1919–1929*, Berlin, 1930
―――, *The Social Consequences of Economic Depression*, London/Geneva, 1936
Wunderlich, Frieda and Ernst Fraenkel, *German Labor Courts*, Chapel Hill, NC, 1948
Wunderlich, Frieda, *Farm Labor in Germany 1820–1945*, Princeton, NJ, 1961
Youngson, A. J., *The British Economy 1920–1957*, London, 1960
Ziebura, Gilbert (ed.), *Grundfragen der deutschen Aussenpolitik seit 1871*, Darmstadt, 1975
Zischka, Anton, *Sieg der Arbeit*, Leipzig, 1941
Zumpe, Lotte, *Wirtschaft und Staat in Deutschland 1933 bis 1945*, East Berlin, 1980

4. Articles and Unpublished Theses

Abendroth, Wolfgang, 'Historische Funktion und Umfang des Widerstandes der Arbeiterbewegung gegen das Dritte Reich', *Festschrift für Otto Brenner zum 60. Geburtstag*, ed. Peter von Oertzen, Frankfurt am Main, 1967
Agnoli, Johannes, 'Zur Faschismus-Diskussion', *Berliner Zeitschrift für Politologie*, vol. 9 (2, 3), 1968
Andic, Süphan and Jindrich Ververka, 'The Growth of Governmental Expenditure in Germany Since Unification', *Finanzarchiv*, new series, vol. 23 (2), January 1964
Anon., 'The Reduction of the Working Week in Germany', *International Labour Review*, vol. XXIX (6), June 1934
Anon, 'The Reform of Workers' Compulsory Pension Insurance in Germany',

Bibliography

International Labour Review, vol. XXXI (3, 4), April/May 1935

Anon, 'Labour Problems in Time of War', *International Labour Review*, vol. XL (5), November 1939

Applegate, Jeffrey M, 'Sociologists and National Socialism: An Historical Study of English Language Writing on the Sociology of National Socialism, 1933–1945', B. Litt. thesis, Oxford, 1974

Das Argument, nos. 30, 32, 33, 41, 47, 58

Bagel-Bohlan, Elke Anja, 'Die industrielle Kriegsvorbereitung in Deutschland von 1936–1939', Ph.D. thesis, Bonn, 1973

Bahne, Siegfried, '"Sozialfaschismus" in Deutschland. Zur Geschichte eines politischen Begriffes', *International Review of Social History*, vol. 10, 1965

Balogh, Thomas, 'The National Economy of Germany', *Economic Journal*, vol. 48, September 1938

———, 'The Economic Background in Germany', *International Affairs*, vol. 18, 1939.

Barkai, Avraham, 'Die Wirtschaftsauffassung der NSDAP', *Aus Politik und Zeitgeschichte: Beilage zur Wochenzeitung Das Parlament*, 1975, no. 9

Baumgart, Winfried, 'Zur Ansprache Hitlers vor den Führern der Wehrmacht am 22. August 1939', *Vierteljahrshefte für Zeitgeschichte*, vol. 16 (2), April 1968

Beier, Gerhard, 'Einheitsgewerkschaft. Zur Geschichte eines organisatorischen Prinzips der deutschen Arbeiterbewegung', *Archiv für Sozialgeschichte*, vol. XIII, 1973

———, 'Zur Entstehung des Führerkreises der vereinigten Gewerkschaften Ende April 1933' (Documentation), *Archiv für Sozialgeschichte*, vol. XV, 1975

Benz, Wolfgang, 'Vom freiwilligen Arbeitsdienst zur Arbeitsdienstpflicht', *Vierteljahrshefte für Zeitgeschichte*, vol. 16 (4), October 1968

Berghahn, Volker R., 'NSDAP und "geistige Führung" der Wehrmacht 1939–1943', *Vierteljahrshefte für Zeitgeschichte*, vol. 17 (1), January 1969

Birkenfeld, Wolfgang, 'Stalin als Wirtschaftspartner Hitlers (1939–1941)', *Vierteljahrschrift für Sozial- und Wirtschaftsgeschichte*, vol. 53, 1966

Blaich, Fritz, 'Wirtschaftspolitik und Wirtschaftsverfassung im Dritten Reich', *Aus Politik und Zeitgeschichte: Beilage zur Wochenzeitung Das Parlament*, 20 February 1971

———, 'Wirtschaft und Rüstung in Deutschland', *Sommer 1939. Die Grossmächte und der europäische Krieg*, ed. Wolfgang Benz and Hermann Graml, Stuttgart, 1979

Bleyer, Wolfgang, 'Der geheime Bericht über die Rüstung des faschistischen Deutschlands vom 27. Januar 1945', *Jahrbuch für Wirtschaftsgeschichte*, 1969, part II

Böhme, Helmut, 'Emil Kirdorf. Überlegungen zu einer Unternehmerbiographie', *Tradition*, vol. 13, 1968

Bibliography

Böker, Karl, 'Entwicklung und Ursachen des Krankenstandes der west-deutschen Arbeiter', *Das Argument*, no. 69, 1971

Bracher, Karl-Dietrich, 'Die Speer-Legende', *Neue Politische Literatur*, vol. XV(4), 1970

Braunthal, Gerard, 'The German Free Trade Unions during the Rise of Nazism', *Journal of Central European Affairs*, vol. 15 (4), 1956

Bridenthal, Renate, 'Beyond Kinder, Kirche, Küche: Weimar Women at Work', *Central European History*, vol. 6 (2), 1973

Broszat, Martin, 'Die Anfänge der Berliner NSDAP 1926/27', *Vierteljahrshefte für Zeitgeschichte*, vol. 8 (1), January 1960

Brozek, Andrzej, 'Ostflucht aus Schlesien (1933 bis 1939)', *Jahrbuch für Wirtschaftsgeschichte*, vol. 8 (1), January 1969, part I

Buhl, Horst, 'Ausgangspunkte und Entwicklungslinien der freiwilligen sozialen Leistungen in industriellen Unternehmungen', Ph.D. thesis, FU Berlin, 1965

Bullock, Alan, 'Hitler and the Origins of the Second World War', *Proceedings of the British Academy*, vol. LIII, 1967.

Burdick, Charles, 'Die deutschen militärischen Planungen gegenüber Frankreich 1933–1938', *Wehrwissenschaftliche Rundschau*, vol. 6 (12), 1964

Caplan, Jane, 'The Civil Servant in the Third Reich', D. Phil. thesis, Oxford, 1973 [*Goverment Without Administration. State and Civil Service in Weimar and Nazi Germany*, Oxford, 1988]

——, 'Theories of Fascism: Nicos Poulantzas as Historian', *History Workshop Journal*, no. 3, 1977.

Castell Rüdenhausen, Adelheid Gräfin zu, '"Nicht mitzuleiden, mitzukämpfen sind wir da!" Nationalsozialistische Volkswohlfahrt im Gau Westfalen-Nord', *Die Reihen fast geschlossen*, ed. Detlev Peukert and Jürgen Reulecke, Wuppertal, 1981

Carnegie, D., 'Some Economic and Social Effects of Rearmament', *International Affairs*, vol. 18, 1939

Childers, Thomas, 'The Social Bases of the National Socialist Vote', *Journal of Contemporary History*, no. 4, October 1976

Chilston, Viscount, 'The Rearmament of Britain, France and Germany down to the Munich Agreement of 30 Sept. 1938', *Survey of International Affairs*, 1938, vol. III, ed. V. M. Toynbee, London, 1953

Cole, Taylor, 'The Evolution of the German Labor Front', *Political Science Quarterly*, vol. 52, 1937.

Crumb, N., 'The Economics of the Third Reich', *Journal of the Royal Statistical Society*, vol. 102, 1939

Cullity, John P., 'The Growth of Governmental Employment in Germany 1882–1950', *Zeitschrift für die gesamte Staatswissenschaft*, vol. 123 (2), April 1967

Czollek, Roswitha, 'Zwangsarbeit und Deportationen für die deutsche Kriegsmaschine in den baltischen Sowjetrepubliken während des Zweiten Weltkrieges', *Jahrbuch für Wirtschaftsgeschichte*, 1970, part II

_____, and Dietrich Eichholtz, 'Zur wirtschaftspolitischen Konzeption des deutschen Imperialismus beim Überfall auf die Sowjetunion', *Jahrbuch für Wirtschaftsgeschichte*, 1968, part I

Deist, Wilhelm, 'Die Aufrüstung der Wehrmacht', Wilhelm Deist, Manfred Messerschmidt, Hans-Erich Volkmann and Wolfram Wette, *Das deutsche Reich und der Zweite Weltkrieg*, Stuttgart, 1979, vol. 1: *Ursachen und Voraussetzungen der Deutschen Kriegspolitik*

Dixon, J. M., 'Gregor Strasser and the Organization of the Nazi Party 1925–1932', Ph.D. thesis, Stanford, 1966

Doering, Dörte, *Die deutsche Aussenwirtschaftspolitik 1933–1935*, Ph.D. thesis, FU Berlin, 1969

Draper, Theodore, 'The Ghost of Social Fascism', *Commentary*, 47, February 1969

Dülffer, Jost, 'Der Beginn des Krieges 1939: Hitler, die innere Krise und das Mächtesystem', *Geschichte und Gesellschaft*, vol. 2 (4), 1976

Eichholtz, Dietrich, 'Probleme einer Wirtschaftsgeschichte des Faschismus in Deutschland', *Jahrbuch für Wirtschaftsgeschichte*, 1963, part III

_____, 'Die IG-Farben-Friedensplanung. Schlüsseldokumente der faschistischen "Neuordnung des europäischen Grossraums"', *Jahrbuch für Wirtschaftsgeschichte*, 1966, part III

_____, 'Zur Lage der deutschen Werktätigen im ersten Kriegsjahr 1939/1940', *Jahrbuch für Wirtschaftsgeschichte*, 1967, part I

_____, 'Zum Anteil des IG-Farben-Konzerns an der Vorbereitung des Zweiten Weltkrieges', *Jahrbuch für Wirtschaftsgeschichte*, 1969, part II

_____, '"Wege zur Entbolschewisierung und Entrussung des Ostraumes". Empfehlungen des IG-Farben-Konzerns für Hitler im Frühjahr 1943', *Jahrbuch für Wirtschaftsgeschichte*, 1970, part II

_____, 'Alte und "neue" Konzeptionen. Bürgerliche Literatur zur Wirtschaftsgeschichte des Faschismus in Deutschland', *Jahrbuch für Wirtschaftsgeschichte*, 1971, part III

_____, 'Manager des staatsmonopolistischen Kapitalismus', *Jahrbuch für Wirtschaftsgeschichte*, 1974, part III

_____, and G. Hass, 'Zu den Ursachen des Zweiten Weltkrieges und den Kriegszielen des deutschen Imperialismus', *Zeitschrift fur Geschichtswissenschaft*, vol. 15, 1967

Emig, Dieter and Rüdiger Zimmermann, 'Das Ende einer Legende: Gewerkschaften, Papen und Schleicher. Gefälschte und echte Protokolle', *Internationale wissenschaftliche Korrespondenz zur Geschichte der deutschen Arbeiterbewegung*, vol. 12 (1), 1976

Eschenburg, Theodor, 'Streiflichter zur Geschichte der Wahlen im Dritten Reich' (Documentation), *Vierteljahrshefte für Zeitgeschichte*, vol. 3 (3), July 1955

Eucken, W., 'On the Theory of the Centrally Administered Economy: An Analysis of the German Experiment', *Economica*, 15, 1948

Farquharson, J. E., 'The NSDAP and Agriculture in Germany 1928–1938',

Ph.D. thesis, Univ. of Kent, Canterbury, 1972. [*The Plough and the Swastika: The NSDAP and Agriculture in Germany 1928–1945*, London/Beverly Hills, 1976]

Feldman, Gerald D., 'The Social and Economic Policies of German Big Business 1918–1929', *American Historical Review*, vol. LXXV (1), October 1969

Fetscher, Iring, 'Die industrielle Gesellschaft und die Ideologie der Nationalsozialisten', *Gesellschaft, Staat, Erziehung*, vol. 7 (1), 1962

———, 'Zur Kritik des sowjetmarxistischen Faschismusbegriffs', *Politische Vierteljahresschrift*, 1962, no. 3

Flanders, Alan, 'Collective Bargaining: a Theoretical Analysis', *British Journal of Industrial Relations*, vol. VI (1), 1968

Friedensburg, Ferdinand, 'Die sowjetischen Kriegslieferungen an das Hitler-Reich', *Vierteljahreshefte für Wirtschaftsforschung*, 1962, no. 4

Gackenholz, Hermann, 'Reichskanzlei 5. November 1937', *Forschungen zu Staat und Verwaltung. Festgabe für Fritz Hartung*, Berlin, 1958

Garraty, John A., 'The New Deal, National Socialism and the Great Depression', *American Historical Review*, vol. 78 (4), 1973

Geck, L.H.A., 'New Trends in Social Policy in Germany', *International Labour Review*, vol. XXXVI (1), July 1937

Gewerkschaftliche Monatshefte, vol. 26 (7), 1975

Geyer, Michael, 'Rüstungsbeschleunigung und Inflation. Zur Inflationsdenkschrift des Oberkommandos der Wehrmacht vom November 1938', *Militärgeschichtliche Mitteilungen*, 1981, no. 2

———, 'Zum Einfluss der nationalsozialistischen Rüstungspolitik auf das Ruhrgebiet', *Rheinische Vierteljahrsblätter*, vol. 45, 1981

———, 'Krieg als Gesellschaftspolitik', *Archiv für Sozialgeschichte*, vol. 36, 1986

Giess, Horst, 'R. Walther Darré und die nationalsozialistische Bauernpolitik in den Jahren 1930 bis 1933', Ph.D. thesis, Frankfurt am Main, 1968

Gossweiler, Kurt, 'Der Übergang von der Weltwirtschaftskrise zur Rüstungskonjunktur in Deutschland 1933/1934', *Jahrbuch für Wirtschaftsgeschichte*, 1968, part II

Grebler, Leo, 'Work Creation Policy in Germany 1932–1935', *International Labour Review*, vol. XXXV (3, 4), March–April 1937

Grumbach, Franz and Heinz König, 'Beschäftigung und Löhne in der deutschen Industriewirtschaft 1888–1954', *Weltwirtschafts-Archiv*, 1957, 1

Grünfeld, J., 'Rationalization and the Employment and Wages of Women in Germany', *International Labour Review*, vol. XXIX (5), May 1934

Gurland, A. R. L., 'Technological Trends and Economic Structure under National Socialism', *Studies in Philosophy and Social Science*, vol. IX (2), 1941

Hachtmann, Rüdiger, 'Von der Klassenharmonie zum regulierten Klassenkampf', *Soziale Bewegungen, Jahrbuch 1: Arbeiterbewegung und Faschismus*, Frankfurt am Main/New York, 1984

Heberle, Rudolf, 'Zur Soziologie der nationalsozialistischen Revolution. Notizen aus dem Jahre 1934', *Vierteljahrshefte für Zeitgeschichte*, vol. 13 (4), October, 1965

Hennig, Eike, 'Industrie und Faschismus', *Neue Politische Literatur*, vol. XV (4), 1970

Herbert, Ulrich, 'Apartheid nebenan. Erinnerungen an die Fremdarbeiter im Ruhrgebiet', *Die Jahre weiss man nicht, wo man die hinsetzen soll' Faschismuserfahrungen im Ruhrgebiet*, ed. Lutz Niethammer, Berlin/Bonn, 1983

———, 'Arbeit und Vernichtung. Ökonomisches Interesse und Primat der "Weltanschauung" im Nationalsozialismus', *Ist der Nationalsozialismus Geschichte?*, ed. Dan Diner, Frankfurt am Main, 1987

Herbst, Ludolf, 'Die Krise des nationalsozialistischen Regimes am Vorabend des Zweiten Weltkrieges und die forcierte Aufrüstung. Eine Kritik', *Vierteljahrshefte für Zeitgeschichte*, vol. 26 (3), July 1983

———, 'Die Mobilmachung der Wirtschaft 1938/39 als Problem des national-sozialistischen Herrschaftssytems', *Sommer 1939. Die Grossmächte und der europäischen Krieg*, ed. Wolfgang Benz and Hermann Graml, Stuttgart, 1979

Hetzer, Gerhard, 'Die Industriestadt Augsburg. Eine Sozialgeschichte der Arbeiteropposition', *Bayern in der NS-Zeit*, ed. Martin Broszat, vol. 3, Munich/Vienna, 1981

Hildebrand, Klaus, 'Monokratie oder Polykratie? Hitlers Herrschaft und das Dritte Reich', *Der 'Führerstaat': Mythos und Realität*, ed. Gerhard Hirschfeld and Lothar Kettenacker, Stuttgart, 1981

Hillgruber, Andreas, 'Forschungsstand und Literatur zum Ausbruch des Zweiten Weltkrieges', *Sommer 1939. Die Grossmächte und der europäische Krieg*, ed. Wolfgang Benz and Hermann Graml, Stuttgart, 1979

Hillman, H., 'The Comparative Strength of the Great Powers', *Survey of International Affairs: The World in March 1939*, ed. A. Toynbee and F. T. Ashton-Gwatkin, London, 1952

Hitler, Adolf, 'Warum musste ein 8. November kommen?', *Deutschlands Erneuerung*, IV, 1924

Hüllbusch, Ursula, 'Gewerkschaften und Staat: Ein Beitrag zur Geschichte der Gewerkschaften zu Anfang und zu Ende der Weimarer Repulik', Ph.D. thesis, Heidelberg, 1958

———, 'Die deutschen Gewerkschaften in der Weltwirtschaftskrise', *Die Staats- und Wirtschaftskrise des Deutschen Reiches 1929/33*, ed. Werner Conze and Hans Raupach, Stuttgart, 1967

Hutton, Graham, 'German Economic Tensions: Causes and Results', *Foreign Affairs*, vol. 17 (3), April 1939

Jäger, Jörg-Johannes, 'Sweden's Iron-Ore Exports to Germany 1933–1944', *Scandinavian Economic History Review*, vol. XV (1, 2), 1967

Jannen, William, Jr, 'National Socialists and Social Mobility', *Journal of Social*

History, vol. 9 (3), Spring 1976

Jeck, Albert, 'The Trends of Income Distribution in West Germany', *The Distribution of National Income*, ed. J. Marchal and B. Ducros, London/New York, 1968

Kaiser, David, 'Germany, "Domestic Crisis" and War in 1939: Comment 1', *Past and Present*, no. 122, February 1989

Karlbom, R., 'Sweden's Iron-Ore Exports to Germany 1933–1944', *Scandinavian Economic History Review*, vol. XIII (1), 1965; vol. XVI (2), 1968

Keese, Dietmar, 'Die volkswirtschaftliche Gesamtgrossen für das Deutsche Reich in den Jahren 1925–1936', *Die Staats- und Wirtschaftskrise des Deutschen Reiches 1929/33*, ed. Werner Conze and Hans Raupach, Stuttgart, 1967

Kettenacker, Lothar, 'Sozialpsychologische Aspekte der Führer-Herrschaft', *Der 'Führerstaat': Mythos und Realität*, ed. Gerhard Hirschfeld and Lothar Kettenacker, Stuttgart, 1981

Kirchberg, Peter, 'Typisierung in der deutschen Kraftfahrzeugindustrie und der Generalbevollmächtigte für das Kraftfahrwesen', *Jahrbuch für Wirtschaftsgeschichte*, 1969, part II

Kluke, Paul, 'Hitler und das Volkswagenprojekt', *Vierteljahrshefte für Zeitgeschichte*, vol. 8 (4), October, 1960

Koehl, R., 'Feudal Aspects of National Socialism', *American Political Science Review*, vol. LIV (4), December 1960

Köhler, Henning, 'Arbeitsbeschaffung, Siedlung und Reparationen in der Schlussphase der Regierung Brüning', *Vierteljahrshefte für Zeitgeschichte*, vol. 17 (3), July 1969

Krause, Heinz, 'Some Aspects of the Problem of the Industrial Workers on the Land', *International Labour Review*, vol. XXXII (6), December 1935

Kutsche, Lothar, 'Die NS-Gemeinschaft "Kraft durch Freude" innerhalb der "Deutschen Arbeitsfront", 1933–1939', paper, TU Hanover, 1974

Livchen, R., 'Wartime Developments in German Wage Policy', *International Labour Review*, vol. XLVI (2), August 1942

Loewenberg, Peter, 'The Psychohistorical Origins of the Nazi Youth Cohort', *American Historical Review*, vol. 76 (5), December 1971

Ludwig-Bühler, Ulrike, 'Im NS-Musterbetrieb. Frauen in einem Textilunternehmen an der Schweizer Grenze', *'Wir kriegen jetzt andere Zeiten'. Auf der Suche nach der Erfahrung des Volkes in nachfaschistischen Länder*, ed. Lutz Niethammer, Berlin/Bonn, 1985

Lükemann, Ulf, 'Der Reichsschatzmeister der NSDAP', Ph.D. thesis, FU Berlin, 1963

Maier, Charles, 'Between Taylorism and Technocracy', *Journal of Contemporary History*, vol. V (2), 1970

Martin, Bernd, 'Friedens-Planungen der multinationalen Grossindustrie (1932 bis 1940) als politische Strategie', *Geschichte und Gesellschaft*, vol. 2 (1), 1976

Mason, Timothy W., 'Some Origins of the Second World War', *Past and Present*, no. 29, December 1964

———, 'Labour in the Third Reich 1933–1939', *Past and Present*, no. 33, April 1966

———, 'Der antifaschistische Widerstand der Arbeiterbewegung im Spiegel der SED-Historiographie', *Das Argument*, no. 43, July 1967

———, 'Women in Germany, 1925–1940: Family, Welfare and Work', *History Workshop – a Journal of Socialist Historians*, nos. 1 and 2, 1976. (Abbreviated version in *Gesellschaft. Beiträge zur Marxschen Theorie*, vol. 6, ed. H. G. Backhaus *et. al.*, Frankfurt am Main, 1976)

———, 'National Socialist Policies towards the German Working Classes 1925 to 1939', D. Phil. thesis, Oxford, 1971

———, 'The Coming of the Nazis', *Times Literary Supplement*, 1 February 1974

———, 'Zur Entstehung des Gesetzes zur Ordnung der nationalen Arbeit vom 20. Januar 1934', *Industrielles System und politische Entwicklung in der Weimarer Republik*, Hans Mommsen, Dietmar Petzina and Bernd Weisbrod (eds.), Düsseldorf, 1974

———, 'Innere Krise und Angriffskrieg 1938/1939', *Wirtschaft und Rüstung am Vorabend des Zweiten Weltkrieges*, ed. Friedrich Forstmeier and Hans-Erich Volkmann, Düsseldorf, 1975

———, 'Zur Funktion des Angriffskrieges', *Grundfragen der deutschen Außenpolititk seit 1871*, ed. Gilbert Ziebura, Darmstadt, 1975

———, 'Open Questions on Nazism', *People's History and Socialist Theory*, ed. Raphael Samuel, London, 1981

———, 'The Workers' Opposition in Nazi Germany', *History Workshop Journal*, no. 11, 1981

———, 'Intention and Explanation: A Current Controversy about the Interpretation of National Socialism', *Der 'Führerstaat': Mythos und Realität*, ed. G. Hirschfeld and L. Kettenacker, Stuttgart, 1981

———, 'Die Bändigung der Arbeiterklasse im nationalsozialistischen Deutschland', *Angst, Belohnung, Zucht und Ordnung*, Carola Sachse *et al.*, Opladen, 1982

———, 'Massenwiderstand ohne Organisation. Streiks im faschistischen Italien und im NS-Deutschland', *Aufstieg des Nationalsozialismus, Untergang der Republik, Zerschlagung der Gewerkschaften*, ed. Ernst Breit, Cologne, 1984

———, 'Gli scioperi del marzo 1943', *L'Italia nella Seconda Guerra Mondiale e nella Resistenza*, ed. F. Tosi, G. Grassi and M. Legnani, Milan, 1988

———, 'Germany, "Domestic Crisis" and War in 1939: Comment 2', *Past and Present*, no. 1, 22, February 1989

Matthias, Erich 'Resistance to National Socialism: The Example of Mannheim', *Past and Present*, no. 45, 1969

Maurette, F., 'A Year of Experiment in France', *International Labour Review*, vol. XXXVI (1), July 1937

Bibliography

Meinck, Gerhard, 'Der Reichsverteidigungsrat', *Wehrwissenschaftliche Rundschau*, 1966, 6

Messerschmidt, Manfred, 'Aussenpolitik und Kriegsvorbereitung', Wilhelm Deist, Manfred Messerschmidt, Hans-Erich Volkmann and Wolfram Wette, *Das deutsche Reich und der Zweite Weltkrieg*, Stuttgart, 1979 vol. 1: *Ursachen und Voraussetzungen der Deutschen Kriegspolitik*

Milward, Alan S., 'German Economic Policy towards France 1942–1944', *Studies in International History*, ed. K. Bourne and D. C. Watt, London 1967

———, 'Could Sweden have stopped the Second World War?', *Scandinavian Economic History Review*, vol. XV (1, 2), 1967

———, 'French Labour and the German Economy', *Economic History Review*, vol. XXIII (2), 1970

Morsch, Günter, 'Streik im "Dritten Reich"', *Vierteljahrshefte für Zeitgeschichte*, vol. 36 (4), October 1988, 4

———, 'Arbeitsniederlegungen im "Dritten Reich". Eine quellenkritische Dokumentation der Jahre 1936 und 1937', Hasso Spode, Heinrich Volkmann, Günter Morsch and Rainer Hüdemann, *Statistik der Streiks und Aussperrungen in Deutschland* (forthcoming)

Mühlberger, Detlef W, 'The Rise of National Socialism in Westphalia 1920–1933', D. Phil. thesis, Univ. of London, 1975

Müller, Klaus-Jürgen, 'Militärpolitik in der Krise. Zur Militärpolitischen Konzeption des deutschen Heeres- Generalstabes 1938', *Deutschen Konservatismus im 19. und 20. Jahrhundert*, ed. Dirk Stegmann, Bernd-Jürgen Wendt and Peter-Christian Witt, Bonn, 1983

Noakes, Jeremy, 'Nazism and Eugenics: The Background to the Nazi Sterilization Law of 14 July 1933', *Ideas Into Politics*, ed. R. J. Bullen, H. Pogge von Strandmann and A. Polonsky, London, 1984

Nolte, Ernst, 'Zur Phänomenologie des Faschismus', *Vierteljahrshefte für Zeitgeschichte*, vol. 10 (4), October 1962

van Ooyen, Wilhelm, 'Die Errichtung des Vertrauenstrates', D. Jur. thesis, Cologne, 1938

Overy, R. J., 'Transportation and Rearmament in the Third Reich', *Historical Journal*, vol. XVI (2), 1973

———, 'Hitler's War and the German Economy: A Reinterpretation', *Economic History Review*, 2nd ser., vol. 35 (2), 1982

———, 'Germany, "Domestic Crisis" and War in 1939', *Past and Present*, no. 116, August 1987

———, '"Blitzkriegswirtschaft"? Finanz, Lebensstandard und Arbeitseinsatz in Deutschland 1939–1945', *Vierteljahrshefte für Zeitgeschichte*, vol. 36 (3), July 1988

———, 'Germany, "Domestic Crisis" and War in 1939: Reply', *Past and Present*, no. 122, February 1989

Parsons, Talcott, 'Some Sociological Aspects of the Fascist Movements', in T. Parsons, *Essays in Sociological Theory*, Glencoe, Ill., 1964

————, 'Democracy and Social Structure in Pre-Nazi Germany', in T. Parsons, *Essays in Sociological Theory*, Glencoe Ill., 1964

Pelcovits, N.A., 'The Social Honor Courts of Nazi Germany', *Political Science Quarterly*, vol. 58, 1938

Peterson, E.N., 'The Bureaucracy and the Nazi Party', *Review of Politics*, vol. 28, 1966

Petrick, Fritz, 'Eine Untersuchung zur Beseitigung der Arbeitslosigkeit unter der deutschen Jugend in den Jahren von 1933 bis 1935', *Jahrbuch für Wirtschaftsgeschichte*, 1967, part I

————, '"Jugenddienst" und "Jugendschutz" im faschistischen Deutschland', *Jahrbuch für Wirtschaftsgeschichte*, 1969, part II

Petzina, Dietmar, 'Der nationalsozialistische Vierjahresplan von 1936', Ph.D. thesis, Mannheim, 1965

————, 'Hitler und die deutsche Industrie', *Geschichte in Wissenschaft und Unterricht*, vol. 17, 1966

————, 'Hauptprobleme der deutschen Wirtschaftspolitik 1932/33', *Vierteljahrshefte für Zeitgeschichte*, vol. 15 (1), January 1967

————, 'Materialien zum sozialen und wirtschaftlichen Wandel in Deutschland', *Vierteljahrshefte für Zeitgeschichte*, vol. 17 (3), July 1969

————, 'Germany and the Great Depression', *Journal of Contemporary History*, vol. 4 (4), October 1969

————, 'Die Mobilisierung deutscher Arbeitskräfte vor und während des Zweiten Weltkrieges', *Vierteljahrshefte für Zeitgeschichte*, vol. 18 (4), October 1970

Peukert, Detlev, 'Arbeitslager und Jugend-KZ: die Behandlung "Gemeinschaftsfremder" im Dritten Reich', *Die Reihen fast geschlossen*, ed. Detlev Peukert and Jürgen Reulecke, Wuppertal, 1981

————, 'Das "Dritte Reich" aus der "Alltags"-Perspektive', *Archiv für Sozialgeschichte*, vol. XXVI, 1986

————, 'Alltag und Barbarei. Zur Normalität des Dritten Reiches', *Ist der Nationalsozialismus Geschichte?*, ed. Dan Diner, Frankfurt am Main, 1987.

Radkau, Joachim, 'Entscheidungsprozesse und Entscheidungsdefizite in der deutschen Aussenwirtschaftspolitik 1933–1940', *Geschichte und Gesellschaft*, vol. 2 (1), 1976

Rämisch, Raimund, 'Die berufsständische Verfassung in Theorie und Praxis des Nationalsozialismus', Ph.D. thesis, FU Berlin, 1957

————, 'Der berufsständische Gedanke als Episode in der nationalsozialistischen Politik', *Zeitschrift für Politik*, new series, vol. 4, 1957

Ramm, Thilo, 'Nationalsozialismus und Arbeitsrecht', *Kritische Justiz*, 1968

Reichardt, Hans J., 'Die Deutsche Arbeitsfront', Ph.D. thesis, FU Berlin, 1956

————, 'Neu Beginnen', *Jahrbuch für die Geschichte Mittel- und Ostdeutschlands*, vol. 12, 1963

Saage, Richard, 'Zum Verhältnis von Nationalsozialismus und Industrie', *Aus Politik und Zeitgeschichte: Beilage zur Wochenzeitung Das Parlament*, 9, 1975

Bibliography

Sachse, Carola, 'Hausarbeit im Betrieb. Betriebliche Sozialarbeit unter dem Nationalsozialismus', *Angst, Belohnung, Zucht und Ordnung*, Carola Sachse *et al.*, Opladen, 1982

Salter, Stephen, 'Structures of Consensus and Coercion: Workers' Morale and the Maintenance of Work Discipline, 1939–1945', *Nazi Propaganda*, ed. David Welch, London, 1983

———, 'The Mobilisation of German Labour, 1939–1945', D. Phil. thesis, Oxford, 1983

Sanmann, Horst, 'Daten und Alternativen der deutschen Wirtschafts- und Finanzpolitik in der Ära Brüning', *Hamburger Jahrbuch für Wirtschafts- und Gesellschaftspolitik*, 10, 1965

Sauer, Wolfgang, 'National Socialism: Totalitarianism or Fascism?', *American Historical Review*, vol. LXXIII (2), December 1967

Schafhausen, Kurt, 'Probleme unserer staatlichen Lohnpolitik im Weltkrieg und im neuen Krieg', Ph.D. thesis, Univ. of Cologne, Mönchengladbach, 1941

Schindler, E., 'Handicrafts in Germany', *International Labour Review*, vol. XXXV (1), January 1937

Schlicker, Wolfgang, 'Arbeitsdienst-Bestrebungen des deutschen Monopol-kapitals in der Weimarer Republik unter besonderer Berücksichtigung des Deutschen Instituts für technische Arbeitsschulung', *Jahrbuch für Wirtschaftsgeschichte*, 1971, part III

Schröder, Hans-Jürgen, 'Deutsche Südosteuropapolitik 1929–1936. Zur Kontinuität deutscher Aussenpolitik in der Weltwirtschaftskrise', *Geschichte und Gesellschaft*, vol. 2 (1), 1976

Schwarz, Johannes, 'Wie haben sich die Preise und Preisspannen im national-sozialistischen Festpreissystem gegenüber der früheren freien Preisbildung entwickelt? Eine Untersuchung für Niedersachsen für die Jahre 1927–1936', D. Jur. thesis, Göttingen, 1938

Schweitzer, Arthur, 'Der ursprüngliche Vierjahresplan', *Jahrbücher für Nationalökonomie und Statistik*, vol. 168, 1956

———, 'Die wirtschaftliche Wiederaufrüstung Deutschlands von 1934 bis 1936', *Zeitschrift für die gesamte Staatswissenschaft*, vol. 114 (4), 1958

———, 'Organisierter Kapitalismus und Parteidiktatur 1933–1936', *Schmollers Jahrbuch*, vol. 79 (1), 1959

———, 'Business Power in the Nazi Regime', *Zeitschrift für Nationalökonomie*, vol. 20 (3/4), 1960

———, 'The Foreign Exchange Crisis of 1936', *Zeitschrift für die gesamte Staatswissenschaft*, vol. 118 (2), April 1962

———, 'Parteidiktatur und überministerielle Führergewalt', *Jahrbuch für Sozialwissenschaft*, vol. 21 (1), 1970

———, 'Plans and Markets, Nazi Style', *Kyklos. International Review for Social Sciences*, vol. 30, 1977

Simpson, Amos E., 'The Struggle for Control of the German Economy 1936–37', *Journal of Modern History*, vol. 31 (1), 1959

Skrzypczak, Henryk, 'Fälscher machen Zeitgeschichte. Ein quellenkritischer Beitrag zur Gewerkschaftspolitik in der Ära Papen und Schleicher', *Internationale wissenschaftliche Korrespondenz zur Geschichte der deutschen Arbeiterbewegung*, vol. 11 (4), 1975

Sohn-Rethel, Alfred, 'Die soziale Rekonsolidierung des Kapitalismus (September 1932). Ein Kommentar nach 38 Jahren', *Kursbuch*, no. 21, Berlin, 1970

Stegmann, Dirk, 'Zum Verhältnis von Grossindustrie und Nationalsozialismus 1930–1933', *Archiv für Sozialgeschichte*, vol. XIII, 1973

Steinwarz, Herbert, 'The Amenities of Industry and Labour in Germany', *International Labour Review*, vol. XXXVI (6), December 1937

Stolleis, Michael, 'Gemeinschaft und Volksgemeinschaft. Zur juristischen Terminologie im Nationalsozialismus', *Vierteljahrshefte für Zeitgeschichte*, vol. 20 (1), January 1972

Steubel, H., 'Die Finanzierung der Aufrüstung im Dritten Reich', *Europa-Archiv*, June 1951

Tacke, Bernhard, 'Erinnerungen um den 1. Mai 1934', *Gewerkschaftliche Monatshefte*, vol. 26 (7), 1975

Tenfelde, Klaus, 'Proletarische Provinz. Radikalisierung und Widerstand in Penzberg/Oberbayern', *Bayern in der NS-Zeit*, ed. Martin Broszat *et al.*, vol. 4, Munich/Vienna, 1981

Teppe, Karl, 'Zur Sozialpolitik des Dritten Reiches am Beispiel der Sozialversicherung', *Archiv für Sozialgeschichte*, vol. XVII, 1977

Thompson, E.P., 'Time, Work-Discipline and Industrial Capitalism', *Past and Present*, no. 38, December 1967

Treue, Wilhelm (ed. and introd.), 'Hitlers Denkschrift zum Vierjahresplan 1936', *Vierteljahrshefte für Zeitgeschichte*, vol. 3 (3), July 1955

_____, (ed.), 'Hitlers Rede vor der deutschen Presse (10 November 1938)', *Vierteljahrshefte für Zeitgeschichte*, vol. 6 (2), April 1958

_____, 'Die Einstellung einiger deutscher Großindustrieller zu Hitlers Aussenpolitik', *Geschichte in Wissenschaft und Unterricht*, vol. 17, 1966

_____, 'Die deutschen Unternehmer in der Weltwirtschaftskrise 1928 bis 1933', *Die Staats- und Wirtschaftskrise des Deutschen Reiches 1929/33*, ed. Werner Conze and Hans Raupach, Stuttgart, 1967

Trevor-Roper, H. R., 'Hitlers Kriegsziele', *Vierteljahrshefte für Zeitgeschichte*, vol. 8 (2), April 1960

Turner, Henry A., Jr, 'Hitler's Secret Pamphlet for Industrialists 1927', *Journal of Modern History*, vol. 40 (3), September 1968

_____, 'Emil Kirdorf and the Nazi Party', *Central European History*, vol. 1, 1968

_____, 'Big Business and the Rise of Hitler', *American Historical Review*, vol. LXXV (1), October 1969

_____, 'The "Ruhrlade": Secret Cabinet of Heavy Industry in the Weimar Republic', *Central European History*, vol. 3, 1970

Bibliography

———, 'Fritz Thyssen und "I paid Hitler"' *Vierteljahrshefte für Zeitgeschichte*, vol. 19 (3), July 1971

———, 'Hitlers Einstellung zu Wirtschaft und Gesellschaft vor 1933', *Geschichte und Gesellschaft*, vol. 2 (1) 1976

———, 'Großunternehmertum und Nationalsozialismus 1930–1933', *Historische Zeitschrift*, vol. 221, 1975

Vierhaus, Rudolf, 'Auswirkungen der Krise um 1930 in Deutschland: Beiträge zu einer historisch-psychologischen Analyse', *Die Staats- und Wirtschaftskrise des Deutschen Reiches 1929/33*, ed. Werner Conze and Hans Raupach, Stuttgart, 1969

Voges, Michael, 'Klassenkampf in der "Betriebsgemeinschaft". Die Deutschland-Berichte der Sopade (1934–1940) als Quelle zum Widerstand im Dritten Reich', *Archiv für Sozialgeschichte*, vol. XXI, 1981

Volkmann, Hans-Erich, 'Die NS-Wirtschaft in Vorbereitung des Krieges', Wilhelm Deist, Manfred Messerschmidt, Hans-Erich Volkmann and Wolfram Wette, *Das deutsche Reich und der Zweite Weltkrieg*, Stuttgart, 1979, vol. 1: *Ursachen und Voraussetzungen der Deutschen Kriegspolitik*

Vollweiler, H., 'The Mobilization of Labour Reserves in Germany', *International Labour Review*, vol. XCI (4), October 1968

Vorländer, Herwart, 'NS-Volkswohlfahrt und Winterhilfswerk des deutschen Volkes', *Vierteljahrshefte für Zeitgeschichte*, vol. 34 (3), July 1986

Wächtler, Eberhard, 'Die bergbauliche Tradition als Bestandteil der antikommunistischen Politik des deutschen Imperialismus', *Jahrbuch für Wirtschaftsgeschichte*, 1969, part III.

Waelbroeck, P. and I. Bessling, 'Some Aspects of German Social Policy under the National Socialist Regime', *International Labour Review*, vol. XLIII (2), February 1941

Walesch, Anne, 'Das Amt 'Schönbeit der Arbeit' in der NS-Organisation 'Kraft durch Freude', 1933–1939', paper, TU Hanover, 1973

Wehler, Hans-Ulrich, 'Sozialökonomie und Geschichtswissenschaft', *Neue Politische Literatur*, vol. 14 (3), 1969

———, 'Bismarck's Imperialism 1862–1890', *Past and Present*, no. 48, August 1970

Weil, Felix, 'Neuere Literatur zur deutschen Wehrwirtschaft', *Zeitschrift für Sozialforschung*, vol. 7, 1938

Weindling, Paul, 'Compulsory Sterilisation in National Socialist Germany', *German History*, no. 5, Autumn 1987

Winkler, H. A., 'Unternehmerverbände zwischen Ständeideologie und Nationalsozialismus', *Vierteljahrshefte für Zeitgeschichte*, vol. 17 (4), October 1969

———, 'Der entbehrliche Stand. Zur Mittelstandspolitik im "Dritten Reich"', *Archiv für Sozialgeschichte*, vol. XVII, 1977

———, 'Vom Mythos der Volksgemeinschaft', *Archiv für Sozialgeschichte*, vol. XVII, 1977

Bibliography

Wisotzky, Klaus, 'Der Ruhrbergbau am Vorabend des Zweiten Weltkrieges', *Vierteljahrshefte für Zeitgeschichte*, vol. 30 (3), July 1982

Wörtz, Ulrich, 'Programmatik und Führerprinzip. Das Problem des Strasser-Kreises in der NSDAP. Eine historisch-politische Studie zum Verhältnis von sachlichem Programm und persönlicher Führung in einer totalitären Bewegung', Ph.D. thesis, Erlangen/Nuremberg 1966

Wynn, A., 'A Note on German Agriculture', *Economic Journal*, vol. 43, 1933

Zimmermann, Michael, 'Ausbruchshoffnung. Junge Bergleute in den Dreissiger Jahren', *'Die Jahre weiss man nicht, wo man die hinsetzen soll.'* *Faschismuserfahrungen im Ruhrgebiet*, ed. Lutz Niethammer, Berlin/ Bonn, 1983

Zumpe, Lotte, 'Die Textilbetriebe der SS im Konzentrationslager Ravensbrück', *Jahrbuch für Wirtschaftsgeschichte*, 1969, part I

―――, 'Arbeitsbedingungen und Arbeitsergebnisse in den Textilbetrieben der SS im Konzentrationslager Ravensbrück', *Jahrbuch für Wirtschaftsgeschichte*, 1969, part II

―――, 'Ein Beitrag zur Wirtschafts- und Sozialgeschichte des deutschen Faschismus', *Jahrbuch für Wirtschaftsgeschichte*, 1979, part IV

Index

Action Committe for the Protection of German Labour, 75
ADGB. *See* Free Trade Unions
agricultural labour, 232, 324, 345, 355
agriculture, 47, 48, 54, 58, 79, 112, 125, 130, 131, 140, 147, 185, 189, 194, 195, 196, 201, 204, 220, 228, 232, 234, 238, 240, 242, 246, 265, 296, 309, 318, 322, 348
anti-Semitism, *see also* racism, 1, 5, 45n, 71, 267, 278
AOG. *See* Labour Organization Law
Ardennes, 13, 15, 17
armaments industry, *see also* rearmament, 33, 113, 127, 128, 135, 141, 190, 191, 196, 201, 203, 203n, 208, 240, 240n, 243, 247, 248, 252, 253, 353
Arnhold, Karl, 170n
artisans. *See* handicrafts
Auschwitz, 1
Austria, 15, 203, 207n, 224, 238, 239, 262, 324
automotive industry, 217, 218

Bavaria, 15, 43, 49n, 143
'Beauty of Labour' (*Schönheit der Arbeit)*, 154, 162, 163–164, 173n, 215
Berlin, 8, 9, 12, 13, 15, 28n, 30, 44, 60, 63, 68n, 75, 120, 120n, 137, 159, 190, 191, 274, 354
Betriebsgemeinschaft. *See* factory community
Betriebsrat. *See* factory council
Bismarck, Otto von, 23
Bliztkrieg strategy, 31, 182, 207, 347, 360

and domestic policy, 255–58
Boehm (Admiral), 180n, 264n
Bolshevik Revolution, 21
Bormann, Martin, 8, 9, 177
bottleneck, 185, 189, 190, 317
    commissions, 347
    economic, 206
    in dairy industry, 194
    in labour market, 189
    production, 186
von Brauchitsch, Walther (General), 270, 271
Braun, Otto (Prussian Prime Minister), 85
Britain, 2, 3, 183, 256, 258, 294, 295, 300, 301n, 302, 320, 324
Brucker, Ludwig, 41
Brüning, Heinrich (Chancellor) 68, 81, 84, 132
building industry, 114, 123, 124, 127, 138, 139, 185, 188, 190n, 198n, 203n, 226, 244, 324
Bürckel, Josef, 175, 217

Central Economic Parliament, 48
Chamber of Labour, 169, 220, 221
Chamber of Commerce and Industry, 217
Chamber of the Economy, 168
Chamberlain, Neville, 300
chemical industry, 187, 201
Churchill, Winston, 8, 17, 32
civil servants, 59, 95, 104, 118n, 139, 141n, 142, 148, 174n, 193, 297, 306, 307
civilian conscription, 125, 187, 234, 244, 246-49, 249n, 253, 260, 268, 319, 335, 337, 341, 345, 346, 355
clothing industry, *see also* textile